Health at Older Ages

**A National Bureau
of Economic Research
Conference Report**

Health at Older Ages
The Causes and Consequences
of Declining Disability
among the Elderly

Edited by **David M. Cutler and
David A. Wise**

The University of Chicago Press

Chicago and London

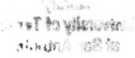

DAVID M. CUTLER is the Otto Eckstein Professor of Applied Economics in the Department of Economics and at the John F. Kennedy School of Government, Harvard University, and a research associate of the National Bureau of Economic Research.

DAVID A. WISE is the John F. Stambaugh Professor of Political Economy at the John F. Kennedy School of Government, Harvard University, and director of the Programs on Aging and Health Care at the National Bureau of Economic Research.

The University of Chicago Press, Chicago 60637
The University of Chicago Press, Ltd., London
© 2008 by the National Bureau of Economic Research
All rights reserved. Published 2008
Printed in the United States of America

17 16 15 14 13 12 11 10 09 08   1 2 3 4 5

ISBN-13: 978-0-226-13231-0 (cloth)
ISBN-10: 0-226-13231-5 (cloth)

Library of Congress Cataloging-in-Publication Data

Health at older ages : the causes and consequences of declining
    disability among the elderly / edited by David M. Cutler and
    David A. Wise
        p. ; cm. — (National Bureau of Economic Research conference
        report)
    Includes bibliographical references and index.
    ISBN-13: 978-0-226-13231-0 (cloth : alk. paper)
    ISBN-10: 0-226-13231-5 (cloth : alk. paper) 1. Older people—
    Health and hygiene—United States—Statistics. 2. Older people
    with disabilities—United States—Statistics. I. Cutler, David M.
    II. Wise, David A. II. Series.
        [DNLM: 1. Aged—United States. 2. Geriatric Assessment—
    United States. 3. Chronic Disease—economics—United States.
    4. Chronic Disease—prevention & control—United States.
    5. Disabled persons—United States. 6. Health Services for the
    Aged—trends—United States. WT H433402 2008]
        RA408.A3H33   2008
        618.97—dc33

2008008844

♾ The paper used in this publication meets the minimum requirements of the American National Standard for Information Sciences— Permanence of Paper for Printed Library Materials, ANSI Z39.48-1992.

Library
University of Texas
at San Antonio

Relation of the Directors to the Work and Publications of the National Bureau of Economic Research

1. The object of the NBER is to ascertain and present to the economics profession, and to the public more generally, important economic facts and their interpretation in a scientific manner without policy recommendations. The Board of Directors is charged with the responsibility of ensuring that the work of the NBER is carried on in strict conformity with this object.

2. The President shall establish an internal review process to ensure that book manuscripts proposed for publication DO NOT contain policy recommendations. This shall apply both to the proceedings of conferences and to manuscripts by a single author or by one or more co-authors but shall not apply to authors of comments at NBER conferences who are not NBER affiliates.

3. No book manuscript reporting research shall be published by the NBER until the President has sent to each member of the Board a notice that a manuscript is recommended for publication and that in the President's opinion it is suitable for publication in accordance with the above principles of the NBER. Such notification will include a table of contents and an abstract or summary of the manuscript's content, a list of contributors if applicable, and a response form for use by Directors who desire a copy of the manuscript for review. Each manuscript shall contain a summary drawing attention to the nature and treatment of the problem studied and the main conclusions reached.

4. No volume shall be published until forty-five days have elapsed from the above notification of intention to publish it. During this period a copy shall be sent to any Director requesting it, and if any Director objects to publication on the grounds that the manuscript contains policy recommendations, the objection will be presented to the author(s) or editor(s). In case of dispute, all members of the Board shall be notified, and the President shall appoint an ad hoc committee of the Board to decide the matter; thirty days additional shall be granted for this purpose.

5. The President shall present annually to the Board a report describing the internal manuscript review process, any objections made by Directors before publication or by anyone after publication, any disputes about such matters, and how they were handled.

6. Publications of the NBER issued for informational purposes concerning the work of the Bureau, or issued to inform the public of the activities at the Bureau, including but not limited to the NBER Digest and Reporter, shall be consistent with the object stated in paragraph 1. They shall contain a specific disclaimer noting that they have not passed through the review procedures required in this resolution. The Executive Committee of the Board is charged with the review of all such publications from time to time.

7. NBER working papers and manuscripts distributed on the Bureau's web site are not deemed to be publications for the purpose of this resolution, but they shall be consistent with the object stated in paragraph 1. Working papers shall contain a specific disclaimer noting that they have not passed through the review procedures required in this resolution. The NBER's web site shall contain a similar disclaimer. The President shall establish an internal review process to ensure that the working papers and the web site do not contain policy recommendations, and shall report annually to the Board on this process and any concerns raised in connection with it.

8. Unless otherwise determined by the Board or exempted by the terms of paragraphs 6 and 7, a copy of this resolution shall be printed in each NBER publication as described in paragraph 2 above.

Contents

Preface

This volume consists of papers presented at a conference held in Jackson Hole, Wyoming, in October 2004. Most of the research was conducted as part of the program on the Economics of Aging at the National Bureau of Economic Research and was sponsored by the U.S. Department of Health and Human Services, through National Institute on Aging grants P30-AG12810 and R01-AG19805 to the National Bureau of Economic Research, and by a grant from the Mary Woodard Lasker Charitable Trust and Michael E. DeBakey Foundation. Any other funding sources are noted in the individual papers.

Any opinions expressed in this volume are those of the respective authors and do not necessarily reflect the views of the National Bureau of Economic Research or the sponsoring organizations.

Introduction

David M. Cutler, David A. Wise, and
Richard G. Woodbury

An accumulating body of research has identified significant and ongoing improvements over time in the functional ability of older people, both in the United States and throughout the world. The implications of declining disability are enormous, and measurable in both social and economic terms. This volume is part of a continuing NBER project to understand the foundations of disability decline, what might be done to extend and even accelerate future improvements in functional ability, and how the benefits of disability decline can be evaluated and quantified in economic terms. Why is this so important?

The quality of later life. People are living longer than at any time in history. But will those increased years of life be characterized by functional disability or functional independence? Declining disability into the future will assure not just more years of life, but a better quality of later life.

Population aging. In addition to living longer as individuals, the baby boom generation is approaching retirement age. Thus the fastest-growing population groups in the future will be the oldest—those in their seventies, eighties, and nineties. Declining disability will moderate the economic and social challenges of a growing older population.

Disability and work. Disability is a major reason that people retire from the labor force. Disability declines will enable people to work longer, earn

David M. Cutler is the Otto Eckstein Professor of Applied Economics at Harvard University, and a research associate of the National Bureau of Economic Research. David A. Wise is the John F. Stambaugh Professor of Political Economy at the John F. Kennedy School of Government, Harvard University, and director of the program on aging at the National Bureau of Economic Research. Richard G. Woodbury is associated with the program on aging at the National Bureau of Economic Research.

1

income longer, and contribute longer to the economic productivity of the labor market.

Caregiving. Informal caregiving within families, formal long-term care services, and residential care in nursing homes and other long-term care facilities together represent a major cost of disability. Declining disability will reduce all of the social, psychological, and economic costs associated with caregiving.

Medical care. The amount spent on medical care for individuals with disabilities is several times larger, on average, than the amount spent on medical care for those without disabilities. While many factors will play into future medical care costs in the United States, future disability rates are a significant factor. Medical advances and medical spending also have an important role in causing reductions in disability.

The value of functional health to individuals, caregivers, society, and the economy would be hard to overstate. By understanding the root causes of past disability decline, one can begin to look forward at likely future disability trends and factors that might stimulate further improvements in functional ability. One can also begin to quantify the value of disability decline, which encompasses all of these benefits: better quality of life, the ability to work and earn income longer, and the potential savings in caregiving and medical costs.

A Framework for Studying Disability

To conceptually organize the complexity of issues involved in a comprehensive study of disability, we have structured our investigation in a way that considers together the causes, characteristics, and consequences of disability trends. The individual studies reported in this volume deal with smaller pieces of a larger and more integrated project effort. Figure 1 illustrates the structural framework around which we have organized this larger project effort, and some of the significant components that make up that larger effort.

The structural framework laid out in figure 1 categorizes factors that have contributed to disability decline (the causes), the multiple dimensions through which disability is measured or characterized (the characteristics), and some important implications of disability trends (the consequences). Each of the chapters in this volume fits into the overall framework, focusing in some way on a cause of disability or disability decline, an improved understanding of how health conditions relate to functional independence, or a consequence of disability decline. The framework is not so much a blueprint for the project, but rather a conceptual structure that relates individual investigations of disability issues in an integrated way.

The characterization of disability (the center section of fig. 1) is a partic-

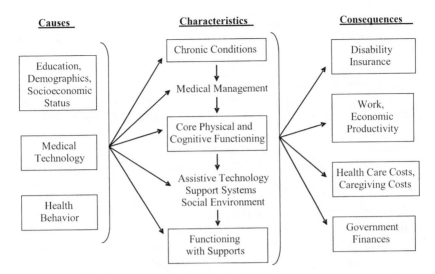

Fig. 1   A framework for studying disability

ularly important foundation for our inquiry, because it highlights the multiple dimensions through which one can analyze health and disability. One basis for analyzing disability is the presence of a chronic health condition. Thus, trends in the prevalence of chronic illnesses matter. However, the impact of chronic illness on core physical and cognitive functioning also changes over time, as we find ways to better manage the symptoms associated with chronic illness. So a second, more relevant measure of disability is core physical and cognitive functioning, independent of any chronic illness.

A third measure is our ability to live and function independently—to successfully accomplish the activities of daily living—despite our underlying physical and cognitive capacity, and using whatever assistive devices and social and environmental support systems that might be available. Trends in the technology, availability, and use of assistive devices are an important factor, as are broader changes in technology, such as remote control devices, microwave cooking technology, automation technologies, and mobile telephones. Social and community support systems also matter, such as transportation support, home delivery, Meals On Wheels (Association of America), and other services. The increasing options and variability in living arrangements, which combine housing and support services in innovative ways, also contribute to functional independence.

A fourth measure of disability focuses on the functional ability of individuals to work productively in the labor force. It highlights the critical interactions between functional ability, decisions about work and retirement, income, economic productivity, and the role of disability insurance.

Each of these measures of disability means something a little bit different, and points to the complexity of what we mean by *disability*. Thus one direction of project research has sought to better characterize disability in its many dimensions, and how disability rates are changing over time.

After taking account of the multiple dimensionality of disability, we can then explore with better focus the causes of disability, the pathways through which individuals develop disabilities, the relationships between specific health conditions and disability, and the reasons behind disability trends. Among the factors contributing to disability trends are improvements in the diagnosis, prevention, and treatment of disabling illnesses; improved management of the disabling effects of chronic illness; improved treatment of mental illness; improvements in cognitive health; pharmaceutical innovations; healthier lifestyles and health-related behaviors; decreases in hazardous exposures and improved workplace safety; the emergence of a continuum of living arrangement options; improved and more widespread use of assistive devices and technologies that enable people with disabling conditions to function more effectively; improved and expanded environmental accommodations and social systems to support older and functionally disabled people; and societal changes that make physical and mental disabilities less of an impediment to independence.

The strong relationship between education and functional ability is also clear, suggesting an important role of education in preventing or deferring disability. In short, the factors contributing to disability decline are a complex combination of physiological, medical, economic, social, and environmental influences.

We can also explore with better focus the consequences of disability and disability trends for such issues as disability insurance, capacity for work and economic productivity, health care costs, caregiving costs, and government finances.

This volume reports on the early stages of a more comprehensive research agenda that investigates in some detail these relationships. In the remainder of this introduction, we summarize the fifteen chapters in the volume, drawing heavily on the authors' own descriptions of their work. The fifteen chapters cover a breadth of topics, drawing on various research methods, data sources, and definitions of disability and study populations. To organize this collection of research, we have divided the volume into five sections: (a) disability trends, (b) pathways to disability, (c) medical advances and disability, (d) work disability, and (e) assistive technology and caregiving.

Disability Trends

The first section of the volume explores disability trends, focusing initially on long-term historical changes in health and functional ability. In chapter 1, "The Health of Older Men in the Past," Dora Costa details the long-term improvements in health and longevity over the past century. This chapter is based on the health records of Union Army veterans, and considers three broad disease categories—heart conditions, musculoskeletal problems, and loss of cognitive functioning.

The results show that in the past, occupation was an important determinant of valvular heart disease, congestive heart failure, and joint and back problems, suggesting that higher socioeconomic status protected against mechanical wear and tear and that it purchased less crowding and therefore less infectious diseases such as rheumatic fever. The high probability of physical injury on the job and in the home, the high rates of infectious disease, and incomes that were too low to purchase uncrowded housing all explain why chronic disease rates were so high among men in the past. Declining disease rates and the shift from blue-collar to white-collar jobs explain a significant part of the decline in both valvular heart disease and arthritis. Additional potential explanations include the mechanization of blue-collar jobs and reductions in work injuries within jobs, innovations in medical care and the diffusion of accurate medical knowledge to individuals, and improvements in the food supply.

Declines in infectious disease rates resulted from many factors, including advances in medical technology, rising incomes and living standards, public health reforms, and improved personal hygiene. Public health reforms have included investments in sewage, clean water, clean milk supplies, and iron fortification. Cities also invested in disease reporting and quarantining systems and, in conjunction with private philanthropists, in well-baby and child health care (including vaccination) and in campaigns against specific diseases such as syphilis.

Chapter 2 also looks at the long-term historical foundations of disability decline, but with a focus on arthritis. In "Arthritis: Changes in Its Prevalence during the Nineteenth and Twentieth Centuries," Paula Canavese and Robert Fogel compare the prevalence of arthritis among Union Army veterans with arthritis among men at the end of the twentieth century. The study finds that the current prevalence rate of arthritis is lower than it was in the late nineteenth century and the beginning of the twentieth century. The average age of onset of arthritis is eleven years later, and the proportion of men who ever get arthritis is substantially lower than it used to be.

One explanation suggested in the study is the progress of medicine during the last century, which has encompassed many new forms of treatment for arthritis. Also relevant are changes in public health, lifestyle, and the distribution of occupations. The tremendous change in public health infrastructure (e.g., improvements in the water supply, better sewage systems, cleaning of the milk supply) has reduced the probability of developing arthritis at later ages by reducing adverse health experiences during earlier years of life. Also, for those people who have it, arthritis is less severe now, partly because of many interventions that are used today, but that were not available in the late nineteenth century. Medical advances have alleviated the severity of the condition, both through drugs and by advocating changes in lifestyle.

Chapters 1 and 2 provide a longer-term context for studying more recent disability trends. While the long-term historical foundations of disability decline may differ in detail from those that matter now, the major categories of influence are much the same. Medical advances, public health initiatives, improved health behaviors, improved economic conditions, and higher education attainment all were relevant then—and are still relevant today.

The focus of chapter 3 is on trends in health disparities over the past two decades. Health, disability, and mortality are highly correlated with socioeconomic and demographic factors. The question is whether health and functional ability are improving at different rates for different population groups, and thus whether the disparities in health status across groups are getting larger or smaller over time. In "Socioeconomic and Demographic Disparities in Trends in Old-Age Disability," Robert Schoeni, Vicki Freedman, and Linda Martin document changes in disparities in old-age disability across socioeconomic and demographic groups, including education, income, race/ethnicity, age, gender, marital status, and region of residence. They find that old-age disability rates among all major socioeconomic and demographic groups declined over the past two decades, but the magnitude of the fall was larger for those who have higher income, have more years of education, are married, and are younger. For example, the decline in disability rates for those with a college degree was 2.5 percent annually, while the decline for those with less than eight years of education was 0.9 percent annually. The decline for those in the highest income quartile was 3.1 percent annually, compared with 1.4 percent in the lowest income quartile. The decline for married people was 4.0 percent annually, while the decline for singles was 1.4 percent annually. And the decline in disability at younger ages (seventy to seventy-four) was 2.8 percent annually, while the decline at older ages (eighty-five and older) was 1.1 percent. As a result of these differences in disability trends across population groups, disparities in disability rates have increased, rather than decreased.

The importance of education is highlighted in this study, as in others. Investigators suggest that education, among other things, may represent the lifelong effects of mediating factors, including early childhood experiences, access to medical care throughout the lifecourse, health behaviors, and ability to navigate the health care system and implement complex medical regimens. They suggest that to identify the causes of the declines in disability and shifts in the gaps in disability rates across demographic groups, we must look to these mediating effects as well as other factors not directly linked to educational attainment. Taken together, the factors causing a relationship between socioeconomic and demographic characteristics and disability are likely to be a complex mix of medical, social, and behavioral influences.

Pathways to Disability

Another direction of our research, and the topic of chapters 4 and 5, focuses on the pathways through which individuals become disabled. A common framework for understanding pathways to disability is from an identifiable health condition that may develop over time to a physiological limitation to an inability to perform one or more activities of functional independence. By focusing on the pathway, one can also isolate points along it where interventions might make a difference. For example, one may effectively reduce disabilities anywhere along the pathway by preventing adverse health conditions and events before they develop, by early diagnosis, through medical treatment of the condition, by managing more effectively the symptoms of the condition, through the technological development and use of effective assistive devices, or through social and environmental supports that facilitate independent functioning despite a physiological limitation.

One is better positioned to identify the most efficient interventions if one knows the pathways through which disabilities develop. Thus, our research has tried to identify those pathways to disability that are most common, as well as the broader distribution of health pathways across healthy and less healthy circumstances. This can be done looking forward or backward in time. For example, what is the likelihood that a person in excellent health at age sixty will become disabled by age seventy, eighty, or ninety? How do these probabilities compare with someone who was in fair health at age sixty? Or what is the likelihood that someone with a particular health condition at age seventy-five was in poor, fair, good, or excellent health at age fifty-five?

This approach was the basis for research reported in chapter 4, "Pathways to Disability: Predicting Health Trajectories," by Axel Börsch-Supan, Florian Heiss, Michael Hurd, and David Wise. Their basic finding is that differences in self-reported health at any age lead to dramatic differences in the likelihood of developing a subsequent disability. Health and disability at younger ages are strongly related to future health and disability paths as people age. This finding parallels the strong relationship between self-reported health and subsequent mortality. Reversing the analysis, they also find that survival to older ages (eighty or ninety) provides substantial information about health and disability status at younger ages.

Chapter 4 also highlights the very significant variation in pathways to disability across individuals with different education backgrounds, different incomes or wealth, or between those who are married and those who are single. At age fifty, for example, people with eight or fewer years of education are about four times more likely to be in poor health than people with sixteen or more years of education. The difference in rates of poor health between the low-education and high-education groups increases in parallel to about age seventy, when the two groups start to converge. There is a similar pattern in the mortality rates of the two groups, but shifted to older ages. This, too, reflects the latter stages of the pathway from poor health to mortality. In continuing research, the investigators plan to consider other socioeconomic attributes, as well as the role of specific medical conditions.

The pathway to disability from specific medical conditions is already the focus of chapter 5, "Clinical Pathways to Disability," by Mary Beth Landrum, Kate Stewart, and David Cutler. In this study, the investigators aim to disentangle the major clinical pathways through which the health of older people declines. Dementia is highlighted in the study as a leading precursor to disability. Other chronic and acute conditions that often lead to disability include cardiovascular disease (particularly heart failure and stroke), fractures, Parkinson's disease, and arthritis. There is also a category of individuals who do not attribute their disability to any specific health condition, but instead cite symptoms or simply old age as the source of their disability.

In addition to identifying the major pathways, the study compares conditions that may be less common but have a major impact on disability (such as dementia) with conditions that are more common, but have a smaller impact on disability (such as arthritis). The study also differentiates between disability in mobility-related tasks, disability in complex tasks requiring cognitive capabilities, and disability in basic personal care tasks.

The investigators point to significant differences in costs, the nature and severity of disability, the types of functional limitations, and the types of help and assistive services that are used, depending on the clinical pathway that leads to disability. For example, while respondents with dementia had relatively low rates of hospitalizations and physician visits, almost half were institutionalized. The heavy reliance on personal assistance with Activities of Daily Living (ADL) and Instrumental Activities of Daily Living (IADL) tasks among disabled respondents with dementia also suggests potential caregiver burden among this cohort. In contrast, newly disabled respondents with arthritis were relatively infrequent users of intensive inpatient or nursing home care, but had higher than average use of medications and physician visits. In addition, arthritis was most strongly associated with the use of assistive equipment alone. Those attributing their disability to symptom causes or old age tended to have less severe disability, use fewer supportive services, and use less health care more generally.

Both chapters 4 and 5 help to understand the process through which individual health evolves, enabling more careful targeting of interventions toward individual pathways that lead to disability. The direct relationships between specific clinical conditions, and the development of particular functional disabilities—with particular needs for management, treatment, and assistive care—should facilitate more effective targeting of both medical and nonmedical interventions.

Medical Advances and Disability

The third section of the volume is a natural extension of the first two. Medical advances are an important factor in explaining the improvements in health and longevity that have occurred over time, as emphasized in the research on disability trends. Medical advances are also a means to delay or prevent the development of a functional limitation among individuals, as emphasized in the research on pathways to disability. In this section, therefore, we look at some of the effects of medical advances on specific health conditions and in turn, the effect of improving health on medical care spending.

Chapters 6 and 7 are condition-specific studies. Specific medical advances (such as cataract surgery, antidepressant medication, beta blockers, or hip replacements) have been most important in treating or preventing the functional limitations associated with specific health conditions. Thus, understanding the relationships between specific medical advances, individual health conditions, and functional limitations (and how these relationships have evolved over time), is critical to understanding the deeper causes of disability decline.

Cardiovascular disease is a natural candidate for condition-specific analysis because it is the most common cause of death in the United States, because treatment technology has evolved considerably, and because more is spent on cardiovascular disease than on any other condition. Therefore, it is a condition where medical care could really matter. In chapter 6, "Intensive Medical Care and Cardiovascular Disease Disability Reductions," David Cutler, Mary Beth Landrum, and Kate Stewart look at the particular role of improvements in cardiovascular disease treatment in the overall composition of disability decline in the United States.

Their analysis has three parts. In the first part, they examine basic trends in disability associated with cardiovascular disease. They show that reduced disability for people with cardiovascular disease incidents is a major part of the reduction in overall disability in the United States, accounting for between one-fifth and one-third of the total reduction in disability. The second part of the chapter considers the role of advances in medical care in reducing disability from cardiovascular disease. In this part of the analysis, Cutler, Landrum, and Stewart estimate that the use of improved treatments for heart attacks, including prescriptions of beta-blockers, aspirin, and ace-inhibitors at discharge—as well as use of reperfusion and other surgical procedures—increased the probability that elderly patients survive an acute cardiovascular event in a nondisabled state by 14 to 22 percent between 1984 and 1994. As one might expect, patients living in regions with high use of appropriate medical therapies had better health outcomes than patients living in low-use areas.

The third part of chapter 6 attempts to quantify the long-term health and financial impacts of improved care for people with cardiovascular disease. The study estimates that preventing disability after an acute event can add as much as 3.7 years of quality-adjusted life expectancy, or perhaps $316,000 of value. The cost of this change is much smaller. The initial treatment costs range from $8,610 to $16,332, depending on procedure use. Further, recent cost analyses reported that annual Medicare spending was lower for the nondisabled compared to the disabled, which suggests that higher treatment costs may be offset by lower future spending among a more healthy population. Therefore, by virtually any measure, improved medical technology after acute cardiovascular episodes is worth the cost.

An important question is whether these conclusions extend to other conditions beyond cardiovascular disease. Chapter 7 focuses on arthritis and mobility-related disabilities. In "Are Baby Boomers Aging Better than Their Predecessors? Trends in Overweight, Arthritis, and Mobility Difficulty," Suzanne Leveille, Christina Wee, and Lisa Iezzoni look in an integrated way at trends in arthritis prevalence, being overweight, and having a mobility-related disability. As with most other functional limitations, mobility-related disability appears to be declining over time. The significant advances in medical treatment for arthritis and other mobility-impairing conditions, including both pharmacological and surgical advances, are no doubt related to the decreasing prevalence of mobility-related disabilities and can be compared qualitatively with the impact of medical advances on disability from cardiovascular conditions, as explored in the previous chapter. Countering these positive trends, however, are the significant increases in the population of Americans who are overweight or obese— conditions that are associated with increased mobility difficulty. Chapter 7 is an exploratory compilation of these interrelated issues and trends.

The study quantifies the prevalence of overweight, arthritis, and mobility disability across successive waves of the National Health and Nutrition Examination Surveys (NHANES), comparing women and men born in ten-year intervals: 1926–1935, 1936–1945, 1946–1955, and 1956–1965. The proportion of Americans who are overweight was found to increase substantially. When the two older cohorts were aged thirty-five to forty-four years, 38–42 percent of women were overweight (Body Mass Index [BMI] >25). When the two younger cohorts were aged thirty-five to forty-four, 50–60 percent of women were overweight. Despite this increase, the prevalence of mobility difficulty (measured in the two most recent waves of the NHANES) declined in each successive birth cohort. That suggests that other factors, such as medical advances and changes in the distribution of occupations in the workforce, have offset the potentially detrimental effects of being overweight. How these trends will evolve and interact going forward, however, is a question for continuing research.

A common thread in chapters 6 and 7 is the important role of medical advances as a major influence on disability trends, whether focused on cardiovascular disease, arthritis, or other conditions. Medical advances are likely an important factor in reducing almost any form of disability, and almost any health condition associated with disability. How all of this relates to health care costs is a question raised in chapter 8. Of course, developing and using new medical technologies and treatments costs money. On the other hand, those who are healthier and less functionally disabled spend less on medical care than those who are not. How these offsetting influences affect health care costs on balance is an open question.

In chapter 8, "Disability and Spending Growth," Michael Chernew, Dana Goldman, Feng Pan, and Baoping Shang analyze spending trends by those with and without functional limitations. The primary finding is that the rate of growth in medical spending is faster for those who are not disabled than it is for those who have functional disabilities. The argument is made, therefore, that there is some convergence in health care spending across disability categories and, if such a convergence continues, savings accruing to improved disability status may have less of an impact on overall spending than analysis of current spending patterns would suggest.

A fundamental question raised in the chapter is whether this convergence will continue. Related questions are whether the increases in spending among those who spend very little are economically significant relative to the spending of those who spend a lot, how medical and pharmacological advances relate to costs, and the influence of disability trends on the lifetime medical expenditures of individuals. These are topics for continuing research.

Work Disability

The next section of this volume focuses on work-related disability. In addition to the personal burden of disability and the expense of medical and assistive care, an important economic consequence of disability results from lost earnings. In this section, we look at the measurement of work disability, the extent of disability risk, and the growing number of recipients of disability insurance benefits.

The section begins with a methodological study on the measurement of work disability. Self-reported disability is influenced by many factors, including how people interpret survey questions, based on the phrasing of the question, the frame of reference of the respondent, or on cultural or social norms. These factors may have nothing to do with underlying health. For example, Americans are four times more likely to state that they are in excellent health than the Dutch—a discrepancy that could not possibly result from differences in actual health status between the two populations.

In chapter 9, "Work Disability is a Pain in the *****, Especially in England, the Netherlands, and the United States," James Banks, Arie Kapteyn, James Smith, and Arthur van Soest investigate the wide variation across these countries in self-reported work disability. The diversity in reported work disability stands in sharp contrast to the relative similarity across these countries in standards of living and in more objective health measures. The authors investigate in particular the role of pain as a factor leading to work disability in the Netherlands, the United Kingdom, and the United States.

They find that pain is by far the most important factor leading to reports of work disability in all three countries. However, respondents who appear to be suffering from similar degrees of pain respond very differently to questions on work disability, depending on which country they are from. These differences in the relationship between pain and work disability do not appear to be related to differential use of painkillers or differential degrees of work accommodation across countries. The authors suggest instead that the differences in self-reported work disability result primarily from differences in thresholds, or response scales that relate to work disability. Similar differences in response scales were found within countries, based on gender, education, and age.

Based on a new research methodology known as *vignettes*, in which respondents are asked to evaluate the health of a hypothetical person described in the survey, the findings from chapter 9 suggest that a significant part of the observed difference in reported work disability between the two countries is explained by the fact that residents use different response scales in answering the standard questions on whether they have a work disability. Essentially for the same level of actual work disability, Dutch respondents have a lower response threshold in claiming a work disability. The vignette methodology helps to calibrate differences in self-reports across cultural, socioeconomic, or cross-national groups.

Chapter 10 focuses on the economic risk associated with a work disability. The onset of disability has significant economic as well as lifestyle consequences. Disability generally leads to greater medical and caregiving expenses, and in some cases, dramatically higher expenses. At the same time, it can require a departure from the labor force and a loss of earnings. The combination of lost earnings and increased expenses can impose a very significant financial burden, not only on individuals who become disabled, but their families as well. The limited probability of a very high cost occurrence makes disability risk a natural circumstance for insurance. In chapter 10, "Disability Risk and the Value of Disability Insurance," Amitabh Chandra and Andrew Samwick consider the magnitude of the disability risk, the extent of precautionary saving for potential disability, and the value of disability insurance.

Part of their work analyzes the decline in disability in the working age population over the past two decades (i.e., focusing on people under age sixty-five). In the early 1980s, disability rates of working-age men were about two percentage points higher than those of women. But over the period from 1980 to 2003, they find a substantial decline in work-limiting disability among men (but not for women), so that men and women now have similar disability rates at the end of their working lives. For men, the declines in disability are particularly significant among those age fifty-five to sixty-four, rather than at younger ages. As in other studies, Chandra and Samwick find that the largest disparities in disability rates are found across educational groups: by age sixty-two, about 17 percent of those without a college education have a work-limiting disability, compared to about 5 percent of those with a college education.

Based on this risk analysis, Chandra and Samwick then consider the relative value of precautionary saving and insurance against the risk of disability. They estimate that no more than 20 percent of preretirement savings is precautionary saving against the risk of disability for any demographic group. (The average precautionary saving for disability risk among all demographic groups is closer to 4 percent of saving.) Compared to other motives for saving, like saving for retirement, or saving for routine income fluctuations over a working career, disability risk generates comparatively little additional saving. The investigators suggest that because the probability of work disability is small and the average size of the loss—conditional on becoming disabled—is large, disability risk is not effectively insured through precautionary saving.

They find that disability risk is addressed much more effectively through disability insurance. They estimate that a typical consumer would be willing to pay about 5 percent of his or her lifetime consumption toward disability insurance. About 2 percentage points reflect the impact of disability on expected lifetime earnings; the remaining 3 percentage points are attributable to the uncertainty associated with the disability risk. Thus, the value of disability insurance is likely to be very high.

Chapters 11 and 12 look at the dramatic growth in recent years in the number of people receiving disability insurance benefits, despite the apparent declines in disability rates. During the last two decades, the fraction of nonelderly adults receiving Social Security Disability Insurance (SSDI) benefits increased by 76 percent. In chapter 11, "Why Are the Disability Rolls Skyrocketing? The Contribution of Population Characteristics, Economic Conditions, and Program Generosity," Mark Duggan and Scott Imberman consider three categories of explanation: the characteristics of individuals insured by the DI program, the state of the economy, and the generosity of program benefits.

One explanation for the increasing number of DI recipients is the changing age structure in the U.S. population, highlighted by the aging of the baby boom generation into a period of life when one might expect a large increase in DI receipt. Duggan and Imberman find that age demographics explain about 15 percent of the increase in DI receipt among men and about 4 percent for women. The increasing coverage of women under the disability program (resulting from the increased labor force participation of women) explains another 24 percent of the growth in DI receipt among women. A second explanation is that adverse economic shocks affected applications. Confirming this explanation, the study finds that the recessions of 1991 and 2001 can explain 24 percent of the growth in DI receipt among men and 12 percent of the growth among women.

A third explanation is DI benefit generosity. Because of the interactions between rising income inequality and the progressive benefit formula used by the Social Security Administration (SSA), low-skilled individuals can now replace a much larger fraction of their earnings with DI benefits than they could have two decades ago. The findings suggest that rising replacement rates can explain 28 percent of the growth in DI receipt among women and 24 percent of the growth for men. A fourth explanation is the more liberal definition of disability used to determine DI eligibility. These changes differentially increased the probability that individuals with mental disorders or musculoskeletal conditions (e.g., back pain, arthritis) were awarded DI benefits, with the fraction of DI awards to these two conditions increasing from 28 percent in 1983 to 52 percent twenty years later. The findings suggest that the liberalized eligibility criteria can explain 38 percent of the growth in DI receipt among women and 53 percent for men. Duggan and Imberman conclude the chapter with a forecast of the changes in disability recipiency that will occur during the upcoming years, arguing that the growth in DI rolls is likely to continue and perhaps accelerate going forward.

Chapter 12 looks at the particular impact of depression on disability enrollment. Since the early 1990s, mental illnesses are the fastest-growing cause of new claims for income support from the DI and the SSI programs, making up 30 percent of DI awards in 2000. In chapter 12, "Early Retirement and DI/SSI Applications: Exploring the Impact of Depression," Rena Conti, Ernst Berndt, and Richard Frank look at the potential effects of one major mental health condition, depression, and its dual effect on work-related activity. Depression may have both a direct effect on work, reducing an individual's interest and productivity in the workplace, and an indirect effect, through its interaction with physical illnesses and other life events. To examine the direct impact, the study focuses on individuals who experience an incident case of depression and compares these people to similar individuals who did not experience a new episode of depression. To estimate the indirect effects, the study compares the work activity responses to adverse health events (and other life events, such as widowhood) for people likely to have depression and a similar group of people without significant symptoms of depression.

The results of both estimation strategies indicate that depression decreases work, increases early retirement, and increases DI/SSI applications. Depression alone induces some DI applications. Depression also works in combination with other medical illnesses and widowhood to increase DI applications. The magnitude of the effects appears to be of the same order of magnitude to that of physical illness. These findings have important implications for interpreting disability levels and trends, partly because of the direct effect of depression on disability, and partly through the significant indirect interactions between depression and physical illness. Similar to cardiovascular disease, there have been significant advances in the treatment of depression over the past two decades. A final aspect of chapter 12 is to estimate roughly the returns to depression treatment, assuming treatment returns an individual to the likelihood of employment status enjoyed by a nondepressed individual. The receipt of guideline treatment for depression in the study population is estimated to result in a three to fifteen percent point reduction in adverse employment outcomes. Thus, the impact of treatment for depression on work disability may be substantial, and represents an important area for continuing study.

Assistive Technology and Caregiving

The last section of this volume looks at how people function with physiological limitations. One way is through the use of assistive devices. Advances in assistive technology and increasing use of assistive devices and equipment are an important component of increasing functional independence in the population. Another way is through paid medical and caregiving services, or through unpaid caregiving within families. Chapters 13 through 15 deal with three diverse questions under this broader theme: trends in the use of assistive technologies, how those with functional limitations feel about their health care, and how the burden of caregiving affects spouses.

In chapter 13, "Trends in Assistance with Daily Activities: Racial/Ethnic and Socioeconomic Disparities Persist in the U.S. Older Population," Vicki Freedman, Linda Martin, Jennifer Cornman, Emily Agree, and Robert Schoeni explore older U.S. population trends in forms of assistance with daily activities and disparities in assistance by race/ethnicity and socioeconomic status. A core finding from the study is a substantial increase between 1992 and 2001 in the independent use of assistive technology (without help from another person). In general, similar trends are found across demographic groups. Still, some socioeconomic groups are more likely to use assistive technology without help than others. Notably, higher levels of education are associated with higher probabilities of using technology independently to carry out daily activities. Among those with difficulty with one or more daily activities, all else equal, there has been a persistent five percent point gap in the independent use of assistive technology between those with more than a high school education and those with eight or fewer years of completed education. Even larger gaps by education are evident among those reporting difficulty bathing—reaching eight percent in 2001. The investigators report a number of limitations in their analysis. First,

questions about assistive devices were limited to those individuals reporting that they experienced difficulty with a particular task, omitting those
individuals who benefit from an assistive technology but who do not report
a difficulty. Second, the study only analyzed technologies that are specifically designed for day-to-day tasks, excluding related advances that have
also improved quality of life and independence. Third, the analysis considers only personal care activities, setting aside for future research the role
of technology in reducing IADL limitations. Each of these limits suggests
an even larger impact of assistive technologies on the quality of life and the
functional independence of individuals as they age. The scope of applications for assistive technologies, the development of new technologies, and
the dissemination and increased use of assistive technologies contribute
significantly to disability trends.

In chapter 14, "How Do Medicare Beneficiaries with Physical and
Sensory Disabilities Feel about Their Health Care?," Lisa Iezzoni, Jane
Soukup, and Suzanne Leveille consider how people with specific sensory
and physical impairments perceive various aspects of their health care.
The Medicare Current Beneficiary Survey (MCBS) asks respondents
twenty questions about their health care experiences that fit generally into
three broad dimensions: access to care, (including costs of care), technical
quality of care, and interpersonal quality of care.

The study finds that the vast majority of Medicare beneficiaries with or
without disabilities perceive their physicians as competent and well trained
and hold favorable views of their overall quality of care. Along most other
dimensions of care, 80 to 90 percent of persons report satisfaction, regardless of disability. However, after accounting for various demographic and
other respondent attributes, Medicare beneficiaries with major sensory and
physical disabilities are significantly more likely to be dissatisfied with the
care they receive. Their concerns include difficulties accessing care, perceived incomplete understanding by physicians of patients' clinical histories and conditions, lack of thoroughness, and inadequate communication.
These findings held across disabling conditions. People with disabilities are
much more likely than others to lack confidence in their doctors.

The study suggests some of the reasons for dissatisfaction, as well as approaches to care that might improve satisfaction, including facilitating
transportation, communication, and time spent with a physician. Four factors may lead patients with disabilities to need more time with their physicians than patients without disabilities: complex underlying medical conditions, extra knowledge, skill, sensitivity, or time required by clinicians
because of the disabling condition itself; the need to employ special means
to ensure effective communication, such as sign language interpreters or
assistive listening devices; and discordant perceptions and expectations
between physicians and patients, especially around the experience of disability. Other suggestions to improve patient satisfaction include environ-

mental accommodations (e.g., ramps, widened doorways, automatically adjustable examination tables), specialized resources (e.g., large print and Braille written materials, readily available sign language interpreters), and flexible practice policies (e.g., longer appointment times).

Completing the volume, chapter 15 analyzes the possibility that improvements in functional ability may have multiplier effects beyond their impact on those who might otherwise become disabled. In chapter 15, "Interspousal Mortality Effects: Caregiver Burden Across the Spectrum of Disabling Disease," Nicholas Christakis and Paul Allison explore the possible externalities of health and disability on caregivers and others who may be affected by those who are ill or functionally impaired. They hypothesize that the process of caregiving for a loved one, the process of sharing in the illness of a loved one, and even the process of dying have spillover effects from one person to another. The spillover effects might result from the stress imposed by a partner's illness, or the loss of social support that is provided by the partner. The implication of the theory is that improvements to health and functional ability have a multiplier benefit well beyond the individuals affected directly.

To test the theory, Christakis and Allison look at the effect of serious illness on the health and mortality of spouses. They find that certain serious illnesses (stroke, the onset of dementia, and psychiatric disease) can have a significantly detrimental effect on the spouses of those who become ill or functionally impaired. The health impact of being in a caregiving role varied according to the duration of the role, with periods of greatest impact occurring within a few months of spousal hospitalization and a year or more afterward. Christakis and Allison conclude that it may be almost as bad for someone's health to have his or her partner fall ill, especially with certain diseases, as it is for that partner to die. Cancer is less burdensome to caregiving spouses than other conditions, such as dementia.

The results reported in chapter 15 support the idea of an externality, or multiplier impact of illness and disability beyond the individual affected directly, extending to those who care for them. This means that efforts to reduce disease, disability, and death can be self-reinforcing, that medical care has a social value larger than the value to the individual patient, and that the cost-effectiveness of medical interventions should account for both the direct impact on patients and the indirect impact on those who care for them.

Future Research

While there is no shortage of important topics for continuing research, we highlight several themes from the research reported in this volume. One of those themes is the important influence of education on disability trends. Across many of the investigations reported in this volume, education is consistently identified as a significant contributing factor to disability trends. Future work should be done to figure out why education is so important to the likelihood of becoming disabled, and what the strong relationship suggests for future disability trends.

The second theme is to disentangle the complex interrelationship between medical costs and disability trends, an issue that is complicated by the complexity of the causal relationships between them. On the one hand, medical spending is an important causal factor in improving functional health, as advances in medicine and the provision of medical care services prevents, delays, or alleviates the symptoms of potentially disabling medical conditions. Throughout this volume are examples of what medical advances have done to reduce disabilities. Thus, it is clear from our research that medical spending has a role in buying declining disability. On the other hand, those who are less disabled require less medical care, at least in the short term, than those who are more disabled. From the reverse perspective, therefore, better functional health may lead to reduced medical spending in the population as a consequence of disability decline. Both factors are almost certainly part of the relationship, and disentangling them is an important objective of our continuing research effort.

A third theme is to consider more comprehensively the relationship between disability trends and work. Many of the economic costs of disability result from the loss of productive capacity, the loss of income, and the reduced labor force participation of those who develop functional limitations. To what extent might we expect declining disability, in conjunction with modifications to retirement policies, to change work and retirement behavior at older ages? To what extent can the ability to work longer moderate the economic and financial pressures of an aging population?

The fourth and related theme of continuing research is the effect of disability on government finances. For example, what will be the financial impact on Social Security, Disability Insurance, and other income-support programs of enabling people to stay in the workforce longer? Will there be financial benefits to Medicare, Medicaid, and other health programs as a result of lower medical costs and lower caregiving costs from a healthier older population? How will the broader economic and tax implications of a healthier population affect government finances more generally?

The important relationships between education and disability, medical advances and disability, work, population aging, government finances, and the economy are core topics of continuing research interest.

I

Disability Trends

1

The Health of Older Men in the Past

Dora L. Costa

1.1 Introduction

The population of the United States has been rapidly aging—slowly at first, more rapidly recently. In 1910, only 4 percent of the population was older than sixty-four. By 1940 the figure was 7 percent, and by 1990, 13 percent. By 2050 the figure is projected to rise to at least 20 percent (Costa 1998). If life expectancies increase faster than expected, the percentage of the population older than sixty-four in 2050 will be even greater. Vaupel (1991) has argued that children alive today may live ninety on average, or even one hundred years.

What are the consequences of mortality declines for older-age health? Gruenberg (1977) and Verbrugge (1984) have argued that rising longevity may increase both chronic disease and disability rates. Fries' (1980, 1989) theory of the aging process implies that the onset of chronic disease and disability rates can be postponed until the limit of life is reached, thus implying that both chronic disease and disability rates are decreasing. Manton (1982) has argued that even though declines in mortality may increase the prevalence of chronic disease, the rate of progression of chronic disease and therefore of disability may fall.

The empirical evidence available thus far shows that, on the whole, population aging has been accompanied by improvements in elderly chronic disease, disability, and functional limitation rates (for a review of recent

Dora L. Costa is a professor of economics at the University of California, Los Angeles, and a research associate of the National Bureau of Economic Research.

I thank the National Institute on Aging grants P30 AG12810 and R01 AG19805, and the Mary Woodard Lasker Charitable Trust and Michael E. DeBakey Foundation, NIH grants AG19637 and AG10120, the Robert Wood Johnson Foundation, and the Center for Advanced Study in the Behavioral Sciences.

trends see Freedman, Martin, and Schoeni [2002]). Costa (2000) finds that the average decline in chronic respiratory problems, valvular heart disease, arteriosclerosis, and joint and back problems was about 66 percent from the 1900s to the 1970s and 1980s, a decline of 0.7 percent per year. Costa and Steckel (1997) document that weight adjusted for height for older men has increased from dangerously low levels at the turn of the twentieth century. Costa (2002) finds that among men age sixty to seventy-four, functional limitations declined by 0.6 percent per year between 1910 and the 1990s. Improvements in functional limitation rates and also in disability rates accelerated since the 1980s. Functional limitation rates declined by 1.5 percent per year between 1992 and 1996 (Waidmann and Liu 2000) and by 1.3 to 1.6 percent per year between 1984 and 1993 or 1995 (Freedman and Martin 1998, 1999, 2000). Manton, Corder, and Stallard (1997) find that between 1982 and 1989 disability among older individuals declined by 1.1 percent per year and between 1989 and 1994 by 1.5 percent per year. In exactly comparable data for 1994 and 1999, disability declined by 2.1 percent per year (Manton and Gu 2001). Using different data sources and different measures of disability, Cutler and Richardson (1997) find declines of 0.5 to 1.0 percent per year between 1980 and 1990; Freedman and Martin (1998) observe declines of 0.9 to 2.3 percent per year between 1984 and 1993; and Crimmins, Saito, and Reynolds (1997) observe a disability decline of 0.9 percent per year between 1982 and 1993. Comparing the offspring of individuals in the Framingham study with the original cohort shows that among those age fifty-five to seventy, disability has fallen substantially between 1977 and 1994 (Allaire et al. 1999).

This improvement in health has not necessarily been continuous. Costa and Steckel (1997) report that chronic disease rates at older ages were higher for cohorts born between 1840 and 1849 than for those born between 1820 and 1829. Cycles may be present in more recent years as well. Although clinicians' reports document steady improvements in health since the 1970s (Waidmann, Bound, and Schoenbaum 1995), self-reported health declined during the 1970s and 1980s (Freedman and Martin 2000; Chirikos 1986; Colvez and Blanchet 1981; Crimmins 1990; Verbrugge 1984), suggesting either that health awareness has increased or that disability has fallen since the 1980s because of declines in the debilitating effects of chronic conditions. Nonetheless, the overall trend appears to be one of improving health.

This paper uses the records of Union Army veterans to document disease rates in the past and to examine why these disease rates were so high. It focuses on three broad disease states—heart conditions, musculoskeletal problems, and loss of cognitive functioning. Heart conditions and musculoskeletal problems represented the bulk of chronic conditions in the past (and still do today) and mental impairments today represent a large percentage of all medical expenditures. Understanding why disease rates were so high in the past will help us understand why the health and longevity of different cohorts has been rising in the United States and can inform our forecasts of morbidity and mortality trends.

Fogel and Costa (1997) argue that the recent increases in health and in longevity are too rapid to have been caused by genetic or evolutionary change, and that explanations should focus on changes in the physical environment. Many factors could account for changes in the physical environment, including the increased efficacy of medical care, lifestyle changes, rising incomes, and rising educational levels. My focus will be on the role of infectious disease and of occupational stress. My findings thus have implications for countries still undergoing an epidemiological transition, many of whom suffer from the same infectious diseases as the United States in the past and, like the United States in the past, have a high proportion of their population employed as manual laborers.

1.2 Environmental Conditions and Disease Etiology

I study three broad disease states—heart conditions, musculoskeletal problems, and loss of cognitive functioning.[1] Loss of cognitive functioning includes memory loss (which I also consider as a separate category), dementia, senility, depression, psychosis, and hallucinations, as well as other mental problems. The musculoskeletal problems that I consider are arthritis and back problems. The heart diseases that I examine are valvular heart disease, arteriosclerosis, and congestive heart failure. I also examine several symptoms and signs, namely, murmurs, tachycardia, bradycardia, irregular heartbeat, and a bounding pulse.

The diagnosed heart disease of the nineteenth and early twentieth century was primarily valvular, a disease involving any dysfunction or abnormality of the heart valves. In developed countries today ischemic heart disease (involving a weakened heart pump, either due to previous heart attacks or to current blockages of the coronary arteries) is the most common form of heart disease. However, it is unclear whether ischemic heart disease rates were low in the past or were often undiagnosed. Arteriosclerosis, a thickening and hardening of the artery walls, is commonly used as a term for atherosclerosis, in which fat, cholesterol, and other substances accumulate in the walls of arteries, forming plaques, which, when they rupture, cause heart attacks and stroke. However, arteriosclerosis can arise from other disease states such as diabetes mellitus or systemic or local inflammation. Congestive heart failure is a disorder in which the heart loses its ability to pump blood efficiently and which could arise from hypertension, coronary artery disease, or valvular heart disease. Arrythmias such as tachycardia (a

---

1. Details about specific conditions, including common causes, are available from Medlineplus.

faster than normal heartbeat) and bradycardia (a slow heartbeat) can be life threatening and are more likely to occur in individuals with coronary heart disease or heart valve disorders. A bounding (strong and forceful) pulse can indicate high blood pressure or fluid overload, which in turn can be caused by congestive heart failure or aortic valve regurgitation, among other factors. An irregular heartbeat may indicate cardiac rhythm disorders or various other conditions, such as an overactive thyroid, metabolic or respiratory disorders, or even simply stress or anxiety.

Infectious disease plays a role in all three of the disease states that I examine. Rheumatic fever and infective endocarditis are the most common infections causing valvular heart disease. Group A streptococcal bacteria can cause both scarlet fever and acute rheumatic fever (which may follow scarlet fever). Rheumatic heart disease—the acute involvement of the heart (carditis)—results from rheumatic fever, but in about half of all cases will develop in the absence of any history of acute rheumatic fever, having been initiated by streptococcal infection (Benedek 1993). Those with a history of rheumatic fever are at greater risk of infective endocarditis, an infection and inflammation of the inner membrane of heart tissue. The end result of rheumatic fever or rheumatic heart disease is damage to the heart valves, primarily the mitral and aortic valve.

Both scarlet fever and rheumatic fever were common childhood illness in the United States in the nineteenth and early twentieth century, and rheumatic fever was the second most common cause of death among children age ten to nineteen as late as 1940 (Wolff 1948). Death rates from rheumatic and scarlet fever were very high at the beginning of the twentieth century, fluctuating considerably from year to year, but then falling beginning in the mid-1910s (see figs. 1.1 and 1.2). However, death rates from rheumatic fever remained high among children throughout the 1910s and 1920s. Salicylic acid was shown to be effective in the treatment of rheumatic fever in 1876 and was replaced by the better-tasting aspirin, first manufactured in 1889 (Vane 2000). From 1940 onward, as the link between streptococcal infections (treated with sulfa drugs and later with penicillin) and rheumatic fever became well established, deaths from rheumatic fever fell steadily for all age groups. Collins (1946) shows that the case rate of scarlet fever did not change from circa 1900 to 1945, but that case fatality rates fell sharply with the introduction of sulfa drugs in the late 1930s. Chapin (1926) hypothesized that earlier declines may have been due to decreases in the virulence of scarlet fever, perhaps because the adoption of effective isolation practices eliminated the more severe strains.

Special surveys and military examinations provide information about the incidence, history, and prevalence of scarlet fever, rheumatic fever, rheumatic heart disease, and valvular heart disease. Survey data from 1928–1931 reveal that 12 percent of those age twenty to twenty-four had ever had scarlet fever, most commonly prior to age fifteen (see table 1.1).

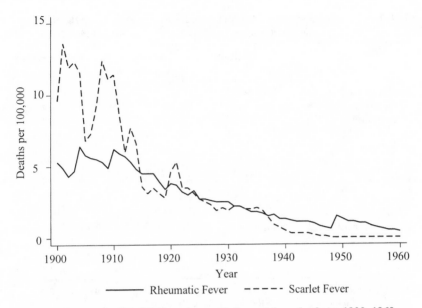

Fig. 1.1 Deaths per 100,000 from rheumatic fever and scarlet fever, 1900–1960

Note: Deaths are for death registrations states only. From various issues of *Vital Statistics of the United States.*

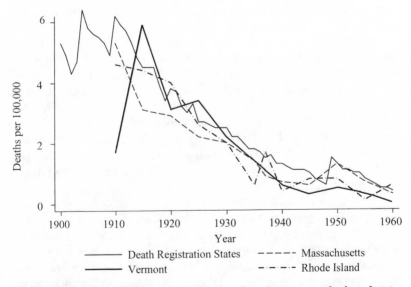

Fig. 1.2 Deaths from rheumatic fever, death registration states and selected states

Note: From various issues of *Vital Statistics of the United States.*

Table 1.1   Incidence and history of rheumatic fever, scarlet fever, and heart disease
                   among white children (rates per 1000), 1928–1931 and 1935–1936

	Ever had, living	Ever had, living and dead	Annual incidence in survey year
Rheumatic fever, 1935–1936			
Age 20–24	6.9	8.5	0.3
Age 15–19	5.3	6.0	0.4
Under age 15	3.2	3.4	5.6
Scarlet fever, 1928–1931			
Age 20–24	118.7		
Age 15–19	129.7		
Scarlet fever, 1935–1936			
Age 15–19	112.0		2.1
Under age 15	78.0		10.8
Heart disease, 1935–1936			
Age 20–24			0.8
Age 15–19			0.8
Under age 15			0.9

Notes: The rates for ever had for 1928–1931 are based upon a survey of 9,000 families as reported in Collins (1938) and those for 1935–1936 are based upon mother's answers to the survey question of the 1936 Communicable Disease Study as reported in Collins (1946, 1947) and Collins and Councell (1943). Past histories of rheumatic fever are for the children of the native-born. The living and dead category includes children who died of rheumatic fever and who, if they had survived, would have been age 20–24 in 1936. Annual incidence rates in the survey year are based both the 1936 Communicable Disease Study and upon the 1935–1936 National Health Survey as reported in Collins (1946, 1947) and Collins and Councell (1943). Annual incidence rates for heart disease are based upon the National Health Survey as reported in Collins (1947).

Table 1.1 also shows that less than 1 percent of those age twenty to twenty-four in 1935–1936 reported ever having had rheumatic fever. However, physical examinations of Connecticut seventh graders in 1934 and 1940 suggest much higher rates of rheumatic heart disease—4 percent in industrial cities, 3 percent in semi-industrial cities, and 1 percent in rural towns (Paul and Deutsch 1941). Among the young men examined for military service, 3 percent had valvular heart disease during World War I and 2 percent had either valvular heart disease or rheumatic heart disease during World War II (see table 1.2).

Other infectious diseases that affect cardiac functioning include late-stage syphilis, measles, and typhoid fever. Studies of typhoid and measles patients in developing countries reveal electrocardiogram abnormalities (Khosla 1981; Olowu and Taiwo 1990). Measles and diphtheria can lead to myocarditis. Tertiary (late-stage) syphilis can result in aortitis and aneurisms. Infections that have been implicated in atherosclerosis include helicobacter pylori, a bacterium that causes gastritis and stomach ailments; chlamdyia pneumonia, a bacterium that causes acute upper and lower respiratory infections; Coxsackie B4 virus, generally causing symptoms no

Table 1.2   Rheumatic heart disease and valvular heart disease rates per 1,000 men
                  examined for military service, World War I and World War II

	Acute rheumatic fever	Rheumatic heart disease	Valvular heart disease
WWI			32.1
WWII			
19,923 men prior to May 31, 1941		2.5	18.2
Nov. 1940–Sept. 1941			
All races	0.1	3.5	12.6
Whites	0.1	3.8	12.7
Blacks	0.0	1.5	11.7
Apr. 1942–Dec. 1943		3.6	12.9
All races		3.6	12.9
Whites		4.0	12.6
Blacks		1.2	15.0

Sources: Love and Davenport (1920); U. S. Selective Service System (1941, 1943, 1944).

Note: Valvular diseases of the heart include aortic insufficiency, aortic stenosis, mitral insufficiency, mitral stenosis, combined aortic and mitral lesions, pulmonic lesions, tricuspid lesions, and unclassified valvular lesions. This category excludes unspecified murmurs. Adding unspecified murmurs would increase the rate per 1,000 from 12.6 to 24.9 for Nov. 1940–Sept. 1941.

more serious than a common cold or sore throat; and some herpes viridae (see reviews by Lindholt et al. 1999; Valtonen 1991; Wong, Gallagher, and Ward 1999). The evidence linking chlamdyia pneumonia to atherosclerosis is the strongest; however, helicobacter pylori infection may be especially harmful when folate absorption is reduced, either because of decreased consumption of ascorbic acid or of folates (Markle 1997).

Estimates of prevalence rates in the first half of the twentieth century exist for some of the commonly recognized infections. Among those older than sixty-four interviewed in health surveys conducted in 1928–1931, 11 percent reported having had typhoid fever at some point in their lives and 8 percent reported having had diphtheria (Collins 1936, 1937). These numbers are probably underestimates. Tests in three cities in the 1920s showed that nearly 60 percent of adults had acquired immunity to diphtheria prior to any artificial immunization (cited in Collins 1937). Venereal disease was also widespread. At least 3 percent of men examined for military service during World War I had venereal diseases (Love and Davenport 1920) and reexaminations yielded higher prevalence rates, showing that 5 percent of men entering the army had syphilis and 23 percent had gonorrhea (Brandt 1987). The more careful examinations done by the military services during World War II included serological tests, and found that 4 percent of men had syphilis (U.S. Selective Service System 1943).

The writings of settlers allow us to trace the history of what has been described as "*the* United States disease of the late nineteenth century"—malaria (Innes 1993). Often confused with typhoid fever, even in the early twentieth century, and sometimes even confused with yellow fever and influenza, two malarial strains were common in the United States. Vivax malaria, introduced to local mosquitoes by European colonists in the early seventeenth century, spread into the upper Mississippi Valley as far north as Canada. The more malignant falciparum malaria, introduced by African slaves in the late seventeenth century, became the dominant strain in southern states such as South Carolina or Georgia that were south of the thirty-fifth parallel (Innes 1993; Humphreys 2001). Settlement of the Midwest caused an initial upsurge in malaria, followed by stability in the 1850s, and then another upsurge as the Civil War brought men into endemic regions and returned them to their local communities as carriers to start epidemics in areas that had been free of malaria for many years. By the 1880s and 1890s malaria in the upper Mississippi Valley began to recede as drainage efforts reduced mosquito breeding sites, the installation of screens on homes reduced transmission to human hosts, a growing livestock population diverted mosquitoes from human to animal hosts, and as transportation moved from water to rail (Ackernecht 1945; Humphreys 2001). Malaria then became solely a problem of the South, where it remained a problem in rural areas even into the 1940s. By World War II, blood tests of men examined for military service revealed that zero percent of the U.S. population was infected (U.S. Selective Service System 1943).

In modern populations lasting cardiac damage due to malaria is rare, but in some cases falciparum malaria can lead to myocarditis and persistent tachycardia (Charles and Bertrand 1982). Excessive doses of quinine, widely used in the nineteenth century to alleviate recurrent attacks of vivax malaria (but which only cures falciparum), can lead to fatal cardiotoxicity and produces cardiac symptoms such as tachycardia and bradycardia, particularly in patients with renal insufficiency or hypokaliemia (Charles and Bertrand 1982).

Both infectious disease and mechanical work stress play a role in musculoskeletal conditions. The joint inflammation of arthritis can result from a bacterial or viral infection, an autoimmune disease (rheumatoid arthritis), mechanical injury to a joint, or mechanical wear and tear that breaks down the joint cartilege (osteoarthritis). Musculoskeletal symptoms are common with many infections, including malaria, syphilis, rheumatic fever, influenza, variola, vaccinia, gonorrhea, mumps, and tuberculosis. With some injuries and diseases, the inflammation may never go away or may cause permanent damage.

Disease and injury can also cause brain damage. Common causes of memory loss include stroke, head trauma, epileptic seizures, brain infections such as herpes encephalitis, and Alzheimer's disease. Less common causes include cerebral malaria, which often results in damage to the subcortical white matter and the fronto-temporal areas of the neocortex, leading to depression, poor memory, personality change, and irritability and violence (Varney et al. 1997). Typhoid fever is accompanied by delirium, hallucinations, fluctuating moods, confusion, attention deficit disorder, and encephalitis (in rare cases) Ali et al. 1997). Encephalitis is also a rare complication of measles (Bergen 1998). Tuberculosis can involve the central nervous system in the form of subacute meningitis or intracerebral granulomas and result in focal epilepsy (Bergen 1998). Tyas et al. (2001) found that individuals who had received vaccinations for either influenza, tetanus, polio, or diphtheria faced less risk of Alzheimer's disease. Another cause of long-term memory loss is exposure to poisonous fumes (Tyas et al. 2001; Kishi et al. 1993). In addition, most studies find that individuals with fewer years of schooling are at greater risk of Alzheimer's disease (e.g., Tyas et al. 2001) and are less able to recover cognitive functioning after a stroke.

Some of the risk factors for memory loss were greater among Americans of the nineteenth and early twentieth centuries than among Americans today. Risk of death from violence fell from 1900 to 1960, regardless of whether homicide deaths are counted, suggesting that the risk of injury in both the workplace and the home has declined. Mortality from stroke in the past was also high. Ten percent of Union Army veterans age fifty to sixty-four in 1900 were dead of stroke by 1917. In contrast, a seventeen-year follow-up of Americans of the same age alive in the early 1970s showed no stroke deaths (Costa 2003). Stroke survival in 1900 was rare, but those who did survive were much more disabled than stroke survivors today. Having had a stroke increased the probability of paralysis by 0.7 among Union Army veterans age sixty to seventy-four in 1910, but among Americans in the late 1980s and early 1990s this probability increased by only 0.1 (Costa 2002).

Higher socioeconomic status has historically enabled men to buy less-crowded housing, cleaner food and water, warmer clothes and shelter, more and better food, and less work away from home for pregnant women or mothers with small children. However, the evidence on the impact of income on mortality (for which I have much more extensive information than health) in historical United States populations is mixed. Wealth conveyed no systematic advantage for the survival of women and children in households matched in the 1850 and 1860 censuses (Steckel 1988). Preston and Haines (1991) used the question on the number of children ever born and the number of children still living in the 1900 census to report that place of residence and race were the most important correlates of child survival in the late nineteenth century, much more important than fathers' occupation. In contrast, early researchers emphasized the importance of social class. Rochester (1923) reported that within the high disease environment of U.S. cities there was a steep gradient between infant mortality and family income. Chapin (1924) reported that in Providence, Rhode Island in

1865 the annual crude death rate for taxpayers was eleven per thousand, while the corresponding rate for nontaxpayers was twenty-five per thousand. Recent research has also emphasized the importance of social class to mortality in past populations. Costa and Lahey (2005) found that among Union Army veterans observed at ages sixty to seventy-four, those of higher lifelong socioeconomic status were favored in survival. Ferrie (2003) linked households in 1850 and 1860 to one-year mortality rates as reported in the 1850 and 1860 censuses of mortality, and found a wealth gradient in rural areas of the United States. Those with greater personal property wealth were less likely to die from any cause and were less likely to die from consumption, a disease associated with crowding and poor housing. They were not more likely to die of cholera, a disease spread through contaminated water supplies, at a time when individuals did not know how to protect themselves.

The sample that I study—Union Army veterans—faced many unnatural situations during the course of their military service. The total number of deaths in the Civil War equaled the total number killed in almost all other U.S. wars combined, and more than one out of every five white men participating died, over half of them from disease (Vinovskis 1990). Union Army veterans who lived to 1910 had seen, on average, 13 percent of the men within their companies die during the war. In one company over half of the men died during the war. In addition, 4 percent of these survivors had personally experienced head injuries and had also experienced very high disease incidence. Twenty-nine percent of them had had diarrhea, 14 percent had had respiratory ailments, 12 percent had had rheumatic fever or experienced rheumatic athropathies, 6 percent had had measles, and another 6 percent had had typhoid (see table 1.3). Although according to wartime records only 4 percent of men had had malaria, records of the examining surgeons suggest that by 1910 7 percent had had malaria and 8 percent another fever (see table 1.3). Infectious diseases acquired in the army may have been more severe than those acquired in civilian life if repeated rapid passage increased the virulence of infectious agents. Contemporary observers noted that measles among Civil War troops was a much severer infection than that witnessed in the civilian population, often followed by such complications as chronic bronchitis, pneumonia, pleurisy, chronic diarrhea, and general debility (Cliff, Haggett, and Smallman-Raynor 1993).

Men who had been prisoners of war, as was true for 9 percent of those who survived to 1910, may have been at particularly high risk. Studies of World War II and Korean War POWs suggest that some of the sequelae of acute malnutrition include higher risks of death from ischemic heart disease, particularly after age seventy-five (Page and Brass 2001; Page and Ostfeld 1994), greater prevalence rates for duodenal ulcer and strongyloidiasis (Goulston et al. 1985), for neurological disorders (Gibberd and

Table 1.3   **History of infectious disease (rates per 1000), Union Army veterans age
60–79 in 1910**

	Rate/1,000
During War	
Diarrhea	292.7
Malaria	35.4
Respiratory	141.5
Measles	63.4
Tuberculosis	16.9
Typhoid	60.8
Rheumatic fever or rheumatic athropathies	115.0
Stomach ailments	15.7
Syphilis	13.6
Ever noted by examining surgeon	
Malaria	69.0
Any fevers, including scarlet fever, but excluding those due to malaria, typhoid, measles, rubella, mumps, and meningitis	75.5

Simmonds 1980), and for psychiatric problems, particularly psychoneurosis (Beebe 1975).

Thus far I have stressed the positive relationship between early life conditions and chronic disease at older ages, but the relationship could be negative as well. If genetic susceptibility to death from infectious disease or other insults at early ages is positively correlated with genetic susceptibilty to develop chronic disease at older ages, then, because fewer genetically frail individuals survive to old age, the morbidity rate of such a cohort may be lower relative to a cohort in which more genetically frail individuals survive. Additionally, cohorts who survive infectious disease may acquire partial or complete immunity and therefore may have lower mortality rates. Lee (2003) finds that under the extreme disease conditions of Union Army camp life, growing up in a large city (an extremely unhealthy locale circa 1860) relative to an isolated rural area had a beneficial mortality effect, because men from isolated areas lacked immunities to the diseases that ravaged Union Army camps. However, Costa (2003) and Costa and Lahey (2003) find that among soldiers who survived until 1900 or 1910, those who had grown up in a large city faced a shorter old age.

1.2.1   Data

The data used in this paper are drawn from the military records of the Union Army and from the Union Army pension program.[2] This pension program was the most widespread form of assistance to the elderly prior to

2. The data are available from http://www.cpe.uchicago.edu/ and were collected by a team led by Robert Fogel.

Social Security, covering 90 percent of all veterans by 1910 and benefiting an estimated 25 percent of the population older than sixty-four, whether as a couple consisting of the former soldier and his wife, the single or widowed veteran, or the widows of veterans (Costa 1998).

The Union Army pension program began in 1862, when Congress established the basic system of pension laws, known as the General Law pension system, to provide pensions to both regular and volunteer recruits who were severely disabled as a direct result of military service (see Costa 1998) for a history of the Union Army pension program). The Union Army pension program became a universal disability and old-age pension program for veterans with the passage of the Act of June 27, 1890, which specified that any disability entitled the veteran to a pension. Even though old age was not recognized by statute law as sufficient cause to qualify for a pension until 1907, the Pension Bureau instructed the examining surgeons in 1890 to grant a minimum pension to all men at least sixty-five years of age unless they were unusually vigorous. Veterans, however, had every incentive to undergo a complete examination, because those with a severe chronic condition, particularly if it could be traced to wartime experience, were eligible for larger pensions. The surgeons rated the severity of specific conditions using detailed guidelines provided by the Pension Bureau.

Copious records were generated by the Union Army pension program. Pension applications included detailed medical examinations, both for men whose pension application or bid for a pension increase was rejected and for men whose applications were accepted. These records have been linked to the 1900 and 1910 censuses, which provide occupational information. The sample was drawn as a cluster sample of companies (roughly 100 men) and includes all enlisted men within a company. All men were linked to military records, which provide information on stress at young adult ages, such as prisoner of war status, whether the soldier was ever discharged for disability, and such illnesses as measles, diarrhea, tuberculosis, typhoid, rheumatism, acute respiratory infections (e.g., pneumonia, bronchitis), malaria, and war injuries. About 2 percent of these men were not yet collecting a pension in 1910, either because their applications had been rejected or because they had not yet applied for a pension. A surgeon's exam is available for 93 percent of all men who had a pension in 1910. Men for whom a surgeon's exam is missing tended to be men who entered at a late age and received a pension on the basis of age. I restrict the sample to men with a surgeon's record because I am interested in analyzing the effect of a specific condition as noted by the examining surgeon on later health outcomes. When I redefine my health outcome variables by assuming that men without a surgeon's exam had no chronic conditions, the conclusions I draw from my regression analyses about the importance of infectious disease, socioeconomic factors, and other variables remain unchanged.

Men who entered the Union Army were probably healthier than the population as a whole. An examination of men who were rejected for military service suggests that mean height for the population was about 0.18 inches less than the mean of the recruits. Once men entered the service, rural farmers, who were the better-nourished segment of society, were more likely to die, because they lacked immunities to such common camp diseases as measles and typhoid (Lee 1997). However, men who survived the war (regardless of occupation) were only 0.02 inches shorter than all recruits at enlistment, suggesting that the war itself induced minimal survivorship selection on the basis of height and hence on early net nutritional status. Increased exposure to disease probably left men in worse health than when they entered the army, but by age fifty even men who had grown up in rural areas and had not served had probably been exposed to as many infectious diseases as veterans because of increased migration. Although little is known about the experience of Union Army veterans from the time they left the service until they appear on the pension rolls, several tests indicate that this sample is representative of the general population before the war in terms of wealth and circa 1900 in terms of mortality experience.[3]

I use the descriptions of the examining surgeons for heart, musculoskeletal, neurological, and infectious disease disorders. For heart disease the physician described pulse rate and heartbeat characteristics; whether a murmur was present and its timing, type, and location, and which valves were involved; whether there was enlargement, oedema, cyanosis, dyspnoea, or arteriosclerosis. I define valvular heart disease as any mention of either mitral or aortic valve murmurs. I define congestive heart failure as the contemporaneous mention of edema, cyanosis, and dyspne.[4] Note that arteriosclerosis refers to peripheral arteriosclerosis (symptomatic not just of atherosclerosis but also of diabetes or inflammation). Descriptions of rheumatism include where the rheumatism was located and whether pain, tenderness, swelling, or crepitation was associated with the joint. Descriptions of nervous system disorders include descriptions of balance, aphasia, paralysis, reflexes, neuralgia, vertigo, headaches, seizures, memory loss, and any indications of loss of mental power, including mental illness. Descriptions of infectious disease include both diseases suffered while in the army and also diseases suffered while out of the army, including current ill-

3. Among all adult males age twenty and over in the households to which recruits were linked in the 1860 census, mean wealth was similar to that found in a random sample, suggesting that military service was not very selective of men of lower socioeconomic status. In fact, 95 percent of the sample consisted of volunteers. Cohort life expectancies of veterans who reached age sixty between 1901 and 1910 resemble the cohort life expectancies found in genealogies, and the distribution of deaths from specific causes for all veterans who died between 1905 and 1915 does not differ significantly from the distribution of expected number of deaths from those causes in the death registration states in 1910 (Costa 1998).

4. Although more restrictive definitions are possible (e.g., in the case of congestive heart failure, including cardiomegaly as a criterion and excluding coexisting respiratory infection and asthma), the results are robust to minor variations in definitions.

nesses. I use these descriptions of infectious disease as explanatory variables, classifying them into malaria and into descriptions of any fever, including scarlet fever.

With the exception of my infectious disease category, the symptoms, signs, and conditions that I examine did not require any diagnostic equipment that was unavailable to late nineteenth-century physicians. Because nineteenth-century definitions were looser and because nineteenth-century physicians were more accustomed to direct observation, this may bias past prevalence rates upward relative to recent prevalence rates. However, after 1907, when men received a pension on the basis of age, prevalence rates in the Union Army sample are likely to be understated. Prevalence rates may also be underestimated in the Union Army sample because men may have developed a condition between the time of the last exam and 1910 (see Costa 2000 and 2002 for a discussion of potential biases).

The disease reports from soldiers' military records tend to be terse, one- or two-word descriptions. I classify rheumatic fever and rheumatic athropathies as one category because the common description *rheumatism* could refer to either rheumatic fever, an underlying chronic condition, traumatic arthritis, or any viral infection accompanied by arthritic symptoms. The reports submitted by camp doctors to the surgeon general distinguish between acute and chronic rheumatism, and these suggest that 40 percent of all cases of rheumatism were acute and were mainly caused by rheumatic fever. However, some of the chronic cases may have been prolonged acute rheumatic fever (Bollet 1991).

Health Trends at Older Ages

Union Army veterans were already disabled by chronic conditions by age fifty. Among those on the pension rolls and with a surgeon's exam by 1895 (when program eligibility had already been broadened), 16 percent of men age fifty to fifty-nine had valvular heart disease and 44 percent of men in that age group had joint problems. As Union Army veterans aged, the burden of disability rose. By ages sixty-five to seventy-four, 29 percent had valvular heart disease, 10 percent had congestive heart failure, 13 percent had arteriosclerosis, 59 percent had joint problems, 51 percent had back problems, and 4 percent had memory loss (see table 1.4).

Compared to white men examined in the National Health and Nutrition Examination Surveys (NHANES), Union Army veterans aged prematurely by ten to twenty years. By ages sixty-five to seventy-four, Union Army veterans had the congestive heart failure rates of seventy-five to eighty-four-year-old men in the 1988–1994 NHANES III. Their rates of valvular heart disease at ages fifty to fifty-nine were already more than twice those of sixty-five to seventy-four-year olds in the 1976–1980 NHANES II (see fig. 1.3). At ages fifty-five to sixty-four, Union Army veterans looked like seventy-five to eighty-four-year-old men in 1988–1994 in

Table 1.4　　　　　Prevalence rates (%) among Union Army veterans by year and age

	Year (Age)						
	1895 (50–59)	1900 (55–64)	1905 (60–69)	1910 (65–74)	1915 (70–79)	1920 (75–84)	1925 (80–89)
Heart							
Murmur	26.99	35.34	42.42	44.77	44.24	44.48	51.48
Valvular	15.49	21.76	27.16	28.93	28.64	28.66	33.27
Congestive heart failure	0.59	3.82	7.99	10.18	10.20	10.05	11.61
Arteriosclerosis	0.95	2.12	6.57	10.79	12.79	14.93	28.44
Tachycardia	20.11	24.71	29.96	31.83	31.26	31.49	32.87
Bradychardia	2.58	3.67	5.00	5.70	6.17	5.98	7.38
Bounding pulse	8.77	12.19	16.49	17.35	17.17	16.77	15.75
Irregular heart rate	31.18	40.65	48.52	51.01	51.33	51.39	57.87
Musculoskeletal							
Joint problems	43.56	51.64	57.77	59.06	58.72	58.26	59.94
Back problems	36.00	43.57	49.58	50.91	50.62	50.65	49.80
Cognitive							
All mental problems	6.54	8.16	10.30	11.31	11.19	12.89	20.18
Memory loss	1.38	2.35	3.39	3.54	3.76	4.63	6.20

Note: Estimated for all men who were on the pension rolls in 1895 and with a surgeon's exam by 1895.

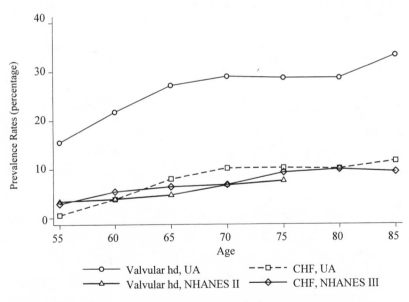

Fig. 1.3　Heart disease rates by age, Union Army veterans and white men in NHANES II and III

Note: Valvular heart disease rates in NHANES II are physician-reported. Congestive heart failure rates in NHANES III are self-reported. Disease rates in the Union Army are physician-reported. All NHANES rates are weighted using examination or interview weights. Ages are centered at the marks around a ten year age interval.

terms of joint problems (see fig. 1.4). At age fifty to fifty-nine they looked like sixty-five to seventy-four-year-old men in 1976–1980 in terms of back problems (see fig. 1.5).

Variation in chronic disease prevalence rates within the Union Army sample by infectious disease rates and by occupational class was even greater than variation in prevalence rates across the Union Army and more recent samples. Figures 1.6–1.8 show that men who were professionals and proprietors circa 1900 had the lowest rates of valvular heart disease, joint problems, and back problems at all ages than all other occupational groups. In the case of joint and back problems, at no age did professionals and proprietors ever resemble those in manual labor in terms of chronic conditions. Figures 1.9–1.11 show that those men who had had rheumatic fever during the war faced much higher prevalence rates of valvular heart disease, joint problems, and back problems at all ages than those who had not had rheumatic fever. A sixty-year-old man who had had rheumatic fever had a slightly higher prevalence rate of valvular heart disease than a seventy-year-old man who had not had rheumatic fever. A sixty-five-year-old man who had had rheumatic fever had a slightly higher prevalence rate than an eighty-five-year-old who had not had rheumatic fever. In the case of joint and back problems, at no age did those who had not had rheumatic fever have prevalence rates as high as those who had had rheumatic fever.

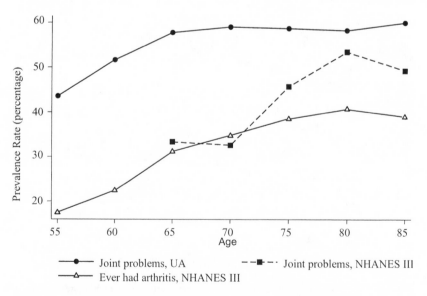

Fig. 1.4   Joint problems by age, Union Army veterans and white men in NHANES III

Note: Joint problems are physician-reported. "Ever had arthritis" is self-reported. Disease rates in the Union Army are physician-reported. All NHANES figures are weighted using examination or interview weights. Ages are centered at the marks around a ten year age interval.

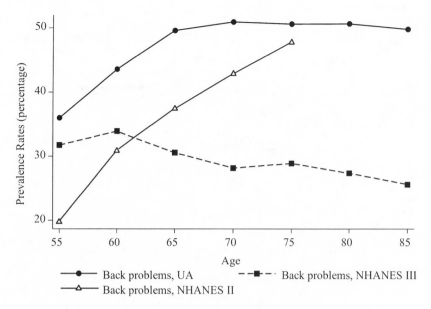

Fig. 1.5 Back problems by age, Union Army veterans and White Men in NHANES II and NHANES III

Note: Back problems in NHANES II are physician-reported. Back problems in NHANES III are self-reported. Disease rates in the Union Army are physician-reported. All NHANES figures are weighted using examination or interview weights. Ages are centered at the marks around a ten year age interval.

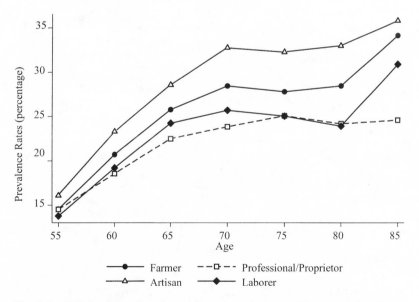

Fig. 1.6 Valvular heart disease prevalence rates by age and by occupational class circa 1900

Note: Ages are centered at the marks around a ten year interval.

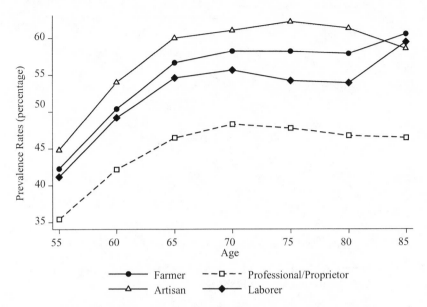

Fig. 1.7   Joint problems prevalence rates by age and by occupational class circa 1900

Note: Ages are centered at the marks around a ten year age interval.

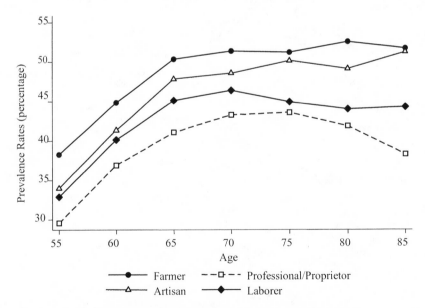

Fig. 1.8   Back problems prevalence rates by age and by occupational class circa 1900

Note: Ages are centered at the marks around a ten year age interval.

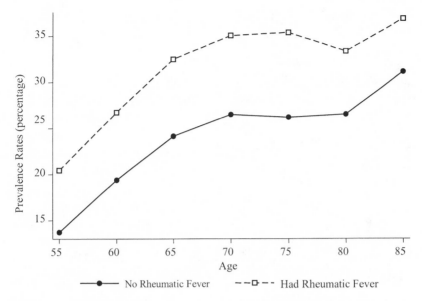

Fig. 1.9   Valvular heart disease prevalence rates by age and whether had rheumatic fever during the Civil War

Note: Ages are centered at the marks around a ten year age interval.

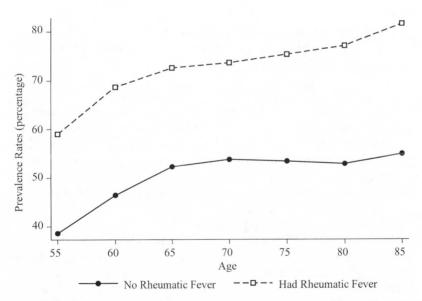

Fig. 1.10   Joint problems prevalence rates by age and whether had rheumatic fever during the Civil War

Note: Ages are centered at the marks around a ten year age interval.

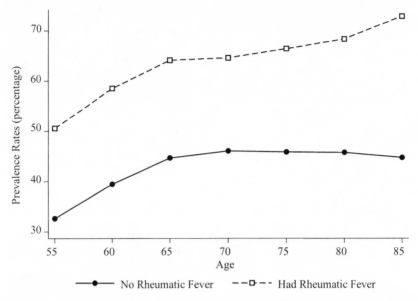

Fig. 1.11   Back problems prevalence rates by age and whether had rheumatic fever during the Civil War

Note: Ages are centered at the marks around a ten year age interval.

Results

I use probit regressions to determine what factors predicted the probability that a veteran would have one of three disease states in 1910. That is, I run regressions of the form

$$\Pr(I = 1) = \Pr(\varepsilon < X' \beta) = \Phi (X' \beta)$$

where $I = 1$ if a veteran had a specific chronic condition, sign, or symptom associated with one of the three disease states, $\Phi()$ is a standard normal cumulative distribution function, and **X** is a vector of control variables. The dependent variables are equal to 1 if the veteran has one of the following specific chronic conditions, signs, or symptoms: a heart murmur, valvular heart disease, arteriosclerosis, congestive heart failure, an irregular pulse, tachycardia, bradychardia, a bounding pulse, joint problems, back problems, any mental problems, and memory loss.

Rheumatic fever during wartime and an examining surgeon's record of either malaria or other infectious diseases increase the probability of heart disease, signs, or symptoms for all of our disease states among Union Army veterans age sixty to seventy-nine in 1910 (see tables 1.5 and 1.6). Having had rheumatic fever during the war increased the probability of valvular heart disease by 0.08 and the probability of both arteriosclerosis and congestive heart failure by 0.05. Having had malaria increased the

Table 1.5 Selected cardiovascular condition probits (marginal effects), Union Army veterans age 60–79 in 1910

	Murmur		Valvular		Arteriosclerosis		CHF	
	$\dfrac{\partial P}{\partial x}$	Standard Error	$\dfrac{\partial P}{\partial x}$	Standard Error	$\dfrac{\partial P}{\partial x}$	Standard Error	$\dfrac{\partial P}{\partial x}$	Standard Error
Dummy = 1 if occupation at enlistment								
Farmer								
Professional or proprietor	-0.062***	0.023	-0.042*	0.022	-0.027*	0.015	-0.032**	0.013
Artisan	-0.075***	0.018	-0.043**	0.017	-0.009	0.011	-0.017	0.010
Laborer	-0.039**	0.016	-0.005	0.017	0.012	0.011	-0.010	0.011
Dummy = 1 if occupation circa 1900								
Farmer								
Professional or proprietor	-0.040**	0.017	-0.032**	0.016	-0.006	0.011	-0.017*	0.010
Artisan	0.031*	0.019	0.034*	0.019	-0.000	0.013	-0.009	0.011
Laborer	-0.000	0.016	-0.008	0.014	0.007	0.009	-0.008	0.009
Logarithm of personal wealth in 1860	-0.003	0.003	0.003	0.003	-0.000	0.002	-0.004**	0.002
Dummy = 1 if writes	-0.010	0.026	-0.043*	0.023	-0.016	0.016	-0.012	0.017
Dummy = 1 if city size								
50,000+	0.007	0.017	-0.018	0.016	0.005	0.009	0.018*	0.011
25,000–50,000	-0.018	0.033	-0.005	0.031	0.009	0.019	-0.000	0.020
2,500–25,000	0.011	0.018	-0.007	0.018	0.028***	0.011	0.009	0.011
< 2,500								
Dummy = 1 if in war had								
Diarrhea	0.023*	0.014	-0.002	0.012	0.002	0.007	0.007	0.007
Malaria	-0.018	0.032	0.011	0.029	-0.010	0.017	0.003	0.018

(continued)

Table 1.5 (continued)

	Murmur		Valvular		Arteriosclerosis		CHF	
	$\frac{\partial P}{\partial x}$	Standard Error	$\frac{\partial P}{\partial x}$	Standard Error	$\frac{\partial P}{\partial x}$	Standard Error	$\frac{\partial P}{\partial x}$	Standard Error
Respiratory infection	0.035**	0.017	0.035**	0.016	0.002	0.011	0.023*	0.011
Measles	−0.034	0.023	−0.022	0.021	−0.008	0.014	−0.016	0.013
Tuberculosis	0.062	0.040	−0.016	0.035	0.011	0.027	0.022	0.027
Typhoid	0.011	0.027	0.023	0.024	0.000	0.014	0.012	0.015
Rheumatic fever	0.112***	0.019	0.075***	0.018	0.053***	0.012	0.051***	0.013
Stomach ailments	0.077	0.047	0.039	0.043	0.065**	0.035	0.038	0.033
Syphilis	0.031	0.053	−0.027	0.043	0.039	0.034	−0.037	0.023
Dummy = 1 if surgeons found evidence								
Malaria	0.161***	0.023	0.137***	0.022	0.042***	0.017	0.058***	0.020
Other infections	0.071***	0.021	0.084***	0.019	0.042***	0.013	0.045***	0.015
Proportion of company who died	0.046	0.080	0.034	0.091	−0.029	0.051	0.010	0.052
Dummy = 1 if POW	0.045**	0.022	0.057***	0.021	0.013	0.014	0.009	0.014
Pseudo R^2	0.022		0.018		0.020		0.027	
Observed P	0.436		0.285		0.103		0.095	
Observations	7,349		7,349		7,349		7,349	

Note: Robust standard errors, clustering on the company. Additional control variables include a dummy equal to 1 if the veteran was ever wounded in the war, dummies for quarter of birth, a dummy if occupation circa 1900 was unknown, and dummies if the individual was not linked to the 1900 or 1860 census.

*** Significant at the 1 percent level.
** Significant at the 5 percent level.
* Significant at the 10 percent level.

Table 1.6 Selected heart rate and pulse characteristic probits (marginal effects), Union Army veterans age 60–79 in 1910

	Irregular		Tachycardia		Bradycardia		Bounding	
	$\frac{\partial P}{\partial x}$	Standard Error	$\frac{\partial P}{\partial x}$	Standard Error	$\frac{\partial P}{\partial x}$	Standard Error	$\frac{\partial P}{\partial x}$	Standard Error
Dummy = 1 if occupation at enlistment								
Farmer								
Professional or proprietor	-0.044	0.028	0.022	0.027	-0.009	0.010	-0.041**	0.017
Artisan	-0.081***	0.022	0.006	0.019	-0.021***	0.007	-0.014	0.015
Laborer	-0.025**	0.021	-0.039***	0.016	0.004	0.008	-0.017	0.014
Dummy = 1 if occupation circa 1900								
Farmer								
Professional or proprietor	-0.047***	0.019	-0.005	0.017	-0.005	0.008	0.037***	0.013
Artisan	-0.005	0.022	0.010	0.019	0.007	0.009	0.004	0.015
Laborer	-0.022*	0.017	0.016	0.015	0.000	0.007	0.010	0.012
Logarithm of personal wealth in 1860	-0.012***	0.003	-0.010***	0.003	-0.002*	0.001	-0.004*	0.002
Dummy = 1 if writes	-0.038	0.027	-0.017	0.023	-0.004	0.011	-0.014	0.019
Dummy = 1 if city size								
50,000+	-0.017	0.018	-0.010	0.016	-0.001	0.007	0.008	0.012
25,000–50,000	-0.101***	0.028	-0.099***	0.032	-0.000	0.014	-0.001	0.024
2,500–25,000	-0.020	0.021	-0.003	0.017	0.000	0.007	0.017	0.015
< 2,500								
Dummy = 1 if in war had								
Diarrhea	0.029**	0.013	0.010	0.012	0.004	0.006	0.011	0.009
Malaria	-0.000	0.036	-0.002	0.029	0.001	0.013	-0.026	0.019
Respiratory infection	0.037**	0.017	0.036***	0.015	0.005	0.008	0.025	0.013

(continued)

Table 1.6 (continued)

	Irregular		Tachycardia		Bradycardia		Bounding	
	$\frac{\partial P}{\partial x}$	Standard Error	$\frac{\partial P}{\partial x}$	Standard Error	$\frac{\partial P}{\partial x}$	Standard Error	$\frac{\partial P}{\partial x}$	Standard Error
Measles	0.001	0.023	0.008	0.023	0.007	0.011	0.018	0.019
Tuberculosis	0.047	0.044	0.034	0.041	-0.015	0.016	0.007	0.034
Typhoid	0.028	0.024	0.019	0.024	-0.007	0.010	0.011	0.018
Rheumatic fever	0.101***	0.018	0.070***	0.018	0.016*	0.009	0.049***	0.016
Stomach ailments	0.104**	0.049	0.060	0.044	-0.012	0.017	0.085**	0.040
Syphilis	-0.029	0.050	0.052	0.045	-0.027	0.014	0.013	0.037
Dummy = 1 if surgeons found evidence								
Malaria	0.126***	0.024	0.122***	0.024	0.017	0.012	0.069***	0.019
Other infections	0.088***	0.021	0.079****	0.020	0.030***	0.012	0.037***	0.016
Proportion of company who died	0.062	0.096	0.136*	0.082	0.020	0.034	0.027	0.061
Dummy = 1 if POW	0.053**	0.024	0.039*	0.021	-0.004	0.008	0.007	0.017
Pseudo R^2	0.026		0.018		0.019		0.019	
Observed P	0.492		0.302		0.054		0.165	
Observations	7,349		7,349		7,349		7,349	

Note: Robust standard errors, clustering on the company. Additional control variables include a dummy equal to 1 if the veteran was ever wounded in the war, dummies for quarter of birth, a dummy if occupation circa 1900 was unknown, and dummies if the individual was not linked to the 1900 or 1860 census.

*** Significant at the 1 percent level.

** Significant at the 5 percent level.

* Significant at the 10 percent level.

probability of valvular heart disease by 0.14 and having had another infection increased this probability by 0.08.

Other infectious disease conditions and proxies for infectious disease conditions affected selected heart conditions. Respiratory infections while in the army were statistically significant predictors of murmurs, valvular heart disease, congestive heart failure, irregular heartbeat, and tachycardia. Stomach ailments while in the army increased the probability of arteriosclerosis. Men who had faced the severe malnutrition and harsh disease environment of POW camps were more likely to have valvular heart disease and to exhibit murmurs, irregular pulse, and tachycardia.

Rheumatic fever and malaria were also strong predictors of joint and back problems (see table 1.7). Rheumatic fever while in the army increased the probability of joint problems by 0.17 and of back problems by 0.15. Malaria noted by an examining surgeon increased the probability of joint problems by 0.10 and of back problems by 0.12. Other infections increased the probability of back problems by 0.05.

Wartime typhoid fever, tuberculosis, malaria, or other infectious diseases as noted by the examining surgeons predicted mental problems (see table 1.8). Those who had had typhoid fever saw their probability of all mental problems increase by 0.03, and those who had had tuberculosis saw their probability of memory loss increase by 0.03. Malaria increased the probabilty of all mental problems by 0.04 and of memory loss by 0.02. Other infections increased the probability of mental problems by 0.06 and of memory loss by 0.02.

Other predictors of all mental problems and of cognitive functioning included having had a head wound during the war, having had a stroke at older ages, having epilepsy, and, in the case of memory loss, wartime stress as measured by the percentage of the company who died during the war. A head wound during the war increased the probability of all mental problems by 0.09 and of memory loss by 0.06. Having had a stroke increased the probability of all mental problems by 0.45 and of memory loss by 0.28. Having epilepsy increased the probability of all mental problems by 0.42 and of memory loss by 0.22. An increase of a standard deviation (0.086) in the percentage of the company that died increased the probability of memory loss by 0.006.

I find that socioeconomic factors were important predictors of all of the three disease categories that I study. Controlling for occupation circa 1900, men who were professionals and proprietors at enlistment were significantly less likely to have valvular heart disease, arteriosclerosis, congestive heart failure, and back problems compared to men who were farmers or laborers. Controlling for occupation at enlistment, men who were professionals and proprietors circa 1900 were significantly less likely to have valvular heart disease, congestive heart failure, and joint or back problems than men who were farmers or laborers circa 1900. Men with

Table 1.7 Musculoskeletal characteristic probits (marginal effects), Union Army veterans age 60–79 in 1910

	Joint Problems		Back Problems	
	$\dfrac{\partial P}{\partial x}$	Standard Error	$\dfrac{\partial P}{\partial x}$	Standard Error
Dummy = 1 if occupation at enlistment				
Farmer				
Professional or proprietor	−0.033	0.026	−0.064**	0.027
Artisan	−0.002	0.017	−0.048**	0.020
Laborer	0.035*	0.019	0.002	0.020
Dummy = 1 if occupation circa 1900				
Farmer				
Professional or proprietor	−0.094***	0.019	−0.067***	0.017
Artisan	0.018	0.020	−0.006	0.020
Laborer	−0.005	0.016	−0.001	0.017
Logarithm of personal wealth in 1860	−0.001	0.003	0.006**	0.003
Dummy = 1 if writes	0.027	0.025	0.025	0.025
Dummy = 1 if city size				
50,000+	0.011	0.015	−0.004	0.016
25,000–50,000	0.007	0.028	−0.010	0.033
2,500–25,000	0.013*	0.017	−0.006	0.018
< 2,500				
Dummy = 1 if in war had				
Diarrhea	−0.009	0.012	0.013	0.014
Malaria	0.024	0.030	0.012	0.033
Respiratory infection	−0.036**	0.018	−0.031*	0.017
Measles	−0.023	0.022	0.001	0.024
Tuberculosis	−0.004	0.042	−0.023	0.043
Typhoid	−0.027	0.026	−0.011	0.024
Rheumatic fever	0.170***	0.017	0.147***	0.017
Stomach ailments	−0.008	0.047	0.054	0.041
Syphilis	0.038	0.050	−0.001	0.048
Dummy = 1 if surgeons found evidence				
Malaria	0.099***	0.023	0.121***	0.023
Other infections	0.005	0.021	0.050***	0.021
Proportion of company who died	−0.121*	0.074	−0.081	0.082
Dummy = 1 if POW	0.011	0.019	−0.009	0.023
Pseudo R^2	0.024		0.020	
Observed P	0.615		0.518	
Observations	7,349		7,349	

Note: Robust standard errors, clustering on the company. Additional control variables include a dummy equal to one if the veteran was ever wounded in the war, dummies for quarter of birth, a dummy if occupation circa 1900 was unknown, and dummies if the individual was not linked to the 1900 or 1860 census.

*** Significant at the 1 percent level.
** Significant at the 5 percent level.
* Significant at the 10 percent level.

Table 1.8   **Cognitive characteristic probits (marginal effects), Union Army veterans age 60–79 in 1910**

	All mental problems		Memory loss	
	$\dfrac{\partial P}{\partial x}$	Standard Error	$\dfrac{\partial P}{\partial x}$	Standard Error
Dummy = 1 if occupation at enlistment				
Farmer				
Professional or proprietor	0.019	0.017	0.008	0.009
Artisan	0.014	0.013	0.009	0.007
Laborer	0.002	0.011	−0.004	0.004
Dummy = 1 if occupation circa 1900				
Farmer				
Professional or proprietor	0.026**	0.012	−0.001	0.005
Artisan	0.017	0.013	−0.003	0.005
Laborer	0.007	0.010	0.005	0.005
Logarithm of personal wealth in 1860	−0.002	0.002	−0.002**	0.001
Dummy = 1 if writes	−0.060***	0.018	−0.015*	0.010
Dummy = 1 if city size				
50,000+	0.016	0.010	0.005	0.004
25,000–50,000	0.018	0.022	−0.003	0.008
2,500–25,000	0.004	0.011	0.002	0.005
< 2,500				
Dummy = 1 if in war had				
Diarrhea	0.018**	0.009	−0.004	0.004
Malaria	−0.018	0.017	0.003	0.009
Respiratory infection	−0.014*	0.011	0.001	0.005
Measles	−0.002	0.016	−0.001	0.006
Tuberculosis	0.016	0.031	0.027*	0.020
Typhoid	0.029*	0.018	−0.004	0.006
Rheumatic fever	−0.007	0.011	−0.001	0.005
Stomach ailments	0.045	0.034	0.017	0.020
Syphilis	0.044	0.035	0.014	0.018
Dummy = 1 if surgeons found evidence				
Malaria	0.044***	0.017	0.016**	0.009
Other infections	0.060***	0.017	0.016***	0.007
Dummy = 1 if head wound in war	0.086***	0.023	0.064***	0.017
Proportion of company who died	0.050	0.049	0.070***	0.019
Dummy = 1 if POW	0.008	0.014	−0.002	0.005
Dummy = 1 if had stroke	0.464***	0.031	0.277***	0.029
Dummy = 1 if epilepsy	0.419***	0.057	0.217***	0.042
Pseudo R^2	0.136		0.249	
Observed P	0.117		0.039	
Observations	7,349		7,349	

Note: Robust standard errors, clustering on the company. Additional control variables include a dummy equal to one if the veteran was ever wounded in the war, dummies for quarter of birth, a dummy if occupation circa 1900 was unknown, and dummies if the individual was not linked to the 1900 or 1860 census.
*** Significant at the 1 percent level.
** Significant at the 5 percent level.
* Significant at the 10 percent level.

higher personal property wealth in 1860 were significantly less likely to have developed congestive heart failure and arrythmias by 1910 and to have experienced memory loss. The illiterate were more likely to have mental problems or memory loss by 1910.

Predicting Declines in Chronic Conditions

How much of the difference in chronic disease rates between Union Army veterans and men in the late twentieth century is explained by infectious disease prevalence and socioeconomic conditions? In this section, I consider the case of valvular heart disease and of arthritis, both of which exhibited remarkable declines in prevalence rates. Among white men age sixty to seventy-nine in the 1988–1994 NHANES, the prevalence of arthritis was 38.4 percent compared to a predicted prevalence of 61.5 among Union Army veterans. Among white men age sixty to seventy-four (older age groups were not examined) in the 1976–1980 NHANES, the prevalence of valvular heart disease was 5.4 percent, compared to a predicted prevalence of 28.5 among Union Army veterans.

I use the regressions for Union Army veterans to calculate lower-bound estimates of the declines due to differences in the disease environment and to changes in the occupational distribution. Thus I assume that I could decrease rheumatic fever rates from 11.5 percent to only 0.7 percent, equal to the percentage age twenty to twenty-four who in 1935–1936 reported ever having rheumatic fever (see table 1.1). I also assume that I could decrease malaria rates from 6.9 to 0.3 percent, equal to the percentage of individuals in the 1928–1931 health surveys who reported having had malaria in the past twelve months (Collins 1944). Because, as previously noted, the case fatality of scarlet fever declined sharply, I further assume that the coefficient on fever becomes zero, but that the other coefficients remain unchanged. Finally, I increase the proportion of white collar workers in our sample and decrease the proportion of laborers and of farmers by assuming that the occupational distribution of Union Army veterans at enlistment was the same as that of men in 1940 and that the occupational distribution of Union Army veterans circa 1900 was the same as that of men in 1980. Table 1.9 presents the results of my prediction exercise for Union Army veterans.

Table 1.9 shows that decreases in the prevalence of the specific infectious diseases that I examine and changes in the occupational distribution would decrease the prevalence of valvular heart disease from 28.5 to 23.6 percent and of arthritis from 61.5 to 55.9 percent. Given that the prevalence of valvular heart disease fell by roughly 22.5 percentage points and that the prevalence of arthritis fell by 23.1 percentage points, I can explain roughly 22 percent of the decline in valvular heart disease and 24 percent of the decline in arthritis. The effects of disease declines and of occupational shifts are of roughly similar magnitudes.

Table 1.9   **Predicted prevalence of valvular heart disease and arthritis among Union Army veterans age 60–79 in 1910**

	Valvular heart disease (%)	Arthritis (%)
Predicted, based upon actual values	28.5	61.5
If decline in rheumatic fever from 11.5% to 0.7%	27.7	59.6
If decline in malaria from 6.9% to 0.3%	27.5	60.7
If the coefficient on fever becomes 0	27.8	61.5
Predicted, all of above three effects	25.9	58.7
Shift in occupational distribution	26.1	58.8
Infectious disease changes and occupational distribution	23.6	55.9

Note: Based upon the regressions shown in tables 1.5 and 1.7. See the text for details.

1.3   Conclusion

Past populations who lived at a time when medical care was ineffective at best provide us a unique opportunity to study the effects of untreated infectious disease and physical injuries on chronic disease. I have shown that in the past, occupation was an important determinant of valvular heart disease, congestive heart failure, and joint and back problems, suggesting that higher socioeconomic status protected against mechanical wear and tear and that it purchased less crowding and therefore less infectious disease, such as rheumatic fever. Infectious diseases such as rheumatic fever and malaria predicted various heart and musculoskeletal conditions. Prisoner of War (POW) status, perhaps a proxy for both nutritional deprivation and infectious disease, predicted various heart conditions, including valvular heart disease. In addition, respiratory disease predicted various heart conditions, and typhoid, tuberculosis, and malaria predicted mental problems. Stroke was a particularly important predictor of mental problems and of memory loss, illustrating the value of stroke therapies. Additional predictors of memory loss included illiteracy, head wounds, and the percentage of a veteran's company who had died during the war, suggesting that wartime trauma also played a role.

My findings suggest that the high probability of physical injury on the job and in the home in the past, the high rates of infectious disease, and incomes that were too low to purchase uncrowded housing all explain why chronic disease rates were historically so high among men. Declining disease rates and the shift from blue-collar to white-collar jobs explain at least 22 percent of the decline in valvular heart disease since 1900 and 24 percent of the decline in arthritis. What accounts for the remaining three-quarters of the decline? I am probably underestimating the portion of the decline due to infectious disease because I cannot observe childhood illnesses. Additional potential explanations include the mechanization of blue-collar jobs and reductions in work injuries within jobs, innovations in medical care, and the diffusion of accurate medical knowledge to individuals, and improvements in the consumed food supply.

Why did infectious disease rates, which played such an important role in the decline in chronic disease rates, fall? Early work emphasized advances in medical technology, rising incomes and living standards, public health reforms, improved personal hygiene, and natural factors such as the declining virulence of pathogens (United Nations 1953 and 1973). McKewon (1976), arguing by a process of elimination, upset this consensus view and claimed that because mortality declines began prior to any changes in medical technology or in public health reforms, the primary explanation had to be improved nutrition. Fogel (1997) argued for the importance not of nutrition per se, but rather of net nutrition—that is, the difference between food intake and the demand made on that intake by disease, climate, and work. Those with parasitic diseases suffer depletion of iron supplies despite their consumption of an otherwise healthy diet. Recurrent sufferers from gastrointestinal diseases cannot digest all of the ingested nutrients.

Recent work on public health reforms that has utilized microdata or city-level data has emphasized the efficacy of these reforms. While there may have already been a declining trend in such water-borne diseases as typhoid or diarrhea, cities' sanitary reforms led to substantial declines in death rates and disproportionately benefited the poor because they had neither the knowledge nor the income to protect themselves in a high-disease environment (Cain and Rotella 2001; Troesken 2004; Costa and Kahn 2006). In addition to large investments in sewage, clean water, and a clean milk supply, cities also invested in disease reporting and quarantining systems and, in conjunction with private philanthropists, in well-baby and -child care (including vaccination), and in campaigns against specific diseases such as syphilis. While doctors may not have been able to prescribe penicillin or antibiotics, they did learn how to quarantine patients to prevent diseases from quickly spreading and hence also from becoming particularly virulent as they jumped from patient to patient. Public health efforts were not limited to large cities. There were various health campaigns in rural areas, the most notable that against hookworm in the rural South, a campaign that also disproportionately benefited the poor (Bleakley 2007). Foods were fortified with iron. There is clearly much more work to be done quantifying the contributions of various health campaigns and innovations in care. Only when this quantification is complete will we be able to determine with certainty why infectious disease rates fell.

References

Ackerknecht, E. H. 1945. *Malaria in the upper Mississippi Valley, 1760–1900.* Baltimore, MD: The Johns Hopkins Press.

Ali, G. S., M. A. Rashid, P. A. Kamli, Shah, and G. Q. Allagaband. 1997. Spectrum of neuropsychiatric complications in 791 cases of typhoid fever. *Tropical Medicine and International Health* 2 (4): 314–8.

Allaire, S. H., M. P. LaValley, S. R. Evans, G. T. O'Connor, M. Kelly-Hayes, R. F. Meenan, D. Levy, D. T. Felson. 1999. Evidence for decline in disability and improved health among persons aged 55 to 70 Years: The Framingham Heart Study. *American Journal of Public Health* 89 (11): 1678–83.

Beebe, G. W. 1975. Follow-up studies of World War II and Korean War prisoners. II. Morbidity, disability, and maladjustments. *American Journal of Epidemiology* 101 (5): 400–422.

Benedek, Thomas G. 1993. Rheumatic fever and rheumatic heart disease. In *The Cambridge world history of human disease*, ed. Kenneth F. Kiple, 970–77. Cambridge: Cambridge University Press.

Bergen, D. C. 1998. Preventable neurological diseases worldwide. *Neuroepidemiology* 17 (2): 67–73.

Bleakley, Hoyt. 2007. Disease and development: Evidence from hookworm eradication in the American South. *Quarterly Journal of Economics* 122, 1:73–117.

Bollet, Alfred Jay. 1991. Rheumatic diseases among Civil War troops. *Arthritis and Rheumatism* 34 (9): 1197–1203.

Brandt, Allan M. 1987. *No magic bullet: A social history of venereal disease in the United States since 1880*. New York: Oxford University Press.

Cain, Louis P., and Elyce J. Rotella. 2001. Death and spending: Urban mortality and municipal expenditure on sanitation. *Annales De Demographie Historique* 1:139–54.

Chapin, Charles V. 1924. Deaths among taxpayers and non-taxpayers, income tax, Providence, 1865. *American Journal of Public Health* 14:647–51.

———. 1926. Changes in type of contagious disease with special reference to smallpox and scarlet fever. *Journal of Preventive Medicine* 1 (September): 1–29.

Charles, D., and E. Bertrand. 1982. Coeur et paludisme. *Medicine tropicale: Revue du corps de Sante Colonial* 42 (4): 405–9.

Chirikos, T. N. 1986. Accounting for the historical rise in work-disability prevalence. *The Milbank Quarterly* 64:271–301.

Cliff, Andrew, Peter Haggett, and Matthew Smallman-Raynor. 1993. *Measles: An historical geography of a major human viral disease from global expansion to local retreat, 1840–1990*. Oxford, UK: Blackwell Reference.

Collins, Selwyn D. 1936. History and frequency of typhoid fever immunizations and cases in 9,000 families. Based on nation-wide periodic canvasses, 1928–31. United States Public Health Service. *Public Health Reports* 51 (28): 897–926.

———. 1937. History and frequency of diptheria immunizations and cases in 9,000 families. Based on nation-wide periodic canvasses, 1928–31. United States Public Health Service. *Public Health Reports* 51 (51): 1736–73.

———. 1938. History and frequency of clinical scarlet fever cases and of injections for artificial immunization among 9,000 families. Based on nation-wide periodic canvasses, 1928–31. United States Public Health Service. *Public Health Reports* 53 (11): 409–27.

———. 1944. The incidence of illness and the volume of medical services among 9,000 canvassed families. Washington, DC: Federal Security Agency, United States Public Health Service.

———. 1946. Diptheria incidence and trends in relation to artificial immunization, with some comparative data for scarlet fever. United States Public Health Service. *Public Health Reports* 61 (7): 203–40.

———. 1947. The incidence of rheumatic fever as recorded in general morbidity surveys of families. United States Public Health Service. *Public Health Reports. Supplement.* No. 198.

Collins, Selwyn D., and Clara Councell. 1943. Extent of immunization and case histories for diptheria, smallpox, scarlet fever, and typhoid fever in 200,000 surveyed families in 28 large cities. United States Public Health Service. *Public Health Reports* 58 (30): 1121–51.

Colvez, A., and M. Blanchet. 1981. Disability trends in the United States population 1966–76: Analysis of reported causes. *American Journal of Public Health* 71 (5): 464–71.

Costa, Dora L. 1998. *The evolution of retirement: An American economic history, 1880–1990*. Chicago: University of Chicago Press.

———. 2000. Understanding the twentieth-century decline in chronic conditions among older men. *Demography* 37 (1): 53–72.

———. 2002. Changing chronic disease rates and long-term declines in functional limitation among older men. *Demography* 39 (1): 119–38.

———. 2003. Understanding mid-life and older age mortality declines: Evidence from Union Army veterans. *Journal of Econometrics* 112 (1): 175–92.

Costa, Dora L., and Matthew E. Kahn. 2006. Public health and mortality: What can we learn from the past? In *Public policy and the income distribution*, Alan J. Auerbach, David Card, and John M. Quigley, ed. New York: Russell Sage Foundation.

Costa, Dora L., and Johanna N. Lahey. 2005. Becoming oldest-old: Evidence from historical U.S. data. *Genus* 61 (1): 125–26.

Costa, Dora L., and Richard H. Steckel. 1997. Long-term trends in health, welfare, and economic growth in the United States. In *Health and welfare during industrialization*, ed. R. Floud and R. H. Steckel, 47–89. Chicago: University of Chicago Press.

Crimmins, E. M. 1990. Are Americans healthier as well as longer-Lived? *Journal of Insurance Medicine* 22:89–92.

Crimmins, E. M., Y. Saito, and S. L. Reynolds. 1997. Further evidence on trends in the prevalence and disability and incidence of disability among older americans from two sources: The LSOA and the NHIS. *Journals of Gerontology, Series B, Pyschological Sciences and Social Sciences* 52 (2): S59–S71.

Ferrie, Joseph P. 2003. The rich and the dead: Socioeconomic status and mortality in the United States, 1850–1860. In *Health and labor force participation over the life cycle: Evidence from the past,* ed. D. L. Costa, 11–50. Chicago: The University of Chicago Press.

Fogel, Robert W. 1997. Secular trends in nutrition and mortality. In *Handbook of population and family economics* Vol. 1A, ed. Mark R. Rosenzweig and Oded Stark, 434–81. Amsterdam: Elsevier.

Fogel, Robert W., and Dora L. Costa. 1997. A theory of technophysio evolution, with some implications for forecasting population, health care costs, and pension costs. *Demography*, 34 (1): 49–66.

Freedman, Victoria A., and Linda G. Martin. 1998. Understanding trends in functional limitations among older Americans. *American Journal of Public Health* 88 (10): 1457–62.

———. 2000. The contribution of chronic conditions to aggregate changes in old-age functioning. *American Journal of Public Health* 90 (11): 1755–60.

Freedman, Victoria A., Linda G. Martin, and Robert F. Schoeni. 2002. Recent trends in disability and functioning among older adults in the United States: A systematic review. *Journal of the American Medical Association* 288 (24): 3137–46.

Fries, J. F. 1980. Aging, natural death, and the compression of morbidity. *New England Journal of Medicine* 303:130–36.

Fries, J. F. 1989. The compression of morbidity: Near or far? *Milbank Quarterly* 67 (2): 208–32.

Gibberd, F. B., and J. P. Simmonds. 1980. Neurological disease in ex-far-east prisoners of war. *Lancet* 2 (8186): 135–37.

Goulston, K. J., O. F. Dent, P. H. Chapuis, G. Chapman, C. I. Smith, A. D. Tait, and C. C. Tenant. 1985. Gastrointestinal morbidity among World War II prisoners of war: 40 years on. *Medical Journal of Australia* 143 (1): 6–10.

Gruenberg, E. M. 1977. The failures of success. *Milbank Memorial Fund Quarterly* (Winter): 3–24.

Humphreys, Margaret. 2001. *Malaria: Poverty, race, and public health in the United States*. Baltimore, M. D. and London: The Johns Hopkins University Press.

Innes, Frank C. 1993. The geography of human disease: North America. In *The Cambridge world history of human disease*, ed. Kenneth F. Kiple, 519–34. Cambridge: Cambridge University Press.

Khosla, S. N. 1981. The heart in enteric (typhoid) fever. *Journal of Tropical Medicine and Hygiene* 84 (3): 125–31.

Kishi, R., R. Doi, Y. Fukuchi, H. Satoh, T. Satoh, A. Ono, F. Moriwaka, K. Tashiro, and N. Takahata. 1993. Subjective symptoms and neurobehavioral performances of ex-mercury miners at an average of 18 years after the cessation of chronic exposure to mercury vapor. Mercury Workers Study Group. *Environmental Research* 62 (2): 289–302.

Lee, Chulhee. 1997. Socioeconomic background, diesase, and mortality among Union recruits: Implications for economic and demographic history. *Explorations in Economic History* 34:27–55.

Lindholt, J. S., H. Fasting, E. W. Henneberg, and L. Ostergaard. 1999. A review of chlamydia pneumoniae and atherosclerosis. *European Journal of Vascular and Endovascular Surgery* 17 (4): 283–89.

Love, Albert G., and Charles B. Davenport. 1920. *Defects found in drafted men. Statistical information compiled from the draft records showing the physical condition of the men registered and examined in pursuance of the requirements of the Selective-Service Act*. Washington, D.C.: Government Printing Office.

Manton, Kenneth G. 1982. Changing concepts of morbidity and mortality in the elderly population. *Milbank Memorial Fund Quarterly* 60 (2): 183–244.

Markle, H. V. 1997. Coronary artery disease associated with helicobacter pylori infection is at least partially due to inadequate folate status. *Medical Hypotheses* 49 (4): 289–92.

Medlineplus. n.d. Medical Encyclopedia. United States National Library of Medicine and United States National Institutes of Health. http://www.nlm.nih.gov/medlineplus/

McKewon, Thomas. 1976. *The modern rise of population*. London: Edward Arnold.

Olowu, A. O., and O. Taiwo. 1990. Electrocardiographic changes after recovery from measles. *Tropical Doctor* 20 (3): 123–26.

Page, W. F., and A. M. Ostfeld. 1994. Malnutrition and subsequent ischemic heart disease in former prisoners of war of World War II and Korean conflict. *Journal of Clinical Epidemiology* 47 (12): 1437–41.

Page, W. F., and Brass, L. M. 2001. Long-term heart disease and stroke mortality among former American prisoners of war of World War II and the Korean conflict: Results of a 50-year follow-up. *Military Medicine* 166 (9): 803–8.

Paul, John R., and Joyce V. Deutsch. 1941. Rheumatic fever in Connecticut: A general survey. In *Rheumatic fever in Connecticut*, 1–33. Hartford, CT: Connecticut State Department of Health.

Preston, Samuel H., and Michael R. Haines. 1991. *Fatal years: Child mortality in late nineteenth-century America*. Princeton: Princeton University Press.

Rochester, Anna. 1923. *Infant mortality: Results of a field study in Baltimore, MD. Based on births in one year*. U.S. Department of Labor, Children's Bureau. Bureau Publication no. 119. Washington, D.C.: Government Printing Office.

Steckel, Richard H. 1998. The health and mortality of women and children, 1850–60. *Journal of Economic History* 48 (2): 333–45.

Troesken, Werner. 2004. *Water, race, and disease.* Cambridge, MA: MIT Press.

Tyas, Suzanne L., Jure Manfreda, Laurel L. Strain, and Patrick R. Montgomery. 2001. Risk factors for Alzheimer's Disease: A population-based longitudinal study in Manitoba, Canada. *International Journal of Epidemiology* 30 (3): 590–97.

United Nations. 1953. The determinants and consequences of population trends. *Population Studies,* no. 17. New York: United Nations.

———. 1973. The determinants and consequences of population trends. *Population Studies,* no. 50. New York: United Nations.

United States Selective Service System. 1941. *Analysis of reports of physical examination: Summary of data from 19,923 reports of physical examination.* Medical Statistics Bulletin no. 1. Washington DC: U.S. Selective Service System.

———. 1943. *Causes of rejection and incidence of defects: Local board examinations of selective service registrants in peacetime. An analysis of reports of physical examination from 21 selected states.* Medical Statistics Bulletin no. 2. Washington DC: U.S. Selective Service System.

———. 1944. *Physical examinations of selective registrants during wartime: An analysis of reports for the continental United States and each state. April 1942–December 1943.* Medical Statistics Bulletin no. 3. Washington DC: U.S. Selective Service System.

Valtonen, V. V. 1991. Infection as a risk factor for infarction and atherosclerosis. *Annals of Medicine* 23 (5): 539–43.

Vane, Sir John. 2000. Aspirin and other anti-inflammatory drugs. *Thorax* 55 (Suppl 2): S3–S9.

Varney, N. R., R. J. Roberts, J. A. Springer, S. K. Connell, and P. S. Wood. 1997. Neuropsychiatric sequelae of cerebral malaria in Vietnam veterans. *The Journal of Nervous and Mental Disease* 185 (11): 695–703.

Vaupel, James H. 1991. *The impact of population aging on health and health care costs: Uncertainties and new evidence about life expectancy.* Odense, Denmark: Odense University, Center for Health and Social Policy.

Verbrugge, L. M. 1984. Longer life but worsening health? Trends in health and mortality of middle aged and older persons. *Milbank Quarterly* 62:475–519.

Vinovskis, Maris. 1990. Have social historians lost the Civil War? Some preliminary demographic speculations. In *Toward a history of the American Civil War,* ed. Maris Vinovskis, 1–30. Cambridge: Cambridge University Press.

Waidmann, T., J. Bound, and M. Schoenbaum. 1995. The illusion of failure: Trends in self-reported health of the US elderly. *Milbank Quarterly* 73 (2): 253–87.

Waidmann, T. A., and K. Liu. 2000. Disability trends among elderly persons and disability trends for the future. *The Journals of Gerontology, Series B, Psychological and Social Sciences* 55 (5): S298–307.

Wolff, George. 1948. *Childhood mortality from rheumatic fever and heart disease.* Federal Security Agency. Social Security Administration. Children's Bureau Pub. 322. Washington D.C.: Government Printing Office.

Wong, Y. K., P. J. Gallagher, and M. E. Ward. 1999. Chlamydia pneumoniae and atherosclerosis. *Heart* 81 (3): 232–38.

Arthritis:
Changes in Its Prevalence
during the Nineteenth and
Twentieth Centuries

Paula Canavese and Robert W. Fogel

2.1 Introduction

In this chapter we analyze the prevalence of arthritis and its progress over the lifecycle among Union Army veterans. We also compare patterns in arthritis among Union Army veterans with those among adult white males during the last quarter of the twentieth century.

The disease and its symptoms are described in section 2.2. Section 2.3 describes the data used to calculate the prevalence rates, and the results of our calculations are shown in section 2.4. Section 2.5 discusses factors that could affect the probability of having arthritis and the time survived with this disease. Section 2.6 summarizes our conclusions.

2.2 A Brief History of the Classifications and Treatment of Arthritis

Arthritis[1] is defined as a deforming disease of the joints, regarded by most authorities as distinct from gout and rheumatism,[2] and characterized

Paula Canavese received a Ph.D. in economics from the University of Chicago in 2005 and is currently a Manager at Deloitte Tax LLP. Robert W. Fogel is director of the Center for Population Economics and Charles R. Walgreen Distinguished Service Professor, Graduate School of Business at the University of Chicago, and a research associate of the National Bureau of Economic Research.

This work is part of the NBER Project on Disability, which is supported by National Institute on Aging grants P30 AG12810 and R01 AG19805, and the Mary Woodard Lasker Charitable Trust and Michael E. DeBakey Foundation. The views expressed are those of the authors and not necessarily those of the Center for Population Economics. We would like to thank Claudia Linares for help in arranging the Surgeon's Certificates data and other CPE members for helpful comments. This work was supported by the National Institutes of Health under program project grant P01 AG10120.

1. From the Greek *arthron*, meaning "joint."
2. The terms *rheumatism* and *rheumatic diseases* are still sometimes used to describe a range of different conditions that affect the muscles, tendons, and other nonjoint tissues of the body.

by destructive changes in the cartilage and bone and by bony outgrowths restricting the motion of the joint.

The first written reference to arthritis was in 123 AD in a text from India called *Caraka Samhita,* which describes a disease where swollen, painful joints initially occur in the hands and feet, then spread to the body, causing loss of appetite, and occasionally fever (Underwood 2000).

In thirteenth century Europe any joint ailment was called *gutta*[3] for a noxious humor falling drop by drop into the joint. Gout and gouty diathesis were used as broadly as the term arthritis is used today (Kiple 1993).

Physicians such as Sydenham (1633), Musgrave (1763), Haller (1764), and de Sauvages (1768) alluded to the characteristic changes in the bone due to arthritis deformans, but the first correct description was read by Landre Beauvais before the Paris Academy of Medicine in 1800, under the name "Goute Asthenique Primitive." William Heberden, Sr. (1710–1801) of England was, however, the first to recognize its true clinical position as a condition distinct from gout. John Haygarth's 1805 paper, "Nodosity of the Joints," describes the disease clinically, and he remarked upon the peculiar incidence of its occurrence among women (Kiple 1993).

In 1891, Arbuthnot Lane attached much importance to mechanical wear and tear in the production of lesions. In 1897, James Stewart of Montreal read a paper supporting an infectious origin of the disease before the Section of Medicine of the British Medical Association. In 1951 Guillaume de Baillou, a French physician and dean of the University of Paris medical faculty, wrote one of the first books on arthritis, using the term *rheumatism* to describe a condition characterized by inflammation, soreness, stiffness in the muscles, and pain in and around the joints (Underwood 2000).

In 1680 doctors began treating rheumatism with a Peruvian bark that contains the antimalarial agent quinine. In 1763, another weapon was found to fight rheumatism: willow bark, which contains salicylate, the active ingredient in aspirin.[4] Still another drug emerged in 1929 when periodic injections of gold salts were first used to relieve muscle pain (Underwood 2000).

The first autoimmune theory of arthritis was introduced in 1939. Sir Mc-Farlane Burnet, head of the Research Institute of Melbourne, Australia, found that autoimmunity, the process by which the body's defense system malfunctions and attacks its own tissues, causes many arthritic conditions.

The development of x-rays in 1895, the surgical pin[5] in 1907, and the ball and cup artificial hip joint in 1931 led to the formation of the American Academy of Orthopedic Surgeons in 1933 (Underwood 2000).

It was not until 1859 that rheumatoid arthritis gained its own classifica-

3. From the Latin, meaning "a drop."
4. The Bayer Company took the willow bark treatment one step further in 1897, manufacturing acetylsalicylic acid, better known as aspirin.
5. Used as a bone screw.

tion, when Sir Alfred Garrod, a London physician, coined the clinical term
rheumatoid arthritis (Underwood 2000). Rheumatoid arthritis is an inflammatory disease that causes pain, swelling, stiffness, and loss of function in the joints. It has several special features that make it different from
other kinds of arthritis. For example, rheumatoid arthritis generally occurs
in a symmetrical pattern. This means that if one knee or hand is afflicted,
the other is also. The disease often affects the wrist joints and the finger
joints closest to the hand, but can also affect other parts of the body. Some
remissions do occur, but the illness progresses to produce permanent damage and deformity. Rheumatoid arthritis occurs in all races and ethnic
groups. It often begins in middle age and occurs with increased frequency
in older people (NIAMS 1998).

Osteoarthritis[6] was commonly used as a synonym for rheumatoid arthritis beginning in the 1860s. A clear distinction between the two ailments began to emerge at the turn of the century with the development of x-rays. In
1904, Boston physician Joel E. Goldthwait described differences revealed
by x-rays. Osteoarthritis is a joint disease that mostly affects the cartilage,
which is the slippery tissue that covers the ends of bones in a joint. With
this disease, the surface layer of the cartilage breaks down and wears away.
This allows bones under the cartilage to rub together, causing pain,
swelling, and loss of motion of the joint. Today, osteoarthritis is the most
common type of arthritis, especially among older people, and one of the
most frequent causes of disability among adults (NIAMS 2002).

Migratory arthritis refers to pain and swelling in a specific joint that has
a fairly rapid onset, disappears in the course of twenty-four or thirty-six
hours, and then is followed by similar symptoms elsewhere that are usually
asymmetric (Barth 1997).

2.2.1   The Diagnosis of Arthritis

Arthritis is very difficult to diagnose in its early stages, for several reasons.
First, there is no single test for the disease. Second, symptoms differ from
person to person and can be more severe in some people than in others.
Third, the full range of symptoms develops over time, and only a few symptoms may be present in the early stages. As a result, doctors use a variety
of tools to diagnose the disease and to rule out other conditions. These tools
include the medical history (the patient's description of symptoms and
when and how they began), physical examination, laboratory tests, and
x-rays.

The method used to diagnose arthritis has not changed much in history.[7]
The appearance of x-rays and the development of laboratory tests such as

---

6. From the Greek *osteon*, meaning "bone."
7. Since the method of diagnosing arthritis has not changed much over time, comparing
prevalence rates for this disease at different points in time seems plausible.

blood tests have only helped to make a distinction between different kinds of arthritis. The most important tool for the diagnosis of arthritis, however, has always been the medical history.

The history probably provides 80 percent of the necessary information, whereas the physical examination provides 15 percent, and laboratory tests and x-rays, 5 percent. Moreover, the history influences many of the decisions to order laboratory tests and x-rays. The type of symptom onset is highly informative. The history may also reveal the presence of morning stiffness, a common symptom in many patients with rheumatic complaints. The duration and extent of morning stiffness are helpful guides to the degree of inflammation that may be involved. For example, in cases of rheumatoid arthritis, morning stiffness typically extends for several hours, affects the whole body, and is associated with afternoon fatigue. In cases of noninflammatory joint problems such as osteoarthritis, morning stiffness may be brief and is usually limited to the affected joint (Barth 1997).

In a physical examination, helpful points of differentiation include the number of joints involved, their location, and, when multiple joints are involved, whether they are symmetric or asymmetric. The duration of symptoms and changes over time are important considerations. Age and gender should be noted in the office evaluation because they can provide clues to rheumatic diseases seen more frequently in one age or gender group than another.

Classic signs and symptoms that can be readily diagnosed by the primary care physician accompany many musculoskeletal complaints. Others are much less obvious: in the office evaluation of patients with musculoskeletal complaints, the least helpful elements are laboratory tests. Although available tests are sensitive to the presence of rheumatic diseases, they are not specific for any of them. Thus, the most commonly used laboratory tests for rheumatic diseases should be considered helpful but not diagnostic. They must be ordered and interpreted in the context of the history and the physical examination findings (Barth 1997).

X-rays for a new joint complaint are helpful only in certain situations. They show bone best, but they are less helpful in showing changes in soft tissue. It may take a long time for some symptoms to cause erosion visible by conventional radiography.

Scientists do not yet know what causes the disease, but they suspect a combination of factors, including being overweight, aging, joint injury, stresses on the joints from certain jobs and sport activities, and environmental factors. Also, scientists have found that certain genes that play a role in the immune system are associated with a tendency to develop certain kinds of arthritis. Thus, an infection followed by an altered or sustained immunologic response could be instrumental for development of the disease (NIAMS 1998, 2002).

Patients with infectious arthritis frequently have underlying conditions such as neoplasia, liver disease, and chronic renal failure. Migratory arthritis is most common in patients with viral diseases, acute rheumatic fever, and bacterial endocarditis. Other symptoms of arthritis could be psoriasis, Reiter's syndrome, and inflammatory bowel disease. These conditions can cause inflammation of the joints. Another related disease is gout. Arthritis patients are often diagnosed as also having gout (Barth 1997).

2.3 Data

We have used three different samples to explore the evolution of the prevalence for arthritis among the U.S. population from the late nineteenth century to today.

To calculate prevalence rates during the late nineteenth century and the beginning of the twentieth century, we have used the data in the Surgeon's Certificates. This dataset contains 87,223 medical exam records from 1862 to 1940 for 17,721 Union Army pensioners with a documented birthdate (Fogel 2000, 2001). Each Civil War veteran received a thorough medical examination when he originally applied for a pension and every time he asked for an increase in the pension amount. These examinations were performed by a board of physicians appointed by the Bureau of Pensions. The physicians would assess the veteran's general health (as well as diagnose any specific impairment) and record the symptoms. The majority of these exams occurred between 1885 and 1920 (Linares 2001).

The conditions in this dataset are classified by disability groups. Those groups include cardiovascular, ear, eye, gastrointestinal, genito-urinary, respiratory, musculoskeletal, and liver/spleen/gallbladder conditions, as well as infectious diseases and fevers, injuries, neoplasms/tumors, nervous disorders, disorders of the rectum/hemorrhoids, varicose veins, hernias, and general appearance (conditions involving mainly blood, nutrition, and skin, gum, teeth, and muscles). Specifically, the musculoskeletal group is defined by any one of the following conditions: rheumatism, sciatica, and spinal curvature. In this study we examine the rheumatism variable among these three conditions, since it generally describes arthritis cases by specifying the part of the body in which inflammation of the joint or muscle was detected.[8]

To compare the Union Army prevalence rates with recent ones, we use the National Health and Nutrition Examination Survey (NHANES) conducted by the National Center of Health Statistics (NCHS). This survey includes data on the health status of U.S. residents as well as a number of demographic and socioeconomic variables. There are four phases of the

---

8. The sciatica variable is identified when the claimant had pain or tenderness of the sciatic nerve. The spinal curvature variable conveys information about the location of kyphosys, scoliosis, or lordosis.

NHANES that have been released so far: NHANES I was conducted from 1971 to 1975, NHANES II from 1976 to 1980, NHANES III from 1988 to 1994, and NHANES IV from 1999 to 2000.

Finally, the other data source used to calculate current prevalence rates comes from the National Health Interview Survey (NHIS). The NHIS is a multipurpose health survey also conducted by the NCHS and is the principal source of information on the health of the civilian, noninstitutionalized household population of the United States. The NHIS has been conducted annually since its beginning in 1957 and public use data is released on an annual basis. The NHIS questionnaire items are revised every ten to fifteen years, with the last major revisions having occurred in 1982 and in 1997.

In these two surveys one of the health conditions the individuals are asked about is arthritis. However, except in the last two NHANES, the type of arthritis is not specified.

Although the NHIS has been conducted since 1957, suitable data on arthritis are available only since 1990. The variables referring to the health status of the population in the NHIS are self-reported. By contrast, in the NHANES the questions referring to health conditions specifically ask, "Has a doctor ever told you that you have . . . ?"

Another disadvantage of using the NHIS to study changes in prevalence rates over time is the fact that the questionnaire has changed significantly over the years. Specifically, the 1997 revision has changed the question from "did you ever have arthritis?" to "does arthritis cause any limitation?" Because of this, we only use the available years for the NHIS prior to 1997.

Since the Surgeon's Certificates contain information only for Civil War Union Army veterans, we limit the calculations in the NHANES and the NHIS to adult white males in order to compare results across the different data sets.

Also, to make the NHANES and the NHIS samples representative of the adult white male U.S. population, we use weighted data.

2.4   Prevalence Rates and Duration of Arthritis

By calculating prevalence rates for white males with arthritis for the Union Army sample, as well as for the NHANES and NHIS samples, we try to analyze how the life cycle pattern of this specific disease has changed over time.

For each individual observation that reports an arthritic condition in any of the datasets used, a dummy variable coded 1 was created. If no arthritis is found, the arthritis dummy variable was coded 0. The arthritis prevalence rate is defined as the number of individuals with arthritis divided by the total number of individuals at risk in a given group.

First, in figure 2.1, we graph the prevalence rates for birth cohorts over the years between 1873 and 1910. Then, in figure 2.2, we graph the

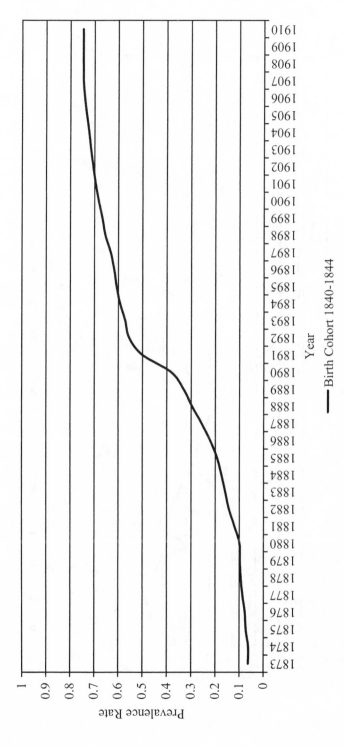

Fig. 2.1   Arthritis prevalence rate among Union Army veterans by selected birth cohorts, 1873–1910

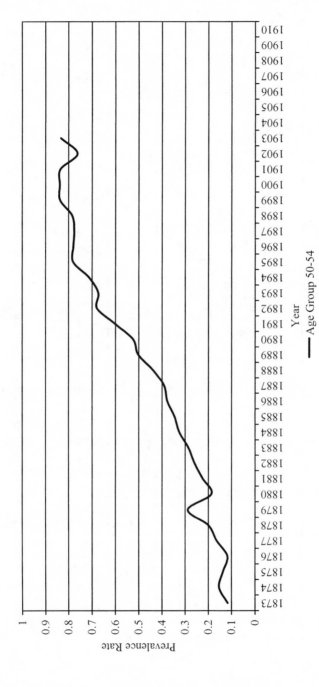

Fig. 2.2 Arthritis prevalence rate among Union Army veterans by selected age groups, 1873–1910

prevalence rates for veterans of a given age at each year between 1873 and 1910.[9] This second way of looking at prevalence rates helps to assess the impact of changes in pension law and practices on the calculated rates.

Figure 2.1 shows that the rate of increase in prevalence rates was greater before 1892 than after that year. For example, the cohort born between 1840 and 1844 had a prevalence rate below 10 percent in 1875, when it was between ages thirty-one and thirty-five. A decade later, its prevalence rate was double, and in 1890 was 40 percent. Finally, when the cohort was aged sixty-one to sixty-five, its prevalence rate was over 70 percent. In other words, the prevalence rate of this cohort increased more rapidly before 1892 than afterward. Note particularly the sharp acceleration in the prevalence rates between 1890 and 1892. This acceleration is very likely due to the law of 1890, which removed the restriction that a veteran was eligible for a pension only if his arthritis was war related. Under the law of 1890, having arthritis, regardless of its cause, was sufficient to warrant admission to the pension system.

The suspicion that administrative decisions influenced the prevalence rates is confirmed by figure 2.2. Here, the line shows the prevalence rate of veterans between fifty and fifty-four years old for each year between 1873 and 1903, after which the line ends because all veterans were over age fifty-four by then. Notice that in 1875 the prevalence rates among these veterans was less than 15 percent, but in 1895 the prevalence rate was over 70 percent. Since public health in the cities deteriorated badly between 1830 and 1860, one would expect the increased insults at developmental ages to be reflected in higher prevalence rates at middle ages, but one would hardly expect a ten-fold increase. Most of the increase in the prevalence rates of veterans between fifty and fifty-four years old reflects changes in pension policy.

How, then, should figure 2.1 be interpreted? Prevalence rates are too low before 1890. They are biased downward most sharply before 1880, after which the pension officials became more liberal in interpreting whether arthritis was war related. Hence the acceleration in the arthritis rates between 1881 and 1890 is exaggerated. The further acceleration between 1890 and 1892 reflects the impact of the 1890 law. After 1892, the prevalence rates appear to be unbiased by administrative decisions. Notice also that the difference in prevalence rates by birth cohort in any given year remain consistent and do not appear to have been affected by administrative directives. At late ages, all of the cohorts show prevalence rates of arthritis between 70 and 80 percent. These extremely high prevalence rates at the end of the nineteenth century suggest poor environmental, socioeconomic, and health conditions during this period.

---

9. We choose to graph only one birth cohort and only one age group, since the behavior of all of them is very similar. The birth cohort and the age group chosen are the largest.

To clarify this interpretation, we calculate the prevalence rates by age group and birth cohort for the NHANES survey. Table 2.1 shows the prevalence rate by age group, as well as the average duration of arthritis in years, for each of the first three phases of the NHANES survey,[10] as well as for these phases aggregated together. Here, the prevalence rate is generally decreasing over time for the same age group. For example, for individuals aged between sixty and sixty-four the prevalence for the period 1971–1975 is greater (35 percent) than the prevalence for the period 1988–1994 (29 percent). Table 2.1 shows that between 1971–1975 and 1988–1994, prevalence rates continued to fall at most ages. The maximum prevalence rate is 41 percent at ages seventy-five to seventy-nine in NHANES III, which is almost half the rate in the Union Army sample at the same age. Thus, over the past century, prevalence rates of arthritis have decreased by about half.

We calculate the prevalence rate by cohort for each five-year age interval when the three reported phases of the NHANES are aggregated together. Figure 2.3 shows the line that represents the evolution of arthritis prevalence for the cohort born before 1920. The lines representing other cohorts are not shown, since most recent cohorts are not numerous enough to graph. Although the prevalence rate increases with age, the rise is modest compared with the Union Army cohort.

The peak at age eighty in figure 2.3 is 41 percent, which again is almost half that for the Union Army cohort.

Table 2.2 shows the prevalence rates for different stages of the NHIS survey as well as for all these stages aggregated. Even when the prevalence rate increases with age, the level of the prevalence rates in this case is lower than for the NHANES. Self-reporting seems to undercount the prevalence of arthritis. It might be that with over-the-counter painkillers widely available, people do not feel as if they have arthritis. This undercounting is present across all age groups. Consequently, the NHANES is a more appropriate dataset to work with.

The results suggest that aging was and continues to be a very important factor in the prevalence of arthritis in an individual's life. However, when observing the life cycle evolution, the pronounced increase in the prevalence of arthritis with age during the late nineteenth century moderated during the twentieth century, as reflected in the NHANES and NHIS data.

A more interesting question that is possible to analyze only with the Union Army data is the average number of years a person lives after first being diagnosed with the disease. Table 2.3 shows the average number of years lived with arthritis by age groups for the Union Army veterans. For people diagnosed with the disease at earlier ages, its duration was greater

10. The data released for NHANES IV contain very few observations, and thus we obtained no reliable results to compare with the prevalence rates for the other phases of the NHANES.

Table 2.1 Arthritis prevalence rate and average duration in years among U.S. white males, 1971–1994

Age group	NHANES I (1971–1975)		NHANES II (1976–1980)		NHANES III (1988–1994)		Total NHANES (1971–1994)	
	Prevalence rate	Average duration	Prevalence rate	Average duration	Prevalence rate	Average duration	Prevalence rate	Average duration
Less than 50	0.054	6.974	0.048	7.256	0.070	8.573	0.052	7.489
50 to 54	0.261	9.424	0.195	10.026	0.181	9.924	0.211	9.393
55 to 59	0.280	11.558	0.300	12.065	0.167	11.860	0.263	11.649
60 to 64	0.352	11.816	0.333	11.253	0.290	11.167	0.323	11.248
65 to 69	0.354	13.137	0.345	13.030	0.332	12.163	0.352	12.943
70 to 74	0.382	13.519	0.360	15.695	0.368	14.236	0.375	14.172
75 to 79					0.411	14.509	0.411	14.509
80 to 84					0.399	15.913	0.399	15.913
85 to 89					0.363	14.535	0.363	14.535
Total number of persons	6,336		7,466		6,439		20,241	
Total number of persons w/ Arthritis	1,094		1,228		1,165		3,487	

Source: Authors' calculations from NHANES I, NHANES II, and NHANES III.

Note: White males are divided into five-year age groups according to their age at the time of the survey.

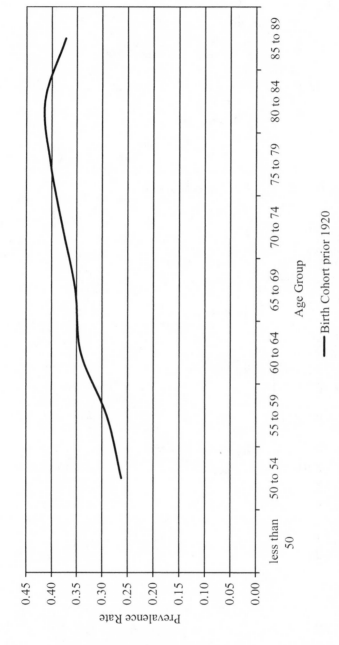

Fig. 2.3 Arthritis prevalence rate among U.S. white males by selected birth cohorts, 1971–1994

Table 2.2   Arthritis prevalence rate among U.S. white males, 1990–1994

Age group	1990 NHIS Prevalence rate	1991 NHIS Prevalence rate	1992 NHIS Prevalence rate	1993 NHIS Prevalence rate	1994 NHIS Prevalence rate	1990–1994 (Total NHIS) Prevalence rate
Less than 50	0.043	0.046	0.044	0.048	0.043	0.045
50 to 54	0.091	0.119	0.101	0.092	0.108	0.103
55 to 59	0.118	0.157	0.137	0.153	0.144	0.141
60 to 64	0.183	0.174	0.184	0.176	0.145	0.171
65 to 69	0.177	0.194	0.189	0.197	0.202	0.191
70 to 74	0.191	0.189	0.198	0.189	0.224	0.196
75 to 79	0.195	0.229	0.209	0.209	0.209	0.214
80 to 84	0.198	0.258	0.209	0.240	0.234	0.231
85 to 89	0.166	0.282	0.224	0.231	0.163	0.203
90 to 94	0.208	0.209	0.153	0.195	0.235	0.212
95 to 99	0.169	0.346	0.393	0.388	0.000	0.222
Total number of persons	15,626	14,481	15,691	13,675	14,233	73,706
Total number of persons w/ Arthritis	1,559	1,579	1,631	1,461	1,477	7,707

Source: Authors' calculations from NHIS.

Note: White males are divided into five-year age groups according to their age at the time of the survey.

Table 2.3   Years lived with arthritis among Union Army veterans

Age group		Years lived with Arthritis after first diagnosis			
	N	Mean	Std. dev.	Minimum	Maximum
Less than 50	4,088	24.320	10.561	1.000	58.000
50 to 54	2,644	19.531	9.028	1.000	42.000
55 to 59	2,044	16.410	8.356	1.000	39.000
60 to 64	1,484	13.501	7.592	1.000	37.000
65 to 69	711	11.274	6.766	1.000	30.000
70 to 74	243	9.531	6.461	1.000	27.000
75 to 79	59	6.305	4.477	1.000	20.000
80 to 84	16	5.313	5.606	1.000	20.000
85 to 89	5	4.600	3.578	1.000	9.000

Source: Authors' calculations from Surgeon's Certificates.
Note: Recruits are divided into five-year age groups according to their age at the first diagnosis of arthritis.

than if the diagnosis occurred later in life. For example, people diagnosed with arthritis when they were between fifty and fifty-four years lived with the disease for another twenty years, while people first diagnosed when they were seventy to seventy-four years old had arthritis for almost ten years. It follows that people who got arthritis later in life had a longer lifespan than those who developed it earlier.[11]

In order to obtain a more reliable evaluation of the effect of arthritis on longevity, it is necessary to run a set of regressions analyzing the impact of various diseases and socioeconomic factors.

Table 2.1 has data on the duration of the disease for the NHANES survey.[12] Here, the average duration is defined as the number of years a person had lived with arthritis at the time of the interview. However, this duration is defined differently from the one reported for the Union Army in table 2.3.

Table 2.1 shows that duration increases with age. But increase in duration is less than the increase in age. For example, for NHANES I, people aged sixty to sixty-four had had arthritis for almost twelve years on average when interviewed, and people aged sixty-five to sixty-nine had had arthritis an average of approximately thirteen years. Thus, people aged sixty-five to sixty-nine had had arthritis only one more year than people aged sixty to sixty-four, despite the fact that they were five years older. This means that an increasing number of people get arthritis later in life. This is another fact that suggests that the age-specific and the birth-cohort longitudinal increase in prevalence rates of arthritis is less in the NHANES than in the Union Army.

Table 2.4 shows the average number of years Union Army veterans had

11. We consider arthritis a chronic condition, so once diagnosed, the disease will be present all the remaining years of life.
12. In the NHIS no similar data is available on the duration of arthritis.

Table 2.4   **Duration of arthritis by age among Union Army veterans, 1895**

	Duration of arthritis in years				
Age group	N	Mean	Std. dev.	Minimum	Maximum
Less than 50	4,088	5.599	3.782	1.000	32.000
50 to 54	17,312	6.512	5.077	1.000	32.000
55 to 59	12,719	7.128	5.095	1.000	32.000
60 to 64	7,349	7.438	5.150	1.000	32.000
65 to 69	4,672	8.332	5.661	1.000	32.000
70 to 74	2,423	9.304	6.288	1.000	32.000
75 to 79	1,360	11.835	7.515	1.000	32.000
80 to 84	87	11.667	5.724	3.000	26.000
85 to 89	24	11.250	6.771	4.000	24.000

Source: Authors' calculations from Surgeon's Certificates.

lived with arthritis in 1895. Even though this is a lower-bound estimate of the duration of arthritis in the Union Army (because it is possible that veterans had the disease even before applying for a pension), this table is comparable with table 2.1. Duration of the condition increases with age, but it is lower than in the NHANES sample for all age groups.

2.5   What Affects the Probability of Having Arthritis?

We have demonstrated that the current prevalence rate of arthritis is lower than in the late nineteenth century and beginning of the twentieth century. The question to be answered now is what is the possibility that prevalence rates will continue to decline.

To assess whether this trend is continuing, we run some logistic regressions trying to identify the factors influencing the odds of having arthritis. To do so, we estimate the effect of different health and socioeconomic variables on the probability of being diagnosed with arthritis, using the data from the Union Army records described before.

First, we construct as a dependent variable a dummy that takes the value 1 if the veteran had arthritis at some point in his life and 0 if he never had been diagnosed with the disease.

As independent variables we include the number of disabilities the veteran had during his life, the age at the first physical exam for the pension application process, the BMI at that exam,[13] the number of battles the veteran participated in, and the number of years enlisted in the army. We also include some socioeconomic factors that could be related to this disease. Some of these factors affecting the probability of having arthritis could be

13. We group the BMIs in four categories: underweight (BMI less or equal to twenty), normal (between twenty and twenty-five), overweight (between twenty-five and thirty) and obese (more than thirty).

the number of inhabitants in the place where the individual lives, marital status, level of income, and occupation.

We construct dummy variables for veterans' residence and birth places. We group the United States into four regions: Northeast, Midwest, West, and South.[14] Using these regions, we create a set of five dummies for being resident at enlistment in any of them or outside these regions, either unspecified or outside the United States. We also classify the place of birth, using six dummies indicating whether the veteran had been born in one of the four regions of the United States, in an unspecified place, or outside the United States (i.e., this indicates whether the veteran was an immigrant).

We create a set of dummies reflecting the veteran's occupation at enlistment by dividing the different occupations into five categories: farmers, professionals, artisans, manual laborers, and all other occupations. Also, another variable included is a dummy taking the value 1 if the veteran was ever married, and zero otherwise.

For data from the 1900 census, we construct a similar set of dummies reflecting the veteran's place of residence and occupation in 1900 as well as two dummy variables to capture any change in place of residence or occupation since time of enlistment. However, none of these variables had a significant effect when included in the regression analysis.

A weakness of this dataset is that it contains no information on education and scarce information on personal wealth. Even when some data describing wealth is included in the estimation, the number of observations is too small and thus not statistically significant.

Table 2.5 shows the summary statistics of the variables included in the logistic regression. The results of the logistic regression are shown in table 2.6.

These results suggest that older people had a greater probability of having arthritis; age increased the probability of getting the disease at a decreasing rate. This is corroborated by the positive coefficient on the total number of disabilities over life. A person with a greater number of disabilities generally was older and the probability of having arthritis increased.

Those veterans who were enlisted for a longer period of time had a lower probability of getting arthritis. Those men who were in the army for a longer period were probably healthier, since those who were sick would have had to leave the army. Those that resided in the Northeast, were manual laborers, or had higher BMIs had a greater probability of developing the disease. This suggests that residing in more populated places could

---

14. These are the regions used by the Bureau of the Census. The Northeast comprises: Connecticut, Massachusetts, Vermont, New Hampshire, Rhode Island, Maine, New Jersey, New York, and Pennsylvania. The Midwest comprises: North Dakota, South Dakota, Nebraska, Kansas, Missouri, Iowa, Minnesota, Wisconsin, Illinois, Indiana, Michigan, and Ohio. The South comprises: Oklahoma, Texas, Arkansas, Louisiana, Mississippi, Alabama, Tennessee, Kentucky, Florida, Georgia, South Carolina, North Carolina, Virginia, West Virginia, District of Columbia, Maryland, and Delaware. The West comprises: Washington, Oregon, California, Arizona, Nevada, Idaho, Montana, Wyoming, Utah, Colorado, New Mexico, Hawaii, and Alaska.

Table 2.5   **Descriptive summary statistics, Union Army veterans**

Variable	N	Mean	Std. dev.	Minimum	Maximum
Dummy = 1 if ever had arthritis	17,702	0.518	0.500	0.000	1.000
Age at first exam	16,586	47.322	10.462	16.000	85.000
Total number of conditions diagnosed over life	16,574	7.055	3.538	0.000	19.000
Number of years enlisted	15,945	2.477	0.901	0.083	9.000
Dummy = 1 if BMI at first exam					
Less than 20	14,697	0.120	0.325	0.000	1.000
20–25	14,697	0.642	0.479	0.000	1.000
26–30	14,697	0.198	0.398	0.000	1.000
More than 30	14,697	0.041	0.198	0.000	1.000
Dummy = 1 if place of residence at enlistment					
Northeast	17,339	0.295	0.456	0.000	1.000
Midwest	17,339	0.568	0.495	0.000	1.000
South	17,339	0.084	0.277	0.000	1.000
West	17,339	0.047	0.212	0.000	1.000
Not in U.S. or unspecified	17,339	0.006	0.078	0.000	1.000
Dummy = 1 if occupation at enlistment					
Farmer	17,476	0.562	0.496	0.000	1.000
Professional	17,476	0.065	0.247	0.000	1.000
Artisan	17,476	0.191	0.393	0.000	1.000
Manual laborer	17,476	0.130	0.337	0.000	1.000
Other	17,476	0.051	0.220	0.000	1.000

Source: Authors' calculations from Surgeon's Certificates and Union Army records.

have a positive effect on the odds of contracting this disease. Those veterans who were residents of less populated areas had a lower expected chance of getting the disease than those living in densely populated areas. At that time, rapid urbanization, especially in the Northeast, made cities a less healthy environment due to overcrowding, the absence of sewage systems, no water filtration, and other poor sanitary conditions. However, since the coefficient for those residing in the South is also positive and significant, we may be in the presence of a weather effect at the same time. Even though the relationship between weather and arthritis is still not proved, it is well known that under some weather conditions the pain is more severe.

Nutrition, as predicted by the theory of technophysio evolution, seems to have had a large impact on the odds of the disease during the post-Civil War period. Those with higher BMIs had a greater risk of getting arthritis, since the excess weight could affect the joints.

The fact that those veterans in nonfarming occupations had a greater probability of being diagnosed with arthritis suggests that the physical characteristics needed to perform certain jobs had a significant effect on this disease.

The logistic analysis shows that aging has a very important effect on this disease.

Table 2.6   **Logit model, Union Army veterans**

Constant	−5.118
	(0.433)***
Total number of conditions diagnosed over life	0.119
	(0.005)***
Age at first exam	0.153
	(0.017)***
Age at first exam square	−0.001
	(0.0002)***
Number of years enlisted	−0.130
	(0.02)***
Dummy = 1 if place of residence at enlistment	
Northeast	0.237
	(0.043)***
Midwest	omitted
South	0.237
	(0.067)***
West	−0.138
	(0.084)*
Not in U.S. or unspecified	0.257
	(0.216)
Dummy = 1 if occupation at enlistment	
Farmer	omitted
Professional	−0.051
	(0.078)
Artisan	0.027
	(0.050)
Manual laborer	0.091
	(0.057)*
Other	0.186
	(0.088)**
Dummy = 1 if BMI at first exam	
Less than 20	−0.405
	(0.057)***
20–25	omitted
26–30	0.263
	(0.047)***
More than 30	0.307
	(0.093)***
Observations	13,485
Pseudo R^2	0.055

Notes: The dependent variable is a dummy indicating whether the veteran ever had arthritis. Between brackets the standard error for each coefficient is shown. Information comes from surgeon's certificates and Union Army records.

*** Significant at the 1 percent level.

** Significant at the 5 percent level.

* Significant at the 10 percent level.

At the beginning of the twentieth century, residing in a less healthy environment, such as the overpopulated cities of that time, had a greater impact on the diagnosis of arthritis. So it is very likely that the decline of the prevalence rates over time is related to the improvements in sanitary conditions. Also, improvements in occupational conditions could have been in part responsible for the decline of arthritis prevalence rates. Finally, it seems that obesity and malnutrinition are two problems that cannot be ignored when trying to reduce the prevalence rate of this particular disease.

2.6 Conclusions

Disability caused by arthritis has decreased over time when extending the time horizon further than the beginning of twentieth century. One possible explanation is based on the progress of medicine during the century. This has brought many new forms of treatment for arthritis that have affected the severity of this condition since the late nineteenth century.

Moreover, contemporary prevalence rates are lower than in the late nineteenth century, reflecting changes in public health, lifestyle, and the distribution of occupations.

The tremendous change in public health infrastructure (improvements in the water supply, better sewage systems, cleaning of the milk supply) has reduced the probability of developing arthritis at later ages by reducing insults during earlier years of life. Also, for those people who have it, arthritis is less severe now, partly because of many interventions that were not available in the late nineteenth century. Finally, the accomplishment's of modern medicine has led to the alleviation of the severity of the condition, both through drugs and by advocating changes in lifestyle.

The aging process is critical for this condition, and is one of the main reasons that older people suffer more from this disease. Over the life cycle of each individual, arthritis prevalence is increasing at any point in time.

The results obtained confirm the fact that, historically, older men had a worse health status than they have today.[15] Age-specific prevalence rates are declining, and the average age of onset is eleven years later; moreover, the contemporary proportion of males who ever get arthritis is substantially lower than the historical record.

References

Barth, W. 1997. Office evaluation of the patient with musculoskeletal complaints. *American Journal of Medicine* 102 (Suppl. no. 1A): 3S–10S.

15. See D. Costa (2004) in this volume.

Costa, D. Forthcoming. Heart, joints, and mind: Why were older men in the past in such poor health? NBER.

Fogel, R. W. 2000. *Public use tape on the aging of veterans of the Union Army: Military, pension, and medical records, 1860–1940, Version M-5.* Chicago: University of Chicago, Center For Population Economics. Available at www.cpe.uchicago.edu.

———. 2001. *Public use tape on the aging of veterans of the Union Army: Surgeon's certificates, 1862–1940, Version S-1 Standardized.* Chicago: University of Chicago, Center For Population Economics.

Kiple, K. 1993. *The Cambridge world history of human disease.* Cambridge: Cambridge University Press.

Linares, C. 2001. History of the Civil War pension laws. In *Public use tape on the aging of veterans of the Union Army: Surgeon's certificates, 1862–1940, Version S-1 Standardized.* Chicago: University of Chicago, Center For Population Economics.

National Center for Health Statistics. Data File Documentation, National Health Interview Survey, 1990 (machine readable data file and documentation). Hyattsville, MD: National Center for Health Statistics, Centers for Disease Control and Prevention.

———. Data File Documentation, National Health Interview Survey, 1991 (machine readable data file and documentation). Hyattsville, MD: National Center for Health Statistics, Centers for Disease Control and Prevention.

———. Data File Documentation, National Health Interview Survey, 1992 (machine readable data file and documentation). Hyattsville, MD: National Center for Health Statistics, Centers for Disease Control and Prevention.

———. Data File Documentation, National Health Interview Survey, 1993 (machine readable data file and documentation). Hyattsville, MD: National Center for Health Statistics, Centers for Disease Control and Prevention.

———. Data File Documentation, National Health Interview Survey, 1994 (machine readable data file and documentation). Hyattsville, MD: National Center for Health Statistics, Centers for Disease Control and Prevention.

———. 2000. Data File Documentation, National Health Interview Survey, 1997 (machine readable data file and documentation). Hyattsville, MD: National Center for Health Statistics, Centers for Disease Control and Prevention.

National Institute of Arthritis and Musculoskeletal and Skin Diseases (NIAMS). 1998. *Handout on Health: Rheumatoid Arthritis.*

———. 2002. *Handout on Health: Osteoarthritis.*

Tyson, J. 1903. *The Practice of Medicine.* Philadelphia: P. Blakiston's Son & Co.

Underwood, T. 2000. *The History of Rheumatoid Arthritis.* Available at arthritis insight.com.

U.S. Department of Health and Human Services (DHHS). National Center for Health Statistics. *First National Health and Nutrition Examination Survey (NHANES I), 1971–1975.* Hyattsville, MD: Centers for Disease Control and Prevention.

———. *Second National Health and Nutrition Examination Survey, (NHANES II), 1976–1980.* Hyattsville, MD: Centers for Disease Control and Prevention.

———. 1996. *Third National Health and Nutrition Examination Survey, (NHANES III), 1988–1994.* Hyattsville, MD: Centers for Disease Control and Prevention.

———. *National Health and Nutrition Examination Survey, (NHANES IV) 1999–2000.* Hyattsville, MD: Centers for Disease Control and Prevention.

3

Socioeconomic and Demographic Disparities in Trends in Old-Age Disability

Robert F. Schoeni, Vicki A. Freedman, and
Linda G. Martin

3.1 Introduction

Socioeconomic and demographic disparities in health status are substantial. Disparities are greatest in midlife, but gaps in old age remain large (House et al. 1990; House et al. 1994). Among people ages sixty-five and older, minority and socioeconomically disadvantaged populations are much more likely than other groups to experience disability and the physical, cognitive, and sensory limitations that underlie it (Freedman and Martin 1999; Freedman, Aykan, and Martin 2001; Manton and Gu 2001). Disability prevalence increases rapidly with age, and women, including widows, have much higher prevalence rates. The burden of disability clearly falls disproportionately on less-advantaged groups.

In the 1980s, research revealed that population health and disability were worsening (Colvez and Blanchet 1981; Verbrugge 1984). Subsequent research questioned that conclusion (Waidmann, Bound, and Schoenbaum 1995), and studies of the elderly, in particular, began to find significant reductions in disability (Manton, Corder, and Stallard 1993). Based on a stream of research on the topic starting in the late 1990s, the current

Robert F. Schoeni is a research professor at the Survey Research Center and Population Studies Center, Institute for Social Research, and professor of economics and public policy at the University of Michigan. Vicki A. Freedman is a professor in the Department of Health Systems and Policy at the University of Medicine and Dentistry of New Jersey, School of Public Health. Linda G. Martin is a senior fellow at the RAND Corporation.

Corresponding author: Robert F. Schoeni, Institute for Social Research, University of Michigan, 426 Thompson Street, Ann Arbor, MI 48109, (734) 763-5131, (734) 936-3809 (fax), bschoeni@umich.edu. Freedman, Martin, and Schoeni acknowledge support from the U.S. National Institute on Aging, grant numbers R01-AG021516, P30 AG12810, and R01 AG19805, the Mary Woodard Lasker Charitable Trust and Michael E. DeBakey Foundation, and from the National Bureau of Economic Research.

evidence suggests that old-age disability has declined by roughly 1.5 percent per year during the past two decades (Freedman, Martin, and Schoeni 2002). Declines of this magnitude have wide-ranging implications for individuals and society, including the potential for substantial savings in health and long-term care spending (Waidmann and Liu 2000).

Disparities in health and disability have historically been large, and disability has declined recently, but only a handful of studies have explored whether disparities in disability have widened or narrowed (for a review see Freedman, Martin, and Schoeni 2002). Moreover, exploring whether the gains have been experienced widely or only among certain socioeconomic and demographic groups may provide insights into determinants of the decline.

The goal of this study is to document changes in disparities in old-age disability across the most salient socioeconomic and demographic groups, including education, income, and race/ethnicity, as well as age, sex, marital status, and region of residence. The chapter begins with a description of the data and methods, followed by a statement of the results and a discussion of the implications of the findings.

3.2   Data and Methods

The analysis is based on the National Health Interview Survey (NHIS), which is a repeated cross-sectional survey of the noninstitutionalized population in the United States. Conducted annually by the National Center for Health Statistics, the NHIS includes in each year a sample of roughly 8,000 adults age seventy and older. The analysis uses data from each year 1982 to 2002, resulting in a sample of 172,227 men and women ages seventy and older during this period.[1] These large samples allow relatively precise estimates of disability prevalence among elderly persons for each year, including estimates for some major subgroups. The sampling plan follows a multistage area probability design that permits the representative sampling of households. The *final basic weights*, which have been post-stratified to represent the civilian noninstitutional population, are used in all estimation. The statistical software program SUDAAN is used to adjust statistical tests for the complex nature of the survey design.

Disability is measured in different ways across the major national surveys, and empirical evidence finds that some measures have changed at varying rates (Freedman et al. 2004). The defining dimension of disability in the two questions in the NHIS is need for personal help. The first question asks about help with activities of daily living (ADL): "Because of any impairment or health problem, does _____ need help of other persons with

---

1. People age seventy in 1982 are not included because they were not asked the same disability questions.

personal care needs, such as eating, bathing, dressing, or getting around this home?" Those who answered no to this question were then asked about limitations with instrumental activities of daily living (IADL): "Because of any impairment or health problem, does _____ need help of other persons in handling routine needs, such as everyday household chores, doing necessary business, shopping, or getting around for other purposes?" Prior to 1982 the questions were substantially different. The questions were slightly modified in 1997, with the introductory phrase using the following alternative language: "Because of a physical, mental, or emotional problem, does . . ." Estimates of disability prevalence are reported for any disability (i.e., either ADL or IADL disability).[2]

Disparities are examined by education, income, race/ethnicity, age, sex, marital status, and region. Education is classified into five groups: zero to eight, nine to eleven, twelve, thirteen to fifteen, and sixteen or more years. Disability prevalence is also reported for year-specific quartiles in the total family income distribution. Unlike education, then, the proportion of the population in each income group remains the same across each year. In survey years 1982–1996 (1997–2002), family income is reported by the respondent as being in one of twenty-six (eleven) categories. In order to stratify prevalence estimates by income quartiles, we calculated a continuous income amount within categories, using a three-step procedure. First, for each year 1982 to 2002, we used the seventy-and-older population from the March Current Population Survey (CPS)—which is the U.S. Census Bureau's source for official estimates of income and poverty—to estimate family income as a function of sociodemographic variables and the family income categories appearing in the NHIS. For respondents missing income information altogether, we estimated a separate prediction equation without the income bracket indicators. Second, we used parameter estimates from these models along with demographic and income bracket information from the NHIS to calculate an estimate of family income within category for each NHIS respondent. Finally, we grouped individuals in each year of the NHIS into income quartiles. We evaluated the procedure by comparing the March CPS and calculated NHIS income distributions and trends and found they were substantially similar. The appendix provides a complete description of the procedures used.

Non-Hispanic whites are compared to all other racial/ethnic groups combined. There remain substantial differences in culture, socioeconomic status, and other factors within these racial/ethnic groups, but further dis-

---

2. Prior to 1997 the NHIS considered the respondent to have a disability only if the condition associated with the limitation was chronic or lasted three months. This chronicity restriction is not imposed in the public use disability indicator in 1997 and beyond. Therefore, for the post-1996 data, information in the public use data files that indicates whether the associated condition has lasted at least three months is combined with the disability indicator to mimic the procedure that was used prior to 1997.

aggregation of the minority group led to imprecise estimates. Moreover, comparisons between blacks and nonblacks, and whites and nonwhites led to similar conclusions. Four age groups are considered: seventy to seventy-four, seventy-five to seventy-nine, eighty to eighty-four, and eighty-five and older. Men and women, including currently married and unmarried elderly, are also examined. Finally, geographic disparities are examined for the four regions identifiable in the NHIS public use data: South, West, Midwest, and Northeast.

Unadjusted estimates of the disparities in the prevalence of disability for the population seventy and older are presented graphically for each year 1982 to 2002. The graphs depict trends in the difference in disability for selected groups for each of the socioeconomic and demographic factors. Some factors have too many categories to display the full range of comparisons; for these factors the categories with the highest and lowest disability prevalence in 1982 are shown. For education, for example, the difference in the prevalence for people with zero to eight years and sixteen or more years is displayed for each year. In addition, for each graph a third-order polynomial was fit to the data and displayed.

Two sets of graphs are presented. The first set (fig. 3.3) presents the simple difference in the disability rate across the groups for each year, 1982 to 2002. The second set of graphs (fig. 3.4) presents the relative difference across the groups (i.e., the difference in the disability rate between the group with the highest rate and the group with the lowest rate, divided by the latter, multiplied by 100) across the groups for each year, 1982 to 2002. It is important to consider trends in both measures of the gaps in disability because the disability rate in 1982 is quite different across the socioeconomic and demographic groups.

The second set of graphs is more consistent in approach with the logistic models that are estimated to test for trends and disparities in trends after adjusting for various factors. Statistical tests for adjusted trends and disparities in trends are based on a set of logistic regression models estimated from all years of data combined. The key explanatory factor is a linear trend variable that takes the value of zero in 1982 and increases by 1 in each subsequent year, with maximum value of 20 in 2002. This parsimonious linear specification was adopted because the second- and third-order polynomial terms were not consistently significant. The control variables in all models include age (represented by categories for seventy to seventy-four, seventy-five to seventy-nine, eighty to eighty-four, and eighty-five and older), sex, and indicators for whether the response was given by a proxy. Proxy is also interacted with an indicator for whether the interview was taken after 1996, because the proxy rules in the NHIS changed after 1996.

The first model includes the trend variable along with all of the control variables except age. Model two adds the control for age to demonstrate the importance of age adjustment. The subsequent models, model three through model nine, add the socioeconomic and demographic factors individually; that is, the direct effect of the factor is included as well as inter-action terms between the trend and the variables of interest. A final model includes all of the factors simultaneously.

An estimate of the average annual percent change in disability, the parameter of central interest, is calculated as the estimated odds ratio on the trend variable minus 1, multiplied by one hundred. Tests for differences across groups in the average annual percent change are evaluated by significance levels of interaction terms.

Finally, as a robustness check, all of the multivariate models were reestimated using ordinary least squares (OLS) instead of logistic models. The OLS estimates provide the regression analog of the simple differences reported in figure 3.3. The OLS estimates (appendix table 3.1) lead to the same substantive conclusion as the logistic models. The primary exception to this conclusion is the change in the disparity across age groups, and this point is described when referring to unadjusted disparities in figures 3.3 and 3.4.

3.3   Results

Disparities in health and disability are well documented in the population as a whole, and the magnitude of the disparities in disability for the population age seventy and older are displayed in figure 3.1. That is, the percentage of the population age seventy and older who report needing help with a daily activity in 1982 (the beginning of our time period) is displayed for each of the socioeconomic and demographic factors. Appendix table 3.2 reports the proportion of this population that falls into each of these groups in each year.

Socioeconomic differentials (panel A) are large, with disability rates of 27 percent for people with zero to eight years versus 15 percent for people with sixteen or more years. The lowest income quartile has a disability rate that is 38 percent higher than the highest income quartile (29 versus 21 percent), with similar differences between non-Hispanic whites and all other racial/ethnic groups.

Demographic disparities in disability are also substantial. The disparities in favor of men over women (8 percentage points), married over not married (11 percentage points), and residents in the West over the South (10 percentage points) are all at least as large as the disparity that exists for the highest versus the lowest income quartiles. Obviously age is strongly related to disability, with a rate of 15 percent for the seventy to seventy-four year-old age group and 42 percent for those ages eighty-five and older.

Unadjusted trends in old-age disability are reported in figure 3.2. At the beginning of the period, 22.7 percent had either an ADL or IADL disability. There was a steep drop in the subsequent five years, but then the rate was virtually unchanged for the next ten years, 1986 to 1996. The rate fell quickly during the following six-year period, from 19.3 percent in 1996 to

Panel A: Education, Income, and Race/Ethnicity

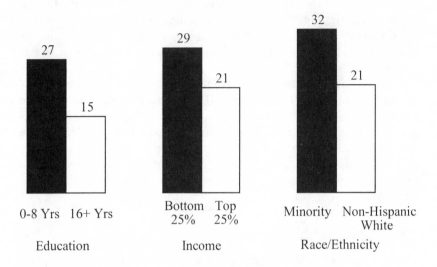

0-8 Yrs	16+ Yrs	Bottom 25%	Top 25%	Minority	Non-Hispanic White
Education		Income		Race/Ethnicity	

Panel B: Age, Sex, Marital status, Region

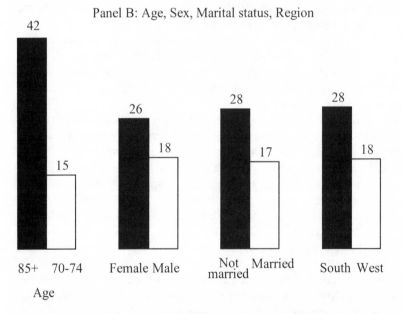

85+	70-74	Female	Male	Not married	Married	South	West
Age							

Fig. 3.1   Percent of the population seventy and older who have a disability, by socioeconomic and demographic characteristics: 1982

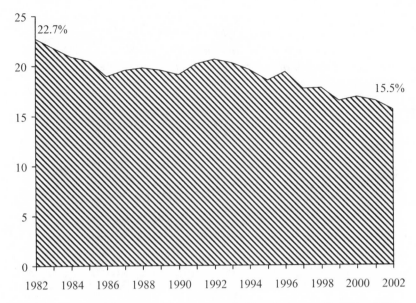

Fig. 3.2   Percent of the population seventy and older who have a disability: 1982 to 2002

15.5 percent in 2002. Taken as a whole, the 32 percent reduction in disability (i.e., 7.2 percentage point decline divided by 22.7 percent disability rate in 1982) over the twenty year period translates into a–1.39 percent annual change in disability.

Figure 3.3 displays the difference in the percentage that have a disability between the groups with the highest and lowest disability rates in 1982. For example, at the beginning of the period people with zero to eight years of schooling were roughly 10 percentage points more likely to have a disability than were people with sixteen or more years of schooling. The disparity increased to nearly 15 percentage points by the end of the twenty year period. Income disparities were smaller than the educational disparity but experienced a roughly similar increase through 2002. At the same time, racial/ethnic disparities were cut in half, from about 10 percentage points to 5 percentage points.

Disparities by age and sex were fairly constant during the twenty year period. The advantage in favor of married people shows a modestly increasing trend through 2002. Regional differences declined, specifically between the South and the West. The South had the highest disability rate in 1982—a rate that was 10 percentage points higher than in the West—but this gap was eliminated by 2002. During this period, the seventy-and-older population shifted toward both of these regions by somewhat similar magnitudes and away from the Northeast and Midwest (appendix table 3.2).

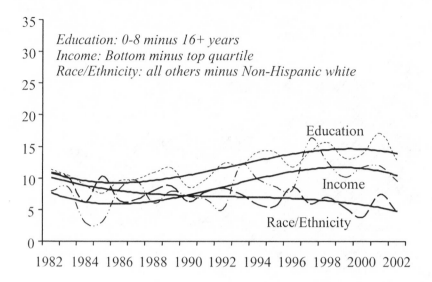

Panel A: Education, Income, Race/Ethnicity

Education: 0-8 minus 16+ years
Income: Bottom minus top quartile
Race/Ethnicity: all others minus Non-Hispanic white

Education

Income

Race/Ethnicity

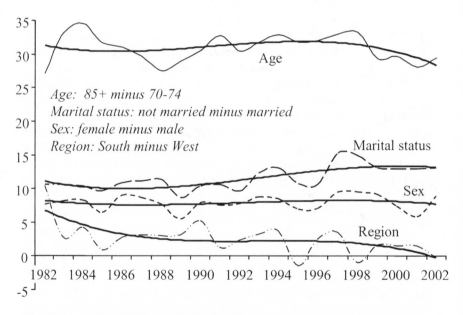

Panel B: Age, Sex, Marital Status, Region

Age

Age: 85+ minus 70-74
Marital status: not married minus married
Sex: female minus male
Region: South minus West

Marital status

Sex

Region

Fig. 3.3   Unadjusted difference in the disability rate: Low versus high socioeconomic and demographic groups: 1982 to 2002

Note: In each year for each variable, the disability rate for the category with the lowest rate (as of 1982) is subtracted from the rate for the category with the highest rate (as of 1982). A cubic trend is displayed on top of estimates for each factor.

The trends in relative disability (fig. 3.4) are similar to the trends in the simple difference in disability (fig. 3.3). That is, regardless of the measure of disparity in disability, the differences by education, income, and marital status increased, and the differences by region decreased. The most notable exception is for age. There was little change in the simple difference in disability prevalence across age groups, but because the disability rate is much lower for the younger age groups, the relative difference increased substantially, which indicates a widening gap. Specifically, the disability rate in 1982 was roughly 200 percent higher for people eighty-five and older than people seventy to seventy-four. But the gap increased to nearly 400 percent by 2002 (fig. 3.4). The trend in the gap between racial/ethnic groups is also somewhat sensitive to whether relative or simple differences are examined; both measures indicate some decline in the racial/ethnic gap, but the simple difference measure in figure 3.3 shows a larger decline than the relative difference measure, which is expected, given the fact that minorities experienced a larger absolute decline in disability than non-Hispanic whites over the twenty year period.

3.3.1 Multivariate Analyses

The estimates from model one in table 3.1 replicate the graphical analysis in figure 3.4 but control for sex and proxy response and parameterize the trend as linear. The odds ratio of 0.9845 implies an annual change of −1.55 percent per year ([0.9845–1.0] × 100), which is close to the unadjusted estimate of –1.39 percent based on the change in the prevalence at the endpoints 1982 and 2002, discussed previously.

The age distribution of the population seventy and older became only slightly older. However, because of the strong relationship between age and disability, adjusting for age (model two versus model one) increases (in absolute value terms) the estimated rate of change in disability to –2.15 percent per year. The estimate is also very precise, with the 95 percent confidence interval ranging from 0.9751 to 0.9820, or in average annual percentage terms from –1.80 to –2.49.

The multivariate estimates are consistent with the graphical depiction of the trends in disparities between education and income groups. The odds ratios imply a larger decline for the higher income and education groups. For example, the lowest education group experienced a change of just –0.88 percent per year, while the most educated group experienced a change of –2.53 percent per year. Moreover, the trend exhibits an almost fully monotonic increase with education and income; at all levels, the higher the education and income, the greater the decline. The differences between the higher groups and the lowest group are statistically significant and substantively important in most cases as well.

The age-adjusted decline is somewhat greater for minorities than for non-Hispanic whites, although the difference is not statistically significant.

Panel A: Education, Income, Race/Ethnicity

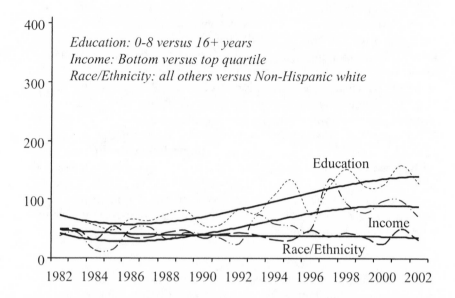

Education: 0-8 versus 16+ years
Income: Bottom versus top quartile
Race/Ethnicity: all others versus Non-Hispanic white

Panel B: Age, Sex, Marital Status, Region

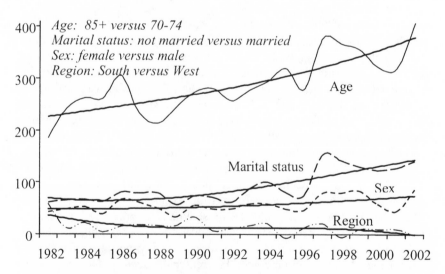

Age: 85+ versus 70-74
Marital status: not married versus married
Sex: female versus male
Region: South versus West

Fig. 3.4   Unadjusted relative disability rate: Low versus high socioeconomic and demographic groups: 1982 to 2002

Note: In each year for each variable, the difference between the disability rate for the category with the highest rate (as of 1982) and the disability rate for the category with the lowest rate (as of 1982) is divided by the rate for the latter category, and multiplied by 100. A cubic trend is displayed on top of estimates for each factor.

Table 3.1 Odds ratios from logistic models allowing trend to differ by socioeconomic and demographic characteristics

	Model 1		Model 2		Model 3		Model 4		Model 5	
	OR	95% CI	OR	95% CI	OR	95% CI	OR	95% CI	OR	95% CI
Trend	0.9845	0.9811–0.9879	0.9785	0.9751–0.9820						
Trend * Education										
0–8 years					0.9912	0.9862–0.9962				
9–41 years					0.9916	0.9852–0.9981				
12 years					0.9839**	0.9789–0.9891				
13–15 years					0.9833*	0.9756–0.9911				
16+ years					0.9747***	0.9669–0.9826				
Trend * Income										
Quartile 1							0.9862	0.9812–0.9912		
Quartile 2							0.9735***	0.9679–0.9791		
Quartile 3							0.9694***	0.9639–0.9750		
Quartile 4							0.9689***	0.9634–0.9744		
Trend * race/ethnicity										
Non-Hispanic white									0.9782	0.9747–0.9818
All others									0.9743	0.9675–0.9811
Controls										
Age 75–79			1.5855	1.5275–1.6457	1.5415	1.4853–1.5999	1.5533	1.4963–1.6124	1.6000	1.5411–1.6610
Age 80–84			2.8030	2.6937–2.9167	2.6464	2.5424–2.7546	2.6901	2.5837–2.8008	2.8487	2.7372–2.9648
Age 85+			5.6906	5.4451–5.9472	5.1957	4.9685–5.4332	5.3614	5.1291–5.6043	5.8057	5.5553–6.0675
Female	1.8859	1.8302–1.9433	1.7403	1.6874–1.7949	1.7475	1.6943–1.8023	1.6437	1.5927–1.6963	1.7329	1.6802–1.7873
Any Proxy	1.9600	1.8812–2.0421	1.9596	1.8823–2.0401	1.9178	1.8415–1.9973	2.1526	2.0683–2.2403	1.9140	1.8388–1.9924
Any Proxy * Post-1996	0.6723	0.6291–0.7184	0.6955	0.6517–0.7422	0.6902	0.6465–0.7368	0.7673	0.7178–0.8202	0.6952	0.6514–0.7420
DK Proxy	1.4411	1.2212–1.7006	1.3228	1.1092–1.5776	1.1356	0.9455–1.3638	1.3112	1.0943–1.5712	1.3027	1.0920–1.5540
DK Proxy * Post-1996	0.6602	0.3156–1.3810	0.8961	0.3967–2.0243	1.0167	0.4603–2.2455	1.1140	0.4969–2.4976	0.8533	0.3754–0.9400
Main effects										
Education 9–11 years					0.7696	0.7113–0.8327				
Education 12 years					0.6486	0.6038–0.6967				
Education 13–15 years					0.6148	0.5524–0.6844				
Education 16+ years					0.6467	0.5779–0.7237				
Income quartile 2							0.7594	0.7060–0.8169		
Income quartile 3							0.7200	0.6646–0.7800		
Income quartile 4							0.7112	0.6541–0.7733		
Non-Hispanic whites									0.6024	0.5493–0.6605

(continued)

Table 3.1 (continued)

	Model 6 OR	Model 6 95% CI	Model 7 OR	Model 7 95% CI	Model 8 OR	Model 8 95% CI	Model 9 OR	Model 9 95% CI
Trend * Age								
Age 70–74	0.9720	0.9667–0.9773						
Age 75–79	0.9742	0.9691–0.9792						
Age 80–84	0.9812***	0.9758–0.9867						
Age 85+	0.9893***	0.9839–0.9947						
Trend * Sex								
Female			0.9795	0.9759–0.9831				
Male			0.9763	0.9713–0.9813				
Trend * Marital status								
Married					0.9596	0.9547–0.9646		
Not married					0.9864***	0.9828–0.9901		
Trend * Interview region								
South							0.9722	0.9662–0.9782
Northeast							0.9768	0.9703–0.9854
Midwest							0.9836***	0.9774–0.9899
West							0.9846***	0.9778–0.9914
Controls								
Age 75–79	1.5541	1.4518–1.6637	1.5857	1.5277–1.6459	1.5244	1.4684–1.5824	1.5884	1.5303–1.6488
Age 80–84	2.5511	2.3603–2.7573	2.8035	2.6942–2.9172	2.5648	2.4637–2.6700	2.8131	2.7034–2.9273
Age 85+	4.7250	4.3412–5.1429	5.6908	5.4453–5.9474	4.8483	4.6358–5.0707	5.7415	5.4935–6.0006
Female	1.7412	1.6884–1.7958	1.6830	1.5923–1.7789	1.4396	1.3937–1.4871	1.7438	1.6909–1.7984
Any Proxy	1.9622	1.8851–2.0425	1.9556	1.8777–2.0368	2.1337	2.0480–2.2231	1.9539	1.8770–2.0339
Any Proxy * Post-1996	0.6967	0.6528–0.7437	0.6990	0.6543–0.7467	0.8102	0.7572–0.8670	0.6974	0.6535–0.7442
DK Proxy	1.3294	1.1154–1.5844	1.3229	1.1093–1.5776	1.2836	1.0766–1.5304	1.3098	1.0947–1.5672
DK Proxy * Post-1996	0.9087	0.3979–2.0752	0.8973	0.3969–2.0284	1.0985	0.4833–2.4966	0.8937	0.3940–2.0272
Married					0.7775	0.7313–0.8266		
Northeast region							1.0026	0.8842–1.1367
Midwest region							1.0120	0.8897–1.1382
South region							1.3652	1.2150–1.5340

Notes: OR = Odds Ratio; CI = Confidence Interval; DK = Do not know; N = 172,227. Sample is all persons aged seventy (seventy-one in 1982) and older in the NHIS. To account for the complex nature of the sample design, variance estimation was conducted using SUDAAN software. Reference groups for models 1–5 are: zero to eight years, quartile 1, "all others." Reference groups for models 6–9 are: seventy to seventy-four, female, married, South. *, **, *** indicate a statistical significant trend relative to the trend for the reference group at the 0.10, 0.05, and 0.01 level, respectively.

While changes were substantial for the older age groups (–1.07 percent per year for people eighty-five and older) the declines were much larger for the younger group. The rate of change was –2.80 percent and –2.58 percent per year for the two youngest groups, respectively.

For the population seventy and older between 1982 and 2002, male mortality improved more than female mortality. If it were the case that the relatively strong improvements for males resulted in keeping alive people who had a disability, then it would be expected that disability declines would be greater for women. But this is not the case; the declines in disability are not statistically significantly different between the sexes.

The changes are much larger among married elderly: –4.04 percent versus –1.36 percent per year for the unmarried. Recall that these estimates adjust for the direct effect of marriage, and the marital status distribution did not change substantially during the twenty years. The South has the highest initial disability rate among the four regions, but it is also the region that experienced the largest declines in disability.

All factors simultaneously.

Can the trends for various groups be explained by changes in the composition of the sample over the twenty-year period? We explore this issue by estimating models identical to those in table 3.1, but for each model add controls for the direct effects of all of the socioeconomic and demographic factors. The first column of table 3.2 replicates the estimates reported in table 3.1, but instead of reporting the odds ratio it reports the average annual percentage change in disability (i.e., the odds ratio minus 1, multiplied by 100). Each set of rows separated by a horizontal line is based on its own logistic model, as in table 3.1. The second column contains the estimate of the average annual percentage change based on the models that include the additional factors. For example, the average annual percentage change without controlling for any factors other than age, sex, and proxy is –2.15. If all of the socioeconomic and demographic factors are accounted for, the change is reduced to –1.86. In logistic models not reported in the tables, it was found that education accounted for virtually all of the change in the estimate.

The estimated changes in disability for most socioeconomic and demographic groups were not altered substantially when the additional factors were accounted for. For example, the trend for people seventy to seventy-four is –2.80 without additional controls and –2.63 with additional controls. For income, the trends are slightly lower for each group when controls are added, but all trends remain statistically significant, and the trend for the two highest income quartiles remains more than twice as large as the decline among the lowest income quartile. For education, trends are strengthened for each group, with especially large increases for the least educated: the change is –0.88 without controls and –1.52 with controls. Again, however,

Table 3.2   **Estimated average annual percent change in disability controlling for all socioeconomic and demographic factors simultaneously**

	Based on estimates reported in models 2–9 in Table 3.1 (1)	Same as (1) but also controls for direct effect of all socioeconomic and demographic factors (2)
Trend	−2.15	−1.86
Trend * Education		
0–8 years	−0.88	−1.52
9–11 years	−0.84	−1.35
12 years	−1.61**	−1.92
13–15 years	−1.67*	−2.01
16+ years	−2.53***	−2.85***
Trend * Income		
Quartile 1	−1.38	−1.10
Quartile 2	−2.65***	−2.05***
Quartile 3	−3.06***	−2.57***
Quartile 4	−3.11***	−2.34***
Trend * Race/ethnicity		
Non-Hispanic white	−2.18	−1.76
All others	−2.57	−2.36***
Trend * Age		
Age 70–74	−2.80	−2.63
Age 75–79	−2.58	−2.22
Age 80–84	−1.88***	−1.40***
Age 85+	−1.07***	−0.91***
Trend * Sex		
Female	−2.05	−1.78
Male	−2.37	−2.03
Trend * Marital Status		
Married	−4.04	−3.41
Not married	−1.36***	−1.10***
Trend * Interview region		
South	−2.78	−2.39
Northeast	−2.32	−1.99
Midwest	−1.64***	−1.18***
West	−1.54***	−1.56*

Notes: All models include controls for age, sex, and proxy factors listed in table 3.1. All estimates of trends are significant at the 0.05 level. Reference groups are: zero to eight years, quartile 1, non-Hispanic white, seventy to seventy-four female, married, South. Estimates in each set of rows are based on a separate logistic model. *, **, *** indicate a statistical significant trend relative to the trend for the reference group at the 0.10, 0.05, and 0.01 level, respectively.

the declines are much larger for those with more education. However, statistically significant racial/ethnic differences in trends in favor of minorities emerge once the other controls are added. And declines in disability among older people living in the South remain significantly greater than those for people living in the West and Midwest.

3.3.2 Institutionalized Population

We explored sensitivity to the omission of the institutional population using data from the National Nursing Home Survey (NNHS). The NNHS is used to add in the nursing home population to the estimates based on the noninstitutional population from the NHIS. One of the limitations of this approach is that some assisted living facilities are most likely not included in either the NHIS or the NNHS. Although the exact number of elderly persons living in such facilities is unknown, it is believed to be small but increasing.

Table 3.3 displays the disability rate for the noninstitutional population (NHIS) and for the noninstitutional population combined with the nursing home population (NHIS+NNHS) in each year in which the NNHS was conducted: 1985, 1995, 1997, and 1999. The NNHS does not contain data on income and education of nursing home residents, but race/ethnicity, age, sex, marital status, and region are measured. All of the underlying estimates that are needed to combine the NHIS and NNHS estimates into a single estimate are contained in table 3.3 for the entire population seventy and older, and, as an illustration, for the two racial/ethnic groups. In calculating these estimates, it is assumed that all nursing home residents have either an ADL or IADL disability.

The central issue is whether the trends in disparities in disability are different when the nursing home population is folded into the estimates of disability. This is addressed in figures 3.5 and 3.6, which display the exact same disparities displayed in figures 3.3 and 3.4 for the population living in the community (i.e., the NHIS estimates), but also shows the disparities after the nursing home population is included into the analysis. The general finding is that adding in the nursing home population does not alter the estimated trend in disparities. For example, the cubic trend in the gap between racial/ethnic groups based on the estimates from the community-dwelling sample in the NHIS (fig. 3.5) runs almost exactly through the large square data points representing the racial/ethnic disparity once the nursing home population is included. The disparities by marital status and age are larger when the nursing home population is included, which is exactly what would be expected given the fact that unmarried and older persons are much more likely to be living in nursing homes than married and younger persons. However, the trends in disparities are quite similar regardless of the inclusion of the nursing home population: the disparity between the married and unmarried increased between 1985 and the later periods; dispari-

Table 3.3 Disability rate with and without the nursing home population included, by race/ethnicity

	All Persons			Non-Hispanic white			All other racial/ethnic groups		
	Number of people	Number with any disability	Proportion with any disability	Number of people	Number with any disability	Proportion with any disability	Number of people	Number with any disability	Proportion with any disability
	National Nursing Home Survey (NNHS)								
1985	1,234,301	1,234,301	1.0000	1,119,917	1,119,917	1.0000	114,383	114,383	1.0000
1995	1,359,583	1,359,583	1.0000	1,137,779	1,137,779	1.0000	221,804	221,804	1.0000
1997	1,403,624	1,403,624	1.0000	1,153,462	1,153,462	1.0000	250,163	250,163	1.0000
1999	1,396,921	1,396,921	1.0000	1,144,488	1,144,488	1.0000	252,434	252,434	1.0000
	National Health Interview Survey (NHIS)								
1985	17,753,893	3,627,120	0.2043	15,666,083	3,011,021	0.1922	2,087,810	616,530	0.2953
1995	21,689,083	4,016,818	0.1852	18,659,629	3,310,218	0.1774	3,029,454	706,772	0.2333
1997	22,410,160	3,959,875	0.1767	19,258,332	3,114,072	0.1617	3,151,828	697,500	0.2213
1999	23,286,508	3,821,316	0.1641	19,795,256	2,969,288	0.1500	3,491,252	711,168	0.2037
	NNHS + NHIS								
1985	18,988,194	4,861,421	0.2560	16,786,000	4,130,938	0.2461	2,202,193	730,914	0.3319
1995	23,048,666	5,376,401	0.2333	19,797,408	4,447,997	0.2247	3,251,258	928,576	0.2856
1997	23,813,784	5,363,499	0.2252	20,411,794	4,267,534	0.2091	3,401,991	947,662	0.2786
1999	24,683,429	5,218,237	0.2114	20,939,744	4,113,776	0.1965	3,743,686	963,602	0.2574

Panel A: Race/Ethnicity, Marital Status

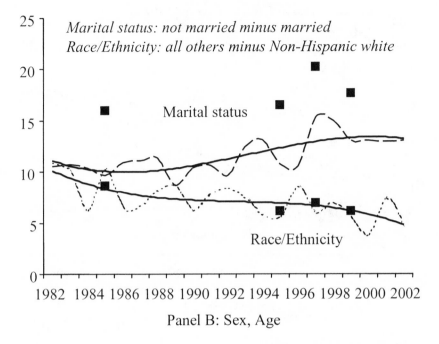

Panel B: Sex, Age

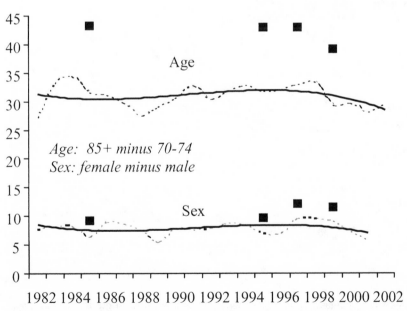

Fig. 3.5   Unadjusted difference in disability rate with and without the nursing home population: 1982 to 2002

Note: In each year for each variable, the disability rate for the category with the lowest rate (as of 1982) is subtracted from the rate for the category with the highest rate (as of 1982). A cubic trend is displayed on top of estimates for each factor. Square marks = with nursing home population; dashed lines = without nursing home population.

Panel A: Race/Ethnicity, Marital Status

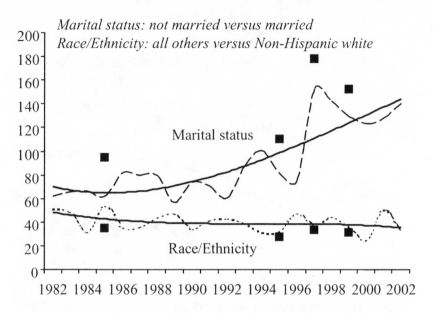

Panel B: Sex, Age

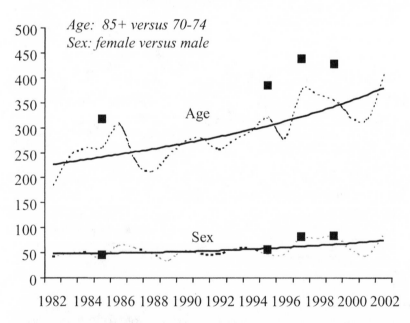

Fig. 3.6 Unadjusted relative disability rate with and without the nursing home population: 1982 to 2002

Note: In each year for each variable, the difference between the disability rate for the category with the highest rate (as of 1982) and the disability rate for the category with the lowest rate (as of 1982) is divided by the rate for the latter category, and multiplied by 100. A cubic trend is displayed on top of estimates for each factor. Square marks = with nursing home population; dashed lines = without nursing home population.

ties between non-Hispanic whites and all others did not increase and showed some signs of declining, although the estimates were not significant; disparities between men and women changed very little; when measured by the simple difference in disability rates, age disparities were flat between 1985 and 1997 and then fell somewhat, but when measured by the relative differences the age disparities increased (fig. 3.6).

3.4 Discussion

Old-age disability rates among all socioeconomic and demographic groups declined over the past two decades, but the magnitude of the decline was larger for several groups with lower risk of having disability—those who had higher income, had more years of education, were married, and were younger. As a result, disparities in disability generally have increased.

Two noteworthy exceptions involve regional and racial/ethnic patterns. First, once all other factors were controlled, there was a narrowing of the disability disparity between non-Hispanic whites and others. Second, because declines were greatest in the southern states, gaps in disability between the South and West and between the South and Midwest narrowed over this time period.

These findings extend previous studies of trends in disability gaps in several ways. Prior studies have typically limited exploration of gaps to disparities by age, sex, race, and education and have often omitted important statistical tests (Freedman, Martin, and Schoeni 2002). The only study to consistently include statistical tests (Schoeni, Freedman, and Wallace 2001) drew upon the same dataset we use here (the NHIS), but was limited to fifteen years, from 1982 to 1996. In that analysis it was found, as we find here, that educational and marital status differences were widening and regional differences narrowing over time. Unlike that prior analysis, however, we have here documented growing disparities by income quartiles, narrowing of racial gaps, and relative increases in the age gap.

What has caused these trends? Our analysis suggests that trends cannot be attributed to changes in the size or makeup of the nursing home population. And, with the exception of age disparities, we find trends and disparities therein are robust whether we consider absolute differences in prevalence across groups or relative differences. Nor can we attribute declines completely to shifts in the demographic composition of the older population. Indeed, we found that sociodemographic and economic factors are highly correlated with disability in old age, and along many of these dimensions the composition of the older population has changed. Population groups that have lower disability rates—those who are married, male, more educated, and for example—have become more prevalent among the elderly. But we find that together, changes in these factors and others explain little of the net improvement in disability.

We also find, like others (Freedman and Martin 1999; Waidmann and Liu 2000), that shifts in the education distribution in particular explain a substantial portion (but not all) of the decline in disability. Education may represent, among other things, the lifelong effects of mediating factors including early childhood experiences, access to medical care throughout the lifecourse, health behaviors, and ability to navigate the health care system and implement complex medical regimens. To identify the causes of the declines in disability and shifts in the gaps we must look to these mediating effects as well as other factors not directly linked to educational attainment.

Late-life disability is influenced by a variety of factors, many of which are modifiable and are linked to demographic characteristics and socioeconomic status (Stuck 1999). Here we speculate about the relevance of three domains: behavioral and biologic risk factors, medical care, and the physical environment. These factors may assert their effects in different stages of the lifecourse, including early life and midlife (Barker 1994; Blackwell, Hayward, and Crimmins 2001; Elo and Preston 1992; Kuh and Ben-Shlomo 1997).

Risk factors for lifestyle-related diseases have been linked to disability and have been shown to vary by demographic and socioeconomic status (Berkman and Mullen 1997; DeLew and Weinick 2000). The contribution of risk factors to trends has been explored for the adult population in other countries (Ahacic et al. 2007; Galobardes et al. 2003), where increases in socioeconomic status have been linked to declines in disability through mediating health behaviors and biologic risk factors. To our knowledge, in the United States nationally representative population-based evidence linking trends in risk factors to late-life disability for various demographic and socioeconomic groups is not available. However, insight into this relationship may be gleaned from more selective studies and from studies with too few older people to stratify by demographic and socioeconomic status. For example, Allaire and colleagues (1999) show for the (largely white) Framingham Heart Study that offspring have fewer risk factors for disability (i.e., were more physically active and less likely to smoke or consume high amounts of alcohol) than their parents. Vita and colleagues (1998) have demonstrated for a cohort of college graduates that individuals with a low-risk profile in terms of smoking, body mass index, and exercise patterns live longer and experience fewer years of disability compressed at the end of life. At the same time, data from the fifty state Behavioral Risk Factor Surveillance System suggests health-related quality of life and self-rated health status has improved for people ages sixty-five and older (Zack et al. 2004) despite worsening trends for other age groups. Analysis of changes in health behaviors between 1990 and 2000 suggest that older Americans in 2000 were more likely to exercise, consume more fruits and vegetables daily, and to have recently obtained a routine medical checkup and less likely to smoke tobacco or drink any alcohol (Mokdad et al. 2004).

Another domain of speculation that may be particularly relevant is changes in the use of medical care. There also are important differentials, for example, in access to medical care and health care information (AHRQ 2003). Although few studies provide evidence of gaps over time in medical care, limited evidence is available on trends by race and on cross-sectional patterns by region. Escarce and McGuire (2004), for example, find that between 1986 and 1997 the white–black gap in use of medical procedures and diagnostic tests under Medicare narrowed. Findings have been mixed, however, with respect to specific medical procedures and services. For example, Groeneveld, Heidenreich, and Garber (2005) found declines in racial disparities in the use of implantable cardiac defribillators, while Crystal and colleagues (2003) found increases in depression treatment were larger for whites than for Hispanics. Regional variation in medical care is substantial, even for narrowly defined conditions (Baicker et al. 2004; Wennberg and Cooper 1999; Weinstein et al. 2004). Fisher and colleagues (2003) find that per capita Medicare spending is particularly high for hospital referral areas in the southern region, and Lin and Zimmer (2002) have identified higher rates of disability in southern states, but how these patterns have changed over the last two decades and whether they are linked needs further exploration.

Changes over time in the physical environment in which older people live and work may also be influencing disability rates differentially by demographic and socioeconomic status. Less advantaged groups often live in poorer-quality older housing and face more environmental barriers (Gitlin et al. 2001; Tomita et al. 1997; Newman 2003) and are less likely to turn to assistive technologies for difficulty with daily activities (Agree, Freedman and Sengupta 2004). At the same time, socioeconomically advantaged groups are more likely to live in homes with features in place that facilitate aging (e.g., retirement communities built with wide hallways, railings, and accessible bathrooms). Recent studies suggest a strong trend toward the use of assistive technology as the sole form of assistance—that is, without help from another person (Freedman et al. 2004; Spillman 2004)—and increases in the presence of home modifications among older people reporting a housing-related disability. Differentials in these trends have been explored for the first time elsewhere in this volume by Freedman and colleagues, who show that disparities in assistive technology use by race and socioeconomic status have persisted through 2001. They also show, however, that only among those with more than a high school education have increases in assistive technology offset declines in the chances of receiving help. Such evidence is consistent with the divergent disability trends by education we found here.

Understanding the underlying cause of the disparities in disability and the reasons for the changes in this gap are pressing social and policy concerns. The causal factors are likely to consist of a mixture of medical, social, and behavioral influences. Interdisciplinary teams are needed to make significant headway on these unresolved issues. Moreover, a broad population-level perspective, as opposed to focusing on a single cause or subgroup, is likely to be a more effective approach.

Appendix

Income Quartile Estimation

To determine a value for total family income for the NHIS 1982–2002 person data, we used the following imputation method. A regression model of total family income was estimated using the March Current Population Survey (CPS) data for each year, 1982–2002, for persons aged seventy and older. The March CPS is the Census Bureau's official source for income and poverty estimates. The explanatory variables include characteristics measured in both the CPS and the NHIS: age, years of education completed, ethnicity and race, marital status, sex, region, and family size. In addition, dummy variables were constructed to reflect whether a respondent was in a given income bracket, with the income brackets being the NHIS-defined categories. For 1982–1996 there were twenty-six NHIS income brackets and for 1997–2002 there were eleven. Years of education were grouped into three categories: zero to eight years, nine to twelve years, and thirteen and over years. Hispanic ethnicity and race were combined to form four categories: Hispanic, non-Hispanic whites, non-Hispanic blacks, and non-Hispanic other. Four variables represented family size: 1, 2, 3, and 4 or more. Region was defined as Northeast, Midwest, South, and West. All sociodemographic factors were interacted with the income brackets when the width of the bracket was not equal to $5,000. For example, for years 1982–1996, interactions were included for family income between $20,000 and $49,999, family income of $50,000 or over, and family income over $20,000. For years 1997–2002, interactions were included for family income between $25,000 and $74,999, family income of $75,000 or more, and family income over $20,000.

The NHIS person data contain some missing observations for total family income. Therefore, a separate model was estimated that had all of the explanatory variables previously described except the income categories, since these were unknown in the NHIS for some NHIS respondents.

Finally, using the parameter estimates from the CPS models for each year, a predicted income value was generated for each person in the NHIS sample. After calculating the predicted value of total family income for each respondent in the NHIS, tests were run to determine if the predicted value fell within the NHIS-defined income bracket that they reported. For all but five of the 172,227 cases estimated, income values fell within the actual reported income bracket.

Table 3A.1 OLS regression allowing trend to differ across socioeconomic and demographic factors

	Model 1		Model 2		Model 3		Model 4		Model 5	
	Coefficient	Standard error	Coefficient	Standard error	Coefficient	Standard error	Coefficient	Standard error	Coefficient	Standard error
Trend	-0.0023	0.0003	-0.0030	0.0003						
Trend * Education										
0–8 years					-0.0014	0.0004				
9–11 years					-0.0011	0.0005				
12 years					-0.0021	0.0003				
13–15 years					-0.0020	0.0005				
16+ years					-0.0026	0.0005**				
Trend * Income										
Quartile 1							-0.0022	0.0004		
Quartile 2							-0.0035	0.0004**		
Quartile 3							-0.0038	0.0004***		
Quartile 4							-0.0038	0.0004***		
Trend*Race/ethnicity										
Non-Hispanic white									-0.0030	-0.0003
All others									-0.0044	0.0006**
Controls										
Age 75–79			0.0523	0.0022	0.0480	0.0021	0.0492	0.0022	0.0533	0.0022
Age 80–84			0.1426	0.0031	0.1332	0.0031	0.1359	0.0031	0.1443	0.0031
Age 85+			0.2963	0.0042	0.2803	0.0042	0.2859	0.0042	0.2979	0.0042
Female	0.0911	0.0021	0.0752	0.0021	0.0753	0.0021	0.0661	0.0021	0.0744	0.0021
Any proxy	0.1105	0.0039	0.1046	0.0035	0.1003	0.0035	0.1156	0.0035	0.1011	0.0035
Any proxy * Post-1996	-0.0705	0.0055	-0.0619	0.0051	-0.0620	0.0050	-0.0526	0.0051	-0.0611	0.0050
DK proxy	0.0581	0.0148	0.0426	0.0147	0.0138	0.0151	0.0407	0.0149	0.0402	0.0146
DK proxy * Post-1996	-0.0618	0.0463	-0.0138	0.0479	0.0103	0.0468	0.0105	0.0477	-0.0197	0.0480
Main effects										
Education 9–11 years					-0.0467	0.0063				
Education 12 years					-0.0698	0.0055				
Education 13–15 years					-0.0775	0.0074				
Education 16+ years					-0.0732	0.0079				
Income quartile 2							-0.0500	0.0060		
Income quartile 3							-0.0578	0.0064		
Income quartile 4							-0.0583	0.0068		
Non-Hispanic whites									-0.0862	0.0081

(continued)

Table 3A.1   (continued)

	Model 1		Model 2		Model 3		Model 4	
	Coefficient	Standard error	Coefficient	Standard error	Coefficient	Standard error	Coefficient	Standard error
Trend * Age								
Age 70–74	−0.0025	0.0003						
Age 75–79	−0.0034	0.0003**						
Age 80–84	−0.0036	0.0005**						
Age 85+	−0.0029	0.0006						
Trend * Sex								
Female			−0.0033	0.0003				
Male			−0.0026	0.0003**				
Trend * Marital Status								
Married					−0.0044	0.0003		
Not married					−0.0022	0.0003***		
Trend * Interview Region								
South							−0.0041	0.0005
Northeast							−0.0031	0.0005
Midwest							−0.0023	0.0004***
West							−0.0021	0.0005***
Controls								
Age 75–79	0.0613	0.0045	0.0522	0.0022	0.0467	0.0022	0.0524	0.0022
Age 80–84	0.1542	0.0066	0.1426	0.0031	0.1296	0.0031	0.1429	0.0031
Age 85+	0.3005	0.0085	0.2963	0.0042	0.2724	0.0042	0.2971	0.0042
Female	0.0752	0.0021	0.0819	0.0039	0.0499	0.0021	0.0753	0.0021
Any Proxy	0.1046	0.0035	0.1050	0.0036	0.1168	0.0035	0.1039	0.0035
Any Proxy * Post-1996	−0.0621	0.0050	−0.0629	0.0051	−0.0467	0.0051	−0.0614	0.0050
DK Proxy	0.0424	0.0146	0.0426	0.0146	0.0363	0.0146	0.0411	0.0148
DK Proxy * Post-1996	−0.0143	0.0479	−0.0142	0.0479	0.0135	0.0469	−0.0142	0.0479
Main effects								
Married					−0.0506	0.0045		
Northeast region							0.0006	0.0091
Midwest region							0.0019	0.0086
Southern region							0.0478	0.0089

Notes: DK = Do not know; N = 172,227. Sample is all persons aged seventy (seventy-one in 1982) and older in the NHIS. To account for the complex nature of sample design, variance estimation was conducted using SUDAAN software. The reference groups are: seventy to seventy-four, female, married, South. *, **, *** indicate a statistical significant trend relative to the trend for the reference group at the 0.10, 0.05, and 0.01 level, respectively.

Table 3A.2   Weighted descriptive statistics: 1982 to 2002

	1982	1983	1984	1985	1986	1987	1988	1989	1990	1991	1992	1993	1994	1995	1996	1997	1998	1999	2000	2001	2002
Disabled	0.227	0.218	0.209	0.204	0.189	0.195	0.198	0.195	0.191	0.201	0.206	0.202	0.195	0.185	0.193	0.170	0.170	0.158	0.163	0.159	0.155
Years of education																					
0–8	0.464	0.416	0.398	0.396	0.373	0.346	0.334	0.325	0.308	0.297	0.276	0.269	0.252	0.246	0.220	0.213	0.202	0.191	0.186	0.181	0.171
9–11	0.155	0.163	0.169	0.164	0.157	0.163	0.164	0.163	0.165	0.148	0.164	0.152	0.159	0.152	0.158	0.171	0.162	0.153	0.148	0.152	0.135
12	0.210	0.239	0.256	0.253	0.264	0.283	0.287	0.297	0.306	0.315	0.326	0.331	0.335	0.344	0.353	0.322	0.330	0.329	0.346	0.332	0.343
13–15	0.083	0.087	0.091	0.100	0.107	0.106	0.110	0.109	0.114	0.123	0.120	0.124	0.135	0.131	0.130	0.166	0.175	0.180	0.183	0.184	0.193
16+	0.087	0.095	0.087	0.087	0.100	0.101	0.104	0.105	0.106	0.117	0.114	0.125	0.120	0.126	0.139	0.128	0.132	0.146	0.138	0.152	0.158
Non-Hispanic white	0.885	0.875	0.878	0.882	0.870	0.878	0.881	0.879	0.875	0.863	0.886	0.863	0.858	0.860	0.865	0.859	0.850	0.850	0.847	0.841	0.839
Age																					
70–74	0.359	0.416	0.415	0.417	0.416	0.411	0.411	0.410	0.407	0.414	0.407	0.405	0.401	0.400	0.394	0.380	0.368	0.373	0.371	0.356	0.357
75–79	0.322	0.295	0.306	0.293	0.297	0.297	0.298	0.299	0.291	0.285	0.280	0.288	0.287	0.286	0.298	0.299	0.301	0.305	0.303	0.305	0.302
80–84	0.197	0.177	0.170	0.179	0.176	0.175	0.176	0.177	0.184	0.182	0.186	0.185	0.188	0.184	0.179	0.191	0.196	0.185	0.197	0.203	0.200
85+	0.122	0.112	0.109	0.112	0.111	0.118	0.115	0.114	0.118	0.119	0.126	0.123	0.123	0.130	0.129	0.130	0.135	0.138	0.129	0.137	0.141
Female	0.615	0.607	0.613	0.608	0.605	0.607	0.605	0.607	0.602	0.597	0.598	0.595	0.598	0.602	0.595	0.594	0.594	0.590	0.591	0.587	0.590
Married	0.471	0.482	0.483	0.481	0.495	0.499	0.504	0.502	0.511	0.513	0.512	0.509	0.509	0.511	0.517	0.498	0.517	0.507	0.512	0.501	0.523
Region																					
South	0.325	0.323	0.334	0.345	0.336	0.335	0.344	0.335	0.343	0.340	0.343	0.341	0.329	0.344	0.336	0.347	0.343	0.343	0.341	0.345	0.358
West	0.174	0.184	0.183	0.162	0.163	0.176	0.178	0.184	0.180	0.191	0.186	0.194	0.193	0.188	0.205	0.185	0.200	0.189	0.194	0.194	0.195
Midwest	0.262	0.254	0.255	0.253	0.259	0.246	0.248	0.241	0.254	0.245	0.249	0.246	0.250	0.252	0.235	0.247	0.238	0.251	0.243	0.242	0.242
Northeast	0.240	0.240	0.228	0.239	0.242	0.242	0.229	0.240	0.223	0.225	0.223	0.219	0.228	0.216	0.224	0.220	0.218	0.217	0.221	0.219	0.205
Proxy																					
Any proxy	0.197	0.206	0.203	0.194	0.191	0.195	0.202	0.203	0.198	0.215	0.204	0.213	0.207	0.207	0.213	0.330	0.342	0.337	0.333	0.334	0.348
DK if proxy	0.004	0.004	0.008	0.006	0.008	0.012	0.013	0.008	0.008	0.012	0.011	0.008	0.012	0.012	0.009	0.001	0.004	0.001	0.001	0.000	0.001
Any proxy * post-1996	0.000	0.000	0.000	0.000	0.000	0.000	0.000	0.000	0.000	0.000	0.000	0.000	0.000	0.000	0.000	0.330	0.342	0.337	0.333	0.334	0.348
DK proxy * post-1996	0.000	0.000	0.000	0.000	0.000	0.000	0.000	0.000	0.000	0.000	0.000	0.000	0.000	0.000	0.000	0.001	0.004	0.001	0.001	0.000	0.001
Number of observations	6724	7650	7793	7035	4749	9522	9917	9457	9693	10175	10082	9038	10025	8168	4921	8239	7920	7799	7983	7757	7580

References

Agency for Healthcare Research and Quality (AHRQ). 2003. *National Healthcare Disparities Report*. Rockville, MD: AHRQ.

Agree, E. M., V. A. Freedman, and M. Sengupta. 2004. Factors influencing the use of mobility technology in community-based long-term care. *Journal of Aging Health* 16(2): 267–307.

Ahacic, K., I. Kåreholt, M. Thorslund, and M. G. Parker. 2007. Relationships between symptoms, physical capacity and activity limitations in 1992 and 2002. *Aging Clinical and Experimental Research* 19(3): 187–93.

Allaire, S. H., M. P. La Valley, S. R. Evans, G. T. O'Connor, M. Kelly-Hayes, R. F. Meenan, D. Levy, and D. T. Felson. 1999. Evidence for decline in disability and improved health among persons aged 55 to 70 years: The Framingham Heart Study. *American Journal of Public Health* 89:1678–83.

Baicker, K., A. Chandra, J. S. Skinner, and J. E. Wennberg. 2004. Who you are and where you live: How race and geography affect the treatment of Medicare beneficiaries. *Health Affairs*. Available at http://content.healthaffairs.otg/cgi/content/full/hltfaff.var33/DC3

Barker, D. J. P. 1994. *Mothers, Babies, and Disease in Later Life*. London: BMJ Publishing Group.

Berkman, L. F., and J. F. Mullen. 1997. How health behaviors and the social environment contribute to health differences between black and white older Americans. In *Racial and Ethnic Differences in the Health of Older Americans*, ed. L. G. Martin, B. J. Soldo, 163–82. Washington, DC: National Academy Press.

Blackwell, D. L., M. D. Hayward, and E. M. Crimmins. 2001. Does childhood health affect chronic morbidity in later life? *Social Science and Medicine* 52:1269–84.

Colvez, A., and M. Blanchet. 1981. Disability trends in the United States population: 1966–1976: Analysis of reported causes. *American Journal of Public Health* 71:464–71.

Crystal, S., U. Sambamoorthi, J. T. Walkup, and A. Akincigil. 2003. Diagnosis and treatment of depression in the elderly Medicare population: Predictors, disparities, and trends. *Journal of the American Geriatrics Society* 51(12): 1718–28.

De Lew, N., and R. Weinick. 2000. An overview: Eliminating racial, ethnic, and SES disparities in health care. *Health Care Financing Review* 21(4): 1–7.

Elo, I. T., and S. H. Preston. 1992. Effects of early-life conditions on adult mortality: A review. *Population Index* 58(2): 186–212.

Escarce, J. J., and T. G. McGuire. 2004. Changes in racial differences in use of medical procedures and diagnostic tests among elderly persons: 1986–1997. *American Journal of Public Health* 94(10): 1795–9.

Fisher, E. S., D. E. Wennberg, T. A. Stukel, D. J. Gottlieb, F. L. Lucas, and E. L. Pinder. 2003. The implications of regional variations in Medicare spending. Part 1: The content, quality, and accessibility of care. *Annals of Internal Medicine* 138(4): 273–87.

Freedman, V. A., and L. G. Martin. 1999. The role of education in explaining and forecasting trends in functional limitations among older Americans. *Demography* 36(4): 461–73.

Freedman, V. A., H. Aykan, and L. G. Martin. 2001. Aggregate changes in severe cognitive impairment among older Americans: 1993 and 1998. *Journals of Gerontology: Psychological Sciences and Social Sciences* 56B: S100–S111.

Freedman, V. A., L. G. Martin, and R. F. Schoeni. 2002. Recent trends in disability and functioning among older Americans: A critical review of the evidence. *Journal of the American Medical Association* 288(24): 3137–46.

Freedman, V. A., E. Crimmins, R. F. Schoeni, B. Spillman, H. Aykan, E. Kramarow, K. Land, J. Lubitz, K. Manton, L. G. Martin, D. Shinberg, and T. Waidmann. 2004. Resolving inconsistencies in old-age disability trends: Report from a technical working group. *Demography* 41(3): 417–41.

Galobardes, B., M. C. Costanza, M. S. Bernstein, C. Delhumeau, and A. Morabia. 2003. Trends in risk factors for lifestyle-related diseases by socioeconomic position in Geneva, Switzerland, 1993–2000: Health inequalities persist. *American Journal of Public Health* 93:1302–09.

Gitlin, L. N., W. Mann, M. Tomita, and S. M. Marcus. 2001. Factors associated with home environmental problems among community-living older people. *Disability and Rehabilitation* 23(17): 777–87.

Groeneveld, P. W., P. A. Heidenreich, and A. M. Garber. 2005. Trends in implantable cardioverter defibrillator racial disparity: The importance of geography. *Journal of the American College of Cardiology* 45(1): 72–8.

House, J. S., R. C. Kessler, A. R. Herzog, R. P. Mero, A. M. Kinney, and M. J. Breslow. 1990. Age, socioeconomic status, and health. *The Milbank Quarterly* 68(3): 383–411.

House, J. S., J. M. Lepkowski, A. M. Kinney, R. P. Mero, R. C. Kessler, and A. R. Herzog. 1994. The social stratification of aging and health. *Journal of Health and Social Behavior* 35(3): 213–34.

Kuh, D., and Y. Ben-Shlomo. 1997. *A life course approach to chronic disease epidemiology*. Oxford: Oxford University Press.

Lin, G., and K. Zimmer. 2002. A geographic analysis of spatial differences in mobility and self-care limitations among older Americans. *International Journal of Population Geography* 8:395–408.

Manton, K. G., L. S. Corder, and E. Stallard. 1993. Estimates of change in chronic disability and institutional incidence and prevalence rates in the U.S. elderly population from the 1982, 1984, and 1989 National Long Term Care Survey. *Journals of Gerontology* 48(4): S153–66.

Manton, K. G., and X. L. Gu. 2001. Changes in the prevalence of chronic disability in the United States black and nonblack population above age 65 from 1982 to 1999. *Proceedings of the National Academy of Sciences of the United States of America* 98:6354–59.

Mokdad, A. H., W. H. Giles, B. A. Bowman, G. A. Mensah, E. S. Ford, S. M. Smith, and J. S. Marks. 2004. Changes in health behaviors among older Americans, 1990 to 2000. *Public Health Reports* 119(3): 356–61.

Newman, S. J. 2003. The living conditions of elderly Americans. *Gerontologist* 43(1): 99–109.

Schoeni, R. F., V. A. Freedman, and R. B. Wallace. 2001. Persistent, consistent, widespread, and robust? Another look at recent trends in old-age disability. *Journals of Gerontology: Psychological Sciences and Social Sciences* 56(4): S206–18.

Spillman, B. C. 2004. Changes in elderly disability rates and the implications for health care utilization and cost. *The Milbank Quarterly* 82:157–94.

Stuck, A. E. 1999. Risk factors for functional status decline in community-living elderly people: A systemic literature review. *Social Science and Medicine* 48:445–69.

Stuck, A. E., J. M. Walthert, T. Nikolaus, C. J. Bula, C. Hohmann, and J. C. Beck. 1999. Risk factors for functional status decline in community-living elderly people: A systematic literature review. *Social Science and Medicine* 48(4): 445–69.

Tomita, M. R., W. C. Mann, L. F. Fraas, and L. L. Burns. 1997. Racial differences of frail elders in assistive technology. *Assistive Technology* 9(2): 140–51.

Verbrugge, L. 1984. Longer life but worsening health? Trends in health and mortality of middle-aged and older persons. *Milbank Memorial Fund Quarterly* 62:475–519.

Vita, A. J., R. B. Terry, H. B. Hubert, and J. F. Fries. 1998. Aging, health risks, and cumulative disability. *New England Journal of Medicine* 338(15): 1035–41.

Waidmann, T., J. Bound, and M. Schoenbaum. 1995. The illusion of failure: Trends in the self-reported health of the U.S. elderly. *Milbank Memorial Fund Quarterly* 73:253–87.

Waidmann, T., and K. Liu. 2000. Disability trends among the elderly and implications for the future. *Journal of Gerontology: Social Sciences* 55B: S298–S307.

Weinstein, J. N., K. K. Bronner, T. S. Morgan, and J. E. Wennberg. 2004. Trends: Trends and geographic variations in major surgery for degenerative diseases of the hip, knee, and spine. *Health Affairs* Web Exclusive, accessed at http://content.healthaffairs.org/webexclusives

Wennberg, J. E., and M. M. Cooper. 1999. *The Dartmouth Atlas of Health Care in the United States.* Health Forum Incorporated.

Zack, M. M., D. G. Moriarty, D. F. Stroup, E. S. Ford, and A. H. Mokdad. 2004. Worsening trends in adult health-related quality of life and self-rated health-United States, 1993–2001. *Public Health Reports* 119(5): 493–505.

II

Pathways to Disability

4

Pathways to Disability
Predicting Health Trajectories

Florian Heiss, Axel Börsch-Supan, Michael Hurd,
and David A. Wise

4.1. Introduction

The aging of populations and the prospect of a rising number of disabled persons has generated an increasing interest in understanding the causes and precursors of disability. A perhaps countervailing motivation to understand disability has been the finding by some analysts of declining age-specific disability rates over the past two or three decades, in the United States in particular. Declining age-specific disability rates could moderate the projected increase in the incidence of disability due to aging populations.

In contrast to the finding of declining health disability, there has been an increase in participation in the Disability Insurance (DI) program in the United States (see Duggan and Imberman, chapter 11 in this volume). The participation rate in disability insurance programs has also increased in some European countries. Moreover, DI participation rates vary dramati-

Florian Heiss is an assistant professor of economics at the University of Munich. Axel Börsch-Supan is a professor of economics at the University of Mannheim, director of the Mannheim Research Institute for the Economics of Aging, and a research associate of the National Bureau of Economic Research. Michael Hurd is senior economist and director, RAND Center for the Study of Aging, and a research associate of the National Bureau of Economic Research. David A. Wise is the John F. Stambaugh Professor of Political Economy at the John F. Kennedy School of Government, Harvard University, and research associate and director of the program on the economics of aging at the National Bureau of Economic Research.

Acknowledgments: We thank participants in the NBER workshops in Charleston, SC, Cambridge, MA, and Jackson Hole, WY. Financial support from the National Institute on Aging through grants P30 AG12810, R01 AG19805, R01 AG16772-05, and P01 AG005842, the Mary Woodard Lasker Charitable Trust and Michael E. DeBakey Foundation, and the sponsors of MEA, including the State of Baden-Wuerttemberg and the German Association of Insurers, is gratefully acknowledged.

cally across the industrial countries (Aarts, Burkhauser, and de Jong 1996; Börsch-Supan 2005). The differences across countries, however, are almost surely explained in large part by differences in the provisions of disability insurance programs (Gruber and Wise 1999, 2004).

In this chapter, we explore the pathways to disability in the United States. Our analysis is based on data in the Health and Retirement Study (HRS). We exploit the rich information in the HRS to shed light on transitions into and out of disability and on the relationship of disability to self-reported health. We consider health precursors of disability and consider how disability is related to education and other socioeconomic circumstances of individuals. Our hope is that by advancing our understanding of the precursors and the correlates of disability we will be in a better position to project future disability rates and to perhaps even understand how the incidence of disability might be reduced.

By way of introduction to the HRS data, we show the responses to two questions, one pertaining to disability and the other to health status. Figure 4.1 shows responses to this question: "Do you have any impairment or health problem that limits the kind or amount of paid work you can do?" The figure shows the steady increase in work-related disability from about 20 percent at age fifty to about 60 percent at age eighty-five and above.

Figure 4.2 shows the proportion of persons who say they are in poor or fair health (as distinct from good, very good, or excellent health). By comparing figures 4.1 and 4.2, it can be seen that the HRS data show a close correspondence between work-related disability and self-reported health. (The HRS data for the United States differ from European data that show a divergence between trends in self-reported disability and trends in self-reported health.[1])

To understand health and disability transitions, of course, panel data like those in the HRS are required. Several avenues of prior work help to inform our analysis. The most widely used measure of health has been self-rated health because of its predictive power for the onset of disease and mortality (Idler and Kasl 1995; Burstrom and Fredlund 2001; Borg and Kristensen 2000; Hurd, McFadden, and Merrill 2001; Power, Mathews, and Manor 1998), and because of its wide availability in social science surveys such as the HRS.

Models of health dynamics typically begin with estimation of a first-order Markov transition equation

$$P(H_t \mid H_{t-1}, X_{t-1})$$

where H_t is health status at time t and X_{t-1} are covariates that are thought to influence the rate of transition of health between $t-1$ and t. This relationship can be estimated on panel data. Separate estimates by age can

1. See Börsch-Supan (2005).

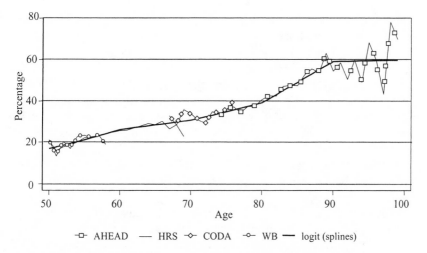

Fig. 4.1   Work-related disability in the Health and Retirement Study

Note: Share of respondents who report a disability which limits their ability to work.

Source: Authors' calculations based on the Health and Retirement Study, merged data of AHEAD, CODA, HRS, and WB cohorts. For cohort and variable definition, see section 4.2.

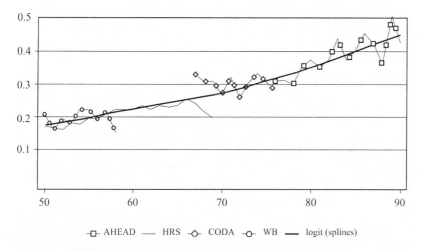

Fig. 4.2   Prevalence of poor and fair health in the Health and Retirement Study

Note: Share of respondents who self-assess their health as fair or poor.

Source: Authors' calculations based on the Health and Retirement Study, merged data of AHEAD, CODA, HRS, and WB cohorts. For cohort and variable definition, see section 4.2.

reveal whether the effect of X on the transition probability varies with age. In prior research, the determinants X of the relationship between socioeconomic status (SES) and health have included income, wealth, education, occupation, and social class.[2]

However, unobserved heterogeneity that has an influence both on X and on H_t conditional on H_{t-1} will cause biased estimation of the causal relationship between H and X. For example, unobserved heterogeneity may be traced to differences in early childhood circumstances. Such differences appear to affect the rate of onset of disease later in life (Feinstein 1993; Goldman 2001; Richards and Wadsworth 2004; Ravelli et al. 1998; Barker 1997). Childhood circumstances are also likely a determinant of SES later in life.

In models of health transitions, accounting for unobserved heterogeneity often produces substantially different results from models that do not account for heterogeneity. For example, Halliday (2005) used the waves of the Panel Study of Income Dynamics (PSID) from 1984–1997 to study the evolution of self-rated health. He distinguished healthy and unhealthy persons and considered their transition probabilities between the states of ill (self-rated health fair or poor) and well (self-rated health excellent, very good, or good). He found that the transition rates varied substantially between the two groups and that the change in the transition rates with age also varied between the two groups. These differences led Halliday to conclude that investments in childhood health would have substantial health payoffs later in life. Models that do not permit heterogeneity could not have come to this conclusion.

Contoyannis and Jones (2004) allow unobserved heterogeneity to influence the choice of healthy and unhealthy behaviors, as well as health status itself. They find that in a model that allows for heterogeneity and controls for the correlation between behaviors and unobserved health characteristics, the effect of behaviors on health is substantially increased. They conclude that ". . . over 75 percent of the total effect of lifestyle on the social class gradient [in health] is masked when unobserved heterogeneity is ignored" (p. 986).

On the other hand, Michaud and van Soest (2004) consider whether SES causes health or whether health causes SES, as Adams et al. (2003) had done. They find that controlling for heterogeneity does not substantially alter their results. But whereas Adams et al. conditioned health and wealth changes on as many as nineteen health conditions and behaviors, Michaud and van Soest used a first-order Markov model and summarized health by the first-principle component of a large number of health conditions. In es-

---

2. Meer, Miller, and Rosen 2003; Smith 2004; Adams et al. 2003; Hurd and Kapteyn 2003; Wadsworth and Kuh 1997; Marmot 1999; Adda, Chandola, and Marmot 2003; Michaud and van Soest 2004.

timation there is some similarity between first-order Markov models that control for a number of health states and first-order Markov models with unobserved heterogeneity. Unobserved health heterogeneity can be at least partially observed. Indeed, the results of Michaud and van Soest are similar to those of Adams et al. with respect to the causal flows between SES and health.

The method used by Halliday (2005) is similar in spirit to the method we propose in this chapter. Our estimations model, however, sets out a more complex error structure than his and includes a heterogeneity specification that allows for more extreme levels of health and disability. In addition, we study an older age group and use data from a different time period. We consider higher-order Markov processes and use simulation methods to explore the implications of heterogeneity.

The remainder of this chapter is organized in the following way. In section 4.2 we describe the data and variables that we use. In section 4.3 we present descriptive data on changes in self-reported health and self-reported work-related disability during the eight years between the first wave of the HRS in 1992 and the fifth wave in 2000. In section 4.4 we use data on sequences of self-reported health status to demonstrate that to correctly model health transitions, it is critical to account for state dependence, heterogeneity, and classification errors in self-reported categorical assessment of health. In section 4.5 we present a model of health transitions based on a latent (hidden) continuous measure of health. The model allows for unobserved heterogeneity, state dependence, and classification error in self-reported health and disability. In section 4.6 we present results, through simulations based on the model. Section 4.7 provides a summary of results and suggests further analysis based on the model developed in this chapter.

4.2   Data and Variable Definition

This chapter is based on all four cohort components of the Health and Retirement Study (HRS):

1. The original HRS cohort, comprising age-eligibles—persons between fifty-one and sixty years of age at the time of the first HRS wave in 1992—plus their (potentially younger or older) spouses. The age-eligibles therefore represent the birth cohorts born between 1931 and 1941.

2. The AHEAD cohort (Survey of Asset and Health Dynamics of the Oldest Old), comprising all persons age seventy or older in 1994, at the time of the first AHEAD wave (birth cohorts born before 1923), plus their spouses.

3. The cohort comprising Children of the Depression Age (CODA), born between 1924 and 1930 (and their spouses) filling the gap between the HRS and the AHEAD birth cohorts.

4. The cohort of War Babies (WB) was added in 1998 and included persons who became age eligible since the beginning of the HRS in 1992. The WB cohorts comprise the birth cohorts born between 1942 and 1947.

Respondents were reinterviewed every two years. Attrition due to various reasons and death were recorded separately, and deaths were ascertained with the help of the National Death Index. Figure 4.3 shows the age coverage of the longitudinal data in each of the HRS cohorts.

Work-related disability and self-reported health are the key outcome variables in our analysis. Work-related disability is available in all waves for all cohorts, except for the first two waves of the AHEAD cohort (1994 and 1996). Work-related disability is constructed from the question, "Do you have any impairment or health problem that limits the kind or amount of paid work you can do?" (See fig. 4.1.)

Self-reported health is available in all waves for all cohorts. It is constructed from the question, "Would you say your health is excellent, very good, good, fair, or poor?" Although five categorical choices are allowed—excellent, very good, good, fair, and poor—in most of our analyses, we group excellent, very good, and good in one category, and fair and poor in a second category, as in figure 4.2.

Work-related disability and self-reported heath are very closely related in our data. A simple cross-sectional logit regression of work-related disability on various health measures shows strong associations between disability and health. Table 4.1 shows the odds of having a work-related disability compared to persons who say their health is very good or excellent for the pooled data of wave 1 through 5. For example, persons who say they are in poor or fair health are 4.53 times as likely to have a work-related

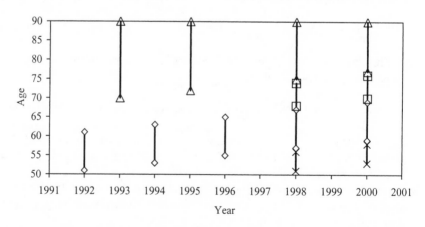

HRS: 1931-1941   AHEAD: 1890-1923   CODA: 1924-1930   WB: 1942-1947

Fig. 4.3   Longitudinal data

disability as persons who say they are in very good or excellent health. Persons who have an additional IADL are 1.813 times more likely to have a work-related disability. And so forth.

In addition, a similar logit regression of mortality on lagged disability and health shows that even after controlling for other health measures, work-related disability is a strong predictor of mortality, as shown in table 4.2. The table shows that persons who say they have a work-related disability are 1.76 times more likely to die before the interview for the next wave than people who say they are in very good or excellent health, even after controlling for the other measures of health in the regression.

In summary, self-reported work disability as measured in the Health and

Table 4.1   Work-related disability as function of self-reported health

	Odds ratio	p-value
Age (splines)	—	0.000
Female	0.771	0.000
Number health conditions	1.264	0.000
Number fine motor skills	1.159	0.008
Number gross motor skills	0.791	0.000
Number mobility problems	1.598	0.000
Number large muscle activities	1.513	0.000
Number ADLs	1.235	0.000
Number IADLs	1.813	0.000
Health very good or excellent	1.000	—
Health good	1.944	0.000
Health poor/fair	4.530	0.000

Source: Authors' calculations based on the HRS.

Table 4.2   Work-related disability as predictor of mortality

	Odds ratio	p-value
Age (splines)	—	0.000
Female	0.524	0.000
Disabled	1.760	0.000
Number health conditions	1.254	0.000
Number fine motor skills	1.011	0.874
Number gross motor skills	1.024	0.754
Number mobility problems	1.210	0.000
Number large muscle act.	0.813	0.000
Number ADLs	1.014	0.842
Number IADLs	1.220	0.000
Health very good or excellent	1.000	—
Health good	1.310	0.005
Health poor/fair	2.146	0.000

Source: HRS cohort.

retirement study is strongly related to future longevity. This relationship is unlikely to hold in all countries, in particular those where the underlying health of the population is close to that of the United States, but a much larger fraction of older people are receiving benefits from a disability program. For example, there is a very limited correlation between work-related disability and self-reported health as reported in the German Socio-Economic Panel.[3]

4.3 Health Transitions in the HRS: From 1992 to 2000

In this section, we present descriptive data on health and disability transitions. These descriptive data, as well as the data in the next section, are intended to inform the more formal analysis in sections 4.4 through 4.6 and to motivate the econometric specification that underlies that analysis.

Respondents in the first wave of the HRS in 1992 were between fifty-one and sixty-one years of age. Table 4.3 shows transitions by self-reported health status. About 78 percent of respondents reported that they were in good health or better (excellent, very good, good) and 22 percent were in fair or poor health. Eight years later, their health had deteriorated, with only 68 percent of the respondents reporting that they were in good or better health and 22 percent reporting that they were in fair or poor health; 10 percent had died (excluding persons who were no longer in the sample—attrition). The table also shows that the transition to poor or fair health and the transition to death vary enormously by health status in 1992. For example, of those who were in good or better health in 1992, only 11 percent were in poor or fair health in 2000 and only 5 percent had died. Of those who were in poor or fair health in 1992, over 43 percent stayed in poor or fair health in 2000 and almost 21 percent had died.

Table 4.4 shows transitions by self-reported disability status. The transitions between 1992 and 2000 are very similar to the self-reported health transitions. That is, the transitions for those who report a work disability are very similar to those who report that they are in fair or poor health, and the transitions for those who report no work disability are very similar to those who say that they are in good or better health. In addition, the share reporting work-related disabilities in 1992 is almost identical to the share reporting poor or fair health in 1992 (78.73 percent compared to 78.17 percent). (Attrition rates show little correlation with initial health status or with initial work disability status.)

Tables 4.5 and 4.6 show transition rates by health status, by age in 1992, and by gender. Transition rates by health status are in table 4.5 and by disability status in table 4.6. These tables show, as expected, that death rates are substantially higher for men than for women. For example, of men who report that they are disabled in 1992, over 23 percent have died by 2000,

---

3. Börsch-Supan (2001).

Table 4.3   **Eight year transitions for self-reported health in the HRS**

	Status in 2000				
Status in 1992	Health good or better	Health poor or fair	Dead	Attrition	Total
Health good or better	6,052	1,037	465	1,506	9,060
	66.8	*11.45*	*5.13*	*16.62*	*100*
Health poor or fair	511	1,090	526	403	2,530
	20.2	*43.08*	*20.79*	*15.93*	*100*
Total	6,563	2,127	991	1,909	11,590
	56.63	*18.35*	*8.55*	*16.47*	*100*

Source: Authors' calculations from HRS.
Note: Italic font denotes percentages.

Table 4.4   **Eight year transitions for work-related disability in the HRS**

	Status in 2000				
Status in 1992	Not disabled	Disabled	Dead	Attrition	Total
Not disabled	5,735	1,295	500	1,551	9,081
	63.15	*14.26*	*5.51*	*17.08*	*100*
Disabled	517	1,094	490	352	2,453
	21.08	*44.60*	*19.98*	*14.35*	*100*
Total	6,252	2,389	990	1,903	11,534
	54.2	*20.71*	*8.58*	*16.5*	*100*

Source: Authors' calculations from the HRS.
Note: Italic font denotes percentages.

whereas of women who report they are disabled in 1992 only about 16 percent have died by 2000. Again, these detailed data show a striking relationship between health status and death rates at all ages, and between disability status and death rates at all ages. For example, for men age sixty-one who reported that they were disabled in 1992, over 38 percent had died by 2000; for those who reported that they were not disabled, only about 8 percent had died by 2000.

   Tables 4.7 and 4.8 show the progression of health status and disability status over the first five waves of the HRS. Each table has three panels: One for persons who were age fifty-one in 1992, one for persons age sixty-one, and one panel for all ages in 1992. Each panel shows data for men and for women separately. Table 4.7 shows progression of health status, by health status in 1992; table 4.8 shows progression of disability, by disability status in 1992. For each combination of age in 1992, health or disability status in 1992, gender, and health or disability status in 2000, there are four values. The four values are for health or disability status in wave 2, wave 3, wave 4,

Table 4.5   Eight year health transitions in the HRS, by age and sex

Age at wave 1	Men					Women				
	Observations	Health good+	Poor/fair	Dead	Attrition	Observations	Health good+	Poor/fair	Dead	Attrition
Health in wave 1 = good or better										
50	86	66.28	12.79	3.49	17.44	117	72.65	11.97	3.42	11.97
51	340	67.35	10.88	2.94	18.82	390	73.33	11.28	2.82	12.56
52	336	63.99	9.82	6.25	19.94	364	75.00	11.54	1.10	12.36
53	359	60.45	15.04	5.29	19.22	340	70.59	11.76	4.41	13.24
54	302	64.90	10.26	5.30	19.54	352	69.89	11.65	4.55	13.92
55	301	65.78	11.30	5.32	17.61	350	73.14	11.14	4.57	11.14
56	314	64.01	13.06	3.50	19.43	344	77.03	7.85	4.65	10.47
57	311	64.95	11.58	5.14	18.33	307	71.99	12.70	4.23	11.07
58	267	66.29	10.11	8.61	14.98	310	75.81	10.97	3.55	9.68
59	252	61.90	13.49	9.92	14.68	292	73.29	13.36	4.11	9.25
60	297	64.31	9.43	9.76	16.50	294	67.01	14.63	5.78	12.59
61	179	63.69	12.29	7.26	16.76	219	73.52	8.22	7.31	10.96
Total	3,344	64.38	11.60	6.04	17.97	3,679	72.82	11.42	4.10	11.66
Health in wave 1 = poor/fair										
50	18	22.22	44.44	16.67	16.67	33	15.15	63.64	15.15	6.06
51	73	17.81	36.99	30.14	15.07	92	25.00	57.61	8.70	8.70
52	66	22.73	37.88	19.70	19.70	99	16.16	57.58	13.13	13.13
53	79	16.46	44.30	13.92	25.32	98	24.49	41.84	16.33	17.35
54	72	18.06	37.50	25.00	19.44	103	16.50	57.28	13.59	12.62
55	82	19.51	39.02	28.05	13.41	109	24.77	57.80	9.17	8.26
56	76	19.74	40.79	21.05	18.42	95	25.26	44.21	18.95	11.58
57	87	25.29	39.08	24.14	11.49	109	23.85	43.12	22.94	10.09
58	94	14.89	46.81	24.47	13.83	108	22.22	60.19	12.96	4.63
59	84	22.62	32.14	27.38	17.86	105	24.76	46.67	18.10	10.48
60	77	23.38	35.06	31.17	10.39	117	23.93	42.74	23.08	10.26
61	67	13.43	29.85	40.30	16.42	62	20.97	45.16	20.97	12.90
Total	875	19.54	38.51	25.60	16.34	1,130	22.39	50.88	16.11	10.62

Source: Authors' calculations based on the HRS cohort.

Table 4.6 Eight year disability transitions in the HRS, by age and sex

	Men					Women				
Age at (wave 1)	Observations	Not disabled	Disabled	Dead	Attrition	Observations	Not disabled	Disabled	Dead	Attrition
Not disabled in wave 1										
50	85	64.71	14.12	3.53	17.65	114	67.54	11.40	4.39	16.67
51	341	66.28	10.26	5.28	18.18	406	64.04	17.24	2.22	16.50
52	329	57.75	15.81	5.47	20.97	374	66.58	14.97	1.60	16.84
53	360	62.50	11.94	5.28	20.28	356	61.52	13.48	3.93	21.07
54	309	61.49	12.94	5.18	20.39	350	60.57	14.00	4.29	21.14
55	304	62.50	12.83	8.22	16.45	362	63.81	16.85	4.70	14.64
56	305	63.61	13.77	2.95	19.67	340	62.94	16.76	3.82	16.47
57	314	60.51	16.24	6.05	17.20	298	66.11	13.42	3.02	17.45
58	270	61.85	12.96	11.11	14.07	320	66.25	16.56	3.75	13.44
59	238	62.61	13.03	10.08	14.29	304	63.49	18.09	3.62	14.80
60	290	65.86	8.28	9.31	16.55	306	62.09	16.01	7.19	14.71
61	181	62.98	13.81	8.29	14.92	210	62.86	15.24	5.71	16.19
Total	3,326	62.57	12.90	6.70	17.83	3,740	63.80	15.59	3.88	16.74
Disabled in wave 1										
50	18	33.33	33.33	16.67	16.67	36	25.00	55.56	8.33	11.11
51	72	20.83	41.67	19.44	18.06	74	18.92	55.41	13.51	12.16
52	72	22.22	40.28	22.22	15.28	83	9.64	62.65	10.84	16.87
53	74	13.51	50.00	14.86	21.62	82	18.29	45.12	15.85	20.73
54	64	15.63	40.63	28.13	15.63	104	24.04	51.92	13.46	10.58
55	78	17.95	46.15	17.95	17.95	96	29.17	46.88	9.38	14.58
56	83	8.43	51.81	21.69	18.07	92	26.09	43.48	22.83	7.61
57	83	21.69	40.96	21.69	15.66	111	21.62	45.05	22.52	10.81
58	90	26.67	38.89	17.78	16.67	95	25.26	55.79	8.42	10.53
59	97	17.53	39.18	24.74	18.56	89	24.72	47.19	20.22	7.87
60	84	19.05	39.29	30.95	10.71	101	17.82	49.50	18.81	13.86
61	65	12.31	27.69	38.46	21.54	68	25.00	39.71	23.53	11.76
Total	880	18.30	41.48	23.07	17.16	1,031	22.11	49.56	16.00	12.32

Source: Authors' calculations based on the HRS cohort.

Table 4.7   Progression of health status by 1992 status, by age and sex

		Male, wave:				Female, wave:			
Health 1992	Status	2	3	4	5	2	3	4	5
		Initial age = 51							
Good+	Good+	0.874	0.824	0.700	0.674	0.854	0.795	0.695	0.703
	Fair–	0.056	0.065	0.126	0.109	0.100	0.105	0.156	0.103
	Dead	0.003	0.012	0.018	0.029	0.000	0.010	0.021	0.028
	Attrition	0.068	0.100	0.156	0.188	0.046	0.090	0.128	0.167
Fair-	Good+	0.356	0.315	0.192	0.178	0.293	0.337	0.174	0.239
	Fair–	0.507	0.397	0.438	0.370	0.674	0.543	0.652	0.543
	Dead	0.096	0.178	0.219	0.301	0.011	0.043	0.054	0.087
	Attrition	0.041	0.110	0.151	0.151	0.022	0.076	0.120	0.130
		Initial age = 61							
Good+	Good+	0.832	0.782	0.659	0.637	0.831	0.772	0.685	0.694
	Fair–	0.123	0.117	0.173	0.123	0.119	0.132	0.142	0.082
	Dead	0.006	0.028	0.050	0.073	0.005	0.009	0.050	0.068
	Attrition	0.039	0.073	0.117	0.168	0.046	0.087	0.123	0.155
Fair-	Good+	0.194	0.149	0.179	0.134	0.274	0.226	0.210	0.210
	Fair–	0.612	0.507	0.418	0.299	0.597	0.613	0.532	0.452
	Dead	0.119	0.224	0.269	0.403	0.081	0.113	0.145	0.210
	Attrition	0.075	0.119	0.134	0.164	0.048	0.048	0.113	0.129
		Averaged over all ages:							
Good+	Good+	0.840	0.764	0.676	0.644	0.850	0.795	0.708	0.696
	Fair–	0.086	0.097	0.131	0.116	0.095	0.099	0.137	0.107
	Dead	0.009	0.026	0.042	0.060	0.006	0.014	0.026	0.037
	Attrition	0.064	0.113	0.151	0.180	0.049	0.092	0.129	0.160
Fair-	Good+	0.221	0.246	0.181	0.195	0.255	0.284	0.204	0.212
	Fair–	0.643	0.502	0.480	0.385	0.655	0.565	0.566	0.482
	Dead	0.077	0.145	0.192	0.256	0.041	0.073	0.112	0.154
	Attrition	0.059	0.107	0.147	0.163	0.050	0.077	0.118	0.151

Source: Authors' calculations based on the HRS cohort.

and wave 5 of the HRS. The wave 5 values correspond to the eight years transitions between 1992 and 2000.

For example, consider the progression of health in table 4.7 for men who were age sixty-one in 1992 and in good or better health. The progression of the proportion that reported they were in good or better health over the next four waves of the HRS are shown in the top row of numbers for men. The proportion in good or better health was .87 in the second wave, .82 in the third wave, .70 in the fourth, and .67 in the fifth wave.

In almost all cases, there is a consistent decline in the proportion in good or better health. And there is a consistent increase in the proportion that has died. On the other hand, the proportion in fair or poor health does not follow a consistent pattern. The reason is the relationship between death and health status. For example, consider men of all ages who were in fair or poor health in 1992 (see table 4.7). The proportion that had died in-

Table 4.8   **Progression of disability status by 1992 status, by age and sex**

		Male, wave:				Female, wave:			
Status 1992	Status	2	3	4	5	2	3	4	5
		Initial age = 51							
Not disabled	Not disabled	0.848	0.767	0.696	0.663	0.860	0.748	0.705	0.640
	Disabled	0.082	0.118	0.115	0.103	0.101	0.156	0.149	0.172
	Dead	0.009	0.024	0.035	0.053	0.000	0.007	0.017	0.022
	Attrition	0.062	0.091	0.153	0.182	0.039	0.089	0.129	0.165
Disabled	Not disabled	0.208	0.181	0.208	0.208	0.253	0.176	0.189	0.189
	Disabled	0.653	0.542	0.486	0.417	0.680	0.676	0.608	0.554
	Dead	0.069	0.125	0.139	0.194	0.013	0.068	0.081	0.135
	Attrition	0.069	0.153	0.167	0.181	0.053	0.081	0.122	0.122
		Initial age = 61							
Not disabled	Not disabled	0.840	0.718	0.669	0.630	0.826	0.741	0.676	0.629
	Disabled	0.122	0.188	0.177	0.138	0.122	0.165	0.162	0.152
	Dead	0.006	0.033	0.055	0.083	0.000	0.009	0.043	0.057
	Attrition	0.033	0.061	0.099	0.149	0.052	0.085	0.119	0.162
Disabled	Not disabled	0.092	0.108	0.138	0.123	0.206	0.209	0.209	0.250
	Disabled	0.692	0.523	0.415	0.277	0.676	0.627	0.522	0.397
	Dead	0.123	0.215	0.262	0.385	0.088	0.104	0.149	0.235
	Attrition	0.092	0.154	0.185	0.215	0.029	0.060	0.119	0.118
		Averaged over all ages:							
Not disabled	Not disabled	0.836	0.743	0.683	0.626	0.831	0.756	0.690	0.638
	Disabled	0.092	0.117	0.122	0.129	0.113	0.135	0.146	0.156
	Dead	0.011	0.030	0.047	0.067	0.006	0.015	0.029	0.039
	Attrition	0.061	0.109	0.148	0.178	0.051	0.094	0.135	0.167
Disabled	Not disabled	0.175	0.185	0.181	0.183	0.183	0.187	0.224	0.221
	Disabled	0.684	0.564	0.490	0.415	0.729	0.669	0.570	0.496
	Dead	0.069	0.128	0.173	0.231	0.044	0.073	0.109	0.160
	Attrition	0.073	0.123	0.155	0.172	0.043	0.071	0.097	0.123

Source: Authors' calculations based on the HRS cohort.

creased from .08 to .15 to .19 to .26, but the proportion in fair or poor health *declined* from .64 to .50 to .48 to .39. The implication is that those in poor health were more likely to die, so that of those remaining fewer and fewer were in fair or poor health. This relationship highlights the strong selection effect that disproportionately leaves healthier persons in the sample as age increases. Similar relationships can be seen for the progression of disability, as shown in table 4.8.

4.4   Modeling Health Transitions: What are the Difficulties?

The tables in section 4.3 show transition probabilities over an eight-year period and from wave to wave in the HRS. Can these transition probabilities be used to project health and disability status into the future? The apparent relationship between health (or disability) and death revealed in tables 4.7 and 4.8 suggests that the answer is no. Those who remain in the sample are likely to be healthier than those who die. This section demonstrates this and additional features of the data that must be accounted for to adequately specify transitions models of self-reported health and work-related disability. Since most of this section serves to demonstrate the key issues, most of the presentation pertains to our binary indicator of self-reported health (good or better versus fair or worse) and to men only.

The transition probabilities from wave to wave in the HRS are shown in table 4.9, for men who were in good or better health in the first wave. The entries in the table represent the average transition probabilities over all waves, by initial age. There are 308 observations of men initially aged fifty in good or better health in waves 1 through 4. Overall, 83.6 percent of them remain in good health in the subsequent wave, while for 11.2 percent health deteriorates, 0.3 percent die, and 4.9 percent cannot be interviewed in the following wave.

An important question is whether these two year transitions can be used to predict the evolution of health in the long run. A simple estimate of an eight year transition probability is the two year transition probability raised to the power four. Using this procedure to estimate health status in 2000, given the health status in 1992 does not work well, however. The results are shown in table 4.10. The actual proportion of respondents in good health is substantially greater than the predicted probability at all ages. The actual proportion in poor or fair health is substantially less than the simulated probability at all ages.

There are several potential reasons why this procedure predicts actual probabilities poorly. One reason is the simplistic first-order Markov as-

Table 4.9   **Average two year transition probabilities: Men, lagged health = good or better**

Age (wave 1)	Observations	Health good+	Poor/fair	Dead	Attrition
50	308	83.55	11.18	0.33	4.93
51	1,237	85.55	8.13	0.99	5.34
52	1,181	83.79	8.94	1.58	5.70
53	1,226	82.16	11.47	0.84	5.53
54	1,072	84.91	8.08	1.17	5.84
55	1,058	84.18	9.59	1.34	4.89
56	1,110	83.04	10.51	0.83	5.62
57	1,115	84.19	9.47	1.19	5.15
58	941	82.99	11.12	1.64	4.25
59	887	82.26	12.33	1.61	3.80
60	1,051	84.65	8.65	1.85	4.86
61	627	82.77	11.76	1.61	3.86
Total	11,813	83.75	9.91	1.27	5.07

Source: Authors' calculations from the HRS.

Table 4.10 **Projection of 1992–2000 health changes based on two year average transition probabilities—men in good or better health in wave 1**

Age (wave 1)	Actual probabilities				Predicted probability			
	Good+	Poor/fair	Dead	Attrition	Good+	Poor/fair	Dead	Attrition
50	0.663	0.128	0.035	0.174	0.617	0.165	0.041	0.178
51	0.674	0.109	0.029	0.188	0.624	0.130	0.058	0.189
52	0.640	0.098	0.063	0.199	0.583	0.142	0.072	0.203
53	0.604	0.150	0.053	0.192	0.553	0.189	0.053	0.205
54	0.649	0.103	0.053	0.195	0.586	0.143	0.065	0.205
55	0.658	0.113	0.053	0.176	0.588	0.163	0.075	0.174
56	0.640	0.131	0.035	0.194	0.580	0.170	0.052	0.199
57	0.650	0.116	0.051	0.183	0.591	0.162	0.067	0.179
58	0.663	0.101	0.086	0.150	0.565	0.189	0.093	0.153
59	0.619	0.135	0.099	0.147	0.561	0.185	0.104	0.150
60	0.643	0.094	0.098	0.165	0.591	0.140	0.103	0.166
61	0.637	0.123	0.073	0.168	0.554	0.183	0.109	0.155

Source: Authors' calculations from the HRS cohort.

sumption that underlies the predictions. State dependence may be more complicated; the value in wave t may depend on the value not only in wave $t-1$, but on prior waves as well. A second reason is heterogeneity. If there are two populations, for instance, one intrinsically healthier than the other, the transition probability averaged over both subpopulations will underestimate the proportion in good health after eight years and will overestimate the proportion in fair or poor health after eight years. In the following discussion we show descriptive evidence of both state dependence and heterogeneity. A third reason is measurement error, in this case misclassification of a respondent into the wrong categorical health status. We will also show descriptive evidence of this problem.

To demonstrate that health outcomes in wave 3 depend on health in wave 1 as well as wave 2, we show in table 4.11 a complete "tree" of health status probabilities in waves 1, 2, and 3. These probabilities are based on 513 men who were aged fifty-one in wave 1. The first column (wave 1) simply shows the proportions in good and poor health at wave 1. Column 2 (wave 2) shows the distribution of health status in wave 2, given health status in wave 1. The third column (wave 3) shows the evidence on state dependence. Health in wave 3 depends not only on health in wave 2, but also on health in wave 1. For example, 91.25 percent of men who are in good health in wave 2 *and* in wave 1 are in good health in wave 3. But only 61.54 percent of men who are in good health in wave 2 *and* in fair health in wave 1 are in good health in wave 3. Also, 36.84 percent of men who are in good health in wave 1 and in fair health in wave 2 are in fair health in wave 3. On the other hand, 59.46 percent of men who are in fair health in *both* wave 1 and in wave 2 are in fair health in wave 3. That is, health status in wave 3

Table 4.11   Health transitions in the first three waves of the HRS cohort, for men age 51 in wave 1

Wave 1		Wave 2		Wave 3	
Good +	82.32	Good +	87.35	Good +	91.25
				Poor/fair	5.05
				Dead	0.67
				Attrition	3.03
		Poor/fair	5.59	Good +	47.37
				Poor/fair	36.84
				Dead	5.26
				Attrition	10.53
		Dead	0.29		
		Attrition	6.76		
Poor/fair	17.68	Good +	35.62	Good +	61.54
				Poor/fair	26.92
				Dead	3.85
				Attrition	7.69
		Poor/fair	50.68	Good +	18.92
				Poor/fair	59.46
				Dead	13.51
				Attrition	8.11
		Dead	9.59		
		Attrition	4.11		

Source: Authors' calculations based on the HRS cohort.

depends not only on health in the preceding wave 2, but also on health in the prior wave 1. Thus a second-order Markov process would describe these transitions much better than a first-order Markov process.

The underlying reason for such state dependence may, however, be population heterogeneity. Indeed, table 4.12 shows the results of a regression of change of health status between each pair of successive waves on a host of individual characteristics in the first of the two waves. The table shows the individual characteristics of a substantial effect on the transition. Thus, substantial heterogeneity is attributable to observed individual characteristics, suggesting substantial heterogeneity over unobserved characteristics as well. The marital status is interacted with gender; the reference group is married males. Particularly striking are the estimated coefficients on the upper and lower wealth and income quartiles. They indicate a significantly lower probability of remaining in poor health if a person is in the top wealth quartile or in the top income quartile.

To see whether these covariates improve the long-run predictive power of the two year transitions, we use the predicted transition probabilities to project health status in 2000, beginning with health status in 1992. One such specification is shown in table 4.12. We again compare the predicted probabilities of the outcomes in 2000 with the actual probabilities. We are interested in how much closer the predicted probabilities are to the actual

Table 4.12   Regression of health in second of two waves based on observable characteristics in first wave

Attribute in the first of the two waves	Wave 1→2			Wave 2→3			Wave 3→4			Wave 4→5		
	Health poor/fair	Dead	Attrition	Health poor/fair	Dead	Attrition	Health poor/fair	Dead	Attrition	Health poor/fair	Dead	Attrition
Fair or poor health	2.894***	2.948***	1.029***	2.865***	2.917***	1.194***	2.933***	2.982***	0.557***	2.728***	2.672***	-0.483***
	(41.23)	(16.26)	(8.40)	(39.94)	(16.68)	(9.10)	(39.20)	(17.68)	(4.02)	(37.95)	(16.39)	(3.48)
Age	0.026**	0.099***	-0.020	0.009	0.042*	-0.040**	-0.009	0.074***	-0.016	0.009	0.076***	-0.032**
	(2.47)	(3.67)	(1.35)	(0.86)	(1.67)	(2.39)	(0.89)	(2.92)	(1.15)	(0.84)	(3.19)	(2.48)
Single male	-0.047	0.030	-0.059	-0.083	0.607**	-0.184	-0.056	-0.278	-0.168	-0.068	0.187	-0.063
	(0.35)	(0.10)	(0.32)	(0.57)	(2.43)	(0.81)	(0.39)	(0.85)	(0.89)	(0.45)	(0.71)	(0.37)
Single female	-0.235**	-0.644***	-0.574***	-0.195+	-0.564**	-0.799***	-0.066	-0.334	-0.357***	-0.330***	-0.729***	-0.403***
	(2.33)	(2.71)	(3.71)	(1.86)	(2.36)	(4.16)	(0.64)	(1.42)	(2.51)	(3.02)	(3.17)	(3.08)
Married female	-0.133+	-0.932***	-0.268**	-0.086	-0.962***	-0.196+	-0.077	-0.462**	-0.151	-0.156+	-0.670***	-0.189**
	(1.71)	(4.22)	(2.45)	(1.09)	(4.46)	(1.68)	(1.01)	(2.43)	(1.53)	(1.91)	(3.58)	(2.06)
1 child	0.139	0.813+	-0.346	0.229	0.099	0.044	0.102	0.240	-0.007	0.195	-0.327	0.039
	(0.84)	(1.88)	(1.64)	(1.33)	(0.26)	(0.17)	(0.60)	(0.61)	(0.03)	(1.06)	(0.92)	(0.20)
2 children	-0.176	0.246	-0.525***	0.017	0.160	-0.149	0.008	-0.215	-0.238	0.161	-0.276	-0.217
	(1.23)	(0.61)	(3.04)	(0.12)	(0.50)	(0.67)	(0.06)	(0.60)	(1.32)	(1.01)	(0.95)	(1.32)
3 or more children	0.114	0.651*	-0.631***	0.046	0.103	-0.197	0.125	0.164	-0.224	0.245+	-0.238	-0.196
	(0.86)	(1.76)	(3.95)	(0.33)	(0.35)	(0.93)	(0.92)	(0.52)	(1.33)	(1.66)	(0.91)	(1.27)
1st wealth quartile	0.524***	0.748***	0.471***	0.442***	0.179	0.064	0.450***	0.481**	0.540***	0.417***	0.208	0.652***
	(6.57)	(3.70)	(3.91)	(5.29)	(0.92)	(0.44)	(5.46)	(2.54)	(4.85)	(4.80)	(1.14)	(6.30)
4th wealth quartile	-0.448***	0.144	0.106	-0.308***	-0.005	0.091	-0.359***	-0.500*	-0.101	-0.449***	-0.512**	-0.046
	(4.49)	(0.57)	(0.86)	(3.08)	(0.02)	(0.69)	(3.86)	(1.95)	(0.88)	(4.38)	(2.18)	(0.44)
1st income quartile	0.601***	0.708***	0.508***	0.481***	0.474**	0.414***	0.525***	0.300	0.128	0.582***	0.794***	0.463***
	(7.43)	(3.48)	(4.20)	(5.65)	(2.43)	(2.95)	(6.26)	(1.53)	(1.09)	(6.58)	(4.29)	(4.35)
4th income quartile	-0.474***	-0.203	-0.242+	-0.305***	-0.318	-0.255+	-0.343***	-0.348	-0.408***	-0.395***	0.005	-0.188+
	(4.53)	(0.72)	(1.86)	(2.98)	(1.22)	(1.83)	(3.64)	(1.38)	(3.47)	(3.81)	(0.02)	(1.77)
Constant	-3.691***	-10.749***	-1.068	-2.846***	-6.757***	-0.407	-1.445**	-8.253***	-1.037	-2.897***	-8.102***	-0.033
	(6.13)	(6.84)	(1.26)	(4.59)	(4.64)	(0.43)	(2.40)	(5.58)	(1.32)	(4.53)	(5.89)	(0.05)
Observations	9024			8355			8044			7724		
Log likelihood	-5588.88			-5146.94			-5814.33			-5702.05		
Pseudo-R²	0.23			0.22			0.20			0.20		

Note: Absolute value of z statistics in parentheses.

Source: Authors' calculations based on the HRS cohort.

*** Significant at the 1 percent level.

** Significant at the 5 percent level.

* Significant at the 10 percent level.

probabilities when more individual attributes in the first wave are controlled for, in addition to health status in the first of the two waves. We used three specifications:

- Specification (1) includes only age and gender.
- Specification (2) is the one shown in table 4.12.
- Specification (3) refines the description of health by adding to specification (2) the RAND summary indices for the number of conditions, and indices of gross and fine motor activities and mobility that significantly correlate with disability, as shown in table 4.1.

Controlling for initial values of covariates improves the predictions substantially. Still, even specification (3) understates the proportion of persons who were in poor or fair health in 1992 who are in poor or fair health in 2000. While 44.07 percent of these persons are in poor or fair health in 2000, the predicted percent is only 36.67 percent. However, specification (3) does much better than specification (1) or specification (2), which control for fewer individual attributes. Specification (3) also predicts much better than specification (1) or (2) the percentage of persons who were in good or better health in 1992 who are in good or better health in 2000. The improvement in fit, displayed in the second column of table 4.13, is measured by the average simulated probability of the observed outcome. Thus, better control for individual heterogeneity improves the transition predictions substantially.

Finally, we consider misclassification error. We assume that underlying health (or disability) is continuous, ranging from persons with the worst health to those with the best health. The measure of health status reported in the HRS, however, is discrete, allowing for five self-reported categories (which we often condense even further into only two categories). Measured disability allows for only two categories. These categories are not precisely defined. Respondents may therefore misclassify their health or disability status because they report a different category than others who have the same underlying health status.

Misclassifications are likely to be particularly frequent in situations in which true underlying health status is on the borderline between categories. This may explain sequences that exhibit a frequent back-and-forth movement from one category to the other (such as 01010 in the binary disability categories). Another type of misclassification is simple error. Sequences that show a single deviation from an otherwise constant pattern (such as 00100) may reflect such errors, although they may also indicate for example, a temporary illness.

Table 4.14 shows the frequencies of each sequence of self-reported health in the HRS data. In each of the five waves between 1992 and 2000, zero represents good or better health, 1 fair or poor health, and x either death or attrition. The sequences are ordered in descending frequency. The

Table 4.13   Prediction of 1992–2000 health changes, controlling for observable characteristics

			Wave 5 health							
			Actual				Simulated			
Specification	"Fit"	Initial health	Good+	Poor/fair	Dead	Attrition	Good+	Poor/fair	Dead	Attrition
(1)	0.413	Good+	67.12	11.13	4.83	16.92	60.47	16.77	5.88	16.89
		Poor/fair	20.50	43.99	19.85	15.66	43.81	24.26	16.16	15.76
(2)	0.436	Good+	67.12	11.14	4.83	16.91	61.88	15.58	5.64	16.91
		Poor/fair	20.51	44.01	19.86	15.62	38.89	28.48	17.01	15.62
(3)	0.469	Good+	67.17	11.10	4.82	16.91	64.95	13.07	4.89	17.09
		Poor/fair	20.56	44.07	19.71	15.66	29.06	36.67	19.28	15.00

Note: The slight differences in the actual distributions are due to missing values for some of the covariates.
Source: Authors' calculations based on the HRS cohort.

Table 4.14   Sequences of health status, 1992–2000

Sequence	Frequency	Percent	Cumulative	Sequence	Frequency	Percent	Cumulative	Sequence	Frequency	Percent	Cumulative
00000	4048	44.84	44.8	11110	67	0.74	88.2	10xxx	27	0.30	97.3
11111	578	6.40	51.2	10111	61	0.68	88.9	010xx	25	0.28	97.6
0xxxx	449	4.97	56.2	11000	56	0.62	89.5	10100	23	0.25	97.8
00xxx	327	3.62	59.8	01011	51	0.56	90.1	10110	23	0.25	98.1
000xx	267	2.96	62.8	11010	51	0.56	90.7	0111x	21	0.23	98.3
00010	257	2.85	65.6	01110	48	0.53	91.2	101xx	20	0.22	98.5
00001	243	2.69	68.3	10011	48	0.53	91.7	0011x	18	0.20	98.7
1xxxx	221	2.45	70.8	11101	45	0.50	92.2	110xx	17	0.19	98.9
0000x	211	2.34	73.1	01010	41	0.45	92.7	1001x	16	0.18	99.1
00011	144	1.60	74.7	00101	40	0.44	93.1	10101	16	0.18	99.3
11xxx	143	1.58	76.3	001xx	39	0.43	93.5	1000x	13	0.14	99.4
10000	128	1.42	77.7	0001x	38	0.42	94.0	1011x	10	0.11	99.5
01111	126	1.40	79.1	10010	33	0.37	94.3	0110x	8	0.09	99.6
00111	120	1.33	80.5	11001	33	0.37	94.7	1101x	8	0.09	99.7
01000	113	1.25	81.7	10001	32	0.35	95.1	0100x	7	0.08	99.8
00100	103	1.14	82.8	01001	31	0.34	95.4	0010x	5	0.06	99.8
111xx	101	1.12	84.0	11100	30	0.33	95.7	1110x	5	0.06	99.9
1111x	96	1.06	85.0	00100	29	0.32	96.0	1100x	4	0.04	99.9
01xxx	80	0.89	85.9	011xx	29	0.32	96.4	0101x	3	0.03	100.0
00110	75	0.83	86.7	01101	27	0.30	97.0	1010x	3	0.03	100.0
11011	69	0.76	87.5								
Total								9,028		100	

Source: Authors' calculations from the HRS cohort.

most striking feature of the data is the stability of self-reported health status. Almost 45 percent of all respondents reported that their health was good or better in all five waves. Another 6.4 percent reported that their health was fair or poor in all five waves. Including incomplete histories (noted by x), 71.3 percent of respondents never changed their self-reported health status. Another 13.7 percent changed their self-reported health status only once, mostly from good or better to fair or poor.

Self-reported health sequences with changes from good or better to fair or poor, or the reverse, are relatively rare. Thus, these data provide prima facie evidence suggesting that misclassification cannot dominate self-reported health categorization. Self-reported sequences with three or four changes make up only 3.7 percent of all sequences. Single-change sequences are more frequent, accounting for 6.6 percent of all sequences. And it is not clear how many of these reflect true one-spell illnesses. Thus we should perhaps be less concerned about errors in the data than about the reduction in information inherent in the discrete coding of an underlying continuous variable.

The sequences also provide some information that helps to distinguish true state dependence from unobserved heterogeneity. We calculate the probability of a bad health state in wave 5, conditional on a sequence in the first four waves of the HRS. The data are reported in table 4.15. In this representation, we assume that heterogeneity is held constant by conditioning on the total number of past bad health states, regardless of order. State dependence in this representation is suggested if the sequence of past health states determines health status in wave 5, but the number of past bad health states does not determine health status in wave 5.

Thus we first order the entries in the table by the number of bad health states, and then by the number of waves over which the most recent health state was observed without change. Not surprisingly, the probability of being in bad health in wave 5 increases with the number of prior bad states. In addition, there is also a distinct time lag effect: The more recent a bad health status, the higher the probability of being in bad health in wave 5.

Comparing sequence 1 to sequence 2, we see clearly that even health status fives waves earlier affects health status in wave 5. With no prior bad health states, the probability of bad health in wave 5 is 0.06; if the only change is that health status five waves earlier is bad (but good in the subsequent three waves), the probability of bad health in wave 5 is increased from 0.06 to 0.19. This change suggests heterogeneity. The comparison of sequences 3 with 6 tells the same story. So does the comparison of sequences 4 and 7.

Comparison of sequences 2, 3, and 4 shows that, holding the number of past bad health states constant, the more recent the bad health state the greater the probability that health status in wave 5 will be bad. This suggests state dependence. Obviously, there is more going on than simple het-

Table 4.15   Probability of bad health in wave 5, conditional on sequence of health states in waves 1 through 4

Number	Initial sequence in waves 1 through 4	Frequency of initial sequence	Number of past bad health states	Lag since last bad health state	Probability of bad health in wave 5
1	0000	5,572	0	—	0.06
2	1000	209	1	4	0.19
3	0100	185	1	3	0.21
4	0010	183	1	2	0.28
5	0001	538	1	1	0.38
6	1100	110	2	3	0.38
7	1010	46	2	2	0.39
8	0110	75	2	2	0.51
9	0101	125	2	1	0.55
10	1001	108	2	1	0.61
11	0011	249	2	1	0.61
12	1110	93	3	2	0.58
13	1101	157	3	1	0.61
14	0111	216	3	1	0.73
15	1011	106	3	1	0.73
16	1111	799	4	1	0.90
Total		8,771			0.25

Source: Authors' calculations from HRS cohort.

erogeneity. State dependence may overlay differences in self-reported health status due to heterogeneity. Similar conclusions follow from comparing sequence 6 to sequence 7, and sequence 7 to sequence 8. In each sequence, there are two bad health states. But the more recent the last of these bad health states, the greater the probability that health status in wave 5 will be bad. One explanation for this state dependence is a drift in the underlying continuous health variable that underlies our coarse binary health indicator. We will return to this issue in our more refined model in section 4.5.

The number of bad health states (as a measure of heterogeneity) and the number of waves since the last bad health state (as a measure of state dependence) are close to a sufficient statistic for the initial sequences. The probability of bad health in wave 5 is very closely approximated by these two measures. Table 4.16 shows logit regression estimates of health status in wave 5 regressed on these two measures (based on the first four waves). This specification cannot be rejected versus a specification with a full set of dummies for the sixteen sequences in table 4.15 (p = 0.5409).

Table 4.17 shows the fitted probabilities of bad health in wave 5 based on the regression above, together with the actual probabilities, for each of the sequences in table 4.15. It is clear that the fitted values are close to the actual values.

Table 4.16   **Probability of bad health in wave 5 based on summary measures of health status in the prior 4 waves**

Logit estimates	Odds ratio	Standard error	Z	P > |z|
Number bad states = 0	1.00		(Reference)	
Number bad states = 1	4.06	0.50	11.29	0.00
Number bad states = 2	8.40	1.61	11.11	0.00
Number bad states = 3	11.92	3.17	9.33	0.00
Number bad states = 4	39.24	13.18	10.93	0.00
wave status wave 1 = bad	1.00		(Reference)	
wave status wave 2 = bad	1.06	0.15	0.43	0.67
wave status wave 3 = bad	1.44	0.17	2.99	0.00
wave status wave 4 = bad	2.24	0.26	6.85	0.00
Number of observations	Log likelihood	LR chi2(7)	Pseudo R2	Prob > chi2
8,771	−3,049.0437	3,698.25	0.3775	0.00

Source: Authors' calculation based on the HRS cohort.

Table 4.17   **Predicted versus actual probability of health status in wave 5**

Sequence in waves 1–4	Actual	Predicted
0000	0.061	0.061
0001	0.385	0.372
0010	0.279	0.276
0011	0.606	0.638
0100	0.205	0.219
0101	0.552	0.565
0110	0.507	0.455
0111	0.731	0.727
1000	0.187	0.209
1001	0.611	0.551
1010	0.391	0.441
1011	0.726	0.715
1100	0.382	0.367
1101	0.611	0.649
1110	0.581	0.542
1111	0.897	0.897
Total	0.246	0.246

Source: Authors' calculations based on HRS cohort.

4.5   An Econometric Model Based on Continuous Latent ("Hidden") Health Status

The descriptive analysis presented in section 4.5 suggests that self-reported health status in all waves prior to wave 5 contains information about wave 5 health status. That is, health status in wave 5 depends on health status in all prior waves. There are at least three explanations for this:

- State dependence: past health states directly affect the risk of a current (good or bad) state.
- Heterogeneity: past states contain information on individual-specific risk that is correlated over time.
- Misclassification: categorical coding induces error in self-reported health status.

Thus to predict future health status, we use an econometric model that accounts for each of these features of the data.[4] The key idea is to model true underlying health status as a continuous latent variable. The categorical self-assessed indicators of health (or work disability) are determined by this latent health. The underlying continuous latent health variable is correlated over time and thus induces correlation over time in the observed responses to the categorical self-assessment of health status and disability. In addition, the probability of death is assumed to depend on the hidden health measure, thus allowing for correlation between health status and selection into the group of persons who survive from one period to the next. The key features of the specification are illustrated in figure 4.4. It relates a categorical self-assessed health indicator y to true latent health h and a set of observed covariates x.

The diagram describes the evolution of latent heath, the measured health indicators y, and mortality m over time—in periods 0, 1, 2, and so forth. Latent health h depends on observed individual covariates x and on unobserved individual attributes a, which are correlated over time. In addition to the random unobserved variable a, which directly influences h, self-reported health or disability y, and mortality, depend on two additional stochastic shocks. One shock, u, represents classification error in self-reported health as well as unmeasured variables that affect self-reported health. Another shock, e, reflects unobserved determinants of mortality.

More precisely, the model used to describe health (or disability) transitions and mortality is represented by the following equations:

(1) Latent (hidden) health:

$$h_{iw} = x_{iw}\gamma + a_{iw}$$

(2) Unobserved determinants of latent health (heterogeneity):

$$a_{iw} \sim N(0,\sigma_a^2)$$

$$a_{iw} \mid a_{iw-1} \sim N\left[\rho^{t(w)-t(w-1)}a_{iw-1}, \sigma_a^2(1 - \rho^{2[t(w)-t(w-1)]})\right]$$

(3) Categorical self-reported health measure y:

$$\Pr(y_{iw} = y \mid x_{iw}, h_{iw}) = \Lambda(\alpha_y - h_{iw} - x_{iw}\beta) - \Lambda(\alpha_{y-1} - h_{iw} - x_{iw}\beta)$$

$$= \Lambda[\alpha_y - (x_{iw}\gamma + a_{iw}) - x_{iw}\beta] - \Lambda[\alpha_{y-1} - (x_{iw}\gamma + a_{iw}) - x_{iw}\beta]$$

---

4. Details can be found in Heiss (2005, Ch. 3).

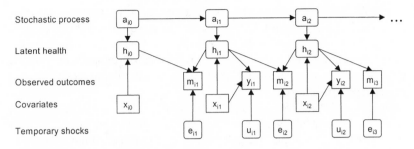

Fig. 4.4   **Modeling a hidden health process**

(4) Mortality hazard rate:

$$\lambda_{it(w)} = \exp\left(\alpha + \delta h_{iw}\right)$$
$$= \exp[\alpha + \delta\left(x_{iw}\gamma + a_{iw}\right)]$$

(5) Survival probability from HRS wave w - 1 to wave w:

$$S_i[t(w)|t(w-1)] = \exp\left\{-[t(w) - t(w-1)]\frac{\lambda_{it(w)} - \lambda_{it(w-1)}}{\delta(h_{iw} - h_{iw-1})}\right\}$$

Equation (1) describes the key latent health variable. Latent health of individual i in wave w is determined by two components: a deterministic part that is a function of the explanatory variables x_{iw}, and an unobserved component a_{iw} which persists from period to period and provides for heterogeneity among respondents. The persistence of the unobserved determinant of latent health is described in equation (2). The a_{iw} follow a first-order autoregressive process defined in continuous time.[5] The marginal distribution of a_{iw} is normal with zero mean and variance σ^2. Conditional on a previous realization d time units ago, where d may be continuous, its distribution is normal with mean $\rho^d a_{iw-d}$ and variance $\sigma^2(1 - \rho^{2d})$. (Simpler specifications [such as independent realizations or random effects] can be specified as special cases of equation 2.)

The observed categorical self-reported health or work disability responses are determined by the ordered logit functional form described in equation (3). The logit probabilities depend on the covariates x_{iw} and on the latent health measure h—which in turn is also a function of the measured covariates x_{iw} and the unobserved determinant a_{iw} of latent health (equation 1)—and by transitory shocks u_{iw}, which are independent and follow a logistic distribution. The cumulative distribution function (c.d.f.) of the logistic distribution is $\Lambda(\cdot)$, with $\alpha_0 = -\infty$ and $\alpha_5 = \infty$. The threshold parameters α_1 through α_4 are cutoff values of latent health that indicate the switch

---

5. An Ornstein-Uhlenbeck process.

points from one categorical response y to another. They are estimated in the model. In the case of a binary specification, equation (3) reduces to a simple logit model. Notice that from equation (3) alone, both of the parameters γ and β cannot be identified. But mortality depends only on the covariates x through latent health and thus allows separate identification of γ, as described next.

Equations (4) and (5) describe the mortality process that induces sample selection, distinguishing persons who remain in the sample from those who die and leave the sample. We start with a straightforward formulation of the mortality hazard rate (equation 4), which depends only on latent health h_{iw}. We then use an approximation formula to integrate this expression over time to obtain the survival function (equation 5). The parameters α and δ are estimated.

The underlying health process and the selection process due to mortality are obviously related. The health change of a typical respondent between two waves is confounded by the fact that this comparison is possible only for the relatively healthy who survive from one wave to the next. A similar problem arises, for example, when back-casting the health at age fifty of a respondent who was interviewed at age eighty. The fact that a person survived until eighty tells us that he or she was probably healthier than the average respondent at age fifty.

In our model, the correlation between health and mortality is generated through latent health h, which in turn depends on observed covariates x as well as the unobserved component of latent health a. So conditional on the covariates x, mortality risk and health are allowed to be correlated through a. In order to identify the model, we assume that conditional on the covariates *and* the unobserved determinants of latent health, the self-reported health measures and mortality are independent. Hence, once we know the covariates x *and* latent health h, there is no additional information in the self-reported health measures of an individual that we could use to make a better prediction of the individual's life expectancy. Our core identifying assumption is that all such information is contained in the latent health variable.

The model is estimated by simulated maximum likelihood. Conditional on the sequence of unobserved persistent health shocks a_{iw}, all calculations are straightforward—the probabilities of self-reported health are given in equation (3) and the survival/mortality probabilities are given in equations (4) and (5). We then integrate over the sequence of health shocks a_{iw} using Monte-Carlo simulation. Their joint distribution is given by equation (2). We account for the fact that selectivity through mortality has gone on before the first wave by integrating not over the unconditional distribution of a_{iw} but over the distribution conditional on survival up to the first interview—see figure 4.7.

This method results in asymptotically efficient parameter estimates if certain regularity conditions hold and the number of replications rises fast enough with the number of individuals. For details on these simulation methods see Hajivassiliou and Ruud (1994). Alternative simulation schemes for this and similar models, such as nonlinear filtering, are discussed by Heiss (2006).

4.6   Results

We have estimated the different joint model of the health status and mortality on the first six waves (1992–2002) of the HRS (using all four cohorts). As previously discussed, the health outcomes we consider are the five categories of self-reported health (SRH) and the two categories of work disability (WD).

We begin with a model that includes only age splines. Age enters the latent health equation and the SRH and WD outcome equations. (Age does not separately enter the mortality equation and latent health enters the outcome equations with a normalized weight of 1. In this way, the age effects in the latent health equation are identified.)

Table 4.18 presents the estimation results for the SRH and WD outcomes. The unobserved heterogeneity (the standard deviation of a) is substantial. The standard deviation of a is estimated to be 3.2 in the SRH model and 4.7 in the WD model. The correlation of a over time is close to 1 in both models, although significantly less than 1. The estimated correlation over one year translates into a correlation between values twenty years apart of 0.7 in the SRH model and 0.5 in the WD model. Consequently, the hypothesis of no heterogeneity ($\sigma = 0$) and the random effects hypothesis ($\rho = 1$) are rejected. Results from these models can be requested from the authors.[6]

4.6.1   Simulations with Age Only

Given the parameter estimates for self-reported health (SRH) and work disability (WD) shown in table 4.18, we can simulate future paths of survival and health (and disability) conditional on health earlier in life. This is done by simulating not over the unconditional distribution of latent health shocks (a) but over the distributions conditional on survival or observed health outcomes. Figure 4.7 presents such conditional distributions for survival up to different ages.

The simulated survival rates conditional on survival up to age fifty for the whole population is shown and compared with the life tables for 1997 (National Center for Health Statistics: National Vital Statistics Report, Vol. 47, no. 28) in figure 4.5. Our simulated survival probabilities tend to be

---

6. The transitory shocks u in the categorical health equations are normalized to $(\pi/\sqrt{3}) \approx 1.8$, as is implicit in the logit model.

Table 4.18 **Estimation results with age only**

	Self-reported health estimate	Standard error	Work disability estimate	Standard error
Latent Health (h):				
Standard deviation of a (σ)	3.2411	0.0153	4.6886	0.0429
1-year correlation of a (ρ)	0.9817	0.0006	0.9663	0.0005
Covariates (γ): Age	−0.5908	0.0425	−0.4644	0.0141
Age spline 60+	0.3012	0.0573	0.1424	0.0303
Age spline 70+	−0.0128	0.0443	−0.0436	0.0394
Age spline 80+	−0.2429	0.0390	−0.2841	0.0382
Age spline 90+	−0.0974	0.0501	−0.0771	0.0539
Health measure (y):				
Latent health	(Enters with weight normalized to 1)			
Covariates (β): Age	0.4610	0.0434	−0.2421	0.0162
Age spline 60+	−0.2504	0.0573	0.0627	0.0299
Age spline 70+	−0.0694	0.0431	0.0631	0.0383
Age spline 80+	0.1837	0.0374	−0.0701	0.0381
Age spline 90+	0.0325	0.0496	0.0202	0.0580
Other	4 ordered logit cut points		constant	
Mortality (m):				
Baseline (α)	−6.8642	0.0846	−8.0584	0.0905
Latent health (δ)	−1.0721	0.0163	−0.4387	0.0055
Number individuals	25,497		25,050	
Number observations (health)	103,250		88,798	
Number parameters	18		15	
Log-likelihood	−150,438.0		−60,269.9	

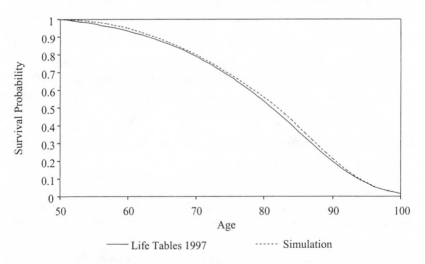

Fig. 4.5 Survival probabilities—simulation versus life tables

slightly higher than the numbers from the life tables. This might be because the HRS samples only individuals who are initially noninstitutionalized.

Both health and disability are strongly related to mortality, as shown in figure 4.6. The figure shows this relationship by comparing future survival probabilities conditional on self-reported health (or disability) at the age of fifty. The differences are striking: for example, only 48.5 percent of respondents who report poor health at age fifty survive until age seventy, whereas 91.6 percent of those reporting excellent health at age fifty survive until age seventy. A similar pattern is revealed with respect to work disability.

Two technical aspects of figure 4.6 are noteworthy. First, the inner and outer 95 percent confidence bands represented by the two lines for each of the three simulations are very close to each other, indicating a rather precise fit. We therefore will not show confidence bands in the sequel of this chapter. Second, and as shown in figure 4.5, the unconditional simulation is not significantly different from the actual life tables.

Figure 4.7 illustrates the selection effect induced by differential mortality. The figure shows the distribution of the unobserved component a of latent health given survival to selected ages. (These are weighted kernel-density estimates and are scaled by survival probabilities, so that the curves integrate to the share of surviving population at the respective ages.) Those who are in the left part of the distributions with relatively poor latent health are more likely to be selected out, so the distribution shifts to the right with the survival age.

To simplify the presentation of simulated paths of health (or disability) we collapse the five point scale of self-reported health into two groups—good or better and fair or poor. Figure 4.8 shows three different health or disability paths. Part a pertains to the proportion of the population in fair or poor health, from age fifty to age one hundred. Part b pertains to the proportion of the population that reports a work disability. The path labeled *unconditional path* shows the hypothetical path of fair or poor health (or work disability) if there were no deaths; or perhaps more meaningful, it shows the path of poor health in the surviving population if poor health and mortality were independent. Because persons in poor health have a much higher mortality rate than persons in good health, health of the surviving population is much better than the hypothetical health shown by the *unconditional path*. The path labeled *survivors* shows poor health among persons who survive to a given age. The difference between the unconditional path and the survivor path represents the selection effect—persons in poor health are more likely to die and thus are less likely to be in the sample at older ages.

Figure 4.8 also shows the actual proportion of persons in poor health (or disabled), based on self-reported health (or disability) responses among persons of a given age in the HRS. Of course, the survey can only interview

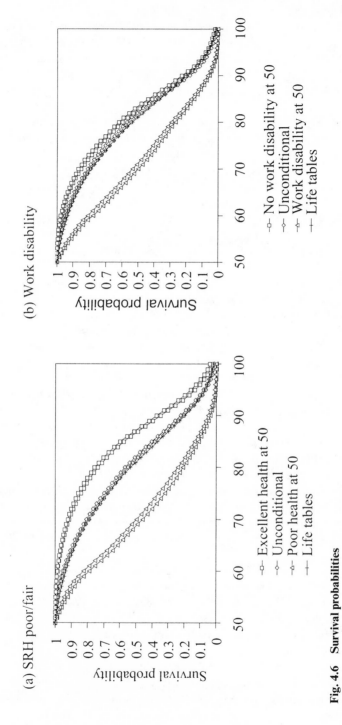

(a) SRH poor/fair

Survival probability

- Excellent health at 50
- Unconditional
- Poor health at 50
- Life tables

(b) Work disability

Survival probability

- No work disability at 50
- Unconditional
- Work disability at 50
- Life tables

Fig. 4.6 Survival probabilities

Note: The two lines for each series represent the inner and outer 95 percent confidence bands.

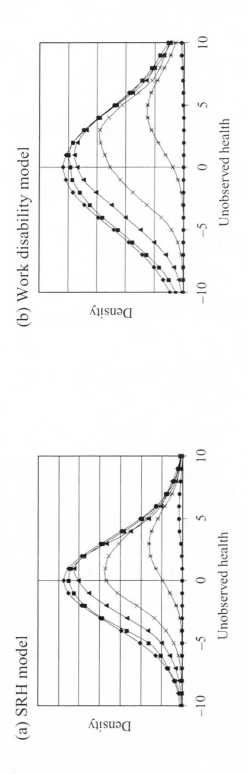

Fig. 4.7   Distribution of unobserved health given survival to selected ages

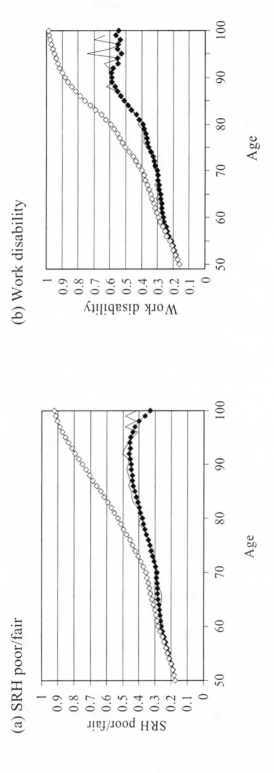

Fig. 4.8   Paths of health measures and the selection effect

(a) SRH poor/fair

SRH poor/fair

Age

(b) Work disability

Work disability

Age

◇ Unconditional path   ◆ Survivors   — Raw data

survivors. The path determined by the actual response at each age is also shown in the figure. If the model represents an appropriate description of poor health and mortality, and their dependence, the simulated poor health path for the surviving population should correspond closely to the actual self-reported poor health levels of persons who survived to a given age. Figure 4.8 shows that the two paths correspond very closely for both poor health and for work disability. Only at very old ages do the two paths diverge noticeably. The actual data at these older ages is very sparse, however.

Because of the mortality selection, the survival of a respondent provides information about the person's health at younger ages. The model can be used to simulate the health status at earlier ages of persons who survive to a given age. Figure 4.9 shows the simulated evolution of health (or disability), conditional on survival to at least age eighty, or to at least age ninety. Because of the strong relationship between health and mortality and the large intertemporal correlation of health, the two conditional paths differ substantially. To understand the relationship, consider the four poor-health paths shown in figure 4.9. The unconditional path and the survivor path are the same as those shown in figure 4.8. The proportion of all persons who are in poor or fair health at age fifty is about 0.18, as shown by the "survivors" path. The proportion of persons who are in poor health at age fifty among those who will survive until age eighty is about 0.09. Of those who survive until age ninety, the proportion in bad health at age fifty is only about 0.06. The proportions with respect to disability are similar to those for health—about 0.16, 0.08, and 0.05, respectively.

Perhaps more striking is the comparison of health at age eighty of persons who survive until at least eighty with the health at age eighty of those who survive until at least ninety. At age eighty, about 40 percent of persons who survive until at least eighty are in poor health. On the other hand, only about 20 percent of persons who survive until at least age ninety are in poor health at age eighty. A comparable comparison for disability shows similar values.

The model could also be used to simulate more detailed information about the health status at younger ages of persons who survive to a given age, like the distribution over all health states at age fifty.

What does self-reported health status tell us about underlying latent health? Figure 4.10 shows the distribution of latent health at age fifty, given self-reported health at age fifty. The distribution of latent health is very different, depending on self-reported health status. Panel a of figure 4.10 shows the distribution of latent health for persons who reported they were in poor health and for persons who reported they were in excellent health. These distributions hardly overlap. The different distributions, together with the high persistence of latent health over time, generate substantial persistence of health outcomes.

The distributions conditional on disability are somewhat different. The

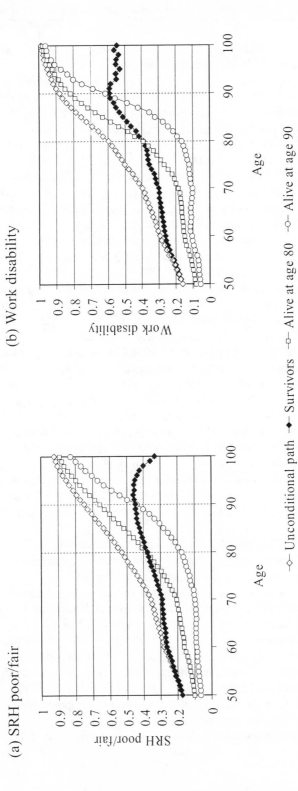

(a) SRH poor/fair

(b) Work disability

Fig. 4.9   Health paths conditional on survival to age 80 and 90

—◇— Unconditional path   —◆— Survivors   —□— Alive at age 80   —○— Alive at age 90

(a) SRH

(b) Work disability

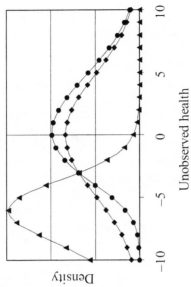

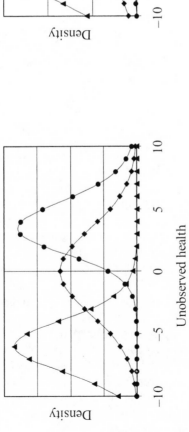

Fig. 4.10 Distribution of latent health at age 50

distribution of latent health for persons who report a work disability at age fifty is clearly over the left tail of the distribution of latent health for all persons at age fifty. But knowing that a person reports no disability at age fifty provides only limited information to distinguish this group from all persons at age fifty. The distribution of latent health for the no-disability group is only slightly to the right of the distribution of latent health for all persons. The reason is that at age fifty most respondents classify themselves in the no-disability group, and thus there can be little difference between the no-disability group and all respondents.

Figure 4.11 shows future health (and disability) conditional on self-reported health at age fifty. Conditional on self-reported health, two paths are shown—one for all persons that does not account for selection due to mortality, and one for survivors. Panel a of figure 4.11 shows the proportion in poor or fair health. Panel b of figure 4.11 shows the proportion with a work disability. Note that because of self-reported classification errors, the health path for those who report they are in poor health at age fifty does not start at zero. And the path for those who say they are in excellent health does not start at 1. A similar explanation pertains to the work disability paths.

Self-reported health is highly persistent—the two paths converge only slowly. Consider the two survivor paths. Until age seventy or eighty the two paths remain far apart. The paths only start to converge rapidly after age ninety. For persons surviving until age 100, the mortality selection effect leaves survivors with approximately the same health status at age 100, no matter what their reported health status at age fifty. (The selection effect is much less pronounced for persons with excellent initial health. The paths of the total and the surviving population diverge more slowly for this group than for the group with poor reported health at age fifty.) For work disability, the results are similar. Persistence with respect to disability, however, is not as strong as persistence with respect to poor versus excellent health. This is because poor and excellent health at age fifty are very distinct outcomes, which contain significant information about latent health, as shown in figure 4.10. Work disability versus no work disability contains less information, also shown in figure 4.10.

Figure 4.12, instead of showing the future path of persons conditional on reported health at age fifty (as in figure 4.11), shows the reverse paths for persons who survive until at least age eighty and report their health status at age eighty. The pure information about health provided by survival through age eighty is shown in figure 4.9. Conditioning on reported health at age eighty obviously also conditions on survival to at least age eighty. Survival to age eighty and health status at age eighty may provide countervailing information, however. Survival is good news; bad health is bad news. Bad self-reported poor health at age eighty outweighs the good information on survival through age eighty. Back-casting SRH from age

(a) SRH poor/fair

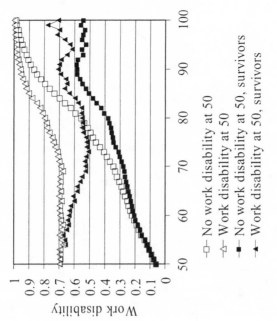

Excellent health at 50
Poor health at 50
Excellent health at 50, survivors
Poor health at 50, survivors

(b) Work disability

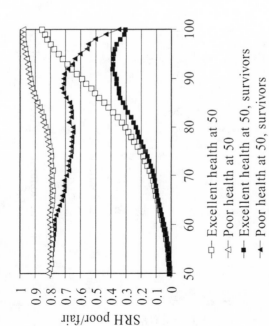

No work disability at 50
Work disability at 50
No work disability at 50, survivors
Work disability at 50, survivors

Fig. 4.11 Health paths by initial health at age 50

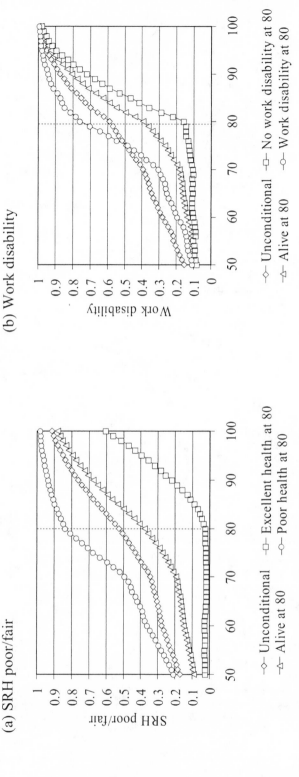

Fig. 4.12 Health paths by initial health at age 80

eighty to age fifty, the unconditional poor health risk at fifty is 17.8 percent. Conditional on survival to age eighty, the likelihood of poor health decreases to 10 percent. Of those who survive until age eighty and report poor health at age eighty, 20.3 percent are simulated to be in poor or fair health at age fifty. Of those who survive to age eighty and report excellent health at age eighty, only 2.1 percent are predicted to be in poor or fair health at age fifty.

On the other hand, information about work disability at age eighty, given survival to at least age eighty, provides little information about disability status at age fifty, as suggested by figure 4.10.

4.6.2 Simulations: Conditioning on Sociodemographic Characteristics

In addition to the model in which we only conditioned on age, we estimate a model for SRH with additional covariates—gender, race, and education and also interactions of these variables with age—in the latent health and the self-reported health outcome equations. Table 4.19 shows the parameter estimates. Note that the covariates enter both the latent health equation and the SRH equation. Thus, the covariates in the SRH equation capture the additional effects on SRH that are not captured by latent health (which also enters the SRH equation). Females have higher latent health (a lower mortality risk) at age fifty, and this effect increases at higher ages.[7] On the other hand, given latent health (mortality risk), the SRH of women is much worse. This might be due to different response scales or different health conditions, such as arthritis, that affect subjective health status more than mortality. Respondents have a higher latent health and report better SRH given latent health.

Figure 4.13 shows the relative mortality hazards for males versus females, nonwhite versus white respondents, and low- versus high-education respondents. While the mortality risk of males relative to females is more or less constant over all ages, mortality differences by race and education diminish at older ages. This apparently results from the mortality selection effect, with those in better health more likely to survive until older ages no matter what their race or education.

The next three figures show the likelihood of fair or poor SRH (sometimes referred to as *poor health*) by gender, race, and education, respectively. Figure 4.14 shows health paths by gender. The paths labeled "male" and "female" show unconditional health paths of men and women. The paths labeled "male survivors" and "female survivors" show the health of the survivors and account for the strong relationship between poor health and mortality. At age fifty, both men and women report about the same level of poor health. As discussed previously, latent health is better for

---

7. The variable age is actual age minus fifty.

Table 4.19   Estimation results with age and sociodemographics

	Latent health (h)		SRH	
	Estimate	Standard error	Estimate	Standard error
Latent Health (h):				
Standard deviation of a (σ)	2.9894	0.0386		
1-year correlation of a (ρ)	0.9787	0.0006		
Covariates (γ): Age	−0.4844	0.0319	0.4130	0.0299
Age spline 60+	0.2228	0.0422	−0.1717	0.0413
Age spline 70+	−0.0164	0.0415	−0.0589	0.0402
Age spline 80+	−0.2369	0.0368	0.1713	0.0351
Age spline 90+	−0.1028	0.0464	0.0549	0.0470
Female	1.0897	0.2388	−1.3104	0.2282
Education	0.2128	0.0385	0.1883	0.0358
Nonwhite	−2.6672	0.2768	1.1884	0.2626
Hispanic	0.0114	0.4468	−0.5425	0.4222
Female * age	0.0277	0.0083	−0.0027	0.0080
Education * age	−0.0033	0.0012	−0.0023	0.0012
Nonwhite * age	0.0586	0.0104	−0.0377	0.0099
Hispanic * age	0.0118	0.0167	0.0064	0.0155
Other			4 ordered logit cut points	
Mortality (m):				
Baseline (α)	−5.8253	0.1904		
Latent health (δ)	−0.3541	0.0039		
Number individuals	25,497			
Number observations (health)	103,250			
Number parameters	34			
Log-likelihood	−148,652.8			

women, but SRH conditional on latent health is worse. On balance, these two effects roughly cancel out. Poor health increases more rapidly for men than for women, as shown by the "male" and "female" paths. On the other hand, selection due to mortality is greater for men than for women, and more men than women reporting poor health leave the sample. Thus the self-reported health of men and women survivors is about the same through age eighty-five. After age eighty-five, the health of women is worse than the health of men. This results entirely from differential mortality.

Figure 4.15 shows poor health by race. The figure shows poor health paths for white and African American men with twelve years of education. At age fifty, African Americans are much more likely than whites to be in poor health. Through age seventy, the slopes of the poor health paths (not accounting for mortality) for African American and for white respondents are about the same, but mortality is much higher for African Americans. Thus, the paths for African American and white survivors converge. As

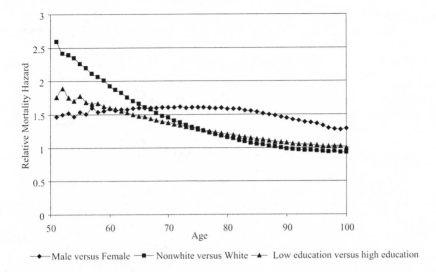

Fig. 4.13 Relative mortality hazards

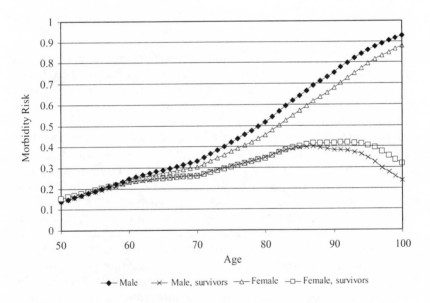

Fig. 4.14 Poor health by gender
Note: All simulations are for white respondents with twelve years of education.

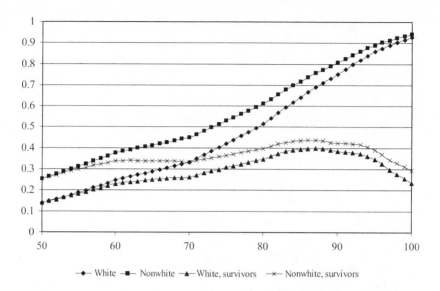

Fig. 4.15   Poor health by race
Note: All simulations are for male respondents with twelve years of education.

shown in figure 4.15, the mortality differences between African Americans and whites diminish at older ages. On the other hand, the true poor health paths start to converge after age seventy. Thus, the poor health paths of survivors remain roughly parallel at older ages, with poor health more likely for African Americans than for whites.

Figure 4.16 shows poor health paths by education level—eight years of schooling (low education) and sixteen years (high education). At age fifty, the likelihood of poor health for the low-education group is about four times as high as for the high-education group. The true poor health levels of the two groups increase in parallel to about age seventy and thereafter the true poor health levels of the two groups start to converge. In addition, as shown in figure 4.15, the difference between the mortality rates of the two groups declines at older ages. Thus, the difference in the poor health levels of low- and high-education survivors starts to converge after age seventy, although the poor health level of the low-education group remains substantially higher than for the high-education group.

4.7   Conclusions

To help understand pathways to disability, we have explored the relationship between health (and disability) at younger ages and health (and disability) at older ages. In particular, we developed an econometric model

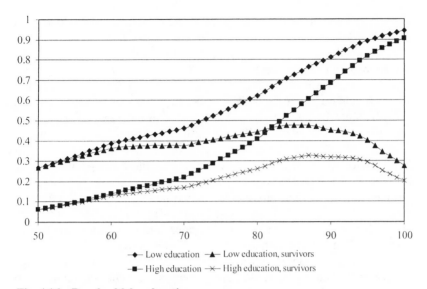

Fig. 4.16   Poor health by education

Note: All simulations are for white male respondents.

designed to take account of three key features of the data that characterize the health and disability of persons as they age:

- State dependence: all past states directly affect the risk of a current bad state.
- Heterogeneity: past states contain information on the individual risk that is correlated over time.
- Misclassification: categorical coding of self-reported health and disability induces classification errors.

The key idea of the model is to consider true underlying health status, specified as a continuous latent variable. The categorical self-assessed indicators of health (or work disability) are determined by this latent health. The underlying continuous latent health variable is correlated over time and thus induces correlation over time in the observed responses to the categorical self-assessment of health status and disability. In addition, the probability of death is assumed to depend on the hidden latent health measure, thus allowing for correlation between health status and selection into the group of persons who survive from one period to the next.

The analysis is based on the four cohorts of the Health and Retirement Study (HRS, AHEAD, CODA, and WB). We used the econometric model to simulate future mortality and the future health and disability paths of survivors, conditional on health or disability at younger ages (age fifty).

We find that health and work disability correspond very closely (in the HRS data). We find a very strong relationship between health and disability and mortality. We find that future paths of health and disability are very strongly related to health and disability at age fifty. Reversing the process, we find that survival to older ages (eighty or ninety) provides substantial information about health and disability status at younger ages.

In addition, the interplay between health and mortality of persons as they age can be studied in detail using simulations based on the econometric model. For example, at age fifty, the poor health level of persons with eight or fewer years of education is about four times as high as the poor health level of those with sixteen or more years of education. The true poor health levels of the two groups increase in parallel to about age seventy and thereafter the true poor health levels of the two groups start to converge. But the difference between the mortality rates of the two groups declines at older ages. Thus the difference in the poor health levels of low- and high-education survivors starts to converge after age seventy, although the poor health level for the low-education group remains substantially higher than the level for the high-education group. Similar decomposition of mortality and poor health is presented by race and by gender.

To date, we have used only a few individual socioeconomic attributes in the model. Many more attributes, such as specific medical conditions, could be incorporated in the model. The onset of particular medical conditions could be held to explain, for example, the differences between the health and disability paths of low-education and high-education groups or the differences between the health and disability paths by race or ethnic group. Such analysis may also help to understand how future medical technology may change the prevalence of disability.

References

Aarts, L. J. M., R. V. Burkhauser, and P. R. de Jong, eds. 1996. *Curing the Dutch disease: An international perspective on disability policy reform.* Aldershot: Avebury.
Adams, P., M. D. Hurd, D. McFadden, A. Merrill, and T. Ribeiro. 2003. Healthy, wealthy, and wise? Tests for direct causal paths between health and socioeconomic status. *Journal of Econometrics* 112:3–56.
Adda, J., T. Chandola, and M. Marmot. 2003. Socioeconomic status and health: Causality and pathways. *Journal of Econometrics* 112:57–63.
Barker, D. J. P. 1997. Maternal nutrition, fetal nutrition, and diseases in later life. *Nutrition* 13 (9): 807–13.
Borg, V., and T. S. Kristensen. 2000. Social class and self-rated health: Can the gradient be explained by differences in lifestyle or work environment? *Social Science and Medicine* 51 (7): 1019–30.
Börsch-Supan, A. 2001. Incentive effects of Social Security under an uncertain dis-

ability option. In *Themes in the economics of aging*, ed. D. A. Wise, 281–310. Chicago, London: University of Chicago Press.

Börsch-Supan, A. 2005. Work disability and health. In *Health, aging, and retirement in Europe: First results from SHARE*, eds. A. Börsch-Supan, A. Brugiavani, H. Jurges, J. Mackenbach, J. Siegrist, and G. Weber, 253–59. Mannheim: MEA-Press.

Burström, B., and P. Fredlund. 2001. Self rated health: Is it as good a predictor of subsequent mortality among adults in lower as well as in higher social classes? *Journal of Epidemiology and Community Health* 55:836–40.

Contoyannis, Paul, and Andrew M. Jones. 2004. Socio-economic status, health, and lifestyle. *Journal of Health Economics* 23:965–95.

Feinstein, J. 1993. The relationship between socioeconomic status and health: A review of the literature. *The Milbank Quarterly* 71 (2): 279–322.

Goldman, N. 2001. Social inequalities in health: Disentangling the underlying mechanisms, in *Population Health and Aging—Strengthening the Dialogue Between Epidemiology and Demography*. Maxine Weinstein, Albert I. Hermalin, and Michael A. Stoto, eds. *Annals of the New York Academy of Sciences* 954:118–39.

Gruber, J., and D. Wise, eds. 1999. *Social Security and retirement around the world.* Chicago: University of Chicago Press.

———. 2004. *Social Security and retirement around the world: Micro estimation.* Chicago: University of Chicago Press.

Hajivassiliou, V. A., and P. A. Rund. 1994. Classical estimation methods for LDV models using simulation. In *Handbook of econometrics Vol. IV*, ed. Robert F. Engle and Daniel L. McFadden, 2383–2441. Amsterdam: Elsevier.

Halliday, T. J. 2005. Heterogeneity, state dependence and health. University of Hawaii at Manoa, Department of Economics. Working Paper no. 200503.

Heiss, F. 2005. *Essays on specification and estimation of latent variable models.* Ph.D. diss. University of Mannheim.

Heiss, F. 2006. *Nonlinear state-space models for microeconometric panel data.* University of Munich, Department of Economics. Discussion Papers in Economics no. 1157.

Hurd, M. D., and A. Kapteyn. 2003. Health, wealth and the role of institutions. *Journal of Human Resources* 38 (2): 386–415.

Hurd, M. D., D. McFadden, and A. Merrill. 2001. Predictors of mortality among the elderly. In *Themes in the economics of aging*, ed. David Wise, 171–97. Chicago: University of Chicago Press.

Idler, E., and S. Kasl. 1995. Self-ratings of health: Do they also predict change in functional ability? *Journal of Gerontology* 50 (6): S344–53.

Marmot, M. 1999. Multi-level approaches to understanding social determinants. In *Social epidemiology*, ed. Lisa Berkman and Ichiro Kawachi. Oxford: Oxford University Press.

Meer, J., D. L. Miller, and H. S. Rosen. 2003. Exploring the health-wealth nexus. *Journal of Health Economics* 22:713–30.

Michaud, P. C., and A. van Soest. 2004. Health and wealth of elderly couples: Causality tests using dynamic panel data models. Discussion paper IZA 1312 and CentER 2004–81.

Power, C., S. Mathews, and O. Manor. 1998. Inequalities in self-rated health: Explanations from different states of life. *Lancet* 351:1009–14.

Ravelli, A. C. J., J. H. P. van der Meulen, R. P. J. Michels, C. Osmond, D. J. P. Barker, C. N. Hales, and O. P. Bleker. 1998. Glucose tolerance in adults after prenatal exposure to famine. *Lancet* 351:173–76.

Richards, M., and M. E. J. Wadsworth. 2004. Long term effects of early adversity on cognitive function. *Archives of Disease in Childhood* 89:922–27.

Smith, James P. 2004. Unraveling the SES-Health Connection. In *Aging, health, and public policy: Demographic and economic perspectives,* ed. Linda J. Waite. *Population and Development Review* Suppl. 30:108–32.

Wadsworth, M. E. J., and D. J. L. Kuh. 1997. Childhood influences on adult health: A review of recent work from the British 1946 National Birth Cohort Study, the MRC National Survey of Health and Development. *Pediatric and Perinatal Epidemiology* 11:2–20.

5

Clinical Pathways to Disability

Mary Beth Landrum, Kate A. Stewart,
and David M. Cutler

5.1 Introduction

While disability declined over the course of the 1980s and 1990s (Crimmins, Saito, and Reynolds 1997; Freedman and Martin 1998; Waidmann and Liu 2000; Cutler 2001; Manton and Gu 2001; Schoeni, Freedman, and Wallace 2001; Freedman, Martin, and Schoeni 2002; Freedman, Crimmons et al. 2004; Spillman 2004), the prevalence of disability among the elderly remains high (Waidmann and Liu 2000; Schoeni, Freedman, and Wallace 2001; Manton, Gu, and Lamb 2006). Moreover, disability is associated with poor quality of life (Lamb 1996), high medical spending (Komisar, Hunt-McCool, and Feder 1997; Liu, Wall, and Wissoker 1997; Fried et al. 2001; Guralnik et al. 2002; Chernew et al. 2005), and increased mortality (Manton 1988; Guralnik et al. 1991; Ferrucci et al. 1996). Thus, it is critical to understand the major clinical pathways through which the health of the elderly declines to be able to develop effective interventions to prevent or minimize disability in the elderly population.

In this paper, we analyze data from the National Long Term Care Survey (NLTCS)—a longitudinal survey on a nationally representative sample of Medicare beneficiaries that has been linked to Medicare administrative

Mary Beth Landrum is an associate professor of biostatistics in the Department of Health Care Policy at Harvard Medical School. Kate A. Stewart is a researcher at Mathematica Policy Research, Inc., and was a PhD candidate in Health Policy at Harvard Medical School when this research was completed. David M. Cutler is the Otto Eckstein Professor of Applied Economics and Dean for the Social Sciences at Harvard University and an affiliate of the National Bureau of Economic Research.

This work was funded by the National Institute of Aging (P30 AG12810 and R01 AG19805) and the Mary Woodard Lasker Charitable Trust and Michael E. DeBakey Foundation.

data—to identify the major pathways through which the elderly become disabled. We compare two methods of identifying disabling conditions. First, using administrative billing data, we evaluate thirty-one potentially disabling clinical conditions and estimate the proportion of incident disability attributable to each condition. In order to better understand the association between medical conditions and disability, we consider both simple binary measure of any disability in addition to measures that reflect severity (i.e., the total number of Activities of Daily Living [ADL] and Instrumental Activities of Daily Living [IADL] disabilities) and types of limitations (i.e., mobility-related, cognitive, or self-care). We also examine the relationship between medical conditions and the use of supportive and medical services. We hypothesize that different medical conditions lead to disability of varying severity, type, and need for assistance. Identifying these differences may help to prioritize medical conditions for interventions to prevent or delay disability and to help design appropriate interventions for different types of disability.

In the second part of the chapter, we compare these empirical results to respondents' self-reported causes. We find that an important subset of newly disabled elderly did not report a chronic condition or an acute medical event when asked to identify the cause of their disability; rather, they cited symptoms or simply attributed their disability to old age. We explore whether respondents who attributed their disability to old age or symptoms differed from respondents who cited chronic or acute medical conditions in both patterns of disablement and health care utilization, to better understand whether old age and symptom causes represent pathways to disability independent of diseases and conditions.

Our chapter is structured as follows. First we discuss prior literature relevant to our analyses. We then describe our data and analytic methods and present our results. Finally, we summarize our conclusions and discuss implications of our findings.

5.2   Background

5.2.1   Heterogeneity in the Disablement Process

Disability in an elderly, nonworking population is typically defined as the need for assistance[1] with one or more or self-care tasks (such as bathing or eating) called Activities of Daily Living (ADLs), or tasks required to live independently (such as grocery shopping or preparing meals) called Instrumental Activities of Daily Living (IADLs). National surveys measuring disability in the elderly typically ask respondents about their ability to perform a set of ADL and IADL tasks, and often also ask respondents

---

1. Some surveys ask respondents about the level of difficulty without assistance.

about physical limitations, such as difficulty walking long distances, going up stairs, or grasping small objects.

Previous research has demonstrated that disability may develop as the result of a catastrophic event such as a stroke or a hip fracture, or as a progressive process associated with chronic and sometimes degenerative conditions such as arthritis or dementia (Ferrucci et al. 1996; Ferrucci et al. 1997; Wolff et al. 2005). Depending on the cause of disability, many elderly may recover from disability (Gill, Robinson, and Tinetti 1997; Gill et al. 2006; Gill et al. 2006) or they may progress to more severe states of disability. Among those who do not recover from disability, both theoretical and empirical work (Katz et al. 1963; Kempen and Suurmeijer 1990; Verbrugge and Jette 1994; Ferrucci et al. 1998) has suggested a hierarchy in physical limitations and ADL and IADL tasks where an elderly person typically progresses from first having physical limitations to needing assistance with complex tasks (such as cooking, grocery shopping, or managing money), progressing to needing assistance with some personal care needs (such as getting out of bed and bathing), and then finally needing assistance with the most basic personal tasks, such as toileting and feeding. However, there is disagreement across studies about the exact nature of the disablement process (Siu, Reuben, and Hays 1990; Lazaridis et al. 1994; Dunlop, Hughes, and Manheim 1997; Jagger et al. 2001), which may be attributable to differing patterns of onset (i.e., catastrophic versus progressive) and likelihood of recovery.

Researchers have also demonstrated that disability, regardless of its cause, may be characterized as a continuum of difficulty and dependency (Fried et al. 1991; Fried et al. 1996; Gill, Robinson, and Tinetti 1998; Fried et al. 2000; Fried et al. 2001). For example, Gill, Robinson, and Tinetti (1998) examined the relationship between difficulty and dependence in specific tasks and demonstrated that separate questions about the use of assistance and difficulty could be used to classify respondents into three ordered categories: independent without difficulty, independent with difficulty, and dependent. Similarly, the work by L.P. Fried et al. (2000, 2001) identified a state of preclinical disability where respondents denied difficulty with a task, but nevertheless reported having modified their performance of the task because of health or physical problems. Respondents with preclinical disability were found to have intermediate levels of physical functioning between that of respondents who reported difficulty with tasks and those who reported neither difficulty nor modification, suggesting that modification without reported difficulty represents early manifestations of functional declines and a less severe form of disability.

Other empirical studies have conducted factor analyses to identify the number and types of underlying dimensions of disability (Fried et al. 1994; Spector and Fleishman 1998). For example, Spector and Fleishman (1998) found a great deal of correlation among seven ADL and nine IADL measures in approximately 3,000 disabled respondents to the 1989 National Long Term Care Survey, so that a single factor that combined fifteen of the sixteen items adequately described the observed patterns. Fried et al. (1994) examined seventeen physical limitations, ADL and IADL items, in 5,201 community-based elderly adults living in one of four U.S. communities; they found that self-reported difficulty with these seventeen items could be partitioned into four factors representing mobility problems, difficulty with complex tasks, difficulty with self-care, and upper extremity limitations. These four factors explained 48 percent of the total variance in the seventeen items. Researchers have also used grade-of-membership models, an extension of latent class models that hypothesize different underlying types of respondents with different patterns of disability, to examine profiles of disability (Lamb 1996; Manton, Stallard, and Corder 1998).

Prior research has also documented specificity in the associations between conditions and specific types of limitations. Arthritis has generally been found to be strongly associated with functional limitations and moderate ADL limitations (Verbrugge, Lepkowski, and Konkol 1991; Fried et al. 1994; Guccione et al. 1994; Manton, Stallard, and Corder 1998) while stroke and dementia have been consistently linked with both IADL limitations and more severe disability in self-care tasks (Fried et al. 1994; Guccione et al. 1994; Manton, Stallard, and Corder 1998). Similar patterns are found in respondents' self-reports of the causes of their limitations (Ford et al. 1988; Ettinger et al. 1994; Valderrama-Gama et al. 2002). Arthritis was most often cited as the cause of limitations in mobility-related tasks, including getting out of bed and getting around inside. Heart and lung diseases were the most often cited causes for aerobic tasks, such as walking half a mile, while stroke and dementia were most often associated with cognitive and self-care tasks.

In this chapter, we evaluate the association of specific diseases and conditions with varying types and severity of disability to better understand the association between medical conditions and the disablement process. We also use the total number of limitations as a proxy for severity of disability, and evaluate whether severity varies across conditions. We further examine reported medical care and assistive services used by disabled respondents, hypothesizing that greater use of medical care and assistive services may reflect more severe disability.

5.2.2   Chronic Conditions Leading to Disability

A large body of research has demonstrated the importance of chronic disease as the primary contributor to disability (Kosorok et al. 1992; Guccione et al. 1994; Boult et al. 1996; Ferrucci et al. 1997; Aguero-Torres et al. 1998; Dunlop et al. 2002; Wolff et al. 2005; Song Chang, and Dunlop 2006). However, these studies often limit attention to the noninstitutionalized elderly population—thus omitting important conditions such as dementia—or focus on a small number of conditions. Further, studies were often conducted on nonrepresentative samples. In this chapter, we extend these prior results by examining the share of disability attributable to a wide range of clinical conditions in a nationally representative sample.

5.2.3   Characteristics of Disabled Respondents Attributing Disability to Symptoms or Old Age

The prior literature provides conflicting evidence on whether chronic disease is responsible for the majority of disability attributed to old age or symptoms by elderly respondents, or whether these respondents are identifying a pathway to disability that is largely independent of chronic disease. Research supporting the idea that the elderly may attribute declines in health related to chronic conditions to old age or symptoms include a study of 230 community-dwelling elderly that found that those who attributed their disability to old age were similar to those not reporting old age as the cause of their disability in terms of age, gender, and race, but were more likely to have chronic conditions, such as arthritis, heart disease, or hearing difficulties (Williamson and Fried 1996). In addition, several regional studies (Ettinger et al. 1994; Williamson and Fried 1996; Leveille, Fried, and Guralnik 2002; Leveille et al. 2004) demonstrated strong relationships between specific diseases and symptoms. For example, elderly who cited pain as a primary cause of their disability were also likely to cite arthritis when asked for a condition cause, and they had a high prevalence of arthritis confirmed by clinical examination; disability attributed to fatigue and shortness of breath was associated with lung and heart disease.

In contrast, Leveille, Fried, and Guralnik (2002) found that women who were unable to cite specific chronic conditions causing their disability were often better able to name symptom causes. They also found little association between certain symptoms, such as fear of falling and general weakness, and chronic conditions, suggesting that at least some of the disability attributed to symptoms or old age is not directly related to common disabling chronic conditions. The literature on frailty generally supports the notion of a pathway to disability that is not a direct result of chronic disease, but instead is associated with age-related loss of physical condition and reserve. For example, Guralnik et al. (1995) found that objective measures of physical functioning among nondisabled elderly predicted subsequent disability even after controlling for chronic conditions (Guralnik et al. 1995). Other authors have argued for the importance of frailty as a separate concept from comorbidity and have found that frailty is associated with disability independently of chronic disease (Ferrucci et al. 1996; Lunney et al. 2003; Fried et al. 2004).

In this chapter, we seek to resolve some of this conflict by further analyzing the characteristics of respondents who attribute disability to either old age or symptom causes as opposed to chronic or acute medical conditions. In particular, we compare severity of disability and use of medical and assistive services to identify systematic differences across these populations that may suggest a pathway to disability independent of diseases and conditions.

5.3 Data and Methods

We used data from the National Long Term Care Survey (NLTCS). The NLTCS is a longitudinal, nationally representative survey of the Medicare population that was designed to study changes in the health and functional status of elderly Americans. Starting in 1982, a random sample of approximately 20,000 Medicare beneficiaries completed a screening interview. Those found to have a chronic disability[2] were then asked to complete a detailed survey. Follow-up surveys were conducted in 1984, 1989, 1994, and 1999. Chronically disabled respondents who survived until the next survey were automatically contacted for detailed follow-up surveys. In addition, at each subsequent wave of the survey, a subsample of nondisabled respondents from the previous wave were contacted for a new screener interview and those found to be chronically disabled were asked to complete the detailed survey. Finally, at each wave a random sample of approximately 5,000 Medicare beneficiaries who reached age sixty-five between waves of the survey were screened in order to maintain a nationally representative sample of the Medicare population. Over the 5 waves of the survey, more than 90,000 screening interviews were performed, leading to over 32,000 detailed interviews (Manton and Gu 2001). Approximately 20 percent of 1994 and 1999 surveys were completed by proxy respondents (Freedman et al. 2004).

The NLTCS has several important strengths. First, the longitudinal design with age-in cohorts allows us to obtain national estimates. Second, response rates for both screener interviews and detailed surveys were over 95 percent in each wave. In addition, survey data has been linked to Medicare administrative data, providing detailed information on the existence of clinical conditions for which respondents were receiving care.

5.3.1 Study Cohorts

Our analyses are based on nondisabled respondents from the 1994 survey whose disability and vital status is known in 1999. From the cohort of 12,366 participants in the 1994 survey who were not chronically disabled,

2. Defined as residence in a long-term care facility, the inability to perform one of nine ADLs (eating, getting in or out of bed, getting in or out of chairs, walking around inside, going outside, dressing, bathing, getting to the bathroom, or using the toilet, and controlling bowel movements or urination) without personal assistance or special equipment, or one of seven IADLs (preparing meals, laundry, light housework, shop for groceries, manage money, take medicines, and use the telephone) without help because of disability or health problem for at least ninety days.

we excluded (a) 1,568 participants who were not sixty-five years old on January 1, 1992, in order to assure complete claims data in the baseline period prior to 1994, (b) ten participants who could not be matched to Medicare data, (c) 1,231 respondents whose disability status was unknown in 1999 because they were not resampled ($n = 752$) or lost to follow-up ($n = 479$), and (d) 1,830 participants enrolled in an HMO for six months or longer, leaving an analytic cohort of 7,727 participants.

5.3.2 Disability Measures

Subjects were considered newly disabled if they reported any ADL or IADL limitations in the 1999 detailed survey[3] or if they were institutionalized at the time of the 1999 survey. Limitations on six specific ADL tasks (eating, getting in and out of bed, getting around inside, dressing, bathing, and toileting) were obtained from the detailed interviews of both community-based and institutionalized respondents. Limitations on eight specific IADL tasks (light housework, laundry, preparing meals, shopping for groceries, getting around outside, managing money, taking medications, and using the telephone) and nine functional limitations (difficulty climbing a flight of stairs, walking across a room, bending to put on socks, lifting a ten pound object, reaching above the head, using fingers to grasp and handle small objects, seeing well enough to read newsprint, speaking, and hearing) were also obtained from the detailed interviews with community-based respondents.

We grouped the fourteen individual ADL and IADL tasks into categories for several analyses. To explore the empirical relationships between the specific tasks, we fit a principal component model to the 5,787 nondisabled respondents in the 1994 NLTCS who survived to 1999 and completed a screener interview. We found that three factors could explain 85 percent of the total variance in the fourteen items. Similar to Fried et al. (1994), one of these factors was strongly associated with more complex IADL tasks requiring cognitive abilities (cooking, laundry, light housekeeping, grocery shopping, managing money, and using the telephone). Also as in the Fried et al. analysis, difficulty getting around outside (typically considered an IADL) was more strongly related to mobility-related ADL tasks than the other IADL tasks. Thus, we used the aggregation of tasks employed by Fried et al. (1994) to summarize our fourteen ADL and IADL measures into three major types of disability: (1) mobility disability (getting out of bed, walking inside and walking outside the home), (2) disability in complex tasks (cooking, laundry, light housework, grocery shopping, managing money, and using the telephone) and (3) disability in self-care tasks

---

3. Respondents were classified as disabled on an ADL task if they reported that someone helped them perform the task, if someone stayed nearby in case they needed help, or if they used special equipment to perform the task. Respondents were classified as disabled on an IADL task if they report that they cannot do the task because of disability or health problem.

(eating, dressing, toileting, and bathing). Following theoretical and empirical work suggesting hierarchies in the disablement process, we consider disability in basic self-care tasks to represent the most severe type of disability, and mobility disability to represent early manifestations of loss of functional abilities.

Detailed interviews of the community-based disabled also asked respondents to report the heath conditions they believed were the cause of their disability. Respondents were able to list up to ten conditions, and 89 percent of the community-based respondents ($n = 892$) provided at least one response. We developed a coding scheme that summarized free-text responses into: (a) chronic conditions, (b) acute events, (c) physical symptoms that were not directly linked to a clinical condition (such as weakness, lack of balance, or pain), or (d) old age. These categories were not mutually exclusive, as respondents often reported multiple causes. We also coded a set of binary indicators of specific chronic conditions and acute events and modified a recently validated taxonomy of self-reported symptom causes to classify symptom causes as pain, balance, weakness, endurance, or other symptoms, (Leveille et al. 2004). Both authors independently coded the free-text responses. Agreement was high, with kappas ranging from 0.7 to 1.0 for chronic and acute conditions. Agreement was slightly lower for symptom causes (ranging from 0.3 for upper extremity pain to 1.0 for hearing). Final coding was based on consensus when there was disagreement.

5.3.3   Other Variables

Mortality and information about the existence of thirty-one chronic conditions[4] were obtained from Medicare administrative data. We examined the prevalence of chronic conditions over two time frames. Participants were coded as having the clinical condition at baseline if there was at least one inpatient claim or two nonhospital claims (outpatient, home health, SNF, or hospice) with a primary or secondary diagnosis of interest between January 1, 1992, and December 31, 1994[5]. Similarly, participants were coded as developing the condition between surveys if they had at least

---

4. These mutually exclusive categories were previously defined on the basis of prevalence of ICD-9 diagnosis and their observed relationship with disability (McClellan and Yan 2000; Cutler 2005). See table 5.A1 in the Appendix for list of clinical conditions and associated ICD-9 codes.

5. We examined several alternative coding schemes for clinical conditions. First we considered rules that considered a respondent to have the condition if there were any claims for the condition (inpatient, outpatient, SNF, home health, or hospice). In addition, we examined a two-year window (January 1, 1993–December 31, 1994) for conditions existing prior to baseline. Based on examination of the prevalence of conditions, the persistence of conditions across time frames, and the association with self-reported conditions, in addition to an examination of prior literature, we determined that a three-year look-back for the baseline period and the requirement of at least two noninpatient diagnoses provided the best compromise between sensitivity and specificity for a majority of the conditions.

one inpatient claim or two nonhospital claims with a primary or secondary diagnosis of interest between January 1, 1995, and December 31, 1999. We then combined these two time frames and examined the impact of having the condition either at baseline or developing the condition between the surveys on the likelihood of developing disability[6].

Demographic variables (age, gender, race, and marital status) were obtained from the screener surveys. Detailed interviews with community-based disabled respondents provided information on the use of health care and assistive services: this includes any nursing home stays; hospitalizations in the past year; visits in the past month to the emergency room; physicians; physical, occupational, speech, or hearing therapists; home health services in the past month; and the number of prescription medications obtained in the previous month. The detailed survey also asked respondents about their living arrangements, including whether they were living in an assistive living setting with board and/or personal care services available.

5.4   Analyses

5.4.1   Empirical Pathways to Disability

We fit multinational regression models to estimate the relative importance of the thirty-one clinical factors in explaining any disability and differing types of disability. We fit four separate models for any disability, mobility disability, disability in complex tasks, and disability in self-care tasks. In each case, the dependent variable was a categorical variable with three levels: disabled in at least one specific task in the group, alive and not disabled in at least one task in the group, or died before the 1999 survey. All regression models included age (in five-year categories), gender, marital status in 1994, race (coded as white, black, or other), the set of thirty-one indicators variables for each of the clinical conditions and a binary variable equal to 1 if the respondent did not have any medical claims during the study period. In addition, we examined interaction terms to understand the extent to which combinations of diseases have synergistic effects on disability. To focus the exploration of interactive effects, we included all pairwise interactions of conditions that were each estimated to cause at least 5 percent of incident of any type disability as measured by the adjusted attributable fraction.

---

6. We included conditions developed between the surveys in order to study conditions such as dementia that may be disabling over a short time frame. The associations between conditions and disability should be interpreted cautiously, as we do not know when the participant became disabled and thus some of the new conditions may follow or even be a result of declining functional status (for example, a fracture may be the result of weakness and/or loss of balance). However, for a majority of these conditions, the more likely scenario is that the condition led to functional limitations and resulting disability.

We used results from the multinomial regression models to compute adjusted attributable fractions (Greenland and Drescher 1993). Attributable fractions estimate the importance of the condition from a population perspective by combining the prevalence of the factor with the strength of the association between the factor and future disability status. Specifically, for each condition we estimated the reduction in each type of disability that could be achieved by preventing the condition as the average predicted probability of becoming disabled if none of the participants had the condition, holding all other covariates at their observed values. A few clinical conditions were found to be protective for mortality, disability, or both. As these effects are likely markers for either improved access to treatments or relative health that allows for treatment of milder chronic conditions (Jencks, Williams, and Kay 1988; Iezzoni et al. 1992), we did not estimate attributable fractions for conditions that were protective of both disability and death. In cases where a condition was estimated to be protective for death but positively associated with disability, we computed attributable fractions for disability by setting all negative mortality coefficients equal to zero and rescaling the intercept terms to match observed overall proportions in our data.

5.4.2   Characteristics of Pathways

We examined how the empirical pathways differed in terms of number of limitations and use of medical and assistive services to understand whether various pathways are associated with more intensive medical and social service needs. We focused on the conditions that were each responsible for at least 5 percent of incident disability. Note these groups are not mutually exclusive, and in fact, there is a great deal of co-occurrence of disabling diseases in this population. In these descriptive analyses, for each of the major pathways, we compared disabled respondents with the condition to those without evidence of the condition in their medical claims.

5.4.3   Self-Reported Causes of Disability

Our second set of analyses describes self-reported causes of disability in the newly disabled community-dwelling cohort (institutionalized respondents were not asked to report the cause of their disability). We also examined the distribution of the number of functional limitations and limitations in IADL and ADL tasks, and described reported use of medical and assistive services. In all analyses, we compared newly disabled community-dwelling respondents reporting old age or symptom causes to those who reported only medical conditions as the cause of their disability.

Analytic weights that account for complex sampling scheme were used in all analyses to provide estimates that reflect the national population of nondisabled Medicare beneficiaries aged sixty-seven and older in 1994. Specifically, cross-sectional weights that accounted for complex sampling scheme and nonresponse to the 1994 survey were augmented to account for subsampling of healthy respondents for a screener interview in 1999, nonresponse to the 1999 screener interview, and exclusion of patients enrolled in an HMO by redistributing weights for healthy respondents in 1994 who were excluded from our analyses to the respondents in our sample within cells defined by age and sex. Statistical tests and standard errors were also corrected for the complex survey design using approximations based on Taylor series linearizations.

5.5 Results

5.5.1 Empirical Pathways to Disability

Sixty-six percent of nondisabled respondents in 1994 survived and remained nondisabled to 1999, while 15.1 percent became disabled over the five-year period and 18.9 percent died between survey waves. Out of the nondisabled respondents to the 1994 survey, 12, 10, and 11 percent developed one or more mobility-related, complex task, or self-care disabilities, respectively, between survey waves. Death and incident cases of disability were more common among older, African American, and unmarried respondents (table 5.1). Females were more likely to become disabled but less likely to have died compared to males. Hip and pelvic fractures, dementia, Parkinson's and related diseases, depression, and stroke had the strongest association with new cases of disability. Most disabling conditions were also associated with death.

Regression models with main effects for the thirty-one conditions identified six clinical conditions—arthritis, infectious disease, dementia, heart failure, diabetes, and stroke—that contributed to at least 5 percent of new cases of disability. Only 17 percent of elderly respondents did not have one of these six conditions, and a majority (54 percent) had two or more.

Our final regression models included fifteen pairwise interactions between the six largest contributors to overall disability. Regression results are presented in table 5.2. Several interactions were found to be important in these analyses. For any disability, the interaction between diabetes and arthritis was positive, suggesting that these two conditions have synergistic effects such that having both conditions was more disabling than would be expected by the effects of each individual condition. In contrast, two interactions with dementia were negative (stroke/dementia and heart failure/dementia), suggesting that in the presence of a highly disabling condition like dementia, other conditions have effects that are dampened relative to what would be expected when the disease occurs in isolation. These general patterns were found in the analysis of each type of disability, although the strength of the interactions (and their statistical significance) varied some across the three types. In addition, several new interactions were important

Table 5.1   Health status at follow-up according to demographic and clinical characteristics of study cohort

	% of cohort (N = 7727)	Status at 1999 Interview (%)			
		Newly disabled	Deceased	Alive and nondisabled	P value
All respondents	100	15.1	18.9	65.9	
Age in 1994					< 0.001
67–69	22.5	8.8	11.1	80.2	
70–74	34.3	10.5	13.9	75.6	
75–79	23.6	18.6	20.9	60.5	
80–84	13.0	25.6	28.5	45.9	
85–89	5.3	29.4	43.4	27.2	
90 and over	1.3	21.5	57.5	21.0	
Race					0.008
White	91.7	15.1	18.7	66.2	
Black	6.6	16.3	24.1	59.7	
Other	1.7	9.6	12.3	78.2	
Gender					< 0.001
Female	56.7	17.7	15.6	66.7	
Male	43.3	11.7	23.3	65.0	
Marital status in 1994					< 0.001
Married	56.5	12.4	16.3	71.3	
Widowed	32.0	19.4	21.6	59.0	
Divorced/separated/never married	9.0	18.2	21.2	60.5	
Unknown	2.5	11.5	36.2	52.3	
Clinical conditions[a]					
Hip and pelvic fracture	6.1	34.6	28.8	36.6	< 0.001
Dementia and organic brain diseases	15.3	33.9	36.5	29.6	< 0.001
Paralysis, Parkinson's, and related diseases	10.7	30.3	34.8	34.9	< 0.001
Depression	13.3	27.1	22.7	50.3	< 0.001
Stroke	29.9	23.5	25.7	50.9	< 0.001
Other mental disorders	24.2	22.3	24.6	53.1	< 0.001
Chronic renal failure	6.9	22.1	44.3	33.6	< 0.001
Peripheral vascular disease	32.5	21.9	23.6	54.5	< 0.001
Heart failure and arrhythmia	44.2	20.9	29.9	49.2	< 0.001
Diabetes	28.0	20.3	21.8	58.0	< 0.001
Infectious diseases[‡]	47.9	20.2	22.5	57.3	< 0.001
Respiratory failure	23.1	20.0	37.6	42.4	< 0.001
Anemia	42.1	19.6	24.2	56.3	< 0.001
Other blood diseases	16.3	19.1	29.5	51.4	< 0.001
Thyroid disorders	30.6	18.9	17.4	63.7	< 0.001
Arthritis and arthropathy	58.6	18.5	16.4	65.1	< 0.001
Ischemic heart disease	49.8	18.5	23.0	58.6	< 0.001
Back/neck pain	50.9	18.2	16.3	65.5	< 0.001
COPD and related diseases	49.6	17.4	21.7	61.0	< 0.001
Hypertension	75.2	17.0	18.8	64.2	< 0.001
Respiratory diseases	71.8	16.9	21.4	61.7	< 0.001

Table 5.1   (continued)

	% of cohort (N = 7727)	Status at 1999 Interview (%)			
		Newly disabled	Deceased	Alive and nondisabled	P value
Other circulatory diseases	76.1	16.8	20.9	62.3	< 0.001
Acute renal failure and insufficiency	4.7	16.8	60.8	22.5	< 0.001
Other metabolic and immunity disorders	70.7	16.6	19.5	64.0	< 0.001
Musculoskeletal disorders	84.5	16.5	18.8	65.8	< 0.001
Gastrointestinal diseases	73.1	16.3	20.1	63.7	< 0.001
Colorectal and lung cancer	7.7	16.3	43.7	40.0	< 0.001
Glaucoma and cataract	70.9	16.2	15.5	68.4	< 0.001
Genitourinary diseases	77.2	16.1	18.8	65.1	< 0.001
Other cancers	60.7	14.8	19.6	65.6	0.14
Breast and prostate cancer	13.0	13.4	22.4	64.2	0.006
No condition (no claims)	5.4	9.0	16.1	74.9	0.001

Notes: Not including pneumonia, acute respiratory infections, or influenza. All percentages based on weighted sample size. Statistical tests account for complex survey design. Conditions are ordered based on strength of their relationship with disability. COPD = chronic obstructive pulmonary disease

[a] Respondents are considered to have the condition if there was at least one inpatient claim or two non-hospital claims (outpatient, home health, SNF, or hospice) with a primary or secondary diagnosis of interest between Jan 1, 1992 to December 31, 1999.

for disability in complex tasks. In particular, stroke exacerbated the effects of both diabetes and heart failure in disability in complex tasks.

Dementia in the absence of heart failure, stroke, arthritis, infectious disease, or diabetes had the strongest association with new disability of all types in multinomial regression models (odds ratio [OR] for any disability relative to remaining alive and health = 8.0; 95 percent CI = [4.6, 13.8]). Other conditions with strong relationships with incident disability included Parkinson's and related disorders (OR for any disability = 2.3 [1.8, 3.0]), hip and pelvic fractures (OR for any disability = 2.1 [1.6, 2.9]), colorectal and lung cancer (OR for any disability = 1.9 [1.4, 2.4]), acute renal failure (OR for any disability = 1.7 [1.1, 2.7]), and heart failure in the absence of stroke, arthritis, infectious disease, diabetes, or dementia (OR for any disability = 1.6 [1.1, 2.4]). While many conditions were strongly related to all three types of disability, the strength of the association varied for many of these conditions. For example, infectious disease, heart failure, and arthritis had the strongest relationship with complex task disability, while hip and pelvic fractures were strongly associated with mobility and self-care disability.

In adjusted models, divorced, separated, or never married respondents and females were more likely to become disabled. Race was not significantly associated with future status after controlling for the other factors.

Table 5.2   Multinomial regression estimates of the association between clinical conditions and any mobility, complex task, and self-care disability

Variable	Any disability vs. health coefficient (SE)	Mobility disabled v. Healthy coefficient (SE)	Complex task disabled vs. healthy coefficient (SE)	Self-care disabled vs. healthy coefficient (SE)
Diseases/conditions				
Dementia and organic brain diseases	2.08 (0.28)**	2.00 (0.28)**	2.67 (0.29)**	1.79 (0.28)**
Paralysis, Parkinson's, and related diseases	0.84 (0.14)**	0.98 (0.15)**	1.14 (0.14)**	1.07 (0.13)**
Hip and pelvic fracture	0.76 (0.15)**	0.75 (0.16)**	0.58 (0.17)**	0.90 (0.17)**
Colorectal and/or lung cancer	0.62 (0.14)**	0.61 (0.16)**	0.63 (0.18)**	0.53 (0.17)**
Acute renal failure and insufficiency	0.54 (0.24)**	0.58 (0.26)**	0.74 (0.25)**	0.47 (0.24)**
Heart failure and arrhythmia	0.48 (0.19)**	0.41 (0.20)**	0.99 (0.27)**	0.44 (0.23)*
Arthritis and arthropathy	0.40 (0.18)**	0.44 (0.19)**	0.71 (0.24)**	0.56 (0.22)**
Respiratory failure	0.38 (0.09)**	0.37 (0.11)**	0.43 (0.12)**	0.56 (0.11)**
Chronic renal failure	0.32 (0.16)**	0.43 (0.17)**	0.31 (0.18)*	0.34 (0.17)*
Depression	0.30 (0.11)**	0.39 (0.12)**	0.38 (0.12)**	0.33 (0.12)**
Other mental disorders	0.27 (0.10)**	0.30 (0.11)**	0.31 (0.13)**	0.23 (0.11)**
Infectious diseases	0.22 (0.21)	0.41 (0.27)	0.65 (0.24)**	0.33 (0.24)
Peripheral vascular disease	0.14 (0.08)*	0.22 (0.09)**	0.20 (0.11)*	0.14 (0.09)
Respiratory disease	0.14 (0.10)	−0.04 (0.12)	0.17 (0.13)	0.11 (0.12)
Stroke	0.13 (0.22)	0.02 (0.25)	−0.10 (0.27)	0.39 (0.25)
Anemia	0.12 (0.10)	0.11 (0.11)	0.00 (0.11)	0.03 (0.12)
Other blood disease	0.10 (0.11)	0.17 (0.12)	0.28 (0.13)**	0.04 (0.11)
COPD and related diseases	0.05 (0.09)	0.09 (0.09)	0.06 (0.10)	0.02 (0.10)
Back/neck pain	0.05 (0.10)	−0.01 (0.09)	−0.02 (0.10)	0.02 (0.10)
Hypertension	0.05 (0.12)	0.18 (0.13)	0.04 (0.14)	0.02 (0.12)
Ischemic heart disease	0.04 (0.09)	0.02 (0.10)	−0.02 (0.11)	0.12 (0.11)
Musculoskeletal disorders	−0.01 (0.18)	−0.01 (0.20)	−0.11 (0.21)	0.09 (0.21)

Diabetes	−0.02 (0.22)	0.03 (0.25)	0.30 (0.28)	−0.06 (0.28)
Genitourinary diseases	−0.04 (0.11)	−0.12 (0.12)	−0.15 (0.14)	0.03 (0.13)
Thyroid Disorders	−0.04 (0.09)	−0.13 (0.09)	−0.11 (0.10)	0.01 (0.09)
Breast and/or prostate cancer	−0.06 (0.13)	0.04 (0.13)	−0.16 (0.15)	−0.12 (0.13)
Other metabolic and immunity disorders	−0.11 (0.13)	−0.20 (0.14)	−0.18 (0.13)	−0.10 (0.13)
Other circulatory diseases	−0.13 (0.11)	0.07 (0.12)	−0.27 (0.15)*	−0.18 (0.15)
Gastrointestinal diseases	−0.20 (0.10)**	−0.30 (0.10)**	−0.15 (0.12)	−0.14 (0.11)
Glaucoma and cataract	−0.24 (0.11)**	−0.40 (0.12)**	−0.17 (0.13)	−0.23 (0.11)**
Other cancers	−0.26 (0.08)**	−0.20 (0.09)**	−0.30 (0.10)**	−0.19 (0.09)**
No diseases or conditions	0.12 (0.26)	0.05 (0.32)	0.37 (0.28)	0.23 (0.29)
Interactions				
Infectious diseases and diabetes	0.22 (0.19)	0.21 (0.19)	0.03 (0.22)	0.26 (0.22)
Infectious diseases and dementia	−0.02 (0.19)	−0.06 (0.21)	0.02 (0.23)	0.21 (0.22)
Infectious diseases and heart failure	0.24 (0.19)	0.27 (0.20)	−0.02 (0.23)	0.21 (0.21)
Infectious disease and arthritis	−0.20 (0.19)	−0.28 (0.21)	−0.45 (0.22)**	−0.25 (0.23)
Diabetes and dementia	−0.23 (0.19)	−0.22 (0.22)	−0.58 (0.21)**	−0.28 (0.24)
Diabetes and heart failure	−0.11 (0.19)	−0.09 (0.22)	−0.28 (0.26)	0.09 (0.24)
Diabetes and arthritis	0.43 (0.19)**	0.47 (0.21)**	0.24 (0.24)	0.33 (0.27)
Dementia and heart failure	−0.50 (0.22)**	−0.48 (0.22)**	−0.60 (0.22)**	−0.22 (0.24)
Dementia and arthritis	−0.38 (0.24)	−0.25 (0.27)	−0.38 (0.26)	−0.18 (0.24)
Arthritis and heart failure	−0.07 (0.21)	−0.03 (0.22)	−0.35 (0.27)	−0.14 (0.23)
Stroke and infectious disease	0.15 (0.20)	0.07 (0.22)	0.11 (0.25)	−0.13 (0.22)
Stroke and diabetes	0.07 (0.19)	0.09 (0.21)	0.44 (0.24)*	−0.09 (0.23)
Stroke and dementia	−0.41 (0.20)**	−0.33 (0.21)	−0.31 (0.20)	−0.44 (0.20)**
Stroke and heart failure	0.28 (0.18)	0.29 (0.21)	0.44 (0.22)**	0.29 (0.22)
Stroke and arthritis	−0.14 (0.18)	0.01 (0.20)	−0.16 (0.20)	−0.28 (0.20)

(continued)

Table 5.2 (continued)

Variable	Any disability vs. health coefficient (SE)	Mobility disabled v. Healthy coefficient (SE)	Complex task disabled vs. healthy coefficient (SE)	Self-care disabled vs. healthy coefficient (SE)
	Demographic characteristics in 1994			
Age 70–74	0.09 (0.15)	−0.01 (0.17)	0.11 (0.19)	0.28 (0.17)
Age 75–79	0.77 (0.15)**	0.77 (0.16)**	0.84 (0.18)**	0.87 (0.19)**
Age 80–84	1.31 (0.16)**	1.33 (0.18)**	1.46 (0.19)**	1.44 (0.21)**
Age 85–89	1.74 (0.19)**	1.75 (0.20)**	1.97 (0.23)**	1.76 (0.22)**
Age 90 +	1.78 (0.37)**	2.02 (0.39)**	2.12 (0.40)**	2.06 (0.42)**
Widowed	0.10 (0.09)	0.15 (0.10)	0.06 (0.10)	0.13 (0.11)
Divorced, separated, or single	0.45 (0.15)**	0.47 (0.16)**	0.24 (0.18)	0.35 (0.15)**
Missing marital status	−0.41 (0.28)	−0.30 (0.28)	−0.33 (0.34)	−0.24 (0.27)
Black	0.04 (0.21)	0.10 (0.20)	0.28 (0.22)	−0.10 (0.20)
Other race	−0.29 (0.28)	−0.48 (0.38)	0.11 (0.40)	−0.08 (0.31)
Female	0.28 (0.09)**	0.31 (0.10)**	0.06 (0.11)	0.22 (0.11)**

Notes: Reference groups were individuals "age 65–69" for age categories, "married" for marital status indicators, and "white" for race variables. Conditions are ordered based on strength of their relationship with overall disability. Standard errors account for complex survey design.

* Significant between 0.05 and 0.10.

** Significant at less than 0.05.

We found some differences in the effect of demographic characteristics on disability. In particular, women were more likely than men to report new disabilities in mobility and self-care tasks, but not with complex tasks.

Age, even after adjusting for a set of thirty-one clinical conditions and interactions among the top six contributors, was strongly associated with disability. For example, the adjusted odds of becoming disabled relative to remaining alive and nondisabled was 3.7 (95 percent CI = [2.7, 5.1]) times higher for eighty to eighty-four-year-olds compared to sixty-seven to seventy-year-olds. This represents a 23 percent decline in the effect of age relative to a model that controlled only for demographic factors.

5.5.2   Largest Contributors to Disability

Figures 5.1–5.4 display adjusted attributable fractions for each type of disability based on regression results. Attributable fractions, a combination of the prevalence of the conditions and their association with disability, estimate the proportion of disability that was explained by each condition, holding all other characteristics of the respondents constant. Although arthritis was only moderately associated with incident disability (OR for any new disability = 1.5 [1.1, 2.1]), because it is a common condition it was the largest contributor, accounting for 13 percent of any new disability. Five other conditions—infectious diseases, dementia, heart failure and arrhythmia, diabetes, and stroke—contributed to at least 5 percent of new cases of disability, and these six top conditions together explained almost half (48 percent) of new cases.

We observed some heterogeneity in these pathways across the different types of disability (figs. 5.2–5.4). Arthritis was the largest contributor to impairments in mobility (explaining 17 percent of this type of disability), but played a much less prominent role in disability in complex tasks. Similarly, stroke contributed most to less severe forms of disability and explained only 4 percent of disability associated with self-care tasks. Dementia was a large contributor to overall disability, was responsible for almost a quarter of disability in completing complex tasks, and was also the largest contributor to the most severe form of disability, dependence in self-care tasks. Ischemic heart disease, which was not found to be a prominent contributor to overall disability, explained more than one in twenty cases of new disability in self-care tasks. Not all diseases, however, demonstrated such specificity. For example, heart failure and infectious disease played a prominent role in all three types of disability, each explaining between 10 percent and 15 percent of each type of disability.

5.5.3   Characteristics of Pathways

Almost all (96 percent) of newly disabled respondents had at least one of the top six conditions leading to disability—dementia, stroke, heart failure, infectious diseases, arthritis, or diabetes. Moreover, there was sub-

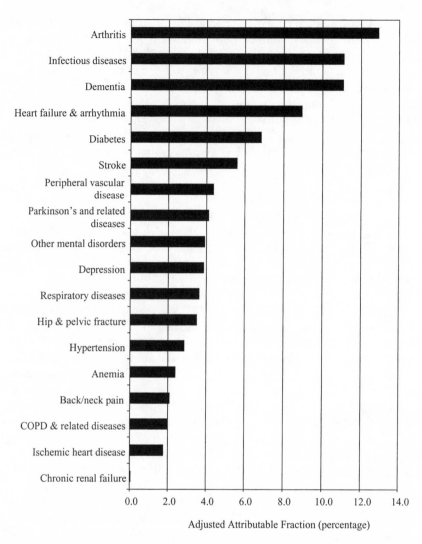

Fig. 5.1   Estimated percentage of any new disability attributable to each condition

stantial overlap among the six pathways: only 12 percent of the newly disabled cohort had only one of the six conditions, and two-thirds had three or more.

Figure 5.5 displays the average number of functional limitation, IADL limitations, and ADL limitations in newly disabled respondents according to diagnoses in their medical claims (table 5.A2 in the appendix provides information on specific limitations). The newly disabled cohort had a large number of each type of limitation. Physical limitations in particular were

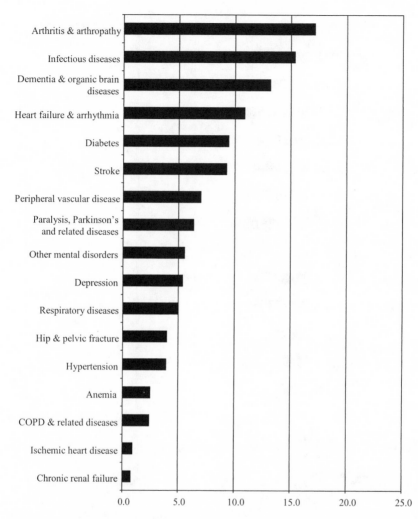

Fig. 5.2   Estimated percentage of mobility disability attributable to each condition

quite prevalent, with community-dwelling respondents reporting 3.3 limitations on average. Even the most severe forms of disability—inability to perform ADL tasks—were prevalent, with respondents reporting on average 2.6 ADL limitations. Newly disabled respondents with dementia reported the largest number of limitations of each type, including more than four IADLs on average. Newly disabled respondents with each of the top six conditions were more likely to report functional limitations compared to those not reporting the condition, and most of the conditions (dementia, stroke, heart failure, and infectious diseases) were associated with a higher number of limitations of each type. However, neither arthritis nor

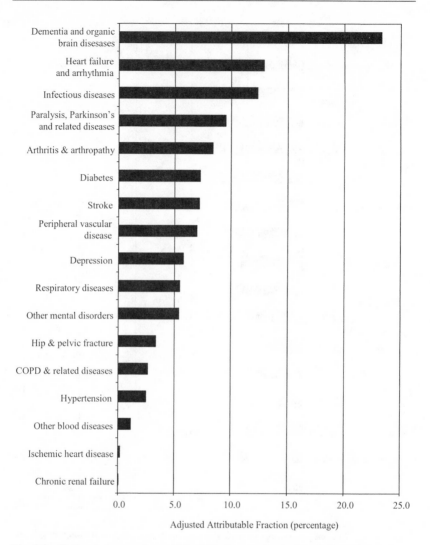

Fig. 5.3   Estimated percentage of disability in complex tasks attributable to
each condition

diabetes was associated with higher numbers of IADL limitations, and diabetes was not associated with a higher number of ADL limitations.

We present self-reported utilization of health care and assistive services
in table 5.3. Approximately 20 percent of the newly disabled cohort was institutionalized. Of those living in the community 12 percent reported past
nursing home stays; however, only a small number reported living in assistive living facilities. Institutionalization and nursing home stays were most
likely among newly disabled respondents with dementia, stroke, heart fail-

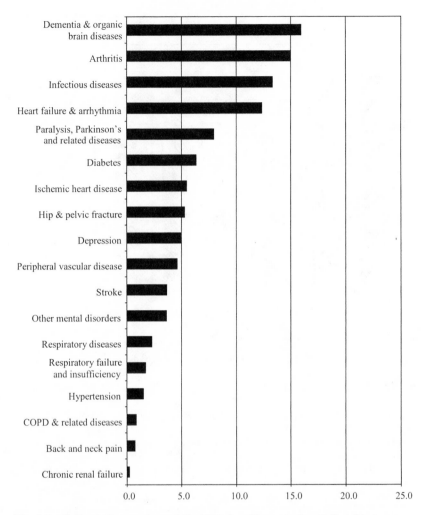

Fig. 5.4   Estimated percentage of disability in self-care tasks attributable to each condition

ure, or infectious diseases. Those with dementia were also most likely to receive supportive services, including physical and occupational therapy and home health services. In addition, health care use was high among this cohort. Approximately half of newly disabled respondents reported a physician visit in the prior month, over a third reported a hospitalization in the prior year, and they reported filling an average of four prescriptions in the past month. Health care utilization was highest among respondents with stroke, heart failure, and diabetes, and lowest among respondents with dementia and arthritis.

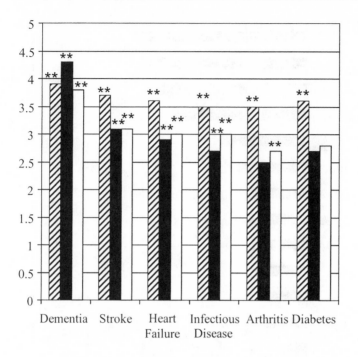

Dementia   Stroke   Heart   Infectious Arthritis Diabetes
                     Failure   Disease

▨ Number of functional limitations   ■ Number of IADLs   □ Number of ADLs

Fig. 5.5   Number of limitations among newly disabled respondents by conditions in medical claims

* Marginally significantly different from respondents without evidence of condition in their medical claims ($0.05 < p$-value < 0.10).

** Significantly different from respondents without evidence of condition in their medical claims (p-value < 0.05).

Institutionalized respondents are excluded from calculations of average numbers of functional limitations and IADL tasks.

5.5.4   Self-Reported Causes of Disability

Over half of the newly disabled community-dwelling respondents reported that a chronic condition was a factor in their limitations, while 30 percent reported an acute event (table 5.4). Musculoskeletal problems and cardiovascular diseases were the most common reported cause of disability. Dementia, lung diseases, diabetes, eye diseases, surgeries, fractures, and falls were also commonly cited causes of disability. While a majority of respondents reported chronic or acute medical conditions as the cause of their disability, 30 percent reported symptoms that were not directly linked to a chronic or acute health problem, and 14 percent of respondents reported that old age contributed to their disability.

Respondents often cited multiple causes, and those citing symptoms and old age often cited specific acute and chronic conditions as well. We report

Table 5.3   Self-reported utilization of health and assistive services by conditions in medical claims

	All newly disabled	Dementia	Stroke	Heart failure	Infectious disease	Arthritis	Diabetes
N	1,264	450	598	781	808	911	449
% of cohort	100	34.2	46.4	61.2	63.8	71.7	37.5
Institutionalized (at time of survey)	20.3	45.9**	26.9**	23.1**	26.1**	21.2	21.2
Hospitalization (in the past year)	37.1	42.9**	47.2**	45.6**	42.1**	39.4**	42.8**
Of those in community:							
Past nursing home stay (ever)	11.8	18.3**	15.5**	14.0**	14.8**	11.5	11.5
Assisted living (at time of survey)	2.8	5.6**	3.4	2.5	2.5	2.0**	3.5
Home health care (in the past month)	11.7	20.1**	15.3**	15.6**	13.9**	11.9	13.8
Physical, occupational, speech or hearing therapy (in the past month)	8.4	11.8**	12.2**	8.5	9.5	8.9	8.1
Emergency room visit (in the past month)	6.6	5.7	6.4	8.3**	6.3	6.2	7.2
Physician visit (in the past month)	49.8	44.8*	51.5	52.2	49.7	52.1**	53.4
Number of prescriptions (in the past month)	3.9	3.5*	4.5**	4.7**	4.4**	4.1**	4.7**

*Marginally significantly different from respondents without evidence of condition in their medical claims (0.05 < p-value < 0.10).

**Significantly different from respondents without evidence of condition in their medical claims (p-value < 0.05).

conditions cited by these respondents in table 5.5. Among respondents reporting symptoms, 44 percent and 21 percent reported at least one chronic or acute condition, respectively, while the remaining 41 percent reported only symptoms. Heart disease was the most frequently reported condition among those citing symptom causes. Only 8 percent of those reporting symptom causes also cited old age as a contributor. Old age was the only reported cause for 46 percent of respondents attributing their disability to old age. About a third of respondents citing old age as a cause of their disability also cited a chronic condition and 13 percent cited acute causes. Arthritis was the most commonly cited condition among those attributing disability to old age.

Table 5.6 reports characteristics of newly disabled respondents according to self-reported cause of disability. Respondents citing old age were more likely to be female, African American, and widowed at the time of the 1999 survey and were approximately four years older (80.2 versus 75.8 years old) than those citing only medical causes. However, they were no

Table 5.4   **Self-reported causes of disability among the newly disabled cohort residing in the community (N = 892)**

Cause	N†	%
Chronic condition	489	54.8
Arthritis	186	22.2
Heart or circulatory disease (not including heart failure)	91	10.0
Dementia/memory problems	88	9.2
Lung disease (asthma, emphysema)	38	4.7
Diabetes	36	3.9
Eye disease (cataract, glaucoma, macular degeneration)	38	3.6
Cancer	30	3.4
Heart failure	23	2.8
Osteoporosis	19	2.4
Hypertension	21	2.4
Parkinson's	14	1.7
Depression/other mental illness	6	0.7
Back disease	6	0.4
Other chronic condition	64	8.0
Acute event	275	32.1
Stroke	83	10.1
AMI or bypass surgery	42	5.4
Hip/knee replacement	40	4.1
Other surgery	33	4.6
Hip fracture	36	3.6
Other fracture or fall	42	4.0
Amputation	7	1.0
Other acute event	34	3.9
Symptom not linked to condition	266	30.2
Pain/Discomfort (includes pain, swelling, stiffness, and other problems)	105	11.8
Hips/knees	44	5.1
Back	30	3.4
Legs	25	3.0
Feet/ankle	13	1.5
Upper extremities	4	0.4
Other pain/discomfort	6	0.8
Balance	40	4.4
Unsteady/balance problems	31	3.4
Dizziness	12	1.5
Endurance	22	2.8
Shortness of breath	15	2.0
Fatigue	8	0.9
Weakness	37	3.7
General weakness	23	2.2
Lower body weakness	14	1.4
Other symptoms	105	12.3
Vision/blindness	48	5.6
Hearing	16	2.0
Fear/security	9	1.1
Other symptom	38	4.3
Old age	133	14.0

Note: Respondents were able to list up to ten causes for their disability. *N* represents the number of respondents who reported the condition or symptom as at least one cause of their disability. All percentages based on weighted sample size.

Table 5.5   Chronic condition cited by community-dwelling newly disabled respondents who also cite symptoms or old age as a cause of their disability.

	All newly disabled	Old age	Symptom
N	892	133	266
% of cohort	100	14.0	30.2
Chronic conditions	54.8	32.8	43.5
Arthritis	22.2	17.1	12.0
Heart disease	12.5	6.1	15.7
Lung disease	4.7	3.1	5.5
Dementia	9.2	6.2	4.8
Diabetes	3.9	1.5	5.4
Eye disease	3.6	0.0	2.6
Acute conditions	32.1	12.8	20.5
Hip fracture	3.6	0.9	2.5
Heart attack or open heart surgery	5.4	4.2	3.2
Stroke	10.1	4.6	5.9
Old age	14.0	100.0	8.4
Old age only	6.5	46.0	0.0
Symptom	30.2	18.1	100.0
Symptom only	12.5	0.0	41.4
Pain	11.8	2.0	39.2
Balance	4.4	1.4	15.5
Endurance	2.8	5.0	9.1
Weakness	3.7	5.4	12.1
Other symptom	12.3	7.2	40.8

more likely to have any of the most disabling clinical conditions, and in fact were less likely to have diagnoses of arthritis, diabetes, Parkinson's and related diseases, and respiratory diseases compared to respondents who did not cite old age as a cause of their disability. Respondents reporting symptoms were also often less likely to have disabling conditions compared to those reporting chronic conditions or acute event. However, patients reporting pain/discomfort or weakness as a cause of their disability were more likely to have evidence of arthritis. Respondents citing weakness were more likely to be female. However, the sample sizes were small in several of these categories, making precise inference difficult.

5.5.5   Types and Severity of Limitations

We report the number of functional limitations, IADL limitations, and ADL limitations according to self-reported cause of disability in figure 5.6 (table 5.A3 in the appendix provides information on specific limitations). Newly disabled respondents reporting only chronic or acute conditions reported more functional limitations than respondents who reported old

Table 5.6   **Characteristics of newly disabled cohort according to self-reported cause of disability.**

	Medical only[a]	Old age	Symptom	Pain	Balance	Endurance	Weakness
N	518	133	266	105	40	22	37
% of cohort	58.3	14.0	30.2	11.8	4.4	2.8	3.7
Average age	75.8	80.2**	76.4	76.3	76.2	77.2	77.0
Female	63.5	71.5*	67.2	68.2	55.4	61.2	88.7**
Race		*					
White	92.9	87.3	95.0	96.3	90.7	96.1	85.0
Black	6.0	9.6	4.4	3.2	9.3	3.9	11.3
Other	1.1	3.1	0.6	0.4	0.0	0.0	3.8
Marital status (1994)							
Married	51.5	45.1	50.9	43.7	55.8	55.8	34.1
Widowed	37.2	43.0	36.3	44.5	30.5	28.4	44.1
Not married	10.1	10.5	11.1	11.8	10.3	7.2	21.7
Missing	1.3	1.5	1.6	0.0	3.4	8.6	0.0
Marital status (1999)		**					
Married	39.6	26.6	39.1	33.0	49.9	47.0	30.4
Widowed	51.8	68.8	52.1	57.3	44.1	37.3	63.4
Not married	8.6	3.7	8.7	9.7	5.9	15.8	6.3
% with conditions/ diseases:[b]							
Arthritis and arthropathy	74.5	61.6**	69.9	80.9**	59.8	67.4	71.9
Infectious disease	61.1	51.1	58.1	63.7	47.4	54.2	42.4
Dementia and organic brain diseases	25.3	23.8	16.4**	13.2**	16.5	22.4	7.0[a]
Heart failure and arrhythmia	58.4	58.5	63.2	61.5	61.1	72.9	61.2
Diabetes	37.3	24.8**	40.8	41.7	39.2	24.6	38.0
Stroke	43.6	40.9	42.9	44.6	50.3	43.8	39.1
Peripheral vascular disease	44.6	41.1	44.0	39.3	35.7	45.2	52.7
Paralysis, Parkinson's	22.5	9.3**	12.4**	12.5	15.5	16.2	3.6[a]
Depression	21.8	19.2	12.8**	10.9**	6.6	20.4	5.6
Other mental disorders	31.7	32.1	28.7	23.6	39.3	18.3	28.6
Respiratory diseases	80.5	72.2**	82.1	84.9	84.9	77.0	80.7
Hip and pelvic fracture	14.0	11.5	9.4	9.4	6.0	14.6	7.2

[a]Respondents who reported chronic or acute causes of their disability without citing either symptoms or old age.

[b]Based on diagnoses in respondents medical claims.

*Marginally significantly different from respondents reporting only medical causes ($0.05 < p$-value < 0.10).

**Significantly different from respondents reporting only medical causes (p-value < 0.05).

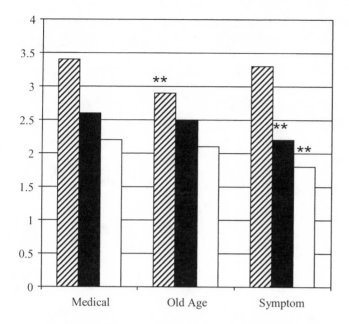

◪ Number of functional limitations   ■ Number of IADLs   ▢ Number of ADLs

Fig. 5.6   Number of limitations among newly disabled respondents by self-reported cause of disability
* Marginally significantly different from respondents reporting only medical causes ($0.05 < p$-value < 0.10).
** Significantly different from respondents reporting only medical causes (p-value < 0.05).

age, and significantly more ADL and IADL than respondents who reported symptoms.

5.5.5   Medical and Assistive Services

We present self-reported utilization of health care and assistive services in table 5.7. Past nursing home stays were highest among those who reported clinical causes and lowest among those citing symptoms. Respondents citing symptom causes were also less likely to report use of physical or occupational therapy services. Consistent with the observation that respondents citing old age or symptoms were less likely to have evidence of clinical conditions in their medical claims, these respondents have lower levels of health care utilization (physician visits, medications, and hospitalizations). However, health care use was high in all groups. Forty percent of respondents citing old age reported a physician visit in the past month and a quarter reported being hospitalized in the previous year, suggesting sufficient contact with the health care system to receive care for chronic conditions.

Table 5.7   **Self-reported utilization of health and assistive services by self-reported cause of disability**

	Medical only[a]	Old age	Symptom	Pain	Balance	Endurance	Weakness	Other symptom
N	518	133	266	105	40	22	37	105
% of cohort	58.3	14.0	30.2	11.8	4.4	2.8	3.7	12.3
Past nursing home stay (ever)	15.1	9.7	6.5**	5.5**	8.4	4.4	4.7*	9.4
Assisted living (now)	3.0	3.7	2.1	2.8	4.7	0.0	0.0	3.2
Home health care (in the past month)	11.9	11.1	10.7	8.6	9.0	21.9	16.4	9.9
Physical, occupational, speech, or hearing therapy (in the past month)	10.3	9.3	4.9**	5.9	7.5	9.6	5.4	2.2**
Emergency room visit (in the past month)	5.7	8.1	8.4	9.2	12.8	0.0	10.3	6.9
Hospitalization (in the past year)	36.6	25.1**	36.5	36.3	37.7	30.4	34.0	39.0
Physician visit (in the past month)	52.3	41.8*	50.1	52.2	57.6	36.8	63.2	45.5
Number of prescriptions (in the past month)	4.2	3.0**	3.7	3.6	3.3*	3.5	4.2	3.7

[a] Respondents who reported chronic or acute causes of their disability without citing either symptoms or old age.

* Marginally significantly different from respondents reporting only medical causes ($0.05 < p$-value < 0.10).

** Significantly different from respondents reporting only medical causes (p-value < 0.05).

5.6   Discussion

Analyzing thirty-one clinical conditions, we estimate that arthritis, dementia, infectious diseases, heart failure, diabetes, and stroke each explained at least 5 percent of incident disability. These top six conditions together explained almost half of new disability (48 percent). Consistent with these findings, arthritis, stroke, dementia, and heart disease were the conditions most often mentioned among respondents who reported an acute or chronic condition as a cause of their limitation.

We also found that newly disabled respondents with these six conditions typically experience problems in multiple categories of functional limitations, ADL, and IADL tasks. Elderly patients with any of these six conditions were also more likely to have been hospitalized in the past year and had a greater average number of prescription drugs in the past month compared to the average newly disabled patient. However, there were differences across these pathways in the types of disability experienced and in the use of services. For example, dementia represents the pathway most strongly associated with the most severe types of disability and the largest number of reported limitations. Newly disabled respondents with dementia were also the heaviest users of supportive services, including nursing home residence. In contrast, arthritis, while being the largest contributor to overall disability, was associated most strongly with mobility limitations, and newly disabled respondents with arthritis used relatively few supportive and medical services.

Our comparison of newly disabled respondents who attributed their disability to old age or symptoms to those citing chronic or acute medical conditions also demonstrated important differences. First, we found that those who reported age as a cause of their disability had similar or lower levels of disabling conditions compared to those who reported a clinical condition. In addition, newly disabled respondents attributing disability to symptom causes or old age tended to have less severe disability and use fewer supportive services. While those citing old age had lower use of health care, there were sufficient interactions with clinicians (42 percent report visit with a physician in prior month) to have had chronic disease diagnosed. These results suggest that those reporting old age or symptoms represent a different pathway; that is, frailty or preclinical disease that lead to their disability. The importance of infectious diseases in our empirical models also suggests a role for heightened vulnerability in the elderly, as past diagnoses of infectious diseases may be a marker for frailty.

We found that self-reported causes and empirical analyses of claims-based measures provided complementary information. Claims-based diagnoses were available on all respondents, and empirical models allowed us to estimate the fraction of disability attributable to each condition independently of the other conditions. However, binary measures of diagnoses from medical claims may not adequately capture disease severity. In addition, claims-based analyses did not capture most visual and hearing impairments, which have been shown to be important correlates of disability here and in other studies (Kosorok et al. 1992; Dunlop et al. 2002). Analyses based on self-reported causes, which were only collected from community-based respondents, may underestimate the effect of highly disabling conditions like dementia. Given the differing strengths and weaknesses of clinical data and self-reports, future attempts to measure causes of disability should combine the two approaches.

These analyses have important implications. First, an understanding of the major contributors to disability in the late 1990s provides insight into potential future trends in the health of the elderly. We found that conditions without effective medical treatments—dementia in particular—were major contributors to disability in older persons. Alzheimer's and other forms of dementia are highly disabling progressive diseases with few effective interventions to slow their progression (Cummings and Cole 2002). Until effective treatments are found, dementia-related disability is likely to increase in importance. In contrast, many conditions—stroke, heart disease, and arthritis—in particular—are amenable to both medical and lifestyle interventions, suggesting that increased use of effective medical therapies and control of risk factors could lead to continued improvement in the health of the elderly (Manton 1989; Boult et al. 1996; Singer and Manton 1998). However, obesity rates continue to rise and obesity is a risk factor for four of the six most important pathways in our analysis (arthritis, heart failure, stroke, and diabetes). The increase in obesity rates in the elderly and nonelderly population, coupled with increases in disability rates in younger populations, have led others to suggest that disability rates in older persons will increase in the future (Lakdawalla, Bhattacharya, and Goldman 2004; Leveille, Wee, and Iezzoni 2005). Moreover, a recent study found that obesity contributed to an increasing number of cases of arthritis between 1971 and 2002 (Leveille, Wee, and Iezzoni 2005).

Second, our results suggest potential avenues for medical and other interventions to alleviate dependence in the elderly. We found that various diseases and conditions are specific to different types of disability. This suggests that interventions to prevent or reduce disability may be targeted to different types of tasks, depending on the medical condition experienced by the patient. Interventions likely need to be targeted to multiple ADL and IADL tasks within a category of disability, as the six diseases and conditions were associated with limitations in multiple tasks.

In addition, medical care and assistive service utilization varied across conditions, suggesting that there may be variation in opportunities to intervene through medical and nonmedical services. For example, while respondents with dementia had relatively low rates of hospitalizations and physician visits, almost half were institutionalized and 20 percent were using home health services. Until effective medical interventions are available for dementia patients, current interventions may be best targeted through supportive care services and within their living environment. In contrast, newly disabled respondents with arthritis were relatively infrequent users of intensive inpatient or nursing home care, but had higher than average use of medications and physician visits, suggesting that interventions for disability assessment and prevention services among these patients may be most effectively conducted by physicians. For all diseases and conditions studied, improved medical care in the future may help to reduce disability.

Our analyses of newly disabled respondents attributing their disability to old age or symptoms suggest a greater focus on physician-based assessment of preclinical disease and treatment of symptoms in order to prevent disability. The large number of disabled respondents in the community who cited old age as a cause of disability may also imply that elderly respondents have low expectations for interventions, either medical or otherwise, to help them function independently. Physician-based interventions may help to educate patients about expectations for functioning and additional medical care treatments and interventions to minimize disability.

In conclusion, we identified six major clinical pathways to disability that account for almost half of incident disability, but differ in both the types of disability experienced and use of medical and assistive services. These results have important implications for future trends in the health of the elderly population, highlighting substantial challenges to continued improvement in disability.

Appendix

Table 5A.1   Clinical conditions

Condition	ICD-9-CM Codes
Infectious diseases	001.*–139.*, 320.*–323.*, V09.*
Colorectal and lung cancer	153.*, 154.*, 162.*
Breast and prostate cancer	174.*–175.*, 185.*
Other cancers	140.*–239.* (~#2, #3), 611.72, V10
Diabetes	250.*, 251.3
Thyroid disorders	240.*–259.* (~#5)
Other metabolic and immunity disorders	270.*–273.*, 275.*–279.*
Anemia	280.*–285.*
Other blood diseases	285.*–289.*
Dementia and organic brain diseases	290.*, 294.*, 310.*, 330.*, 331.*
Depression	296.* (~296.9), 298.0, 300.4, 311.*
Other mental disorders	290.*–319.* (~#10, #11), 797.*
Paralysis, Parkinsons's, and related diseases	332.*, 340.*–344.*, 438.*
Stroke	362.34, 430.*, 431.*, 432.9, 433.*–436.*
Glaucoma and cataract	365.*–366.*, 743.2–743.3
Chronic renal failure	403.01, 403.11, 403.91, 404.02, 404.12, 404.92, 585.*–586.*, V45.1, V56.*
Hypertension	401.*–405.* (~#16), 437.0, 437.9
Ischemic heart disease	410.*–414.* (~414.11, 414.19), 429.5–429.7
Heart failure and arrhythmia	425.*, 427.1, 427.3–427.5, 428.*, 429.1, 429.3
Peripheral vascular disease	440.*, 442.*, 443.* (~443.2), 444.*, 446.*, 447.* (~447.6), 451.*, 453.1
Other circulatory diseases	391.*–459.* (~#13, #14, #16, #17, #18, #19, #20), 786.5, V717.*
Chronic obstructive pulmonary diseases and related diseases	466.*, 490.*–496.*, 518.12
Respiratory failure	518.*, 799.1
Respiratory diseases	460.*–519.* (~#22, #23), 786.0, 786.1, 786.52, 793.1
Gastrointestinal disease	530.*–579.*, 789.0, 787.0, 787.7
Acute renal failure and insufficiency	584.*, 587.*, 588.*
Genitourinary diseases	580.*–629.* (~#4, #16, #25, #26), 788.* (~788.3, 788.4), 793.8, V44.5–V44.6, V55.5–V55.6
Arthritis and arthropathy	274.*, 390.*, 710.*–716.*
Back/neck pain	720.*–724.*, 839.0–839.5, 846.*, 847.*
Hip and pelvic fracture	808.*, 820.*
Musculoskeletal disorders	717.*–739.* (~#29), 800.*–999.* (~#29, #30)

Table 5A.2   Self-reported limitations in newly disabled cohort according to conditions in their medical claims

	All newly disabled (n = 1264)	Dementia (n = 450)	Stroke (n = 598)	Heart failure (n = 781)	Infectious disease (n = 808)	Arthritis (n = 911)	Diabetes (n = 449)
Functional limitations (among noninstitutionalized)							
Going up stairs	78.9	84.1	82.2	84.4	81.5	81.5	85.3
Walking across room	41.1	51.0	46.1	45.1	43.8	42.7	46.6
Bending	52.9	59.1	59.4	56.7	56.2	56.7	58.7
Lifting ten pound package	62.4	72.8	70.3	67.7	67.0	64.0	67.0
Reaching above head	36.6	43.9	44.0	40.9	39.7	38.4	39.3
Grasping small objects	32.7	38.9	36.5	34.8	35.1	33.3	34.9
Seeing to read newsprint	20.2	25.7	24.7	21.9	22.5	20.9	22.5
Speaking	2.0	3.4	3.8	2.4	2.6	1.7	1.8
Hearing	6.5	14.2	6.5	6.1	6.6	7.1	8.3
IADLs (among noninstitutionalized)							
Light housework	22.4	40.9	30.9	27.0	25.2	22.1	25.9
Laundry	27.9	51.6	37.0	32.6	31.1	28.7	29.8
Cooking	24.3	52.6	32.2	28.9	26.8	24.1	25.8
Grocery shopping	42.6	63.4	52.3	48.5	45.9	41.3	45.7
Managing money	23.1	54.6	30.1	24.9	23.4	22.0	22.0
Taking medications	28.6	57.1	38.1	33.7	30.6	27.1	31.9
Using telephone	12.7	32.2	15.7	14.1	12.3	11.9	10.3
Getting around outside	72.9	76.6	78.2	76.3	76.9	75.4	79.8
ADLs (all respondents)							
Eating	18.4	37.3	25.6	22.0	22.6	17.7	17.6
Getting out of bed	45.2	65.8	55.8	50.8	50.8	47.6	50.6
Getting around inside	55.3	69.7	65.2	62.0	60.8	59.1	59.0
Dressing	33.4	62.2	43.6	39.8	40.5	35.2	37.9
Bathing	67.2	81.5	74.0	72.5	71.7	69.0	69.0
Toileting	42.8	63.6	50.4	48.7	50.1	45.8	43.7

Table 5A.3 Self-reported limitations in community-dwelling newly disabled cohort according to self-reported cause of disability

	All newly disabled (n = 892)	Medical only (n = 518)	Old age (n = 133)	Symptom (n = 266)	Pain (n = 105)	Balance (n = 40)	Endurance (n = 22)	Weakness (n = 37)	Other symptom (n = 105)
Functional limitations									
Going up stairs	79.8	80.3	69.5	82.6	92.2	81.3	70.6	87.4	78.8
Walking across room	40.1	41.4	38.9	37.8	44.5	45.6	45.7	22.5	31.5
Bending	52.9	55.9	40.6	51.4	62.9	47.4	24.8	49.7	51.6
Lifting ten pound package	62.0	62.6	56.8	62.6	68.3	47.1	69.8	77.3	61.3
Reaching above head	35.9	38.7	31.7	32.0	32.5	25.2	19.9	30.0	37.6
Grasping small objects	32.7	34.3	29.9	29.1	29.8	33.8	20.2	14.8	33.7
Seeing to read newsprint	20.4	20.0	16.9	24.1	12.0	18.0	16.7	16.9	41.5
Speaking	1.7	2.5	0.0	0.8	0.0	0.0	0.0	0.0	2.0
Hearing	6.7	6.8	4.1	7.2	5.5	4.0	0.0	1.9	14.8
IADLs									
Light housework	20.5	22.3	21.8	14.5	13.1	10.5	23.7	9.2	17.2
Laundry	26.3	28.4	27.9	21.5	20.3	18.3	41.2	16.4	21.9
Cooking	22.5	24.4	25.6	17.8	16.9	20.4	23.2	11.2	20.0
Grocery shopping	41.4	44.1	39.7	38.5	35.0	39.5	53.0	37.1	41.2
Managing money	22.3	25.5	24.1	14.3	6.0	13.3	24.1	10.6	24.8
Taking medications	27.2	28.5	26.6	24.5	22.3	22.6	16.4	12.5	34.0
Using telephone	11.9	12.2	9.9	11.8	4.5	12.0	6.5	7.3	21.9
Getting around outside	71.7	71.1	70.8	73.5	82.4	86.2	79.9	71.1	66.8
ADLs									
Eating	12.2	13.1	12.8	10.6	11.2	5.0	7.3	1.6	17.3
Getting out of bed	33.6	35.1	34.9	30.0	37.9	29.2	36.0	13.3	27.8
Getting around inside	47.0	48.4	48.2	44.1	51.3	44.3	38.3	59.0	40.1
Dressing	20.3	23.5	17.6	15.1	11.5	12.4	11.4	11.3	22.6
Bathing	60.0	64.7	60.0	52.2	49.5	42.3	52.2	57.8	57.2
Toileting	33.9	35.3	32.3	31.6	37.0	30.2	18.4	19.8	34.6

References

Aguero-Torres, H., L. Fratiglioni, Z. Guo, M. Vitanen, E. von Strauss, and B. Winblad. 1998. Dementia is the major cause of functional dependence in the elderly: Three-year follow-up data from a population-based study. *American Journal of Public Health* 88 (10): 1452–56.

Boult, C., M. Altmann, D. Gilbertson, C. Yu, and R. L. Kane. 1996. Decreasing disability in the 21st century: The future effects of controlling six fatal and nonfatal conditions. *American Journal of Public Health* 86 (10): 1388–93.

Chernew, M. E., D. P. Goldman, F. Pan, and B. Shang. 2005. Disability and health care spending among Medicare beneficiaries. *Health Affairs* 24 (2): W5R42–W5R51.

Crimmins, E. M., Y. Saito, and S. L. Reynolds. 1997. Further evidence on recent trends in the prevalence and incidence of disability among older Americans from two sources: The LSOA and the NHIS. *Journals of Gerontology: Psychological Sciences and Social Sciences.* 52 (2): S59–71.

Cummings, J. L., and G. Cole. 2002. Alzheimer Disease. *Journal of the American Medical Association.* 287 (18): 2335–38.

Cutler, D. M. 2001. Declining disability among the elderly. *Health Affairs* 20 (6): 11–27.

———. 2005. Intensive medical technology and the reduction in disability. In *Analyses in the Economics of Aging*, ed. D. A. Wise, 161–84. Chicago: The University of Chicago Press.

Dunlop, D. D., S. L. Hughes, and L. M. Manheim. 1997. Disability in activities of daily living: Patterns of change and a hierarchy of disability. *American Journal of Public Health* 87 (3): 378–83.

Dunlop, D. D., L. M. Manheim, M.-W. Sohn, X. Liu, and R. W. Chang. 2002. Incidence of functional limitations in older adults: The impact of gender, race, and chronic conditions. *Archives of Physical Medicine and Rehabilitation* 83 (7): 964–71.

Ettinger, W. H., Jr., L. P. Fried, T. Harris, and L. Shemanski. 1994. Self-reported causes of physical disability in older people: The Cardiovascular Health Study. CHS Collaborative Research Group. *Journal of the American Geriatrics Society* 42 (10): 1035–44.

Ferrucci, L., J. M. Guralnik, F. Cecchi, N. Marchionni, B. Salini, J. Kasper, R. Celli, et al. 1998. Constant hierarchic patterns of physical functioning across seven populations in five countries. *Gerontologist* 38 (3): 286–94.

Ferrucci, L., J. M. Guralnik, M. Pahor, M. C. Corti, and R. J. Havlik. 1997. Hospital diagnosis, Medicare charges, and nursing home admissions in the year when older persons become severely disabled. *Journal of the American Medical Association* 277 (9): 728–34.

Ferrucci, L., J. M. Guralnik, E. Simonsick, M. E. Salive, C. Corti, and J. Langlois. 1996. Progressive versus catastrophic disability: A longitudinal view of the disablement process. *Journals of Gerontology. Series A, Biological Sciences and Medical Sciences* 51 (3): M123–30.

Ford, A. B., S. J. Folmar, R. B. Salmon, J. H. Medalie, A. W. Roy, and S. S. Galazka. 1988. Health and function in the old and very old. *Journal of the American Geriatric Society* 36:187–97.

Freedman, V. A., E. M. Crimmons, R. F. Schoeni, B. C. Spillman, H. Aykan, E. Kramarow, K. Land, et al. 2004. Resolving inconsistencies in trends in old-age disability: Report from a technical working group. *Demography* 41 (3): 417–41.

Freedman, V. A., and L. G. Martin. 1998. Understanding trends in functional limitations among older Americans. *American Journal of Public Health* 88 (10): 1457–62.

Freedman, V. A., L. G. Martin, and R. F. Schoeni. 2002. Recent trends in disability and functioning among older adults in the United States: A systematic review. *Journal of the American Medical Association* 288 (24): 3137–46.

Fried, L. P., K. Bandeen-Roche, P. H. Chaves, and B. A. Johnson. 2000. Preclinical mobility disability predicts incident mobility disability in older women. *Journal of Gerontology: Medical Sciences* 55: M43–52.

Fried, L. P., K. Bandeen-Roche, J. D. Williamson, P. Presada-Rao, E. Chee, S. Tepper, and G. S. Rubin. 1996. Functional decline in older adults: Expanding methods of ascertainment. *Journals of Gerontology: Biological Sciences and Medical Sciences* 51 (5): M206–14.

Fried, L. P., W. H. Ettinger, B. Lind, A. B. Newman, and J. Gardin. 1994. Physical disability in older adults: A physiological approach. *Journal of Clinical Epidemiology* 47 (7): 747–60.

Fried, L. P., L. Ferrucci, J. Darer, J. D. Williamson, and G. Anderson. 2004. Untangling the concepts of disability, frailty, and comorbidity: Implications for improved targeting and care. *Journals of Gerontology. Series A, Biological Sciences and Medical Sciences* 59 (3): M255–63.

Fried, L. P., S. J. Herdman, K. E. Kuhn, G. Rubin, and K. Turano. 1991. Preclinical disability: Hypotheses about the bottom of the iceberg. *Journal of Aging and Health* 3:285–300.

Fried, L. P., Y. Young, G. Rubin, and K. Bandeen-Roche. 2001. Self-reported preclinical disability identifies older women with early declines in performance and early disease. *Journal of Clinical Epidemiology* 54:889–901.

Fried, T. R., E. H. Bradley, C. S. Williams, and M. E. Tinetti. 2001. Functional disability and health care expenditures for older persons. *Archives of Internal Medicine* 161:2602–07.

Gill, T. M., H. G. Allore, S. E. Hardy, and Z. Guo. 2006. The dynamic nature of mobility disability in older persons. *Journal of the American Geriatrics Society* 54 (2): 248–54.

Gill, T. M., E. A. Gahbauer, H. G. Allore, and L. Han. 2006. Transitions between frailty states among community-living older persons. *Archives of Internal Medicine* 166 (4): 418–23.

Gill, T. M., J. T. Robinson, and M. E. Tinetti. 1998. Difficulty and dependence: Two components of the disability continuum among community-living older persons. *Annals of Internal Medicine* 128 (2): 96–101.

———. 1997. Predictors of recovery in activities of daily living among disabled older persons living in the community. *Journal of General Internal Medicine* 12 (12): 757–62.

Greenland, S., and K. Drescher. 1993. Maximum likelihood estimation of the attributable fraction from logistic models. *Biometrics* 49 (3): 865–72.

Guccione, A. A., D. T. Felson, J. J. Anderson, J. M. Anthony, Y. Zhang, P. W. Wilson, M. Kelly-Hayes, P. A. Wolf, B. E. Kreger, and W. B. Kannel. 1994. The effects of specific medical conditions on the functional limitations of elders in the Framingham Study. *American Journal of Public Health* 84 (3): 351–58.

Guralnik, J. M., L. Alecxih, L. G. Branch, and J. M. Wiener. 2002. Medical and long-term care costs when older persons become more dependent. *American Journal of Public Health* 92 (8): 1244–45.

Guralnik, J. M., L. Ferrucci, E. M. Simonsick, M. E. Salive, and R. B. Wallace. 1995. Lower-extremity function in persons over the age of 70 years as a predictor of subsequent disability. *New England Journal of Medicine* 332:556–61.

Guralnik, J. M., A. Z. LaCroix, L. G. Branch, S. V. Kasl, and R. B. Wallace. 1991. Morbidity and disability in older persons in the years prior to death. *American Journal of Public Health* 92:443–47.

Iezzoni, L. I., S. M. Foley, J. Daley, J. Hughes, E. S. Fisher, and T. Heeren. 1992. Comorbidities, complications, and coding bias: Does the number of diagnosis codes matter in predicting in-hospital mortality? *Journal of the American Medical Association* 267 (16): 2197–2203.

Jagger, C., A. J. Arthur, N. A. Spiers, and M. Clarke. 2001. Patterns of onset of disability in activities of daily living with age. *Journal of the American Geriatrics Society* 49:404–9.

Jencks, S. F., D. K. Williams, and T. L. Kay. 1988. Assessing hospital-associated deaths from discharge data: The role of length of stay and comorbidities. *Journal of the American Medical Association* 260: 2240–46.

Katz, S., A. B. Ford, R. W. Moskowitz, B. A. Jackson, and M. W. Jaffe. 1963. Studies of illness in the aged. The index of ADL: A standardized measure of biological and psychosocial function. *Journal of the American Medical Association* 185:914–19.

Kempen, G. I., and T. P. Suurmeijer. 1990. The development of a hierarchical polychotomous ADL-IADL scale for noninstitutionalized elders. *Gerontologist* 30 (4): 497–502.

Komisar, H. L., J. Hunt-McCool, and J. Feder. 1997. Medicare spending for elderly beneficiaries who need long-term care. *Inquiry* 34(4): 302–10.

Kosorok, M. R., G. S. Omenn, P. Diehr, T. D. Koepsell, and D. L. Patrick. 1992. Restricted activity days among older adults. *American Journal of Public Health* 82:1263–67.

Lakdawalla, D. N., J. Bhattacharya, and D. P. Goldman. 2004. Are the young becoming more disabled? *Health Affairs* 23 (1): 168–76.

Lamb, V. L. 1996. A cross-national study of quality of life factors associated with patterns of elderly disablement. *Social Science and Medicine* 42 (3): 363–77.

Lazaridis, E. N., M. A. Rudberg, S. E. Furner, and C. K. Cassel. 1994. Do activities of daily living have a hierarchical structure? An analysis using the longitudinal study of aging. *Journal of Gerontology* 49 (2): M47–M51.

Leveille, S. G., L. P. Fried, and J. M. Guralnik. 2002. Disabling symptoms: What do older women report? *Journal of General Internal Medicine* 17:766–73.

Leveille, S. G., L. P. Fried, W. McMullen, and J. M. Guralnik. 2004. Advancing the taxonomy of disability in older adults. *Journals of Gerontology. Series A, Biological Sciences and Medical Sciences* 59A (1): 86–93.

Leveille, S. G., C. C. Wee, and L. I. Iezzoni. 2005. Trends in obesity and arthritis among baby boomers and their predecessors, 1971–2002. *American Journal of Public Health* 95 (9): 1607.

Liu, K., S. W. Wall, and D. A. Wissoker. 1997. Disability and Medicare costs of elderly persons. *Milbank Quarterly* 75 (4): 461–93.

Lunney, J. R., J. Lynn, D. J. Foley, S. Lipson, and J. M. Guralnik. 2003. Patterns of functional decline at the end of life. *Journal of the American Medical Association* 289 (18): 2387–92.

Manton, K. G. 1988. A longitudinal study of functional change and mortality in the United States. *Journal of Gerontology* 43 (5): S153–61.

———. 1989. Epidemiological, demographic, and social correlates of disability among the elderly. *Milbank Quarterly* 67 Suppl 2 Pt. 1:13–58.

Manton, K. G., and X. Gu. 2001. Changes in the prevalence of chronic disability in the United States black and nonblack population above age 65 from 1982 to

1999. *Proceedings of the National Academy of Sciences of the United States of America* 98 (11): 6354–59.

Manton, K. G., X. Gu, and V. L. Lamb. 2006. Change in chronic disability from 1982 to 2004/2005 as measured by long-term changes in function and health in the U.S. elderly population. *Proceedings of the National Academy of Sciences of the United States of America* 103 (48): 18374–9.

Manton, K. G., E. Stallard, and L. Corder. 1998. The dynamics of dimensions of age-related disability 1982 to 1994 in the U.S. elderly population. *Journals of Gerontology: Biological Sciences and Medical Sciences* 53 (1): B59–70.

McClellan, M., and L. Yan. 2000. Understanding disability trends in the U.S. elderly population: The role of disease management and disease prevention. Unpublished paper. Stanford University, Department of Economics.

Schoeni, R. F., V. A. Freedman, and R. B. Wallace. 2001. Persistent, consistent, widespread, and robust? Another look at recent trends in old-age disability. *Journal of Gerontology* 56B (4): S206–18.

Singer, B. H., and K. G. Manton. 1998. The effects of health changes on projections of health service needs for the elderly population of the United States. *Proceedings of the National Academy of Sciences of the United States of America* 95 (26): 15618–22.

Siu, A. L., D. B. Reuben, and R. D. Hays. 1990. Hierarchical measures of physical functioning in ambulatory geriatrics. *Journal of the American Geriatrics Society* 38 (10): 1113–19.

Song, J., R. W. Chang, and D. D. Dunlop. 2006. Population impact of arthritis on disability in older adults. *Arthritis and Rheumatism* 55 (2): 248–55.

Spector, W. D., and J. A. Fleishman. 1998. Combining activities of daily living with instrumental activities of daily living to measure functional disability. *Journal of Gerontology* 53B (1): S46–S57.

Spillman, B. C. 2004. Changes in elderly disability rates and the implications for health care utilization and cost. *Milbank Quarterly* 82 (1): 157–94.

Valderrama-Gama, E., J. Damian, A. Ruigómez, and J. M. Martin-Moreno. 2002. Chronic disease, functional status, and self-ascribed causes of disability among noninstitutionalized older people in Spain. *Journal of Gerontology* 57A (11): M716–21.

Verbrugge, L. M., and A. M. Jette. 1994. The disablement process. *Social Science and Medicine* 38 (1): 1–14.

Verbrugge, L. M., J. M. Lepkowski, and L. L. Konkol. 1991. Levels of disability among U.S. adults with arthritis. *Journal of Gerontology* 46 (2): S71–S83.

Waidmann, T. A., and K. Liu. 2000. Disability trends among elderly persons and implications for the future. *Journal of Gerontology* 46 (5): S298–S307.

Williamson, J. D., and L. P. Fried. 1996. Characterization of older adults who attribute functional decrements to "Old Age." *Journal of the American Geriatrics Society* 44 (12): 1429–34.

Wolff, J. L., C. Boult, C. Boyd, and G. Anderson. 2005. Newly reported chronic conditions and onset of functional dependency. *Journal of the American Geriatrics Society* 53 (5): 851–55.

III

Medical Advances and Disability

6

Intensive Medical Care and Cardiovascular Disease Disability Reductions

David M. Cutler, Mary Beth Landrum, and Kate A. Stewart

Disability among the elderly has declined markedly in the United States in the past two decades. In 1984, 25 percent of the elderly population reported difficulty with activities associated with independent living.[1] By 2004 and 2005, the share had fallen to below 20 percent, a decline of one fifth.

Although these basic facts are well known, the interpretation of these facts is not clear. Is the reduction in disability a result of improved medical care, individual behavioral changes, or environmental modifications that allow the elderly to better function by themselves? Will the trend continue, or is it time limited? What does the reduction in disability mean for years of healthy life and labor force participation? We explore these issues in this chapter.

To make progress, we focus on disability caused by a specific set of medical conditions—cardiovascular disease. Focusing on one condition is helpful because it allows us to analyze health shocks and their sequelae in some detail. Cardiovascular disease (CVD) is a natural condition to pick because it is the most common cause of death in the U.S. (and most other developed

David M. Cutler is the Otto Eckstein Professor of Applied Economics and Dean for the Social Sciences at Harvard University and an affiliate of the National Bureau of Economic Research. Mary Beth Landrum is an associate professor of Biostatistics in the Department of Health Care Policy at Harvard Medical School. Kate A. Stewart is a researcher at Mathematica Policy Research, Inc., and was a Ph.D. candidate in Health Policy at Harvard Medical School when this research was completed.

We are grateful to the National Institute on Aging grants P30 AG12810 and R01 AG19805, and the Mary Woodard Lasker Charitable Trust and Michael E. DeBakey Foundation for research support.

1. The data are from the National Long-Term Care Survey, a survey we describe later and use in this chapter.

countries), and more is spent on cardiovascular disease than any other condition. Thus, this is a case where medical care could really matter.

Our analysis has three parts. In the first part, we examine basic trends in disability associated with cardiovascular disease. We show that reduced disability for people with cardiovascular disease incidents is a major part of reductions in overall disability, accounting for between one fifth and one third of the total reduction in disability. The second part of the chapter considers the role of advances in medical care in reducing disability from cardiovascular disease. We show that medical technology in the treatment of cardiovascular disease is a major factor in reduced disability. We estimate that use of recommended treatments for heart attacks, including prescriptions of beta-blockers, aspirin, and ace-inhibitors at discharge, as well as use of reperfusion and other surgical procedures may have increased the probability that elderly patients survive an acute cardiovascular event in a nondisabled state by up to 50 percent between 1984 and 1994. The third part of the chapter considers the long-run health and financial impacts of improved care for people with cardiovascular disease.

6.1 Background on Cardiovascular Disease

Cardiovascular diseases are diseases of the heart and blood vessels, which carry oxygen to the body's major organs. Ischemic heart disease is the most common manifestation of cardiovascular disease. When the arteries supplying blood to the heart become occluded, the heart does not get enough oxygen. Like any muscle, oxygen is essential for the heart's performance. Constriction of the coronary arteries will result in chest pain on exertion, or perhaps at rest. A person with such constriction might be unable to engage in activities such as walking for a prolonged period (for example, to get to a grocery store) or engaging in light or heavy housework (cleaning, cooking, etc.)

A blockage of the arteries to some or all of the heart is termed a *myocardial infarction,* or *heart attack.* The equivalent in other extremities, especially the legs, is termed *peripheral vascular disease.* Heart attacks can be fatal and can lead to substantial disability if survived. A person who survives a heart attack might be unable to shop or cook, might have difficulty walking up stairs or entering a raised bathtub, and might have difficulty keeping house. Peripheral vascular disease can lead to the same types of impairments.

Medical advances have made tremendous strides in preventing and treating coronary events. Several risk factors for heart disease are well known. Traditional risk factors include smoking, hypertension or high blood pressure, high cholesterol, obesity, family history, age, and diabetes. Since the early 1970s, standard recommendations for people at risk have been behavioral changes (stop smoking, reduce weight, cut back on fat intake, and exercise) combined with medical therapy (antihypertensive medication, and more recently, cholesterol-reducing medications). Cutler and Kadiyala (2003) show significant reductions in the incidence of heart disease over time attributable to reductions in these risk factors, especially reduced smoking and better blood pressure control.

There have also been technological changes in the treatment available for people with severe heart disease. Bed rest was once standard therapy for people with heart attacks. Today, therapy for a heart attack—and often heart disease in earlier stages of progression—generally starts with drugs such as aspirin, which help dissolve clots and restore blood flow to the heart. Beta-blockers are also given to reduce the workload of the heart and thus reduce the demand for oxygen. In addition, ace-inhibitors are prescribed to help reduce the workload of the heart by lowering blood pressure. Statins are prescribed to help process and break down cholesterol in the arteries (American Heart Association 2006).

Finally, there have been significant advances in acute care and invasive surgical procedures for treating coronary blockage. Thrombolytics are a class of drugs that may be used to help dissolve the clot. Percutaneous coronary intervention (PCI) is used to clear out blockages of the coronary arteries. These procedures are now frequently accompanied by use of a stent to keep the occluded artery open. A more invasive option is coronary artery bypass grafting (abbreviated CABG, and pronounced like the vegetable).

Each of these technologies has been shown to increase survival after a heart attack among patients without contraindications for treatment (Krumholz et al. 1995; Hennekens et al. 1996; Krumholz et al. 1996; Soumerai et al. 1997; Gottlieb, McCarter, and Vogel 1998; Krumholz et al. 1998; Freemantle et al. 1999; Shlipak et al. 2001; Braunwald et al. 2002; Antman et al. 2004; Vitagliano et al. 2004; Stukel, Lucas, and Wennberg 2005). They have an ambiguous effect on disability, however, with the increase in survival among those with serious heart damage possibly offsetting the improved health among traditional survivors (Crimmins, Saito, and Ingegneri 1989; Crimmins, Hayward, and Saito 1994; Waidmann, Bound, and Schoenbaum 1995).

Cerebrovascular disease, or stroke, is the second major form of cardiovascular disease. Ischemic strokes are the most common type of stroke and are similar to heart disease: an artery in the brain becomes blocked, and a part of the brain is denied oxygen. Disability is quite common after a stroke, particularly among the elderly (Pohjasvaara et al. 1997; Prencipe et al. 1997; Zhu et al. 1998). Recent studies report that 39 percent to 54 percent of stroke survivors are disabled three months after the stroke (Henon et al. 1995; Zhu et al. 1998; Glader et al. 2003). The high level of disability can persist among survivors. One study found that 37 percent of stroke survivors were disabled one year after the event (Appelros, Nydevik, and Viitanen 2003). In addition, stroke is associated with increased odds of cognitive impairment, both with and without dementia (Pohjasvaara et al. 1997; Prencipe et al. 1997; Zhu et al. 1998).

Thrombolytic medication may be given after a stroke, but the benefit is far less certain than in heart disease. Clinical trials show that thrombolytics are effective only if given in the first three hours after an acute event (National Institute of Neurological Disorders, 1995; Clark et al. 1999; Adams et al. 2005). Revascularization procedures such as carotid endarterectomy may be performed in patients with certain types of stroke—including transient ischemic attacks—after the patients have recovered from the acute phase of the stroke. A small share of strokes are hemorrhagic strokes, where a blood vessel bursts and there is bleeding in the skull. Little therapy is generally available in such cases, and death is common.

Heart failure and arrhythmias are other types of cardiovascular disease that cause substantial morbidity and mortality among the elderly. Heart failure occurs when the heart's ability to pump blood is impaired. Patients may experience breathlessness and fatigue that makes it difficult to keep up usual activities, fluid retention and edema, coughing, memory loss, and heart palpitations. An arrhythmia is an irregular heartbeat that can cause the heart to pump blood less effectively. Patients with heart failure and/or arrhythmias may also be at substantial risk for stroke and other complications (American Heart Association 2006). Treatment for heart failure includes ace-inhibitors or angiotensin II receptor blockers, beta-blockers, and diuretics. Appropriate patients may also undergo valve replacement surgery or other revascularization. Patients with arrhythmias often receive pacemakers and occasionally receive implantable cardioverter defibrillators along with antiarrhythmic drugs and blood thinners.

Other cardiovascular diseases, generally with smaller prevalence, include rheumatic heart disease, aneurysms, acute pulmonary heart disease, other diseases of the endocardium, capillary diseases, and problems with veins (e.g., varicose veins).

6.2   The Importance of Cardiovascular Disease
     for Reductions in Disability

Like every multidimensional concept, there is no perfect measure of disability. We follow the lead of most researchers in measuring disability as the presence of impairments in Activities of Daily Living (ADLs) and Instrumental Activities of Daily Living (IADLs). Our data source, the National Long-Term Care Survey of 1984–1999 (NLTCS) includes information on six ADL measures: eating, getting in or out of bed, walking around inside, dressing, bathing, and getting to the toilet or using the toilet. Questions are also asked about eight IADL measures: doing light housework, laundry, preparing meals, shopping for groceries, getting around outside, managing money, taking medications, and making telephone calls.

The NLTCS is a nationally representative longitudinal survey of the health and disability profile population aged sixty-five and over. The first NLTCS survey wave was conducted in 1982 and subsequent surveys were administered in 1984, 1989, 1994, and 1999. Each survey wave began with a screener that collected information on whether the respondent reported inability to conduct the six ADLs and eight IADLs without help (i.e., help from another person or special equipment), and whether these limitations had lasted or was expected to last at least three months. The screener also collected demographic information on marital status, race, and age.

Respondents who reported inability to perform any ADLs or IADLs for at least three months on the screener were asked to complete a detailed survey. Disability status was determined by responses to questions about use of help and inability to conduct the ADLs and IADLs on the detailed survey. Sampling and weighting issues are described fully elsewhere (Manton, Corder, and Stallard 1993; Manton, Corder, and Stallard 1997; Manton, Stallard, and Corder 1997; Singer and Manton 1998; Manton and Gu 2001).

We obtained Medicare-linked data for all NLTCS participants, including data on date of death from the denominator files. We used inpatient claims for all analyses because Medicare claims files for Part B and other nonhospital services were incomplete prior to 1991. We also obtained data on zip code of residence at the most recent interview for all NLTCS survey respondents.

Basic data on disability among the elderly population is shown in figure 6.1. For reasons that will become clear shortly, we report disability for the population that is aged seventy and older in each of three years: 1989, 1994, and 1999. The share of the elderly population that is disabled declined

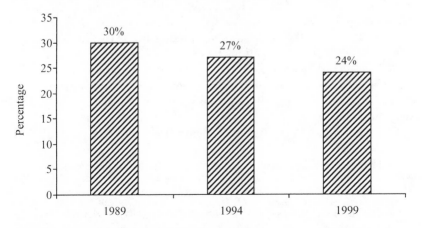

Fig. 6.1   Share of population 70+ who are disabled

Note: Disability is defined as any difficulty conducting Activities of Daily Living or Instrumental Activities of Daily Living without help.

markedly in the 1990s. The cumulative decline was 6.3 percentage points, or 2.1 percent per year.

To examine the role of cardiovascular disease in explaining this reduction in disability, we form a population sample likely affected by the condition. We start by looking at the population aged seventy and older in the 1989, 1994, and 1999 surveys. For each of these cohorts, we group all hospitalizations over the preceding five years into one of thirty-two categories (the five-year look back is the reason for the restriction to people over seventy). These categories were designed to pick up relatively homogenous clinical conditions that would be predictive of disability. The set of thirty-two categories is shown in table 6.1, along with the rate of disability for people hospitalized with each condition from the 1989 survey cohort. The relevant categories for cardiovascular disease are stroke, hypertension, ischemic heart disease, heart failure and arrhythmia, peripheral vascular disease, and other circulatory diseases.[2]

Figure 6.2 reports the share of people with a hospitalization for any of these conditions. Twenty-two percent of people were admitted to a hospital with some cardiovascular disease. Ischemic heart disease is the most common admission. Stroke and heart failure are also common, as are other circulatory diseases. Admissions for peripheral vascular disease and hypertension are much less common.

A person who had a hospital admission for cardiovascular disease and is disabled may or may not have been disabled because of that condition. The NLTCS does not reliably determine the precise condition that leads to each disability. We make two alternative assumptions about the probability of being disabled by cardiovascular disease. The first assumption, a less restrictive assumption, labels someone as disabled from cardiovascular disease if he or she was admitted to a hospital with cardiovascular disease in the previous five years. The more restrictive assumption subsets this group to those for whom the most disabling condition was cardiovascular disease,[3] where the list of conditions by disability status is reported in table 6.1. Thus, a person who had a stroke and hip fracture would be termed disabled because of cardiovascular disease by the first measure, but not by the second measure. Fortunately, our results are very similar regardless of the definition used.

Figure 6.3 shows the probability of being disabled by cardiovascular dis-

2. ICD-9 codes are as follows: stroke: 362.34, 430, 431, 432.9, 433–436; hypertension: 401–402, 405, 437.0, 437.9; ischemic heart disease; 4.10–4.14, 429.5–429.7, excluding 414.11 and 414.19; heart failure and arrhythmia: 425, 427.1, 427.3–427.5, 428, 429.1, 429.3; peripheral vascular disease: 440, 442, 443.0–443.1, 443.8–443.9, 444, 446, 447.0–447.5, 447.8–447.9, 451, 453.1; circulatory diseases: 391–400, 406–409, 414.11, 414.19, 415–424, 426, .427.2, 427.6, 427.8, 427.9, 429.2, 429.4, 429.8, 429.9, 432.1–432.8, 437.1–437.8, 439, 441, 443.2, 445, 447.6, 448–450, 452–453.0, 453.2–459, 786.5, V717.

3. Note even this more restrictive assumption may underestimate the importance of disabling diseases, such as arthritis or dementia, that are not common causes of hospitalizations.

Table 6.1   Most disabling conditions

Condition	% disabled	Rank
Chronic renal failure	88.9	1
Dementia and organic brain diseases	83.1	2
Paralysis, Parkinson's, etc.	82.5	3
Hip and pelvic fracture	80.2	4
Acute renal failure and insufficiency	68.1	5
Other metabolic and immunity disorders	67.0	6
Other blood diseases	66.5	7
Respiratory failure and insufficiency	66.5	8
Anemia	65.9	9
Diabetes	64.1	10
Thyroid disorders	59.9	11
Stroke	59.5	12
Infectious diseases	59.2	13
Respiratory diseases	56.8	14
Depression	56.2	15
Peripheral vascular disease	55.4	16
Composite category	54.8	17
Musculoskeletal disorders	53.2	18
Heart failure and arrhythmia	51.5	19
Chronic obstructive pulmonary diseases and related diseases	51.0	20
Other mental disorders	49.9	21
Glaucoma and cataract	48.8	22
Hypertension	48.4	23
Gastrointestinal disease	45.2	24
Arthritis and arthropathy	45.0	25
Circulatory diseases	42.0	26
Colorectal and lung cancer	40.0	27
Back/neck pain	39.2	28
Ischemic heart disease	38.7	29
Genitourinary diseases	38.7	30
Other cancers	37.6	31
Breast and prostate cancer	28.9	32

Notes: Analyses conducted using 1989 cohort, and based on primary hospitalization diagnosis codes in the proceeding five years. Composite category includes hospitalizations for any diagnoses other than the thirty-one specific categories above.

ease. Using the less restrictive measure, the decline in disability is 1.4 percentage points, or 22 percent of the 6.3 percentage point total reduction in disability. Using the more restrictive measure, the decline is 0.9 percentage points, or 14 percent of the total decline. In each case, cardiovascular disease is a substantial share of the total decline.

As previously noted, the conclusion that cardiovascular disease is a substantial share of disability decline contradicts an earlier literature that suggested that marginal survivors contribute to an increase in disability. If more people survive strokes, the argument went, the share of the elderly

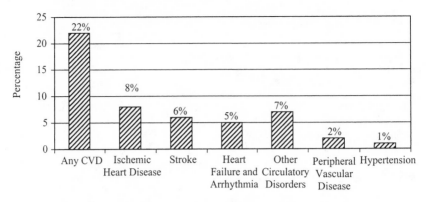

Fig. 6.2   Clinical conditions for people age 70+ with cardiovascular disease
Note: The sample is NLTCS survey respondents with at least one CVD hospitalization in the five years prior to the survey, for all three survey years pooled.

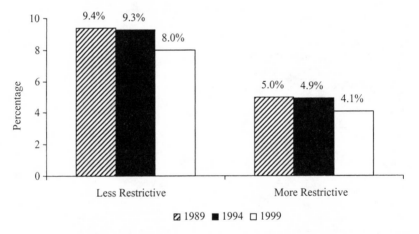

Fig. 6.3   Probability of being disabled because of cardiovascular disease
Note: Cross-sectional analyses based on hospitalizations in the five years prior to the survey.

with disabilities would rise. The finding of a reduction in disability suggests, in contrast, two other hypotheses: either fewer people are suffering cardiovascular disease events, or those who have always survived such events are less disabled now than they were formerly (i.e., the incidence of disability among cardiovascular disease patients is falling). These possible effects are demonstrated in equation (1):

(1) Pr (Disabled from CVD) = Pr (Had CVD Incident)
$$\times \text{ Pr (Survive | Had Event)}$$
$$\times \text{ Pr (Disabled | Had Event, Survival)}$$

The first term on the right hand side is the incidence of events. The second term is the survival rate, and the third term is the health effect among survivors. The change in disability rates is arithmetically related to the change in one or more of these factors.[4] The marginal survivors theory focuses on the second term: the change in the probability of survival after an acute event (i.e., as more patients survive acute events, the pool of people at risk of disability expands). The other theories focus on the first and third terms (i.e., either reduced incidence of disease or better health among survivors).

Table 6.2 shows cardiovascular disease event probabilities, survival rates, and conditional disability rates for each of our three time periods. To measure the cardiovascular disease event rate, we consider the population surveyed at the beginning of the five year interval, and look at events in those five years. For example, the cardiovascular disease event rate for the 1989 cohort is the share of the population aged sixty-five and older in 1984 that had a cardiovascular disease hospital admission in the subsequent five years.[5]

The first row shows that the share of people who had a hospitalization for cardiovascular disease was relatively constant over the time period, at about 26 percent. This is somewhat surprising given the reduction in event rates noted in other surveys such as the Framingham Heart Study (Sytkowski et al. 1996) and the Minnesota Heart Survey (McGovern et al. 1996; McGovern et al. 2001). It may be that some of the admissions among the later cohorts in our study were done explicitly to perform surgical operations such as angioplasty or bypass surgery, and thus contribute to an increased reporting of cardiovascular disease. However, another recent U.S. study of subjects aged thirty-five to seventy-four reported little change in the incidence of first myocardial infarction between 1987 and 1994 (Rosamond et al. 1998). Alternatively, it may be that less severe cases of these conditions are being diagnosed over time.[6]

In addition, the Framingham and Minnesota studies included patients younger than sixty-five, and results from these studies may have been driven by a decline in heart disease among the younger population. A Finnish study of coronary heart disease between 1978–1980 and 2000–2001 reported decreased prevalence of coronary heart disease among men and women aged forty-five to sixty-four, no change in prevalence among men and women aged sixty-five to seventy-four, and increased incidence

---

4. There are covariance terms as well, but these are generally small.
5. Were the NLTCS a fixed panel survey, the sample of people at the starting year (e.g., 1984) would be only those for whom the disability status is known five years later plus those who died in the interim. The NLTCS did not interview the entire sample every year, however, so some people are lost to follow-up. To generate a nationally representative sample, we analyzed only those people whose health and mortality status were known at follow-up for each survey year, and reweighted the sample weights to reflect the age-sex distribution of all respondents to the 1999 survey.
6. Clinical trials published in 1996 showed that a blood test for troponin, a protein released from damaged heart tissue, can be used to diagnose heart attacks. This likely led to greater diagnosis of smaller heart attacks and may also have led to increased hospitalizations, depending on how frequently these patients were previously admitted.

Table 6.2   Decomposing changes in cardiovascular disease disability

	Cohort (%)			Change, 1984–89 to 1994–99 (%)
	1984–1989	1989–1994	1994–1999	
Share with CVD event	26.5	29.0	26.3	–0.2
Share with an event who survive	57.2	58.4	61.5	4.3
Share of survivors who are disabled	47.6	43.7	39.4	–8.2

Source: Authors tabulations from the National Long-Term Care Survey.
Note: Data are based on respondents with a CVD hospitalization in between survey waves, and known health status at the second survey. Weights were adjusted to the age and sex distribution of the 1999 NLTCS survey population, and account for unknown follow-up status at the second survey.

among people aged seventy-five and over (Kattainen et al. 2004). Our results may reflect similar trends in age-related incidence of heart disease.

The second row of the table shows a significant increase in the survival rate to the next survey for people admitted to a hospital with cardiovascular disease. The survival rate increased by 4.3 percentage points, or about 7.5 percent. By itself, this would have led to an increase in disability from cardiovascular disease. This effect is overwhelmed, however, by the substantial reduction in disability among survivors, shown in the third row of the table. The share of CVD survivors who are disabled fell from 48 percent in 1989 to 39 percent in 1999, a 19 percent reduction. It is this massive reduction in event-specific disability that needs to be explained.

6.3   Medical Care and CVD-Related Disability

Before estimating formal statistical models to address the role of medical care in reduced CVD-related disability, we consider a less structural analysis of the role of medical care. Specifically, we look at how disability changed in the period shortly after the cardiovascular disease event relative to the period several years later. If the reduction in disability followed immediately after the cardiovascular event, it strongly suggests that medical treatment of the acute event was the major factor responsible for the reduction in disability. A future disability reduction might be attributable to medical intervention, but other factors, such as better coping with limitations due to improved environmental factors, could be important as well.

Figure 6.4 shows the change in disability rates for people whose cardiovascular disease event happened within six months of the survey, by type of event. The rate of disability declined from 1984–1989 cohort to the 1994–1999 cohort for people with hospitalizations for ischemic heart disease, heart failure and arrhythmia, stroke, and other cardiovascular disease. For heart failure and arrhythmia patients as well as other cardiovascular diseases, there were increases in the disability rate from the

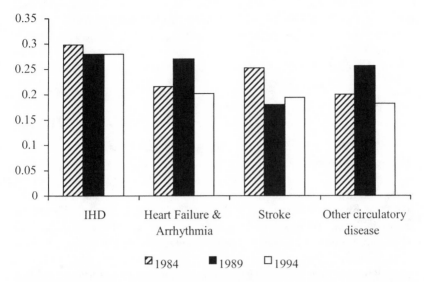

1984   ■1989   □1994

Fig. 6.4   Likelihood of reporting disability among respondents with specific cardiovascular disease events in the six months prior to survey

1984–1989 to 1989–1994 cohorts that need further explanation.[7] Overall, though, it seems that medical advances could have some role in this decline in disability between 1984–1989 and 1994–1999.

6.3.1   Empirical Methodology

To examine the role of medical technology changes in event-related reductions in disability more formally, we estimate regression models for the health of patients who have been admitted to a hospital with cardiovascular disease. Our sample is formed from each of the three cohorts. We select people who were admitted to a hospital with cardiovascular disease in 1984–1989, 1989–1994, and 1994–1999. In each case, the sample includes all people for whom we know health status at the beginning and end of the five-year period. There are three possible health states at the end of each period, that is, at the time of follow-up survey: dead, alive and nondisabled, and alive and disabled. We denote these possible outcomes with the subscript k.

Consider for the moment a single measure of medical treatments, which we wish to relate to the change in disability. For concreteness, assume that the variable is the share of people in an area who receive a surgical proce-

7. For example, the average severity of heart failure hospitalizations may have increased over time if physicians and patients were better able to manage heart failure in the outpatient setting.

dure that has been shown to be effective in improving health for people with that condition. The treatment rate for area j in time period t is denoted $T_{j,t}$. We model the probability that person i in period t will be in health state k using a multinomial logit formulation:

$$(2) \quad \text{Pr (health state } k)_{i,j,t} = \frac{\exp{(X_{i,t}\beta_k + \gamma_k T_{j,t} + \Delta_k \text{cohort}_t)}}{(1 + \exp)(\Sigma X_{i,t}\beta_1 + \gamma_1 T_{j,t} + \Delta_1 \text{cohort}_t)}$$

where $X_{i,t}$ is a set of demographic and baseline health variables, and γ_ks are the coefficient of interest. Our control variables include: age/sex (five-year age groups differentiated by gender); disability status at the baseline interview; dummy variables for other cardiovascular disease hospitalizations (with the exception of the all-CVD model, which does not require indicator variables for other CVD diagnoses); a modified Charlson index (i.e., without cardiovascular disease diagnoses) (Deyo, Cherkin, and Ciol 1992); marital status at the beginning of the five-year window (married, widowed, divorced/separated, or missing marital status); race (white and nonwhite); and zip code-level education and poverty measures (respondents' education and income were only available from the detailed interview).

One issue that comes up in any estimation involving an equation like (2) is the issue of causality. If treatments are not randomly assigned, estimates of γ will be biased. We address this issue in several ways. The most important is to use area-level variation in treatments, rather than individual-level variation. Whether any individual receives a treatment is dependent on the physician's perception of that patient's underlying health. If the underlying severity of disease is relatively constant across areas and over time, however, variations in treatment at the area level will be good markers for exogenous changes in the use of medical care. As is standard in the literature (O'Connor et al. 1999; Fisher et al. 2003a; Fisher et al. 2003b; Stukel, Lucas, and Wennberg 2005), we group individuals into areas based on the Hospital Referral Region (HRR) they live in. Hospital Referral Regions are groups of zip codes where the bulk of patients go to the same set of hospitals and include at least one hospital with a tertiary cardiovascular or neurological surgical center. For example, the HRR for Chicago includes zip codes 60601–60712; within this area, the vast majority of people who are hospitalized get admitted to a hospital in that region.

6.3.2   Measures of Medical Treatment

We use several measures of medical care to predict disability. The first variable is the share of people who receive surgical interventions. To define relevant procedures, we identify treatments for each specific diagnosis that the medical literature has identified as being efficacious (generally in reducing mortality) for at least some subsets of patients with that diagnosis. These procedures are detailed in table 6.3. For hypertension, there are no

Table 6.3   **Relevant procedures for cardiovascular disease admissions**

Condition	Appropriate procedures (CPT-4 Code)
Stroke	Incision, excision, and occlusion of vessels (38)
Hypertension	—
Ischemic heart disease	Operations on vessels of heart (36)
	Other operations on heart and pericardium (37)
Heart failure and arrhythmia	Other operations on heart and pericardium (37)
	Conversion of cardiac rhythm (99)
Peripheral vascular disease	Incision, excision, and occlusion of vessels (38)
	Operations on vessels (39)
	Other procedures on musculoskeletal system (84)
Other circulatory diseases	Operations on valves and septa of heart (35)
	Other operations on heart and pericardium (37)
	Incision, excision, and occlusion of vessels (38)

generally accepted surgical therapies. There are one or more therapies for the other conditions, of which the most common appropriate procedures are "other operations on heart and pericardium" (CPT code 37), which includes PCI (angioplasty), heart replacement procedures and insertion of pacemakers, and "incision, excision and occlusion of vessels" (CPT code 38), which includes endarterectomies. CABG procedures for ischemic heart disease patients are coded under CPT code 36, "operations on vessels of heart."

Table 6.4 shows the average rate of procedure use over time across hospital referral regions for all cardiovascular disease patients and by specific conditions. In the 1984–1989 cohort, the average procedure rate was only 21 percent across regions. The average procedure rate was highest for other circulatory diseases (30 percent), followed by ischemic heart disease (23 percent), stroke (13 percent) and heart failure and arrhythmia (11.3 percent). By 1994–1999, the average procedure rate for all patients across all regions increased to 34 percent. The average procedure rate for ischemic heart disease patients jumped to 48 percent. Average procedure rates increased to 43 percent for other circulatory diseases, 25 percent for stroke, and 14.2 percent for heart failure and arrhythmia. These increases reflect the greater belief among physicians about the efficacy of therapy, and advances in the therapy itself.[8]

Our other measures of medical technology involve use of pharmaceuticals for patients with acute myocardial infarction. As noted in the previous section, these pharmaceuticals have been shown to improve survival, although the overall effect of pharmaceutical treatment on both improved survival and disability in the elderly has not been well established. Ran-

---

8. For example, catheters used in surgery have improved, and stents were developed for use in angioplasty in the mid-1990s.

Table 6.4   Average rates of procedures and pharmaceuticals

Measure	1984–1989	1989–1994	1994–1999
Share of people receiving relevant procedure, % (SD)	21.1 (0.4)	26.1 (0.5)	34.2 (0.6)
By specific conditions			
Ischemic Heart Disease	22.6 (0.9)	33.2 (1.0)	47.9 (1.3)
Stroke	13.0 (0.8)	17.1 (0.9)	24.8 (1.0)
Heart Failure	11.3 (0.6)	11.9 (0.8)	14.2 (0.9)
Other Circulatory Diseases	29.7 (1.1)	32.5 (1.2)	43.0 (1.3)
Beta-blockers	—	50.7 (1.0)	—
Reperfusion		67.1 (0.8)	
Aspirin		76.4 (0.6)	
Ace-inhibitors		60.0 (0.6)	

Note: Based on respondents with a CVD hospitalization between survey waves. The procedure figures are the averages across HRRs, consistent with the CCP data.

domized studies comparing various treatments for ischemic heart disease on functional status and quality of life reported improvements for most outcome measures for both medical and surgical therapies (Rogers et al. 1990; Strauss et al. 1995; Hlatky et al. 1997; Pocock et al. 2000; Borkon et al. 2002; Pfisterer et al. 2003). However, most of these studies included patients under age sixty-five who may be more likely to improve than elderly patients (Rogers et al. 1990; Strauss et al. 1995; Hlatky et al. 1997; Pocock et al. 2000; Borkon et al. 2002). A recent trial comparing medical and surgical management of elderly patients with coronary artery disease reported improved quality of life at one year for both treatment arms (Pfisterer et al. 2003), suggesting that treatment likely reduces disability in the elderly population. However, no studies to date have estimated the effect of increased use of appropriate pharmaceutical treatments over time on disability rates in the elderly population.

Pharmaceutical use is not captured in Medicare claims. Thus, we do not have time series data on the use of pharmaceuticals by area. We do have a snapshot of data on pharmaceutical use, taken from a survey of medical records in the mid-1990s. The Cooperative Cardiovascular Project (CCP) abstracted medical record data on 186,800 Medicare patients hospitalized for an AMI between February 1994 and July 1995, including data on appropriateness for and receipt of guideline-recommended treatments (Marciniak et al. 1998).

Use among patients most suited for treatment ranged from 51 percent for beta-blockers in the immediate postmyocardial infarction treatment to 76 percent for aspirin. Average utilization rates for the mid-1990s are shown in table 6.4. Researchers at Dartmouth have calculated the average use rate of each of these pharmaceuticals at the HRR level, which we employ in our analysis (O'Connor et al. 1999).

While not known at the area level, use of these pharmaceuticals did increase during our study time frame. Reported use of aspirin for heart attack patients in 1985 and between 1998 and 2000 was 30 percent and 85 percent, respectively, and over the same time, use of beta-blockers was 48 percent and 72 percent, thrombolytics was 9 percent and approximately 80 percent, and ace-inhibitors was 0 percent and 71 percent, respectively (Jencks et al. 2000; Heidenreich and McClellan 2001; Vaccarino et al. 2005). The change in ace-inhibitors use from this study was based only on changes in the Worcester, Massachusetts area and may not reflect changes in use nationally.

The lack of time series data on pharmaceutical use at the area level requires us to modify our analyses. Equation (2) assumes that we have time-varying data on procedures and pharmaceuticals. Since we can only assign patients to true area levels for pharmacological treatments in 1994–1995, we estimated a model with all CCP variables on the 1994–1999 cohort only. We estimate a separate model using the panel data and time-varying procedures variables based on equation (2).

From our models, we estimate the likelihood of being disabled, dead, alive, and nondisabled at follow-up if all respondents lived in HRRs that provided relevant procedures and pharmaceuticals from the 10th to the 90th percentiles of care, holding all other covariates at their observed levels. We further estimate how much of the change in disability and death over time may be explained by increased use of appropriate treatments that were significantly associated with lower disability and death, based on average use of procedures during each cohort period and estimates from the literature of average use in 1985 and 1999 (i.e., between 1998 and 2000). We defined appropriate treatments for these analyses as those treatments with class IA recommendations from recent guidelines. These include the relevant procedures for Ischemic Heart Disease (IHD) and heart failure as well as all of the pharmacological treatments for IHD, reperfusion and aspirin for stroke, and beta-blockers and ace-inhibitors for heart failure and arrhythmia (Braunwald et al. 2002; Antman et al. 2004; Hunt et al. 2005; Adams et al. 2007). We did not estimate a separate model for other circulatory diseases, because this category includes multiple diagnoses and has no guidelines.

6.3.3   Estimation Results

Table 6.5 shows demographic characteristics of our cohort by year of baseline survey. The proportion of respondents disabled at baseline declined over time, from 32 percent in 1984 to 25.9 percent in 1994. This 6 percentage point decline in disability at baseline is consistent with other analyses using the NLTCS (Manton and Gu 2001). In addition, there was a slight increase in the mean modified Charlson index score from 0.94 in 1984 to 1.07 in 1994.

Table 6.5   Demographic characteristics of CVD cohort, by year of baseline survey

	1984 N = 4,146 wN = 6,403,326	1989 N = 3,671 wN = 7,935,884	1994 N = 3,676 wN = 7,723,454
Age groups, %			
65–69	20.0	21.6	21.0
70–74	24.8	24.3	22.7
75–79	23.2	23.4	24.0
80–84	17.2	16.7	17.1
85+	14.8	14.1	15.2
Male, %	45.0	45.7	45.4
Nonwhite, %	8.0	7.9	8.8
Marital status, %			
Married	51.3	51.1	51.3
Widowed	39.6	37.8	36.7
Divorced, separated, or single	8.1	10.0	9.5
Unknown marital status	1.1	1.1	2.4
Disabled at baseline survey, %	32.2	30.0	25.9
Modified Charlson comorbidy index[a], mean (SD)	0.94 (0.02)	1.04 (0.02)	1.07 (0.02)

Note: Estimates adjusted to the age and sex distribution of the 1999 population of Medicare beneficiaries.
[a] Hospitalizations for cardiovascular disease events were excluded from the Charlson index.

Disability and death at follow-up declined over time for patients with any of the CVD conditions, except for heart failure and arrhythmia patients who had slightly increased probability of disability over time (table 6.6). The share of patients alive and nondisabled at follow-up increased over time for all CVD conditions, including heart failure and arrhythmia; the increase ranged from 8 percent among circulatory disease patients to 32 percent for stroke patients.

Coefficients and standard errors from our estimation results are shown in tables 6.7–6.10 for models with all CVD patients, ischemic heart disease, stroke, and heart failure patients. Each table includes a panel data model with covariates for baseline survey year and area-level relevant procedures as well as a model on the 1994–1999 cohort with covariates for area-level appropriate pharmaceutical use and relevant procedures, with the exception of the stroke table, which only includes the model on the 1994–1999 cohort.

All-CVD

Area-level use of relevant procedures was not significantly associated with lower disability or death in the model with panel data nor in the model

Table 6.6	Health outcomes at follow-up over time, by CVD condition			
	1984–1989	1989–1994	1994–1999	% change, 1984–1989— 1994–1999
Disabled at follow-up, %				
All CVD	26.1	25.3	24.0	–8.1
IHD	23.3	22.2	21.5	–8.0
Stroke	31.0	31.7	29.5	–4.8
Heart failure and arrhythmia	21.8	23.5	22.9	5.5
Other circulatory disease	28.6	30.2	26.0	–9.1
Dead at follow-up, %				
All CVD	41.7	42.2	39.3	–5.8
IHD	39.2	36.8	32.2	–17.9
Stroke	47.4	46.0	42.1	–11.2
Heart failure and arrhythmia	57.0	55.0	51.3	–9.9
Other circulatory disease	31.0	33.2	30.3	–2.2
Alive and nondisabled at follow-up, %				
All CVD	32.2	32.5	36.7	14.0
IHD	37.4	41.0	46.3	23.8
Stroke	21.6	22.4	28.4	31.6
Heart failure and arrhythmia	21.3	21.6	25.7	20.8
Other circulatory disease	40.4	36.6	43.7	8.1

Table 6.7	All CVD: Multinomial regression models for health status outcome five years after baseline survey			
	Model 1: Panel data		Model 2: 1994 cohort only	
Coefficients (SEs)	Disability	Death	Disability	Death
Relevant procedures	–0.000 (0.004)	–0.006 (0.003)	–0.001 (0.005)	–0.006 (0.005)
Beta-blockers	—	—	–0.012 (0.006)**	–0.017 (0.005)***
Aspirin	—	—	0.002 (0.011)	0.001 (0.010)
Reperfusion	—	—	–0.019 (0.007)***	–0.006 (0.007)
Ace-inhibitors	—	—	0.012 (0.006)**	0.013 (0.006)**
Model Statistics				
N	11,491		3,676	
F-test	56.26		14.78	
P-value	P < 0.0001		P < 0.0001	

Note: Models also adjust for age and sex interactions, disability status at the baseline interview, marital status, race (white versus other), Charlson comorbidity score, and zip code-level measures of education and poverty.

*** Significant at or below the 1 percent level.

** Significant at or below the 5 percent level.

Table 6.8   **Ischemic heart disease: Multinomial regression models for health status outcome five years after baseline survey**

Coefficients (SEs)	Model 1: Panel data		Model 2: 1994 cohort only	
	Disability	Death	Disability	Death
Relevant procedures	−0.005 (0.004)	−.013 (.003)***	−0.007 (0.005)	−0.013 (0.005)**
Beta-blockers	—	—	−0.020 (0.010)**	−0.020 (0.008)**
Aspirin	—	—	−0.009 (0.018)	−0.010 (0.018)
Reperfusion	—	—	−0.014 (0.012)	−0.010 (0.011)
Ace-inhibitors	—	—	0.008 (0.012)	0.008 (0.011)
	Model statistics			
N	3,842		1,202	
F-test	15.39		5.99	
P-value	$P < 0.0001$		$P < 0.0001$	

Note: Models also adjust for age and sex interactions, disability status at the baseline interview, marital status, race (white versus other), zip code-level measures of education and poverty, Charlson comorbidity score, and hospitalizations for stroke, hypertension, heart failure, peripheral vascular disease, and circulatory diseases.

*** Significant at or below the 1 percent level.

** Significant at or below the 5 percent level.

Table 6.9   **Stroke: Multinomial regression models for health status outcome five years after baseline survey**

Coefficients (SEs)	Model 2: 1994 cohort only	
	Disability	Death
Relevant procedures	—	—
Beta-blockers	—	—
Aspirin	0.009 (0.023)	−0.019 (0.021)
Reperfusion	−0.040 (0.014)**	−0.021 (0.016)
Ace-inhibitors	—	
	Model Statistics	
N	1,066	
F-test	3.94	
P-value	$P < 0.0001$	

Note: Model also adjusts for age and sex interactions, disability status at the baseline interview, marital status, race (white versus other), zip code-level measures of education and poverty, Charlson comorbidity score, and hospitalizations for ischemic heart disease, hypertension, heart failure, peripheral vascular disease, and circulatory diseases.

** Significant at or below the 5 percent level.

Table 6.10   **Heart failure and arrhythmia: Multinomial regression models for health status outcome five years after baseline survey**

Coefficients (SEs)	Model 1: Panel Data		Model 2: 1994 cohort only	
	Disability	Death	Disability	Death
Relevant procedures	–0.001 (0.006)	0.002 (0.005)	–0.003 (0.010)	0.005 (0.008)
Beta-blockers	—	—	–0.023 (0.009) **	–0.019 (0.008)**
Aspirin	—	—	—	—
Reperfusion	—	—	—	—
Ace-inhibitors	—	—	0.027 (0.012)**	0.024 (0.011)**
		Model Statistics		
N		3,752		1,228
F-test		16.61		5.45
P-value		$P < 0.0001$		$P < 0.0001$

Note: Models also adjust for age and sex interactions, disability status at the baseline interview, marital status, race (white versus other), zip code-level measures of education and poverty, Charlson comorbidity score, and hospitalizations for stroke, hypertension, ischemic heart disease, peripheral vascular disease, and circulatory diseases.
**Significant at or below the 5 percent level.

on the 1994–1999 cohort, after adjusting for baseline survey year, demographics, and health characteristics. In the 1994–1999 cohort model, beta-blockers were significantly associated with lower disability and mortality, and reperfusion was associated with significantly lower disability. Ace-inhibitors were significantly associated with worse outcomes in this model, including increased disability and death.

Predicted event rates by percentiles of beta-blocker and reperfusion use for all CVD patients are shown in figure 6.5. We estimate that disability and death at follow-up would decline 5 percent and 19 percent, respectively, if all patients moved from areas providing beta-blockers at the 10th percentile level to areas providing beta-blockers at the 90th percentile level. Based on average use in 1984 (48 percent) and 1999 (72 percent), we estimate that increased use of beta-blockers may have led to a 12 percent decline in mortality (from 39.2 percent to 34.5 percent) and a 3 percent decline in disability (from 23.7 percent to 22.9 percent). These declines in mortality and disability associated with increased beta-blocker use represent approximately 194 percent and 38 percent of the observed declines in mortality and disability, respectively, between 1984 and 1999.

The effect of reperfusion on disability across the percentiles of care is quite large. The probability of disability at follow-up declines approximately 22 percent from 27 percent to 21 percent if all patients moved from 10th percentile areas for reperfusion to 90th percentile areas. Based on average use over the study time frame, we estimate that increased use of reperfusion may have led to a 51.5 percent decline in disability, from 41.8 per-

5a. Beta-Blockers

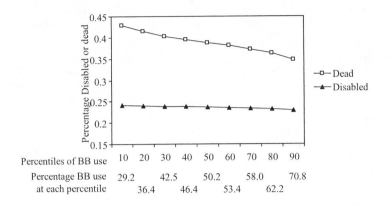

Percentiles of BB use	10	20	30	40	50	60	70	80	90
Percentage BB use at each percentile	29.2		42.5		50.2		58.0		70.8
		36.4		46.4		53.4		62.2	

5b. Reperfusion

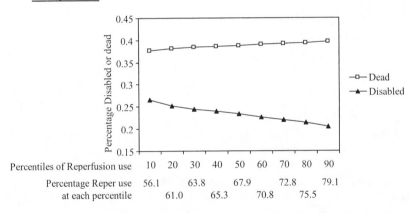

Percentiles of Reperfusion use	10	20	30	40	50	60	70	80	90
Percentage Reper use at each percentile	56.1		63.8		67.9		72.8		79.1
		61.0		65.3		70.8		75.5	

Fig. 6.5   All CVD: Adjusted probability of death and disability at follow-up by percentiles of beta-blocker and reperfusion use

cent to 20.3 percent. The decline in disability associated with reperfusion is substantially greater than the observed decline in disability. However, because of the substantial increase in the use of reperfusion over this time frame, these calculations involve out-of-sample projections and should be viewed cautiously.

Ischemic Heart Disease

In both the panel data model and the model on the 1994–1999 cohort, relevant procedures were associated with significantly lower mortality. The coefficient on the relevant procedures variable in both models was approximately the same (–0.013), suggesting the effect of the procedures on death may not be confounded by inclusion or exclusion of the pharmacological treatments in the two models. In the model on the 1994–1999 cohort, beta-blockers were significantly associated with lower disability and death.

Figure 6.6 shows predicted event rates based on percentiles of relevant procedures and beta-blocker use. If all patients lived in 10th percentile areas (0 percent procedure use), approximately 40 percent would die by follow-up compared to only 28 percent if all patients lived in 90th percentile regions (70 percent procedure use). If all patients were treated at the

6a. Relevant Procedures*

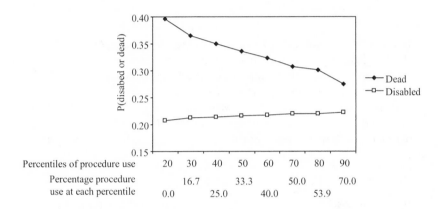

6b. Beta Blockers

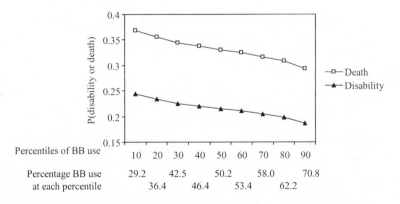

*Adjusted probabilities based on panel data model

Fig. 6.6   IHD: Adjusted probability of death and disability at follow-up by percentiles of invasive procedures and beta-blocker use

average level in 1984 (23 percent) and in 1999 (48 percent), the percentage dead at follow-up would fall from 35.4 percent to 31.1 percent, which accounts for approximately 61 percent of the decline in IHD mortality over time. For beta-blockers, the share disabled and dead at follow-up would decline by approximately 23 percent and 20 percent, respectively, if all patients moved from 10th percentile to 90th percentile treatment areas (29.2 percent versus 70.8 percent). If all patients were treated at the average levels in 1984 (48 percent) and 1999 (72 percent), disability would decline from 21.8 percent at the 1984 level to 18.6 percent at the 1994 level. Mortality would also fall from 33.5 percent to 29.1 percent. These figures represent more than 100 percent of the observed disability decline and 63 percent of the decline in mortality.

Stroke

In the 1994–1999 model with stroke patients, reperfusion was associated with significantly lower disability at follow-up. Predicted event rates for stroke patients, based on percentiles of reperfusion use, are shown in figure 6.7. Increasing reperfusion use from 10th to 90th percentile levels would lower disability approximately 34 percent from 35 percent to 23 percent. Based on the increase in average use from 1984 to 1999, reperfusion explains more than 100 percent of the decline in disability among stroke patients.

Heart Failure and Arrhythmia

In the panel data model, heart failure and arrhythmia patients were significantly less likely to die in 1994–1999 cohort compared to 1984–1989

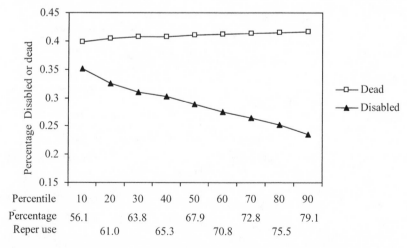

Fig. 6.7   Stroke: Adjusted probability of death and disability at follow-up by percentiles of reperfusion use

(table 6.10). Relevant procedures were not associated with disability or death in either the panel data model or the model on the 1994-1999 cohort. Beta-blockers were associated with lower disability and death, and ace-inhibitors were associated with increased mortality and disability. We estimate that moving all patients from 10th percentile to 90th percentile levels of beta-blocker treatment would lower disability by 21 percent and mortality by 9 percent (fig. 6.8). We also find that increased use of beta-blockers from average levels in 1984 to 1999 would have led to a decline in disability among heart failure patients, in contrast to the observed increase in disability. In addition, this would have led to a 6 percent decline in death over time from 50.6 percent to 47.6 percent, and would explain approximately 53 percent of the observed decline in mortality.

6.4   Interpreting the Results

Use of effective treatments contributed to the decline in disability and death among cardiovascular disease patients. With the exception of ace-inhibitors in the heart failure and arrhythmia and all-CVD models, increased use of effective treatments was associated with improved health outcomes. In particular, increased use of beta-blockers explained more than 100 percent of the decline in disability among IHD and heart failure patients, as well as 63 percent to 53 percent of the decline in mortality over time. Stroke patients benefited from increased use of reperfusion between 1984 and 1999, which explained over 100 percent of the decline in disability. Invasive procedures were important for IHD patients and explained

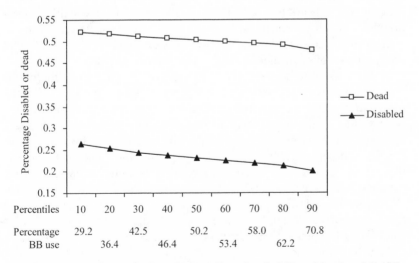

Fig. 6.8   Heart failure and Arrhythmia: Adjusted probability of death and disability at follow-up by percentiles of beta-blocker use

approximately 60 percent of the decline in mortality over the study time frame. The role of beta-blockers in explaining more than 100 percent of the decline in disability for IHD and heart failure patients as well as reperfusion for disability among stroke patients may seem overstated. However, adverse trends in risk factors for cardiovascular disease morbidity and mortality not included in our models, such as diabetes and obesity, were increasing over this time frame (Cooper et al. 2000; Villareal et al. 2005; Cowie et al. 2006). Our results suggest that the excess reduction in disability attributable to improved treatments may be explained by increased risk for morbidity in the elderly population over time.

Improved medical treatment after an acute cardiovascular event resulted in improved survival and reductions in disability. It may also affect medical spending. While we cannot do a complete evaluation of the impact of these changes, we can provide some information. We begin with the change in quality-adjusted life expectancy. To consider how reductions in disability in one year translate into long-term changes in quality-adjusted life expectancy, we estimate regression models for future survival and disability status as a function of disability in a base year. For a cohort in year t, we estimate linear probability models of the form:

$$(3) \qquad \Pr (\text{Alive in year } t + k)_i = \mathbf{X}_{i,t}\, \beta + \gamma\, \text{Disability}_{i,t} + e_{i,t}.$$

The coefficient γ indicates how changes in disability in year t affect long-term health outcomes, and $\mathbf{X}_{i,t}$ is a set of demographic and health status variables. The identifying assumption in equation (3) is that people who are not disabled because of medical treatment are subsequently equivalent in their health to those who never had an incident. This may or may not be the case. If this is not true, and survivors of events are less healthy, conditional on disability status, we will overstate the benefits of reductions in disability. Thus, one should properly view these estimates as an upper bound on the impact of medical interventions to reduce disability.

Figure 6.9 shows the survival rate by year, conditional on disability status in the base survey year. We report the results for the ten years after the survey for the 1989 cohort, and the five years after the survey for the 1994 cohort due to data limitations on long-term follow-up. Not surprisingly, survival for the disabled is below that for the nondisabled by a large margin. The difference is about 20 percentage points, and remains at that level throughout the decade. To forecast mortality beyond the ten-year observation window, we assume that the mortality hazard estimated in 1997–1999 prevails in all subsequent years. Making this assumption, we estimate that those not disabled in 1989 have an average life expectancy of 7.8 years while those disabled in 1989 were expected to live only another 5.1 years on average (table 6.11).

This calculation does not account for the difference in subsequent disability in the next decade. Table 6.12 shows the disability rate for the 1989

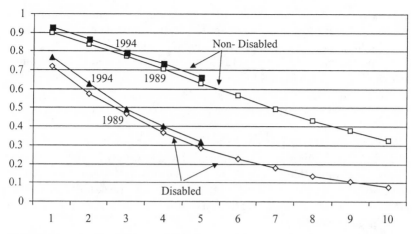

Fig. 6.9   Survival by disability and year

Table 6.11   **The persistence of disability status across surveys**

Cohort	Not disabled at baseline	Disabled at baseline
1989 Cohort		
Pr [Disabled in 1994]	31.4	79.1
Pr [Disabled in 1999]	36.9	72.1
1994 Cohort		
Pr [Disabled in 1999]	25.2	83.9

Note: Disability frequencies are conditional on being alive at follow-up.

Table 6.12   **Life expectancy by disability status**

Measure	Not disabled	Disabled	Difference
Life expectancy	7.8	5.1	2.7
Quality-adjusted life expectancy	6.7	3.0	3.7

Source: Details about the calculations are described in text.

cohort in the 1994 and 1999 surveys, and the disability rate for the 1994 cohort in 1999. In each case, we condition disability status on being alive at the end date. Seventy-nine percent of people who were disabled in 1989 and still alive in 1994 were also disabled in 1994, compared to 31 percent of those not disabled in 1989. This pattern repeats itself in 1999 and is true for the 1994 cohort as well.

To estimate quality-adjusted life expectancy, we interpolate disability rates between 1989 and 1994, and 1994 and 1999. In each case, we assume that disability rates change at a common rate each year of the interval. We also extrapolate disability rates after 1999, using the annual change between 1994 and 1999. As a rough approximation, we assume that one year in a disabled state is equivalent to 0.5 quality-adjusted life years.

As the second row of table 6.12 shows, quality-adjusted life expectancy is lower in each case than is life expectancy, but the difference between the disabled and nondisabled is similar to the unadjusted estimates. The increase in quality-adjusted life expectancy associated with not being disabled is 3.7 years.

The value of this improvement in life expectancy depends on the value of a year of life. Following a substantial recent literature (Viscusi and Aldy 2003), we assume that a year of life in good health is worth $100,000 (in 1992 dollars). We also assume that future values are discounted at a 3 percent real rate of interest. Using these assumptions, we estimate the value of disability prevention to be $316,000.

These benefits need to be weighed against the cost of reducing disability. These costs have two parts. The first is the initial treatment cost that led to the reduction in disability. To measure these costs, we use data on hospitalization spending for the 1989 cohort in the year after the CVD admission.[9] The one-year interval is relatively common in studying acute treatment for cardiovascular disease (Cutler and McClellan 2001; Skinner, Staiger, and Fisher 2006). The limitation to hospital costs is because only those data are reliable prior to 1991. We inflated all costs to a common year of 1992 using the implicit GDP Price Deflator (Economic Report of the President 1997). We estimate that in the year after the CVD event, hospital spending averages $8,610 for patients who do not receive relevant procedures and $16,332 for patients receiving relevant procedures.

Although treatment costs are approximately twice as high for respondents receiving appropriate treatments, these costs may be offset by lower yearly spending in subsequent years among survivors. A previous study of 1982 and 1984 NLTCS respondents found annual per capita spending by Medicare for respondents without any ADL or IADL limitations was approximately $3,275, compared to $7,400 for respondents with at least four ADL and five IADL impairments, and $13,100 for institutionalized respondents. These data suggest that the costs of intensive medical treatments that prevent or delay disability may be offset by lower annual average spending among healthier beneficiaries.

More recent studies using the Medicare Current Beneficiary Survey found similar lifetime spending between nondisabled and disabled seventy-year-olds, but life expectancy was approximately 2.7 years longer among the nondisabled (Lubitz et al. 2003). This provides further evidence that av-

9. By definition, all participants in the 1989 cohort had at least one CVD admissions between 1984 and 1989. We averaged costs across all CVD hospitalizations for respondents with multiple relevant hospitalizations.

erage annual spending may be lower among the nondisabled relative to the disabled. However, another recent study found spending on the nondisabled is growing faster than spending on the disabled (Chernew et al. 2005). Whether increased spending on intensive medical care treatments, such as those for cardiovascular disease, continues to increase life expectancy and reduce average annual yearly spending among the nondisabled relative to the disabled will require further investigation.

6.5 Conclusions

Examining disability associated with cardiovascular disease leads to several important results. Reduced disability associated with cardiovascular disease accounts for a significant part of the total reduction in disability— between 19 and 22 percent. The evidence suggests that improvements in medical care, including both increased use of relevant procedures and pharmaceuticals, led to a significant part of this decline.

While precise data on the implications of reduced disability are lacking, the possible impact of disability reductions is staggering. We estimate that preventing disability after an acute event can add as much as 3.7 years of quality-adjusted life expectancy, or perhaps $316,000 of value. The cost of this change is much smaller. The initial treatment costs range from $8,610 to $16,332, depending on procedure use. Further, recent cost analyses report that annual Medicare spending was lower for the nondisabled compared to the disabled, which suggests that higher treatment costs may be offset by lower future spending among a more healthy population. By virtually any measure, therefore, medical technology after acute cardiovascular episodes is worth the cost.

The major issue raised by our results is whether these conclusions extend to other conditions. Disability reductions are complex, and will certainly involve medical as well as nonmedical factors. Sorting these out for other conditions is a high priority for future research.

References

Adams, H., R. Adams, G. Del Zoppo, and L. B. Goldstein. 2005. Guidelines for the early management of patients with ischemic stroke. 2005 Guidelines Update: A scientific statement from the stroke council of the American Heart Association/ American Stroke Association. *Stroke* 36:916–21.

Adams, H. P., Jr., G. Del Zoppo, M. J. Alberts, D. L. Bhatt, L. Brass, A. Furlan, R. L. Grubb, et al. 2007. Guidelines for the early management of adults with ischemic stroke: A guideline from the American Heart Association/American Stroke Association Stroke Council, Clinical Cardiology Council, Cardiovascular Radiology and Intervention Council, and the Atherosclerotic Peripheral

Vascular Disease and Quality of Care Outcomes in Research Interdisciplinary Working Groups: The American Academy of Neurology affirms the value of this guideline as an educational tool for neurologists. *Stroke* 38:1655–1711.

American Heart Association. 2006. Medication information and drug classification http://www.americanheart.org/presenter.jhtml?identifier=70.

Antman, E. M., D. T. Anbe, P. W. Armstrong, E. R. Bates, L. A. Green, M. Hand, J. S. Hochman, et al. 2004. ACC/AHA guidelines for the management of patients with ST-elevation myocardial infarction: Executive summary: A report of the ACC/AHA task force on practice guidelines (committee to revise the 1999 guidelines on the management of patients with acute myocardial infarction). *Journal of the American College of Cardiology* 44:671–719.

Appelros, P., I. Nydevik, M. Viitanen. 2003. Poor outcome after first-ever stroke: Predictors for death, dependency, and recurrent stroke within the first year. *Stroke* 34:122–26.

Borkon, A. M., G. F. Muehlebach, J. House, S. P. Marso, and J. A. Spertus. 2002. A comparison of the recovery of health status after percutaneous coronary intervention and coronary artery bypass. *Annals of Thoracic Surgery* 74:1526–30.

Braunwald, E., E. M. Antman, J. W. Beasley, R. M. Califf, M. D. Cheitlin, J. S. Hochman, R. H. Jones, et al. 2002. ACC/AHA 2002 guideline update for the management of patients with unstable angina and non-ST segment elevation myocardial infarction: A report of the American College of Cardiology/American Heart Association task force on practice guidelines (Committee on the management of patients with unstable angina). Accessed at http://www.ncbi.nlrm.nih.gov/pubrmed/12383588

Chernew, M. E., D. P. Goldman, F. Pan, and B. Shang. 2005. Disability and health care spending among Medicare beneficiaries. *Health Affairs* 24(2): W5-R42–W5-R51.

Clark, W. M., S. Wissman, G. W. Albers, J. H. Jhamandas, K. P. Madden, and S. Hamilton. 1999. Recombinant tissue-type plasminogen activator (alteplase) for ischemic stroke 3 to 5 hours after symptom onset. *Journal of the American Medical Association* 282(21): 2019–26.

Cooper, R., J. Cutler, P. Desvigne-Nickens, S. P. Fortmann, L. Friedman, R. Havlik, G. Hogelin et al. 2000. Trends and disparities in coronary heart disease, stroke and other cardiovascular diseases in the United States: Findings of the National Conference on Cardiovascular Disease Prevention. *Circulation* 102:3137–47.

Cowie, C. C., K. F. Rust, D. D. Byrd-Holt, M. S. Eberhardt, K. M. Flegal, M. M. Engelgau, S. H. Sydah, D. E. Williams, L. S. Geiss, and E. W. Gregg. 2006. Prevalence of diabetes and impaired fasting glucose in adults in the U.S. population. *Diabetes Care* 29:1263–68.

Crimmins, E. M., M. D. Hayward, and Y. Saito. 1994. Changing mortality and morbidity rates and the health status and life expectancy of the older population. *Demography* 31 (1): 159–75.

Crimmins, E. M., Y. Saito, and D. Ingegneri. 1989. Changes in life expectancy and disability-free life expectancy in the United States. *Population and Development Review* 15 (2): 235–67.

Cutler, D. M., and S. Kadiyala. 2003. The return to biomedical research: Treatment and behavioral effects. In *Measuring the gains from medical research: An economic approach,* ed. K. M. Murphy and R. H. Topel, 110–162. Chicago: University of Chicago Press.

Cutler, D. M., and M. McClellan. 2001. Is technological change in medicine worth it? *Health Affairs* 20 (5): 11–29.

Deyo, R. A., D. C. Cherkin, and M. A. Ciol. 1992. Adapting a clinical comorbidity index for use with ICD-9-CM administrative databases. *Journal of Clinical Epidemiology* 45 (6): 613–19.

Economic Report of the President. 1997. Accessed at http://www.gpoaccess.gov/usbudget/fy98/pdf/erp.pdf Washington, D.C.: United States Government Printing Office.

Fisher, E. S., D. E. Wennberg, T. A. Stukel, D. J. Gottlieb, F. L. Lucas, and E. L. Pinder. 2003a. The implications of regional variations in Medicare spending. Part 2: Health outcomes and satisfaction with care. *Annals of Internal Medicine* 138:288–98.

————. 2003b. The implications of regional variations in Medicare spending. Part 1: The content, quality and accessibility of care. *Annals of Internal Medicine* 138:273–87.

Freemantle, N., J. Cleland, P. Young, J. Mason, and J. Harrison. 1999. B blockade after myocardial infarction: Systematic review and meta regression analysis. *British Medical Journal* 318:1730–37.

Glader, E.-L., B. Stegmayr, B. Norring, A. Terent, K. Hulter-Asberg, P.-O. Wester, and K. Asplund. 2003. Sex differences in management and outcome after stroke: A Swedish national perspective. *Stroke* 34:1970–75.

Gottlieb, S. S., R. J. McCarter, and R. A. Vogel. 1998. Effect of beta blockade on mortality among high-risk and low-risk patients after myocardial infarction. *New England Journal of Medicine* 339 (8): 489–97.

Heidenreich, P. A., and M. McClellan. 2001. Trends in treatment and outcomes for acute myocardial infarction: 1975–1995. *American Journal of Medicine* 110:165–74.

Hennekens, C. H., C. M. Albert, S. L. Godfried, J. M. Gaziano, and J. E. Buring. 1996. Adjunctive drug therapy of acute myocardial infarction—evidence from clinical trials. *New England Journal of Medicine* 335 (22): 1660–67.

Henon, H., O. Godefroy, D. Leys, F. Mounier-Vehier, C. Lucas, P. Rondepierre, A. Duhamel, and J. P. Pruvo. 1995. Early predictors of death and disability after acute cerebral ischemic event. *Stroke* 26:392–98.

Hlatky, M. A., W. J. Rogers, I. Johnstone, and D. Boothroyd. 1997. Medical care costs and quality of life after randomization to coronary angioplasty or coronary bypass surgery. *New England Journal of Medicine* 336:92–99.

Hunt, S. A., W. T. Abraham, M. H. Chin, A. M. Feldman, G. S. Francis, T. G. Ganiats, M. Jessup, et al. 2005. ACC/AHA 2005 guideline update for the diagnosis and management of chronic heart failure in the adult: Summary article: A report of the American College of Cardiology/American Heart Association task force on practice guidelines (writing committee to update the 2001 guidelines for the evaluation and management of heart failure). *Circulation* 112: e154–e235.

Jencks, S. F., T. Cuerdon, D. R. Burwen, B. Fleming, P. M. Houck, A. E. Kussmaul, D. S. Nilasena, D. L. Ordin, and D. R. Arday. 2000. Quality of medical care delivered to Medicare beneficiaries: A profile at state and national levels. *Journal of the American Medical Association* 284:1670–76.

Kattainen, A., A. Reunanen, S. Koskinen, T. Martelin, P. Knekt, P. Sainio, T. Harkanen, and A. Aromaa. 2004. Secular changes in disability among middle-aged and elderly Finns with and without coronary heart disease from 1978–1980 to 2000–2001. *Annals of Epidemiology* 14:479–85.

Krumholz, H. M., M. J. Radford, E. F. Ellerbeck, J. Hennen, T. P. Meehan, M. Petrillo, Y. Wang, and S. F. Jencks. 1996. Aspirin for secondary prevention after acute myocardial infarction in the elderly: Prescribed use and outcomes. *Annals of Internal Medicine* 124:292–98.

Krumholz, H. M., M. J. Radford, E. F. Ellerbeck, J. Hennen, T. P. Meehan, M. Petrillo, Y. Wang, T. F. Kresowik, and S. F. Jencks. 1995. Aspirin in the treatment of acute myocardial infarction in elderly Medicare beneficiaries. *Circulation* 92:2841–7.

Krumholz, H. M., M. J. Radford, Y. Wang, J. Chen, A. Heiat, and T. Marciniak. 1998. National use and effectiveness of β-blockers for the treatment of elderly patients after acute myocardial infarction: National cooperative cardiovascular project. *Journal of the American Medical Association* 280 (7): 623–29.

Lubitz, J., L. Cai, E. Kramarow, and H. Lentzner. 2003. Health, life expectancy and health care spending among the elderly. *New England Journal of Medicine* 349:1048–55.

Manton, K. G., L. S. Corder, and E. Stallard. 1993. Estimates of change in chronic disability and institutional incidence and prevalence rates in the U.S. elderly population from the 1982, 1984, and 1989 National Long Term Care Survey. *Journal of Gerontology* 48 (4): S153–66.

————. 1997. Chronic disability trends in elderly United States populations: 1982–1994. *Proceedings of the National Academy of Sciences of the United States of America* 94:2593–98.

Manton, K. G., and X. Gu. 2001. Changes in the prevalence of chronic disability in the United States black and nonblack population above age 65 from 1982 to 1999. *Proceedings of the National Academy of Sciences of the United States of America* 98 (11): 6354–59.

Manton, K. G., E. Stallard, and L. S. Corder. 1997. Changes in the age dependence of mortality and disability: Cohort and other determinants. *Demography* 34 (1): 135–57.

Marciniak, T. A., E. F. Ellerbeck, M. J. Radford, T. F. Kresowik, J. A. Gold, H. M. Krumholz, C. I. Kiefe, R. M. Allman, R. A. Vogel, and S. F. Jencks. 1998. Improving the quality of care for Medicare patients with acute myocardial infarction: Results from the cooperative cardiovascular project. *Journal of the American Medical Association* 279 (17): 1351–57.

McGovern, P. G., D. R. Jacobs, E. Shahar, D. K. Arnett, A. R. Folsom, H. Blackburn, and R. V. Luepker. 2001. Trends in acute coronary heart disease mortality, morbidity and medical care from 1985 through 1997: The Minnesota Heart Study. *Circulation* 104:19–24.

McGovern, P. G., J. S. Pankow, E. Shahar, K. M. Doliszny, A. R. Folsom, H. Blackburn, and R. V. Luepker. 1996. Recent trends in acute coronary heart disease: Mortality, morbidity, medical care, and risk factors. *New England Journal of Medicine* 334:884–90.

The National Institute of Neurological Disorders and Stroke rt-PA Stroke Study Group. 1995. Tissue plasminogen activator for acute ischemic stroke. *New England Journal of Medicine* 333 (24): 1581–87.

O'Connor, G. T., H. B. Quinton, N. D. Traven, L. D. Ramunno, T. A. Dodds, T. A. Marciniak, and J. E. Wennberg. 1999. Geographic variation in the treatment of acute myocardial infarction: The Cooperative Cardiovascular Project. *Journal of the American Medical Association* 281 (7): 627–33.

Pfisterer, M., P. Buser, S. Osswald, U. Allermann, W. Armann, W. Angehrn, E. Eeckhout, et al. 2003. Outcome of elderly patients with chronic symptomatic coronary artery disease with an invasive vs optimised medical treatment strategy: One year results of the randomized TIME trial. *Journal of the American Medical Association* 289:1117–23.

Pocock, S. J., R. A. Henderson, T. Clayton, G. H. Lyman, and D. A. Chamberlain. 2000. Quality of life after coronary angioplasty or continued medical treatment for angina: Three-year follow-up in the RITA-2 trial. *Journal of the American College of Cardiology* 35:907–14.

Pohjasvaara, T., T. Erkinjuntti, R. Vataja, and M. Kaste. 1997. Comparison of stroke features and disability in daily life in patients with ischemic stroke aged 55 to 70 and 71 to 85 years. *Stroke* 28:729–35.

Prencipe, M., C. Ferretti, A. R. Casini, M. Santini, F. Giubilei, and F. Culasso. 1997. Stroke, disability, and dementia. *Stroke* 28:531–36.

Rogers, W. J., J. Coggin, B. J. Gersh, L. D. Fisher, W. O. Myers, A. Oberman, and L. T. Sheffield. 1990. Ten-year follow-up of quality of life in patients randomized to receive medical therapy or coronary artery bypass graft surgery: The coronary artery surgery study (CASS). *Circulation* 82:1647–58.

Rosamond, W. D., L. E. Chambless, A. R. Folsom, L. S. Cooper, D. E. Conwill, L. Clegg, C.-H. Wang, and G. Heiss. 1998. Trends in the incidence of myocardial infarction and in mortality due to coronary heart disease, 1987–1994. *New England Journal of Medicine* 339 (13): 861–67.

Shlipak, M. G., W. S. Browner, H. Noguchi, B. Massie, C. D. Frances, and M. McClellan. 2001. Comparison of the effects of angiotensin converting-enzyme inhibitors and beta blockers on survival in elderly patients with reduced left ventricular function after myocardial infarction. *American Journal of Medicine* 110:425–33.

Singer, B. H., and K. G. Manton. 1998. The effects of health changes on projections of health service needs for the elderly population of the United States. *Proceedings of the National Academy of Sciences of the United States of America* 95 (26): 15618–22.

Skinner, J. S., D. O. Staiger, and E. S. Fisher. 2006. Is technological change in medicine always worth it? The case of acute myocardial infarction. *Health Affairs* 25 (2): W34–W47.

Soumerai, S. B., T. J. McLaughlin, E. Speigelman, G. Hertzmark, G. Thibault, and L. Goldman. 1997. Adverse outcomes of underuse of beta-blockers in elderly survivors of acute myocardial infarction. *Journal of the American Medical Association* 277 (2): 115–21.

Strauss, W. E., T. Fortin, P. Hartigan, E. D. Folland, and A. F. Parisi. 1995. A comparison of quality of life scores in patients with angina pectoris after angioplasty compared with after medical therapy. *Circulation* 92:1710–19.

Stukel, T. A., F. L. Lucas, and D. E. Wennberg. 2005. Long-term outcomes of regional variations in intensity of invasive vs. medical management of Medicare patients with acute myocardial infarction. *Journal of the American Medical Association* 293:1329–37.

Sytkowski, P. A., R. B. D'Agostino, A. Belanger, and W. B. Kannel. 1996. Sex and time trends in cardiovascular disease incidence and mortality: The Framingham Heart Study, 1950–1989. *American Journal of Epidemiology* 143(4): 338–50.

Vaccarino, V., S. S. Rathore, N. K. Wenger, P. D. Frederick, J. L. Abramson, H. V. Barron, A. Manhapra, S. Mallik, and H. M. Krumholz. 2005. Sex and racial differences in the management of acute myocardial infarction, 1994 through 2002. *New England Journal of Medicine* 353 (7): 671–82.

Villareal, D. T., C. M. Apovian, R. F. Kushner, and S. Klein. 2005. Obesity in older adults: Technical review and position statement of the American Society for Nutrition and NAASO, The Obesity Society. *American Journal of Clinical Nutrition* 82:923–34.

Viscusi, W. K., and J. E. Aldy. 2003. The value of a statistical life: A critical review of market estimates throughout the world. *Journal of Risk and Uncertainty* 27 (1): 5–76.

Vitagliano, G., J. P. Curtis, P. Jeptha, J. Concato, A. R. Feinstein, M. J. Radford, and H. M. Krumholz. 2004. Association between functional status and use and effectiveness of beta-blocker prophylaxis in elderly survivors of acute myocardial infarction. *Journal of the American Geriatric Society* 52:496–501.

Waidmann, T. A., J. Bound, and M. Schoenbaum. 1995. The illusion of failure: Trends in the self-reported health of the U.S. elderly. *The Milbank Quarterly* 73 (2): 253–87.

Zhu, L., L. Fratiglioni, Z. Guo, H. Aguero-Torres, B. Winblad, and M. Viitanen. 1998. Association of stroke with dementia, cognitive impairment, and functional disability in the very old: A population-based study. *Stroke* 29: 2094–99.

7

Are Baby Boomers Aging Better Than Their Predecessors? Trends in Overweight, Arthritis, and Mobility Difficulty

Suzanne G. Leveille, Christina C. Wee, and
Lisa I. Iezzoni

7.1 Introduction

Several reports describe imminent profound demographic shifts with the aging of the post-World War II Baby Boom generation, persons born from 1946 through 1964 (Day 1993; Centers for Disease Control (CDC) 2003; Kinsella and Velkoff 2001). The elderly population in the United States is expected to double in the thirty years from 2000 to 2030 (Kinsella and Velkoff 2001). Better understanding of the health risk and health status trends of the aging Baby Boomers will enhance our preparations to meet the health care needs of this new generation of elders. The first of the Baby Boomers will reach age sixty-five in the year 2011. Preventing and postponing disability will continue to be important goals for maintaining health in old age for the Baby Boom generation. Although studies have shown declines in disability rates in the older population in recent decades (Freedman, Martin, and Schoeni 2002; Manton, Corder, and Stallard 1997; Manton and Gu 2001), worrisome health behavior trends across all ages in the United States ultimately may reverse the progress in reducing

Suzanne G. Leveille, Ph.D., is Assistant Professor of Medicine, Harvard Medical School, and a Research Associate in the Division of General Medicine and Primary Care, Beth Israel Deaconess Medical Center, Boston. Christina C. Wee, M.D., M.P.H., is Assistant Professor of Medicine, Harvard Medical School, and an Associate in Medicine in the Division of General Medicine and Primary Care, Beth Israel Deaconess Medical Center, Boston. Lisa I. Iezzoni, M.D., M.Sc., is Professor of Medicine, Harvard Medical School, and Associate Director, Institute for Health Policy, Massachusetts General Hospital.

We thank Mary Beth Hamel, M.D., for her valuable contribution. This work was supported by the Arthritis Foundation, the National Bureau of Economic Research with funding from the National Institute on Aging grants P30 AG12810 and R01 AG19805, and the Mary Woodard Lasker Charitable Trust and Michael E. DeBakey Foundation.

disability. It is critical that we closely monitor trends in health in this very large cohort of aging persons in the United States.

Behavioral factors, such as physical activity, weight management, and avoidance of smoking, are key to reducing population disability, often related to musculoskeletal impairments. Unfortunately, these factors, notably physical activity and obesity, are showing hazardous trends, especially among Baby Boomers (Manson et al. 2004; Flegal et al. 2002). Access to better nutrition has improved, but so has access to high fat, high carbohydrate foods, via fast food restaurants and the wide availability of inexpensive prepared foods, endemic to harried lifestyles. Dietary patterns show a substantial increase in carbohydrate and total energy intake in the last thirty years (CDC 2004). Rates of obesity have increased dramatically and physical activity rates have remained unchanged in recent years.

Substantial differences in prevalence of overweight (Body Mass Index [BMI] ≥ 25) have been observed among women but not men across race groups. More than three-quarters of non-Hispanic black women aged twenty and older were overweight in 1999–2002, compared to less than 60 percent of non-Hispanic white women. Prevalence of overweight in Mexican American women was intermediate (72 percent) (Hedley et al. 2004).

In coming decades, these lifestyle factors are likely to contribute to large increases in rates of arthritis, as well as diabetes and cardiovascular disease. Recent projections show that the aging Baby Boomers will double the numbers of persons aged sixty-five and older with arthritis or chronic joint symptoms (CJS) by the year 2030, when the last Baby Boomers will turn sixty-five years old (CDC 2003). However, these calculations assume stability of arthritis prevalence and likely underestimate the impending surge in arthritis rates among more obese Baby Boomers. At the population level, disability and health utilization accompany higher rates of arthritis (Dunlop et al. 2003).

To examine trends in prevalence of overweight, arthritis, and mobility difficulty among Baby Boomers and their predecessors, we analyzed data from successive waves of the National Health and Nutrition Examination Survey (NHANES) from 1971 through 2002. In addition, we studied the relationship between overweight, arthritis, and mobility difficulty among the birth cohorts using recent waves of the NHANES.

7.2 Study Design

We analyzed successive waves of data from the National Health and Nutrition Examination Survey (NHANES), which began in 1971 and is available from the National Center for Health Statistics up through the 1999–2002 survey. These publicly available data were exempted from review by our Institutional Review Board.

The NHANES has collected detailed health information from interviews and medical examinations on nationally representative samples of U.S. residents across age groups. The NHANES uses a complex multistage probability cluster sampling design and provides sophisticated weighting approaches to yield national prevalence estimates. The NHANES I, conducted from 1971 to 1974, included medical history interviews and examinations with 18,836 persons aged twelve to seventy-four years. The NHANES II, conducted from 1976 to 1980, included interviews and examinations of 18,447 persons aged twelve to seventy-four years. The NHANES III was conducted in two three-year phases from 1988 to 1994 and interviewed 20,050 adults aged seventeen and older. In general, examinations took place in the NHANES Mobile Examination Center (MEC), a large trailer equipped with various testing technologies; very few were conducted in participants' homes. The most recent wave of NHANES began in 1999 and continues today in two-year cycles. Data are available on the 1999–2002 interviews of 21,004 persons and include medical conditions interviews of 10,291 adults aged twenty and older.

During each wave of the NHANES, study examiners measured weight and height. For this study, body mass index (BMI: weight in kilograms/ height in meters squared) was calculated and standard cut points were used to classify overweight (BMI $\geq$ 25 kg/m^2) and obesity (BMI $\geq$ 30 kg/m^2). Each wave of the NHANES interviews asked participants if a physician ever told them they had arthritis. Substantial variations across waves of the NHANES in clinical evaluations for arthritis, such as x-rays and physical examinations, precluded our using data other than self-report to determine prevalence of arthritis. For example, NHANES III performed hand and knee x-rays, physician's joint examinations, and physical function tests only on persons aged sixty years and older. Despite limitations of the self-report information, the participant interview question used to assess physician-diagnosed arthritis remained essentially the same over the 4 waves of NHANES that we analyzed.

Mobility difficulty was measured only during the two most recent waves of the NHANES. We classified mobility disability as report of any difficulty or inability in walking 1/4 mile or climbing ten steps without the use of special equipment. These items were not included in the earlier NHANES I and II. Thus, for each of the ten-year birth cohorts, we determined the prevalence of mobility difficulty using NHANES III and 1999–2002 data.

7.2.1   Birth Cohort Analyses

In order to examine birth cohort trends, we grouped the Baby Boom and Silent Generations into four, ten-year birth cohorts (born 1926–1935, 1936–1945, 1946–1955, and 1956–1965). This birth cohort classification, shown in figure 7.1, allowed us to depict trends in prevalence of overweight across waves of the NHANES from 1971 through 2002. For example, we followed the oldest ten-year age group, those born from 1926 to 1935, with

Young Baby Boom (born 1956-1965)
25-34y   35-44y

Older Baby Boom (born 1946-1955)
23-32y   35-44y   45-54y

Young Silent Generation (born 1936-1945)
28-37y   33-42y   45-54y   55-64y

Older Silent Generation (born 1926-1935)
38-47y   43-52y   55-64y   65-74y

1971-74   1976-80   1988-94   1999-2002
NHANES

Fig. 7.1   Birth cohort analysis schema showing the ages of the birth cohorts at the time of each wave of the NHANES

Note: Age ranges were based on interviewees' ages at midpoint of each survey period.

four waves of NHANES data. This birth cohort, the older Silent Generation, was thirty-eight to forty-seven years of age at the time of the first NHANES and sixty-five to seventy-four years of age during the most recent NHANES, in 1999 to 2002. During these same time periods, the next younger birth cohort, the young Silent Generation, was aged twenty-eight to thirty-seven years and fifty-five to sixty-four years, respectively. For the older Baby Boom generation, born from 1946 to 1955, there were only three waves of NHANES during which all members of this cohort were over twenty-one years of age. Data from NHANES I for the older Baby Boom cohort were not used because members of this cohort were below age twenty-one at the time of the survey. The youngest cohort, the young Baby Boom generation, was over age twenty-one only during the two most recent waves, NHANES III and NHANES 1999–2002.

The NHANES datasets included age in years (but not birth date) for all participants. For our analyses, we assumed age at interview was age at the midpoint of the survey for all waves. For NHANES III, which took place over six years from 1988–1994 in two phases of three years each, the longest survey period of the four waves, the dataset included information about whether participants were examined in the first or second phases. Because the six year interval of the NHANES III survey data collection was longer than the other surveys, we added one year to the age of Phase 1 participants and subtracted one year from the age of Phase 2 participants in the NHANES III, then assumed age to be the midpoint of the six year survey period.

We used SAS for Windows version 8.01 (SAS Institute, Cary, NC) for all analyses and SAS-callable SUDAAN version 8 (RTI, Research Triangle Park, NC) for analyses that accounted for cluster design and the complex multistage sampling. Appropriate interview and examination sampling weights were applied in all prevalence estimation. Adjusted odds ratios (OR) and 95 percent confidence intervals (CI) were derived from multivariate logistic regression modeling using SUDAAN, also accounting for weighting and complex sampling design using the Taylor series method. Due to the high prevalence of mobility disability and subsequent concern about overestimating the prevalence ratio, odds ratios were converted to approximate relative risks (RR) using the method described by Zhang and Yu (1998). Multivariate models were adjusted for age, sex, and race/ethnicity.

7.3   Results

The prevalence of overweight increased profoundly according to age among men and women in each of the ten-year birth cohorts during the three decades beginning in 1971 (fig. 7.2). With each younger birth cohort, the proportion with overweight rose markedly at successively younger ages. Specifically, members of the Baby Boom generation had substantially greater prevalence of overweight at younger ages than their predecessors in the Silent Generation, a difference that is most evident in the thirty-five to forty-four year old age range. This was the only age group for which NHANES data was available for the four birth cohorts (fig. 7.2). In the thirty-five to forty-four year age group, 66 percent to 70 percent of the youngest Baby Boomer men were overweight compared to 56 percent to 62 percent of their counterparts in the Silent Generation. Among women in the Baby Boom generation at ages thirty-five to forty-four, 50 percent to 60 percent were overweight or obese compared to 38 percent to 42 percent of same-aged women in the Silent Generation. In both women and men, overweight prevalence in the young Baby Boom cohort at ages twenty-five to forty-four years was comparable to that of the Silent Generation cohorts when they were ten to twenty years older. Overall, the rate of increase in prevalence of overweight among Baby Boomers appeared steeper over the three decades than in the Silent Generation (fig. 7.2).

In general, the prevalence of arthritis increased as expected with age across the birth cohorts, but we did not observe substantial intercohort differences in arthritis prevalence (data not shown). However, the older Baby Boomer cohort may have been too young during the most recent

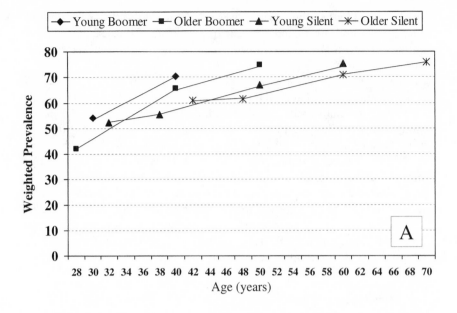

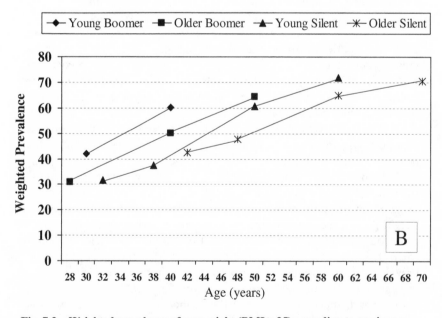

Fig. 7.2 Weighted prevalence of overweight (BMI ≥ 25) according to age in men (*A*) and women (*B*) within ten-year birth cohorts, NHANES 1971–1974, 1976–1980, 1988–1994, 1999–2002

NHANES—average approximately age fifty—to evaluate if they were more likely to have arthritis than previous birth cohorts. Thus, we examined the distribution of BMI among the proportion of each NHANES population that was aged fifty-five to sixty-four years at the time of the respective surveys, an age group that experiences a substantial onset of arthritis (fig. 7.3). Across the waves of the NHANES, more persons aged fifty-five to sixty-four with arthritis were also obese, compared to persons without arthritis. Conversely, the proportion of nonoverweight persons in this age group generally declined over time, but more so among persons with arthritis than without arthritis.

In the decade between NHANES III and NHANES 1999–2002, men and women of both cohorts of the Silent Generation showed substantial increases in prevalence of mobility disability (fig. 7.4). In contrast, the prevalence of mobility disability among the Baby Boomers, all of whom were less than age fifty-five, was essentially unchanged during the ten year period. Of note, the disability prevalence was progressively lower in each of the Baby Boomer cohorts than their same-aged counterparts both in the older Baby Boom cohort and in the Silent Generation. This is portrayed by the gap between the lines in figure 7.4 for the young Baby Boomers and the older Baby Boomers, then also between the older Baby Boomers and the young Silent Generation cohort. For example, when the young Silent Generation women were aged forty-five to fifty-four, 20 percent reported mobility disability, compared to 12.5 percent of the same-aged older Baby Boomer women. Even among the youngest Baby Boom cohort, the proportion with disability at ages thirty-five to forty-four was lower than same-aged women of the older Baby Boom (8.6 percent and 13.1 percent respectively). Similar differences were observed in the men, who had lower disability prevalence than women overall.

To understand the association between arthritis and mobility difficulty among middle-aged adults (aged forty-six to seventy-five years), we examined changes in arthritis prevalence according to disability status. The proportion of persons aged forty-six to seventy-five years with mobility difficulty who reported having arthritis increased from 1990 to 2000 (56 percent to 63 percent), while the proportion without disability who reported arthritis decreased somewhat from 30 percent to 26 percent. Conversely, the likelihood that persons with arthritis would report mobility difficulty increased over the decade from 1990 to 2000 among adults aged forty-six to seventy-five years, from 86 percent to 168 percent (table 7.1), even after adjustment for overweight and obesity. Obesity was strongly associated with mobility disability in the two recent waves of the NHANES in persons aged forty-six to seventy-five years, ages when both arthritis prevalence and disability prevalence climbs dramatically (table 7.1). Persons who were overweight but not obese did not have an increased likelihood of having mobility disability after controlling for self-reported arthritis.

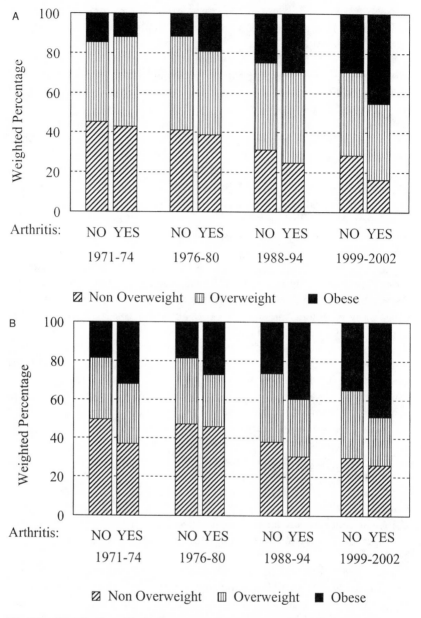

Fig. 7.3 Distribution of body mass categories among men (*A*) and women (*B*) aged 55 to 64 years with and without arthritis, NHANES 1971–2002

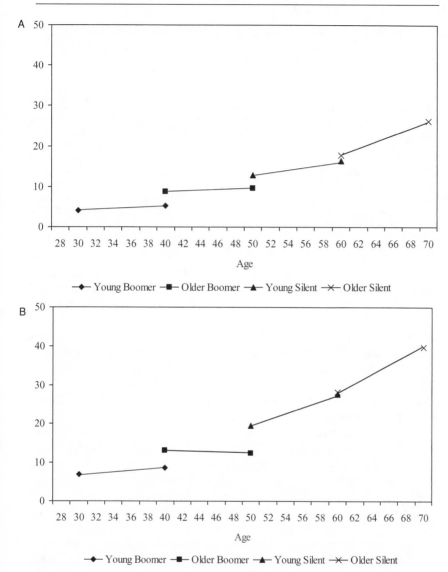

Fig. 7.4   **Weighted prevalence of mobility difficulty in men (*A*) and women (*B*) within ten year age cohorts, NHANES 1988–1994, 1999–2002**

7.4   Discussion

Our findings portray a mixed picture of health and health risks of the Baby Boomer cohort compared to their predecessors. The drastic increases in overweight and obesity in the last two decades raise serious concerns about future health and physical functioning of the aging Baby Boom gen-

Table 7.1   Relationship between overweight, self-reported arthritis and risk
             for mobility difficulty among persons aged 46 to 75 years,
             United States, NHANES

	NHANES III 1988–1994 RR (95% C.I.)[a]	NHANES 1999–2002 RR (95% C.I.)[a]
Overweight (BMI 25–29)	1.08 (0.93–1.26)	1.08 (0.90–1.27)
Obese (BMI ≥ 30)	1.58 (1.32–1.86)	2.02 (1.69–2.40)
Arthritis	1.86 (1.69–2.04)	2.68 (2.34–3.05)

Note: Mobility difficulty defined as any reported difficulty walking 1/4 mile or climbing ten steps.
[a]Derived from logistic regression models adjusted for age, sex, race/ethnicity, accounting for complex sampling design effects; performed using Taylor series method in SUDAAN. The OR's corrected to RR approximation using method of Zhang and Yu (1998).

eration in the United States. Notably, the Baby Boomers will have spent several more years in an overweight or obese condition than their predecessors in the Silent Generation. In their thirties and forties, many more Baby Boomers were overweight or obese than members of the Silent Generation when they were in their thirties and forties. Also, the time trend toward increasing prevalence of overweight shows no evidence of leveling off even among older adults.

Arthritis prevalence may or may not change with the aging of the Baby Boomers. The NHANES data were inconclusive because the Baby Boomer cohort is only now approaching the age when arthritis prevalence begins to climb. Given the risks for arthritis related to obesity, we might have expected to see an indication that arthritis may be increasing more rapidly in the Baby Boomers than compared to the Silent Generation. Subsequent NHANES should yield answers to this question within the next decade. However, other factors may account for a possible lack of change in arthritis prevalence. For example, persons in the Silent Generation may have been subjected to greater occupational hazards that contribute to arthritis or possibly had more injuries that predispose to arthritis in later life. Findings from the first NHANES showed occupational factors to be more important than obesity as a contributor to arthritis prevalence in the early 1970s (Anderson and Felson 1988). More research is needed to determine whether arthritis risk related to occupational factors has decreased in recent years with the shift away from heavy manufacturing jobs toward less physically demanding service and technology sector employment.

Mobility disability is a major concern for the aging Baby Boomers because of their greater rates of overweight and obesity throughout adulthood. Obesity is strongly associated with many chronic conditions and health risk which lead to disability (Mokdad et al. 2003). High BMI is an independent predictor of mobility declines and disability (Stuck et al. 1999; LaCroix et al. 1993). In the most recent NHANES, we found that obese middle-aged and older persons had twice the likelihood of reporting mobility difficulty even after controlling for arthritis. Nonetheless, we also observed that the prevalence of mobility disability was somewhat lower among the Baby Boomers compared to their predecessors. This is notable because the Baby Boomers are not yet in the age group of high disability rates. Even in middle age, we show evidence that mobility disability may be declining in the U.S. population. As we stated in our introduction, others have reported on general declining rates of disability among the elderly (Freedman, Martin, and Schoeni 2002; Manton, Corder, and Stallard 1997; Manton and Gu 2001), but our finding of a decline in disability rates in middle-aged adults as well signals an important continuing trend toward health improvement among Baby Boomers as they approach old age compared to their predecessors. The marked declines in mobility disability in Baby Boomer women is particularly encouraging given that women in old age bear a greater burden of disability overall.

Whether the mobility declines will be reversed as a result of increased hazards from obesity is a question that will require ongoing research. The impact of obesity on life expectancy is another major concern. A recent analysis of the forty year follow-up of the Framingham Study showed that obese forty-year-old non-smokers lost six to seven years of life expectancy compared to normal weight peers (Peeters et al. 2003). Comparable results were found using national data with a shorter follow-up period (Fontaine et al. 2003). Although cardiovascular disease deaths continue to decline (Kochanek and Smith 2004), rates of diabetes mirror the rise in obesity prevalence (CDC 2005) and may predict a reversal in the gains we have witnessed in cardiovascular disease morbidity and mortality.

Figure 7.3, which shows the BMI distribution among persons with self-reported physician-diagnosed arthritis, portrays the differences among the birth cohorts in the relationship between overweight, obesity, and arthritis. A greater proportion of men and women with arthritis were obese in the two most recent waves, compared to earlier waves of the NHANES. It remains unclear whether the increase in obesity prevalence will ultimately lead to an increase in arthritis prevalence among the Baby Boomers compared to the Silent Generation. These data support the probability that obesity will remain a significant risk factor for arthritis among aging Baby Boomers.

This study used a series of cross-sectional surveys; thus we could not conduct statistical tests to compare the prevalence or risk estimates across the birth cohorts. Also, the population was in a dynamic state across the waves of NHANES, and racial and ethnic minorities comprise a growing proportion of the U.S. population. Some of the increase in prevalence of overweight could be due to the changing composition of the population rather than exclusively to weight increases among the stable sectors of the population.

Others have shown the age trends over the past several decades in rising population obesity rates (Flegal et al. 2002). However, our findings suggest that the profound cultural changes leading to the high prevalence of overweight and obesity has progressed rapidly across generations. How will this shift influence life in old age among the Baby Boomers? Arthritis and mobility disability are just two of many obesity-related chronic conditions which could consume considerable health care resources, generate wide-ranging societal costs, and reduce quality of life. Both obesity and arthritis contribute to disability and are especially limiting as comorbid conditions (Jordan et al. 1996; Ettinger et al. 1994). Will the aging of the heavier Baby Boom generation halt or reverse the trend toward decreasing disability that has been observed in the older population in the past decade (Freedman, Martin, and Schoeni 2002; Manton, Corder, and Stallard 1997; Manton and Gu, 2001)? The trends we examined will require continued surveillance as the Baby Boomers continue to age.

The first of the Baby Boom generation will reach age sixty-five in the year 2011. If rates of overweight and obesity continue to climb with the aging of the Baby Boom generation, the consequences for musculoskeletal conditions and disability will place an unprecedented burden on the generation and the society as a whole. Urgent public health and research efforts are needed to develop interventions to mitigate the impact of obesity on chronic disease and disability in older adults.

References

Anderson, J. J., and D. T. Felson. 1988. Factors associated with osteoarthritis of the knee in the first national Health and Nutrition Examination Survey (HANES I): Evidence for an association with overweight, race, and physical demands of work. *American Journal of Epidemiology* 128 (1): 179–89.
Centers for Disease Control and Prevention (CDC). 2003. Public health and aging: Projected prevalence of self-reported arthritis or chronic joint symptoms among persons aged >65 years—United States, 2005–2030. *Morbidity and Mortality Weekly Report (MMWR)* 52:489–91.
———. 2004. Trends in intake of energy and macronutrients—United States, 1971–2000. 53 (4): 80–82.
———. 2005. Prevalence of diagnosed diabetes by age, United States, 1980–2002. Article online available from http://www.cdc.gov/diabetes/statistics/prev/national/figage
Day, J. 1993. *Population projections of the United States, by age, sex, race, and hispanic origin: 1993 to 2050.* Washington, DC: U.S. Bureau of the Census, P25–1104.
Dunlop, D. D., L. M. Manheim, J. Song, and R. W. Chang. 2003. Health care utilization among older adults with arthritis. *Arthritis and Rheumatism* 49 (2): 164–71.
Ettinger, W. H., M. A. Davis, J. M. Neuhaus, and K. P. Mallon. 1994. Long-term physical functioning in persons with knee osteoarthritis from NHANES. I: Effects of comorbid medical conditions. *Journal of Clinical Epidemiology* 47 (7): 809–15.

Flegal, K. M., M. D. Carroll, C. L. Ogden, and C. L. Johnson. 2002. Prevalence and trends in obesity among U.S. adults, 1999–2000. *Journal of the American Medical Association* 288 (14): 1723–27.

Fontaine, K. R., D. T. Redden, C. Wang, A. O. Westfall, and D. B. Allison. 2003. Years of life lost due to obesity. *Journal of the American Medical Association* 289 (2): 187–93.

Freedman, V. A., L. G. Martin, and R. E. Schoeni. 2002. Recent trends in disability and functioning among older adults in the United States: A systematic review. *Journal of the American Medical Association* 288 (24): 3137–46.

Hedley, A. A., C. L. Ogden, C. L. Johnson, M. D. Carroll, L. R. Curtin, and K. M. Flegal. 2004. Prevalence of overweight and obesity among U.S. children, adolescents, and adults, 1999–2002. *Journal of the American Medical Association* 291 (23): 2847–50.

Jordan, J. M., G. Luta, J. B. Renner, G. F. Linder, A. Dragomir, M. C. Hochberg, and J. G. Fryer. 1996. Self-reported functional status in osteoarthritis of the knee in a rural southern community: The role of sociodemographic factors, obesity, and knee pain. *Arthritis Care Res* 9 (4): 273–78.

Kinsella, K., and V. Velkoff. 2001. *An Aging World: 2001.* Washington, DC: U.S. Census Bureau, Series P95/01-1.

Kochanek, K. D., and B. L. Smith. 2004. *Deaths: Preliminary data for 2002. National vital statistics reports.* Hyattsville, MD: National Center for Health Statistics.

LaCroix, A. Z., J. M. Guralnik, L. F. Berkman, R. B. Wallace, and S. Satterfield. 1993. Maintaining mobility in late life. II. Smoking, alcohol consumption, physical activity, and body mass index. *American Journal of Epidemiology* 137 (8): 858–69.

Manson, J. E., P. J. Skerrett, P. Greenland, and T. B. VanItallie. 2004. The escalating pandemics of obesity and sedentary lifestyle. A call to action for clinicians. *Archives of Internal Medicine* 164 (3): 249–58.

Manton, K. G., L. Corder, and E. Stallard. 1997. Chronic disability trends in elderly United States populations: 1982–1994. *Proceedings of the National Academy of Sciences* 94 (6): 2593–98.

Manton, K. G., and X. Gu. 2001. Changes in the prevalence of chronic disability in the United States black and nonblack population above age 65 from 1982 to 1999. *Proceedings of the National Academy of Sciences* 98 (11): 6354–59.

Mokdad, A. H., E. S. Ford, B. A. Bowman, W. H. Dietz, F. Vinicor, V. S. Bales, and J. S. Marks. 2003. Prevalence of obesity, diabetes, and obesity-related health risk factors, 2001. *Journal of the American Medical Association* 289 (1): 76–79.

Peeters, A., J. J. Barendregt, F. Willekens, J. P. Mackenbach, A. Al Mamun, and L. Bonneux. 2003. Obesity in adulthood and its consequences for life expectancy: A life-table analysis. *Annals of Internal Medicine* 138 (1): 24–32.

Stuck, A. E., J. M. Walthert, T. Nikolaus, C. J. Bula, C. Hohmann, and J. C. Beck. 1999. Risk factors for functional status decline in community-living elderly people: a systematic literature review. *Social Science and Medicine* 48 (4): 445–69.

Zhang, J., and K. E. Yu. 1998. What's the relative risk? A method of correcting the odds ratio in cohort studies of common outcomes. *Journal of the American Medical Association* 280 (19): 1690–91.

8

Disability and Spending Growth

Michael E. Chernew, Dana Goldman,
Feng Pan, and Baoping Shang

Almost one of every six elderly Medicare beneficiaries suffers from some disability (U.S. Department of Health and Human Services 2004). Reductions in the prevalence and severity of disability could have dramatic effects on well-being; moreover, because the disabled spend more on health care than the nondisabled, lower rates of disability could reduce medical spending (Liu, Wall, and Wissoker 1997, Chan et al. 2002). For example, using data on Medicare beneficiaries between 1992 and 2000, Chernew et al. (2005) report that on average, the total medical care spending of people with one or two Activities of Daily Living (ADLs) was about twice that of nondisabled elderly. In contrast, people with five or more ADLs incurred four to five times the medical care spending of people without disability. Similarly, Cutler and Meara (1999) report that expenditure for persons with five or more activity limitations was nearly five times the amount incurred by those with Instrumental Activities of Daily Living (IADL) conditions.

Several studies in the health services literature posit that reduced disability levels in the future will lead to considerable cost savings. For example, Waidmann and Liu (2000) suggest that if disability rates continue

Michael E. Chernew is professor in the Department of Health Care Policy at Harvard Medical School, and a research associate of the National Bureau of Economic Research. Dana Goldman holds the RAND Chair in Health Economics and is Director of Health Economics at RAND. He is also a Professor of Health Services and Radiology at University of California, Los Angeles, and a research associate of the National Bureau of Economic Research. Feng Pan is a research associate at the United BioSource Corporation. Baoping Shang is a research associate in the Health Policy Center at the Urban Institute in Washington, D.C.

We are grateful for financial support from the National Institute on Aging grants P30 AG12810 and R01 AG19805, and the Mary Woodard Lasker Charitable Trust and Michael E. DeBakey Foundation.

their current decline, the number of disabled elderly people will not grow either in absolute terms or relative to the size of the working-aged population, even in the face of the dramatic growth in the elderly population. Lubitz et al. (2003) show that the savings of improved health might offset the health care costs associated with longer life. Even though healthier people live longer, their total expected medical care expenses appear to be no greater than those for less healthy persons.

Yet Chernew et al. (2005) report that spending growth among the least disabled was faster than that among the more disabled. After adjustment for a range of covariates including demographic and health status, spending by the nondisabled and beneficiaries with only IADL disability grew 23 percent and 28 percent, respectively. This compares to a 10 percent increase for those with one or two ADLs, a 0.6 percent increase for those with three or four ADLs, and a 10 percent decrease for most disabled. As a result, the ratio of spending among the ADL disabled groups, relative to the nondisabled, declined over the study period. Thus, projections of cost savings based on the current pattern of spending by disability status may overstate the savings associated with improved disability.

This work expands upon the existing literature by exploring the spending trends by disability category for specific types of health care services. If a greater number of major procedures are performed on the less disabled, we would expect to see greater convergence in spending for inpatient services. If less disabled individuals are increasingly receiving expensive diagnostic tests or preventive services, relative to the more disabled, we would expect to see strong convergence in spending for physician and outpatient services. Greater use of medications among the less disabled, perhaps to manage chronic—though not necessarily disabling—conditions, would yield convergence in pharmaceutical spending across disability categories.

The pattern of results suggests that the convergence in spending is driven by reductions in spending for long-term care services. This reflects, in part, the effects of the Balanced Budget Act of 1997, which limited spending on long-term care. Because these services were disproportionately used by the most disabled, this led to a convergence of spending across disability groups. In addition to the effects of long-term care spending, we also find that pharmaceutical spending contributed to the convergence of spending across groups. In contrast to long-term care, where spending growth was constrained, spending on prescription medications was rapid in all disability groups. However, it was most rapid in the least disabled groups, leading to convergence in spending. Finally, we cannot reject the hypothesis that cost growth in inpatient care and provider/outpatient care was the same across disability categories.

8.1   Methods

To estimate the trends in spending by disability group, we model total spending by Medicare beneficiaries (program spending plus beneficiary out-of-pocket spending) as a function of disability, other covariates (including disease burden), and a set of parameters. Estimates are conducted separately for total spending and four subcategories of spending: inpatient payments, outpatient and physician payments, prescription drug payments, and long-term care payments (hospice, home care, skilled nursing home, and facility).

Changes in Medicare spending over time will reflect either changes in the distribution of covariates (including disability) or changes in the coefficients that relate those covariates to spending. We estimate a nonlinear regression model of the form:

$$\mathrm{E}[spending_{it} \mid x_{it}] = \exp(x'_{it}\beta)$$

For services in which more than 90 percent of beneficiaries have some spending (total spending and provider/ outpatient spending), we estimate this model as a single-equation generalized linear model (GLM) where the variance of spending has a Gaussian distribution. In spending categories in which more than 10 percent of beneficiaries had no spending in a year, we estimate spending as a two part model, where the first part is a probit regression predicting positive spending (versus no spending in the category), and the second part is the GLM model described above, estimated on only those individuals with positive spending. Predicted spending by disability category and joint tests of the hypothesis that spending growth did not differ by disability category were based on analysis combining the estimates from both parts of the model.

To examine convergence of spending across disability categories, we include in all models interactions between covariates (most importantly disability category) and a linear time trend. We dropped the time interactions for those domains and disease states in which the estimates for total spending suggested the coefficients were stable over time. These dropped interaction terms include the interactions of time with: age, education, gender, race, region of residence, urban/rural, and marriage status. The dropping of the interaction terms signifies stability of the effects of these variables over time. The corresponding variables not interacted with time were retained in the model and were often important predictors of expenditures.

The GLM specification was based on specification tests of the total spending model. Relative to an Ordinary Least Squares (OLS) model and a similar nonlinear model that assumed a Gamma distribution instead of a Gaussian distribution, our model had lower mean average prediction errors using both a split sample approach and a set of models which were estimated on data from 1992 through a given year (t) and then used results to predict expenditures in periods after t through 2000. We estimated several such models using different years to define t.

Because disability is a marker of disease, a portion of the association between spending and disability may not be causal. Higher spending on individuals with disabilities may reflect efforts to treat the underlying disease that caused the disability. Moreover, if individuals with disabilities are disproportionately in poorer health (in unobserved ways) than other individuals, higher spending may reflect efforts to treat unrelated diseases.

8.2   Data

Our analysis is based on data from the 1992–2000 panels of the Medicare Current Beneficiary Survey (MCBS). The MCBS is a rotating panel survey in which a nationally representative sample of Medicare beneficiaries completes twelve interviews over three years. The survey is designed to ascertain utilization and expenditures for the Medicare population. Our analysis is confined to respondents enrolled in Medicare Part A and/or Part B and over sixty-five years of age. Beneficiaries eighty-five years of age or over are over-sampled. The MCBS provides demographic data including age, sex, race, and educational attainment. It also contains self-reported information on health, including the prevalence of various conditions, and measures of physical limitation in performing ADLs and IADLs.

8.2.1   Measuring Costs

Our measure of spending is based on Medicare claims data, linked to the MCBS and supplemented by respondent self-reports. Total spending includes both program spending and beneficiary out-of-pocket spending (Eppig and Chulis 1997). We include spending for all health care services (inpatient, outpatient, physician, pharmaceutical, nursing home, and home care). For services covered by Medicare, the data captures both the spending by Medicare, other payers including Medicaid, and by the beneficiary. Spending for services not covered by Medicare is based on self-reports and may be underreported. Spending by Medicare beneficiaries enrolled in HMOs is imputed based on measures of service utilization. All spending was converted to 2000 dollars using the consumer price index. The price index conversion will not influence relative spending across service types or disability groups.

8.2.2   Measuring Disability

Our measure of disability is derived from limitations in Activities of Daily Living (ADLs) and Instrumental Activities of Daily Living (IADLs). There are six ADLs: eating, bathing, dressing, transferring, walking, and toileting. There are eight IADLs: telephoning, using transportation, grocery shopping, personal shopping, housekeeping, chores, managing medications, and managing money (Evashwick 2001). Activities of Daily Living and IADLs are measured on a five-point scale ranging from independent, requiring supervision, limited assistance, extensive assistance, or total dependence. Thus, the level of disability may be influenced not only by physical limitations, but also by the respondent's environment and social situation. For an ADL or IADL, we consider any respondent reporting that they require any supervision or assistance to suffer from that ADL. We then aggregate the disability measures into five categories commonly used in the literature: nondisabled, those with IADL only, with one or two ADLs, with three or four ADLs, and those with five or more ADLs (Liu, Wall, and Wissoker 1997; Cutler and Meara 1999; Manton and Gu 2001).

Beneficiaries residing in nursing homes do not report their disability status on a consistent basis. For this reason we treat nursing home residence as a separate category, which though related to disability, is not a direct measure of disability. Some community-dwelling elderly may suffer from greater disability than some nursing home residents.

8.2.3   Measuring Disease

Disease measured in the MCBS is based on self-report of whether the respondent has ever been told by a doctor that he had a list of important conditions. We capture the presence of diabetes, cancer, heart disease, stroke, Alzheimer's disease, hypertension, osteoarthritis, and lung disease using a series of indicator variables.

8.2.4   Other Covariates

We control for a range of demographic information such as age (dummy variables for ages sixty-five to sixty-nine, seventy to seventy-four, seventy-five to seventy-nine, eighty to eighty-four, eighty-five and over), gender, marriage status, race (white, black, Hispanic), education (less than eleven, twelve to fifteen, more than sixteen), region of residence (Midwest, West, Northeast, South, and other [Puerto Rico]). We also control for behavioral markers: current or former smoker; BMI category (obese, overweight, underweight); and supplemental insurance coverage (Part A only, Part B only, Medicaid, employer supplemental, private supplemental, and HMO).

8.3   Results

Each model yields two sets of coefficients. One set measures the effect of the relevant covariate in the base year (1992) and the other set measures how the effect of each covariate changes over time (the coefficients on the time interactions).

The base coefficients consistently indicate that spending rises as disability get worse (table 8.1). This is true for aggregate spending and for each category of spending. Spending on inpatient care exhibits the largest absolute differential in spending between the most disabled community-dwelling

Table 8.1   Parameter estimates: Base year parameters

Level	Total spending	Long-term care		Physician care spending	Inpatient care		Prescription drug	
		Any spending	Spending |any		Any spending	Spending |any	Any spending	Spending |any
Constant	7.661***	-2.371***	4.399***	6.45***	-1.805***	6.549***	-0.196***	5.28***
Age 70–74	0.141***	0.231***	0.217*	0.11***	0.12***	0.08	0.097***	0.055***
Age 75–79	0.058	0.356***	0.165*	0.036	0.158***	-0.051	0.152***	0.023
Age 80–84	-0.003	0.519***	0.132	-0.068	0.196***	-0.138*	0.183***	-0.032
Age 85 and up	-0.061	0.647***	0.148	-0.295***	0.151***	-0.364***	0.076***	-0.139***
Died	-0.041	0.984***	-0.593***	0.269***	1.154***	1.234***	-0.351***	-0.514***
Male	0.064***	0.001	0.027	0.176***	0.112***	0.226***	-0.188***	-0.123***
Black	0.121***	0.023	-0.02	0.176***	0.009	0.297***	-0.149***	-0.204***
Hispanic	0.132***	-0.052	-0.013	0.243***	-0.007	0.242***	0.033	-0.136***
Married	0.002	-0.166***	-0.031	0.018	-0.052***	-0.102*	0.106***	0.071***
High school	0.025	0.013	0.03	-0.004	-0.024*	-0.008	-0.004	0.033*
Some college	0.034	-0.04	-0.009	0.027	-0.055***	0.016	0.027	0.037
College and above	0.028	-0.032	0.12	0.017	-0.1.01***	-0.1	0.023	0.016
Urban	0.212***	0.023	0.2***	0.177***	0.002	0.173***	0.024	0.02
IADL only	0.38***	0.275***	1.181***	0.294***	0.251***	0.443***	0.194***	0.246***
ADL 1–2	0.622***	0.516***	1.841***	0.48***	0.36***	0.605***	0.241***	0.358***
ADL 3–4	1.057***	1.009***	3.063***	0.788***	0.584***	1.042***	0.376***	0.523***
ADL 5+	1.55***	1.543***	4.073***	1.115***	0.784***	1.128***	0.381***	0.568***
Nursing home	2.563***	3.764***	5.545***	1.382***	1.048***	1.181***	-0.783***	-0.705***

Diabetes	0.228***	0.292***	0.192**	0.212***	0.134***	0.16*	0.427***	0.265***
Cancer	0.209***	0.163***	0.095	0.349***	0.164***	0.044	0.203***	0.085**
Coronary heart disease	0.294***	0.126***	-0.029	0.227***	0.343***	0.264***	0.469***	0.418***
Stroke	0.078*	0.219***	0.208	-0.004	0.175***	0.198	0.046	0.034
Alzheimer's	-0.037	0.197**	0.138	-0.051	0.113**	-0.174	0.232***	0.015
HBP	0.077***	0.028	0.008	0.004	0.047**	0.084	0.594***	0.367***
Osteoarthritis	-0.067**	0.026	-0.192**	0.056	0.06***	-0.09	0.233***	0.099***
Lung disease	0.198***	0.233***	-0.041	0.201***	0.14***	0.135	0.368***	0.271***
Ever smoking	0.062*	0.071**	-0.004	0.141***	0.106***	0.215***	0.056	0.013
Obesity	-0.073	-0.065	0.029	-0.079	-0.066*	-0.125	-0.008	-0.029
Overweight	0.069	-0.021	0.129	0.013	-0.018	-0.033	0.039	-0.006
Underweight	0.044	0.013	0.069**	0.015	-0.026	-0.02	0.004	-0.08
Part A only	-0.337	-0.292**	-0.785***	-0.432*	-0.223***	-0.131	-0.282***	-0.021
Part B only	-0.478***	-0.28*	-0.332**	-0.331	-2.0***	-1.432	0.005	-0.41***
Medicaid	0.171***	0.414***	0.054	0.477***	0.186***	0.444***	0.27***	0.372***
Employer insurance	0.155**	0.075	-0.38***	0.623***	0.167***	0.579***	0.532***	0.385***
Private insurance	0.066	0.067	-0.49***	0.552***	0.182***	0.498***	0.475***	0.319***
Member of HMO	-0.344***	-0.143*	-0.368***	-0.266*	0.08	0.24	0.476***	0.092

Note: Coefficients on region omitted.

*** Significant at the 1 percent level.

** Significant at the 5 percent level.

* Significant at the 10 percent level.

beneficiaries (more than five ADLs) and the nondisabled. This is followed closely by the differential for long-term care spending. Because the nondisabled spend so little on long-term care, the ratio of spending by beneficiaries with five or more ADLs, relative to the nondisabled, is greatest for long-term care spending. Specifically, in 1992 adjusted spending for the most disabled community dwelling elderly was over sixty-five times as much as adjusted spending for nondisabled community dwelling. Spending for prescription drugs is the least influenced by disability. The ratio of predicted spending on prescription medications for beneficiaries with five or more ADLs in the base year was only about twice that for the nondisabled.

Though the level of spending for the least disabled was much below that for the most disabled, the second set of coefficients from each model indicates that spending by the least disabled was growing at the fastest rate (table 8.2). As a result, the ratio of spending for the most disabled, relative to the least disabled was falling. Our estimates suggest that in 1992, spending by community-dwelling beneficiaries with five or more ADLs was 4.7 times greater than otherwise comparable nondisabled beneficiaries. That ratio fell to 3.3 by 2000.

Examination of spending patterns reveals that most of this decline is driven by trends in long-term care spending. Estimated spending by the nondisabled remained low, but average annual spending by those with five or more ADLs, adjusted for demographic and other covariates, fell by about 7 percent. Closer examination of the data indicates that this was driven by a decline in home care spending following the Balanced Budget Act (BBA) of 1997. These findings reflect both a drop in the probability of any use and a drop in the amount of spending conditional on use. This is consistent with the study by Spector et al. (2004), which documents a reduction in home care spending overall following the BBA. The decline in home care spending was present for all disability groups, so the decline in the ratio of long-term care spending for the most disabled, relative to the least disabled was reasonably smooth, without a big break around the BBA. This is illustrated in figure 8.1, which reports the ratio of mean spending (unadjusted for covariates), for total long-term care spending and its two largest components, home care and care in short-term facilities. However, because long-term care is more salient for the disabled, the reduction in spending associated with long-term care drives the reduction in the relative spending by the most disabled group.

The estimates for physician services and inpatient services do not reveal a statistically significant differential in the spending trends between the most and least disabled. In fact, for inpatient care the estimates suggest that if other beneficiary traits remained unchanged from 1992, the relative spending gap between the most and least disabled community-dwelling elderly would have risen.

For pharmaceutical spending, growth was rapid among all categories of

Table 8.2   Parameter estimates: Time interaction parameters

Time interaction	Total spending	Long-term care		Physician care spending	Inpatient care		Prescription drug	
		Any spending	Spending | any		Any spending	Spending | any	Any spending	Spending | any
Time	0.022	0.007	0.051**	0.041	0.01	0.001	0.01	0.089***
IADL only	0.002	0.008	0.009	0.015	0.001	-0.015	0.011	-0.008
ADL 1–2	-0.014	0.004	-0.016	-0.002	-0.002	-0.018	0.008	-0.017**
ADL 3–4	-0.027**	-0.003	-0.038**	-0.013	-0.002	-0.041	-0.011	-0.021**
ADL 5+	-0.045***	-0.02*	-0.085***	-0.02	-0.013	-0.022	0.023	-0.016
Nursing home	-0.003	0.094***	-0.027	-0.008	-0.023**	0.023	-0.044***	-0.077***
Part A only	-0.04	-0.002	0.062	-0.085***	0.008	-0.076	0.029	-0.039*
Part B only	0.054**	0.011	0.069**	0.104**	0.069	-0.277***	0.049*	0.044**
Medicaid	-0.014*	-0.02	-0.007	-0.038**	0.001	-0.021	-0.003	-0.009
Employer insurance	0.003	0.006	0.025	-0.026	0	-0.027	0.014	0.009
Private insurance	0.022*	0.015	0.046***	-0.015	0.004	0	0.015	-0.02*
Member of HMO	-0.005	-0.048***	0.01	-0.015	0.001	-0.055	0.011	-0.01
Ever smoking	0	0.001	-0.001	-0.027**	-0.008*	-0.005	-0.004	0.008
Obesity	-0.02**	-0.006	-0.018*	-0.024**	-0.011	-0.033	0.005	0.008
Overweight	-0.027***	-0.015**	-0.026	0.006	-0.012**	-0.02	-0.002	0.002
Underweight	-0.004	0.024**	-0.007	0.019*	0.011	-0.007	-0.005	0.004
Diabetes	0.017***	-0.012*	0.007	0.019**	0.011**	0.02	0.004	-0.004
Cancer	0.006	0.003	0.014*	0.004	0.009**	0.001	0.017**	0
Coronary heart disease	0.019***	0.012*	0.009**	0.019	0.008*	0.051***	0.008	-0.015***
Stroke	0.005	-0.006	0.013***	0	0.005	-0.025	0.016*	0.01
Alzheimer's	-0.009**	0.014	0.004	-0.036***	-0.022***	-0.044**	-0.06***	0.008
HBP	0.008**	0.007	-0.005*	0.023**	0.012***	0.019	0.027***	-0.001
Osteoarthritis	-0.003	-0.001	-0.007***	-0.009	-0.006	0.01	0.015***	0.01*
Lung disease	0.005	-0.019***	0.004	-0.005	0.01*	0.011	0	0.002
Died	-0.026***	0.005	-0.009	-0.02	-0.033***	-0.047*	-0.036***	-0.036**

***Significant at the 1 percent level.
**Significant at the 5 percent level.
*Significant at the 10 percent level.

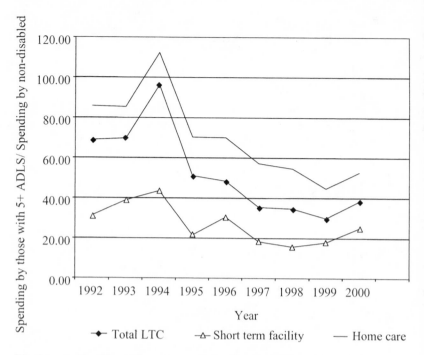

Fig. 8.1   Ratio of Long-Term Care spending, by type of Long-Term Care

disability, but most rapid among the least disabled. Although the coefficient on the interaction between five or more ADLs and time is not statistically significant, the point estimates suggests greater growth in spending for the nondisabled and the coefficients on the time interactions for the other two ADL disability groups are statistically significant. Although the relatively rapid growth in prescription drug spending among the nondisabled contributes to the decline in the ratio of spending by the most disabled, relative to the least disabled, the contribution of prescription drug spending to the overall decline is less than that of long-term care because the share of spending on pharmaceuticals is much lower on average (5 percent of spending for the most disabled and 14 percent for the nondisabled).

   The results comparing the nondisabled to disability groups other than the most disabled reveal a similar pattern of spending ratios for the disabled relative to the nondisabled group. Overall, only the IADL-only group has very similar spending growth as the nondisabled group. In part this is because, like the nondisabled group, the IADL-only group has very limited spending on long-term care, which was the primary driver of the declining relative spending by the most disabled.

The other ADL groups have slower spending growth in aggregate than the nondisabled (and IADL-only) group. Again, this reflects largely less spending on long-term care and somewhat slower growth in pharmaceutical spending relative to the less disabled groups.

8.4 Conclusion

During the 1990s, spending growth for the least disabled exceeded that by the most disabled. This resulted in a convergence of spending between the two groups of beneficiaries. If such a convergence continues, savings accruing to improved disability status may have less of an impact on overall spending than analysis of current spending patterns would suggest.

This analysis reveals that the convergence of spending reflects the reduction in long-term care spending following the BBA. While all disability groups experienced a decline in long-term care spending, the aggregate spending for the most disabled was most affected because long-term care spending is about a quarter of all spending for the most disabled group and less than 5 percent of spending for the nondisabled group.

A fundamental question is whether this convergence will continue. To a large extent the answer depends on decisions by policymakers. The Balanced Budget Act of 1997 was a major reason for the decline in long-term care spending, and thus an important contributor to the convergence in spending. If policymakers can hold the line on long-term care spending, one might expect to continue to observe slower relative spending growth among the most disabled. Moreover, it may be the case that technical innovations that drive spending growth are less salient for long-term care services, suggesting that pressures for increased spending on those services, per beneficiary, will be manageable.

In contrast, technical innovations related to physician, inpatient, and pharmaceutical services appear to affect beneficiaries in all disability groups. In fact, some innovations, such as those related to prescription drugs, were generally more salient for the least disabled group of beneficiaries. As these services consume a growing share of spending, we would forecast greater cost pressures. Like long-term care spending, spending for physician, inpatient, and pharmaceutical services will be sensitive to regulatory changes. Yet historically, constraining the growth of these services has appeared a more difficult task.

As we are faced with a growing number of Medicare beneficiaries, the challenge for policymakers will be to design payment systems and other regulations in a way as to promote efficient delivery of care and allocation of services. The political tradeoffs will be difficult to make and budgetary pressures great. Our analysis suggests that it is unlikely that improved disability status among elderly will eliminate the need for these tough choices.

References

Chan, L., S. Beaver, R. F. Maclehose, A. Jha, M. Maciejewski, and J. N. Doctor. 2002. Disability and health care costs in the Medicare population. *Archives of Physical Medicine & Rehabilitation* 83 (9): 1196–201.
Chernew, M., D. Goldman, F. Pan, and B. Shang. 2005. Disability and health care expenditures among Medicare beneficiaries. *Health Affairs* Web Exclusive, accessed at http://content.healthaffairs.org/webexclusives
Cutler, D. M., and E. Meara. 1999. The concentration of medical spending: An update. NBER Working Paper no. w7279.
Eppig, F., and G. S. Chulis. 1997. Matching MCBS and Medicare data: The best of both worlds. *Health Care Financing Review* 18 (3): 211–29.
Evashwick, C. J. 2001. *The Continuum of Long-Term Care, Second Edition.* Albany, NY: Delmar Thomson Learning.
Liu, K., S. Wall, and D. Wissoker. 1997. Disability and Medicare costs of elderly persons. *Milbank Quarterly* 75 (4): 461–93.
Lubitz, J., L. Cai, E. Kramarow, and H. Lentzner. 2003. Health, life expectancy, and health care spending among the elderly. *New England Journal of Medicine* 349 (11): 1048–55.
Manton, K. G., and X. Gu. 2001. Changes in the prevalence of chronic disability in the United States black and nonblack population above age 65 from 1982 to 1999. *Proceedings of the National Academy of Sciences of the United States of America* 98 (11): 6354–9.
Spector, W. D., J. W. Cohen, and I. Pesis-Katz. 2004. Home care before and after the Balanced Budget Act of 1997: Shifts in financing and services. *Gerontologist* 44 (1): 39–47.
U.S. Department of Health and Human Services. 2004. *Health, United States 200: With chartbook on trends in the health of Americans (Health United States).* Hyattsville, MD: CDC National Center for Health Statistics.
Waidmann, T. A., and K. Liu. 2000. Disability trends among elderly persons and implication for the future. *Journals of Gerontology (B): Psychological Sciences and Social Sciences* 55, no. 5, S298–307.

IV

Work Disability

Work Disability is a Pain in the ****, Especially in England, the Netherlands, and the United States

James Banks, Arie Kapteyn, James P. Smith, and Arthur van Soest

9.1 Introduction

High and rising rates of work disability are a pervasive problem in many industrialized countries (Bound and Burkhauser 1999). But rates of reported work disability vary considerably across countries with similar levels of economic development and comparable medical technology and treatment. Institutional differences in eligibility rules or generosity of benefits no doubt contribute to explaining the differences in disability rolls Haveman, Halberstadt, and Burkhauser (1984). Recent survey data show that significant differences between countries are also found in self-reports of work limiting disabilities and in general health. In comparing such self-reports, account should be taken of measurement issues such as differences in question wordings, as well as differences between and within countries that may exist in the scales that are used in answering questions about work disability.

This chapter investigates in some depth one highly salient—and as it turns out quite important—reason for reporting work disability, which is the presence of some type of pain. Unlike many illnesses of middle age, pain prevalence is very high. It also varies considerably across such key

James Banks is deputy research director at the Institute for Fiscal Studies, and a professor of economics at University College London. Arie Kapteyn is a senior economist at RAND and program director of RAND Labor and Population. James P. Smith is a senior economist at RAND. Arthur van Soest is a senior economist at RAND and a professor of econometrics at Tilburg University.

This research was supported by National Institute on Aging grants P30 AG12810 (to the National Bureau of Economic Research [NBER]) and R01 AG19805 (to the RAND Corporation), and by a Mary Woodard Lasker Charitable Trust and Michael E. DeBakey Foundation grant to the NBER. We thank David Rumpel for his expert programming assistance.

demographic attributes as gender and education. Most importantly for this chapter, amongst all health conditions pain is the most important determinant of work disability.

A unique aspect of this research is that it has a distinct multinational component by using data from three countries: the United States, United Kingdom, and the Netherlands. These three countries differ in a couple of relevant dimensions—observed rates of self-reported work disability, and perhaps national norms about the appropriateness of not working when one is or one claims one is work disabled. However, the countries appear to have similar economic standards of living and similar levels of objectively measured health status of the population. For this reason, international comparisons may be particularly useful in understanding some of the most salient research issues that have dominated the scientific literature on work disability.

Data on pain and its relationship to work disability are not abundant in any of the three countries. In addition to relying on a diverse set of currently available health and economic surveys in each country that do contain relevant information on pain and work disability, we have also been able to remedy that deficiency with new data collection efforts. First, we have had access to some reasonably large Internet samples in two of our countries, allowing us to experiment along several dimensions. These samples are the CentERpanel for the Netherlands and the RAND HRS and RAND MS Internet panels for the United States. For example, we placed experimental disability modules (with alternative forms of disability questions, etc.) and a pain module into these panels. In addition, the recently fielded English Longitudinal Survey on Aging (ELSA) has a detailed set of questions on pain, work disability, and workplace accommodations.

Pain has a subjective as well as objective manifestation, as individuals with the same amount of pain may react to it in very different ways. Another aspect of this chapter is that we utilize the vignette methodology to evaluate—once again in an experimental setting—how people within the same country as well as across countries set thresholds that result in labeling some people work disabled while other people are not so described. Vignette questions have been applied successfully in recent work on international comparisons of health and work disability (King 2004; Kapteyn, Smith, and Van Soest 2007). In this chapter, we will use vignettes on pain to identify systematic differences in self-reported work disability in the Netherlands and the United States.

One reason why pain may have differential impacts on work disability in the three countries is that practices differ on how to limit the effects of pain on people's ability to function effectively in their lives, especially in the workplace. Two aspects of possible cross-country differences will be investigated—the use of medication to relieve pain and the availability of workplace accommodations that lessen its impact on the job.

The remainder of this paper is divided into five sections. Section 9.2 compares and evaluates the impact of some differences in wording of work disability questions both within and across countries on reports of work disability. Section 9.3 summarizes several salient differences and similarities in the type, severity, and duration of pain in our three countries. This section also documents the one-way and multivariate relationship between pain and self-reports of work disability in each country. Section 9.4 examines differences across countries in pain medication and workplace accommodations. Section 9.5 summarizes our results using the vignette methodology, and section 9.6 presents our conclusions.

9.2   Does the Form of the Question Matter?

It is an understatement that there is no agreed upon standard format for asking about work disability. Thus, it is not surprising that the format and wording of questions on work disability vary not only internationally but also across the major social science surveys within a country. For example, in the United States quite different questions are asked in the principal yearly government labor force survey (the Current Population Survey or CPS) and the principal yearly health survey (National Health Interview Survey or NHIS) (Burkhauser et al. 2002). To illustrate, the CPS question is:

> Does anyone in the household have a health problem or disability which prevents them from working or which limits the kind or amount of work they can do? [If so,] who is that? (Anyone else?)

while the NHIS asks instead two questions:

> Does any impairment or health problem now keep you from working at a job or business?
> Are you limited in the kind of amount of work you can do because of any impairment?

To add to the potential domestic confusion, the work disability question in the HRS is

> Do you have any impairment or health problem that limits the kind or amount of paid work you can do?

and for Panel Study of Income Dynamics (PSID) it is:

> Do you have any physical or nervous condition that limits the type of work or the amount of work you can do?

In all cases, the answers permitted are *yes, no, don't know,* or *refuse* so that essentially a dichotomous disability scale can be created.

Some differences between the ways these questions are asked involve language. National Health Interview Survey and Health and Retirement

Study (HRS) use the term impairment; NHIS, HRS, and CPS use health problem; PSID contains only the phrase physical or nervous condition; while the word disability is only used explicitly in CPS. Another potentially important difference is that CPS first asks about anyone in the household and then in a follow-up inquires about whom that might be.

Not surprisingly, survey differences in the manner in which work disability questions are asked are not limited to the United States. For example, the basic work disability question in the Dutch CentERpanel is:

Do you have an impairment or health problem that limits you in the amount or kind of work you can do?

While this sounds very similar to the HRS question format, the possible answers are now arrayed on the following five point scale:

(1) no, not at all, (2) yes, I am somewhat limited, (3) yes, I am rather limited, (4) yes, I am severely limited, and (5) yes, I am very severely limited—I am not able to work.

Finally, in England the disability question used in the British Household Panel Survey (BHPS) is very similar but not identical to the HRS variant— "Does your health limit the type of work or the amount of work you can do?" While ELSA did not have a work disability question in wave 1, the designers placed the following question into the first follow-up: "Do you have any health problem or disability that limits the kind or amount of work you can do?"[1]

This wide variation in the form in which work disability questions are asked both within and between countries raises the question of how important this variation is in creating differences in reported rates of disability prevalence.

9.2.1   Reports of Disability Prevalence

In this project, we conducted several experiments to evaluate the impact of differences in question wording on reporting of disability prevalence. First, we placed the disability questions summarized above from the HRS, CPS, and NHIS into the RAND HRS Internet panel. This panel is based on a sample of about 2,700 respondents in the HRS 2002 wave who had Internet access and who expressed a willingness to participate in an experimental survey on the Internet. This panel allows us to test in a random experimental setting whether the alternative forms of these questions in these three prominent surveys lead to very different measures of disability prevalence using the same population of respondents. Moreover, the reasons for

1. If the answer to this question is yes, ELSA follows the HRS format by asking, "Is this a health problem or disability that you expect to last at least three months?"

Table 9.1   **Disability prevalence**

	Percentage of cases who report disability
NHIS	18.0
HRS	17.4
CPS	24.6
HRS nonmarried	23.5
CPS nonmarried	24.1
NHIS nonmarried	21.4

Note: Sample is from RAND HRS Internet sample.

any differences that emerge can be subsequently explored using the rich information available from the core HRS interviews.[2]

In the RAND HRS Internet panel, we conducted the following experiments: half of the sample was randomly assigned the NHIS form of the disability question while the other half received the CPS variant. To test for mode differences (the Internet versus the telephone in the prior wave), the full RAND HRS Internet sample received the normal HRS question. The principal results are contained in table 9.1.

Contrary to the speculation in the literature, there does not appear to be any difference in estimates of disability prevalence induced by the wordings of these alternative questions. The NHIS and HRS variants produce bang-on estimates. One complication in making these comparisons is that HRS staff has not coded the specific people affected in the CPS question. Fortunately, a fix is available by limiting the comparisons to nonmarried respondents. Table 9.1 shows that in this sample HRS, CPS, and NHIS produce remarkably similar sets of estimates about disability prevalence.

While the PSID disability question was not included in these experiments, one can compare PSID estimates of work disability prevalence with those obtained in the HRS for the same age group. In that case the PSID estimate of work disability was 28.7 percent while it was 26.8 percent in the HRS, about a 2 percentage point difference. This also does not seem to us to be a large difference, but this conclusion must be qualified by the fact that, unlike the numbers in table 9.1, this comparison is not a strict comparison of question wording only, as other factors such as sampling frames likely differ between the surveys in view of the fact that the HRS sample only includes respondents with Internet access.

Similarly, two other British surveys in addition to the British Household Survey (BHPS) ask work disability questions. For example, the Labor

---

2. The HRS respondents with Internet access are a selective sample of the population. However, since we are comparing within sample it seems unlikely that our results are very much affected by this selectivity.

Force Survey (LFS) first asks, "Do you have any health problems or disabilities that you expect will last for more than a year?" If the answer is yes, then respondents are asked in sequence, "Does this health problem affect the KIND of paid work that you might do?" and then, "or the AMOUNT of paid work that you might do?" The other survey is called the Family Resource Survey (FRS), which asks, "Some people are restricted in the amount or type of work they can do, because they have an injury, illness, or disability. Which of these statements comes closest to your own position at the moment? (1) Unable to work at the moment; (2) Restricted in amount or type of work I can do; (3) Not restricted in amount or type of work I can do." In spite of the difference in the manner in which these questions are asked, prevalence rates from the BHPS, LFS, and FRS are remarkably close.

Thus, in our view any conflicts that emerge amongst these surveys in estimates of the prevalence of the work disabled population appear not to be due to the form of the disability questions. One possible explanation is that the greater concentration on health content in the NHIS alerts their respondents to health issues and results in higher reporting of disability, although differences in sampling frames may be a more likely explanation.[3]

Our next set of experiments was conducted using the Dutch CentERpanel, which includes about 2,000 households who have agreed to respond to a set of questions every weekend over the Internet. Unlike the RAND HRS Internet panel, this Dutch sample is not restricted to households with their own Internet access. If they agree to participate and do not currently have Internet access, they are provided Internet access.[4] One advantage of the Dutch Internet panel is that these respondents had already answered many questions about their lives, including questions about their health, demographics, and labor force activity. In this project, we carried out a number of experiments over about a six-month period. These included the vignette experiments, which are reported on below, test-retest experiments, and experiments with question wording. The experiments took place mid-August, mid-October, and mid-December 2003.

For example, in the second round of the CentERpanel vignette disability experiments (mid-October 2003), we conducted another experiment about question wording. Randomly, half of CentERpanel respondents in the second wave of our vignette experiments were given the HRS disability

---

3. Some evidence is available from ELSA which experimented with placing the general health status questions before and after the detailed set of questions that inquired about a long list of possible health problems. There was some tendency to report better general health status when the questions were placed at the end but the principal difference was that there were fewer respondents at either tail of the five point general health scale when the questions were at the end.

4. Providing Internet access may require just a subscription with an Internet provider, but usually it involves the provision of a set-top box which is connected to a TV set and a telephone line to allow Internet access; if needed, a TV set is also provided.

question whereby one answered on a yes no basis to the disability question. In the first round (mid-August 2003), the same question had been asked with a five point response scale, as noted above. Given that the first and second waves of our experiments were only a few months apart so that disability reports should not change that much, for these respondents one can compare the answers to this question to that given on the five point scale a few months earlier.

The results are presented in table 9.2. For all but one row in the five point scale, the correspondence is remarkably close. Ninety-six percent of those who answered they were not at all disabled on the five point scale also said that they were not when using the HRS dichotomous scale. Similarly, more than 90 percent of Dutch respondents who said that they were more than somewhat limited replied that they had a work disability on the U.S. two point scale.

The ambiguity occurs within the somewhat limited category, which splits about fifty/fifty when offered an opportunity to simply respond yes or no about their work disability. These are people who are clearly on the margin in terms of their work disability problems. When offered a stark yes or no choice, some will resist disability labeling. But if given a more nuanced set of alternatives, they report some degree of disability.

Since this somewhat limited group represents just under a quarter of Dutch respondents, the implication is that reports of disability prevalence are considerably lower if the two-point scale is used in place of the five-point scale. Table 9.3 shows reported U.S. disability rates by age (from the PSID) alongside those in the U.K. (from the Labor Force Survey) and the Dutch disability rates using the five and two point scale obtained from CentERpanel. Especially during middle age, the Dutch have the highest rates of self-reported work disability, followed by the British, with the Americans having the lowest rates. While estimates of Dutch disability prevalence using the dichotomous scale are still much higher than that observed in the United States, a significant fraction of the disparity could be explained by the format of the disability scale. However, especially for middle age workers—say those between ages forty-five to sixty-four—

Table 9.2	Correspondence between 5 and 2-point scale in Dutch panel	
5-point work limitations	Percentage in category	marginal Percentage disabled in 2-point scale
Not at all	61.8	4.3
Somewhat limited	22.5	56.1
Rather limited	9.9	91.2
Severely limited	2.2	93.1
Very severely limited	3.6	92.1

Source: Dutch CentERpanel.

Table 9.3   Percentage with work disability by age—United States, United Kingdom, and the Netherlands

	Age group				
	25–34	35–44	45–54	55–64	65+
United States	7.4	11.3	17.6	25.9	38.8
United Kingdom	9.1	12.4	19.4	30.8	n.a.
Netherlands					
5-point scale	25.7	30.3	42.7	44.2	53.6
U.S. 2-point scale	17.2	23.6	38.7	37.4	38.8

Notes: U.S. data are from PSID. U.K. data are from 2001 Labor Force Survey. Due to question routing, the fifty-five to sixty-four group contains women ages fifty-five to fifty-nine and men ages fifty-five to sixty-four. Netherlands data are from CentERpanel. Netherlands 5-point scale is based on report of any limitation. U.S. and U.K. use the 2-point scale. All data are weighted. n.a. = not available.

Dutch rates of reported work disability are still about 15 percentage points higher than those in the United States even when the same question is asked in both countries.

9.3   Pain and Work Disability

In this section, we discuss the central role played by pain as a potential determinant of work disability. The amount and type of pain information available differs in several ways across the countries we study. Rather than going straight to the lowest common denominator by restricting our analysis to information that is available and identical in all three countries, we take the alternative strategy of using the best information that each country has to offer. While comparability across countries will not be exact, this will still provide the most useful information about the relative importance of pain in affecting work disability.

More so than many specific diseases, pain has subjective and objective aspects. Objectively, in a reaction to a variety of stimuli, pain is started when energy is converted into electrical energy (nerve impulses) by sensory receptors called nociceptors. These neural signals are then transmitted to the spinal cord and brain, which perceives them as pain. Some pain medications or analgesics can inhibit nociception and thereby lessen or even eliminate the sensation of pain. Even without medication, individuals differ in how they access, interpret, and tolerate pain so that there may well be a significant subjective component to the reporting of pain, both within and across countries. As shown in the following paragraphs, pain also varies in its severity, duration, and location, all of which may have different implications for the tolerance and perception of pain and for work disability.[5]

5. See the web site of the American Pain Society. Accessed at http://www.ampainsoc.org

With this in mind, table 9.4 provides information about the prevalence and types of pain people experience in the United States, the Netherlands, and the United Kingdom, respectively. Unless otherwise indicated, all data in this table refer to individuals ages twenty-five and over. Pain prevalence rates are also stratified by gender, education, and age. Just like work disability, commonly used questions used to ascertain whether an individual has pain or not also vary a good deal in their format and wording, both across different surveys within countries and across countries. However, unlike the form of questions on work disability, the specific language used in pain questions appears to really matter a lot. For example, the most basic question asked in the National Health Interview Survey (NHIS) in the United States about pain was whether an individual had any recurring pain during the last twelve months, while the most comparable question in the Dutch CentERpanel was, "Are you often troubled by pain?" We will refer to this question form as the recurrent pain question.

Another common form in which pain questions are asked involves inquiring about the presence of pain in specific parts of the body from which an aggregate of pain can be deduced. The American and Dutch surveys used the same parts of the body—neck, back, face or jaw, joints, and headaches. The British survey only asks about migraines. However, these questions tend to ask about the presence of pain over shorter periods of time—for example, in the American NHIS the reference period used is the last three months, while in the Dutch panel the last thirty days are used. We will refer to this question form as the recent pain question.

The situation in England is more complicated. The 1999 British Household Survey (BHPS) contained the SF-36 questionnaire (Ware and Sherbourne 1992). As a consequence all respondents were asked, "How much bodily pain have you had during the past four weeks?" where the allowed responses follow a six-point scale: none, very mild, mild, moderate, severe, and very severe. In addition, a second item of the SF-36 (again delivered to all respondents) asks, "During the past four weeks, how much did pain interfere with your normal work (including both work outside the home and housework)?" where five possible responses are allowed: not at all, a little bit, moderately, quite a bit, and extremely. This SF-36 questionnaire has not yet been delivered again to BHPS respondents. However, in the 2001 wave of the BHPS, respondents were asked, "Are you regularly troubled by pain?" a question that is quite similar to the one asked in the Dutch CentERpanel. Unfortunately, this question was only asked of respondents ages fifty and over. Those reporting yes to this question are asked how often they are troubled by pain (every day, at least once a week, once a month, less often), and how they would describe pain (mild, moderate, or severe). In summary, all BHPS respondents were asked in the 1999 wave a form of the recent pain question while BHPS respondents in the 2001 wave age fifty and over were asked a version of the recurrent pain question.

Table 9.4   Prevalence of types of pain, ages 25+

	All	Men	Women	Education low	Education med.	Education high	Ages 45+	Ages 45–64
United States								
Recurring pain in last 12 months	19.6	17.3	21.5	23.2	20.8	15.1	23.7	23.9
Any pain in last 3 months	51.3	47.3	52.1	55.5	53.1	46.5	56.1	55.0
Neck pain	14.9	12.6	16.8	17.2	15.8	11.6	16.0	17.0
Jaw/face pain	4.7	2.8	6.4	5.3	5.1	3.6	4.6	5.2
Back pain	27.5	25.5	29.0	32.6	28.8	21.9	29.6	30.0
Joint pain	38.7	29.8	42.8	37.7	33.1	26.8	40.9	37.7
Severe headaches/migraines	14.9	9.2	19.9	16.9	15.8	11.7	12.4	15.2
Netherlands								
Often troubled by pain	26.7	20.7	33.1	29.9		19.5	31.6	32.1
Any pain in last 30 days	58.9	51.8	66.4	60.5		55.5	60.5	60.2
Neck pain	20.6	16.2	25.3	22.1		17.3	21.7	23.9
Jaw/face pain	5.7	3.7	7.9	6.4		4.2	5.9	7.9
Back pain	32.9	28.9	37.1	35.9		26.1	34.1	32.6
Joint pain	37.4	34.1	40.8	40.4		30.5	44.3	42.3
Headaches/migraines	25.4	16.9	34.3	25.9		24.1	21.2	27.1
United Kingdom								
Have mild pain or more in last 4 weeks	39.5	33.8	44.1	48.5	33.9	29.7	46.6	41.9
Have moderate pain or more in last 4 weeks	26.5	21.3	30.8	35.1	21.2	17.1	32.6	28.2
Migraines	8.8	4.7	12.2	8.8	9.7	7.1	7.9	9.6

Source: U.S.—National Health Interview Survey (NHIS) 2002. All places of pain are defined over the last three months except joint pain, which is defined over the last thirty days. Any pain in last three months includes the one-month joint pain. Netherlands—CentER panel, December 2004. Each of the specific types of pain are during the last thirty days and any pain in last thirty days means that you had at least one type. United Kingdom—British Household Panel Survey 1999. Units are in percents.

In all three countries, prevalence rates are considerably lower with the recurrent pain than in the recent pain formulation. For example, while one in five adult Americans report some form of recurring pain during the last year, about half of them report having pain somewhere during the last three months. Similarly, while a little more than a quarter of adult Dutch respondents said that they were often troubled by pain, sixty percent of them reported that they had some pain in some place during the last thirty days.

There are several possible reasons for this difference. First, the use of words such as recurring or often may imply a higher pain threshold, especially in its temporal duration, that recent pain questions cannot match. Reflecting a standard result from retrospective memory studies, recent pain may also be more likely to be recalled, thereby increasing its reported prevalence. Finally, any recent pain is calculated by going through specific types of pain like back pain, which because it is less vague and more specific, may stimulate recall. This is quite similar to findings that total consumption measures that are computed by asking about specific consumption items yield higher consumption totals than a catch-all single total consumption question (Browning, Crossley, and Weber 2003).

In whatever form the pain question is asked, there are several key similarities among the countries. In each country, women are much more likely to report that they suffer from pain than men are, pain prevalence declines significantly as education increases, and the age gradient in pain is actually quite muted. If we compare Dutch, Americans, and British using the more comparable recent pain formulation, prevalence levels of pain appear higher in the Netherlands than in the other two countries.

Table 9.4 also documents that pain in the joints and back pain are the most common types of pain that people report in both the Netherlands and the United States. All forms of pain, including joint and back pain, have very pronounced negative gradients across education groups. Finally, all types of pain are more prevalent among women than they are amongst men, and in all three countries, severe headaches or migraines appear to especially be a problem for women. For example, more than a third of Dutch women report that they suffer from headaches compared to less than one in six Dutch men.

Individuals also differ in the severity of the pain that they experience. Table 9.5 summarizes the respondents' assessments of the severity of the pain that they experience, with that assessment placed into three categories—light, moderate, and heavy. While the specific scales used to place individuals within these three groups differ between the countries, the patterns that emerge across groups are quite similar. In each country, there is a great deal of variation amongst people in how they evaluate the severity of the pain that they experience. Women are more likely to say that they experience more severe pain, and in all three countries less-educated individuals are more likely to state that their pain was not light.

Table 9.5   Severity of joint pain in the United States, the Netherlands, and the
                   United Kingdom, ages 25+ (percent distributions)

	All	Men	Women	Education low	Education med.	Education high
			United States			
Light	27.6	31.7	24.2	17.1	25.1	42.1
Moderate	53.2	45.4	52.2	51.4	54.7	50.2
Heavy	19.3	14.0	23.5	31.5	20.3	7.6
			Netherlands			
Light	36.3	38.4	34.2	22.5	n.a.	30.6
Moderate	46.7	49.1	43.4	50.5	n.a.	42.1
Heavy	17.6	12.5	28.3	27.0	n.a.	27.2
			United Kingdom			
Light	52.7	58.0	49.0	44.6	58.6	64.8
Moderate	28.9	26.8	30.3	31.3	27.0	25.3
Heavy	18.4	15.2	20.7	24.1	14.4	9.9

Source: U.S.—National Health Interview Survey (NHIS) 2002. U.S. respondents were asked to rank their pain on a scale of 0–10 with 0 being *no pain* and 10 *very bad pain*. This numerical scale was converted as follows: 0–3 = *light*, 4–7 = *moderate*, 8–10 = *heavy*. Netherlands—CentERpanel, December 2004. Dutch respondents were asked to rank their pain into one of the three categories listed in this table. UK—1999 British Household Panel Survey.

Notes: Respondents were asked to rank from 0 to 5, where 0 = *no pain* in the last 4 weeks. Sample is those who do not report *no pain*. We convert that ranking as follows: 2–3 = *light*, 4 = *moderate*, 5–6 = *heavy*. UK respondents were asked to rank from 1 to 5. We convert that ranking as follows: 1–2 = *light*, 3 = *moderate*, 4–5 = *Heavy*. n.a. = not available.

Using the alternative forms of the definitions of pain used in tables 9.4 and 9.5, table 9.6 documents the relationship between the presence of pain and the report of a work disability. These simple cross-tabular relationships suggest that pain is a very powerful correlate of work disability. No matter which specific definition of pain is used, those who claim that they suffer from pain are much more likely to also say that they have a work disability. To illustrate using the recurrent pain question, Dutch respondents who say that they are often troubled with pain are almost four times as likely to say they are work disabled than those who do not have pain (64.9 percent compared to 16.9 percent). That difference is even larger among Americans (35.7 percent compared to 7.5 percent). Just as in the other two countries, work disability in the United Kingdom is around four times higher for those with general pain than for those without. And as in the other countries, when looking at specific pain, in this case migraines, the differences between those with and without such pain are still apparent although the relative risk of work disability is somewhat lower.

All forms of pain that we measured appear to be strongly associated with work disability. Recurrent pain appears to be somewhat more strongly associated with work disability, and among the alternative types of pain that

Table 9.6 Work disability by presence of pain, ages 25+ (percent distributions)

	All with pain	All without pain	Education low with pain	Education low without pain	Education med with pain	Education med without pain	Education high with pain	Education high without pain
			United States					
Recurring pain in last 12 months	35.7	7.5	52.4	17.0	35.8	7.3	21.4	2.9
Any pain in last 3 months	21.2	7.8	36.5	17.0	21.4	7.7	10.2	2.3
Neck pain	27.4	10.5	45.0	21.2	27.1	10.6	14.6	4.5
Jaw/face pain	31.7	12.1	52.2	22.7	32.6	12.2	12.5	5.5
Back pain	24.3	8.7	39.6	18.3	24.2	8.8	11.7	4.0
Joint pain	25.3	7.2	41.9	15.2	25.1	7.4	13.2	3.0
Severe headaches/migraines	22.7	11.3	40.1	22.2	22.5	11.5	9.6	5.2
Pain light	11.6	n.a.	26.1	n.a.	11.1	n.a.	7.9	n.a.
Pain moderate	24.8	n.a.	37.9	n.a.	25.0	n.a.	15.0	n.a.
Pain heavy	44.4	n.a.	55.2	n.a.	41.8	n.a.	29.3	n.a.
			Netherlands					
Often troubled by pain	64.9	16.9	66.9	18.0			58.0	14.7
Any pain in last 30 days	42.1	11.9	45.7	12.6			33.4	10.4
Neck pain	54.3	23.3	57.7	25.5			44.3	18.7
Jaw/face pain	66.3	27.5	70.1	30.1			53.1	21.8
Back pain	49.9	19.8	53.3	21.1			39.3	17.4
Joint pain	55.0	14.6	58.6	15.0			44.2	13.9
Headaches/migraines	42.3	25.4	46.1	27.9			33.0	20.0
Pain light[a]	27.0	n.a.	28.7	n.a.			23.3	n.a.
	16.1		14.3				19.2	

(continued)

Table 9.6   (continued)

	All with pain	All without pain	Education low with pain	Education low without pain	Education med with pain	Education med without pain	Education high with pain	Education high without pain
Pain moderate[a]	65.3 39.2	n.a.	68.0 42.5	n.a.			54.8 30.7	n.a.
Pain heavy[a]	85.8 66.3	n.a.	89.2 69.3	n.a.			75.5 55.9	n.a.
United Kingdom								
Have mild pain or more in last 4 weeks	40.7	9.7	50.6	14.9	31.1	6.4	25.5	7.2
Have moderate pain or more in last 4 weeks	49.5	12.0	57.7	18.4	39.9	8.0	34.2	8.2
Severe headaches/migraines	30.1	21.1	40.7	31.4	22.7	13.9	19.8	12.1
Pain light	9.7	n.a.	14.9	n.a.	6.4	n.a.	7.2	n.a.
Pain moderate	22.8	n.a.	31.8	n.a.	16.5	n.a.	13.7	n.a.
Pain heavy	47.8	n.a.	55.8	n.a.	38.8	n.a.	34.7	n.a.

Source: U.S.—National Health Interview Survey (NHIS) 2002. All places of pain are defined over the last three months except joint pain which is defined over the last thirty days. Any pain in last three months includes the one-month joint pain. Each cell presents the percentage of respondents with work disability. For instance, the entry 35.7 indicates that among those with recurring pain in the last twelve months, 35.7 percent reports to be work disabled; the entry 7.5 indicates that among those who do not report a recurring pain in the last twelve months, only 7.5 percent reports to be work disabled. Netherlands—CentERpanel, December 2004. Each of the specific types of pain are during the last thirty days and any pain in last thirty days means at least one type. United Kingdom—British Household Panel Survey 1999.

Notes: n.a. = not available.

[a] First number: pain in joints only; second number: most serious types of pain (of the five types: neck pain, jaw/face pain, back pain, joint pain, headaches/migraines).

are included in our surveys, joint pain appears to have the strongest association. Not surprisingly, respondents' report of the severity of pain is quite crucial for whether a work disability is also reported. For example, among Americans those with heavy pain are four times more likely to say that they are work disabled than those who categorize their pain as only light. If anything, this difference is even larger in the Dutch sample. Even after one controls for the degree of pain severity, those in lower education groups are much more likely to report that the pain results in a work disability.

Pain is certainly not the only thing that matters for work disability. Therefore, we next estimated probit models of the probability that a respondent reported having a work disability. The American, Dutch, and British models are presented in table 9.7. In addition to variables that capture some aspect of pain, these models include measures of a standard set of demographic attributes (gender, education, marital status, and age) as well as a list of as many chronic health conditions that are available in the data (hypertension, diabetes, cancer, diseases of the lung, heart problems, stroke, emotional problems, and arthritis).

In each country, three variants of the model were estimated—one with an indicator of pain, the second which categorizes the severity of this pain, and the third of which includes indicators of the location of pain. As mentioned above, places of pain are not available in the United Kingdom, so in its stead we include a second variant where the pain threshold is moderate pain or worse. All tables list estimated coefficients, derivatives, and z values of estimated differences from zero in the three countries.

We first discuss the nonpain variables in these models. The Dutch samples are much smaller than those available in the other two countries. Putting that caveat aside and given the differences in the institutional context in each country, and especially the diverse manner in which the pain questions are formulated, one is struck by the basic similarity in model estimates across the three countries. In these models in all three countries, work disability falls significantly with education level, rises with age, and is lower among married respondents. The only demographic difference that emerges concerns gender. In the United States work disability is lower among women (statistically significant), while it is not different by gender in the other two countries. Finally, all the health problems included in these models appear generally to have independent and statistically significant effects on work disability.

Pain turns out to be the most important predictor of work disability in all three countries. Moreover, pain—in each of the forms in which we measure it (place of pain and its severity)—is a statistically significant independent predictor of work disability.

Our goal with these models is twofold—to uncover the principal factors that led to a report of work disability and to isolate the sources of the international difference in reported work disability. To see how we accomplish

Table 9.7   **Probits for work disability**

	Coefficient	DF/dX	Coefficient	DF/dX	Coefficient	DF/dX
			United States			
High blood pressure	0.149	0.025	0.137	0.024	0.131	0.022
	(6.06)**	(6.06)**	(5.55)**	(5.55)**	(5.28)**	(5.28)**
Diabetes	0.323	0.063	0.308	0.060	0.317	0.061
	(9.23)**	(9.23)**	(8.79)**	(8.79)**	(9.01)**	(9.01)**
Cancer	0.238	0.044	0.240	0.045	0.221	0.040
	(6.71)**	(6.71)**	(6.75)**	(6.75)**	(6.18)**	(6.18)**
Lung disease	0.390	0.079	0.391	0.080	0.347	0.068
	(10.26)**	(10.26)**	(10.20)**	(10.20)**	(8.98)**	(8.98)**
Heart problems	0.391	0.077	0.403	0.081	0.380	0.074
	(13.25)**	(13.25)**	(13.60)**	(13.60)**	(12.77)**	(12.77)**
Stroke	0.585	0.133	0.596	0.138	0.584	0.131
	(10.46)**	(10.46)**	(10.56)**	(10.56)**	(10.32)**	(10.32)**
Arthritis	0.465	0.049	0.368	0.069	0.317	0.057
	(18.85)**	(18.85)**	(13.73)**	(13.73)**	(11.81)**	(11.81)**
Emotional problems	0.694	0.159	0.692	0.160	0.629	0.138
	(22.78)**	(22.78)**	(22.53)**	(22.53)**	(19.95)**	(19.95)**
Pain	0.410	0.072				
	(17.93)**	(17.93)**				
Pain light			0.038	0.006		
			(0.94)	(0.94)		
Pain moderate			0.369	0.072		
			(12.64)**	(12.65)**		
Pain heavy			0.704	0.167		
			(17.93)**	(17.93)**		
Neck pain					0.164	0.028
					(5.33)**	(5.33)*
Back pain					0.289	0.051
					(11.40)**	(11.40)**
Jaw pain					0.156	0.027
					(3.37)**	(3.37)**
Headache					0.171	0.030
					(5.49)**	(5.49)**
Joint pain					0.292	0.050
					(11.38)**	(11.38)**
Female	−0.136	−0.025	−0.130	−0.022	−0.150	−0.024
	(6.07)**	(6.07)**	(5.79)**	(5.79)**	(6.55)**	(6.55)**
Education med.	−0.237	−0.040	−0.232	−0.039	−0.238	−0.039
	(8.88)**	(8.88)**	(8.30)**	(8.30)**	(8.34)**	(8.34)**
Education high	−0.538	−0.074	−0.511	−0.071	−0.529	−0.071
	(14.50)**	(14.50)**	(13.79)**	(13.79)**	(14.06)**	(14.06)**
Age 35–44	0.271	0.049	0.249	0.045	0.260	0.046
	(6.72)**	(6.72)**	(6.19)**	(6.19)**	(6.36)**	(6.36)**
Age 45–54	0.445	0.087	0.401	0.078	0.430	0.082
	(11.11)**	(11.11)**	(10.02)**	(10.02)**	(10.58)**	(10.58)**
Age 55–64	0.606	0.130	0.548	0.116	0.604	0.127
	(14.17)**	(14.17)**	(12.85)**	(12.85)**	(13.95)**	(13.95)**
Age 65+	0.526	0.010	0.445	0.087	0.549	0.108
	(12.23)**	(12.23)**	(10.42)**	(10.42)**	(12.53)**	(12.53)**

	Coefficient	DF/dX	Coefficient	DF/dX	Coefficient	DF/dX
rried	−0.412	−0.068	−0.408	−0.068	−0.412	−0.067
	(18.14)**	(18.14)**	(17.99)**	(17.99)**	(18.03)**	(18.03)**
nstant	−1.633		−1.526		−1.658	
	(34.00)**		(32.50)		(34.40)**	
servations	27,684		27,684		27,684	
served p	0.146		0.146		0.146	
g likelihood	−8,541.1		−8,494.0		−8.403.3	

Netherlands

	Coefficient	DF/dX	Coefficient	DF/dX	Coefficient	DF/dX
h blood pressure	0.007	0.002	−0.028	0.008	0.011	0.003
	(0.07)	(0.07)	(0.28)	(0.28)	(0.11)	(0.11)
betes	0.531	0.180	0.514	0.173	0.602	0.205
	(2.85)**	(2.85)**	(2.70)**	(2.70)**	(3.25)**	(3.25)**
ncer	0.260	0.082	0.127	0.038	0.265	0.082
	(1.31)	(1.31)	(0.62)	(0.62)	(1.32)	(1.32)
ng disease	0.467	0.156	0.513	0.172	0.433	0.141
	(2.79)**	(2.79)**	(3.06)**	(3.06)**	(2.52)**	(2.52)**
art problems	0.931	0.332	0.914	0.324	0.945	0.334
	(6.33)**	(6.33)**	(6.14)**	(6.14)**	(6.39)**	(6.39)**
oke	0.982	0.359	0.875	0.316	0.868	0.311
	(3.08)**	(3.08)**	(2.76)**	(2.76)**	(2.76)**	(2.76)**
hritis	0.719	0.248	0.448	0.146	0.686	0.233
	(5.47)**	(5.47)**	(3.18)	(3.18)	(5.17)**	(5.17)**
otional problems	0.764	0.264	0.842	0.293	0.717	0.243
	(6.35)**	(6.35)**	(6.92)	(6.92)	(5.87)**	(5.87)**
n	1.043	0.352				
	(11.75)**	(11.75)**				
n light			0.407	0.129		
			(3.72)**	(3.72)**		
n moderate			1.200	0.422		
			(11.08)**	(11.08)**		
n heavy			1.793	0.630		
			(9.49)	(9.49		
ck pain					0.218	0.065
					(2.04)**	(2.04)**
ck pain					0.355	0.106
					(3.97)**	(3.97)**
pain					0.380	0.122
					(1.93)	(1.93)
adache					0.077	0.022
					(0.77)	(0.77)
nt pain					0.698	0.212
					(7.70)**	(7.70)**
nale	0.077	0.022	0.095	0.027	0.103	0.030
	(0.93)	(0.93)	(1.13)	(1.13)	(1.23)	(1.23)
ucation med.	−0.057	−0.016	−0.103	−0.029	−0.091	−0.026
	(0.58)	(0.58)	(1.02)	(1.02)	(0.93)	(0.93)

(*continued*)

Table 9.7 (continued)

	Coefficient	DF/dX	Coefficient	DF/dX	Coefficient	DF/dX
Education high	−0.319	−0.089	−0.305	−0.084	−0.326	−0.089
	(3.16)**	(3.16)**	(2.98)**	(2.98)**	(3.21)**	(3.21)*
Age 35–44	−0.192	−0.053	−0.295	−0.079	−0.275	−0.073
	(1.33)	(1.33)	(2.02)**	(2.02)**	(1.89)	(1.89)
Age 45–54	0.030	0.009	−0.186	−0.051	−0.165	−0.045
	(0.22)	(0.22)	(1.33)	(1.33)	(1.17)	(1.17)
Age 55–64	0.174	0.052	0.127	0.037	0.140	0.041
	(1.20)	(1.20)	(0.88)	(0.88)	(0.97)	(0.97)
Age 65+	0.038	0.011	−0.114	−0.032	−0.092	−0.026
	(0.26)	(0.26)	(0.76)	(0.76)	(0.62)	(0.62)
Married	−0.114	−0.034	−0.147	−0.044	−0.106	−0.031
	(1.18)	(1.18)	(1.50)	(1.50)	(1.08)	(1.08)
Constant	−1.137		−1.100		−1.265	
	(6.88)**		(6.68)**		(7.55)**	
Observations	1537		1537		1537	
Observed p	0.254		0.254		0.254	
Log Likelihood	−643.50		−620.20		−635.99	

United Kingdom

	Coefficient	DF/dX	Coefficient	DF/dX	Coefficient	DF/dX
High blood pressure	0.242	0.065	0.239	0.065	0.222	0.059
	(5.19)**	(5.19)**	(5.09)**	(5.09)**	(4.70)**	(4.70)*
Diabetes	0.441	0.131	0.480	0.146	0.456	0.136
	(4.65)**	(4.65)**	(5.06)**	(5.06)**	(4.74)	(4.74)
Cancer	0.977	0.335	0.962	0.330	0.960	0.327
	(7.00)**	(7.00)**	(6.85)**	(6.85)**	(6.76)**	(6.76)*
Heart problems	0.548	0.167	0.566	0.175	0.563	0.172
	(6.96)**	(6.96)**	(7.17)**	(7.17)**	(7.100)**	(7.100)
Stroke	0.637	0.200	0.623	0.197	0.606	0.188
	(7.97)**	(7.97)**	(7.70)**	(7.70)**	(7.43)**	(7.43)*
Arthritis	0.641	0.193	0.627	0.190	0.568	0.168
	(13.57)**	(13.57)**	(13.11)**	(13.11)**	(11.83)**	(11.83)*
Emotional problems	0.660	0.206	0.663	0.208	0.620	0.191
	(10.89)**	(10.89)**	(10.93)**	(10.93)**	(10.00)**	(10.00)*
Pain	0.765	0.205	0.854	0.252		
	(21.21)**	(21.21)**	(22.75)**	(22.75)**		
Pain very mild					0.227	0.061
					(4.21)**	(4.21)*
Pain mild					0.461	0.133
					(8.19)**	(8.19)*
Pain moderate					0.873	0.272
					(17.56)**	(17.56)*
Pain severe					1.285	0.441
					(20.44)**	(20.44)*
Pain very severe					1.374	0.486
					(13.08)**	(13.08)*
Female	−0.049	−0.012	−0.057	−0.014	−0.070	−0.017
	(1.37)	(1.37)	(1.59)	(1.59)	(1.93)	(1.93)

Table 9.7 (continued)

	Coefficient	DF/dX	Coefficient	DF/dX	Coefficient	DF/dX
Education med.	−0.239	−0.058	−0.228	−0.056	−0.214	−0.052
	(5.86)**	(5.86)**	(5.58)**	(5.58)**	(5.19)**	(5.19)**
Education high	−0.235	−0.054	−0.218	−0.051	−0.192	−0.045
	(4.35)**	(4.35)**	(4.05)**	(4.05)**	(3.53)**	(3.53)**
Age 35–44	0.160	0.042	0.149	0.039	0.162	0.042
	(2.66)**	(2.66)**	(2.46)**	(2.46)**	(2.63)**	(2.63)**
Age 45–54	0.258	0.069	0.269	0.073	0.274	0.073
	(4.25)	(4.25)	(4.44)**	(4.44)**	(4.46)**	(4.46)**
Age 55–64	0.324	0.090	0.319	0.089	0.336	0.093
	(4.88)**	(4.88)**	(4.82)**	(4.82)**	(4.99)**	(4.99)**
Age 65+	0.499	0.140	0.508	0.144	0.520	0.146
	(7.73)**	(7.73)**	(7.89)**	(7.89)**	(7.92)**	(7.92)**
Married	−0.114	−0.029	−0.101	−0.026	−0.100	−0.025
	(2.87)**	(2.87)**	(2.53)**	(2.53)**	(2.48)**	(2.48)**
Constant	−1.538		−1.463		−1.624	
	(22.56)**		(21.79)**		(23.06)**	

Note: Robust z statistics in parentheses.
* Significant at the 1 percent level.
Significant at the 5 percent level.

this goal, consider for example an evaluation of the impact of a single health condition j. Let $P(A)$ and $P(B)$ be the (predicted) work disability rates in country A and country B (for a given age group), and let $P(A)^{-j}$ and $P(B)^{-j}$ be the predicted work disabilities in countries A and B for the counterfactual situation that nobody would suffer from health problem j. We can then interpret $P(A) - P(A)^{-j}$ as the work disability rate in country A due to that health problem, and similarly for country B. Note that this assignment of importance to this health condition depends both on the prevalence of the health problem and on the sensitivity of the probability of work disability to that health problem (i.e., on the corresponding coefficients in β_A); we will separate these two below.

The difference in work disabilities in the two countries can be expressed using the following decomposition:

$$P(B) - P(A) = [P(B)^{-j} - P(A)^{-j}] + [P(B) - P(B)^{-j}] - [P(A) - P(A)^{-j}].$$

The first term on the right hand side can be interpreted as the difference between work disability prevalence in the two countries that is *not* due to the chosen health problem. The sum of the second and third term is then the part that is due to the chosen health condition. The latter two terms can be further separated in a *prevalence* effect (the percentage with the health problem) and an *impact* effect (the impact of the health problem on work disability). We can write:

$$P(A) - P(A)^{-j} = \frac{1}{N_A} \sum_{i \in A} [g(x_i, b_A) - g(x_i^{-j}, b_A)]$$

$$= \left(\sum_{i \in A} x_{ij} / N_A \right) \left[\sum_{i \in A, x_{ij}=1} \Delta g(x_j, b_A) / \sum_{i \in A} x_{ij} \right]$$

where $g(x_i, b_A)$ is the probability of having the health condition for an individual with characteristics x_i and parameter vector b_A.

The first factor is the fraction in country A that suffers from the chosen health problem (the quantity effect for country A). In the second term, $\Delta g(x_j, b_A)$ is the marginal effect (partial derivative) for a dummy variable, the difference if it is set to 1 or 0, with other variables set to their values for observation i. Thus, the second term can be seen as the average marginal effect for those who have the health problem.

The same decomposition can be used for all covariates in the model (both health and nonhealth dummy variables), allowing us to compare the importance of each to the reported rates of work disability in each country and the difference between the three countries.

Table 9.8 presents a summary of the relative contributions of different sets of factors toward explaining the differences between the three countries in reported rates of work disability. For this relative assessment, we divide covariates into five groups—the so-called objective health factors (hypertension, diabetes, cancer, diseases of the lung), heart problems and stroke, arthritis, emotional problems, and pain. The first three columns in table 9.8 assess the importance of each factor to explaining work disability in the Netherlands, the United States, and the United Kingdom. The final two columns assess the contribution of each factor toward explaining the differences between countries using the Netherlands as the reference group. Separate assessments are performed for each of the three models estimated for each country in table 9.7.

In each of the three countries, pain is by far the most important factor explaining reported rates of work disability. This is especially true for the Netherlands and the United Kingdom, where observed work disability rates are higher than in the United States. Moreover, as summarized by the "all pain" row in table 9.8, the estimated role of pain rises when we estimate models which differentiate between the degree of pain (light, moderate, and heavy) and the location of pain in the body. Joint pain, and to a somewhat lesser degree back pain, are the most central types of pain in explaining rates of work disability.

The most important columns in table 9.8 are the final two which summarize the role of each set of factors toward explaining differences in work disability between the countries. Once again compared to either the Netherlands or the United Kingdom, pain predicts much lower rates of work disability in the United States. This is in part due to the lower pain

ble 9.8   **Contributions of factors to explaining work disability**

	Netherlands	United Kingdom	United States	Netherlands–U.K.	Netherlands–U.S.
		Model 1			
▸jective health	1.57	2.17	2.64	–0.60	–1.07
▸art problems	2.38	1.61	1.76	0.77	0.62
▸thritis	2.34	2.86	2.74	–0.52	–0.40
▸notional	2.44	1.30	1.72	1.14	0.72
▸in	8.50	6.63	3.05	1.87	5.45
		Model 2			
▸jective health	1.48	2.03	2.52	–0.55	–1.04
▸art problems	2.15	1.57	1.78	0.58	0.37
▸thritis	1.34	2.59	2.19	–1.25	–0.85
▸notional	2.61	1.19	1.68	1.42	0.93
▸in light	1.48	2.08	0.05	–0.60	1.43
▸in moderate	6.37	3.98	1.40	2.39	4.97
▸in heavy	3.19	3.82	1.22	–0.63	1.97
▸ pain (sum of above three rows)	11.04	9.88	2.67	1.16	8.37
		Model 3			
▸jective health	1.60		2.40		–0.80
▸art problems	2.31		1.70		0.61
▸thritis	2.29		1.91		0.38
▸notional	2.25		1.54		0.71
▸ck pain	3.45		1.72		1.73
▸nt pain	7.88		2.13		5.75
▸her Pain	2.28		1.27		1.01
▸ pain (sum of above three rows)	13.61		5.12		8.49

▸te: Units are percentage points.

prevalence in the United States and in part due to the lower effect of pain on work disability in the United States compared to the other two countries. In explaining lower rates of work disability in the United States, pain is by far the most important factor of those listed in table 9.8. Why individuals in the United States respond less to pain than residents of the other two countries will be the central question in the next two sections.

9.4   Pain Medication and Workplace Accommodation

How pain translates into a personal assessment of a work disability may be affected by pain medication and the types of accommodations available in the workplace to deal with any impairment. If pain medication alone sufficiently alleviates the symptoms and severity of the pain, individuals may not feel that they actually have a work disability. Similarly, if accommodations are available at work so that the impairment does not affect the daily routines of work or how productive a worker is, individuals may also believe that their problems are not relevant to their current work situation. In both situations, individuals may answer a question on whether they have a work disability in the negative even though without medication or accommodation they would have one. Moreover, both the use and availability of pain medication or the extent of accommodations available at work may well vary across the three countries we are studying. If they do, these two factors may account for some of the differences in reported work disability across these countries. To investigate this possibility, we present information in this section on the role of pain medication and workplace accommodation in each of our three countries.

9.4.1   Pain Medication

To help answer these questions, we added a pain module to the December 2004 wave of the Dutch CentERpanel. To the question on whether they were often troubled by pain, respondents could answer (1) yes, (2) no, because I use pain medication, and (3) no, and I do not need pain medication. If people respond yes, there was a follow-up question that inquired about whether they used pain medication to combat the pain. That sequence of questions allows us to estimate how many people troubled by pain are using pain medication and how effective that medication is in eliminating the pain.

The results are listed in table 9.9. The use of pain medication is actually very widespread in the Netherlands and the use of this medication affects the reporting of pain. While 26.5 percent of respondents reported that they were often troubled with pain, that fraction would grow to 37.4 percent if we included those whose pain medication eliminated the pain. Among the Dutch respondents who either had pain or would have had pain without medication, 69 percent were taking medication for this pain. Moreover, the use of this medication was quite effective. Within this group, 42 percent of Dutch respondents had no pain at all. Using this definition of effectiveness, pain medication appears equally effective for women and men, but appears to have eliminated pain completely in a larger fraction of the more educated Dutch respondents. This may be due to the fact that their pain was less severe.

Unfortunately, the pain medication questions in the United States and the United Kingdom are not strictly comparable to those in the Netherlands. For the United States we use data from the National Health and Nutrition Examination Survey (NHANES), which asked similar questions about the location of pain (neck, back, headaches, joint, face) during the last three months as described previously for the NHIS. The advantage of

ble 9.9   **The use of pain medication**

	All	Men	Women	Ed low	Ed med	Ed high	Ages 45+	Ages 45–64
I. The Netherlands								
% with pain or taking painkillers	37.4	28.9	46.5	40.8		29.8	41.9	42.9
% of A taking painkillers	68.9	64.7	71.6	69.4		70.6	66.4	67.4
% of B with no pain	41.6	43.9	40.9	39.1		49.1	36.9	37.4
with pain	26.5	20.7	33.1	29.9		19.5	31.6	32.1
II. United States								
% with pain or taking painkillers	61.6	57.1	65.7	64.1	65.1	58.7	65.7	64.3
% of A taking painkillers	41.3	41.0	41.5	37.3	43.8	42.1	54.7	48.4
% of B with no pain	35.5	43.9	29.1	30.6	29.9	41.1	40.3	38.2
with pain	52.6						51.3	52.4
III. United Kingdom								
All 52+								
% with pain	38.3	33.7	41.9	41.9		30.1		
% with moderate/severe pain	27.7	25.7	29.0	28.7		24.4		
% of B taking pain medication	27.3	21.2	31.0	26.6		29.7		
% of B with pain being controlled	60.1	53.2	62.9	59.2		63.1		

ource: Netherlands—CentERpanel, December 2004. United States—NHANES 1999–2000. Pain is efined as some form of pain in the last three months, including neck, face, back, headaches, or joint ain. United Kingdom—ELSA 2004. Sample is aged fifty in 2002.

NHANES is that it also contains a detailed set of questions about all types of medications. The noncomparability with the Dutch sample derives from the fact that we have already demonstrated that this form of the pain question elicits much higher prevalence rates than the recurrent pain question. This expansion in pain prevalence no doubt includes many less serious forms of pain.

For the United Kingdom we use new data from the latest wave of the English Longitudinal Study of Ageing (ELSA), which contains detailed questions on certain types of pain alleviation as part of their questions on the use and efficacy of health care services. In this case the noncomparability arises for three reasons. First, only individuals reporting moderate or severe pain are asked general questions about pain medication. Second, for both general and specific types of pain medication, the ELSA questions relate solely to medication or treatment prescribed by a respondent's doctor or nurse. Finally, the ELSA sample consists of individuals aged fifty and over in 2002, as opposed to being an age-representative sample such as the NHANES or CentERpanel.

These important caveats should be kept in mind when interpreting the second and third panels of table 9.9, illustrating the extent of pain medication in the United States and the United Kingdom respectively. Among those with pain or without the symptoms of pain due to medication, a much smaller proportion of Americans (41.3 percent) are taking pain medication. When they do take medication, it also appears to be less effective in completely eliminating pain symptoms than it was for Dutch respondents. In the United Kingdom, an even lower fraction report receiving medication than in the United States (even when the definition of pain medication in the United States is limited to prescription painkillers only). This effect may even be somewhat underestimated since those in mild pain (who presumably have an even lower rate of medication) are routed out of the ELSA questions. On the other hand, those receiving medication are much more likely than those in both the United States and the Netherlands to report that the medication controls their pain. Once again, comparability of question wording may be an issue here. If controlled pain equates to mild pain, then such cases will be differentially recorded across the different surveys.

Despite the relative lack of comparability of these data, the relevance of their overall message to the questions addressed in this chapter is clear. While we observe a much lower prevalence of work disability and pain in the United States and the United Kingdom compared to the levels observed in the Netherlands, it is not due to a higher rate of (successful) medication in the United States and the United Kingdom. If anything, the differences across countries appear to go the other way.

9.4.2   Workplace Accommodation

In December 2004, we fielded a module on work disability in the Dutch CentERpanel that was based on one already used in ELSA. This module posed a series of questions on workplace accommodations to all respondents who were not self-employed and who had worked during the last decade. These respondents were asked if they had ever asked their employer to make an accommodation, whether their employer had ever offered to make an accommodation, and whether their employer had ever made an accommodation. The types of accommodation inquired about included making work less physically demanding, less mentally demanding/stressful, reducing hours worked/arranging job-sharing, making working hours more flexible, allowing work from home, and providing special equipment and other such adaptations to the workplace that make it easier to keep working.

A unique aspect of this module is that this series of questions were asked of all respondents, whether or not they currently have a work disability. As will be the case with the American and British survey on workplace accommodations discussed below, the standard practice is to restrict these questions to those who said that they had a workplace disability. The advantage of the protocol used in Dutch panels is that it provides a complete description of the availability of workplace accommodations in the work force. For example, if the provision of effective workplace accommodations induced some respondents to say that they did not have a workplace disability, we would never be able to know that with questions limited to those with a workplace disability.

Tables 9.10 and 9.11 summarize the responses from the Dutch respondents from the work accommodation module. Table 9.10 provides the data on the full set of respondents, while table 9.11 is limited to the subset that reports that they have a work disability.

There are no salient differences by age in these patterns of workplace ac-

Table 9.10   Dutch answers on work accommodation for full sample (answers in percents)

Variable	Age 25+	Age 45–64	Age 45+	Men	Women	Low Education	High Education
Currently employed	54.8	53.1	35.1	58.9	50.5	52.4	60.2
Ever employed	94.1	94.3	94.2	97.9	90.7	93.4	95.8
Ever asked employer to change job to							
Less physically demanding	15.6	17.0	15.8	15.7	15.7	19.3	8.2
Less stressful	20.8	21.8	20.9	19.3	22.5	20.7	20.9
Reduce hours	19.2	20.6	19.6	15.6	23.7	18.3	21.1
Make hours flexible	16.8	15.8	15.5	16.3	17.3	15.7	19.0
Work from home	14.2	12.8	12.0	15.6	12.5	11.4	19.8
Provide special equipment	26.1	24.1	22.9	24.4	28.1	28.7	20.9
Other	9.9	12.0	11.3	10.6	9.2	11.2	7.3
Employer ever offered to change job to							
Less physically demanding	17.1	17.0	16.2	16.8	17.4	20.2	10.8
Less stressful	16.0	15.7	15.1	14.5	17.8	16.9	14.1
Reduce hours	13.4	14.3	14.9	12.4	14.6	13.4	13.5
Make hours flexible	16.9	16.0	16.0	17.7	15.9	16.4	18.0
Work from home	11.9	11.7	11.2	13.1	10.3	8.3	19.0
Provide special equipment	26.6	24.0	23.1	25.6	27.9	29.1	21.5
Other	5.0	3.8	3.5	5.4	4.7	5.9	3.2
Employer ever changed jobs to							
Less physically demanding	15.1	14.9	14.4	14.4	15.8	18.2	8.8
Less stressful	11.9	12.8	12.4	9.6	14.7	12.4	10.8
Reduce hours	15.5	15.9	16.2	13.2	18.4	14.3	18.1
Make hours flexible	17.0	16.6	17.2	16.2	18.0	15.8	19.5
Work from home	9.7	10.6	10.0	10.0	9.2	5.7	17.6
Provide special equipment	25.3	22.1	21.8	22.9	28.2	27.3	21.3
Other	3.0	2.2	2.4	2.8	3.2	3.3	2.3
Had adjustment helped	86.2	82.8	83.2	83.8	88.7	86.6	85.4
Would adjustment have helped	23.6	23.3	21.9	23.8	23.2	22.7	25.4

Notes: "Ever Employed": only asked to those who are not current employees. "Physically Demanding, . . . , Other": only asked to current employees and those who have been employees ever since 1996. "Has Adjustment Helped": only asked to those for whom at least one actual adjustment was made. "Would Adjustment Have Helped": only asked to those for whom no adjustments were made.

Table 9.11   Dutch answers on work accommodation for those with current work disability (answers in percents)

Variable	Age 25+	Age 45–64	Age 45+	Men	Women	Low Education	High Educat
Currently employed	33.5	30.9	20.6	34.8	32.4	32.6	36.1
Ever employed	94.9	96.4	95.1	97.9	92.6	95.8	91.9
Ever asked employer to change job to							
Less physically demanding	35.0	34.0	31.9	38.4	31.5	40.2	19.8
Less stressful	30.2	30.1	29.9	28.7	31.8	30.6	29.2
Reduce hours	32.1	33.7	32.9	22.5	25.8	23.8	25.2
Make hours flexible	24.1	24.4	24.4	16.3	17.3	15.7	19.0
Work from home	16.6	10.6	9.8	16.5	16.6	16.9	15.6
Provide special equipment	36.0	32.8	32.1	32.8	39.2	37.5	31.4
Other	18.4	22.7	21.5	22.1	14.7	18.3	18.8
Employer ever offered to change job to							
Less physically demanding	28.4	26.4	25.3	30.7	26.1	32.3	17.0
Less stressful	21.9	20.5	20.2	20.8	23.0	24.8	13.4
Reduce hours	24.1	23.6	23.5	26.2	21.9	24.4	23.0
Make hours flexible	21.8	19.4	19.2	22.6	21.1	22.6	19.6
Work from home	11.0	9.8	9.4	11.4	10.5	10.7	11.6
Provide special equipment	30.2	27.6	27.4	25.5	34.9	32.7	22.8
Other	7.3	3.9	3.9	8.0	6.5	7.0	7.9
Employer ever changed job to							
Less physically demanding	28.0	23.9	23.4	30.6	25.3	32.1	15.9
Less stressful	17.1	18.5	18.0	14.3	19.7	19.0	11.1
Reduce hours	24.9	24.0	24.3	25.6	24.1	25.1	24.2
Make hours flexible	23.1	17.4	18.2	21.6	24.7	23.9	20.8
Work from home	7.8	8.2	7.7	8.4	7.3	7.1	10.1
Provide special equipment	29.7	26.9	27.1	25.0	34.5	33.1	20.0
Other	5.0	3.3	3.7	4.7	5.4	4.0	8.2
Had adjustment helped	78.3	73.7	74.2	74.5	82.4	77.5	81.1
Would adjustment have helped	34.3	31.8	0.0	36.7	32.0	31.9	40.6

Notes: "Ever Employed": only asked to those who are not current employees. "Physically Dema
ing, . . . , Other": only asked to current employees and those who have been employees ever since 19
"Has Adjustment Helped": only asked to those for whom at least one actual adjustment was ma
"Would Adjustment Have Helped": only asked to those for whom no adjustments were made.

commodations. The principal differences that emerge by gender have to do with flexibility of hours where women are more likely to ask and to have had adjustments in their work hours. However, this pattern is only apparent in the full sample, which suggests that the differential gender treatment is largely due to other matters (such as family responsibilities) rather than work disabilities. Within the work disabled subsample, women are more likely to have had adjustments in their physical workplace while men are more likely to have equipment adjustments.

There are much stronger differences by education that appear in both the full and work disability samples. Those in the lower education category are much more likely to have asked for, been offered, and received physical and equipment adjustments in their workplace environment. For example, among those with a work disability, 32 percent of less educated Dutch respondents had a physical adjustment to their workplace compared to only 16 percent of the higher educated respondents.

The final two rows in these tables provide a summary of the Dutch respondents assessment of whether these workplace accommodations were helpful. When there were workplace accommodations, more than three quarters of respondents thought that the adjustments were useful, and when there were no workplace adjustments a third of respondents still believed that the adjustments would have helped if they had been made.

As previously explained, questions on workplace accommodations in American surveys are limited to those with a work disability. Perhaps, the best module was placed into the HRS, where a set of questions was asked about workplace accomodations for those with a work disability. These questions were asked whether or not the individual was currently employed. If not currently employed, the questions referred to the last time of employment.

Table 9.12 (based on the HRS) provides a description of the types of help provided by employers. These data in the HRS sample are most comparable with data from the Dutch samples that are restricted to those with a current work disability and who are older workers (forty-five to sixty-four in the Dutch sample). Similar to the Dutch case, gender differences in workplace accommodation in the United States are small. But in sharp contrast to the Dutch data, there is also almost no education gradient to the use of workplace accommodation in the United States. Most importantly, workplace accommodations are far less common in the American than in the Dutch workplace. This generalization appears to be true across the board,

Table 9.12	Workplace accommodation in the United States (answers in percents)					
	All	Men	Women	Low ed	Med. ed	High ed
Did employer help you	22.4	22.1	22.7	22.4	21.3	24.5
Somewhat helped you out	9.3	8.7	9.5	9.6	9.5	6.9
Shorter work day	6.3	6.4	6.3	6.1	5.8	9.0
Flexible hours	7.3	6.6	7.9	8.6	7.2	9.8
More breaks	8.5	8.5	8.5	8.6	6.5	8.2
Special transportation	1.2	0.9	1.4	1.3	1.3	0.4
Change job	10.1	11.3	8.9	10.2	9.2	11.0
Help learn new skills	3.1	2.5	3.7	3.2	3.1	2.4
Special equipment	2.7	2.6	2.8	2.7	2.8	3.3
Anything else	6.4	6.1	6.7	6.2	6.0	8.6

Note: 1992-HRS baseline ages fifty-one to sixty-one. Sample: all those who said that they had a work disability.

but it is especially pronounced for equipment and physical changes in the workplace.

Since the workplace accommodation questions for our ELSA sample are limited to those who are currently employed, table 9.13 contains the most directly comparable data for all three countries. In this table, both the Dutch and American data are also limited to those who are currently employed. In addition, to preserve some age comparability, the Dutch sample is limited to those forty-five to sixty-four and the American sample to those ages fifty-one to sixty-one. While this is the most comparable comparison possible between all three countries, it is important to note that sample sizes in the Dutch sample become quite small.

The first panel of table 9.13 summarizes the responses from the Dutch respondents from the work accommodation module. To enhance comparability across surveys, we select the sample of older respondents who report a work disability but who were also working at the time of the survey. The principal differences that emerge by gender have to do with the physical nature of work, where women are less likely to have had adjustments, and in flexibility of hours and special equipment, where women are more likely to have had adjustments. Differences by education are also apparent. As before, those in the lower education category are much more likely to have asked for, to have been offered, and to have received physical and equipment adjustments in their workplace environment.

The 2004 wave of the English Longitudinal Study of Ageing contains the same questions on workplace accommodation, although due to the design of the survey, some individuals are routed out of some of the items. In table 9.13 we show similar descriptive statistics to those from the Netherlands for the ELSA sample (which is aged fifty-two and over in 2004). The first three lines of this table establish some basic patterns in the data. As observed in earlier sections of this chapter the prevalence of work disability is high, and higher amongst the low education group than the high education group. In addition, conditional on reporting a work disability, the high education group is substantially more likely to work, but conditional on having a work disability and being in work, the two education groups are equally likely to report that their work disability limits their activities in the current job.

What is apparent from the across-country comparison in table 9.13 is that both overall levels and the patterns across accomodations and across gender and education subgroups are quite different in the United Kingdom from those observed in the Netherlands. Individuals working with a work disability in the United Kingdom are much less likely to have received modifications to their work environment in the United Kingdom. The overall level of accommodations is twice as high in the Netherlands as in the United Kingdom, and the differences are even greater when looking at each individual type of accommodation separately. Perhaps more surprisingly,

	All	Men	Women	Low Education	Med. Education	High Education
Table 9.13					**Workplace accommodation of disability**	
I. Netherlands						
...d employer help you in any way	70.6	77.9	58.5	75.4		59.5
...ysically less demanding	28.3	37.2	13.5	34.2		14.8
...ss stress	25.1	26.0	23.6	29.2		15.9
...orter work day	26.5	27.4	25.0	25.1		29.7
...exible hours	18.4	16.5	21.6	20.0		14.7
...ork from home	10.3	14.3	3.5	7.7		15.9
...ecial equipment or adjustment	33.2	26.4	44.6	34.3		30.9
...ything else	6.3	6.4	6.3	4.6		10.2
II. United Kingdom						
Percent of those aged 52+ reporting a work disability	33.1	33.0	33.2	36.5		25.3
Percent of A who are working	13.3	14.4	12.5	10.4		22.9
Percent of B whose work disability limits type or amount of work in current job	42.9	41.2	44.5	41.9		44.4
All employees reporting a work disability						
...rcent whose employer has either changed or offered to change their work to make it:						
Less physically demanding	9.9	12.3	8.0	9.8		10.0
Less mentally demanding/stressful	2.5	1.6	3.1	2.3		2.7
Fewer hours/job sharing	5.6	4.1	6.8	4.0		8.2
More flexible hours	3.5	2.5	4.3	2.9		4.5
Working from home sometimes	1.8	0.8	2.5	0.6		3.6
Special equipment/workplace adaptation	8.1	5.7	9.9	5.7		11.8
Other	2.1	0.0	3.7	1.7		2.7
Any of the above	25.7	22.1	28.4	21.3		32.7
III. United States						
...d employer help you	29.6	28.4	31.2	32.6	26.0	21.8
...mewhat helped you out	11.6	8.9	15.4	13.8	8.5	6.5
...orter work day	8.3	8.9	7.5	10.0	3.9	6.9
...exible hours	10.1	9.9	10.5	12.9	4.0	5.4
...ore breaks	11.5	11.5	11.6	13.8	6.8	8.2
...ecial transportation	1.5	0.9	2.3	1.7	0.9	1.4
...ange job	16.5	17.4	14.8	19.2	10.5	12.4
...lp learn new skills	4.6	4.8	4.3	5.1	4.8	2.2
...ecial equipment	4.4	5.5	2.8	5.3	3.2	2.3
...ything else	6.8	5.8	8.2	6.8	5.3	8.1

...tes: The Netherlands—2004 CentERpanel ages 45–64. Sample: all those who said that they had a ...rk disability and who were at work at the time of the survey (ninety-one observations). United King-...m—2004 ELSA data ages fifty-two and over—sample all those who said that they had a work dis-...ility and who were at work at the time of the survey. United States—1992 HRS baseline ages fifty-one ... sixty-one. Sample all those who said that they had a work disability and who were at work at the time ... the survey. Data are weighted.

the differences by gender and education are reversed. In the United Kingdom it is women and the highly educated who are most likely to have received workplace accommodations (conditional on working), whereas in the Netherlands these groups have a lower likelihood of workplace accommodation. Once again, evidence from the United States, presented in panel C of table 9.13, reveals similarities between the United States and the United Kingdom and differences to the Netherlands. Table 9.11 (based on the HRS baseline data) provides a description of the types of help provided by employers. The overall level of employer accommodation is lower even than in the United Kingdom (although it should be remembered that the HRS baseline data was collected in 1992, some twelve years before the ELSA data presented for the United Kingdom). As in the United Kingdom, women are more likely to receive accommodations, but as in the Netherlands, it is the more educated that are more likely to receive workplace accommodations in the United States.

This section began by offering the possibility that some of the difference in work disability prevalence among these three countries was due to differences in the use of either pain medications or workplace accommodations. If the use of pain medications or workplace accommodations was more common in the United States that could partially explain the lower rates of reported work disability there. However, if anything, the patterns go the other way with less frequent use of work accommodations and medication in the United States. Apparently, explanations for lower reported rates of work disability in the United States must lie elsewhere.

9.5   Vignettes

If differential use of pain medication and workplace accommodation across countries cannot explain cross country differences in work disability prevalence as documented in section 9.3, what may explain it? In this section we present and apply a new methodology that aims at uncovering differences across countries in their norms and attitudes toward work disability. This new methodology relies on the use of vignettes.

We first provide an intuitive description of the use of vignettes for identifying reporting biases, following King et al. (2004) and Kapteyn, Smith, and Van Soest (2007). Their model shows how vignettes can help to identify systematic differences in response scales between groups (or countries), making it possible to decompose observed differences in, for example, self-reported health in a specific domain into differences due to response scale variation and genuine differences in health. Our analysis applies this model to work limiting disability rather than health. Vignette evaluations were collected in the Netherlands in the fall of 2003, and in the United States in early 2004. Work disability vignettes for the United Kingdom are not available yet. Thus, we can only compare the United States and the Netherlands.

9.5.1. Using Vignettes to Identify Response Scales in Pain

The basic idea of the model is sketched in figure 9.1. It presents the distribution of work-related health in two countries. The density of the continuous health variable in country A is to the left of that in country B, implying that on average, people in country A are less healthy than in country B. The people in the two countries, however, use different response scales if asked to report their health on a five-point scale (for example, poor, fair, good, very good, excellent). In our example, people in country A have a much more positive view on a given health status than people in country B. For example, someone in country A with the health indicated by the dashed line would report to be in very good health, while a person in country B with the same actual health would report fair. The frequency distribution of the self-reports in the two countries would suggest that people in country A are healthier than those in country B—the opposite of the actual health distribution. Correcting for the differences in the response scales, differential item functioning (DIF)—in the terminology of King et al. (2004)—is essential to compare the actual health distributions in the two countries.

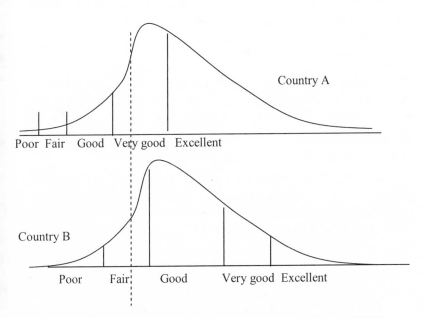

Fig. 9.1   **Comparing self-reported health across two countries in case of DIF**

Vignettes can be used to do the correction. A vignette question describes the health of a hypothetical person and then asks the respondent to evaluate that person's health on the same five-point scale that was used for the self-report. For example, respondents can be asked to evaluate the health of a person whose health is given by the dashed line. In country A, this will be evaluated as very good. In country B, the evaluation would be fair. Since the actual health description of the vignette person is the same in the two countries, the difference in the evaluations must be due to DIF. Vignette evaluations thus help to identify the differences between the response scales in the two countries. Using the scales in one of the two countries as the benchmark, the distribution of evaluations in the other country can be adjusted by evaluating them on the benchmark scale. The underlying assumption is *response consistency*: a given respondent uses the same scale for the self-reports and the vignette evaluations.

The corrected distribution of the evaluations can then be compared to that in the benchmark country—they are now on the same scale. In the example in figure 9.1, this will lead to the correct conclusion that people in country B are healthier than those in country A, on average. King et al. (2004) develop parametric and nonparametric models that make it possible to perform the correction. They apply their method to, for example, political efficacy and visual acuity. Their results strongly support the ability of the vignettes to correct for DIF. For example, in a comparative study of political efficacy of Chinese and Mexican citizens, they find that without correction the Chinese seem to have more political influence than the Mexicans. The conclusion reverses if the correction is applied.[6]

9.5.2   Econometric Model

The model explains respondents' self-reports on work limitations and their reports on work limitations of hypothetical vignette persons. The first is the answer (Y_{ri}, i respondent i) to the question:

Do you have any impairment or health problem that limits the type or amount of work that you can do?

In our data for the United States, the answers are given on a yes/no scale. In the Dutch data, respondents answer this question both on a yes/no scale and on a five points scale, with answers no, not at all ($Y_{ri} = 1$), yes, I am somewhat limited ($Y_{ri} = 2$), yes, I am moderately limited ($Y_{ri} = 3$), yes, I am very limited ($Y_{ri} = 4$) and yes, I am so seriously limited that I am not able to work ($Y_{ri} = 5$).

Table 9.2 suggests that there is some random error in the two-point and/or five-point scale evaluations that is not transferred to the other scale. To account for this, we use the following equations for the respondent's own

---

6. More applications to health are discussed in Salomon, Tandon, and Murray (2004).

work limiting disability, partitioning the error term in a genuine unobserved component of work disability affecting both the two-point and the five-point scale reports, and an idiosyncratic error term affecting only one scale and independent of everything else:

Genuine work disability:

$$Y_{ri}^* = X_i\beta + \varepsilon_{ri}; \varepsilon_{ri} \quad N(0, \sigma_r^2), \varepsilon_{ri} \text{ independent of } X_i, V_i.$$

Five-point scale self-reports:

$$Y_{ri} = j \text{ if } \tau_i^{j-1} < Y_{ri}^* + u_i^5 \le \tau_i^j, j = 1, \ldots, 5.$$

Two-point scale self-reports:

$$Y_{ri} = 0 \text{ if } Y_{ri}^* + u_i^2 \le \tau_i(2)$$

$$Y_{ri} = 1 \text{ if } Y_{ri}^* + u_i^2 > \tau_i(2)$$

$$u_i^2, \quad N(0, \sigma_{u^2}^2); u_i^5 \quad N(0, \sigma_{u^5}^2); u_i^2, u_i^5 \text{ independent of each other}$$
and of other errors (such as ε_{ri}).

The thresholds τ_j^i between the categories of the five-point scale are given by:

$$\tau_i^0 = -\infty, \tau_i^5 = \infty, \tau_i^1 = \gamma^1 V_i, \tau_i^j = \tau_i^{j-1} + \exp(\gamma^j V_i), j = 2, 3, 4.$$

The fact that different respondents can use different response scales is called differential item functioning (DIF). As in the King et al. (2004) model, we assume that response scales can vary only with observed characteristics V_i, including a country dummy and interactions with that country dummy. The exponentials guarantee that the thresholds increase with j.

In order to link the two-point scale and the five-point scale, we use the fact that the cutoff point between *yes* and *no* for the two-point scale is somewhere between the cutoff points between *no* and *mildly* and *mildly* and *moderately* for the five-point scale. In line with this, we model the cutoff point $\tau_i(2)$ on the two-point scale as a weighted mean of the two first cutoff points on the five-point scale:

$$\tau_i(2) = \lambda\tau_i^1 + (1 - \lambda)\tau_i^2$$

We assume that the weight λ does not vary with individual characteristics and is the same in the United States and the Netherlands. Thus, the thresholds on the five-point scale and the thresholds on the two-point scale can have completely different structures in the two countries, but the relation between them is the same. If the Dutch have lower thresholds on the five-point scale, they also have a lower threshold on the two-point scale, etc. This assumption is needed as long as there are no five-point scale self-reports on the five-point scale for the United States. Intuitively, it seems clear that the parameter λ can be identified from the Dutch self-reports on both scales.

In the United States as well as the Netherlands, the questions on work limitations of the vignette persons have the same five answering categories as the five-point scale self-report, and are formulated in the same way ("Does Mr./Mrs. X have any impairment or health problem that limits the type or amount of work that he or she can do?"). The answers will be denoted by Y_{li} where each respondent i evaluates a number of vignettes $l = 1, \ldots, L$.

The evaluations of vignettes $l = 1, \ldots, L$ are modeled using a similar ordered response model:

$$Y_{li}^* = \theta_l + \theta \, \text{Female}_{li} + \varepsilon_{li}$$

$$Y_{li} = j \text{ if } \tau_i^{j-1} < Y_{li}^* \le \tau_i^j, j = 1, \ldots, 5$$

$\varepsilon_{li} \sim N(0, \sigma^2)$, independent of each other, of ε_{ri} and of X_i, V_i.

An important assumption is that the thresholds τ_i^j are the same for the five-point self-reports and the vignettes (*response consistency*). This is the basis for why vignettes help to identify DIF and help to correct for reporting differences.

The second assumption of King et al. (2004) is that Y_{li}^* does not vary with respondent attributes in any systematic way; it only varies with vignette characteristics given in the descriptions of the vignettes (captured by a vignette specific constant θ_l and a dummy for the gender of the vignette person).

Given these assumptions, vignette evaluations can be used to identify β and γ ($= \gamma^1, \ldots, \gamma^5$) if all questions were asked on the five-point scale: from the vignette evaluations alone, $\gamma, \theta, \theta_1, \ldots, \theta_5$ can be identified (up to the usual normalization of scale and location). From the self-reports, β can then be identified in addition. Thus, the vignettes can be used to solve the identification problem due to DIF. The two-step procedure is sketched only to make intuitively clear why the model is identified. In practice, all parameters will be estimated simultaneously by maximum likelihood, which is asymptotically efficient.

Correcting for DIF is straightforward once the parameters are estimated. Define a benchmark respondent with characteristics $V_i = V(B)$. (For example, choose one of the countries as the benchmark country.) The DIF correction would now involve comparing Y_{ri}^* to the thresholds τ_B^j rather than τ_i^j, where τ_B^j is obtained in the same way as τ_i^j but using $V(B)$ instead of V_i. Thus, a respondent's work-related health is computed using the benchmark scale instead of the respondent's own scale. This does not lead to a corrected score for each individual respondent (since Y_{ri}^* is not observed) but it can simulate corrected *distributions* of Y_{ri} for the whole population or conditional upon some of the characteristics in V_i and or X_i. Of course, the corrected distribution will depend upon the chosen benchmark.

9.5.3 Data and Vignette Questions

To estimate the model comparing work disability in the United States and the Netherlands, three data sets are combined: the Dutch CentER-panel (waves 1, 2, and 3 in August, October, and December 2003), the US RAND MS Internet panel, and the US HRS wave 1. They all have different age selections (all age groups in CentERpanel, 40+ in RAND MS Internet Panel, fifty-one to sixty-one in HRS), but since we condition on age, this should not be a problem. CentERpanel and RAND MS have exactly the same vignette questions on pain problems, emotional problems, and cardiovascular disease. HRS wave 1 has no vignettes. In this chapter, we only use the vignettes on pain problems.

In August 2003, we have collected work disability self-reports and vignette evaluations in the Dutch CentERpanel, which allows researchers to include short modules of experimental questions. This feature has been used to collect our data on work disability. The Internet infrastructure makes the CentERpanel an extremely valuable tool to conduct experiments, with possibilities for randomization of content, wording, question and response order, and regular revisions of the design. Production lags are very short, with less than a month between module design and data delivery. Based upon our first analysis, we have fielded a second wave in October with different wordings of the vignette questions. In this chapter, we use the self-reports on work disability collected in the first wave (August 2003) and we use vignette data from both waves (August and October 2003). The vignettes on pain are presented in table 9.14. All of them deal with back pain. The first two describe relatively light problems; the other three describe more serious problems.

The vignette questions in table 9.14 were also fielded in the RAND MS Internet panel, an Internet survey for U.S. respondents aged forty and over. Table 9.15 presents the vignette evaluations in the United States and the Netherlands. In both countries, the frequency distributions of evaluations reflect that vignettes 1 and 2 describe less serious problems than vignettes 3, 4, and 5. Still, there are some substantial differences in the evaluations between the two countries. In particular, for the first two vignettes, the U.S. respondents much more often report that the described persons have no limitation at all, where the Dutch respondents have a larger tendency to use the intermediate categories mildly and moderately. The same tendency towards the extremes in the United States and towards the middle for the Netherlands is seen in the fourth vignette, describing a person with relatively serious work limitations. The U.S. respondents much more often evaluate this person as severely or extremely limited, where the Dutch still tend to use the answer moderately. This suggests that correcting for response scale differences could reduce the difference in self-reported health distributions between the two countries.

Table 9.14   Vignette descriptions on pain problems

1. [Katie] occasionally feels back pain at work, but this has not happened for the last several months now. If she feels back pain, it typically lasts only for a few days.
2. [Catherine] suffers from back pain that causes stiffness in her back (especially at work) but is relieved with low doses of medication. She does not have any pains other than this generalized discomfort.
3. [Yvonne] has almost constant pain in her back and this sometimes prevents her from doing her work.
4. [Jim] has back pain that makes changes in body position while he is working very uncomfortable. He is unable to stand or sit for more than half an hour. Medicines decrease the pain a little, but it is there all the time and interferes with his ability to carry out even day-to-day tasks at work.
5. [Mark] has pain in his back and legs, and the pain is present almost all the time. It gets worse while he is working. Although medication helps, he feels uncomfortable when moving around, holding, and lifting things at work.

Table 9.15   Vignette evaluations in the United States and Netherlands (percent distributions)

	Vignette 1		Vignette 2		Vignette 3		Vignette 4		Vignette 5	
Limited?	NL	U.S.	NL	U.S.	NL	U.S.	NL	U.S.	NL	U.S
Not at all	24.89	38.09	10.52	29.66	0.35	0.15	0.46	0.15	0.46	0.7
Mildly	63.28	49.71	53.46	47.87	6.22	7.35	7.28	2.35	11.94	8.5
Moderately	10.47	10.44	29.44	20.26	26.56	30.44	31.11	15.42	33.79	38.5
Severely	1.32	0.88	6.27	1.47	50.89	46.76	46.28	58.88	43.90	40.9
Extremely	0.05	0.88	0.30	0.73	15.98	15.29	14.87	23.20	9.91	11.2

Sources: Netherlands—CentERpanel, August 2003, 1,977 observations; United States—RAND M Internet Panel, 2003–2004, 681 observations.

9.5.4   Estimation Results

Estimation results of the complete model are presented in table 9.16. The equations for work disability and for the thresholds all include a complete set of interactions with the country dummy for the Netherlands. Vignette evaluation equations and the auxiliary parameters introduced above concerning the transformation from the two-point to the five-point scale do not include such interactions. Panel A of table 9.16 presents the results for the work disability equation in the complete model and in a model without any form of DIF, in which thresholds do not vary by country, individual characteristics, or health conditions. The latter model is clearly rejected against the complete model by a likelihood ratio test.

Education level in the United States is more important according to the complete model than in the model without DIF. The explanation is that the pain vignettes indicate that in the U.S., the higher educated use lower thresholds than the lower educated (i.e., they tend to assign higher work disability to the same vignette person than the lower educated). This is also

Estimation results United States—Netherlands model

Panel A[a] Work disability

	Model without DIF		Complete model	
	est.	s.e	est.	s.e.
onstant	−10.424	1.444*	−11.033	1.560*
ducation med.	−2.425	0.346*	−3.294	0.584*
ducation high	−4.857	0.509*	−5.933	0.809*
ge 15–44	−17.359	6.287*	−15.996	8.365+
ge 45–54	−2.740	1.345*	−1.665	1.620
ge 55–64	−0.844	1.328	−0.677	1.631
Voman	−1.435	0.318*	−0.945	0.506+
Iigh blood	2.687	0.326*	2.843	0.536*
Diabetes	4.103	0.463*	2.832	0.797*
ancer	3.757	0.594*	3.421	0.929*
ung	6.400	0.539*	7.522	0.892*
Ieart	7.679	0.462*	8.496	0.945*
motional	5.995	0.463*	5.597	0.803*
ft pain	11.571	0.447*	11.474	0.618*
	Interactions with dummy NL			
onstant	−0.955	1.745	−3.064	2.031#
ducation med.	2.011	0.883*	2.867	1.025*
ducation high	1.937	0.978*	3.613	1.183*
ge 15–44	14.980	6.369*	12.755	8.431#
ge 45–54	3.736	1.716*	2.462	1.960
ge 55–64	1.761	1.734	1.466	2.006
Voman	2.387	0.756*	1.544	0.874+
Iigh blood	−1.729	0.878*	−2.230	1.001*
Diabetes	1.503	1.613	1.418	1.872
ancer	−1.248	1.521	−0.484	1.742
ung	0.425	1.354	−1.408	1.621
Ieart	1.104	1.287	0.421	1.562
motional	2.000	1.027+	1.485	1.240
ft pain	3.920	0.860*	4.029	0.981*

Panel B Threshold parameters

	γ^1	s.e.	γ^2	s.e.	γ^3	s.e.	γ^4	s.e.
onstant	0.000	0.000	2.017	0.149*	1.988	0.138*	2.101	0.115*
ducation med.	−0.932	0.572#	0.044	0.091	0.022	0.090	−0.022	0.078
ducation high	−1.149	0.755#	0.054	0.116	0.084	0.112	−0.026	0.097
ge 15–44	1.113	0.814#	0.147	0.134	−0.115	0.144	−0.153	0.130
ge 45–54	1.004	0.710#	0.051	0.118	−0.117	0.115	0.066	0.092
ge 55–64	−0.004	0.738	0.108	0.120	−0.110	0.126	0.035	0.091
Voman	0.602	0.469#	−0.065	0.074	−0.123	0.077#	0.028	0.064
Iigh blood	0.402	0.500	−0.155	0.083+	0.118	0.090#	−0.050	0.073
Diabetes	−1.257	0.748+	−0.016	0.121	0.127	0.124	−0.028	0.109
ancer	−0.489	0.871	0.082	0.125	−0.033	0.134	−0.121	0.111
ung	1.528	0.832+	−0.286	0.174+	0.047	0.163	−0.102	0.132

(continued)

Table 9.16   (continued)

	γ^1	s.e.	γ^2	s.e.	γ^3	s.e.	γ^4	s.e.
Heart	0.673	1.058	0.071	0.195	−0.351	0.224#	0.123	0.144
Emotional	−0.409	0.706	−0.005	0.117	−0.075	0.139	0.007	0.087
Oft pain	−0.267	0.492	0.079	0.078	0.002	0.082	0.036	0.069
Interactions with dummy NL								
Constant	−2.849	0.886*	0.376	0.147*	−0.062	0.136	0.118	0.113
Education med.	1.016	0.605+	−0.082	0.094	0.036	0.095	0.046	0.082
Education high	1.789	0.781*	−0.072	0.118	−0.043	0.115	0.096	0.100
Age 15–44	−1.830	0.856*	−0.173	0.138	0.084	0.149	0.051	0.134
Age 45–54	−1.039	0.758#	−0.057	0.122	0.062	0.121	−0.263	0.099
Age 55–64	0.105	0.788	−0.175	0.125#	0.152	0.132	−0.142	0.099
Woman	−1.050	0.498*	0.095	0.076	0.134	0.081+	−0.012	0.067
High blood	−1.012	0.545+	0.223	0.086*	−0.094	0.094	0.044	0.077
Diabetes	−0.641	0.882	0.109	0.131	−0.107	0.139	0.054	0.124
Cancer	0.986	0.961	−0.142	0.136	0.090	0.149	0.222	0.122
Lung	−2.422	0.930*	0.309	0.182+	0.003	0.172	0.117	0.140
Heart	−0.421	1.107	−0.090	0.199	0.308	0.229#	−0.202	0.151
Emotional	−0.669	0.757	0.013	0.122	0.101	0.145	0.037	0.093
Oft pain	0.338	0.528	−0.092	0.081	−0.050	0.087	−0.093	0.074

Panel C Vignette equation

	θ	s.e.
Dummy vig 1	0.800	0.841
Dummy vig 2	5.104	0.863*
Dummy vig 3	16.825	1.098*
Dummy vig 4	16.816	1.097*
Dummy vig 5	14.982	1.052*
V woman	−0.265	0.078*
Sig vig	6.449	0.270*

Panel D Two-point and Five-point scales

	Coefficient	s.e.
λ	0.788	0.046*
σ_{u2}	4.317	0.776*
σ_{u5}	7.213	0.532*

Notes: * denotes $p < 0.01$. + denotes p, 00.05. # denotes p, 0.10.
[a] Normalization: $\sigma_r^2 = 10$.

revealed by the estimates for the first threshold equation (γ^1) in panel B; the other threshold parameters appear not to play a large role here.[7] The complete model corrects for this. In the Netherlands, the correlation between

7. A model in which all thresholds shift with respondent characteristics in a parallel manner is statistically rejected against the model presented here, but gives very similar corrections in the work disability equation.

education level and work disability is much weaker, both before and after correcting for DIF.

Age is insignificant in the complete model. Of course, this is related to the fact that health conditions are controlled for directly. The large coefficients on the youngest age group are somewhat misleading since this group is quite small in the U.S. data. The age group forty-five to fifty-four in the United States uses higher thresholds than the fifty-five and over age groups. This is similar to the finding of Salomon, Tandon, and Murray (2004) for mobility (as a domain of general health, not work related), who explains it from expectations: older respondents may more often expect to have some work disability and adjust their scales accordingly. In the model that does not correct for DIF, this would lead to the conclusion that this age group has significantly lower work disability. The role of gender is also smaller in the model that controls for DIF than in the model without DIF.

Health condition dummies are answers to questions of the form, "has the doctor ever told you that . . . ," except for pain, which is self-reported (e.g., "do you often suffer from pain?"). The same variables were used in section 9.3. They are included as exogenous background variables; we assume that these health conditions do not suffer from reporting errors or other measurement errors. Different health conditions have very different effects on work disability, as in the binary probits in the previous section. This does not change much after correcting for response scale differences.

In section 9.3, we found that the effect of pain on reported work disability is much larger in the Netherlands than in the United States. The results in table 9.16 confirm this result. In the United States, pain has a larger effect on work disability than any other health condition. The significantly positive interaction with the dummy for the Netherlands indicates that the effect is even stronger in the Netherlands. Correcting for DIF hardly changes the effect of pain in either the United States or the Netherlands. Thus, differences in response scales for reporting work disability cannot explain why the effect of pain on reported work disability is so much larger in the Netherlands than in the United States.

Panel C contains the estimates for the vignette equations. The dummies for the five vignettes are in line with the idea that vignettes 3, 4, and 5 describe more serious health problems than vignettes 1 and 2. There appears to be a systematic difference between evaluating male and female vignette persons (the parameter on the dummy female in 0). For a given vignette description, a male vignette person is seen as more work disabled than a female vignette person, by both male and female respondents.[8] The estimated standard deviation of the vignette evaluations is much smaller than that of the self-reports. This is in line with the fact that everyone gets the

---

8. We included an interaction term of respondent gender and gender of the vignette person, but this was insignificant.

same vignette descriptions (apart from the name of the person described, determining the gender). In the self-reports, heterogeneity in respondents' own work disability not explained by gender, education, or age, leads to the much larger variance of the unsystematic part.

Finally, panel D presents the auxiliary parameters related to the transformation between the two-point and the five-point scale. The cut off point for the two-point scale is a weighted mean of the first and second threshold in the five-point scale, with an estimated weight for the first threshold of 0.79. Both idiosyncratic errors in the vignette reports play a role, and are of similar order of magnitude as the unobserved heterogeneity term in true latent work disability, which is common in both reports and has variance 10, by means of normalization.

Table 9.17 compares predictions of work disability for the age group forty-five to sixty-four on the two-point scale of the models with and without DIF (the same two models presented in the first panel of table 9.16). The model without DIF predicts work disability rates of 34.8 percent in the Netherlands and 20.6 percent for the United States, close to the observed work disability rates on the two-point scale for this age group. For the model with DIF, the estimated thresholds for the United States are used. For the U.S. sample, this again closely reproduces the observed work disability rate. This is due to the way the prediction is computed: there is no correction for within U.S. DIF, only for cross-country DIF. For the Netherlands, however, the result is quite different. For every Dutch respondent, the work disability probability is computed as if this respondent would use the threshold of a U.S. respondent with the same characteristics (age, education level, gender, health conditions). The results show that, if the Dutch

Table 9.17   **Predicted work disability and health conditions**

	Model without DIF		Model with DIF	
	NL	U.S.	NL	U.S.
Total work disability	34.81	20.64	27.64	20.64
Work disability explained by				
Hypertension	0.61	2.09	0.36	2.20
Diabetes	0.73	0.94	0.52	0.66
Cancers	0.28	0.46	0.31	0.42
Lung diseases	0.99	1.13	0.99	1.31
Heart diseases	1.97	2.36	1.99	2.58
Emotional diseases	2.70	1.75	2.39	1.63
Pain	15.21	7.63	14.55	7.56
All health conditions	22.49	16.36	21.12	16.36

Notes: Age group forty-five to sixty-four, CentERpanel and HRS; Weighted using respondent weights. First row: total work disability. Other rows: Reduction in total work disability if dummy for given health condition (or dummies for all health conditions) is always zero. In the model with DIF, work disability is predicted using U.S. response scales.

would use the American thresholds, the self-reported work disability rate in the Netherlands would be reduced to 27.6 percent, a difference of about 7.4 percentage points compared to the 34.8 percent in the model without DIF. Thus, correcting for cross-country DIF reduces the gap between the United States and the Netherlands from 14.2 percentage points to 7.0 percentage points, a reduction of about 50 percent.

The other rows in table 9.17 predict how much each health condition contributes to explaining work disability according to both models, again using U.S. response scales for the model with DIF. Work disability is recomputed after setting the dummy for the given health condition equal to zero, and the reduction in work disability compared to the first row is reported. The differences between the two models are small. Pain remains the dominating factor in both countries, and is much more important in the Netherlands than in the United States. Thus we find that there is a considerable difference in response scales between Dutch and U.S. respondents explaining a large part of the observed difference in the work disability rate, but the difference is not related to whether respondents suffer from a health condition or not. All health conditions together explain most of reported work disability according to both models. They explain more in the Netherlands than in the United States, again due to the effect of pain.

Table 9.18 gives the prevalence rates of the health conditions in the age group forty-five to sixty-four and the average marginal effect of each health condition on the probability of work disability. As in table 9.17, the estimated U.S. response scales are used for both the Dutch and the American respondents. Table 9.17 decomposes the contributions to work disability in two components: prevalence and the marginal effect. There are some differences between the models that do and do not correct for DIF across

Table 9.18	Prevalence and marginal effects					
			Average marginal effect (%-points)			
	Prevalence (in %)		Model without DIF		Model with DIF	
	NL	U.S.	NL	U.S.	NL	U.S.
Hypertension	25.38	36.04	2.41	5.80	1.43	6.10
Diabetes	4.64	9.16	15.69	10.24	11.27	7.18
Cancer	4.53	5.25	6.20	8.73	6.85	7.98
Lung disease	6.35	6.84	15.52	16.55	15.67	19.20
Heart disease	8.42	11.69	23.40	20.21	23.67	22.07
Emotional disorder	12.81	11.14	21.10	15.69	18.63	14.66
Pain	32.09	24.07	47.41	31.71	45.35	31.43

Notes: Age group forty-five to sixty-four, CentERpanel and HRS; Weighted using respondent weights. Prevalence: fraction of the sample with the given health condition. Average marginal effect taken over all observations with given health condition.

292   James Banks, Arie Kapteyn, James P. Smith, and Arthur van Soest

countries, but the qualitative conclusions remain the same. Pain has both the largest prevalence rate and the largest marginal effect in both countries, explaining why it has by far the strongest contribution on work disability. In the Netherlands, both prevalence and marginal effect are substantially larger than in the United States, explaining why the contribution of pain to explaining work disability is larger in the Netherlands than in the United States.

9.6   Conclusions

Workers in different industrial western countries report very different rates of work disability. The diversity in reported work disability stands in sharp contrast to the believed relative similarity in their observed health outcomes. This contradiction continues to be seen as a major unresolved puzzle.

In this chapter, we investigated the role of pain as a factor leading to work disability in three countries—the Netherlands, the United Kingdom, and the United States. In all three countries, pain is by far the most important factor leading to reports of work disability. We also find, however, that respondents in these three countries who appear to be suffering from similar degrees of pain respond very differently to questions on work disability. These differences do not appear to be related to differential use of painkillers to alleviate the effects of pain or differential degrees of work accommodation available in the three countries.

Using a new methodology of vignettes which were implemented in Internet surveys in the United States and the Netherlands, our analysis claims that a significant part of the observed difference in reported work disability between the two countries is explained by the fact that residents of the two countries use different response scales in answering the standard questions on whether they have a work disability. Essentially for the same level of actual work disability, Dutch respondents have a lower response threshold in claiming disability than American respondents do. An important follow-up question is what causes these differences in thresholds across countries.

One possibility is that more people in the Netherlands know people who are on work disability programs than is the case for residents of the United States and that this familiarity makes people less tough on what it takes to constitute a work disability. In a recent paper, Van Soest et al. (2007) do find that reference group effects (the fraction of people one knows on work disability) are significant, and contribute substantially to an explanation of why self-reported work disability in the Netherlands is much higher than in the United States. This implies an important role for social interactions and norms on the perception of work limitations.

References

Bound, J., and R. Burkhauser. 1999. Economic analysis of transfer programs targeted on people with disabilities. In *Handbook of labor economics, Vol. 3C*, ed. O. Ashenfelter and D. Card, 3417–3528. Amsterdam: Elsevier.

Browning, M., T. Crossley, and G. Weber. 2003. Asking consumption questions in general purpose surveys. *Economic Journal* 113:F540–67.

Burkhauser, R., M. Daly, A. Houtenville, and N. Nargis. 2002. Self-reported work limitation data—what they can and cannot tell us. *Demography* 39 (3): 541–555.

Haveman, R., V. Halberstadt, and R. Burkhauser. 1984. *Public Policy Toward Disabled Workers.* Ithaca and London: Cornell University Press.

Kapteyn, A., J. P. Smith, and A. van Soest. 2007. Self-reported work disability in the US and the Netherlands. *American Economic Review* 97 (1): 461–73, March 2007.

King, G., C. Murray, J. Salomon, and A. Tandon. 2004. Enhancing the validity and cross-cultural comparability of measurement in survey research. *American Political Science Review* 98 (1): 191–207.

National Center for Health Statistics. Data File Documentation, National Health Interview Survey, 2002 (machine readable data file and documentation). Hyattsville, MD: National Center for Health Statistics, Centers for Disease Control and Prevention.

Salomon, J., A. Tandon, and C. Murray. 2004. Comparability of self rated health: cross sectional multi-country survey using anchoring vignettes. *British Medical Journal* 328 (7434): 258–60.

Van Soest, A., A. Andreyeva, A. Kapteyn, and Smith, J. P. 2007. Self reported disability and reference groups. RAND Working Paper no. WR-409-1.

Ware, J. J., and C. D. Sherbourne. 1992. The MOS 36-item short form health survey (SF-36) I: Conceptual framework and item selection. *Medical Care* 30:473–83.

Disability Risk and the Value of Disability Insurance

Amitabh Chandra and Andrew A. Samwick

10.1 Introduction

As successive generations of Americans have access to healthier life-styles and more advanced medical technologies, we can expect the prevalence of work-limiting disabilities to recede. A decline in disability will have important consequences for the nature of employment at older ages and the optimal design of social insurance programs. In this chapter, we take initial steps toward understanding these consequences by measuring the disability decline in the working age population over the past two decades and assessing its implications for welfare and saving. We focus on consumers' valuation of disability insurance—either as income or as an assistive technology—to protect against the risk of permanent disablement. Because the probability of disablement is small but the loss conditional on the event is large, consumers will find it difficult to self-insure substantially against the risk of disablement through precautionary saving.

To understand changes in the probability of a work-limiting disability, we

Amitabh Chandra is an Assistant Professor of Public Policy at the Kennedy School of Government at Harvard University, and a Faculty Research Fellow at the National Bureau of Economic Research. Andrew A. Samwick is a Professor of Economics and Director of the Nelson A. Rockefeller Center at Dartmouth College, and a Research Associate at the National Bureau of Economic Research.

We are grateful to the National Institute on Aging (grants P30 AG12810 and R01 AG19805) and the Mary Woodard Lasker Charitable Trust and Michael E. DeBakey Foundation for financial support. We are grateful to Andrew Houtenville for generously providing us with access to CPS data that are not publicly available. We thank David Cutler, Doug Staiger, David Wise, and participants at the NBER conference, "The Decline in Disability," for helpful comments. Any errors are our own. Address correspondence to the authors at Amitabh_Chandra@Harvard.edu and Andrew.Samwick@Dartmouth.edu

examine data from twenty-five years of the Current Population Survey (CPS). We begin by documenting the prevalence of disability in the population as a whole, as well as in subpopulations defined by age, gender, education, race, marital status, census region of residence, and metropolitan status of residence. We show that the prevalence of disability has declined substantially for men over the age of fifty-five, for whom the unadjusted declines have ranged from 15 to 25 percent of their levels twenty years ago (corresponding to an absolute decline of about 4 percentage points). Disability rates have been increasing for women, so that by 2004, disability prevalence was roughly equal for men and women. In the cross-section, the largest disparities occur across educational groups: by age sixty-two, about 17 percent of those without a college education have a work-limiting disability, compared to about 5 percent of those with a college education or higher.

We then consider the implications of differences in disability risk for welfare and saving in a stochastic life cycle model of consumption. We model disability as involuntary retirement, focusing on the economic implications of unexpectedly lower income. In this chapter, we do not consider the impact of a decline in health status on the quality of life that can be purchased with that income. We show that a typical consumer would be willing to pay about 5 percent of lifetime expected consumption to remove the average risk of disability found in the CPS, and perhaps another 4 percent to remove the highest risks we observe in our data. Our simulations also show that the share of preretirement wealth attributable to the average disability risk (for those who do not become disabled) is about 4 percent. For no demographic group that we identify in our empirical work do the simulations suggest that disability risk would account for more than 20 percent of preretirement wealth accumulation. Compared to anticipated drops in income at retirement or annual fluctuations in income that generate similar reductions in expected utility, we note that the risk of disability generates less of a saving response. The reason is that saving is a far less effective hedge against low-probability, high-impact events like disablement.

The remainder of the chapter is organized as follows. In section 10.2, we summarize the data on trends in work-limiting disability over the period from 1980–2004 in the working age population as a whole, as well as for large demographic subgroups. In section 10.3, we present graphical analyses based on logistic regressions that decompose the raw data into age profiles for disability prevalence while controlling for other demographics and year-specific shocks to disability rates. To investigate the implications of these patterns for welfare and saving, we develop a stochastic lifecycle model of consumption decisions in section 10.4. In our model, consumers face three reasons for saving: an anticipated income drop at retirement, persistent uncertainty in their annual incomes, and an annual risk of disability prior to retirement. We model disability as permanent, involuntary retirement. In section 10.5, we show that disability risk has a relatively large impact on welfare and a smaller impact on saving compared to the other motives for saving. Section 10.6 concludes and discusses directions for future work. In the appendix to this chapter, we provide a detailed account of trends in work-limiting disability for different demographic groups.

10.2   Data Description

We use data from the March Current Population Survey (CPS) from 1980–2004 for our analysis. The CPS is a monthly survey of the noninstitutionalized population that is conducted by the Bureau of Census for the Bureau of Labor Statistics. In March of each year, the standard CPS survey is supplemented with additional questions on demographic characteristics, income, program participation, employment, and health insurance. Additionally, there are questions that allow researchers to identify persons with disabilities that limit work. For example, in the last ten years of our sample, the survey asks:

59A. (Do you/Does anyone in this household) have a health problem or disability which prevents (you/them) from working or which limits the kind or amount of work (you/they) can do?
59B. If yes to 59A., who is that?

All of the measures of work-limiting disability that we use start with an affirmative answer to this question, because we require a definition of disability that changes little over the period from 1980 to 2004. Note that a measure of disability based solely on this question does not restrict respondents to be out of the labor force in order to have a work-limiting disability. In fact, it is possible for a respondent to give an affirmative response to the above question, yet also claim to be working. Furthermore, this definition allows a respondent to be working full-time but in a job other than what they may have chosen in the absence of disability (the question asks for "the *kind* or amount of work"). Therefore, our estimates of work-limiting disability should not be viewed as providing comprehensive estimates of the phenomenon of disability as defined by Americans with Disabilities Act (ADA) legislation (a definition that would include impairments that may not affect an individual's ability to work).[1] Data from the National Health Interview Survey (NHIS) demonstrate that a large fraction of those with impairments do not report having a work-limiting disability. Many of these respondents are potentially covered by ADA legislation but will not contribute to our measure of work-limiting disability.

---

1. An impairment is a disability under the ADA if it limits a major life activity. Such an activity is not limited to work-related spheres. For example, a college professor who loses the ability to drive a car, sit in a chair, or engage in recreational activities as a result of a back injury would generally be classified as being disabled for the purpose of ADA legislation.

While this restriction causes us to undercount a portion of the disabled population, Burkhauser et al. (2003) demonstrate that some respondents who claim to be work-limited in a single cross-section of the CPS are not permanently work-limited. The authors establish this claim by linking respondents in the CPS in consecutive years and examining the fraction that reported a work limitation in both years. They note that the prevalence of disability as measured by the more stringent two-year restriction results in lower estimates of disability than those obtained by using a single cross-section.

Burkhauser et al. (2003) also demonstrate that even though different surveys such as the CPS, NHIS, and the Survey of Income and Program Participation (SIPP) define disability differently and arrive at different estimates of the *level* of disability in a given year, each of these surveys generates very similar time *trends* in disability. This important finding suggests that there have not been substantial changes since 1980 in the prevalence of impairments (or richer measures of work limitations) that might bias our results. For example, the SIPP solicits information on respondents' Activities of Daily Living (ADLs) and Instrumental Activities of Daily Living (IADLs). These broader questions cover a richer range of limitations concerning mobility, paying bills, and doing light housework and hence raise estimates of measured disability. Therefore, the measurement of disability using SIPP data will yield a higher level of disability prevalence, albeit one with the same trend as that computed using data from the CPS or NHIS.

For the purpose of calibrating our model, we need a measure of disability that corresponds to permanent, involuntary retirement. Our strategy is to start with the work-limitation measure and impose additional conditions to ensure that we are measuring withdrawal from the labor force.[2] An alternative approach to measure permanent disability might use program participation in the Disability Insurance (DI) or Supplemental Security Income (SSI) programs. We are reluctant to pursue this approach; as carefully noted by Autor and Duggan (2003), the DI program has been greatly affected by congressionally mandated changes in the stringency with which DI applicants are screened prior to being classified as bona fide candidates

---

2. Mashaw and Reno (1996) note that there are over twenty definitions of disability in the literature, each being used for a specific purpose. The appropriateness of each definition should be determined by the context in which it is used. Note that our focus on measuring the probability of involuntary retirement is different from quantifying the prevalence of a physical or mental condition. The latter would be of interest if we were trying to understand improvements in (absolute) health status over time. For example, Lakdawalla, Bhattacharya, and Goldman (2004) use the NHIS to examine trends in the fraction of people with personal care and routine needs limitations. Their definition of disability deliberately abstracts from the work decision. As the nature of work becomes less physical, the prevalence of a work-limiting disability will mechanically decline. Lakdawalla, Bhattacharya, and Goldman are careful to choose a definition of disability that is robust to this transformation. In contrast to their work, if changes in the nature of work reduce the probability of involuntary retirement through lower disability rates, then it is a channel that should be measured.

for the program. Similarly, the decision to apply for DI is influenced by the attractiveness of its economic alternatives (such as unemployment, retirement, or other social programs). Changes in the returns to these alternatives could generate large fluctuations in the measured prevalence of disability. The incentives associated with these alternatives also affect our work-related definition of disability, albeit to a lesser degree, because the question that we use does not directly query program participation.

We therefore impose additional criteria to the work-limiting definition of disability to ensure that it closely corresponds to the notion of involuntary retirement. We explore four definitions, where each subsequent definition is more stringent than the previous one:

1. Respondent has a work-limiting disability.
2. Respondent has a work-limiting disability and is not presently working.
3. Respondent has a work-limiting disability, is not presently working, and did not work last year.
4. Respondent has a work-limiting disability, is not presently working, did not work last year, and is covered by Medicare.

Definition one is correlated with the prevalence of involuntary retirement but does not precisely measure it—other research shows that large numbers of respondents who claim to have a work-limiting disability are indeed working.[3] As such, definition one should be viewed as providing an upper bound on the phenomenon of involuntary retirement, overstating the impact of disability on both welfare and saving.[4] Definitions two and three are undertaken in the spirit of previously discussed work by Burkhauser et al. (2003), who recommend using a longer time frame to measure permanent disability. Finally, because SSDI beneficiaries who have been on the program for more than two years are eligible for Medicare benefits, moving from definition three to four provides us with a lower bound on the prevalence of a work-limiting disability.[5] In our empirical

3. Bound and Burkauser (1999) demonstrate that 65 percent of men who responded positively to the work-limiting disability question on the PSID (in two consecutive years) were working; only 35 percent were not working at all. For women, 52 percent of those who had a work-limiting disability in two consecutive years were working, whereas 48 percent were not working at all.

4. The Bound and Burkhauser study also notes that 38 percent of disabled men (as identified by two years of work-limiting disability in the PSID) received government transfers, whereas 26 percent of disabled women received such income. These estimates illustrate the wide range of estimates that one obtains by using alternative measures of disability. In future research, we will utilize the HRS dataset, which has been matched to the longitudinal Social Security histories of its respondents. With these data, we will be able to more precisely distinguish between disability and involuntary retirement.

5. Medicare is a secondary payer for disabled individuals who are also covered through employer-provided health insurance. If respondents forget to note this secondary coverage while responding to the CPS questionnaire we would understate the measured prevalence of disability from definition four. This is another reason for why definition four may constitute an absolute lower bound on the prevalence of a work-limiting disability.

work we focus on definition three and use definitions one and four to inform us of the maximum and minimum disability probabilities. Definitions two and three yield similar disability prevalence rates, but definition three has the advantage of being more conservative. Figure 10.1 shows the (regression-adjusted) age-disability profile for each of these definitions of disability.

We utilize all observations in the CPS for respondents who were aged twenty-two to sixty-four at the time of the survey. We choose twenty-two as our lower bound in order to minimize sampling college students while still being able to provide meaningful estimates of work-limiting disability in younger populations. We end our analysis at sixty-four, since almost all respondents claim to be retired after that age. We extract a sample of 2,166,178 respondents in this age range over the 1980–2004 time period. For a given year, our sample sizes range from 85,133 in 1980 to over 110,000 since 2002.

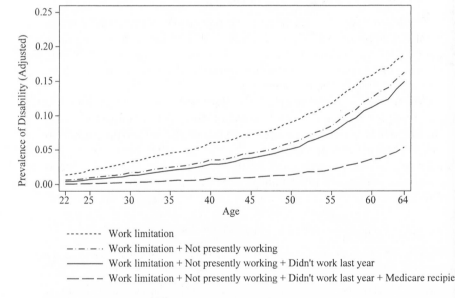

Fig. 10.1   Regression adjusted disability prevalence by age

Notes: Figures report predicted probability of work-limiting disability using alternative definitions from a logistic regression that controls for an unrestricted set of age and year indicator variables, gender, race, and ethnicity (four categories), education (two categories), marital status (three categories), marital status and gender interactions, census region (nine categories), metropolitan status, census division, and metropolitan status interactions, the number of children under the age of eighteen in the family, and the size of the household. The above figure adjusts for all these covariates, except for age. The regression used CPS data from the 1980–2004 files of Annual Demographic Survey (n = 2,166,178).

In table 10.1, we present trends in the prevalence of self-reported disability from 1980–2004.[6] All tables use our third definition of disability, where the respondent has a work-limiting disability, is not presently working, and did not work last year. We present separate estimates by gender and two broad education categories. We also report a regression estimate of the annual, linear trend in disability. Over these two decades, the prevalence of disability increased by 0.5 percentage points for the population aged twenty-two to sixty-four (with an annual increase of 0.036 percentage points per year).[7] For men, work-limiting disability increased by 0.7 percentage points, while it increased by 0.4 percentage points for women. Despite starting at different levels in the early 1980s, the gender gap in disability closed by 2004, with women having slightly higher disability rates than men in the most recent period. Disability rates increased for men and women in both education groups. The increase for less-educated women and the increase for less-educated men were particularly pronounced.

Table 10.1 also separates trends in disability prevalence by race/ethnicity and gender and by marital status and gender. The increase in disability for women, noted above, is similar for white and black women, but it is contrasted with a decline for Hispanic women. Disability prevalence increased more for black men than white men, but there was a decline for Hispanic men.

The last panel of table 10.1 illustrates the importance of focusing on the prevalence of disability within narrowly defined demographic groups. As noted earlier, there was an increase in the overall prevalence of disability for males. The trends described in this panel note that there was no change in disability for married males. The increase for men is the consequence of substantial increases in disability for never married and widowed, separated, or divorced men. Similarly, there has not been a change in disability rates for married women, but there have been larger increases for never married women as well as those who are widowed, separated, or divorced.

6. Our results are similar to other studies that have utilized a single year of the CPS to measure disability. For example, Burkhauser and Daly (1996) note that in 1990, the prevalence of disability among CPS respondents aged twenty-five to sixty-one was 8.1 percent for men, and 7.8 percent for women. Our sample includes respondents aged twenty-two to sixty-four, and the corresponding numbers for men and women are 8.1 and 7.5 percent, respectively. Using a similar question on work-related disability in a single cross-section from the SIPP for the same year provided estimates of 11.4 and 11.3, respectively. As noted by Bound and Burkhauser (1999), the higher rates in the SIPP are the likely consequence of explicitly referring to mental health conditions in contributing to work-limiting disability.

7. Note that an average annual increase of 0.036 percentage points over twenty-five years would result in a 0.9 percentage point increase in disability. Table 10.1 demonstrates that the actual change in disability over this period was 0.5 points. The regression line overpredicts the increase in disability for this time interval, because it imposes a linear time-trend on the data; the true trend in disability is best described by a nonlinear time trend. For most of the demographic groups examined in this chapter, we found it difficult to reject the linear specification. Therefore, we used this specification throughout the chapter.

Table 10.1   Trends in the prevalence of work-limiting disability

| | By education level and gender | | | | | | | | |
| | No college | | | College or more | | | Total | | |
Survey year	Males	Females	Total	Males	Females	Total	Males	Females	Tot
1980–1984	5.9	6.0	5.9	1.2	1.5	1.3	4.7	5.2	5.0
1985–1989	5.8	5.7	5.7	1.1	1.2	1.2	4.5	4.8	4.7
1990–1994	6.0	5.8	5.9	1.1	1.1	1.1	4.7	4.8	4.7
1995–1999	6.5	6.7	6.6	1.3	1.5	1.4	5.1	5.4	5.2
2000–2004	7.0	7.1	7.0	1.4	1.7	1.6	5.4	5.6	5.5
Annual trend	0.060	0.068	0.065	0.017	0.020	0.019	0.040	0.032	0.03

| | By race and ethnicity | | | | | | | | |
| | Whites | | | Hispanic | | | Blacks | | |
	Males	Females	Total	Males	Females	Total	Males	Females	Total
1980–1984	4.2	4.6	4.4	4.6	5.8	5.2	9.0	9.3	9.2
1985–1989	3.9	4.3	4.1	5.1	5.0	5.0	8.8	7.9	8.3
1990–1994	4.1	4.2	4.2	5.2	4.9	5.0	8.8	8.1	8.4
1995–1999	4.4	4.8	4.6	4.9	5.6	5.2	10.3	9.2	9.7
2000–2004	4.9	5.1	5.0	4.3	4.9	4.6	10.3	9.3	9.8
Annual trend	0.041	0.032	0.037	−0.029	−0.021	−0.025	0.087	0.027	0.05

| | By marital status and gender | | | | | | | | |
| | Married | | | Widowed, separated, or divorced | | | Never married | | |
	Males	Females	Total	Males	Females	Total	Males	Females	Tota
1980–1984	4.0	3.8	3.9	8.7	10.4	9.9	5.3	5.1	5.2
1985–1989	3.6	3.5	3.6	8.1	9.5	9.0	5.6	4.3	5.1
1990–1994	3.6	3.4	3.5	8.6	9.5	9.2	5.6	4.5	5.2
1995–1999	3.7	3.9	3.8	9.6	10.6	10.2	6.4	5.4	6.0
2000–2004	3.7	3.8	3.7	10.6	10.9	10.8	6.9	6.2	6.6
Annual trend	−0.009	0.007	*−0.001*	0.116	0.045	0.069	0.088	0.089	0.08

Notes: Tables are constructed from CPS data from the 1980–2004 files of Annual Demographic Surve (n = 2,166,178). Respondents are aged twenty-two to sixty-four at the time of the survey. Whites refer t non-Hispanic whites. Annual trends are calculated as the coefficient on a linear-regression of disabilit for the relevant demographic group on a linear time-trend. Italicized trends are not different from zer at the 5 percent significance level.

In interpreting these estimates, it is important to recognize that the reported trends are not necessarily causal—there is nothing in our analysis that suggests that being unmarried raises the probability of having a work-limiting disability. Rather, the fact that a respondent is unmarried at age fifty-five is better interpreted as being a marker for a particular type of person. Indeed, causality could easily flow in the other direction; it may be the case that because a person is less healthy, he or she is unmarried. With this caveat in mind, we note that the trends documented in table 10.1 (and the next three tables discussed in the following paragraphs) are possibly being driven by compositional shifts in the categorization of workers. This interpretation is best understood by reexamining the results of the first panel in table 10.1. Here, we noted an increase in the disability prevalence of respondents who did not have a college degree. As the fraction of the population with a college degree increases, the group without a college degree is increasingly representative of individuals who are drawn from the lower tails of the skill and health distributions. Such persons are more likely to have attended worse schools, lived in worse neighborhoods, or been affected by credit constraints that restricted investments in health and human capital. As a result, they also may be more likely to be disabled. This framework suggests that even if there were no changes in the prevalence of disability over time conditional on educational attainment, a growth in the college-educated population will manifest itself as increasing disability prevalence for the less-educated.[8]

Age-specific tabulations in table 10.2 demonstrate that the declines in disability have been greatest for the oldest men in our sample. Men are approaching retirement age healthier today than at any point in recent history—the prevalence of work-limiting disability has fallen substantially over the past two decades. In contrast to the declines observed for older populations, there were increases in disability for young and middle-aged men. The results for women show a more modest decline in disability rates in the oldest age group and a comparable increase in disability rates for women aged twenty-two to thirty-nine. In contrast to the results for men, there has been no change in work-limiting disability rates for women aged forty to fifty-nine.[9]

When these age patterns are analyzed by educational attainment in the second panel of table 10.2, we find that among respondents aged twenty-two to thirty-nine, there have been large increases in disability for those without a college degree and no change for the college-educated. For respondents aged forty to fifty-nine, changes in disability prevalence are

8. The same compositional shifts are consistent with the increasing disability rates of those with college educations—the subpopulation of college-educated now includes less healthy people who formerly would have lacked a college education.

9. It is instructive to compare our results to those obtained by Lakdawalla, Bhattacharya, and Goldman (2004), who use alternative measures of disability reported in the National Health Interview Survey (NHIS). Their measure, unlike ours, measures disability prevalence on an absolute scale (by examining prevalence of ADL and IADL limitations). Using these data for the 1984–1996 period, they find no decline in disability rates for those aged sixty to sixty-nine but note a 0.15 percentage point increase for those respondents aged eighteen to twenty-nine. Using the same data for the 1997–2000 period, they note a 0.19 percentage point reduction in disability for those aged sixty to sixty-nine, and a 0.2 percentage point decline for those aged eighteen to twenty-nine.

Table 10.2   Age-specific trends in the prevalence of work-limiting disability, by gender and education

| | By gender | | | | | | | | |
| | Ages 22–39 | | | Ages 40–59 | | | Ages 60–64 | | |
Survey year	Males	Females	Total	Males	Females	Total	Males	Females	Tot
1980–1984	1.7	1.8	1.8	6.2	7.3	6.7	18.2	17.0	17.
1985–1989	2.0	1.7	1.9	5.8	6.6	6.2	16.4	16.1	16.
1990–1994	2.3	2.0	2.2	6.1	6.4	6.2	15.3	14.9	15.
1995–1999	2.5	2.4	2.4	6.5	7.1	6.8	16.1	16.5	16.
2000–2004	2.4	2.4	2.4	6.8	7.1	7.0	13.9	14.8	14.
Annual trend	0.040	0.037	0.039	0.041	*0.008*	0.024	−0.176	−0.085	−0.1

| | By education | | | | | | | | |
| | Ages 22–39 | | | Ages 40–59 | | | Ages 60–64 | | |
	No college	College	Total	No college	College	Total	No college	College	Tot
1980–1984	2.2	0.5	1.8	7.8	1.8	6.7	18.8	8.5	17.
1985–1989	2.4	0.5	1.9	7.5	1.6	6.2	17.9	5.9	16.
1990–1994	2.7	0.4	2.2	7.8	1.4	6.2	16.9	5.9	15.
1995–1999	3.1	0.5	2.4	8.6	1.9	6.8	18.9	5.7	16.
2000–2004	3.2	0.5	2.4	9.0	2.1	7.0	17.2	5.4	14.
Annual trend	0.057	*0.000*	0.039	0.071	0.022	0.024	−0.050	−0.109	−0.1

Notes: Tables are constructed from CPS data from the 1980–2004 files of Annual Demographic Surve (n = 2,166,178). Respondents are aged twenty-two to sixty-four at the time of the survey. Whites refer non-Hispanic whites. Italicized trends are not different from zero at the 5 percent significance level.

driven by an annual trend of 0.07 percentage points for those without college degrees and an annual trend of 0.02 for those with a college degree. For the oldest group in our analysis, those aged sixty to sixty-four, the prevalence of disability fell for persons regardless of educational attainment, but it fell more for the college-educated.

In table 10.3, we disaggregate the trends in disability by age and race in the first panel and by age and marital status in the second. The decline in disability prevalence that was noted for Hispanics is shown to have occurred across all age groups. For blacks, disability rates increased for those below forty and decreased for those above sixty, with the middle age group showing no significant trend. The estimated disability rate of 29.2 percent for blacks aged sixty to sixty-four in 1995–1999 is the single highest estimate in our analysis. By marital status, married people have the lowest rates of disability and the most favorable trends over time. All marital status groups had significant increases in disability rates in the lowest age group.

The most important trend in the labor market relevant to disability over this period is the changing nature of work. As the share of jobs in sectors

Table 10.3 Age-specific trends in the prevelence of work-limiting disability, by race and marital status

By race

Survey year	Ages 22–39				Ages 40–59				Ages 60–64			
	Whites	Hispanics	Blacks	Other	Whites	Hispanics	Blacks	Other	Whites	Hispanics	Blacks	Other
1980–1984	1.4	2.1	4.0	1.4	5.8	8.2	14.0	5.3	16.3	20.5	28.3	15.5
1985–1989	1.5	2.3	3.9	1.3	5.3	7.6	12.4	5.2	14.8	18.9	27.5	13.5
1990–1994	1.8	2.3	4.1	1.9	5.3	7.9	12.1	4.9	13.5	18.8	26.6	12.5
1995–1999	2.0	2.4	4.9	1.8	5.7	8.0	13.5	6.0	14.3	20.6	29.2	15.9
2000–2004	2.2	1.9	4.6	1.7	6.1	7.1	13.1	5.8	12.7	17.9	25.9	11.6
Annual trend	0.043	−0.014	0.046	0.02	0.045	−0.046	−0.005	0.045	−0.154	−0.086	−0.090	−0.091

By marital status

	Ages 22–39			Ages 40–59			Ages 60–64			Total		
	Married	Widowed, separated or divorced	Never married	Married	Widowed, separated or divorced	Never married	Married	Widowed, separated or divorced	Never married	Married	Widowed, separated or divorced	Never Married
1980–1984	0.9	3.2	3.2	5.0	12.1	15.3	14.9	25.2	22.7	3.9	9.9	5.2
1985–1989	0.9	3.1	3.4	4.5	10.7	14.1	13.5	23.6	22.8	3.6	9.0	5.1
1990–1994	1.1	3.6	3.5	4.4	10.7	12.9	12.1	22.7	23.7	3.5	9.2	5.2
1995–1999	1.3	4.0	3.8	4.5	11.4	14.0	12.9	24.8	25.8	3.8	10.2	6.0
2000–2004	1.2	4.2	3.6	4.5	11.6	14.6	10.6	22.9	24.4	3.7	10.8	6.6
Annual trend	0.021	0.066	0.027	−0.021	0.009	0.003	−0.183	−0.070	0.090	−0.001	0.069	0.083

Notes: Tables are constructed from CPS data from the 1980–2004 files of Annual Demographic Survey (n = 2,166,178). Respondents are aged twenty-two to sixty-four at the time of the survey. Whites refer to non-Hispanic whites. Annual trends are calculated as the coefficient on a linear-regression of disability for the relevant demographic group on a linear time-trend.

of the economy with high work-related injuries falls (for example, jobs in manufacturing and mining), it is perhaps unsurprising that the prevalence of work-limiting disability declines for older men. As the nature of work changes and fewer jobs require physical strength and dexterity, it is possible that fewer individuals are work-limited. Kutscher and Personick (1986) document a decline in manufacturing from 25.1 to 18.5 percent of total employment between 1959 and 1984. Mining fell from 0.9 to 0.6 percent of total employment over the same period of time. At the end of 2004, the Bureau of Labor Statistics (2005) reports that manufacturing represents just 10.8 percent of total employment and that mining represents just 0.4 percent of total employment. Of the manufacturing workers, only 70 percent are classified as production workers.

We further consider this hypothesis by examining the trends in disability prevalence by census region in table 10.4.[10] Across all ages, work-limiting disability grew the most in New England and East South Central states. For all regions, there were significant increases in disability rates for respondents aged twenty-two to thirty-nine. Among respondents aged forty to fifty-nine, the only regions not to see a significant increase in disability rates are those in the East North Central and West North Central. For those aged sixty to sixty-four, all regions saw declines in disability rates, though the trends in the New England, Middle Atlantic, and East South Central regions were not significant. For this age group, the largest declines in disability are observed in the Mountain region (comprised of Arizona, Colorado, Idaho, Montana, Nevada, New Mexico, Utah, and Wyoming); this decline is consistent with an interpretation wherein new cohorts of sixty to sixty-four-year-olds are less likely to have been exposed to work in the mining sector. Similarly, for the changing nature of work hypothesis to be true, we should see increases in disability prevalence in regions of the country where manufacturing employment grew in the past twenty years. The East South Central region of the country is one such area (where large Japanese car manufacturers located in the mid-1980s). In this region, we observe an increasing trend in the level of disability (of 0.08 percentage points per year), whose magnitude is larger than that of any other region.

While suggestive, this characterization of the data is not without exceptions. First, note that table 10.1 demonstrates that there were increases in the levels of work-limiting disability for men with a college degree—a group that was never at risk for working in a coal mine or on the assembly line of a manufacturing plant. Disability prevalence has also grown for college-educated women, another group that is at low risk for job-related

10. The nine regions are defined as follows—Mountain: AZ, CO, ID, MT, NV, NM, UT, WY. New England: CT, ME, MA, NH, RI, VT. South Atlantic: DE, DC, FL, GA, MD, NC, SC, VA, WV. West North Central: IA, KS, MN, MO, NE, ND, SD. West South Central: AR, LA, OK, TX. Pacific: AK, CA, HI, OR, WA. East North Central: IL, IN, MI, OH, WI. East South Central: AL, KY, MS, TN. Middle Atlantic: NJ, NY, PA.

Table 10.4

Table 10.4   Age-specific trends in the prevalence of work-limiting disability, by census region

Survey year	N. Eng	Mid Atl	E.N.Cent	W.N.Cent	S.Atl	E.S.Cent	W.S.Cent	Mount.	Pacific
Ages 22–39									
1980–1984	1.7	2.1	1.7	1.3	2.0	2.3	1.5	1.1	1.7
1985–1989	1.2	2.2	2.0	1.2	1.8	2.7	2.0	1.5	1.9
1990–1994	1.7	2.1	2.2	1.5	2.3	3.8	2.2	1.8	2.0
1995–1999	2.4	2.8	2.5	1.6	2.6	3.8	2.3	1.7	2.1
2000–2004	2.9	3.0	2.3	1.7	2.4	3.7	2.2	1.6	2.2
Annual trend	0.075	0.049	0.036	0.028	0.033	0.084	0.036	0.024	0.026
Ages 40–59									
1980–1984	5.3	6.6	6.6	4.9	7.4	10.2	6.9	5.3	6.5
1985–1989	4.9	6.1	6.1	4.5	7.1	9.4	6.4	5.3	5.7
1990–1994	5.0	5.7	6.0	4.3	6.6	11.2	6.9	5.2	5.8
1995–1999	6.8	6.8	6.6	4.6	7.5	10.1	7.1	5.3	6.0
2000–2004	6.3	7.0	6.5	4.8	7.6	10.9	7.4	5.8	6.5
Annual trend	0.078	0.031	*0.008*	*0.003*	0.021	0.037	0.037	0.025	0.014
Ages 60–64									
1980–1984	14.5	15.9	16.5	14.9	19.9	21.3	20.1	17.5	17.6
1985–1989	13.4	14.0	15.9	12.7	17.5	23.8	18.9	15.5	15.6
1990–1994	13.5	13.5	14.6	11.8	16.6	19.4	17.6	14.1	14.5
1995–1999	12.7	15.0	15.4	12.3	18.2	21.6	19.4	14.8	15.6
2000–2004	13.9	14.4	13.3	11.0	14.6	20.9	17.0	11.6	13.4
Annual trend	*-0.033*	-0.055	-0.131	-0.163	-0.208	-0.061	-0.116	0.243	-0.168
All ages									
1980–1984	4.2	5.2	4.8	3.8	5.7	6.9	4.9	3.8	4.6
1985–1989	3.6	4.8	4.7	3.3	5.2	7.1	4.8	3.9	4.2
1990–1994	3.9	4.5	4.7	3.4	5.1	8.0	5.1	4.0	4.3
1995–1999	5.1	5.5	5.2	3.7	5.9	7.9	5.5	4.1	4.5
2000–2004	5.4	5.9	5.2	3.9	5.9	8.6	5.7	4.3	4.9
Annual trend	0.082	0.041	0.027	0.016	0.027	0.084	0.046	0.026	0.023

Notes: Tables are constructed from CPS data from the 1980–2004 files of Annual Demographic Survey (n = 2,166,178). Respondents are aged twenty-two to sixty-four at the time of the survey. Whites refer to non-Hispanic whites. Annual trends are calculated as the coefficient on a linear-regression of disability for the relevant demographic group on a linear time-trend. Italicized trends are not different from zero at the 5 percent significance level.

injuries. Second, the growth in the prevalence of work limitations for women also poses a problem for an explanation of the decline based on the changing nature of work. At first glance, it might be plausible to explain the increase in female disability as stemming from growing female labor force participation (which grew from 51.6 percent in 1980 to 60.2 percent in 2003). While women of all ages increased their participation between 1980 and 2003, the largest absolute increases in participation occurred for women aged forty to fifty-four (for whom labor force participation grew from 61 percent to almost 75 percent). However, disability trends for this group stayed absolutely constant over the 1980s and 1990s (table 10.2, first panel). Finally, we note that the increase in disability in New England states, a group of states that has not witnessed an increase in manufacturing jobs, is comparable to the increase in East Central States. Therefore, no simple explanation is able to reconcile all the facts.

The preceding analysis compares the reported disability rates of respondents of different cohorts at the same age. In results not reported in this chapter, we examined changes in the age-disability profile by birth cohort. Because each cohort is observed at different points in its life cycle, we can compare the prevalence of disability at a certain age for a given cohort to that for another cohort at the same age. By examining the age-disability trend across cohorts, we can assess the extent to which different cohorts have the same age-disability profile. In general, we note only small differences across cohorts in disability through the age of fifty-four. These results are supportive of a common age profile across cohorts—disability rises monotonically with age, and the levels appear to be markedly similar at a given age across cohorts. It does not appear to be the case that a certain group of cohorts is systematically more or less disabled than another cohort, an empirical finding that reduces the potential role of cohort effects in the data.

We conclude our analysis of the trends in disability prevalence by reporting the extent to which there has been convergence (or divergence) in disability rates across the different demographic groups studied above. These results, which provide a succinct summary of the extent to which the levels of disability across different groups are becoming more or less homogeneous over time, are reported in table 10.5. The table is best explained by an example—row 1 of the table indicates that the variance in disability rates across the three age categories that we have focused on is estimated to have fallen by 25 percent in ten years (multiplying the change in variance and its standard error by 2.5 will produce the decline in variance over the twenty-five-year study period). Over the same period, the variance in disability between men and women increased by 8 percent (an estimate not statistically different from zero). Alternatively, in row 8, we note that the variance in disability across age and gender categories (that is, three age categories multiply by two gender categories = six age and gender cate-

Table 10.5   Convergence in disability prevalence by demographic group

Demographic group	Percent change in variance every 10 years	Standard error
1. Age	−25	(4.0)
2. Gender	8	(32.0)
3. Education	46	(3.0)
4. Race	22	(11.0)
5. Marital status	85	(11.0)
6. Census division	17	(15.0)
7. Metropolitan residence	177	(73.0)
8. Age and gender	−25	(4.0)
9. Age and education	−1	(4.0)
10. Age and race	−69	(14.0)
11. Age and marital status	42	(12.0)
12. Age and census division	−25	(4.0)
13. Age and metropolitan status	−32	(4.0)
14. Gender and education	45	(3.0)
15. Gender and race	31	(10.0)
16. Gender and marital status	80	(11.0)
17. Gender and census division	25	(15.0)
18. Gender and metropolitan status	−25	(29.0)

Notes: Table reports the percent change in the variance of disability over time. For each demographic group the table reports the coefficient from a regression of ln (variance of disability) on a linear time-trend. See text for details. There are three categories for age, two for education, four for race, three for marital status, two for metropolitan residence, and nine for census division.

gories) fell by 25 percent. This result implies that disability rates between older and younger men, and older and younger women, are becoming more similar. These estimates were calculated by regressing the natural logarithm of the variance in disability, calculated for each year of the data, across these demographic cells on a linear trend.[11]

The table indicates that there has been dramatic convergence in disability rates by age, but divergence across education, marital status, and metropolitan residence groups. There is no statistically significant change in variance across gender, racial groups, or by census division. In other words, it is not the case that the disability rates for blacks, Hispanics, and whites are becoming more similar, or that disability rates across the nine census regions are more uniform. In rows 8 through 18, we examine convergence in disability rates across more finely defined groupings. We are

11. In this regression, the coefficient on the linear trend measures the percent change in variance *over time*. This interpretation is important to remember, as it implies that the magnitude of the results in table 10.5 say nothing about the level of variance at a point in time. We estimate this regression by using all twenty-five years of the CPS data and computing the variance of disability in each year. We regress the log of this variance on a linear time-trend. We report the coefficient on this trend (multiplied by a factor of 10 to assist in interpretation).

primarily interested in understanding whether the convergence results noted above for age and gender groups persist in conjunction with the convergence or divergence trends for other variables. Rows 8 through 13 demonstrate that the convergence in disability rates across age groups persists even when we examine convergence in disability across age and gender groups, age and race groups, age and census division groups, and age and metropolitan status groups. In contrast, there has been no convergence across age and education groups, and there has been divergence across age and marital status categories. The latter result is unsurprising in light of the fact that there was substantial *divergence* across (univariate) educational and marital status groups, which was partially offset by the convergence across age groups. Rows 14 through 18 of table 10.5 note that there has been divergence in disability rates for groups defined by gender and education, gender and race, and gender and marital status. In other words, the disability rates of black men, white men, black women, and white women are diverging.

10.3   Regression Analysis

The results described in the previous section suffer from an important limitation in that the demographic composition of the population has been changing over time. For example, the age structure of the population has been changing—a large cohort of Baby Boomers born in the years after World War II is moving through their life cycle and affecting the age distribution of the population at each point between 1980 and 2004. Such an effect would contaminate the identification of a declining trend in disability over time, since a secular decline in disability would be partially offset by the increasing age (and consequent disability) of the Baby Boomers. In addition, as documented in section 10.2, there have been changes in education, marital status, and the composition of employment. To account for these factors and thus better understand the relationship between age and the prevalence of a work-limiting disability, we follow a regression-based approach where we estimate the following logistic regression model for the probability of being disabled for individual i, at age j in year t (Δ_{ijt}):

$$(1) \qquad \Pr(\Delta_{ijt} = 1) = F\left(\beta_0 + \mathbf{X}_i' \Theta + \sum_j \gamma_j Age_j + \sum_t \delta_t Year_t\right).$$

In this model, we have included an unrestricted set of age and year dummies, while controlling for factors such as gender, education, race, region of residence, metropolitan residence, marital status, and family size and composition. This specification allows for complete nonparametric identification of the age and year effects. In later specifications, we allow for the age effects to vary by different demographic controls by interacting each of the age indicator variables with different values of the control variables.

We begin by reporting the results of our standard specification (where the age effects are constrained to be the same across all demographic groups) in figure 10.1. The adjusted age-disability profiles (one for each of the four definitions of work-limiting disability), demonstrate a convex and monotonically increasing relationship in age. The age-disability profile that is the focus of this chapter is illustrated with an uninterrupted line. This age-disability profile is what would be observed if secular (i.e., year-specific) changes in disability, as well as in the demographic mix of the CPS sampling frame, were accounted for. The profile starts at approximately 2 percent at the age of twenty-two and increases to 15 percent at the age of sixty-four. The profile increases roughly linearly with age until the age of forty-two, at which point the relationship becomes increasingly convex. Because of the enormous sample sizes available at our disposal, the profile is very precisely estimated (the standard errors are always less than 0.5 for the estimated profiles, even at older ages). For this reason, we suppress the confidence intervals in each of the graphs.

While this model is an improvement over examining unadjusted data, it suffers from two potential criticisms. First, the effect of age on disability may vary over time. This is a testable hypothesis, and we explore its empirical content in figure 10.2. Here, we modify the logistic regression estimated in equation (1) by grouping adjacent years and ages so that we can also include year and age interactions. While these interactions are statistically significant (and have a marginal F-statistic over thirty), the age-disability profile that allows for flexibility over time is seen to be remarkably stable over time. There is a small decline of 1 percentage point in the prevalence of disability of respondents aged sixty to sixty-four over the sample period, but for ages twenty-two to fifty-nine, the profiles are stable. As such, the economic significance of the age-disability profile varying over time is negligible. These results provide persuasive evidence that the age-disability profile has remained stable despite onetime events such as the ADA and more than two complete business cycles. Furthermore, they also demonstrate that the trends in disability noted in tables 10.1 through 10.4 are the consequence of changes in the composition of the labor force. When we control for the demographic characteristics of respondents, the increase in disability for younger populations is entirely eliminated.

A second criticism of the model underlying figure 10.1 is that it is possible that trends in work-limiting disability are a consequence of cohort effects. Such effects would represent cohort-specific changes in the disability profile that are not related to age or period effects. For example, if there is a disease (say, the influenza epidemic of 1918) or medical breakthrough that affects some cohorts but not others, such effects will be cohort-specific. As is well known in the economics literature (Heckman and Robb 1985), it is not possible to separate age, period, and cohort effects simultaneously without further assumptions. For example, in Deaton and Paxson

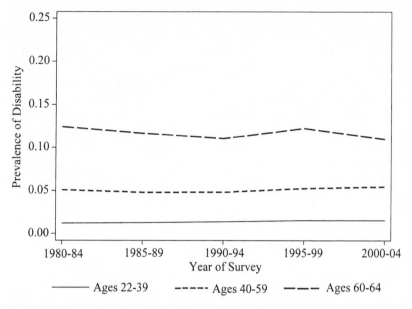

Fig. 10.2   Regression adjusted disability prevalence by age over time

Notes: Figures report predicted probability of work-limiting disability from a logistic regression that controls for an unrestricted set of age and year indicator variables, gender, race, and ethnicity (four categories), education (two categories), marital status (three categories), marital status and gender interactions, census region (nine categories), metropolitan status, census division, and metropolitan status interactions, the number of children under the age of eighteen in the family, and the size of the household. The above figure adjusts for these covariates, except the ones used in the figure. The regression used CPS data from the 1980–2004 files of Annual Demographic Survey (n = 2,166,178).

(1994), the key identifying assumption is that the year effects sum to zero and are orthogonal to a linear time trend. The Deaton-Paxson assumption is plausible for their study of consumption, but is probably inappropriate for the study of disability.

In our analysis, we assume that cohort effects are zero. Our logic is as follows: there is a powerful biological case for including age effects in our models—disability increases with age because of the onset of illness and muscular-skeletal deterioration that is a consequence of the aging process. In addition, the deleterious effects of disability are often cumulative—although not all disabilities are irreversible, many of the more severe ones probably are. Furthermore, we argue that there is also a case for including year effects in our model. Economy-wide changes in the nature of work (for example, from manufacturing and mining jobs to service jobs) will affect the prevalence of disability. Additionally, legislative interventions such as the ADA will manifest themselves through year effects. Therefore, while there are strong a priori reasons for including age and year effects, the case for cohort effects is less clear on a prima facie basis.

Having established that the age-disability profile is stable over time, we explore trends in prevalence of work-limiting disability by gender in figure 10.3. In this figure (and subsequent ones) we allow the age profile to vary by demographic characteristics (here, gender and time.) The graphs adjust for time effects, education attainment, race, marital status, census region of residence, metropolitan residence, and family size and composition. The graphs clearly illustrate the decline in disability for men over the age of fifty-five in the past twenty years. In contrast; the disability profile for women demonstrates the increase in work-related disability for women aged thirty-five to fifty. In the unadjusted data reported in table 10.1, men and women had similar disability rates in 2004, with women reporting substantially larger increases in disability prevalence between 1980 and 2004. In contrast, figure 10.3 demonstrates that those trends are the consequence of compositional changes; after year effects and other demographic characteristics are controlled for, the change in disability profiles for women is not evident. It is interesting to note that these profiles are similar for men and women until the age of fifty. After that, the age-disability profile for men accelerates upwards.

We study differences in the age-disability profile by educational attainment in figure 10.4 and by racial group in figure 10.5. Less-educated workers have a higher level of disability at all points in their life cycle. Additionally, the disability hazard is greater for these workers—at any point in the age distribution, less-educated workers have a larger probability of becoming disabled. Therefore, a small difference in the initial level of

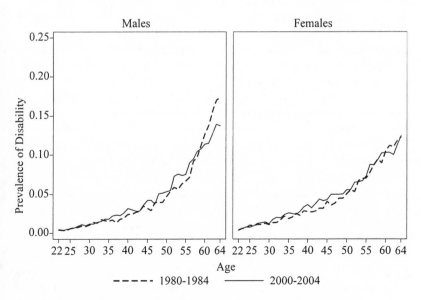

Fig. 10.3   Regression adjusted disability prevalence by gender over time
Note: See note to fig. 10.2.

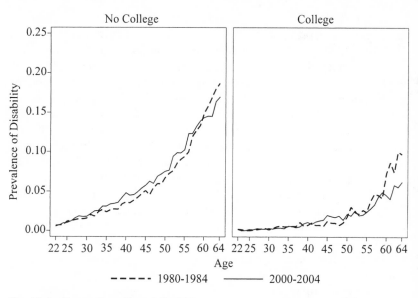

Fig. 10.4   **Regression adjusted disability prevalence by education over time**
Note: See note to fig. 10.2.

disablement at the age of twenty-two is converted to a 10-percentage point difference at the age of sixty-four. For both educational levels, the decline in disability is most pronounced for those over the age of sixty. Figure 10.5 illustrates disability prevalence profiles by racial group. Despite starting at very similar levels at the age of twenty-two, the hazard of reporting a work-limiting disability is much greater for blacks and Hispanics relative to whites (the differences between whites and nonblacks/non-Hispanics, i.e., those grouped together as "other," are not statistically significant). On the eve of retirement, the probability of having a disability for whites is approximately 12 percent in 2004. Yet it is 15 percent for Hispanics and 20 percent for blacks. In the appendix figures, we describe age-disability profiles by marital status, over time (figure 10A.1), marital status and gender (figure 10A.2), education and gender (figure 10A.3), and metropolitan residence (figure 10A.4).

To summarize, the prevalence of a work-limiting disability at a typical age of retirement, across all demographic groups and for the average year in our sample, is 15 percent (fig. 10.1). The lowest prevalence of 6 percent at retirement is observed for college-educated persons in the 2000–2004 period. The highest observed prevalences are 26 percent for never married men (see appendix fig. 10.A2), and 20 percent for black males. These estimates span the range of disablement probabilities and will therefore constitute a central input to our model of intertemporal consumption and saving.

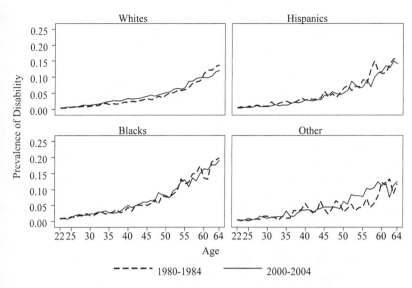

Fig. 10.5   Regression adjusted disability prevalence by race over time
Note: See note to fig. 10.2.

10.4   Optimal Consumption in a Stochastic
Life Cycle Model with Disability

Our empirical work with the CPS documents cross-sectional and time
series differences in disability prevalence. We now seek to quantify the importance of these differences by evaluating their impact on expected utility
(welfare) and saving for representative consumers.

10.4.1   Intuition

Our main analytical tool is a model of household consumption decisions
based on a life cycle framework, in which a primary motivation for saving
is to transfer resources (income) from the working years, when income is
predictably high, to the retirement years, when income is predictably low.
In this model, the household makes a consumption decision in each period
(taken to be a year) based on resources currently available (assets) and expectations of income to be received from continued work and retirement in
the future. The household will be more inclined to consume resources today when it has more assets available or when it has a higher predicted income in the future.

We add to this basic framework two sources of uncertainty in future income, to make it a stochastic life cycle model. The first is the annual variability in income that is attendant to risks of unemployment and the tra-
jectory along which people advance in their careers. Annual variability in

income will lower consumers' well-being if they are risk averse (i.e., if they would be willing to pay a premium for actuarially fair insurance to remove the uncertainty that they face). With a suitable choice of preferences, consumers will also choose to increase their saving in response to increased uncertainty as a way to buffer their consumption against income uncertainty. It is now standard in the economics literature to incorporate this sort of precautionary saving against annual income variability into analyses of consumption and saving.

Unlike the existing literature on consumption and saving, we add a second source of uncertainty to the model in the form of an annual probability that working-age consumers will experience a disabling event that requires them to permanently withdraw from the labor force. The consumer must then rely on accumulated saving and future payments from disability insurance programs to support future consumption. As with annual variability in income, the risk of becoming disabled makes consumers worse off and may elicit higher savings to help mitigate the reduction in future consumption that results from disability.

The remainder of this section presents the more technical specification of the consumption model and a derivation of its key results. The latter are answers to two key questions: by how much are consumers worse off when their risk of disability increases, and by how much do they adjust their saving in response to that higher risk? As a starting point, we develop a stylized model of intertemporal consumption that solves for optimal profiles of consumption while disabled (C_s^d) and nondisabled (C_s^n). The consumer's value function is defined as:

$$V_t(A_t, Y_t, \Delta_t) \equiv \max_{\{C_s^d, C_s^n\}} E_t \sum_{s=t}^{T} \beta^{s-t} [\Delta_s u(C_s^d) + (1 - \Delta_s) u(C_s^u)]$$

such that:

(2) $(a)\, u(C) = \dfrac{C^{1-\gamma}}{1-\gamma}$

$(b)\, A_{s+1} = [1 + r(1 - \tau)][A_s + Y_s(1 - \tau) - C_s]$

$(c)\, A_s \geq 0 \;\forall s$

$(d)\, Pr(\Delta_s = 1) = \begin{cases} 1 - \prod\limits_{q=t}^{s}(1 - \delta_q), \text{ for } \Delta_t = 0 \\ 1, \text{ for } \Delta_t = 1. \end{cases}$

The value function in each period, $V_t(A_t, Y_t, \Delta_t)$, has three state variables: the level of assets (A), the level of income (Y), and an indicator for whether the consumer is disabled (Δ). The value function is equal to the expected discounted utility of consumption in each period from the current period t to the final period T, discounted by a factor of β each period. The rate of time preference is equal to $1/\beta - 1$ and is similar to an interest rate in governing the utility tradeoff across periods. The within-period utility function is assumed to be additively separable in consumption and all other factors that affect utility, including health and leisure, so that these factors can be omitted from the optimization problem. A more detailed model would allow for health and leisure in a given period to affect the willingness of the consumer to spend versus save resources for a later period. As equation (2) makes explicit, our analysis is also predicated on the assumption that agents do not exhibit state-dependent utility. In other words, our calculations are based on the potentially strong supposition that disability shocks do not alter utility from a given level of consumption.[12]

The utility of consumption in each period is assumed to take the Constant Relative Risk Aversion (CRRA) form: $u(C) = C^{1-\gamma}/(1 - \gamma)$, where γ is the coefficient of relative risk aversion. With a utility function such as CRRA that has a convex marginal utility function (i.e., $u'''(C) > 0$), there is a precautionary motive for saving, and greater uncertainty in the income process will induce greater saving.[13]

Assets in the next period are equal to the excess of current assets and income over consumption, augmented at the after-tax interest rate, as in equation (2b). For simplicity, the income tax system is assumed to be linear at a rate, τ, and the portfolio choice is subsumed in the form of a constant interest rate, r. Assets are constrained to be nonnegative in each period. The uncertainty in this model comes from two sources. The first is the risk of becoming disabled. The probability that a nondisabled person becomes disabled in period s is δ_s, thereby leading to the expression in equation (2d) for the probability that a person is disabled in that period. Disability is assumed to be an absorbing state. The second source of uncertainty is the variance in current income while working.

In the equations below, we state the processes that describe income uncertainty and the evolution of current income:

Before retirement or disability:

(3) $(a)\ \ln(Y_s) = \ln(P_s) + u_s$

            $(b)\ u_{s+1} = \rho u_s + \varepsilon_{s+1}$

            $(c)\ \varepsilon_s \sim i.i.d.\ N(0, \sigma^2)$

---

12. Empirical support for our characterization is provided in Gertler and Gruber (2002). In their analysis of Indonesian households on the effect of changes in the disability status of a head of household on changes in per-capita (nonmedical) consumption, they found no evidence for the most plausible manifestations of state-dependent utility. We return to this point in the concluding section of our chapter.

13. The use of the CRRA utility function is standard in both the empirical and theoretical literature on precautionary saving. Constant Relative Risk Aversion utility means that a consumer remains equally willing to engage in gambles over a constant proportion of current wealth as wealth increases. An alternative, and perhaps more realistic assumption, might be that the consumer will accept larger proportional risks as wealth increases. See Kimball (1990) for a discussion and derivation of the key results for precautionary saving.

At retirement or disability:

$$(d) \ Y_{s+1} = g Y_s$$

After retirement or disability:

$$(e) \ Y_{s+1} = Y_s.$$

Prior to retirement or disability, the natural log of current income (Y_s) is equal to the natural log of permanent income (P_s) plus a shock to income (u_s) that follows an autoregressive (AR)(1) process. The innovations to that AR(1) process are assumed to be independently and identically draws from a normal distribution with mean zero and variance σ^2.[14] In the eventuality of either retirement or disablement, income is reduced to a replacement rate (g) of its most recent value. After retirement or disability, income is unchanged at this new level and is no longer uncertain. In the model below, we model life cycle labor supply as the consumer starting work at age twenty-two, retiring at age sixty-two, and living with certainty until age eighty-two (implying that voluntary retirement is taken in the fortieth year out of sixty in the assumed lifetime.)

In this framework, we have included a stylized version of the current Social Security Disability Insurance program. When a worker becomes disabled, he or she gets the same replacement rate that he or she would get at retirement, though calculated on income through the year of disability. In both cases, the real value of benefits stays constant over time. More detailed formulations of both the retirement benefit and the disability benefit are possible, though not without substantially increasing the complexity of the model with an additional state variable (e.g., the average index monthly earnings of the worker to date).

The solution method for stochastic optimization problems with multiple state and control variables is discussed in detail in Carroll (2001). The solution begins in the last period of life, T, when the problem is trivial because the household simply consumes all of its assets and after-tax income, yielding optimal values for the control variables, C_T^d and C_T^n, as a function of the state variables A_T and Y_T. These solutions generate the value function, $V_T(A_T, Y_T, \Delta_T)$, and the partial derivative, $V_T^A(A_T, Y_T, \Delta_T)$, which represents the marginal value of an additional dollar in assets at the beginning of period T.[15] Moving back to the period $T-1$ problem, we can rewrite the objective function as:

$$(4) \quad V_{T-1}(A_{T-1}, Y_{T-1}, \Delta_{T-1}) \equiv \max_{\{C_{T-1}\}} u(C_{T-1}) + \beta E_{T-1}[V_T(A_T, Y_T, \Delta_T)].$$

---

14. In our simulations, we normalize the mean of the lognormal shock to be one in all periods.

15. The partial derivative, $V_T^Y(A_T, Y_T, \Delta_T)$, is not needed, since the value of Y_T is not influenced by the choice variable in period $T-1$.

The problem in period $T - 1$ is a special case, since there is no income uncertainty or further risk of disability. More generally, given the function $V_{t+1}(A_{t+1}, Y_{t+1}, \Delta_{t+1})$ and the associated partial derivatives, the problem at period t is:

(5a) $\qquad V_t(A_t, Y_t, 1) \equiv \max_{\{C_t\}} u(C_t) + \beta E_t[V_{t+1}(A_{t+1}, Y_{t+1}, 1)]$

for disabled consumers or:

(5b) $V_t(A_t, Y_t, 0) \equiv \max_{\{C_t\}} u(C_t) +$

$\qquad \beta E_t[\delta_{t+1} V_{t+1}(A_{t+1}, Y_{t+1}, 1) + (1 - \delta_{t+1}) V_{t+1}(A_{t+1}, Y_{t+1}, 0)]$

for nondisabled consumers. These one-period problems have first-order conditions given by:

(6a) $\qquad u'(C_t) - \beta[1 + r(1 - \tau)] E_t[V_{t+1}^A(A_{t+1}, Y_{t+1}, 1)] = 0$

and

(6b) $u'(C_t) - \beta[1 + r(1 - \tau)]$

$\qquad \cdot E_t[\delta_{t+1} V_{t+1}^A(A_{t+1}, Y_{t+1}, 1) + (1 - \delta_{t+1}) V_{t+1}^A(A_{t+1}, Y_{t+1}, 0)] = 0.$

The first term in each first-order condition is the marginal utility of an additional dollar of consumption in period t. The second term is the expected discounted value of saving that dollar to be used in period $t + 1$. The dollar grows by the after-tax interest rate and has a marginal value of V^A at that time, where in the case of a nondisabled consumer V^A is evaluated at both possibilities for period $t + 1$—disabled or nondisabled—and weighted appropriately by the probability of disability or its complement. The expected marginal utility of a dollar of assets at time $t + 1$ is discounted back to period t utility at a rate β. The difference between the marginal utility of consumption and the expected marginal utility of assets in the next period is zero at the optimal level of consumption.[16]

Once the optimal consumption rules have been obtained, the models can be simulated forward by specifying initial values of the state variables, drawing random shocks to income and disability status, and applying the consumption rules to generate distributions of asset balances in each period. In our simulations, we construct average consumption and asset profiles based on 5,000 independent random draws.

The baseline model consists of assumptions about the income process

16. The solution method is complicated by the liquidity constraint. The constraint that A_{t+1} cannot be negative implies that the maximum amount of consumption in the prior period is $C_t = A_t + Y_t(1 - \tau)$.

and the preference parameters. We assume a starting value of income at age twenty-two of $20,000 and allow permanent income to grow similarly to the profile for noncollege graduates specified in Hubbard Skinner, and Zeldes (1995).[17] We also adopt their parameters of $\rho = 0.95$ and $\sigma = 0.15$ for the AR(1) income process. We specify a replacement rate of 40 percent at retirement or disability, corresponding to a typical replacement rate from the Social Security system. The constant, pretax interest rate, r, is assumed to be 5 percent. The tax rate in the linear tax system, τ, is taken to be 20 percent, applied to both labor and investment income. The after-tax interest rate is therefore 4 percent per year. In alternative models, we consider replacement rates of 20 and 60 percent (with an income standard deviation of 15 percent) and income standard deviations of 10 and 20 percent (with a replacement rate of 40 percent).

There are two main preference parameters. The coefficient of relative risk aversion, γ, is assumed to be 3. In a CRRA model, this results in an intertemporal elasticity of substitution of 1/3. The discount rate, β, takes one of two values: For simulations of a patient consumer, β is assumed to be 1/1.04 percent. For simulations of an impatient consumer, β is assumed to be 1/1.08 percent. In the absence of income uncertainty, an impatient consumer would seek to borrow against future income to finance current consumption, whereas a patient consumer would not. A patient consumer begins saving for retirement early in the life cycle, while an impatient consumer typically engages in buffer stock saving for several periods before saving for retirement. The difference in behavior results from the comparison of the rate of time preference to the interest rate—the patient consumer has $1/\beta = 1 + (1 - \tau)r$, whereas the impatient consumer has $1/\beta > 1 + (1 - \tau)r$. The two values chosen are close to the median estimates of the discount rate in Samwick (1998).

The key parameter that we vary in our simulations is the age-disability profile. For all simulations, we adopt the empirical age profile from figure 10.1 that reflects the regression-adjusted age profile in our CPS data over the period from 1980 to 2004. We smooth out the initial disability prevalence at age twenty-two linearly over all ages, so that the profile starts out at a zero probability of disablement and then rises to the 12 percent prevalence at age sixty-two that we observe in the data. To consider variation around this baseline, we scale the entire profile up or down proportionally to achieve alternative disability rates at age sixty-two, including the values of 0, 6, 12, 18, and 24 percent, with the latter corresponding roughly to the maximum preretirement disability rate that we observe for any of our groups empirically.

17. We approximate this profile by having real income grow at annual rates of 2.5, 1.7, 0.5, and −1.3 percent over the four decades of the working life. Total income growth by the peak (in the thirtieth year of the working life) is about 55 percent, with a subsequent drop of about 12 percent. The choice of the starting income level is immaterial here, as the entire optimization problem scales linearly with income.

Figure 10.6 shows the impact of disability risk on consumption. Each panel graphs the average level of consumption by age for consumers who do not become disabled under each of four different rates of preretirement disability. The top panel is for the impatient consumer, and the bottom panel is for the patient consumer. In each panel, the solid curve indicates the profile that average consumption would take in the absence of a disability risk. Even in this baseline case, it is upward sloping during most of the working life due to the need for precautionary saving against annual income fluctuations in the early years. After the peak, it declines toward the

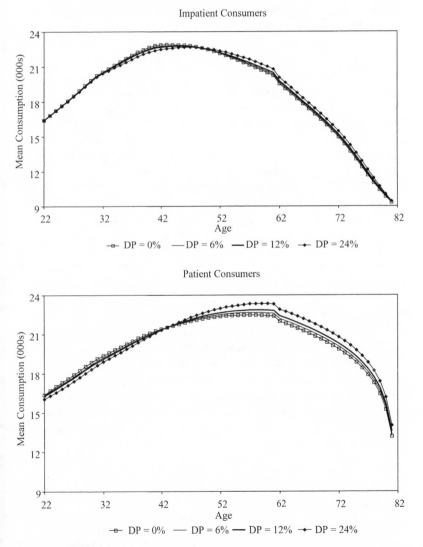

Fig. 10.6   Age-consumption profiles for consumers who do not become disabled

end of the life cycle. There is no important change at retirement in this model, since the voluntary retirement is completely anticipated. The baseline profile is flatter and peaks later for the patient consumer than for the impatient consumer.

As the disability risk increases, the consumption profile starts lower early in life (to allow for more precautionary saving) and remains higher later in life. All of the consumption profiles (in both panels) have the same present value, because the income draws are the same and these are the consumers who do not become disabled before retirement. The distortions in the timing of consumption over the life cycle—induced by the risk of becoming disabled—contribute to the welfare loss discussed in the following paragraphs. The distortions are larger for the patient consumer than for the impatient consumer, because the former reacts more strongly and sooner to the higher risks of preretirement disability.

Figure 10.7 illustrates the effect of a disabling event on the accumulation of assets. Each panel graphs the average asset values by age for preretirement disability risks of 12 and 24 percent. For consumers who do not become disabled before retirement, the asset profiles rise steadily to a peak just prior to retirement, after which they are spent down gradually to zero. Consistent with the consumption profiles, the patient consumer consumes less and accumulates more assets prior to retirement. The graphs also show the asset profiles of consumers who become disabled at age fifty-two, after thirty years of work but ten years prior to voluntary retirement. These profiles track those of those who do not get disabled through that age[18] and are fairly quickly spent down to zero after disablement. It takes about fifteen years for the impatient consumer to exhaust the assets, and about thirty years for the patient consumer to do so. After the assets are exhausted, the consumer simply consumes the income provided by the disability insurance program.

Figure 10.8 shows the range of age-asset profiles corresponding to preretirement disability rates up to 24 percent. In each panel, the solid (bottom) profile corresponds to the baseline case with no disability risk. Preretirement wealth peaks at $87,000 for the impatient consumer and $147,700 for the patient consumer, compared to starting income of $20,000 and peak average income of about $32,000 (at age fifty-two). Successively higher profiles show the effect of increasing the disability risk. With the sample average risk of 12 percent, the peak preretirement wealth rises to $90,100 (3.6 percent) and $154,000 (4.3 percent) for the impatient and patient consumers, respectively.[19]

18. The graphs should overlap exactly prior to disablement. The disparity is due to the small sample variation in income draws for the subset of random draws that first become disabled at exactly age fifty-two.
19. The numbers reported for assets are for the mean profile. Median asset amounts are 15 to 20 percent lower on the eve of voluntary retirement. The increase from zero to 12 percent disability risk raises median assets from $70,200 to $73,900 for the impatient consumer and from $126,300 to $133,300 for the patient consumer.

Impatient Consumers

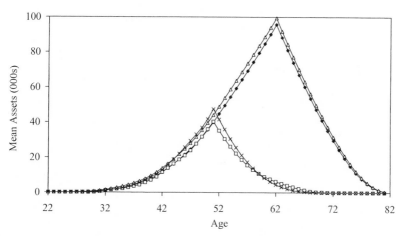

Patient Consumers

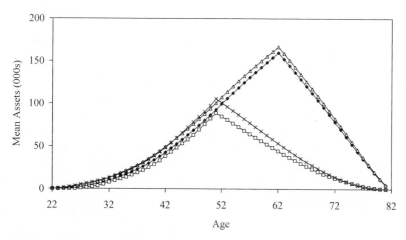

Fig. 10.7   Age-asset profiles by age of disability

10.5   Implications for Expected Utility

Table 10.6 shows the impact of disability risk on the expected lifetime utility and preretirement asset accumulation of the consumer across a range of values for the replacement rate and income uncertainty. The first panel shows the results for our baseline assumptions of a 40 percent replacement rate at retirement or disability and a 15 percent standard devia-

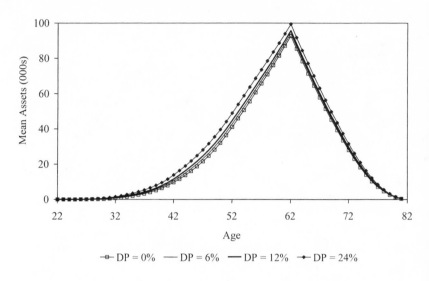

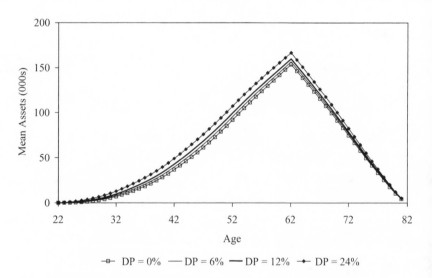

Fig. 10.8   Age-asset profiles for consumers who do not become disabled

tion of the shocks to annual income. The next two panels vary the replacement rate to 20 and 60 percent of preretirement income, and the last two
panels vary the standard deviation of the annual income shock to 20 and
10 percent.

Within each panel, the first column of numbers identifies the probability

Table 10.6   **Impact of disability risk on expected utility and saving**

Preretirement disability rate (%)	Loss in present value of consumption (%)	Equivalent variation (%)		Asset reduction in baseline (%)	
		Impatient	Patient	Impatient	Patient
Replacement rate = 40%, Standard deviation = 15%					
6	1.00	2.34	2.70	1.69	2.01
12	1.92	4.36	5.19	3.47	4.09
18	2.92	6.41	7.58	5.71	6.45
24	3.94	8.05	9.34	7.40	8.27
Replacement rate = 20%, Standard deviation = 15%					
6	1.32	8.41	8.45	5.59	6.33
12	2.60	14.44	13.81	10.66	11.37
18	3.93	19.41	18.27	15.41	15.43
24	5.27	22.29	21.18	19.21	18.40
Replacement rate = 60%, Standard deviation = 15%					
6	0.69	0.76	1.07	0.19	0.47
12	1.27	1.50	2.10	0.41	1.06
18	1.96	2.41	3.10	1.35	2.10
24	2.68	3.12	3.98	1.32	2.45
Replacement rate = 40%, Standard deviation = 20%					
6	1.00	2.02	2.40	1.12	1.19
12	1.89	3.92	4.71	2.33	2.48
18	2.90	5.84	6.86	4.06	4.09
24	3.94	7.20	8.50	4.98	4.95
Replacement rate = 40%, Standard deviation = 10%					
6	0.99	2.22	2.95	2.23	2.65
12	1.93	4.29	5.54	4.57	5.38
18	2.93	6.43	8.04	7.29	8.33
24	3.93	8.26	10.16	9.78	10.94

Notes: Preretirement disability rate is the prevalence of disability in the last period of the working life (here modeled as forty working periods and twenty retirement periods). Loss in PV of consumption is the percent reduction in the present value of expected consumption due to the specified disability risk. Equivalent variation is the percent reduction in consumption relative to the zero-disability case that would reduce expected utility by the same amount as facing the specified disability risk. Asset reduction in the baseline is the percent reduction in asset accumulation in the last period of the working life due to the absence of the specified disability risk. Patient and impatient consumers have rates of time preference equal to 4 and 8 percent, respectively. See the text for a description of the other parameter assumptions.

of becoming disabled prior to the age of anticipated retirement. The numbers range from 6 to 24 percent, with a value of 12 percent corresponding most closely to the average disability prevalence measured in the CPS for those aged sixty to sixty-four. There are several demographic groups with disability prevalence lower than that average, and the highest value of 24 approximates the highest prevalence estimated in the data (fig. 10.A2 demonstrates that is the prevalence of disability for never married men at age sixty-two). The 6 percent number represents the prevalence of a work-limiting disability at age sixty-two for college-educated workers in 2004 (fig. 10.4). The estimate of 18 percent is observed for black men at age sixty-two (fig. 10.5). The impact of shifting disability prevalence across time or group—conditional on our choice of baseline parameters—is therefore captured by the simulations shown in the table.

With a CRRA utility function, multiplying consumption in each period (and disability state) by a constant, k, multiplies expected utility by a factor of $k^{1-\gamma}$. We can therefore compare consumer welfare across two parameterizations by solving for the value of k such that if consumption in the baseline case is multiplied by k, the expected utility would equal the expected utility of the optimal consumption profile under the alternative set of parameters. If k is less (greater) than one, then the consumer is worse (better) off under the alternative parameterization. Since we consider the impact of increases in the disability rate, which necessarily make the consumer worse off, we refer to $1 - k$ as an equivalent variation, because it measures the amount of money (as a share of lifetime consumption in the baseline case) that a consumer would pay to avoid facing the higher disability risk in the alternative parameterization. The middle two columns show the equivalent variations separately for impatient and patient consumers.

Because consumers have a precautionary motive for saving, increasing disability risk will generate an increase in asset accumulation. As a means of calibrating the equivalent variation, the last two columns of the table show the percentage by which asset accumulation is lower in the baseline case with no disability risk compared to the asset accumulation in the alternative case (for those who do not become disabled) with the specified disability risk. Alternatively, this is the percentage of wealth in the alternative case that is attributable to the nonzero risk of disability.

Increasing the preretirement disability risk from zero to the sample average value of 12 percent generates equivalent variations of 4.36 and 5.19 percent for the impatient and patient consumers, respectively. Even though the present value of consumption falls by only 1.92 percent with this disability risk, the consumers would forego about 5 percent of their lifetime consumption to avoid that risk. Recall that disability risk is already partially insured through a stylized DI program in this model—income does not go to zero upon disablement. The 5 percent equivalent variation captures the amount that consumers would be willing to pay to remove the risk that they will ever have to receive payments from that program. The reduction in assets accumulated upon retirement (for those who do not become disabled) is about 1.85 percent in the baseline compared to the alternative.

For every 6-percentage point increase in the risk of disability, the present value of preretirement consumption falls by about 1 percent, the equivalent variation increases by about 2 percentage points, and the gap in preretirement asset accumulation for those who do not become disabled increases by about 2 percentage points. Considering the alternative definitions of disability in figure 10.1, the equivalent variation in the strictest definition, corresponding to the additional requirement of being on Medicare and a disability risk at age sixty-two of 6 percent, is as low as 2.5 percent, with 1 percentage point representing lost consumption. For the least restrictive definition, based solely on the answer to the work-limiting disability question and having a disability risk at age sixty-two of 18 percent, the equivalent variation is about 7 percent, with 3 percentage points representing lost consumption. Alternatively, the different simulations can correspond to the extremes of our data measured using our baseline definition of disability. College-educated workers with only a 6 percent disability risk have equivalent variations of 2.5 percent, while men who never marry have equivalent variations in excess of about 8.5 percent.

The next two panels show the analogous calculations when the replacement rate at retirement or disability is changed by 20 percentage points, to 20 and 60 percent, respectively. Focusing on a preretirement disability risk of 12 percent, cutting the replacement rate in half increases the amount of lost consumption by about 35 percent (from 1.92 to 2.60 percentage points), but the equivalent variation more than doubles to about 14 percent of baseline consumption. The asset reduction in the baseline case also increases to about 11 percent. With the higher replacement rate of 60 percent, the equivalent variation falls to about 1.4 percent and the asset reduction similarly falls to about 0.7 percent. In all cases, the asset reduction in the baseline due to the absence of disability risk is a bit below the equivalent variation.

The bottom two panels show the calculations when the standard deviation of the annual shock to preretirement income is changed by 5 percentage points, to 20 and 10 percent, respectively. The present value of the consumption losses are the same when uncertainty increases (apart from sampling variance), as the shocks are constrained to have a mean of 1. The equivalent variations change very little as income uncertainty changes—the 12 percent disability risk generates an equivalent variation of about 4 to 5 percent, again with about 1 percentage point of difference between impatient and patient consumers. The asset reductions in the baseline case without disability risk are lowest when there is high income uncertainty—the added precautionary saving against annual income fluctuations diminishes the relative importance of precautionary saving against the disability risk.

Table 10.7 shows the impact on expected utility and preretirement asset accumulation of lowering the replacement rate (from 60 to 40 to 20 percent) and increasing the standard deviation of the annual income shock (from 10 to 15 to 20 percent), while holding the preretirement disability risk fixed at 0 or 12 percent. In both sets of comparisons, the changes should serve to decrease expected utility and increase asset accumulation. The results in this table can be used to gauge the magnitudes in table 10.6.

Table 10.7   Impact of replacement rate and income uncertainty on expected utility and saving

Replacement rate or Standard deviation (%)	Loss in present value of consumption (%)	Equivalent variation (%)		Asset reduction in baseline (%)	
		Impatient	Patient	Impatient	Patient
	Disability risk = 0%, Standard deviation = 15%				
RR = 40	2.75	1.50	2.00	44.69	28.42
RR = 20	5.50	2.94	3.69	62.77	44.95
	Disability risk = 12%, Standard deviation = 15%				
RR = 40	3.38	4.36	5.09	46.39	30.62
RR = 20	6.77	15.69	15.21	66.60	50.69
	Disability risk = 0%, Replacement rate = 40%				
SD = 15	0.00	9.81	9.98	30.39	26.16
SD = 20	0.00	22.18	20.92	51.68	44.89
	Disability risk = 12%, Replacement rate = 40%				
SD = 15	−0.02	9.87	9.64	29.59	25.16
SD = 20	−0.04	21.88	20.22	50.54	43.20

Notes: Disability Risk is the prevalence of disability in the last period of the working life (here modeled as 40 working periods and 20 retirement periods). Comparisons in each panel are made relative to the highest replacement rate (60 percent) and the lowest income uncertainty (10 percent). Loss in PV of consumption is the percent reduction in the present value of expected consumption due to the specified change in replacement rate or income uncertainty. Equivalent variation is the percent reduction in consumption relative to the lowest-saving case that would reduce expected utility by the same amount as facing the lower replacement rate or higher income uncertainty. Asset reduction in the baseline is the percent reduction in asset accumulation in the last period of the working life due to the absence of the specified reduction in the replacement rate or increase in income uncertainty. Patient and impatient consumers have rates of time preference equal to 4 and 8 percent, respectively. See the text for a description of the other parameter assumptions.

With no risk of disability, reductions in the replacement rate affect only the level of income received after retirement. Each reduction of 20 percentage points in the replacement rate lowers the present value of consumption by 2.75 percent. However, the equivalent variations show that neither the impatient nor the patient consumer would be willing to forego that amount of consumption—deducted proportionally in each year—to avoid these reductions. The reason is that the consumers can optimally (rather than merely proportionally) adjust their consumption to offset the lower retirement replacement rate by saving more. The last two columns show that there is a substantial savings response to the reductions in the replacement rate, of 45 and 63 percent for the two increments by the impatient consumer and 28 and 45 percent by the patient consumer. (The proportion is lower for the patient consumer, who is doing more life cycle saving in the baseline when the replacement rate is 60 percent.)

The loss in the present value of consumption is 3.38 percent for each 20 percentage point reduction in the replacement rate when the disability risk is increased to the sample average of 12 percent. The equivalent variations increase substantially to 4.4 to 5.1 percent for the drop to a 40 percent replacement rate, and 15.2 to 15.7 percent for the drop to a 20 percent replacement rate. Compared to the zero disability risk case, however, the asset reductions in the baseline increase only 2 to 4 percentage points for the impatient consumer (to 46.4 and 66.6 percent) and 2 to 6 percentage points for the patient consumer (to 30.6 and 50.7 percent).

For changes in the standard deviation of the income shock, the results are comparable for disability risks of zero and 12 percent. In both cases, and for both the impatient and the patient consumer, raising the standard deviation from 10 to 15 percent generates an equivalent variation of 9.6 to 10 percent and asset reductions in the baseline of 25 to 30 percent. An increase in the standard deviation from 10 to 20 percent generates an equivalent variation of about 20 to 22 percent and asset reductions in the baseline of 43 to 52 percent.

The distinction between the impacts of disability risk, income uncertainty, and the replacement rate on saving and expected utility is summarized in figure 10.9. The bottom profile remains the average assets by age for consumers who face a retirement replacement rate of 40 percent, a standard deviation of income shocks of 15 percent, and zero risk of disability. The next lowest profile reflects the impact (on those who do not become disabled) of facing a preretirement disability risk of 36 percent, or three times the sample average risk. In calculations analogous to those shown in table 10.6, the consumer would be willing to forego about 12 percent of consumption in each period to avoid that risk, and about 12 percent of the wealth accumulated at the preretirement peak is attributable to that disability risk.

The top profile in the graphs shows the impact of keeping the disability risk at zero but increasing the standard deviation of the annual income shocks from 15 to 20 percent. The equivalent variation for this shift is about 13 percent, just slightly higher than for the increase in the disability risk to 36 percent. However, about 28 percent of the wealth accumulated at the preretirement peak is attributable to the higher income uncertainty, which is more than twice as much as for the profile that increased the disability risk to 36 percent.

The last profile in the graph, with the shortest dashes, shows the impact of keeping the disability risk at zero and the standard deviation of the income shock at 15 percent, but lowering the replacement rate from 40 to 20 percent. Note that because the disability risk is zero, this reduction affects only the income received after retirement. The peak asset accumulation for this profile is comparable to the peak when income uncertainty is raised to 20 percent. However, the equivalent variation relative to the baseline case is less than 2 percent of lifetime consumption.

What explains these differences? Increases in the disability risk have a large effect on expected utility but a comparatively small effect on asset ac-

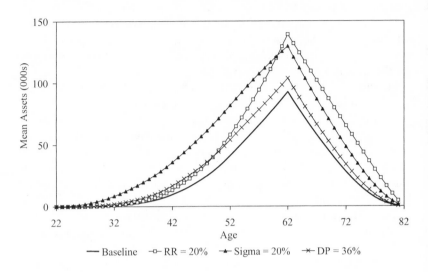

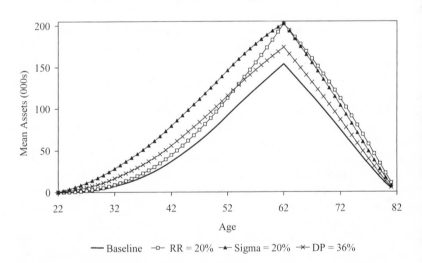

Fig. 10.9   Age-asset profiles for alternative parameterizations for consumers who do not become disabled

cumulation. The reason is that saving is less useful in protecting against a low-probability, high-impact risk than the events in the two alternatives. Saving is a perfect response against the certain drop in income at retirement, and because such an ideal response exists, the equivalent variation of reductions to the retirement replacement rate (when there is no disability risk) is quite small. Additional saving is an effective though imperfect hedge against year-to-year income fluctuations. For a change in parameters of a given equivalent variation, the consumer does less saving against annual income risk than against a planned drop in income, but more saving than against a risk of disability. Preretirement saving is least attractive as a hedge against a disabling risk.

The age-asset profiles also show that when disability or income risk increases, the impact on saving is immediate. The consequences of disability early in life are critical, but the impact on assets fades over time as the number of years over which the disability could occur is reduced and the income level that would be replaced increases. In contrast, when the replacement rate at planned retirement is lowered, the consumer has forty years to overcome the loss. With an upward sloping income profile over the first thirty years of the working life, the lower replacement rate can be accommodated by small reductions in consumption at each age, which accelerate as the date of retirement approaches and income growth slows.

10.6 Conclusion

Using the Current Population Survey over the period from 1980 to 2004, we document the decline in disability over the past two decades, along with cross-sectional differences in the prevalence of disability by gender, education, and other demographic groups. Once we account for compositional changes in demographic characteristics, as well as trends in disability that affect all groups equally, we find that the age-disability profile is fairly stable across time and demographic groups. The exception to this finding is a slight decline in disability prevalence for Americans aged sixty to sixty-four. These findings suggest that demographic changes and year-specific changes in the disability rate (that affect all groups equally) generate the observed changes in the level of disability over time. In our stochastic life cycle model of consumption, we estimate that a typical consumer would be willing to pay a premium equal to about 5 percent of lifetime consumption to avoid the average risk of disability found in our data, even in the presence of a stylized disability insurance program that provides the same replacement rate upon disability as at retirement.

As discussed earlier, our estimates are derived under the assumption that agents do not exhibit state-dependent utility. Under state-dependent utility, the utility of consumption is no longer independent of health. If invalid, this assumption would cause us to either overstate or understate an agent's willingness to pay for insurance against disability. If we assume the utility of consumption if disabled is lower than if nondisabled, which is equivalent to assuming that health and income are complements in consumption, individuals would be willing to pay less for insurance against disability than the situation that we have considered. Alternatively, it could be that the marginal utility of income is higher when disabled since the disabled need more resources to purchase healthcare and assistive technologies. If so, individuals would be willing to pay more for disability insurance. In the absence of evidence that supports state-dependent utility, we have delegated further exploration of this potentially important issue to future work.

Compared to other motives for saving, like an anticipated drop in income at retirement or annual fluctuations in income, disability risk generates little additional saving for a given welfare loss. This is because precautionary saving is less useful as a hedge against low-probability, high-impact events like disability. As a result, it is unlikely that the precautionary saving that occurs specifically due to the empirically observed probabilities of disability is large enough to be of macro- or microeconomic importance. We estimate that no more than 20 percent of assets accumulated before voluntary retirement are attributable to disability risks observed in our data. Because the probability of disablement is too small, and the average size of the loss (conditional on becoming disabled) is large, disability risk is not effectively insured through precautionary saving. Therefore, the value of disability insurance, whether in the form of income or assistive technology, is likely to be high. The magnitude of our finding is consistent with the related work of Fuchs-Schundeln (2003), who estimates that precautionary savings constitute between 5 and 12 of aggregate savings in a calibrated model that measures the welfare effects of uninsured labor risks on consumption.

Our chapter is silent on the specifics of the optimal disability-insurance system. While the value of such an insurance program may be high, and the typical worker is willing to pay for the program, it is important to ensure that its design is actuarially fair by income group. As noted by Bound et al. (2004), the current DI program permits undesirable transfers from low-income able-bodied workers and non-DI-eligible disabled persons to comparatively better off DI beneficiaries. These transfers render the program less fair to low-income persons, a group who would have been predicted to be the greatest beneficiaries of this insurance program.

Throughout our analysis, we have defined disability as a health problem or condition that limits the kind or amount of work that a person can do. This definition is focused on the link between disability and work, but work-limiting disabilities as defined in the CPS may include more conditions than those that lead to involuntary retirement. To mitigate this possibility, our main estimates in the paper follow the methodology of Burkhauser, Houtenville, and Wittenburg (2003) and require that the respondent not be working at present nor have worked in the prior year. Compared to our baseline estimate of a 5 percent equivalent variation, our lower and upper bounds are 2.5 and 7 percent, respectively. Once again, these estimates are in the range obtained by Fuchs-Schundeln (2003), who finds an equivalent variation of 2 to 5 percent of consumption as the welfare consequence of incomplete insurance against idiosyncratic labor shocks.

Relative to the definition of disability chosen in our analysis, other definitions based on health status, such as the inability to perform certain Activities of Daily Living, would suggest an alternative modeling framework in which the impact of disability would lower the utility from a given amount of consumption in addition to its impact on the ability to work. Developing such a model, in which the savings response could differ markedly from that presented here, is an important topic for further research.

Appendix

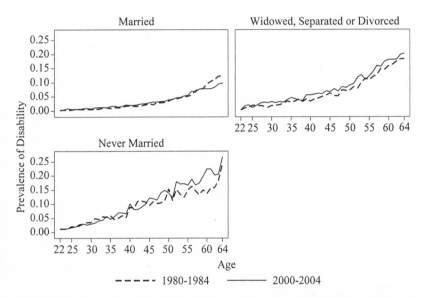

Fig. 10.A1   Regression adjusted disability prevalence by marital status over time

Notes: Figures report predicted probability of work-limiting disability from a logistic regression that controls for an unrestricted set of age and year indicator variables, gender, race and ethnicity (four categories), education (two categories), marital status (three categories), marital status and gender interactions, census region (nine categories), metropolitan status, census division and metropolitan status interactions, the number of children under the age of eighteen in the family, and the size of the household. The above figure adjusts for these covariates, except the ones used in the figure. The regression used CPS data from the 1980–2004 files of Annual Demographic Survey (n = 2,166,178).

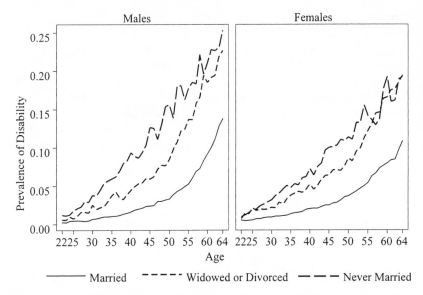

Fig. 10.A2   Regression adjusted disability prevalence by marital status and gender
Notes: See note to figure 10.A1.

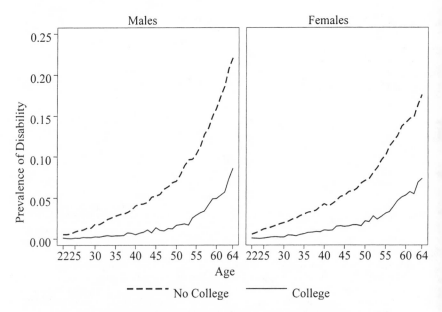

Fig. 10.A3   Regression adjusted disability prevalence by education and gender
Notes: See note to figure 10.A1.

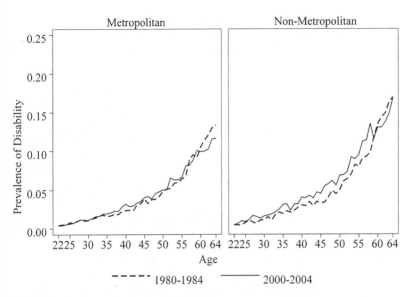

Fig. 10.A4   Regression adjusted disability prevalence by metropolitan status
Notes: See note to figure 10.A1.

References

Autor, David H., and Mark G. Duggan. 2003. The rise in disability rolls and the decline in unemployment. *Quarterly Journal of Economics* 118 (1): 157–206.

Bound, John, and Richard V. Burkhauser. 1999. Economic analysis of transfer programs targeted on people with disabilities. In *Handbook of labor economics, Vol. 3,* ed. Orley Ashenfelter and David Card, 3417–3528. Amsterdam: Elsevier.

Bound, John, Julie Berry Cullen, Austin Nichols, and Lucie Schmidt. 2004. The welfare implications of increasing disability insurance benefit generosity. *Journal of Public Economics* 88 (12): 2487–2514.

Bureau of Labor Statistics. 2005. The Employment Situation: January 2005. Accessed February 4, http://www.bls.gov/ces/

Burkhauser, Richard V., and Mary C. Daly. 1996. Employment and economic well-being following the onset of a disability: The role for public policy. In *Disability, work, and cash benefits,* ed. Jerry Manshaw, Virginia Reno, Richard Burkhauser, and Monroe Berkovitz, 59–102. Kalamazoo, MI: W. E. Upjohn Institute for Employment Research.

Burkhauser, Richard V., Andrew J. Houtenville, and David C. Wittenburg. 2003. A users guide to current statistics on the employment of people with disabilities. In *The decline in employment of people with disabilities,* ed. David C. Stapleton and Richard V. Burkhauser, 23–85. Kalamazoo, MI: W. E. Upjohn Institute for Employment Research.

Carroll, Christopher D. 2001. Lecture notes on solution methods for microeconomic dynamic stochastic optimization problems. Johns Hopkins University, Department of Economics. Unpublished Manuscript, April.

Deaton, Angus, and Christina H. Paxson. 1994. Intertemporal choice and inequality. *Journal of Political Economy* 102 (3): 437–67.

Fuchs-Schundeln, Nicola. 2003. Welfare loss and precautionary savings due to uninsured idiosyncratic labor risk. Harvard University, Department of Economics. Unpublished manuscript.

Gertler, Paul, and Jonathan Gruber. 2002. Insuring consumption against illness. *American Economic Review* 91 (1): 51–70.

Heckman, James J., and Richard Robb. 1985. Alternative methods for evaluating the impact of interventions. In *Longitudinal analysis of labor market data*, eds. James Heckman and Burton Singer, 156–245. New York: Cambridge University Press.

Hubbard, Glenn R., Jonathan S. Skinner, and Stephen P. Zeldes. 1995. Precautionary saving and social insurance. *Journal of Political Economy* 103 (2): 360–99.

Kimball, Miles S. 1990. Precautionary Saving in the Small and the Large. *Econometrica* 58 (1): 53–73.

Kutscher, Ronald E., and Valerie A. Personick. 1986. Deindustrialization and the Shift to Services. *Monthly Labor Review* 109 (6): 3–13.

Lakdawalla, Darius, Jayanta Bhattacharya, and Dana. P. Goldman. 2004. Are the young becoming more disabled? *Health Affairs* 23 (1): 168–76.

Mashaw, Jerry L., and Virginia P. Reno. 1996. Balancing Security and Opportunity: the Challenge of Disability Income Policy. Report of the Disability Policy Panel. Washington, DC: National Academy of Social Insurance.

Samwick, Andrew A. 1998. Discount rate heterogeneity and social security reform. *Journal of Development Economics* 57 (1): 117–46.

Why are the Disability Rolls Skyrocketing? The Contribution of Population Characteristics, Economic Conditions, and Program Generosity

Mark Duggan and Scott A. Imberman

11.1 Introduction

During the last two decades, the fraction of nonelderly adults in the United States receiving Social Security Disability Insurance (hereafter DI) benefits increased by 76 percent, with 6.20 million disabled workers on the program in December of 2004.[1] Recent work has suggested that the growth during this period was to some extent driven by an increase in the financial incentive to apply for DI and by a liberalization of the program's medical eligibility criteria (Autor and Duggan 2003). These changes alone, however, were not the only ones influencing the increase in DI receipt. In this chapter, we estimate the contribution of several factors to the growth in the DI rolls during the past two decades. We divide our determinants into three distinct categories—the characteristics of individuals insured by the DI program, the state of the economy, and the generosity of program benefits.

Mark Duggan is professor of economics at the University of Maryland, and a research associate of the National Bureau of Economic Research. Scott A. Imberman is assistant professor of economics at the University of Houston.

We are grateful to the Mary Woodard Lasker Charitable Trust and Michael E. DeBakey Foundation, and the National Institute on Aging for financial support through grants P30 AG12810 and R01 AG19805. We would also like to thank David Autor, Rona Blumenthal, Amitabh Chandra, David Cutler, Kevin Kulzer, Jeffrey Kunkel, Kalman Rupp, Andrew Samwick, David Wise, and seminar participants at the University of Maryland and at the NBER Disability Conference for their helpful assistance, comments, and suggestions. This work was completed when Scott Imberman was a graduate student at the University of Maryland. All errors remain our own.

1. This does not include an additional 2.7 million nonelderly adults who received disability benefits from the means-tested Supplemental Security Income program but not from DI. Nor does it include the 1.60 million children of disabled workers receiving benefits or the 0.15 million spouses. It does include the 1.3 million nonelderly adults who received disability benefits from both DI and SSI.

We begin with an examination of the changing age structure in the United States (section 11.2). These changes could be important given that DI receipt is so strongly related to age. For example, the probability that a fifty to sixty-four-year-old man receives DI benefits is more than five times greater than the same probability for his counterpart between the ages of twenty and forty-nine. With individuals from the Baby Boom generation now between the ages of forty and fifty-eight (versus twenty and thirty-eight two decades ago), one would expect a large increase in DI receipt. According to our results, the changing age structure of the nonelderly adult population in the United States can explain 15 percent of the increase in DI receipt among men, but just 4 percent for women. This disparity is partly because the growth in DI receipt has been almost twice as large for women as for men during the past two decades, and thus there is less to explain for the latter group.

One explanation for the differential increase in DI receipt among women is the growth in the fraction of women insured by DI. Given that an individual must have twenty quarters of work history during the past ten years to be insured for DI benefits, the substantial increases in female labor force participation in recent decades have increased the fraction of women insured by the program. Our findings suggest that this effect is substantial, as it can explain 24 percent of the growth in DI receipt among women, but just 3 percent among men.

We next turn to the contribution of changes in the health status of nonelderly adults to the growth in DI receipt (section 11.3). On the most widely used measure—mortality—nonelderly adults have become significantly healthier over time. For example, the probability that a male born in 1921 survived to the age of sixty was just 68 percent, whereas a male born twenty years later had a 78 percent chance of surviving to this age. The reductions in mortality were similarly large among women. But this fall in mortality could have a perverse effect on the health of individuals who are alive because marginal survivors may be in poor health. Using data from the National Health Interview Survey covering the years 1984–2001, our findings suggest that near-elderly adults are on average getting healthier whereas health among younger adults has remained roughly constant. Though the measures of health in the NHIS are far from perfect, our findings suggest that changes in health reduced the growth of DI receipt below what it otherwise would have been.

Recent studies have suggested that economic conditions have an important effect on the fraction of individuals receiving DI benefits (Black, Daniel, and Sanders 2002; Autor and Duggan 2003). An examination of the change in DI application rates during the two most recent recessions supports this hypothesis. For example, from 1989 to 1993 the number of applications to DI increased by 45 percent and from 1999 to 2003 by an even larger 58 percent. It is therefore plausible that adverse economic shocks increase the number of individuals applying for and ultimately awarded benefits. Our findings in section 11.4 suggest that the recessions of 1991 and 2001 can explain 24 percent of the growth in DI receipt among men and 12 percent of the growth among women.

Another line of research has emphasized the importance of DI benefit generosity as a determinant of DI application propensities (Parsons, 1980; Bound, 1989; Gruber, 2000). Though the formula used by the Social Security Administration (SSA) to calculate individuals' DI benefits did not change during our study period, individuals' incentives to apply for DI has changed, as shown in section 11.5. Because of the interaction between rising income inequality and the progressive benefit formula used by SSA, low-skilled individuals can now replace a much larger fraction of their earnings with DI benefits than they could have two decades ago. Our findings suggest that rising replacement rates can explain 28 percent of the growth in DI receipt among women and 24 percent of the growth for men.

In section 11.6, the last factor that we consider turns out to be the most important. Because of federal legislation enacted in 1984, the Social Security Administration was required to use a more liberal definition of disability when deciding whether to accept or reject a DI application. For example, the SSA had to use less strict criteria for mental disorders and place greater weight on pain—a condition that might be difficult to verify. These changes differentially increased the probability that individuals with mental disorders or musculoskeletal conditions (e.g., back pain, arthritis) were awarded DI benefits, with the fraction of DI awards to these two conditions increasing from 28 percent in 1983 to 52 percent twenty years later. Our findings suggest that the liberalized eligibility criteria can explain 38 percent of the growth in DI receipt among women and 53 percent for men.

We conclude the chapter (section 11.7) with a forecast of the changes in disability recipiency that will occur during the upcoming years. For at least four reasons, it is likely that the growth in the DI rolls will continue and perhaps accelerate. First, given the average number of awards at present and the average duration of individuals awarded benefits, it is clear that the program is far below its equilibrium size. To reach this equilibrium, the number of recipients would need to increase by 62 percent (to more than 9.8 million). Second, as the Baby Boom generation reaches its sixties, the importance of the age structure effect mentioned previously will increase substantially, with more individuals in these peak disability years. Third, because of reductions in the generosity of Social Security retirement benefits but no corresponding reduction for DI, the program will become relatively more attractive and thus more individuals are likely to apply. And finally, the rising cost of health insurance and the increase in the number who are uninsured suggests that the demand for the Medicare coverage resulting from DI receipt will increase. For all of these reasons, it is likely that the DI rolls will grow substantially above their current level in the absence of any changes to the program.

11.2 Previous Research

A substantial body of previous research has examined the causes and the consequences of the growth in the disability rolls. The vast majority of these works have focused attention on the effect of DI on the labor force participation (LFP) of men. For example Parsons (1980, 1984) argued that virtually all of the fall in male labor force participation during the post-World War II era was caused by the growing generosity of the DI program. However, Haveman and Wolfe (1984) argued that Parsons' model is incorrectly specified and when they redid his analysis, they found little contribution to the drop in male (LFP) from DI. In addition, Bound (1989) later challenged Parsons' estimates after finding that more than one-half of rejected DI applicants in a sample of awardees from the 1970s remained out of the labor force even after their rejections. This study did not claim that DI had no effect on labor market outcomes, but instead that the relationship between DI receipt and labor force exit was much less than one-for-one.

Subsequent studies supported the hypothesis that changes in the generosity of DI benefits and in the medical eligibility criteria influenced labor force participation, with the magnitude varying to some extent across studies and virtually all of these studies focusing exclusively on men (Parsons 1991a, 1991b; Bound 1991; Bound and Waidmann 1992; Gruber and Kubik 1997; Stapleton et al. 1998; Kreider 1999; Bound and Waidmann 2002). These studies had the limitation that because DI is a federal program, there was no obvious control group that could be used to disentangle the effect of changes in DI from other factors. To surmount this obstacle, Gruber (2000) used a substantial change in disability benefits in the Canadian province of Quebec to estimate the effect of DI benefit generosity. In this study, the author uses the other Canadian provinces as a control group and finds that the elasticity of labor force exit to DI benefit generosity is approximately 0.3.

One recent study has emphasized the role of changes in the financial incentive to apply for DI resulting from the interaction of the growth in income inequality and the progressive formula used to determine DI benefits (Autor and Duggan 2003). The authors argue that rising replacement rates (the fraction of one's income that can be replaced with DI benefits) and the more liberal definition of disability used following federal legislation enacted in 1984 increased the likelihood that low-skilled individuals would exit the labor force to apply for DI. The authors stress that both of these factors increased the sensitivity of DI recipiency to economic conditions.

Other studies have examined the contribution of business cycle effects to the growth in DI receipt. For example, Rupp and Stapleton (1995) summarize a series of early papers on the effect of the unemployment rate on DI receipt which find that a 1 percentage point increase in the unemployment rate is associated with up to a 7 percent increase in DI awards (Lewin-

VHI 1995; Stapleton, Coleman, and Dietrich 1995; Hambor 1992, 1975; Levy and Krute 1983; Muller 1982; Lando 1979). A more recent analysis by Black, Daniel, and Sanders (2002) uses plausibly exogenous shocks to the coal mining industry to estimate the effect of economic conditions on DI receipt. Their findings, though not strictly comparable to the studies described in Rupp and Stapleton, suggest an elasticity of DI payments with respect to local earnings of 0.4.

Changing health and population dynamics have also been suggested as possible explanations for the DI increase. Indeed, the aging of the Baby Boom generation has become an important issue for the DI program, since adults who are near retirement age are more likely to apply for and enroll in DI than others. Stapleton et al. (1998) suggest that population growth and aging accounted for a 1.3 percent annual DI growth rate from 1988 to 1992. However, the effects of aging may have been tempered by improvements in health. In particular, improvements in cardiovascular mortality have been dramatic. Cutler and Meara (2001) suggest that 98 percent of mortality reductions since 1960 have been from changes in cardiovascular mortality. Other evidence has shown that overall health amongst nonelderly adults has been improving (Cutler and Richardson 1997).

Whether the prevalence of disabilities has increased or fallen has been an issue of much debate. Crimmins, Saito, and Ingegneri (1989) find that although prevalence of long-term disability has increased, improvements in life expectancy and health care have caused disability-free life expectancy to increase as well. Lakdawalla, Bhattacharya, and Goldman (2004) find disability prevalence to be increasing amongst thirty to fifty-nine-year-olds and remaining stable amongst sixty to sixty-nine-year-olds. Considering that over the time period of their analysis, 1984–1996, all of the Baby Boom generation fell into the thirty to fifty-nine age at some point, the implications of rising disability in this age group for the DI program are enormous. One important limitation to both of these studies is that their measures of health status are based on self-reports and thus may not accurately capture true changes in morbidity over time.[2]

Taken together, past studies suggest that three sets of changes—in the characteristics of individuals insured by DI, in economic conditions, and in the financial incentive to apply for DI—have played an important role in the growth of DI receipt from 1984 to the present. In this study, we

2. There are at least three reasons that self-reporting of disabilities can create biased prevalence estimates. First, increased awareness of conditions could affect people's responses to questions about activity-limiting conditions. For example, it is possible that additional exposure to information about treatments for conditions may make people more aware of whether they are affected by them. Second, the responses to questions on activity limitations are dependent on people's choices regarding which activities they perform and their employment (Lakdawalla, Bhattacharya, and Goldman 2004). Finally, there is the possibility that for some people, whether they say they are work-limited or activity-limited may be causally determined by whether they receive disability benefits.

estimate the contribution of each one of these factors while also forecasting the likely changes in the disability rolls in the years ahead.

11.3   The Impact of Changes in the Age Structure, DI Insured Status, and Health

From December of 1984 to December of 2004, the number of individuals receiving disabled worker benefits from the federal Disability Insurance program increased by 139 percent (from 2.60 million to 6.20 million). Part of this increase was attributable to population growth, with the number of nonelderly adults rising by 29 percent during that same period. But this leaves a substantial portion of the growth unexplained, as evidenced by the increase from 1.91 percent to 3.38 percent in the fraction of twenty to sixty-four-year-old adults on DI during the same period (fig. 11.1). In this section, we explore the contribution of changes in the age distribution, in the fraction of nonelderly adults insured by DI, and in the health of the adult population to the growth in the disability rolls during the past two decades.

11.3.1   Changes in the Age Distribution

Each year, the Social Security Administration publishes data on the number of DI recipients by gender and age category. Combining this information with population data from the Census Bureau, one can investigate how DI receipt varies by gender and age in each year. The first column of table 11.1 provides DI recipiency rates for men and women, respectively, in 1984. As is clear from both panels, the probability that an individual

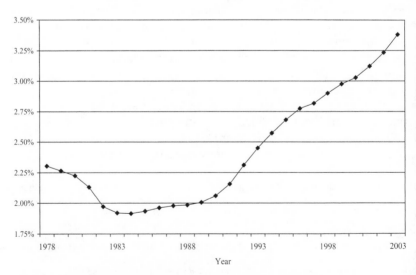

Fig. 11.1   Fraction of population aged 20–64 on DI: 1978–2003
Sources: SSA Office of the Chief Actuary; U.S. Census Bureau.

Table 11.1   Percent of growth in DI recipiency among males and females explained by changes in age structure

	1984 DI recipiency		1984 population		2003 population		Predicted Δ DI 1984–2003			Actual Δ DI 1984–2003		
	% on DI	# on DI	# people	% of pop	# people	% of pop	% on DI 2003	# on DI 2003	Δ in % on DI 1984–2003	% on DI 2003	# on DI 2003	Δ in % on DI 1984–2003
A. Males												
<30[a]	0.38	77	20,370	30.72	20,437	23.6	0.38	77	0.00	0.50	103	0.12
30–39	1.10	198	17,983	27.12	21,176	24.5	1.10	233	0.00	1.51	319	0.41
40–44	1.78	119	6,690	10.09	11,407	13.2	1.78	203	0.00	2.94	335	1.16
45–49	2.60	145	5,582	8.42	10,731	12.4	2.60	279	0.00	4.17	448	1.57
50–54	4.23	224	5,293	7.98	9,313	10.8	4.23	394	0.00	5.91	551	1.68
55–59	7.23	388	5,368	8.10	7,661	8.9	7.23	554	0.00	9.00	689	1.77
60–64	11.93	598	5,014	7.56	5,764	6.7	11.93	687	0.00	13.47	776	1.54
Overall	2.64	1749	66,300	100.00	86,488	100.0	2.81	2,427	0.17	3.73	3,225	1.09
% explained by Δ in pop dist: 15.4%												
B. Females												
<30[a]	0.15	31	20,267	29.4	19,459	22.3	0.15	30	0.00	0.41	79	0.26
30–39	0.47	87	18,388	26.7	20,936	24.0	0.47	99	0.00	1.29	270	0.82
40–44	0.76	53	6,945	10.1	11,555	13.3	0.76	88	0.00	2.41	278	1.65
45–49	1.13	66	5,846	8.5	11,030	12.7	1.13	125	0.00	3.41	376	2.28
50–54	1.92	109	5,664	8.2	9,731	11.2	1.92	187	0.00	4.79	466	2.87
55–59	3.29	197	5,984	8.7	8,133	9.3	3.29	268	0.00	7.03	572	3.74
60–64	5.29	306	5,788	8.4	6,342	7.3	5.29	335	0.00	9.60	609	4.31
Overall	1.23	849	68,882	100.0	87,187	100.0	1.30	1,132	0.07	3.04	2,649	1.81
% explained by Δ in pop dist: 3.6%												

Sources: U.S. Census Bureau Population Estimates, 2003; Decennial Census, 1980–1990; Annual Report of the Social Security Disability Program, 2003; Annual Statistical Supplement of the Social Security Bulletin, 1986.

[a] Population numbers for <30 reflects the twenty to twenty-nine population. All numbers are in thousands.

received DI benefits two decades ago was a steeply increasing function of his or her age. For example, a male in his early sixties was 10.8 times more likely than a male in his thirties to receive DI benefits. This ratio was even larger for women at 11.3. This positive relationship between age and DI receipt is perhaps not surprising given that measures of health such as the probability of survival from one year to the next, likelihood of not having an activity-limiting disability, and self-reported health decline with age (Lakdawalla, Bhattacharya, and Goldman 2004; Case and Deaton 2003; Cutler and Meara 2001).

The first column in this two table also demonstrates the substantial difference between men and women in the probability of DI receipt, with women in each of the six age categories listed less than half as likely as their male counterparts to receive disability benefits. For example, while nearly 12 percent of men in their early sixties were receiving DI benefits in this base year, just 5.3 percent of women in this same age group were on the program.

The third column of this table lists the U.S. population by age group in 1984.[3] The number of individuals in their twenties and thirties in 1984 was substantially greater than the number in either their forties or their fifties for both men and women and accounted for more than 57 percent of all adults aged twenty to sixty-four. This difference was largely driven by the surge in birth rates that occurred in the years following World War II. Almost all of the Baby Boom generation—defined by the U.S. Census Bureau as individuals born between 1946 and 1964—were between the ages of twenty and thirty-nine in 1984.

As previously noted and shown in the first column of table 11.1, DI recipiency rates in 1984 were especially low among young adults. Just 0.4 percent of men in their twenties and 1.1 percent of men in their thirties were receiving DI benefits two decades ago. Because of the positive relationship between DI receipt and age, one would have expected the DI rolls to grow as these individuals reached their forties and fifties. And as the next two columns of the table show, the aging of the Baby Boom generation was associated with a substantial change in age structure, with the fraction of both men and women in their forties and fifties increasing from 35 percent to 46 percent from 1984 to 2003.

In the next three columns we investigate how much of the growth in DI receipt can be explained by the change in population in each age-gender cell from 1984 to 2003. To do this, we take the product of the cell-specific DI recipiency rate in 1984, and the population in that same cell in 2003, and then sum up these predictions across the twelve age-gender groups as specified in the following equation:

---

3. Only individuals between the ages of twenty and sixty-four are listed here given that DI recipients switch to Social Security retirement benefits when they reach sixty-five and because very few people under the age of twenty have sufficient work history to be eligible for DI.

$$\Delta DI_{Sim} = \sum_{a=1}^{6}(\theta_{af,1984} \cdot N_{af,2003}) + \sum_{a=1}^{6}(\theta_{am,1984} \cdot N_{am,2003})$$

with $\theta_{am,1984}$ and $\theta_{af,1984}$ equaling the fraction of men and women, respectively, in age group a who were receiving DI benefits in 1984. The population in each of the six age cells in 2003 is equal to $N_{af,2003}$ for women and $N_{am,2003}$ for men. Using this algorithm, we estimate that the number of men receiving DI would have increased from 1.75 million to 2.43 million from 1984 to 2003 if the rate of DI receipt within each age group had remained the same. The actual number receiving DI in 2003 was 3.22 million, and thus this projection explains 46 percent of the increase in the number of men receiving DI since 1984.

But much of this projection simply captures the fact that the number of men between the ages of twenty and sixty-four is increasing during this period. If one instead only asks how much of the increase in the proportion of men receiving DI can be explained by changes in the age structure, this prediction can explain much less of the increase. Given the changes in age structure from 1984 to 2003, the algorithm described above predicts an increase from 2.64 percent to 2.81 percent in the fraction of men receiving DI. Given the true increase to 3.72 percent, this factor can explain just 15.5 percent of the growth in the likelihood that a nonelderly adult male receives DI benefits.

Among women the contribution of changes in the age structure to the growth in DI receipt has been even smaller, with just 3.6 percent of the increase in DI recipiency rates explained by this factor. This is primarily because the growth has been much more rapid among women than men during this period, with the number of women receiving DI increasing by 212 percent from 1984 to 2003, while the corresponding increase for men was just 84 percent. While it is true that women started from a much lower rate of DI receipt in 1984, this difference remains even if one compares the increase in the fraction of women receiving DI, which grew by 1.81 percentage points versus just 1.08 percentage points for men. One possible reason for the difference is the greater increase among women in the likelihood of being insured by DI, which was itself caused by the rise in female labor force participation. We examine this in the next section.

11.3.2   Changes in DI Eligibility

In order to be insured for DI benefits, an individual between the ages of thirty and sixty-four must have worked in at least five of the ten years before the onset of his or her disability.[4] This standard is relaxed for younger indi-

---

4. More specifically, a person must have at least 20 quarters of coverage during the preceding ten years. The amount of earnings needed to receive 1 quarter of coverage increases from one year to the next. For example, in 1984 a person who earned more than $1,560 during the year would have received credit for 4 quarters, while by 2003 the amount needed had increased to $3,480.

viduals, who must instead have worked in at least half of the years since the age of twenty-one. Part of the reason that men were two times more likely than women to receive DI in 1984 was that they were much more likely to have sufficient work history to be insured. For example, 86 percent of males in their fifties were eligible to receive DI benefits if they developed a disability in 1984, compared to just 53 percent of females in this same age group.

During the subsequent two decades, there was a steady convergence between the fraction of men and women insured by DI as a result of the increase in female labor force participation during this period. This trend is illustrated in figure 11.2, which shows that from 1984 to 2003 eligibility amongst women twenty to sixty-four rose from 62.8 percent to 75.2 percent. In comparison, male eligibility fell slightly from 89.9 percent to 86.2 percent. Given this trend, it is perhaps not surprising that the growth in DI receipt was substantially greater for women than for men during this period.

In table 11.2 we investigate the contribution of the growth in DI insured status for both men and women to the increase in DI receipt from 1984 to 2003. Our method here is similar to the one used in the preceding section. Specifically, we estimate the change in DI receipt that would have occurred from 1984 to 2003 if the fraction of insured individuals in each age cell actually receiving DI benefits remained at its 1984 level.

The first two columns of table 11.2 reveal that the difference between men and women in DI receipt in our base year of 1984 was much smaller if one denominated by the number insured by DI rather than by the total

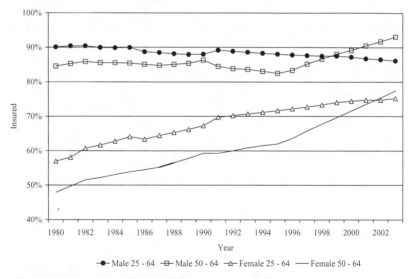

Fig. 11.2   Percent of population DI insured
Sources: SSA Office of the Chief Actuary; U.S. Census Bureau; Annual Statistical Supplement of the Social Security Bulletin.

	1984 DI recipiency			1984 population			2003 population			Predicted Δ DI 2003		Actual Δ DI 2003	
	% pop on DI	% ins on DI	# on DI	# people	# insured	% insured	# people	# insured	% insured	% on DI 2003	# on DI 2003	% on DI 2003	# on DI 2003
A. Males													
<30[a]	0.38	0.41	77	20,370	18,582	91.2	20437	15,935	78.0	0.32	66	0.50	103
30–39	1.12	1.19	198	17,635	16,617	94.2	21176	18,277	86.3	1.03	218	1.51	319
40–44	1.72	1.93	119	6,902	6,156	89.2	11407	10,308	90.4	1.75	199	2.94	335
45–49	2.43	2.89	145	5,957	5,025	84.4	10731	9,806	91.4	2.64	283	4.17	448
50–54	4.02	4.92	224	5,578	4,557	81.7	9313	8,432	90.5	4.45	414	5.91	551
55–59	7.32	8.44	388	5,303	4,598	86.7	7661	6,850	89.4	7.55	578	9.00	689
60–64	12.51	14.10	598	4,781	4,241	88.7	5764	4,903	85.1	12.00	691	13.47	776
Overall	2.63	2.93	1,749	66,525	59,776	89.9	86488	74,511	86.2	2.83	2,450	3.72	3,221
% explained	By Δ in pop dist:			15.4%									
	By Δ in insured:			3.2%									
	By Δ in pop dist and insured%:			18.6%									
B. Females													
<30[a]	0.15	0.21	31	20,267	15,056	74.3	19459	14,613	75.1	0.15	30	0.41	79
30–39	0.48	0.76	87	18,011	11,509	63.9	20936	15,718	75.1	0.57	119	1.29	270
40–44	0.74	1.28	53	7,146	4,128	57.8	11555	8,824	76.4	0.98	113	2.41	278
45–49	1.06	1.91	66	6,246	3,453	55.3	11030	8,599	78.0	1.49	164	3.41	376
50–54	1.82	3.42	109	5,988	3,188	53.2	9731	7,621	78.3	2.68	261	4.79	466
55–59	3.35	6.21	197	5,879	3,171	53.9	8133	5,985	73.6	4.57	372	7.03	572
60–64	5.55	10.70	306	5,518	2,861	51.8	6342	4,190	66.1	7.07	448	9.60	609
Overall	1.23	1.96	849	69,056	43,366	62.8	87187	65,550	75.2	1.73	1,507	3.04	2,650
% explained	By Δ in pop dist:			3.6%									
	By Δ in insured:			24.0%									
	By Δ in pop dist and insured:			27.6%									

[a] Population numbers for <30 reflects the twenty to twenty-nine population, so they reflect the total number of insured under age thirty in 1984 less the number of insured under twenty in 1985. Insured status numbers for 1984 are not available for twenty to twenty-nine.

Sources: U.S. Census Bureau Population Estimates, 2003; Decennial Census, 1980–1990; Annual Report of the Social Security Disability Program, 2003; Annual Statistical Supplement of the Social Security Bulletin, 1999; SSA Office of the Actuary.

population in the age cell. For example, men between the ages of fifty-five and fifty-nine were 2.19 times more likely than women in this same age group to be receiving DI benefits. But this male-female ratio fell to just 1.36 among individuals insured by the program.

The next several columns summarize the change in insurance rates by age and gender from 1984 to 2003. Among men there was very little change in the fraction of individuals eligible for DI during this period, with the patterns differing to some extent across age groups. For example, the fraction of men in their thirties insured by DI fell from 94 percent to 86 percent during this nineteen-year period, while the corresponding shares for men in their fifties increased from 84 percent to 90 percent.[5] Given these offsetting changes, it is not surprising that the change in the fraction of men insured by DI accounted for just 3.1 percent of their total increase in DI receipt during our nineteen-year study period.

For women these changes were much more important. As shown in table 11.2, the fraction of women eligible for DI increased in all age groups during our study period. The increase was especially large for older women. For example, in 1984 less than 54 percent of women in their fifties were eligible for DI, whereas in 2003 this share had increased to 76 percent. Summing up the predicted increases across the different age groups and subtracting out the portion attributable to changes in the age structure, our findings suggest that 24 percent of the increase in the fraction of women on DI can be explained by the growth in their insured status.

11.3.3 Changes in Health Status

In order to qualify for DI, a person must have a medically determinable ailment that is expected to last for at least twelve months or result in death and that prevents him or her from engaging in substantial gainful activity. To the extent that the health of DI-insured individuals has changed over time, this would influence program enrollment even if all other factors remained constant. In this section, we explore the contribution of changes in health status to the rise in the disability rolls during the past two decades. As previous researchers have noted, there is no perfect way to capture changes in health over time. A commonly used measure is mortality, though this has the obvious limitation that it does not capture the incidence of nonlethal but debilitating conditions. Despite this, it has a clear advantage because it is consistently defined over time.

According to this measure, the health of nonelderly adults has improved

---

5. The one outlier group is twenty to twenty-nine-year-olds, whose fraction insured fell substantially from 91 percent to 78 percent. Some of this change is likely due to the considerable increase in college attendance amongst males over this time period (U.S. Department of Education). Since very few people in this age group received DI in 1984, this fall in the fraction of twenty to twenty-nine-year-olds insured likely had only a negligible effect on the total number of DI beneficiaries.

Table 11.3   **Leading causes of death for people aged 50–64, deaths per 100,000 persons**

		1981	1991	2001	Change 1981–2001	% change 1981–2002
A. Male	Circulatory	681.5	470.9	333.8	−347.7	−51
	Cancer	424.3	404.1	313.3	−111.0	−26
	Respiratory	77.1	69.3	54.9	−22.2	−29
	Diabetes	21.8	27.8	34.5	12.8	59
	Suicide	24.3	24.3	22.1	−2.2	−9
	Other	249.7	212.6	221.8	−27.9	−11
	Total	1478.7	1209.0	980.5	−498.2	−34
B. Female	Circulatory	273.3	204.4	156.3	−116.9	−43
	Cancer	311.0	242.7	252.2	−58.8	−19
	Respiratory	39.1	48.6	44.9	5.8	15
	Diabetes	20.3	25.3	25.8	5.5	27
	Suicide	9.5	6.5	6.4	−3.1	−32
	Other	128.7	107.2	127.4	−1.3	−1
	Total	781.8	698.8	613.0	−168.8	−22

Source: Authors' calculations from NCHS Multiple Cause of Death Files and the Decennial Census 1980–2000. Figures do not include U.S. territories, commonwealths, or other outlying areas.

dramatically during the past two decades.[6] The data summarized in table 11.3 list annual mortality rates for both men and women between the ages of fifty and sixty-four in 1981, 1991, and 2001. During the twenty years from 1981 to 2001, annual mortality rates for men and women fell by 34 percent and 22 percent, respectively. Both changes were driven by a substantial decline in the death rate from circulatory disease, which fell by 51 percent for near-elderly males and by 43 percent for females, and accounted for 70 percent and 69 percent of the total drop in mortality rates for men and women, respectively.

As figure 11.3 demonstrates, these reductions in mortality were not limited to the fifty to sixty-four year age group. In this figure, we plot annual mortality rates by age for men and women born in 1921 and 1941. Across the age distribution, mortality has been declining. For example, a forty-year-old male born in 1941 was 20 percent less likely than his counterpart born in 1921 to die during the year, while the corresponding decline for a fifty-year-old male was 35 percent. As a result of these changes, individuals have become more likely to survive to a certain age over time. Just 68 percent of males born in 1921 survived to the age of sixty, while 78 percent of their counterparts born in 1941 did (fig. 11.4).[7] These improvements were

6. See Cutler and Meara (2001) for a detailed analysis of changes in mortality throughout the twentieth century across all age groups.

7. At the time the life tables used in this graph were created (1998), values for ages fifty-nine to sixty-five for the 1941 cohort were projections rather than estimates.

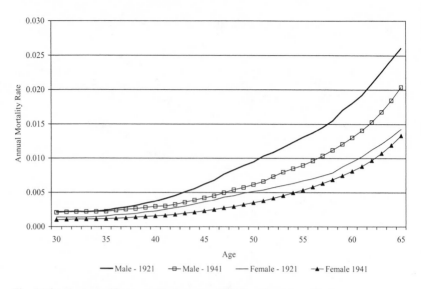

Fig. 11.3   Age-specific mortality by year of birth and gender cohort
Source: SSA Life Tables via Berkeley Mortality Database, 1998.

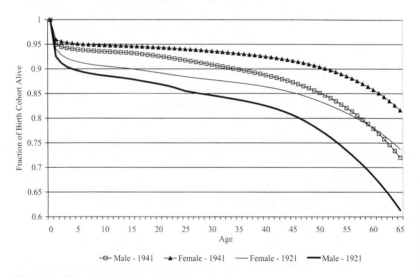

Fig. 11.4   Survival of birth and gender cohorts
Source: SSA Life Tables via Berkeley Mortality Database, 1998.

similarly dramatic for women, with survival rates to this age increasing from 78 percent for the 1921 cohort to 86 percent for women born in 1941.

Thus according to this measure, health among nonelderly adults has improved dramatically in recent years. But these declines in mortality could actually have produced a perverse effect on average health by changing the composition of the nonelderly adult population. Put simply, those individuals surviving to a certain age from the 1941 cohort who would not have survived if born in the 1921 cohort may be less healthy than the average nonelderly adult. Similarly, other factors could have led to changes in health among the nonelderly adult population. For example, the well-documented rise in obesity may have been associated with declines in certain measures of health (Lakdawalla, Bhattacharya, and Goldman 2004).

We therefore turn to an alternative measure—self-reported activity limiting conditions (ALCs)—to estimate changes in health among the nonelderly adult population since 1984. To do this, we utilize data from the annual National Health Interview Survey (NHIS), which includes several questions on activity-limiting conditions. Before describing the results, we must address the benefits and drawbacks of using this data source. The main advantage of using questions about ALCs from the NHIS is that they have been asked in a consistent manner over a long period of time from 1984 to 1996. After the 1996 survey there were major changes in the survey design of the NHIS that altered how some of the limitation questions were asked and how information was recorded.[8] Nonetheless, the questions have remained largely unchanged since then. Thus, we consider these two time periods separately. Despite this consistency in the wording of ALC questions in the NHIS, researchers have raised questions concerning their validity—and the validity of self-reported ALC questions in general—in analyzing condition prevalence and the ability to work (Lakdawalla, Bhattacharya, and Goldman 2004; Burkhauser, Houtenville, and Wittenburg 2003). Thus, even though these are some of the best measures of health status that are publicly available, we must interpret trends in them with some caution.

In table 11.4 panel a, we summarize changes from 1984 to 1996 in four different measures for males and females in three different age groups (thirty to thirty-nine, forty to forty-nine, and fifty to sixty-four). The first column of this table summarizes changes for men and women between the ages of fifty and sixty-four. In all eight cases, the changes from 1984 to 1996 suggest improvements in health for this age group (though just five of the changes are statistically significant at the 10 percent level). For example, the fraction of near-elderly men reporting a work limitation falls from 21.2 percent to 19.6 percent, with a similar decline for women from 21.3 percent to 19.7 percent.

---

8. For example, in the 1984–1996 NHIS, persons were asked whether they were limited in their ability to conduct their major activity and then asked whether they were limited in their ability to conduct any activity. In the 1997–2002 NHIS, people were asked separately whether problems with cognitive functions affect their ability to conduct activities and if any mental, physical, or emotional problem created limitations. The changed working of these questions could have motivated different responses. Similar changes were made in other questions as well.

Table 11.4   Prevalence of Limitations

A. 1984-1996

	Male				Female			
	1984-1985 (%)	1995-1996 (%)	Change (%)	Observations	1984-1985 (%)	1995-1996 (%)	Change (%)	Observations
Age 50–64								
Any activity limitation	25.44	24.30	-1.14*	23,366	26.86	26.06	-0.80	26,214
Any work limitation	21.20	19.62	-1.58***	23,366	21.30	19.71	-1.59***	26,214
Unable to work	13.14	13.15	0.01	23,366	14.11	13.27	-0.84*	26,214
No limitations	74.56	75.70	1.14 *	23,366	73.14	73.94	0.80	26,214
Age 40–49								
Any activity limitation	12.64	14.81	2.17***	21,672	14.42	15.90	1.48***	23,717
Any work limitation	9.34	11.12	1.78***	21,672	10.88	11.41	0.53	23,717
Unable to work	4.36	6.16	1.80***	21,672	5.86	6.17	0.31	23,717
No limitations	87.36	85.19	-2.17***	21,672	85.58	84.10	-1.48***	23,717
Age 30–39								
Any activity limitation	10.54	10.47	-0.07	27,278	9.61	10.49	0.88**	30,185
Any work limitation	7.42	6.90	-0.52	27,278	6.77	7.56	0.79**	30,185
Unable to work	2.91	4.26	1.35***	27,278	2.99	3.96	0.97***	30,185
No limitations	89.46	89.53	0.07	27,278	90.39	89.51	-0.88**	30,185

B. 1997–2002

	Male				Female			
	1997–1998 (%)	2001–2002 (%)	Change (%)	Observations	1997–1998 (%)	2001–2002 (%)	Change (%)	Observations
				Age 50–64				
Any activity limitation	19.05	18.52	-0.53	26,999	20.54	19.37	-1.17**	29,675
Any work limitation	16.03	15.33	-0.70	26,999	17.26	16.00	-1.26***	29,675
Unable to work	10.68	10.27	-0.41	26,999	11.19	10.58	-0.61	29,675
No limitations	80.95	81.48	0.53	26,999	79.46	80.63	1.17**	29,675
				Age 40–49				
Any activity limitation	11.08	9.88	-1.20***	28,147	12.16	11.65	-0.51	30,777
Any work limitation	9.21	8.08	-1.13***	28,147	10.01	9.73	-0.28	30,777
Unable to work	5.48	5.14	-0.34	28,147	5.73	6.28	0.55*	30,777
No limitations	88.92	90.11	1.19***	28,147	87.84	88.35	0.51	30,777
				Age 30–39				
Any activity limitation	7.03	6.66	-0.37	28,886	7.77	7.13	-0.64**	31,965
Any work limitation	5.72	5.14	-0.58**	28,886	6.44	5.90	-0.54*	31,965
Unable to work	3.22	2.98	-0.24	28,886	3.55	3.58	-0.03	31,965
No limitations	92.97	93.33	-0.36	28,886	92.23	92.87	0.64**	31,965

Source: Authors' calculations from NHIS 1997–2002.

*** Significant at the 1 percent level.

** Significant at the 5 percent level.

* Significant at the 10 percent level.

The patterns are quite different for individuals in their forties. For this group, men are significantly more likely to report a work limitation and to report that they are unable to work. For women, reporting of such limitations increase, but not significantly. Work limitations and the complete inability to work seem to have fallen for people in their thirties regardless of gender, with the exception of work limitations for men. If these self-reported measures are accurately capturing true changes in health, this suggests that health is improving for near-elderly adults while it is declining for younger adults.

In panel b of table 11.4, we summarize data from the 1997 to 2002 NHIS to measure the corresponding changes during this six-year period. In contrast to the changes from 1984 to 1996, the changes from 1997 to 2002 are consistent across the age distribution and suggest that health has been improving. For example, individuals in all six age-gender groups are less likely to report a work limitation and more likely to report that they have neither a work limitation nor an activity limitation. Because of the short time frame analyzed here, however, we must be especially cautious about drawing conclusions regarding trends in ALC prevalence.

Nonetheless, the analyses of both periods show that self-reported ALC prevalence has fallen for the near-elderly, suggesting that health among the near-elderly has improved substantially during the past two decades. The evidence for younger adults is somewhat more mixed, with the net change from 1984 to 2002 suggesting little change during this eighteen-year period. But given that approximately 62 percent of DI recipients are between the ages of fifty and sixty-four, changes for this age group will contribute more to the change in DI receipt. It therefore appears that changes in health during the past two decades have slowed rather than added to the growth of the DI rolls. Absent these improvements, the growth in DI enrollment from 1984 to the present would probably have been even greater.

11.4   Economic Conditions

An alternative factor that could influence the number of individuals applying for and ultimately being awarded DI benefits is the business cycle. As economic conditions decline, the value of searching for a new job or continuing in one's current job declines. Theoretically, one would expect this effect to induce some individuals to leave the labor force and apply for DI benefits.[9] Recent research has documented the importance of these business cycle effects, with DI application, award, and enrollment rates increasing substantially in response to adverse economic shocks (Rupp and

9. See Autor and Duggan (2003) for a theoretical model of how job losses affect DI applications.

Stapleton 1995; Stapleton et al. 1998; Black, Daniel, and Sanders 2002; Autor and Duggan 2003).

Nonetheless, little previous work has estimated the contribution of business cycle effects to the recent substantial increase in the disability rolls.[10] A simple examination of changes in DI application rates before and after the two most recent recessions suggests that business cycle effects could be substantial. For example, from 1989 to 1993 the number of DI applications per nonelderly adult increased by 37 percent, while from 1999 to 2003 this increase was even greater at 49 percent. As figure 11.5 demonstrates, the one exception to this occurred during the early 1980s recession, which coincided with a tightening of the medical eligibility criteria for the DI program.

To probe this phenomenon more formally, we next explore the relationship between business cycle conditions and DI application, award, and recipiency rates for the 1984–2003 period by estimating specifications of the following type:

$$\Delta Log(DI\ Applications_t) = \alpha + \beta\ \Delta UnempRate_t + \varepsilon_t.$$

In this regression, the dependent variable is equal to the number of DI applications in the United States in year t divided by the number of individuals aged twenty-five to sixty-four, while the explanatory variable of interest is equal to the unemployment rate for adults ages twenty-five and up.

According to the results summarized in the first column of table 11.5, the business cycle has a significant effect on applications to the DI program. Specifically, a 1 percentage point increase in the unemployment rate is associated with an eight percent increase in the DI application rate. Given the average size of the labor force and of disability applications during our study period, this suggests that for every one-hundred individuals newly unemployed, there are approximately seven new DI applicants. As the second column shows, the coefficient estimate increases slightly if one instead uses the previous period's change in the unemployment rate as the explanatory variable.

In the next two columns we explore this same relationship for the DI award rate. If those who apply for DI because of deteriorating economic conditions are healthier than the average DI applicant, then one would expect DI awards to be somewhat less responsive to the business cycle than DI applications. Unfortunately, the DI award data are not linked to the year of application but instead reflect the year in which the award was made, and thus it is not possible to rigorously test this hypothesis. But given that the estimates for the DI award rate are similar to the ones for the

---

10. To our knowledge, the most recent study to estimate the contribution of economic conditions to overall growth in DI recipiency was Stapleton et al. (1998), which only considers data through 1992. Since that year, the DI rolls have grown by 75 percent.

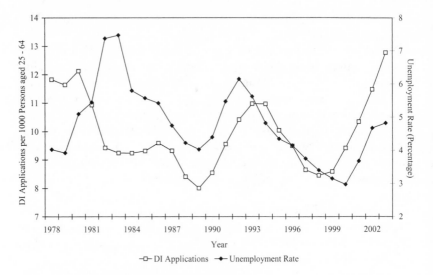

Fig. 11.5   DI applications and unemployment rate
Sources: SSA Office of the Chief Actuary; US Census Bureau; Bureau of Labor Statistics.

Table 11.5   Annual time series regressions of Log DI on unemployment rate 1984–2003

	Δ log applications		Δ log awards		Δ log recipients	
Dependent variable:	(1)	(2)	(3)	(4)	(5)	(6)
Δ unemp (t)	7.93***		8.11***		0.59	
	(1.83)		(1.78)		(0.74)	
Δ unemp (t − 1)		9.04***		5.71**		1.50*
		(1.77)		(2.05)		(0.82)
Const	0.020	0.022	0.029***	0.028**	0.028***	0.030***
	(0.013)	(0.013)	(0.009)	(0.013)	(0.004)	(0.004)
R-Squared	0.38	0.49	0.58	0.29	0.03	0.22
Obs	19	18	19	18	19	18

Notes: Robust standard errors in parentheses. Application, awards, and beneficiaries are per 1,000 persons twenty-five to sixty-four. Unemployment rate is for persons twenty-five and older.
*** Significant at the 1 percent level.
** Significant at the 5 percent level.
* Significant at the 10 percent level.

DI application rate, it appears that the marginal applicants do not have much lower acceptance probabilities than the average DI applicant and thus may be in similarly poor health.

In the final two columns of this table we summarize the results for changes in the DI recipiency rate. Unlike the previous two flow measures, this dependent variable is a stock, and thus one would expect a smaller responsiveness to the unemployment rate in percentage terms; an examination of the coefficient estimates confirms this prediction. The coefficient estimate of interest in the final column suggests that a 1 percentage point increase in the unemployment rate in year t leads to a 1.5 percent increase in DI enrollment in the next year.

Given this finding that the business cycle has a significant effect on DI entry, it is natural to ask how much lower the DI rolls would have been by the end of 2003 if there had been no recession in 1991, or ten years later in 2001. To estimate this, we take the award rate in two years when economic conditions were favorable, linearly interpolate between those two years to estimate the award rate that would have occurred in the absence of business cycle effects, and calculate the difference between this estimate and the actual number of awards in that year. We then combine this with data from the Social Security Administration on the fraction of DI awardees from year t who were still receiving benefits at the end of 2003 to estimate what fraction of these marginal awardees would have still been on the program at the end of our study period.[11] For our base year we choose 1984, a year in which economic growth was strong and the unemployment rate was falling, while for our second year we select 1999, the height of the 1990s expansion. We perform this simulation separately for both men and women given the different trends in DI award rates for the two groups during our study period.

The results of our simulation are summarized in table 11.6. According to this table, male award rates were more affected by the 1991 recession than by the one ten years later, while for women the effects of the two recessions were similar. But for both groups, it is this latter difference that contributes more to the increase in DI enrollment from 1984 to 2003. This is because many of those awarded benefits from 1991 to 1993 were no longer eligible by the end of our study period. As the final rows of this table demonstrate, the changes in the business cycle from 1984 to 2003 have contributed to the growth in the DI rolls, though perhaps not as much as one would have expected. For men, economic conditions can explain 23 percent of the increase in the DI enrollment rate, while for women it can explain just 12 percent.

These estimates are subject to two possible sources of bias. First, many of those who applied for DI in 1992 because of the recession may have applied a few years later in the absence of business cycle effects. This type of effect would lead us to overstate the contribution of economic conditions

---

11. The Social Security Administration publishes data on the fraction of people entitled to receive DI in year t who are still receiving benefits in December of 2003, but publishes no similar data for the year of award. The year of entitlement is typically earlier than the year of award, and we therefore assume that individuals entitled in year t received their award in year $t + 1$ when estimating the fraction of DI awardees in year t still eligible in 2003.

Table 11.6   Simulated business cycle effects

Year	Male Actual	Interpolated	Excess	% On DI in 2003	Excess in 2003	Female Actual	Interpolated	Excess	% On DI in 2003	Excess in 2003
1984	247,833	247,833	0	0.14	0	114,165	114,165	0	0.16	0
1985	274,400	253,904	20,496	0.15	3,155	134,500	124,347	10,153	0.17	1,759
1986	273,700	259,975	13,725	0.17	2,367	135,700	134,530	1,170	0.19	225
1987	265,900	266,046	-146	0.19	-29	143,700	144,712	-1,012	0.22	-227
1988	265,700	272,118	-6,418	0.21	-1,335	147,000	154,894	-7,894	0.25	-1,953
1989	268,600	278,189	-9,589	0.24	-2,285	146,900	165,077	-18,177	0.30	-5,472
1990	293,300	284,260	9,040	0.27	2,433	168,500	175,259	-6,759	0.34	-2,270
1991	322,700	290,331	32,369	0.33	10,580	190,400	185,441	4,959	0.41	2,023
1992	395,600	296,402	99,198	0.32	32,071	241,300	195,624	45,676	0.41	18,683
1993	391,800	302,473	89,327	0.35	31,030	237,900	205,806	32,094	0.46	14,908
1994	379,300	308,544	70,756	0.36	25,737	234,000	215,988	18,012	0.51	9,157
1995	368,400	314,615	53,785	0.40	21,585	263,200	226,171	37,029	0.51	18,933
1996	347,100	320,687	26,413	0.45	11,854	256,900	236,353	20,547	0.56	11,492
1997	311,100	326,758	-15,658	0.55	-8,590	250,200	246,535	3,665	0.62	2,276
1998	331,400	332,829	-1,429	0.54	-778	271,900	256,718	15,182	0.62	9,471
1999	338,900	338,900	0	0.59	0	266,900	266,900	0	0.72	0
2000	329,800	344,971	-15,171	0.71	-10,745	282,400	277,082	5,318	0.79	4,199
2001	364,500	351,042	13,458	0.74	10,010	304,800	287,265	17,535	0.83	14,468
2002	406,336	357,113	49,223	0.80	39,378	343,667	297,447	46,220	0.85	39,287
2003	426,951	363,185	63,766	0.85	54,201	363,157	307,629	55,528	0.90	49,975
Total	—	—	—	Total	220,642	—	—	—	Total	186,934
				Excess					Excess	
				% Excess					% Excess	
Change in beneficiaries 1984–2003				1.09%					1.81%	
				0.26%					0.21%	
				23.4%					11.9%	

Note: Awardee cohorts are proxied by count of year of entitlement cohort. Assume that awards are granted one year after entitlement. For 2002, assumes 80 percent of males and 85 percent of females remain in DI by end of 2003. For 2003, assumes 85 percent of males and 90 percent of females remain on DI by end of 2003.

Source: Authors' calculations based on information in the Annual Statistical Supplement of the Social Security Bulletin, 2004 and Office of the Chief Actuary, SSA.

to the growth in the disability rolls from 1984 to 2003. Second, marginal awardees may be healthier than the typical DI awardee and thus we may understate the actual fraction still on the program by December of 2003 when we use the average for all individuals awarded benefits in a certain year. Given that the effects bias our results in opposite directions, as long as neither effect is too large our estimates should be reasonably accurate.

11.5   Program Changes

Two key determinants of an individual's incentive to apply for DI benefits are the financial generosity of the program and the probability that the application will be successful. Since 1984, there have been important changes in both of these, with these changes serving to increase individuals' incentives to apply for DI benefits. In this section we aim to quantify the contribution of both factors to the growth in the DI rolls during the past two decades.

11.5.1   Changes in Replacement Rates

If an individual has sufficient work history to be insured by DI, his or her potential benefits are a function of earnings in the current year and in most previous working years. The formula used by the Social Security Administration has been in effect since 1978 and consists of two steps. First, the SSA calculates an individual's Average Indexed Monthly Earnings (AIME) in year T as described in the following equation:

$$\text{AIME}_i = \frac{1}{T} \sum_{t=1}^{T} Y_{it} \cdot \max\left(\frac{\overline{Y}_{T-2}}{\overline{Y}_t}, 1\right).$$

In this equation, Y_{jt} represents individual j's nominal monthly earnings in year t that were subject to Old age, survivors, and disability insurance (OASDI) taxes while $\overline{Y}_t$ equals the average national wage in year t. As is clear from the equation, nominal wages from a year before $T - 2$ are inflated using the ratio of average wages in the United States in year $T - 2$ to average wages in year t. Earnings for the two most recent years are not indexed and a person's five lowest years of indexed earnings are dropped from this calculation.[12]

The SSA then uses an individual's AIME to calculate his or her Primary Insurance Amount (PIA), which is equal to the monthly DI benefit in the year that the award is made, as specified in the following equation:

---

12. There are two exceptions to this. First, if an individual has less than five years or just slightly more than five years of earnings then fewer years are dropped from the calculation. Second, if a person has more than forty years of indexed earnings then only the best thirty-five are taken. Thus, for example, SSA would drop nine years of indexed earnings for a person who worked in each year from ages eighteen to sixty-one before applying for DI benefits.

PIA =

$$\begin{cases} 0.9 \times \text{AIME} & \text{if AIME} \in [0, b_1] \\ 0.9 \times b_1 + 0.32 \times (\text{AIME} - b_1) & \text{if AIME} \in [b_1, b_2] \\ 0.9 \times b_1 + 0.32 \times (b_2 - b_1) + 0.15 \times (\text{AIME} - b_2) & \text{if AIME} > b_2 \end{cases}$$

with the bend points b_1 and b_2 rescaled each year by average wage growth in the economy. This formula is progressive as low-income workers enjoy a larger replacement rate than their high-income counterparts. This replacement rate is the most commonly used measure of DI generosity and represents the ratio of DI benefits to recent earnings. In years after the initial award, an individual's PIA is scaled up by the growth in the Consumer Price Index to account for increases in the cost of living.

As emphasized by Autor and Duggan (2003), since the formula was introduced in the late 1970s, DI replacement rates have changed substantially as a result of the increase in earnings inequality. These increases have been important for two reasons. First, because the bend points are scaled up in each year by average wage growth, low-skilled individuals are replacing an ever-greater fraction of their AIME at the 90 percent rate described in the PIA formula. Second, because wages for low-skilled individuals have tended to grow more slowly than the national average, indexed earnings in previous years will be greater than earnings in more recent years.

But rising income inequality has not been the only factor influencing DI replacement rates. An additional force that has tended to increase replacement rates for high-income individuals is the substantial increase in the amount of earnings subject to OASDI taxes. For example, in 1965 average annual wages as calculated by the SSA were equal to $4,659, while social security taxes were paid on just the first $4,800 in earnings. In contrast, by 1985 average wages were equal to $16,823, while an individual paid social security taxes on his or her first $39,600 in wages. The growth in the tax base that accelerated during the 1970s has led to a substantial increase in the AIME for high-income workers.

In table 11.7 we shed some light on the importance of both of these factors while presenting simulated replacement rates in 1984 and in 2002 for males in three different age groups and at different points in the earnings distribution. We must simulate replacement rates because we do not have full earnings histories for males in 1984 and in 2002. To simulate these replacement rates we follow the algorithm used by Autor and Duggan (2003) in which the authors assume that an individual at a certain earnings percentile in his age group in year t is at this same percentile among his age group in year $t - 1$.[13] We consider indexed earnings for the years when the

13. More specifically, a fifty-nine-year-old male at the 25th percentile in the earnings distribution in 2002 is assumed to be a fifty-eight-year-old male at the 25th percentile in 2001, a

Table 11.7   **Changes in replacement rates from 1984–2002**

	Replacement rate (%)		Monthly real wage		Percent change	% earnings taxed	
	1984	2002	1984	2002		1984	2003
			Males 30–39				
10th	48.4	59.4	1,619	1,371	–15	100	100
25th	41.3	49.2	2,476	2,125	–14	100	100
50th	36.2	41.9	3,536	3,250	–8	100	100
75th	29.4	34.7	4,803	4,917	2	98	100
90th	24.1	26.1	6,126	7,500	22	86	99
			Males 40–49				
10th	51.1	55.1	1,659	1,625	–2	100	100
25th	42.7	47.8	2,597	2,460	–5	100	100
50th	33.5	43.3	3,877	3,642	–6	96	100
75th	25.9	33.7	5,224	5,429	4	81	100
90th	19.4	24.8	7,012	8,250	18	64	93
			Males 50–61				
10th	55.2	64.0	1,522	1,573	3	100	100
25th	46.4	55.3	2,360	2,417	2	100	100
50th	34.7	45.9	3,607	3,667	2	87	100
75th	25.6	33.5	5,026	5,636	12	71	95
90th	19.0	23.7	6,782	8,333	23	55	79

Source: Authors' calculations from March Annual Demographic Supplement of the CPS, 1964–2002.

person is twenty-five through his or her current age and are therefore assuming that a person's lowest earnings years occurred before the age of twenty-five.

As is clear from the table, there were substantial increases in replacement rates from 1984 to 2002.[14] For example, among males between the ages of fifty and sixty-one, replacement rates for 10th percentile workers increased from 55.2 percent to 64.0 percent, while for the 25th percentile worker the increase was similar from 46.4 percent to 55.3 percent. Much of the reason for this increase is that a larger fraction of indexed earnings for both individuals were being replaced at the 90 percent rate in 2002 than in 1984. Specifically, the bend points in the PIA formula were—in real terms— scaled up by 19 percent during this eighteen-year period, while real wages for these two groups increased by just 2 to 3 percent. Because these workers

---

fifty-seven-year-old male at the 25th percentile in 2000, and so on. We use data from the 1964–2003 March Current Population Survey for these calculations and consider only nonzero wages in each year.

14. The increases are somewhat smaller than those documented in Autor and Duggan (2003) because they consider 1979 to 1998, and there was a large increase in inequality from 1979 to 1984 (Katz and Autor 1999).

had wages below the OASDI taxable maximum in each year, they paid social security taxes on 100 percent of their past earnings in both 1984 and in 2002. This point is summarized in the last two columns of the table.

But for the other three simulated work histories summarized in these columns of the table, the growth in the OASDI tax base contributed to the increase in the replacement rate from 1984 to 2002. For example, a near-elderly male in 1984 who had remained at the 90th percentile in the earnings history throughout his working years would have paid social security taxes on just 55 percent of his past earnings. His counterpart eighteen years later paid OASDI taxes on a much larger fraction (79 percent) of his earnings, and as a result the replacement rate for the 90th percentile worker increased from 19.0 percent to 23.7 percent during our study period. Interestingly, the largest increase in the replacement rate for near-elderly males occurred for the median worker. This was true because this worker both had very slow wage growth and experienced a mechanical increase in his AIME because of the growing tax base.

The other two panels in this table summarize the change in simulated replacement rates for younger males. As one can see in the table, the increase in earnings inequality is even more striking for men in their thirties and forties during our study period than for near-elderly males. For example, real wages for the 10th percentile male in his thirties fell by 15 percent from 1984 to 2002, while his counterpart at the 90th percentile enjoyed real earnings growth of 22 percent.

Taken together, the replacement rate simulations summarized in table 11.7 strongly suggest that the financial incentive for a typical male worker to apply for DI benefits increased substantially during our study period. Averaging across the five simulated workers in each age group, our findings suggest an increase from 36.2 percent to 44.5 percent for males ages fifty to sixty-one, from 34.5 percent to 40.9 percent for males in their forties, and from 35.9 percent to 42.3 percent for males in their thirties. Averaging across these three age groups, our findings suggest a 20 percent increase (from 35.5 percent to 42.6 percent) in the replacement rate for male workers from 1984 to 2002.

How important have these changes been to the rise in the disability rolls? To estimate this, one needs both the change in replacement rates and the elasticity of DI recipiency to benefit generosity. We use estimates from Bound et. al. (2004), who calculate an elasticity of 0.5.[15] Thus, a 1 percent increase in the DI replacement rate would lead to a 0.5 percent increase in the long-run number of DI recipients. Combining this with the 20 percent increase among males in the average DI replacement rate, this corresponds

15. Their calculation is based off application elasticities from Halpern (1979) and Lando, Coate, and Kraus (1979), information on historical award rates from Bound and Burkhauser (1999), and data from matched Survey of Income and Program Participation/Social Security Administration (SIPP-SSA) earnings data.

to an increase in the fraction of males receiving DI benefits of 0.26 percentage points from 1984 to 2002. Given that the baseline recipiency rate was 2.64 percent, the growth in replacement rates can therefore explain 24 percent of the increase to 3.72 percent in the share of men receiving DI benefits.

The algorithm used above to simulate replacement rates for men is less likely to produce reliable estimates for women given the substantial changes in female labor supply and in DI-insured status during our study period. Additionally, women are more likely to drop out of the labor force for a substantial amount of time than men, and thus the assumption that an Nth percentile earner in year T is an Nth percentile earner in all previous years will more often be violated. To approximate the change in DI replacement rates from 1984 to 2002 among women, we take the admittedly imperfect approach of scaling the increase of 20 percent in male replacement rates by the ratio of female to male DI award value growth over this same period. From 1984 to 2002, the inflation-adjusted DI award amount for women increased by 26 percent, while the corresponding increase for men was just 15 percent.

We therefore estimate that the average replacement rate for women increased by 35 percent during our study period.[16] Combining this with our benefit elasticity from above, this suggests that the growth in replacement rates among women can explain a 17.5 percent increase in the fraction of insured women receiving DI benefits. Scaling this to account for the changes in DI-insured status among women, this factor can explain a 0.50 percentage point increase in the fraction of women receiving DI benefits, thus accounting for 28 percent of the actual increase of 1.81 percentage points in DI receipt among women. This suggests that rising replacement rates have been even more important for women than for men during the last two decades.

11.5.2   Changes in Medical Eligibility Criteria

In 1984, the U.S. Congress passed legislation requiring the Social Security Administration to use a broader definition of disability when deciding whether to accept or reject a DI application. The legislation required SSA to liberalize its screening of mental illness by placing more weight on functional factors (e.g., ability to work) than on medical ones. Additionally, the SSA had to give added weight to pain and related factors that were not previously considered in the disability determination. This latter change influenced certain diagnosis categories much more than others. Applicants with common musculoskeletal conditions such as back pain and arthritis would now have a greater probability of qualifying for DI benefits.

---

16. This likely understates the true increase in replacement rates given that a much smaller fraction would now be equal to zero as a result of the increase in DI-insured status.

Following these changes, the fraction of DI awardees with a mental disorder or a musculoskeletal condition as their primary diagnosis increased
substantially. From 1982 to 1983, just 28 percent of all DI awards went to
individuals in one of these two diagnosis categories, but twenty years later
that share had increased to 52 percent. These changes are summarized in
table 11.8, which lists the fraction of awards by diagnosis category just before the change in medical eligibility criteria and twenty years later. This
table also shows that a much smaller fraction of DI awardees now qualify
because of cancer (neoplasms) or because of circulatory conditions (e.g.,
heart disease, hypertension, stroke, etc.), the two most common diagnoses
in the early 1980s.

In the next column of the table, we summarize data on the average duration of DI receipt by diagnosis category using the results reported in Hennessey and Dykacz (1989). In their study, the authors followed 18,816 DI
awardees from 1972 for seven to eight years to estimate the average length
of time that individuals spent on the program and how this varied across
conditions. The shift from conditions with low average durations such as
neoplasms to those with high average durations (e.g., mental disorders) has
no doubt contributed to the sharp fall in the exit rate from the DI program
that we see in figure 11.6. In every year between 1978 and 1984, the annual

Table 11.8   Percent of awards by diagnosis category

	Awards			Duration estimates of awardees		
	1982–1983	2002–2003	Mean duration[a]	Percent dying within 4 years[b]	Percent remaining after 4 years[b]	Estimate annua exit rate (%
Circulatory system	23.4%	11.7%	7.5	19.8	67.1	12.5
Neoplasms	17.0%	9.6%	3.5	81.0	14.6	47.3
Musculoskeletal system	14.9%	26.3%	10.0	5.3	81.6	6.6
Mental disorders	13.5%	25.7%	15.6	5.4	88.2	4.1
Nervous System and sense organs	8.7%	8.7%	12.5	10.6	80.3	7.1
Respiratory system	6.2%	4.3%	7.3	24.9	63.6	14.0
Injuries	5.3%	3.9%	9.9	6.7	72.0	10.4
Endocrine	4.6%	3.1%	8.3	18.4	73.4	9.8
Digestive system	1.9%	2.3%	7.0	36.9	56.3	17.4
Genitourinary system	1.6%	2.3%	7.5	30.3	60.2	15.6
Infectious and parasitic	1.5%	1.5%	7.6	11.6	79.0	7.6
All other	1.5%	0.7%	12.1	—	—	—
Total	610,021	1,486,089	9.2	21.9	67.9	12.1

[a]From Hennessey and Dykacz (1989). Based on awardees in 1972.
[b]From Hennessey and Dykacz (1993). Based on awardees in 1985.
[c]Authors' calculations based on Hennessey and Dykacz (1993). Based on awardees in 1985.

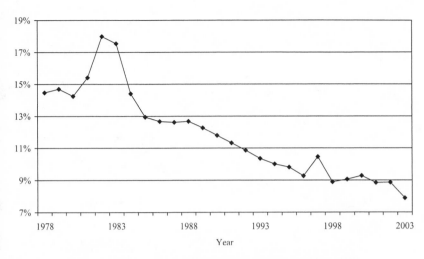

Fig. 11.6   Fraction of DI recipients with benefits terminated: 1978–2003
Sources: Annual Statistical Supplement of the SSB; SSA Office of the Chief Actuary.

exit rate from DI exceeded 14 percent, whereas this same exit rate in 2003 was just 7.9 percent.

Part of the reason for the difference in average durations across conditions is the difference in mortality rates. In two subsequent studies, Hennessey and Dykacz (1992, 1993) followed 34,762 DI awardees from 1985 for four years to determine the fraction that exited the program because of death, retirement (and thus a shift to Old-Age and Survivors Insurance [OASI]), or recovery. As the next column of the table shows, awardees with a mental disorder or with a musculoskeletal condition had a significantly lower probability of death during the subsequent four years than their counterparts with other conditions. This shift from high- to low-mortality diagnoses largely explains the 40 percent fall in the annual mortality rate of DI recipients during the past twenty years.

In figure 11.7 we divide DI awards into three different categories to summarize trends in award rates during our study period. The first group consists of awards with a primary diagnosis of cancer or a circulatory condition, while the second includes those with a mental disorder or a musculoskeletal condition. The final group includes awards with any other condition as the primary diagnosis. Each series in the figure represents the number of awards per 1,000 individuals insured for DI benefits.

As the figure demonstrates, there has been little change over time in the award rate for cancer and heart conditions. For example, in 1983 there were 1.15 awards in one of these two categories per 1,000 individuals insured by DI versus 1.12 twenty years later. This contrasts sharply with the trend in the award rate for mental disorders and musculoskeletal conditions, which

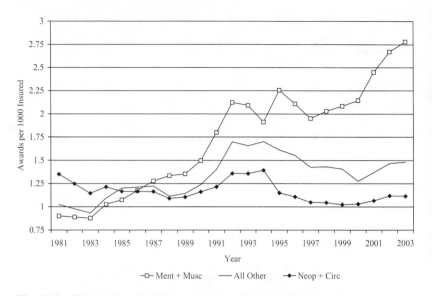

Fig. 11.7   DI awards per 1,000 insured persons by diagnois categories
Sources: Annual Statistical Supplement of the SSB; Annual Statistical Report of the SSDI Program; SSA Office of the Chief Actuary.

increased by more than a factor of three from 0.88 in 1983 to 2.67 twenty years later. The increase in the award rate for all other conditions was much smaller, though still substantial, from 0.93 to 1.47. However, awards for these conditions started to fall in 1994 while musculoskeletal and mental awards continued to rise.

Based on these trends and the description of the 1984 legislation above, it is reasonable to conclude that DI awards for certain conditions were much more affected by the liberalized medical eligibility criteria than others. For example, the changes presumably had little effect on the probability that an applicant with cancer or with a recent stroke would qualify for benefits, while substantially raising this same probability for an applicant with a mental disorder or musculoskeletal condition. This latter effect might have induced more individuals with these conditions to apply or to appeal a rejection.[17]

Reliably estimating the contribution of the liberalized medical eligibility criteria to the growth in the DI rolls is difficult given that other factors were also changing during this same period. As noted above, one would have expected an increase in DI award rates even without the less stringent criteria given the change in the age structure, the recessions in 1991 and in 2001, and

17. More than one-third of DI awards are made on appeal. Thus, while the initial allowance rate is just 33 percent, the probability that an initial application will ultimately result in a successful award is more than 50 percent.

the increase in replacement rates. To control for the effect of these other factors, we make the assumption that DI awards to individuals with mental disorders and musculoskeletal conditions would have grown at the same rate as for all other conditions from 1984 to the present if there were no changes in the medical eligibility criteria. We exclude neoplasms and diseases of the circulatory system from our control group given that there is little change in the award rates for these two conditions over time (suggesting that these conditions are unresponsive to the other factors studied above).

The key identifying assumption is that the responsiveness of DI awards to replacement rates, economic conditions, and changes in the age structure is no different for mental disorders and musculoskeletal conditions than for other conditions such as diseases of the nervous or respiratory system. To the extent that the changes in eligibility criteria affected other diagnoses as well, we will tend to understate the effect of the legislation. On the other hand, it is plausible that individuals with one of these two conditions are more responsive to economic conditions and rising replacement rates, and thus one would have observed a greater increase even without the new criteria. Recognizing these potential limitations, we estimate the effect of the change in criteria as summarized in the following equation:

$$C_T = \sum_{t=1985}^{2003} (A_{mt} - S_{mt})*(1 - r)^{2003-t}.$$

In this equation, A_{mt} is equal to actual awards to individuals with a mental disorder or musculoskeletal condition in year t, S_{mt} is the simulated number of awards (assuming the same growth rate from 1984 to period t as for the other conditions), and r is equal to our estimate of the annual exit rate for these two diagnosis categories. We calculate this last parameter using the annual exit rates implied by Hennessey and Dykacz (1993).[18]

The results of this calculation are summarized in appendix table 11A.1. As the numbers summarized in the final row demonstrate, our estimates suggest that there are an additional 498,887 men and 595,512 women on the program in December of 2003 because of the more liberal screening criteria. Dividing these by the gender-specific nonelderly adult population in 2003, this last factor can explain a 0.57 percentage point increase in the DI recipiency rate among men and a 0.68 percentage point increase among women, thus explaining 53 percent and 38 percent, respectively, of the growth in DI receipt during the last two decades.

18. Let Z be the fraction of people left on DI after four years and assume a constant exit rate. Then the annual exit rate, R, is calculated as $R = Z \char`\^ (1/4)$. This would give us an exit rate of 9.2 percent. In this case, however, such an exit rate is likely to be too low for long-term projections because they are based off of recent awardees, who tend to be younger then the average beneficiary. Thus, we adjust the exit rate to be $R = Z \char`\^ (1/3)$, which gives us a program-wide exit rate of 12.1 percent, which is close to the official beneficiary exit rate of 12.9 percent in 1985.

11.6   Discussion

In the preceding three sections we have estimated the contribution of changing population characteristics, economic conditions, and program generosity to the growth in DI recipiency from 1984 to 2003. In doing this, we have estimated the impact of each factor separately rather than all of them simultaneously. We are therefore essentially assuming that the long-run change in each factor is orthogonal to the change in all other factors. This seems reasonable given that we have in many cases conditioned the change in factor *A* holding constant factor *B*. For example, when estimating the effect of rising replacement rates and more liberal eligibility criteria we were careful to condition on the age structure. If we had not done this an obvious concern would be that estimated contribution of each factor was to some extent driven by the shifting age structure and that we were therefore double counting. An additional limitation with our method is that it does not consider interaction effects. For example, if more liberal eligibility criteria influence the effect of rising replacement rates, we will miss this by assuming a constant elasticity of DI receipt to the replacement rate.

Recognizing these two limitations, table 11.9 summarizes our findings and reports results separately for men and women. Each entry in the table represents our estimate of the contribution of a certain factor to the increase from 1984 to 2003 in the proportion of men or women receiving DI benefits.

As is clear from the table, the more liberal medical eligibility criteria represent the most important factor for both men and women. Their contribution to the growth in DI receipt among men is larger in percentage terms because there is less to explain for this group—recipiency rates for men grew by 1.08 percent versus a 1.81 percent increase for women, while the percentage point increases due to medical eligibility criteria were similar for men and women. The change in DI-insured status is a much more important factor for women because of the substantial increases in female labor supply during our study period. Growing replacement rates accounted for approximately one-fourth of the growth in DI receipt for both groups

Table 11.9   Determinants of DI growth for women and men (%)

Determinant of DI growth	Women	Men
Age structure	4	15
DI-insured status	24	3
Economic conditions	12	24
Replacement rates	28	24
Medical eligibility criteria	38	53
Total explained	106	119

whereas economic conditions were more important for men than for women.

Summing up the contribution of each effect, we can explain 119 percent of the growth in DI receipt among men and 106 percent among women. There are at least two reasons why we may slightly over-explain the growth in DI receipt. First, our findings in 11.3.3 suggest that health has improved among near-elderly men and women during the past two decades. It is therefore likely that the growth in DI would have been even greater were it not for this change. Second, we may to some extent double count when performing our analyses. For example, if mental disorder DI awards were more responsive than other awards to economic conditions, we would count some of these excess awards twice in our calculations. Despite these potential limitations, the fact that our analyses yield a number so close to 100 percent for both groups is striking.

In this chapter, we have not tackled the important question of whether the increase in DI receipt has led to an increase or a reduction in social welfare. As recent research has demonstrated (Bound et al. 2004), this question is inherently difficult because it depends on a reliable estimate for the relative marginal utility of income when a person is disabled. More work on this issue is clearly warranted.

11.7   Will the DI Rolls Continue to Grow?

From 1984 to 2004, the average annual growth rate in the number of nonelderly adults receiving DI benefits was 4.44 percent, with this far outpacing population growth during this same period. For at least four reasons, we expect the rise in the disability rolls to continue and perhaps accelerate in the upcoming years.

11.7.1   Reaching the New Equilibrium

The equilibrium number of individuals on the DI program is equal to the average number of awards in a year divided by the average exit rate from the program. During our study period, the DI award rate has increased while the exit rate from the program has fallen by an even larger amount. Trends in the DI entry and exit rates are summarized in figures 11.6 and 11.8. As the first figure demonstrates, the fraction of individuals awarded benefits was substantially greater during the 1990s than during the 1980s, and the award rate reached its highest level ever in 2003. Even more striking has been the steady decline in the exit rate from the program, which fell from 14.4 percent in 1984 to 7.9 percent by 2003.

The increasing award rate coupled with a declining exit rate explains the rapid growth in DI recipiency during our study period. Given both of these flows, the program is currently far from its equilibrium size. If the number of DI awards remained at its 2003 level during the upcoming years while

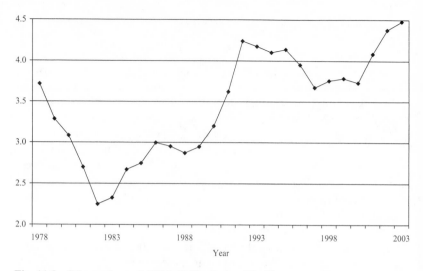

Fig. 11.8   DI awards per 1,000 individuals ages 20–64
Sources: SSA Office of the Chief Actuary; U.S. Census Bureau.

the termination rate stayed just below 8 percent, the number of individuals receiving DI benefits would converge to 9.8 million. This represents an increase of more than 62 percent from the current number of DI recipients. For this reason, it is likely that the rise in the disability rolls will continue and perhaps accelerate during the upcoming years.

11.7.2   Changes in the Age Structure

While DI award rates have increased substantially since the 1980s, the aging of the Baby Boom population suggests that this award rate will grow even more rapidly during the upcoming years. The potential importance of this trend is illustrated in figure 11.9. As is clear from the figure, the number of near-elderly adults is projected to increase substantially in the period from 2000 to 2020. For example, the number of individuals between the ages of sixty and sixty-four—the ages with the highest rate of DI receipt—is projected to increase by more than 92 percent from 2000 to 2020. Thus, absent other changes, the DI rolls will increase substantially as more and more individuals enter their fifties and early sixties.

In table 11.10 we summarize the change in DI receipt that will occur given the projected change in the age structure of the nonelderly adult population and assuming that award rates in each age group remain at their 2003 levels. Here we use the same algorithm as the one described in section 11.3.1 and find that changes in the age structure will lead to a 1.01 percentage point increase in DI receipt among men from 2003 to 2020 and a 0.74 percentage point increase among women. For men this is almost as

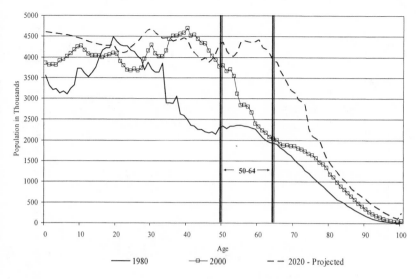

Fig. 11.9   U.S. Population by age—estimates and projections
Source: U.S. Census Bureau.

large as the entire increase from 1984 to 2003, while for women it is almost half as large as the change during this same period. Thus, the aging of the Baby Boom population will lead to substantial increases in DI receipt during the next fifteen years.

11.7.3   The Increase in the Normal Retirement Age

An individual born in 1937 or earlier and with sufficient work history to qualify for OASDI benefits could receive retirement benefits equal to 80 percent of their PIA (Primary Insurance Amount) if they claimed benefits at the age of sixty-two. For each additional month that these individuals waited to claim benefits, they would receive an additional 5/9 percent of their PIA until they could receive the full PIA at the age of sixty-five. Among individuals born in 1937, more than 59 percent of individuals who claimed retirement benefits did so at the age of sixty-two. An additional 19 percent claimed at the age of sixty-three or sixty-four. Thus, just 22 percent of individuals waited until the age of sixty-five or later to claim retirement benefits.

For cohorts born after 1937, the generosity of benefits at the early retirement age of sixty-two will be lower. For example, a person born in 1943 will be able to receive only 75 percent of her PIA if she claims benefits on her sixty-second birthday, while her counterpart born in 1960 or later will receive just 70 percent at this same age. These reductions in benefit generosity at the age of sixty-two are a result of the increase in the normal retirement age in the OASDI program, which is gradually increasing from

Table 11.10   Projected growth in DI recipiency among males and females due to changes in age structure

	2003 DI		2003 population		2020 population		Predicted Δ DI		
	% on DI	# on DI	# people	% of pop	# people	% of pop	% on DI 2020	# on DI 2020	Δ % on DI 2003–2020
A. Males									
<30[a]	0.50	103	20,437	23.6	21,933	22.9	0.50	111	—
30–39	1.51	319	21,176	24.5	22,670	23.6	1.51	341	—
40–44	2.94	335	11,407	13.2	10,363	10.8	2.94	304	—
45–49	4.17	448	10,731	12.4	10,051	10.5	4.17	419	—
50–54	5.91	551	9,313	10.8	10,223	10.7	5.91	605	—
55–59	9.00	689	7,661	8.9	10,664	11.1	9.00	959	—
60–64	13.47	776	5,764	6.7	10,029	10.5	13.47	1,351	—
Overall	3.72	3,221	86,488	100.0	95,933	100.0	4.73	4,090	1.01
Predicted DI growth: 27%									
B. Females									
<30[a]	0.41	79	19,459	22.3	21,179	22.1	0.41	86	—
30–39	1.29	270	20,936	24.0	22,177	23.1	1.29	286	—
40–44	2.41	278	11,555	13.3	10,310	10.7	2.41	248	—
45–49	3.41	376	11,030	12.7	10,168	10.6	3.41	347	—
50–54	4.79	466	9,731	11.2	10,479	10.9	4.79	502	—
55–59	7.03	572	8,133	9.3	11,212	11.7	7.03	788	—
60–64	9.60	609	6,342	7.3	10,827	11.3	9.60	1,039	—
Overall	3.04	2,650	87,187	100.0	96,353	100.4	3.78	3,296	0.74
Predicted DI growth: 24%									

Sources: U.S. Census Bureau Population Estimates, 2003; U.S. Census Bureau Interim Population Projections, 2004; Annual Report of the Social Security Disability Program, 2003.

[a]Population numbers for <30 reflects the twenty to twenty-nine population. All numbers are in thousands.

sixty-five for cohorts born in or before 1937 to sixty-seven for individuals born in 1960 or later.

No similar change is legislated for DI benefits. Thus during the upcoming years, DI benefits will increase from being 25 percent more generous than early retirement benefits to 33.3 percent more generous (for the 1943–1954 cohorts) and eventually to 42.9 percent more generous. These changes are likely to affect DI receipt for at least two reasons. The first is a mechanical one–DI beneficiaries will no longer be shifted to OASI retirement benefits on their sixty-fifth birthday, but instead during the month that they reach their cohort's normal retirement age. Thus, there are currently some sixty-five-year-olds on DI and soon there will be sixty-six-year-olds as well. The second one is behavioral—individuals may choose to apply for DI given the reduction in the relative generosity of OASDI retirement benefits. Estimating the magnitude of this and other behavioral responses resulting from changes to the OASDI program represents an important area for future research.

11.7.4   The Rising Value of Medicare

During the last several years, health insurance premiums have increased by 11 percent per year and the number of individuals without health insurance has increased by more than 10 percent. Both of these changes suggest that the incentive to apply for DI will increase with the rising value of health insurance through Medicare. Some recent research has explored the contribution of health insurance coverage through Medicaid to the rise in the SSI disability rolls and suggested that it can explain as much as 20 percent of the growth in SSI receipt (Yelowitz 1998). Additional research on this issue for the DI program is clearly warranted.[19]

Appendix

Data Sources

1. U.S. Dept. of Commerce, Bureau of the Census. "Current Population Survey: Annual Demographic File, 1964–2003 [Computer File]". Washington, D.C.: U.S. Dept. of Commerce, Bureau of the Census [producer], 2002. Ann Arbor, MI: Interuniversity Consortium for Political and Social Research [distributor], 2003.

---

19. In contrast to the SSI program, DI recipients must wait for two years from the onset of disability before their Medicare coverage begins (Gruber and Kubik 2002). It is therefore plausible that this program is less important for explaining the growth in DI than Medicaid is for the growth in SSI. See Fronstin (2000) for a discussion of the possible effects of Medicare on the DI application decision.

2. U.S. Dept. of Health and Human Services, National Center for Health Statistics. Data File Documentations, Multiple Cause-of-Death, 1979–2001 (machine readable data file and documentation, CD-ROM Series 20, various issues.), Hyattsville, MD: National Center for Health Statistics.

3. U.S. Dept. of Health and Human Services, National Center for Health Statistics. National Health Interview Survey, 1984–2002 [Computer file]. Conducted by U.S. Dept. of Commerce, Bureau of the Census. ICPSR ed. Ann Arbor, MI: Interuniversity Consortium for Political and Social Research [producer and distributor], 2003.

4. U.S. Department of Health and Human Services, Social Security Administration, Office of Research and Statistics. *Annual Statistical Bulletin of the Social Security Bulletin.* Washington, D.C.: 1980–2003. http://www.ssa.gov/policy/docs/statcomps/index.html

5. U.S. Department of Health and Human Services, Social Security Administration, Office of Research and Statistics. *Annual Statistical Report on the Social Security Disability Program.* Washington, D.C.: 2000–2004. http://www.ssa.gov/policy/docs/statcomps/index.html

6. U.S. Department of Health and Human Services, Social Security Administration, Office of the Actuary. "Estimated Number of Workers Insured in the Event of Disability, by Age Group and Sex, on December 31, 1970–2004." June 10, 2004. http://www.ssa.gov/OACT/STATS/table4c2DI.html

7. U.S. Department of Health and Human Services, Social Security Administration, Office of the Actuary. "Disabled Worker Beneficiary Statistics." June 29, 2004. http://www.ssa.gov/OACT/STATS/dibStat.html

8. U.S. Department of Health and Human Services, Social Security Administration, Office of the Actuary. "Social Security Administration Life Tables." Via the Berkeley Mortality Database. July, 1998. http://demog.berkeley.edu/wilmoth/mortality

Table 11A.1   The contribution of liberalized medical eligibility criteria to the growth in DI

Year	All Diagnoses		Mental + Musculoskel		Neoplasms + Circ		All other		Excess mental + Musculoskeletal			
	Men	Women	Men	Women	Men	Women	Men	Women	Men	Still On	Women	Still On
1984	243,949	113,191	72,287	37,617	92,470	37,526	79,192	38,048	0	0	0	0
1985	254,085	123,286	75,857	41,967	90,364	37,520	87,864	43,799	-4346	-1448	-1336	-496
1986	280,342	136,523	114,986	63,557	89,726	36,676	75,630	36,290	45950	16223	27678	10829
1987	273,579	142,269	90,272	54,777	91,316	40,781	91,991	46,711	6302	2357	8595	3543
1988	268,292	141,198	94,875	59,504	90,124	41,219	83,294	40,476	18844	7469	19487	8462
1989	274,677	150,905	96,598	63,319	88,931	41,656	89,148	45,930	15223	6393	17909	8193
1990	300,853	167,124	108,460	71,356	94,230	45,204	98,163	50,564	18856	8390	21365	10297
1991	341,117	195,317	130,460	88,193	99,214	48,449	111,443	58,675	28734	13547	30183	15325
1992	401,102	235,535	155,010	105,978	111,537	55,456	134,555	74,101	32187	16078	32716	17501
1993	395,368	239,870	152,785	107,515	111,590	57,299	130,993	75,056	33214	17579	33309	18772
1994	385,362	246,508	137,359	104,049	113,699	62,177	134,304	80,282	14765	8280	24676	14651
1995	378,526	267,119	160,348	128,858	94,102	53,364	124,076	84,897	47091	27980	44923	28099
1996	355,471	268,783	146,222	128,576	90,379	52,759	118,870	87,448	37717	23745	42119	27755
1997	326,828	260,872	133,621	124,710	86,656	52,154	106,551	84,008	36361	24254	41654	28917
1998	333,032	275,350	140,011	133,338	86,504	54,167	106,517	87,845	42782	30237	46488	34001
1999	337,533	283,026	145,146	140,588	86,199	54,237	106,188	88,201	48217	36108	53386	41136
2000	338,784	282,532	149,793	148,939	87,584	55,959	101,407	77,634	57228	45408	72184	58597
2001	374,355	315,405	172,363	172,854	91,980	58,453	110,012	84,098	71943	60483	89709	76720
2002	406,336	343,667	190,338	190,782	97,743	61,917	118,255	90,968	82394	73393	100844	90859
2003	420,516	357,389	200,400	201,770	96,233	60,605	123,883	95,014	87318	82411	107832	102354
Excess of actual over simulated									720780	498887	813722	595512

Source: Author's calculations from the Annual Statistical Supplement of the Social Security Bulletin 1986–2003 and the Annual Report of the Social Security Disability Program, 2003.

Table 11A.2 Activity-limiting conditions amongst persons 50–64, 1984–1996

	Prevlence of conditions (%)				Percent of people with condition who report work is "Major Activity" (%)			
	1984–1985	1995–1996	Change	Observations	1984–1985	1995–1996	Change	Observations
A. Male								
Musculoskeletal	10.7	11.6	0.9**	23,366	44.3	42.2	-2.1	2,603
Mental	0.8	1.3	0.5***	23,366	9.1	14.4	5.3	240
Circulatory	10.3	7.8	-2.5***	23,366	37.4	32.8	-4.6**	2,185
Respiratory	2.9	2.1	-0.8***	23,366	35.3	28.2	-7.0*	591
Diabetes	2.2	2.1	-0.1	23,366	32.6	25.4	-7.1*	537
Cancer (malignant)	1.0	1.0	0.0	23,366	39.7	31.4	-8.2	235
Any activity limitation	25.4	24.3	-1.1*	23,366	43.8	40.0	-3.8***	5,885
Any work limitation	21.2	19.6	-1.6***	23,366	35.8	31.0	-4.8***	4,873
Unable to work	13.1	13.2	0.0	23,366	11.2	10.7	-0.5	3,121
No limitations	74.6	75.7	1.1*	23,366	85.0	84.1	-0.9	17,481
B. Female								
Musculoskeletal	13.9	14.2	0.3	26,214	24.1	32.6	8.5***	3,763
Mental	0.9	1.6	0.7***	26,214	16.2	13.8	-2.4	311
Circulatory	9.8	6.9	-2.9***	26,214	18.0	19.7	1.6	2,310
Respiratory	2.4	2.9	0.5**	26,214	19.8	20.3	0.6	721
Diabetes	2.7	2.9	0.2	26,214	16.0	17.3	1.3	807
Cancer (malignant)	1.1	1.2	0.1	26,214	22.7	22.5	-0.2	307
Any activity limitation	26.9	26.1	-0.8	26,214	23.3	31.0	7.6***	7,079
Any work limitation	21.3	19.7	-1.6***	26,214	19.8	26.4	6.6***	5,541
Unable to work	14.1	13.3	-0.8*	26,214	6.7	9.3	2.6**	3,710
No limitations	73.1	73.9	0.8	26,214	53.6	64.8	11.2***	19,135

Source: Authors' calculations from NHIS 1984–1996.

*** Significant at the 1 percent level.

Table 11A.3   **Activity-limiting conditions amongst persons 50–64, 1997–2002**

	Prevalence of Conditions			
	1997–1998 (%)	2001–2002 (%)	Change (%)	Observations
	A. Male			
Musculoskeletal	7.7	7.4	–0.2	26,999
Mental	1.9	2.4	0.5 ***	26,999
Circulatory	6.3	5.9	–0.4	26,999
Respiratory	2.0	2.0	0.0	26,999
Diabetes	2.0	2.3	0.3	26,999
Cancer (malignant)	1.0	0.9	–0.2	26,999
Any activity limitation	19.1	18.5	–0.5	26,999
Any work limitation	16.0	15.3	–0.7	26,999
Unable to work	10.7	10.3	–0.4	26,999
No limitations	81.0	81.5	0.5	26,999
	B. Female			
Musculoskeletal	10.0	10.3	0.4	29,675
Mental	2.6	3.1	0.5 **	29,675
Circulatory	5.8	5.3	–0.5 *	29,675
Respiratory	2.1	2.2	0.3	29,675
Diabetes	2.5	2.7	0.3	29,675
Cancer (malignant)	1.1	1.0	–0.1	29,675
Any activity limitation	20.5	19.4	–1.2 **	29,675
Any work limitation	17.3	16.0	–1.3 ***	29,675
Unable to work	11.2	10.58	–0.6	29,675
No limitations	79.5	80.6	1.2 **	29,675

Source: Authors' calculations from NHIS 1997–2002.
*** Significant at the 1 percent level.
** Significant at the 5 percent level.
* Significant at the 10 percent level.

References

Autor, D. H., and M. G. Duggan. 2003. The rise in the disability rolls and the decline in unemployment. *Quarterly Journal of Economics* 118:157–205.

Black, D., K. Daniel, and S. Sanders. 2002. The impact of economic conditions on participation in disability programs: Evidence from the coal boom and bust." *American Economic Review* 92:27–50.

Bound, J. 1989. The health and earnings of rejected Disability Insurance applicants. *American Economic Review.* 79:482–503.

———. 1991. The health and earnings of rejected Disability Insurance applicants: Reply. *American Economic Review.* 81:1427–34.

Bound, J., and Burkhauser, R. 1999. Economic analysis of transfer programs targeted on people with disabilities. In *Handbook of labor economics: Volume 3C*, ed. Orley C. Ashenfelter and David Card, 3417–3528. Amsterdam: Elsevier.

Bound, J., J. B. Cullen, A. Nichols, and L. Schmidt. 2004. The welfare implications

378   Mark Duggan and Scott A. Imberman

of increasing Disability Insurance benefit generosity. *Journal of Public Economics* 88:2487–2514.
Bound, J., and T. Waidmann. 2002. Accounting for recent declines in employment rates among working aged men and women with disabilities. *Journal of Human Resources* 37:231–50.
Burkhauser, R. V., A. J. Houtenville, and D. C. Wittenburg. 2003. A user's guide to current statistics on the employment of people with disabilities. In *The decline in employment of people with disabilities: A policy puzzle,* ed. David C. Stapleton and Richard V. Burkhauser, 23–86. Kalamazoo, Michigan: W. E. Upjohn Institute for Employment Research.
Case, A. C., and A. Deaton. 2003. Broken down by work and sex: How our health declines. NBER Working Paper no. 9821. Cambridge, MA: NBER, July.
Crimmins, E. M., Y. Saito, and D. Ingegneri. 1989. Changes in life expectancy and disability-free life expectancy in the United States. *Population and Development Review* 15:235–67.
Cutler, D. M., and E. Meara. 2001. Changes in the age distribution of mortality over the 20th century. NBER Working Paper no. 8556. Cambridge, MA: NBER, October.
Cutler, D. M., and E. Richardson. 1997. Measuring the health of the U.S. population. *Brookings Papers on Economic Activity: Microeconomics* 1997:217–71. Washington, D.C.: Brookings Institution.
Fronstin, P. 2000. The erosion of retiree health benefits and retirement behavior: Implications for the Disability Insurance program. *Social Security Bulletin* 63 (4): 38–46.
Gruber, J. 2000. Disability Insurance benefits and labor supply. *Journal of Political Economy* 108:1162–83.
Gruber, J., and J. Kubik. 1997. Disability Insurance rejection rates and the labor supply of older workers. *Journal of Public Economics* 64:1–23.
———. 2002. Health insurance coverage and the Disability Insurance application decision. NBER Working Paper no. 9148. Cambridge, MA: NBER, September.
Halpern, J. H. 1979. The Social Security Disability Insurance Program: Reasons for its growth and prospects for the future. *New England Economic Review* (May/June, 1979): 30–48.
Hambor, J. C. 1975. Unemployment and disability: An econometric analysis with time series data. Washington, D.C.: Social Security Administration, Office of Research and Statistics, Staff Paper no. 20.
———. 1992. The role of economic factors in the decline of the DI trust fund. U.S. Department of Treasury, Unpublished Manuscript.
Haveman, R. H., and B. L. Wolfe. 1984. The decline in male labor force participation: Comment. *Journal of Political Economy* 92:532–41.
Hennessey, J. C., and J. M. Dykacz. 1989. Projected outcomes and length of time in the Disability Insurance program. *Social Security Bulletin* 52:2–41.
———. 1992. Comparison of individual characteristics of death rates of disabled-worker beneficiaries entitled in 1972 and 1985. *Social Security Bulletin* 55:24–40.
———. 1993. A comparison of the recovery termination rates of disabled-worker beneficiaries entitled in 1972 and 1985. *Social Security Bulletin* 56:58–69.
Katz, L. F., and D. H. Autor. 1999. Changes in the wage structure and earnings inequality. In *Handbook of labor economics: Volume 3A,* ed. Orley Ashenfelter and David Card, 1463–555. Amsterdam: Elsevier.
Kreider, B. 1999. Social Security Disability Insurance: Applications, awards, and lifetime income flows. *Journal of Labor Economics* 17:784–827.
Lakdawalla, D. N., J. Bhattacharya, and D. P. Goldman. 2004. Are the young becoming more disabled? *Health Affairs* 23:168–76.

Lando, M. E. 1979. Prevalence of work disability by state, 1976. *Social Security Bulletin* 42:41–44.

Lando, M. E., M. B. Coate, and R. Kraus. 1979. Disability benefit applications and the economy. *Social Security Bulletin* 42:3–10.

Lewin-VHI. 1995. Labor market conditions, socioeconomic factors and the growth of applications and awards for SSDI and SSI disability benefits. Final Report. Washington, D.C.: The Office of the Assistant Secretary for Planning and Evaluation, U.S. Department of Health and Human Services and the Social Security Administration.

Levy, J. M., and A. Krute. 1983. The impact of the local economy on the disability process: Further results. Washington, D.C.: Social Security Administration.

Muller, L. S. 1982. The impact of local labor market characteristics on the disability process. Office of Research and Statistics, Working Paper no. 27. Washington, D.C.: Social Security Administration.

Parsons, D. O. 1980. The decline in male labor force participation. *Journal of Political Economy.* 88:117–34.

———. 1984. Disability Insurance and male labor force participation: A response. *Journal of Political Economy* 92:542–49.

———. 1991a. The health and earnings of rejected Disability Insurance applicants: Comment. *American Economic Review* 81:1419–26.

———. 1991b. Self-screening in targeted public transfer programs. *Journal of Political Economy* 99:859–76.

Rupp, K., and D. Stapleton. 1995. Determinants of the growth in the Social Security Administration's disability programs—An overview. *Social Security Bulletin* 58:43–70.

Stapleton, D. C., K. Coleman, and K. Dietrich. 1995. The effects of the business cycle on disability applications and awards. Paper presented at the 1995 annual conference of the Society of Government Economists, Allied Social Sciences Associations' meetings, Washington, D.C.

Stapleton, D. C., K. Coleman, K. Dietrich, and G. Livermore. 1998. Empirical analyses of DI and SSI application and award growth. In *Growth in disability benefits,* ed. Kalmun Rupp and David C. Stapleton, 31–92. Kalamazoo, Michigan: W.E. Upjohn Institute for Employment Research.

Yelowitz, A. 1998. Why did the SSI-Disabled program grow so much? Disentangling the effect of Medicaid. *Journal of Health Economics* 17:321–49.

12

Early Retirement and DI/SSI Applications
Exploring the Impact of Depression

Rena M. Conti, Ernst R. Berndt, and Richard G. Frank

Later middle age is a time of economic stability for most people. This period also begins the transition to reduced health and less active work. The impact of health events in later middle age on employment choices and other indicators of economic well-being has been the focus of a number of recent economic studies (Dwyer and Mitchell 1999; Ettner and Kessler 1997; Ettner 2000; Panzarino 1998; Lerner et al. 2004; Lerner, Berndt, and Adler 2004). This work has contributed to explaining declines in disability associated with later middle age.[1]

The impact of mental health on activities of people in later middle age has been less extensively studied. Evidence suggests that mental disorders negatively affect labor market activity in both men and women (Ettner and Kessler 1997). Mental health may also affect an individual's ability to re-

Rena M. Conti is an instructor in Health Policy and Health Economics, Biological Sciences Division, University of Chicago. Ernst R. Berndt is the Louis B. Seley Professor of Applied Economics at the Sloan School of Management, Massachusetts Institute of Technology, and director of the program on Technological Progress and Productivity Measurement at the National Bureau of Economic Research. Richard G. Frank is the Margaret T. Morris Professor of Health Economics at Harvard University Medical School, and a research associate of the National Bureau of Economic Research.

The authors gratefully acknowledge research support from the Mary Woodard Lasker Charitable Trust and the Michael E. DeBakey Foundation, the National Institute of Aging grants P30 AG12810 and R01 AG19805, and the National Institute of Mental Health (Conti, Frank). The authors are also grateful to David Cutler, Tom McGuire, Joseph Newhouse, Health Policy Research Seminar participants at Harvard University, and members of the NBER Disability Group for helpful comments and suggestions.

1. Most recent work has focused on declining disabilities and improved health among Americans sixty years and older (Cutler 2001; Manton and Gu 2001). A handful of studies have documented declining disability among Americans fifty years and older (Freedman, Martin, and Schoeni 2002; Freedman and Martin 1998; Freedman and Martin 1999). For raw trends see National Center for Health Statistics, 2003.

spond to adverse health events. Recent reports from the Social Security Disability Insurance (DI) and the Supplemental Security Insurance (SSI) programs highlight the disruption of mental disorders to labor market activities. Since the early 1990s, mental illnesses are the fastest-growing cause of new claims for income support from the DI and the SSI programs (U.S. Social Security Administration 2004). These trends appear to be concentrated among middle-aged preretirement adults, ages forty-five to sixty-four.

In this chapter, we attempt to develop a better understanding of the potential effects of one major mental health condition, depression, on work-related activities among people in later middle age. We hypothesize that depression may negatively impact work participation directly by reducing affected individuals' ability to work and interest in employment. Depression may also indirectly affect work through its interaction with physical illnesses and other life events. The analyses focus on three sets of outcomes: employment status, early retirement, and application for DI/SSI benefits. To examine the direct impacts of depression on work-related outcomes, we focus on individuals who experience an incident case of depression and compare these people to similar individuals who did not experience a new episode of depression. To estimate the indirect effects of depression, we compare the work activity responses to incident health events (health shocks) and other life events (widowhood) for people likely to have depression and a similar group of people without significant symptoms of depression.

The chapter is organized as follows. Section 12.1 of this paper presents a brief review of the relevant clinical, epidemiological, and economic literature. Section 12.2 presents our general conceptual approach to studying these issues and reviews the empirical strategies we employ to estimate the direct and indirect effects. Section 12.3 describes the data employed in the analyses. Section 12.4 presents results of simple and more complex empirical analyses and several robustness checks. Section 12.5 discusses study findings and implications for individuals and public policy.

12.1   Background

12.1.2   Depression Impairment, Prevalence, and Factors Associated with Onset in Middle Age

Depression is characterized by melancholy, diminished interest or pleasure in most or all activities, sleep disorders, and feelings of worthlessness. Depression episodes may come and go, last from several weeks to several months, and are followed by periods of relatively normal mood and behavior (Spitzer et al. 1995). There have been substantial advances in the treatment of depression in the past fifteen years. Despite this, depression remains underrecognized and undertreated in the adult U.S. population (U.S. Department of Health and Human Services 1999; McGlynn et al. 2003).

The National Comorbidity Survey Replication (NCS-R) study finds that 6.6 percent of working-aged adults experienced an episode of depression in a given year (Kessler et al. 1994). Individuals aged eighteen to fifty-nine have a higher risk of lifetime major depressive disorder compared with individuals aged sixty and older. Women are also at higher risk for developing major depressive disorder compared with men. Episodes of depression are associated with significant functional impairment (Ormel et al. 1994). Major depression accounts for approximately 30 percent of all current DI/SSI claims.[2]

The indirect impact of depression on individuals' lives has been studied in recent clinical and epidemiological research (Kessler et al. 2003). Depression has been linked to a number of physical illnesses such as heart attacks and heart disease, strokes, diabetes, and cancer (Bruce and Hoff 1994; Carson et al. 2000; Gainotti, Azzoni, and Marra 1999; Surtees et al. 2003; Whyte and Mulsant 2002; Robinson, Morris, and Fedoroff 1990; Bottomley 1998; Spiegel 1996; Zellweger et al. 2004; Rudisch and Nemeroff 2003; O'Connor, Gurbel, and Serebruany 2000; and Musselman et al. 2003). The directionality of these relationships is unclear at this time; some studies suggest depression is an important antecedent risk factor for incident physical illness, while others suggest the opposite causal relationship (Krishnan 2000; Larson et al. 2001; Stewart et al. 2003; Dalton et al. 2002; Wulsin 2004, McMahon and Lip 2002). Regardless of the causal direction, comorbid depression appears to worsen the prognosis, prolong recovery, and may increase the risk of mortality associated with the physical illness (Black, Markides, and Ray 2003; Fultz et al. 2003; House et al. 2001; Jiang et al. 2003; Kotila et al. 1999; Ostir et al. 2002; Ramasubbu and Patten 2003; Williams, Ghose, and Swindle 2004; Carney and Freedland 2003; Rozanski, Blumenthal, and Kaplan 1999). There appears to be important gender differences regarding the negative consequences of depression associated with deteriorating physical health and other factors (Bruce and Hoff 1994; Bruce and Kim 1992). Major life changes, such as widowhood, have also been linked to the onset of depression in middle-aged adults (Perreira and Sloan 2002; Bruce 2002).

The quality of the epidemiological evidence associating depression in middle-aged adults with other social factors varies substantially. In the few studies that appear to use well-defined and reliable measurements of depressive symptoms and social characteristics, small sample sizes and/or highly specific study populations tend to be employed, limiting the statistical power and generalizability of the findings. With respect to life changes,

---

2. Personal communication with SSA research statistician, April 2002.

it is unclear from the epidemiological literature whether these factors affect the severity of illness or are precipitating factors in incident depressive episodes.

12.1.2   Previous Economic Literature

The existing literature focuses exclusively on direct impacts of illness on employment, earnings, and hours of work. A number of studies have documented the direct effects of poor health on contemporaneous labor force participation, DI/SSI applications and benefit receipt, and early retirement (Bazzoli 1985; Bartel and Taubman 1979; Berkovec and Stern 1991; Burtless 1987; Chirikos and Nestel 1985; Quinn 1977; Fenn and Vlachonikolis 1986; Breslaw and Stelcner 1987; Chirikos 1993; Costa 1996). The majority find that poor health is negatively associated with labor force participation and positively correlated with DI/SSI applications. More recent work has focused on declining health's negative impact on employment (Bound et al. 1999; Pelkowski and Berger 2004). Only two studies we identified explicitly decompose health measures into physical and mental illness (Berkowitz and Johnson 1974; Berkovec and Stern 1991). When such distinctions are made, mental illnesses appear to significantly increase the likelihood of labor force exit and disability program application and receipt.

Most of the early literature treated health and health deterioration as exogenous to employment status. In contrast, a growing body of research recognizes that health and labor supply are jointly determined (Dwyer and Mitchell 1999). While the health production framework is well developed, empirical estimation strategies are more varied. When the possible endogeneity of mental health and labor supply is taken into account, there still appears to be significant decrements in employment, earnings, and hours of work for both men and women (Ettner and Kessler 1997; Ettner 2000; Panzarino 1998; Lerner et al. 2004; Lerner, Berndt, and Adler 2004).

Finally, consistent with a handful of recent clinical findings, several studies have viewed retirement as a process rather than a single event, and often that of last resort (Honig and Hanoch 1985; Ruhm 1990). Few studies have estimated the direct effect of health on labor force transitions other than the events of retirement, DI application, and DI receipt (Blau 1998). Two recent studies have investigated the dynamic effects of declining physical health on labor force participation and DI application and receipt in older workers (Bound et al. 1999; Smith 2005). In the first study, the authors report that declines in physical health are strongly associated with labor force exit, job change, and DI applications. In the second, the authors find that negative physical health shocks appear to increase out-of-pocket health care expenses, decrease the extensive margins of labor supply (whether to work or not), increase health insurance access primarily through government programs, and decrease household income.

12.2   Conceptual Framework and Analytical Plan

Taking the human capital model as a point of departure, we hypothesize that incident depression directly decreases labor supply. Based on clinical and epidemiological research, we also hypothesize that depression creates a new vulnerability to other shocks that may also negatively affect labor supply. These proposed pathways are summarized in figure 12.1. In terms of life events, we focus on widowhood, since it appears to be independently and robustly associated with the onset of depression in middle age, is easily and reliably measured in survey data, and is plausibly associated with employment opportunities and outcomes.

We adopt two empirical approaches to estimate these effects and to address the potential endogeneity of depression in labor supply (depicted in the figure as a reverse arrow leading from labor market outcomes to depression). In the first approach, we identify a subset of employed people likely to be depressed at baseline and compare their employment outcomes in subsequent survey waves with those of individuals who are not depressed. We interact baseline depression with incident physical illness (subsequent to the baseline) and widowhood to identify the indirect effects depression may have on the employment outcomes associated with these

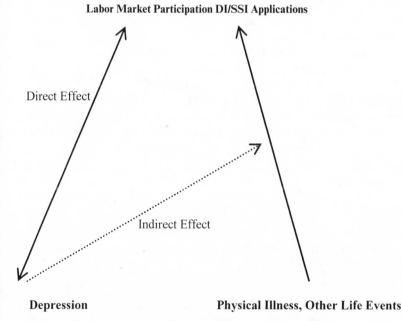

Fig. 12.1   **The direct and indirect effects of depression on labor market participation and disability program application**

life events. To do so, we difference out the independent effect physical illness and life events may have on labor supply decisions. We estimate the indirect effect using a difference in differences approach. For these analyses we control for baseline characteristics of individuals and obtain standard errors that account for the panel structure of the data.[3]

The second method identifies a subset of individuals with no history of psychiatric conditions and no significant symptoms of depression at baseline. Individuals are excluded from the study cohort if they have a physical illness or have lost a spouse at baseline. We estimate the direct effect of incident depression on labor supply and disability program participation. We also estimate the indirect effect of incident depression associated with incident physical illness and widowhood on employment outcomes.

We estimate both models using maximum likelihood. The generalized estimating equations (GEE) model is used to account for the panel structure of the data with non-Gaussian outcomes.[4] To aid in the interpretation of results, we calculate predicted probabilities for each of the outcomes under differing health and mental health states and obtain bootstrapped standard errors. We also perform several sensitivity analyses to assess the robustness of our findings.

We limit our analyses to individuals who are working at baseline to attenuate the possibility that loss of employment may cause an individual to experience depression at baseline or in subsequent periods. We also include regional indicator variables (Northeast, South, West and Midwest) to account for differing economic conditions across the nation. We include an interaction term between region and time dummies to control for differential regional employment and disability application trends. Finally, we include a number of demographic variables in our models that may impact labor market choices, including a respondent's race, educational attainment, and household wealth (total assets and nonhousing total assets).

Given differing labor market participation incentives and opportunities, as well as depression incidence for women and men, we stratify all analyses by gender. We also exclude individuals aged sixty-five years or older in the baseline period in all the analyses. We control for marital status in the baseline period and subsequent changes in marital status excluding widowhood in all empirical analyses. Finally, where possible we check dates of

3. For all analyses reported in the chapter we assume errors are clustered on an individual. We repeated analyses specifying AR1, AR2, AR3, and exchangeable errors terms within individuals. The results of the analyses do not change significantly.

4. We estimated both sets of analyses using conditional logits, and random effect probits in addition to using GEE. We report in this chapter results of the GEE analyses. The results do not significantly differ between estimating procedures. The advantage of GEE over other methodologies is its flexibility in discrete modeling of the error term and its small sample properties. However, GEE has been shown to be biased in estimating causal effects in unbalanced panels. For this reason, we chose to restrict our sample to a continuously enrolled population.

outcomes such as disability application, loss of a job and retirement against interview dates to help control for the possibility of retirement, disability application, and loss of a job preceding the depression episode. All outcomes are assessed at year $t + 1$ when depression occurs in year t.[5]

12.3   Data

The analysis is conducted using data from the Health and Retirement Survey (HRS) (University of Michigan 1999). The survey includes a representative sample of noninstitutionalized men and women born between 1931 and 1941 inclusive, and their spouses or partners. The HRS oversamples blacks, Hispanics, and residents of the state of Florida, and provides population weights for analyses.[6] The first wave was conducted in the spring of 1992 and the winter of 1993 on approximately 7,600 households (12,654 individuals). The first follow up of HRS respondents was fielded approximately two years after the baseline; later waves of the survey have been fielded through 2002 (Juster and Suzman 1995).

The HRS contains extensive measures of income, assets, health insurance coverage, demographic characteristics, and family structure. Among these variables we use measures of employment including full-time and part-time work status, early (pre-age sixty-five) retirement and application for DI/SSI benefits (DI, SSI, and DI/SSI). Since approximately 75 percent of individuals who apply for DI benefits initially are rejected, and approximately 55 percent of these reapply or appeal this initial eligibility determination, often we do not observe the resolution of the application process (U.S. Social Security Administration 2004). Hence, we only include DI/SSI benefit application and appeals in our analyses. Previous studies have suggested that women may be less likely to report being retired when they have exited the labor market than men. Results of a preliminary analysis of the dataset are consistent with this observation; women are less likely to report being retired and more likely to report being not in the labor force conditional on previous employment in comparison to men overall. Therefore, we consider individuals in the main analyses to be retired if they report being retired or left the labor force in response to a survey question regarding self-reported labor force status conditional on previous employment.

The HRS contains an extensive range of health measures, including the prevalence of thirty-nine specific health conditions and a depression index based on the Center for Epidemiologic Studies Depression Scale (CES-D).

5. Responses in the last survey year are the exception. Here we take advantage of the timing of health and employment survey modules. The HRS fields three separate surveys in a given two year survey wave. In the final wave, we use the health responses from the first survey and employment responses from the last survey. The average timing between surveys is nine months.
6. Population weights are used for all analyses.

We employ measures of health conditions linked to depression in the clinical literature, specifically cardiovascular problems (including heart attacks and cardiovascular disease but excluding high blood pressure), stroke, any cancer, and diabetes.

Depression diagnosis is not part of the health conditions specifically identified (Steffick 2000). Therefore, our primary measure of depression is derived from the CES-D. The CES-D is a self-report survey instrument designed to measure the current prevalence of depressive symptoms in the general population (Radloff 1977). A shortened version of the full CES-D questionnaire is administered in the HRS, consisting of eight questions, each scored on a scale of 0–1. A response of zero indicates that the respondent did not experience the symptom in the past year; a score of one indicates the reverse. One major advantage of the CES-D for use in our study is that none of the measures are related to employment or work performance, thereby providing a measure of depression symptomology independent of work outcomes.

Identification of individuals likely suffering from a depressive episode is predicated on the reliability and validity of CES-D cutoff scores. In order to best identify individuals using this score, we relied on an extensive literature on the usefulness of the CES-D in identifying episodes of depression. No equivalent validity and reliability studies for shortened CES-D instruments have been performed in older populations to date. Short forms of the CES-D have been validated for general adult use and shown to be reliable and internally consistent in detecting probable depression (Kohout et al. 1993; Andresen et al. 1994). Several methods have been advanced to convert a cutoff score consistent with probable depression in the full survey (typically 16 out of a total possible score of 60) to the shortened version, each yielding similar results (a score of 2 to 3 out of a possible total score of 8 on the HRS version of the CES-D).[7] One recent work has investigated the validity of the full CES-D for recognizing depression in older community-dwelling populations aged fifty-five and older (Lyness et al. 1997). They report that the optimal cutoff score for identifying major depression in an older adult population using the full CES-D to be 20 to 21 out of a possible total score of 60. A score of 20 to 21 on the full CES-D survey is equivalent to a cutoff score of 4 in the shortened version using the proportionality method advanced by Kohout et al. (1993). We implement this cutoff in our sample; the primary measure of depression that we apply to our sample is an aggregate score of 4 or higher on the shortened CES-D in a given year.

---

7. Several researchers have suggested that findings from younger patient groups regarding the validity and reliably of implementing corresponding cutoffs in the full CES-D for detecting major depression may not apply to older persons. Specifically, older adults tend to underreport depressive symptoms. Comorbid physical illnesses may also confound questions regarding somatic symptoms of depression.

12.3.1   Study Cohort Definitions and Exclusions

For all analyses, we employ survey responses of individuals continuously enrolled between 1994 and 2000 (waves 2 to 5). We concentrate on this time period due to concerns regarding changes in the inclusion of specific CES-D questions in the depression screener and changes in the specific wording of allowable CES-D responses between years 1992 and 1994.[8] Responses from the 1994 survey are considered to be the baseline measures and as such define the before period of our study. Individuals are included in the study sample if they report that they worked during 1994, defined as working part- or full-time, not retired, and not unemployed. In the first set of analyses, we exclude all individuals who reported having diabetes, heart disease, back pain, cancer, or had a stroke in 1994 or earlier. We also exclude all individuals who report being a widow in 1994. In the second set of analyses, individuals who report a history of psychiatric problems or experience depressive symptomology consistent with depression in 1994 are excluded from the sample. We also excluded all individuals who reported having diabetes, heart disease, cancer, or had a stroke in 1994 or earlier. In the second analyses we also exclude individuals who report being a widow in 1994.

12.4   Results

12.4.1   First Analytical Strategy Results

We identified 2,457 men and 2,986 women respondents to the HRS that met our study criterion (table 12.1, panel a). Men were on average approximately two years older than women (54.6 versus 52.3 years of age). Approximately 6 percent of men and 12 percent of women were depressed at baseline based on our CES-D definition. Depressed men and women were more likely to experience a subsequent physical health shock in years 1996–2000 (30.3 percent among men and 18 percent among women) than individuals who were not depressed at baseline (20.3 percent among men and 13.5 percent among women). However, the incidence of widowhood in years 1994–2000 did not appear to be different for individuals depressed and not depressed at baseline (approximately 2.3 percent of men and 7.1 percent of women in each group).

We compared characteristics of depressed and not depressed individuals at baseline. The results are tabulated in table 12.2. Generally, a larger proportion of Hispanic individuals, those having less than a high school education, and poorer individuals (measured by housing and nonhousing as-

---

8. See Jones and Fonda (2004) for a new method to link responses from wave one and wave two in the HRS.

Table 12.1   Description of study population

	Men	Women
A. Strategy #1		
Total N	2,457	2,986
Average age at baseline	54.6	52.3
Percentage depressed at baseline	6%	12%
Percentage depressed at baseline and develop physical illness	30.3%	18%
Percentage depressed at baseline and become widowed	2.3%	7.1%
Percentage develop physical illness, no depression	20.3%	13.5%
Percentage become widowed, no depression	2.3%	7.1%
B. Strategy #2		
Total N	1,345	1,821
Average age at baseline	54.6	52.5
Percentage develop depression	10%	15%
Percentage develop physical illness	18.3%	13%
Percentage become widowed	2.4%	6.6%
Percentage develop depression and physical illness	26.1%	18.7%
Percentage develop depression and become widowed	1.3%	9%

Table 12.2   Comparison of baseline characteristics strategy #1

	Men				Women			
	Not depressed		Depressed		Not depressed		Depressed	
	Mean	SE	Mean	SE	Mean	SE	Mean	SE
Married	**0.88**	**0.007**	**0.7**	**0.04**	**0.74**	**0.009**	**0.67**	0.0
Separated or divorced	0.08	0.008	0.104	0.02	0.11	0.007	0.13	0.0
Less than a high school education	**0.19**	**0.008**	**0.42**	**0.04**	**0.16**	**0.007**	**0.36**	0.0
Black	0.12	0.007	0.12	0.03	0.17	0.007	0.22	0.0
Hispanic	**0.07**	**0.007**	**0.18**	**0.02**	**0.07**	**0.005**	**0.21**	0.0
Has private health insurance	**0.08**	**0.008**	**0.57**	**0.04**	**0.8**	**0.008**	**0.65**	0.0
Nonhousing assets	72147.9	3352.9	64067	6103	61762.31	1639.2	40717	2808

Note: Bold font denotes values significantly different from zero at the 0.05 level.

sets) comprise the depressed than the nondepressed population at baseline. We controlled for these differing baseline characteristics in all analyses.

First differences (the direct effect of depression) and difference in differences (the indirect effect of depression) estimates are presented in table 12.3. Baseline depression alone appears to increase significantly DI/SSI applications and retirement among both men and women. Subsequent physical illnesses are positively associated with increased retirement and DI/SSI applications among men. Subsequent widowhood alone appears to be positively associated with labor force exit for both men and women. The

Table 12.3   Strategy #1 results of first differences and difference in differences by gender

Outcome	Baseline depression		Subsequent physical condition		Interaction baseline depression and physical condition		Subsequent widowhood		Interaction baseline depression and widowhood	
	β	SE	β	SE	β	SE	β	SE	β	SE
Men										
DI/SSI application										
Applies or reapplies for disability insurance	0.45**	0.16	0.46**	0.13	0.32**	0.17	0.09	0.29	0.57	0.5
Employment status										
Works	−0.92	0.88	−0.4**	0.07	−0.16	0.17	−0.007	0.2	−0.77**	0.34
Works at a full-time job	0.06	0.1	−0.3	0.06	−0.35**	0.15	−0.12	0.19	−0.38	0.26
Works at a part-time job	−0.11	0.16	−0.04	0.1	0.12	0.17	0.002	0.29	0.66	0.47
Retirement										
Leaves labor force	0.25**	0.14	0.14**	0.07	0.29**	0.15	0.08	0.2	0.24	0.43
Women										
DI/SSI application										
Applies or reapplies for disability insurance	0.63**	0.14	0.42**	0.11	0.24	0.16	0.002	0.15	0.55**	0.2
Employment status										
Works	−0.74	0.75	−0.25**	0.08	−0.21	0.2	−0.11	0.12	0.03	0.24
Works at a full-time job	−0.08	0.08	−0.09	0.06	−0.21	0.24	−0.21**	0.11	−0.08	0.11
Works at a part-time job	−0.16	0.12	−0.07	0.07	0.14	0.17	0.1	0.12	−0.42**	0.22
Retirement										
Leaves labor force	0.47**	0.15	0.11	0.08	0.1	0.2	0.14	0.12	0.13	0.24

**Significant at the p = 0.05 level.

interaction of baseline depression with subsequent physical illness reduces full-time work for men, but has no significant impact on women's employment status. Baseline depression and subsequent widowhood appears to also have differential effects by gender; increasing retirement among men, but increasing DI/SSI applications and decreasing part-time work and the likelihood of holding a second job among women.

To aid in the interpretation of these findings, we used the regression parameter estimates to construct the predicted mean direct effects of depression alone, physical illness alone, and widowhood alone, and predicted mean indirect effects of depression interacted with incident physical illness and subsequent widowhood, on DI/SSI applications (fig. 12.2) and early retirement (fig. 12.3). All predicted effects are significantly different from zero at the 0.05 level using bootstrapped standard errors depicted as error bars in the figures. Generally, we find baseline depression alone appears to have a greater impact on predicting DI/SSI applications than incident physical illness alone. The interaction of baseline depression and incident physical illness increases the probability of applying for DI/SSI benefits (relative to only baseline depression or only subsequent physical illness) slightly for men. For women, the increase is substantial. For both men and women, while incident widowhood alone has only a small impact on the probability of applying for DI/SSI benefits, when interacted with baseline depression, subsequent widowhood has a large impact. Specifically, the interaction of baseline depression and subsequent widowhood increases both men's and women's likelihood of applying for DI/SSI benefits approximately fourfold over widowhood alone.

With respect to early retirement behavior (fig. 12.3), men appear to be more affected by physical health and widowhood shocks than are women. For men, the effect of physical illness alone on early retirement is larger than baseline depression alone. The interaction of widowhood and baseline depression generates a positive impact on men's early retirement behavior. However, the interaction of baseline depression and subsequent physical illness does not appear to differentially effect retirement. Similarly, the interaction of baseline depression and subsequent physical illness among women has no differential impact from that of subsequent physical illness alone. For women, the combination of baseline depression and subsequent widowhood has large impact on early retirement, but still is smaller than that for men.

12.4.2   Second Analytical Strategy Results

A total of 3,277 respondents to the HRS were included in the second set of analyses: 1,345 men and 1,821 women (table 12.1, panel b). Cumulatively, 139 men (10.1 percent) and 218 women (14.5 percent) experienced an incident episode of depression based on our CES-D definition, while 2.4 percent of men and 6.6 percent of women lost a spouse. Among individu-

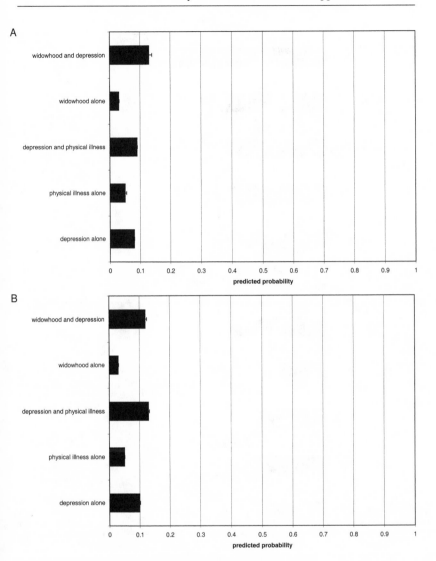

Fig. 12.2   Strategy 1, DI/SSI application: *A*, men; *B*, women

als with subsequent episodes of depression, a larger percentage of men and women also developed an incident physical illness (26.1 percent and 18.7 percent, respectively) than those without subsequent depression (18.3 percent among men and 12.7 percent among women).

The generalized estimating equations (GEE) estimates of the direct and indirect effects of incident depression on various labor market outcomes are presented in table 12.4. For men, incident depression alone and incident physical illness alone appears to increase DI/SSI applications, and

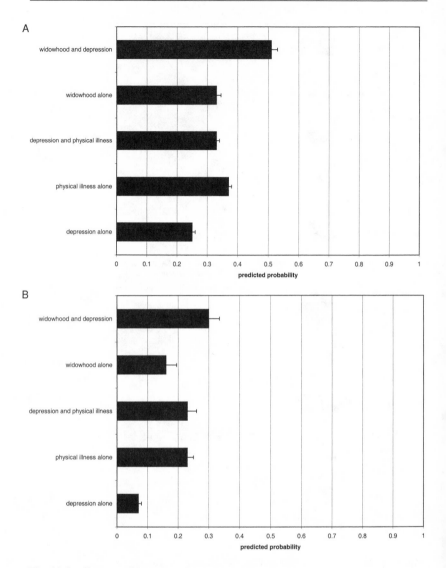

Fig. 12.3   Strategy #1, early retirement: *A*, men; *B*, women

decrease employment overall, by approximately the same amount. The interaction between depression and physical illness increases the likelihood
of DI/SSI application substantially. While subsequent widowhood alone
has little impact on the employment status and DI/SSI application measures, the interaction of depression and widowhood appears to significantly increase DI/SSI application and early retirement among men. For
women, depression alone directly decreases employment overall, and when

Table 12.4 Strategy #2 GEE results by gender

Outcome	Subsequent depression		Subsequent physical illness		Interaction depression and physical illness		Subsequent widowhood		Interaction depression and widowhood	
	β	SE	β	SE	β	SE	β	SE	β	SE
Men										
DI/SSI application										
Applies or reapplies for disability insurance	0.26**	0.12	0.22*	0.11	0.49**	0.19	0.06	0.23	0.67	0.4
Employment status										
Works	−0.26**	0.09	−0.29**	0.1	−0.13	0.18	−0.09	0.23	−0.6	0.32
Works at a full-time job	−0.08	0.07	−0.2**	0.07	−0.32	0.19	−0.15	0.16	−0.5**	0.26
Works at a part-time job	−0.03	0.11	−0.12	0.11	0.33	0.2	−0.06	0.25	0.73	0.46
Retirement										
Leaves labor force	0.12	0.09	0.35**	0.09	0.05	0.17	0.11	0.23	0.62**	0.32
Women										
DI/SSI application										
Applies or reapplies for disability insurance	0.16**	0.1	0.34**	0.1	0.43**	0.17	−0.05	0.12	0.61**	0.17
Employment status										
Works	−0.24**	0.08	−0.22**	0.09	−0.27	0.18	0.04	0.09	−0.2**	0.17
Works at a full-time job	−0.02	0.06	−0.01	0.09	−0.37	0.24	0.04	0.08	−0.08	0.09
Works at a part-time job	−0.22*	0.08	−0.13	0.1	−0.05	0.17	0.03	0.1	−0.14	0.16
Retirement										
Leaves labor force	0.18**	0.08	0.22**	0.09	0.26	0.18	−0.06	0.09	0.23	0.17

**Significant at the p = 0.05 level.

interacted with subsequent physical illness also directly increases the likelihood of DI/SSI applications; this interaction does not appear to have an effect on other measures of employment status or retirement behavior. While by itself subsequent widowhood has no impact on the various employment status measures, the interaction of incident depression with widowhood appears to increase the likelihood of DI/SSI application substantially, but has no significant effect on other employment and retirement outcomes.

To aid in the interpretation of these coefficients, we compute the mean predicted outcomes of the direct effects of depression, physical illness, and widowhood and their interactions on DI/SSI applications and early retirement. Results are reported in figure 12.4 and figure 12.5. All estimated predicted probabilities are significantly different from zero using bootstrapped standard errors (depicted as error bars in the figures).

For men, incident depression alone increases the likelihood of applying for disability benefits by 16 percent. This effect appears to be less than but approximately of the same order of magnitude than incident physical illness (increases DI/SSI applications by 25 percent). The interaction of incident depression and physical illness appears to have a larger effect on the likelihood of men applying for DI/SSI than each illness alone. Widowhood alone increases a man's likelihood of applying for disability benefits by 18 percentage points, similar in magnitude to incident depression and physical illness alone. Interestingly, the interaction of depression and widowhood increases the relative odds of applying for DI/SSI benefits by approximately twofold, to 32 percent, larger than incident depression and incident widowhood alone. For women, the magnitude of the direct effect of depression on DI/SSI applications is equivalent to men. However, incident physical illness alone and its interaction with depression appear to have a larger effect on DI/SSI applications for women in comparison to men. The indirect effect of depression and widowhood appears to be greater for men than for women (14 percent versus 12 percent). The direct effect of incident widowhood on DI/SSI application for women is similar to that of men as is the interaction of incident widowhood and depression, raising the likelihood of applying for DI/SSI benefits substantially more than each condition alone.

With respect to early retirement (fig. 12.5), incident depression appears to have a larger effect on the early retirement for women than physical illness alone, while for men the effects are similar. Women appear to be more likely to retire early due to the effects of incident depression alone than are men. The interaction of incident depression and physical illness increases the likelihood of early retirement more than the direct effects of depression and physical illness alone and are similar for men and women. Finally, while the effect on early retirement of incident widowhood alone is similar for men and women (in both cases being slightly smaller than physical illness

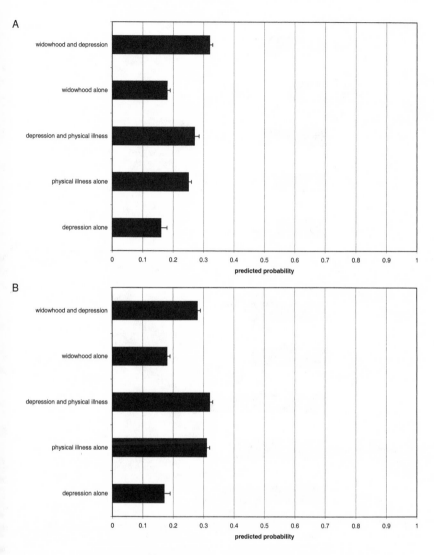

Fig. 12.4   **Strategy #2, DI/SSI applications:** *A*, **men;** *B*, **women**

alone), for men (but not for women) the interaction between incident depression and widowhood is considerably larger than each direct effect and greater than the indirect effect of depression and physical illness combined.

12.4.3   Sensitivity Analyses

To test the robustness of our findings, we performed a series of sensitivity analyses. First, we experimented with the definition of incident physical illness. In one set of analyses, we restricted our definition of incident phys-

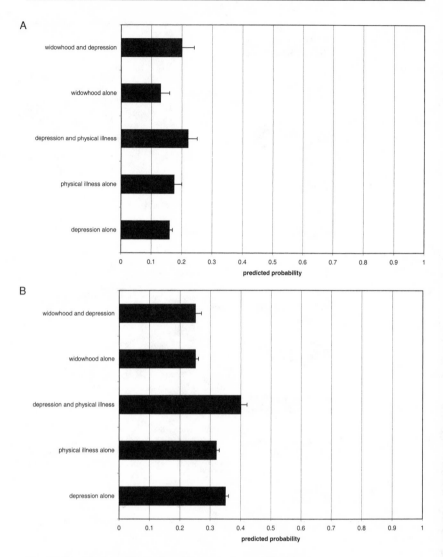

Fig. 12.5   Strategy #2, early retirement: *A*, men; *B*, women

ical illness to include only heart disease, the largest group of incident physical illnesses experienced by the study cohorts. Generally, the significance
of the results reported previously do not change; however, the predicted
probabilities of applying for DI/SSI benefits and early retirement are lower
than those estimated with all physical illnesses included in the models.

The clinical and epidemiological literature has associated pain in general
(and in particular back pain) with depression among older adults (Bair et al.
2003; Eaton and Buka 2004; Larson, Clark, and Eaton 2004). Accounting

for this association may be important to labor market outcomes, particularly DI/SSI applications, since musculoskeletal problems alone are currently the second leading cause of DI/SSI applications (Autor and Duggan 2003). Therefore, in another set of analyses we expanded the definition of incident physical illness to include incident back pain, reestimated the models, and computed predicted mean direct and indirect effects of depression. Generally, for both men and women this addition elevated the predicted probability of applying for DI/SSI benefits and for retiring early over the original definition. Interestingly, this addition appears largely to eliminate the differential results discussed above between genders. This appears to be because more men than women report incident back pain problems.

To address the possibility that our definition of early retirement may be subject to measurement error due to differential reporting by gender correlated with depression and physical illness onset, we reestimated the models using a more exclusive measure of retirement behavior. Specifically, we considered individuals to have exited the labor force if they report being retired in response to a survey question regarding self-reported labor force status. Generally for men, the direction and magnitude of the direct and indirect effects of depression using the more exclusive measure of retirement are consistent with our original findings. However, women are more likely to report being not in the labor force conditional on previous employment in comparison to men overall. Thus, we expected that use of the alternative outcome measure may be particularly sensitive to women's labor market participation. We find that the results are consistent with this expectation: the direct effects of incident depression, incident physical illness, and widowhood alone appear to be approximately half as large with respect to the likelihood of retiring (and remain statistically significant) for women. The indirect effects of depression associated with physical illness and depression associated with widowhood are similarly smaller and remain statistically significant.

The CES-D is an instrument that does not directly provide information on a diagnosis of depression. In particular, it does not contain questions regarding duration and frequency of symptoms that are important diagnostic criteria. Thus, our reliance on the CES-D to determine depression cases may result in misclassification error. In order to assess our identification of cases of depression, we compare case classifications using the CES-D to the onetime fielding of a separate depression assessment tool, the Composite International Depression Instrument (CIDI), in the HRS that directly relates to the DSM-III diagnostic criteria. The HRS fielded the so called CIDI short form in the wave 3 (1996) survey only. A cutoff score of 5 out of 7 corresponds to a DSM-III diagnosis of major depression with high sensitivity and specificity (Steffick 2000).

Applying the CIDI criteria to the second study cohort, we identified a lower percentage of men and women (2.4 percent and 6.6 percent, respectively) with depression compared to that classified as depressed when using the CES-D criteria in wave 3 only (7 percent and 9.6 percent, respectively). In order to determine the overlap in depression cases identified by both surveys we ran a probit regression of CESD cases on CIDI cases at the individual level. We found that determination of depression cases using the CES-D criteria identifies as depressed approximately 79 percent of individuals meeting depression criteria using the CIDI criteria. This represents a relatively high correlation between the two depression measures. The high concordance in depression identification indicated by comparisons between the CES-D and CIDI and the higher numbers of absolute cases attributed to the CES-D criteria suggest that the CES-D does a good job of predicting major depression, but may overidentify cases when duration in particular is not accounted for in the determination process. Therefore, misclassification of depression using the CES-D criteria alone likely results in a downward bias in the estimation of the direct and indirect effects of depression on labor force participation since some transient symptoms of depression are overweighted in the analyses and results.[9]

In our empirical approaches to identifying the direct and indirect roles of depression in determining labor force participation, we have concentrated on defining depression to be incident (in the second analytical strategy) or preexisting (in the first analytical strategy) in an attempt to address concerns regarding the endogeneity of employment and health status. Persistence of depressive symptomology and its potential impact on employment is a challenging issue. For the first strategy, we included in the regression specification a dummy variable if depression occurred in a subsequent survey wave. In the second strategy, once an individual has an incident depressive episode, we examine labor market outcomes in the subsequent survey year. For individuals who have persistent depression (i.e., remain depressed in a subsequent survey wave) we estimate subsequent labor market outcomes for this depression, which may be more properly considered prevalent. Both approaches represent conservative approaches to parameter estimation.

In an effort to evaluate the importance of persistent depressive symptoms in determining employment outcomes, we performed a small cross-sectional analysis using wave 5 (2000) data. Specifically, we created a cumulative measure of depression across the previous survey years (applying the exclusion criteria used to determine the cohorts in the first and second analyses separately). We then estimated the likelihood of DI/SSI application, retirement, and employment status outcomes in the cross section pre-

9. In a separate set of analyses, we applied a more restrictive definition of depression, employing a cutoff score of 5 on the shortened CES-D, to the cohorts and reestimated the models. For several outcomes we were unable to achieve convergence using maximum likelihood when applying this criteria. For the remaining analyses, the results were consistent with reported predicted probabilities discussed previously.

dicted by the number of depressive episodes experienced by an individual in the current and previous waves. In general, the persistence of depressive symptoms is estimated to increase the relative odds of applying for DI/SSI benefits and early retirement for both men and women. The effect of persistent depression is estimated to be monotonically increasing for men in DI/SSI applications and in retirement for both men and women. Notably, the persistence of depressive symptoms appears to be greater in women than in men.

Finally, to assess the robustness of these estimates we projected disability application rates and employment trends for men and women into an out-of-sample survey wave (wave 6, year 2002) using parameter estimates from our model. We then compared these results against actual employment and disability application rates contained in the recently released 2002 HRS data and model predictions applied to the data used in the main analyses.[10] To take into account the changing population surveyed in 2002, we limited our predictions to individuals working in 1994, with no physical illness, depression in 1994, and non-widows who are continuously enrolled in the HRS survey between 1994 and 2002. This yielded a sample of 948 men and 1,460 women.

The projections for the 2002 cohort differ by outcome. For DI/SSI applications, the power of the model is high (96 to 100 percent) in predicting which individuals will not apply for benefits but low (5 to 15 percent) in predicting which individuals will apply for benefits in 2002. On employment status measures (any employment, full-time employment, and part-time employment) the power of the model is high in predicting who will (85 to 98 percent) and will not (95 to 100 percent) work in wave 6. The power of the model is high (95 to 100 percent) in predicting who does not retire, but not very sensitive (4 to 10 percent) in predicting who retires in 2002. In essence, the models are predictive in predicting labor force participation in 2002, but are not reliable in predicting disability insurance applications and retirement among this population. The patterns are similar for men and women.

For interpretation we compare these results to the predictive power of in-sample predictions. On employment status measures (any employment, full-time employment, and part-time employment) and retirement, the predictive power of the model in the sample cohort is highly sensitive (98 to 100 percent) and highly specific (98 to 100 percent). Compared with the out-of-sample predictions, the model does a better job predicting who will and will not work and who will and will not retire in sample years. For DI/SSI applications, our in-sample model predictions are highly specific, predicting

10. Sensitivity is defined as the proportion of individuals predicted to have a positive outcome (i.e., apply for DI/SSI benefits and retire) who actually have these outcomes in 2002; specificity is the proportion of individuals who are predicted to have a negative outcome (i.e., do not apply for DI/SSI benefits, continue to work, do not retire) who actually do in 2002.

accurately 100 percent of men and women who do not apply for benefits and more sensitive than the out-of-sample predictions, predicting approximately 82 to 85 percent of men and women who do apply for benefits.

Differences in the predictive capabilities of the model regarding employment and retirement behavior in and out of sample may be accounted for by several factors. First, macroeconomic conditions in 2001–2002, the time period captured in wave 6, were very different from conditions in 1994–2000; stock market valuations fell substantially in 2000–2002, reducing the value of accrued assets including retirement portfolios, and employment overall fell during this period. Consequently, these changes may have altered the valuation of work relative to retirement among individuals at the margin. In addition, the proximity of Social Security benefit eligibility (simply by observing the cohort aging two more years) may also have altered the valuation of applying for disability benefits among individuals at the margin, given the low likelihood of receiving benefits in a time frame that does not directly compete with social security eligibility. This is consistent with the general trend of disability applications falling among individuals aged sixty-two and older observed in raw data from SSA. Finally, the 2002 data used for this analysis is from the preliminary release version and consequently was not subjected to the same extensive cleaning of the data used for 1994–2000. Therefore, some differences in the power of the model to predict labor market participation and disability outcomes out of sample may be due to data quality differences.

12.5   Interpretation of Findings and Implications

Results of both estimation strategies indicate that symptoms of depression directly increases DI/SSI application and early retirement and decreases work for men and women. This is consistent with the previous economic literature that permitted for distinctions between physical and mental illnesses. This finding is also consistent with recent cost of illness estimates suggesting that the costs of depression associated with workplace outcomes are significant (Wang, Simon, and Kessler 2003). The magnitude of this effect appears to be of the same order of magnitude to that of physical illness both for men and for women and greater than that of widowhood alone.

Depression interacts significantly with physical illness in men and women to increase DI/SSI applications and early retirement and decrease full-time labor force participation. Depression's indirect negative effect on work outcomes through its interaction with widowhood is significant for men and women. Interestingly, this indirect effect appears to be differentially detrimental to men. This finding is consistent with the widower effect documented in the recent sociological literature (Iwashyna and Christakis 2003; Christakis and Iwashyna 2003).

These findings have important implications for interpreting disability levels and trends. First, several recent economic papers have accounted for the role of health in determining DI/SSI applications and other labor force outcomes, but have measured health using changes in aggregate mortality. Aggregate mortality statistics are likely correlated with the morbidity associated with acute and some chronic diseases but represent a rather imprecise measure of the health of the population. In particular, chronic illnesses appear to play an increasingly central role in determining the health of the population. Our results suggest that mental illness alone and in combination with physical illness exert important influences on retirement behavior and DI/SSI applications consistent with recent disability application and recipiency trends. As such, they provide a more complete picture of how chronic disease (and in particular mental illness) impacts employment decisions, retirement, and disability applications.

Second, our results have important implications for interpreting trends in disability overall. The results of the analyses suggest that the interaction between depression and physical illness is substantial and significantly impacts DI/SSI applications. Therefore, holding depression's indirect effect on disability constant, physical illness's role in disability may be decreasing faster than previous research suggests.

There have been significant advances in the treatment of major depression over the past two decades. One major limitation of our dataset is its lack of detailed information on treatment. However, the impact of treatment receipt on individual's lives—related both to their overall health and continued participation in the labor force—may be substantial (Timbie et al. 2005). Research quantifying the impact of treatment on labor market outcomes is an important area for future study and appropriate policy making.

References

Andresen, E. M., J. A. Mamgren, W. B. Carter, and D. L. Patrick. 1994. Screening for depression in well older adults: Evaluation of a short form of the CES-D. *American Journal of Preventive Medicine* 10 (2): 77–84.

Autor, D., and M. Duggan. 2003. The rise in disability recipiency and the decline in unemployment. *Quarterly Journal of Economics* 118 (1): 157–206.

Bair, M. J., R. L. Robinson, W. Katon, and K. Kroenke. 2003. Depression and pain comorbidity: A literature review. *Archives of Internal Medicine* 163 (20): 2433–45.

Bartel, A., and P. Taubman. 1979. Health and labor market success: The role of various diseases. *Review of Economics and Statistics* 61 (1979): 1–8.

Bazzoli, G. J. 1985. The early retirement decision: New empirical evidence on the influence of health. *The Journal of Human Resources* 20 (2): 214–234.

Berkovec, J., and S. Stern. 1991. Job exit behavior of older men. *Econometrica* 59 (1): 189–210.

Berkowitz, M., and W. G. Johnson. 1974. Health and labor force participation. *The Journal of Human Resources* 9 (1): 117–28.

Black, S. A., K. S. Markides, and L. A. Ray. 2003. Depression predicts increased incidence of adverse health outcomes in older Mexican Americans with type 2 diabetes. *Diabetes Care* 26 (10): 2822–28.

Blau, D. M. 1998. Labor Force Dynamics of Older Married Couples. *Journal of Labor Economics* 16 (3): 595–629.

Bottomley, A. 1998. Depression in cancer patients: a literature review. *European Journal of Cancer Care* 7 (3): 181–91.

Bound, J., M. Schoenbaum, T. R. Stinebrickner, and T. Waidmann. 1999. The dynamic effects of health on the labor force transitions of older workers. *Labour Economics* 6 (2): 179–202.

Breslaw, J. A., and M. Stelcner. 1987. The effect of health on the labor force behavior of elderly men in Canada. *The Journal of Human Resources* 22(4): 490–517.

Bruce, M. L. 2002. Psychosocial risk factors for depressive disorders in late life. *Biological Psychiatry* 52 (3): 175–84.

Bruce, M. L., and R. A. Hoff. 1994. Social and physical health risk factors for first onset major depressive episode disorder in a community sample. *Social Psychiatry and Psychiatric Epidemiology* 29 (4): 165–71.

Bruce, M. L., and Kim, K. M. 1992. Differences in the effects of divorce on major depression in men and women. *American Journal of Psychiatry* 149 (7): 914–7.

Burtless, G. 1987. Occupational effects on the health and work capacity of older men. In *Work, health, and income among the elderly,* ed. G. Burtless, 103–50. Washington, D.C.: Brookings Institution.

Carney, R. M., and K. E. Freedland. 2003. Depression, mortality, and physical morbidity in patients with coronary heart disease. *Biological Psychiatry* 54 (3): 241–7.

Carson, A. J., S. MacHale, K. Allen, S. M. Lawrie, M. Dennis, A. House, and M. Sharpe. 2000. Depression after stroke and lesion location: A systematic review. *Lancet* 356 (9224): 122–26.

Chirikos, T. N. 1993. The relationship between health and labor market status. *Annual Review of Public Health* 14:293–312.

Chirikos, T. N., and G. Nestel. 1985. Further evidence on the economic effects of poor health. *Review of Economics and Statistics* 67:61–69.

Christakis, N. A., and T. J. Iwashyna. 2003. The health impact of health care on families: A matched cohort study of hospice use by decedents and mortality outcomes in surviving, widowed spouses. *Social Science and Medicine* 57 (3): 465–75.

Costa, D. 1996. Health and labor force participation of older men, 1900–1991. *Journal of Economics History* 56:62–89.

Cutler, D. M. 2004. *Your money or your life: Strong medicine for America's health care system.* New York: Oxford University Press.

Dalton, S. O., E. H. Boesen, L. Ross, I. R. Schapiro, and C. Johansen. 2002. Mind and cancer. Do psychological factors cause cancer? *European Journal of Cancer* 38 (10): 1313–23.

Dwyer, D. S., and Mitchell, O. S. 1999. Health problems as determinants of retirement: Are self-rated measures endogenous? *Journal of Health Economics* 18 (2): 173–93.

Eaton, W., and S. Buka. 2004. The epidemiology of mental illness. Available at www.jhsph.edu/weaton/pubs

Ettner, S. L. 2000. The relationship between labor market outcomes and physical and mental health: Exogenous human capital or endogenous health production? *Research in Human Capital and Development* 13:1–31.

Ettner, S. L., R. Frank, and R. Kessler. 1997. The impact of psychiatric disorders on labor market outcomes. *Industrial and Labor Relations Review* 51:64–81.

Fenn, P. T., and I. G. Vlachonikolis. 1986. Male labour force participation following illness or injury. *Economica, New Series* 53 (211): 379–91.

Freedman, V. A., and L. G. Martin. 1998. Understanding trends in functional limitations among older Americans. *American Journal of Public Health* 88 (10): 1457–62.

———. 1999. The role of education in explaining and forecasting trends in functional limitations among older Americans. *Demography* 36 (4): 461–73.

Freedman, V. A., L. G. Martin, and R. F. Schoeni. 2002. Recent trends in disability and functioning among older adults in the United States: A systematic review. *Journal of the American Medical Association* 288 (24): 3137–46.

Fultz, N. H., M. B. Ofstedal, A. R. Herzog, and R. B. Wallace. 2003. Additive and interactive effects of comorbid physical and mental conditions on functional health. *Journal of Aging and Health* 15 (3): 465–81.

Gainotti, G., A. Azzoni, and C. Marra. 1999. Frequency, phenomenology, and anatomical-clinical correlates of major post-stroke depression. *British Journal of Psychiatry* 175:163–7.

Honig, M., and G. Hanoch. 1985. Partial retirement as a separate mode of retirement behavior. *Journal of Human Resources* 20 (1): 21–46.

House, A., P. Knapp, J. Bamford, and A. Vail. 2001. Mortality at 12 and 24 months after stroke may be associated with depressive symptoms at 1 month. *Stroke* 32 (3): 696–701.

Iwashyna, T. J., and N. A. Christakis. 2003. Marriage, widowhood, and health-care use. *Social Science and Medicine* 57 (11): 2137–47.

Jiang, W., M. A. Babyak, A. Rozanski, A. Sherwood, C. M. O'Connor, R. A. Waugh, R. E. Coleman, M. W. Hanson, J. J. Morris, and J. A. Blumenthal. 2003. Depression and increased myocardial ischemic activity in patients with ischemic heart disease. *American Heart Journal* 146 (1): 55–61.

Jones, R. N., and S. J. Fonda. 2004. Use of an IRT-based latent variable model to link different forms of the CES-D from the Health and Retirement Study. *Social Psychiatry and Psychiatric Epidemiology* 39 (10): 828–35.

Juster, F. T., and R. Suzman. 1995. An overview of the health and retirement study. *Journal of Human Resources* 30:S7–S27.

Kessler, R. C., K. A. McGonagle, S. Zhao, C. B. Nelson, M. Hughes, S. Eshleman, H. U. Wittchen, and K. S. Kendler. 1994. Lifetime and 12-month prevalence of DSM-III-R psychiatric disorders in the United States. Results from the National Comorbidity Survey. *Archives of General Psychiatry* 51 (1): 8–19.

Kessler, R. C., J. Ormel, O. Demler, and P. E. Stange. 2003. Comorbid mental disorders account for the role impairment of commonly occurring chronic physical disorders: Results from the National Comorbidity Survey. *Journal of Occupational and Environmental Medicine* 45 (12): 1257–66.

Kohout, F. J., L. F. Berkman, D. A. Evans, and J. Cornoni-Huntley. 1993. Two shorter forms of the CES-D depression symptoms index. *Journal of Aging and Health* 5 (2): 179–93.

Kotila, M., H. Numminen, O. Waltimo, and M. Kaste. 1999. Post-stroke depression and functional recovery in a population-based stroke register. The Finnstroke study. *European Journal of Neurology* 6 (3): 309–12.

Krishnan, K. R. 2000. Depression as a contributing factor in cerebrovascular disease. *American Heart Journal* 140 (Suppl. no. 4): 70–6.

Larson, S. L., M. R. Clark, and W. W. Eaton. 2004. Depressive disorder as a long term antecedent risk factor for incident back pain: A 13 year follow-up study from the Baltimore Epidemiological Catchment Area sample. *Psychological medicine* 34:211–19.

Larson, S. L., P. L. Owens, D. Ford, and W. Eaton. 2001. Depressive disorder, dysthymia, and risk of stroke: Thirteen-year follow-up from the Baltimore epidemiologic catchment area study. *Stroke* 32 (9): 1979–83.

Lerner, D., D. A. Adler, H. Chang, E. Berndt, J. T. Irish, L. Lapitsky, M. Y. Hood, J. Reed, and W. H. Rogers. 2004. The clinical and occupational correlates of work productivity loss among employed patients with depression. *Journal of Occupational and Environmental Medicine* 46 (Suppl. no. 6): 545–55.

Lerner, D., E. R. Berndt, and D. A. Adler. 2004. Unemployment, job retention and productivity loss among employees with depression. *Psychiatric Services,* forthcoming.

Lyness, J. M., T. K. Noel, C. Cox, D. A. King, Y. Conwell, and E. D. Caine. 1997. Screening for depression in elderly primary care patients. A comparison of the Center for Epidemiologic Studies-Depression Scale and the Geriatric Depression Scale. *Archives of Internal Medicine* 157 (4): 449–54.

MacMahon, K. M., and G. Y. Lip. 2002. Psychological factors in heart failure: A review of the literature. *Archives of Internal Medicine* 162 (5): 509–16.

Manton, K. G., and X. Gu. 2001. Changes in the prevalence of chronic disability in the United States black and nonblack population above age 65 from 1982 to 1999. *Proceedings of the National Academy of Sciences* 98 (11): 6354–59.

McGlynn, E. A., S. M. Asch, J. Adams, J. Keesey, J. Hicks, A. DeCristofaro, and E. A. Kerr. 2003. The quality of health care delivered to adults in the United States. *New England Journal of Medicine* 348 (26): 2635–45.

Musselman, D. L., E. Betan, H. Larsen, and L. S. Phillips. 2003. Relationship of depression to diabetes types 1 and 2: Epidemiology, biology, and treatment. *Biological Psychiatry* 54 (3): 317–29.

National Center for Health Statistics. 2003. Chartbook on trends in the health of Americans. Hyattsville, MD: National Center for Health Statistics.

O'Connor, C. M., P. A. Gurbel, and V. L. Serebruany. 2000. Depression and ischemic heart disease. *American Heart Journal* 140 (Suppl. no. 4): 63–9.

Ormel, J., M. VonKorff, T. B. Ustun, S. Pini, A. Korten, and T. Oldehinkel. 1994. Common mental disorders and disability across cultures: Results from the WHO collaborative study on psychological problems in general health care. *Journal of the American Medical Association* 272 (22): 1741–48.

Ostir, G. V., J. S. Goodwin, K. S. Markides, K. J. Ottenbacher, J. Balfour, and J. M. Guralnik. 2002. Differential effects of premorbid physical and emotional health on recovery from acute events. *Journal of the American Geriatrics Society* 50 (4): 713–8.

Panzarino, P. J., Jr. 1998. The costs of depression: Direct and indirect; treatment versus nontreatment. *Journal of Clinical Psychiatry* 59 (Suppl. no. 20): 11–4.

Pelkowski, J. M.; and M. C. Berger. 2004. The impact of health on employment, wages, and hours worked over the life cycle. *The Quarterly Review of Economics and Finance* 44 (1): 102–121.

Perreira, K. M., and F. A. Sloan. 2002. Excess alcohol consumption and health outcomes: A 6 year follow-up of men over age 50 from the health and retirement study. *Addiction* 97:301–10.

Quinn, J. F. 1977. Microeconomic determinants of early retirement: A crosssectional view of white married men. *The Journal of Human Resources* 12 (3): 329–46.

Radloff, L. S. 1977. The CES-D scale: A self report depression scale for research in the general population. *Applied psychological measurement* 1 (3): 385–401.

Ramasubbu, R., and S. B. Patten. 2003. Effect of depression on stroke morbidity and mortality. *Canadian Journal of Psychiatry* 48 (4): 250–7.

Robinson, R. G., P. L. Morris, and J. P. Fedoroff. 1990. Depression and cerebrovascular disease. *Journal of Clinical Psychiatry* 51 (Suppl:26–31): discussion 32–3.

Rozanski, A., J. A. Blumenthal, and J. Kaplan. 1999. Impact of psychological factors on the pathogenesis of cardiovascular disease and implications for therapy. *Circulation* 99 (16): 2192–217.

Rudisch, B. and Nemeroff, C. B. 2003. Epidemiology of comorbid coronary artery disease and depression. *Biological Psychiatry* 54 (3): 227–40.

Ruhm, C. J. 1990. Bridge jobs and partial retirement. *Journal of Labor Economics* 8 (4): 482–501.

Smith, J. M. 2005. Transitions in Health and Labor Supply. Paper presented at the Disability and Labor Supply Conference, National Institute on Aging. February 2004, South Carolina.

Spiegel, D. 1996. Cancer and depression. *British Journal of Psychiatry* Suppl (30): 109–16.

Spitzer, R. L., K. Kroenke, M. Linzer, S. R. Hahn, J. B. Williams, F. V. de Gruy, D. Brody, and M. Davies. 1995. Health-related quality of life in primary care patients with mental disorders: Results from the PRIME-MD 1000 study. *Journal of the American Medical Association* 274 (19): 1511–17.

Steffick, D. E. 2000. Documentation of affective functioning measures in the health and retirement study. Ann Arbor, MI: Survey Research Center, University of Michigan. Available at www.umich.edu

Stewart, R. A., F. M. North, T. M. West, K. J. Sharples, R. J. Simes, D. M. Colquhoun, H. D. White, and A. M. Tonkin. 2003. Long-term intervention with pravastatin in ischaemic disease (LIPID) study investigators. Depression and cardiovascular morbidity and mortality: Cause or consequence? *European Heart Journal* 24 (22): 2027–37.

Surtees, P. G., N. W. Wainwright, K. T. Khaw, and N. E. Day. 2003. Functional health status, chronic physical conditions, and disorders of mood. *British Journal of Psychiatry* 183:299–303.

Timbie, J. W., R. G. Frank, M. Horvitz-Lennon, and S. L. Normand. 2005. A meta-analysis of the effect of enhanced care for depression on work-related productivity. Harvard University. Unpublished Manuscript.

U.S. Department of Health and Human Services. 1999. Mental health: A report of the surgeon general—Executive summary. Rockville, MD: U.S. Department of Health and Human Services, Substance Abuse and Mental Health Services Administration, Center for Mental Health Services, National Institutes of Health, National Institute of Mental Health.

U.S. Social Security Administration. 2004. Annual Statistical Supplement 1990–2004. Available at www.ssa.gov

University of Michigan. 1999. Health and Retirement Study: Survey Design. Available at www.umich.edu/~rswww/studydet/desgn.html

Wang, P., S. E. Simon, and R. C. Kessler. 2003. The economic burden of depression and the cost-effectiveness of treatment. *International Journal of Methods in Psychiatric Research* 12 (1): 22–33.

Whyte, E. M., and B. H. Mulsant. 2002. Post stroke depression: Epidemiology, pathophysiology, and biological treatment. *Biological Psychiatry* 52 (3): 253–64.

Williams, L. S., S. S. Ghose, and R. W. Swindle. 2004. Depression and other mental health diagnoses increase mortality risk after ischemic stroke. *American Journal of Psychiatry* 161 (6): 1090–5.

Wulsin, L. R. 2004. Is depression a major risk factor for coronary disease? A systematic review of the epidemiologic evidence. *Harvard Review of Psychiatry* 12 (2): 79–93.

Zellweger, M. J., R. H. Osterwalder, W. Langewitz, and M. E. Pfisterer. 2004. Coronary artery disease and depression. *European Heart Journal* 25 (1): 3–9.

V

Assistive Technology and Caregiving

13

Trends in Assistance with Daily Activities:
Racial/Ethnic and Socioeconomic Disparities Persist in the U.S. Older Population

Vicki A. Freedman, Linda G. Martin,
Jennifer Cornman, Emily M. Agree, and
Robert F. Schoeni

13.1 Introduction

Promoting independence through increased use of assistive technology has been a goal of federal programs and policies, beginning with the passage of the Americans with Disabilities Act over a decade ago, and continuing with the 1998 Assistive Technology Act, and President Bush's New Freedom Initiative. These policies specifically target the removal of environmental barriers and increased access to assistive and universally designed technologies of people of all ages and abilities. Indeed, assistive technology (AT) is playing an increasingly important role in facilitating independence among older Americans (Pew and Van Hemel 2004), particularly those at risk for long-term care, and a growing number of studies sug-

Vicki A. Freedman is a professor in the department of Health Systems and Policy at the University of Medicine and Dentistry of New Jersey's School of Public Health. Linda G. Martin is a senior fellow at RAND Corporation. Jennifer Cornman is an adjunct assistant professor in the department of Health Systems and Policy at University of Medicine and Dentistry of New Jersey's School of Public Health. Emily M. Agree is an associate professor at the Johns Hopkins Bloomberg School of Public Health. Robert F. Schoeni is a research professor at the Survey Research Center and Population Studies Center, Institute for Social Research, and professor of economics and public policy, at the University of Michigan.
An earlier version of this chapter was presented at the Disability Group Meeting, National Bureau of Economic Research, Jackson Hole, WY, October 8–11, 2004, and at the annual meeting of the Gerontological Society of America, Washington, D.C., November 20–22, 2004. We gratefully acknowledge support for this chapter provided by the National Institute on Aging (R01 AG021516, P30 AG12810, R01 AG19805), the Mary Woodard Lasker Charitable Trust and Michael E. DeBakey Foundation, and the National Bureau of Economic Research. The views expressed are those of the authors alone and do not represent those of their employers or funding agencies. Corresponding author: Vicki A. Freedman, Ph.D., Professor, Department of Health Systems and Policy, University of Medicine and Dentistry of New Jersey, School of Public Health, 683 Hoes Lane West, Piscataway, NJ 08854. vfreedman @umdnj.edu

gest devices have a unique role in improving functioning and quality of life even at later ages (Agree and Freedman 2003; Mann et al. 1999; Taylor and Hoenig 2004; Verbrugge et al. 1997). Current estimates suggest that approximately 14 to 18 percent of the U.S. population age sixty-five or older uses assistive devices—most often devices for mobility (canes, walkers) and bathing (grab bars, bath seats, railings) (Cornman, Freedman, and Agree 2005). Among older people reporting difficulty with daily personal care activities, nearly two-thirds report using a device to meet their needs (Agree and Freedman 2000), and about one-third do so but do not receive any help from another person (Agree, Freedman, and Sengupta 2004).

As first reported by Manton and colleagues a decade ago (Manton, Corder, and Stallard 1993), shifts have been occurring in the forms of assistance to cope with disability in late life. In that study, between 1982 and 1989, equipment use increased for older persons with mild chronic impairment and for older people with severe chronic disability as a supplement to personal assistance. During the same time period, reliance on personal care without any supplemental equipment declined. The trend toward using equipment as a sole form of assistance with daily activities has continued through the 1990s (Freedman et al. 2006; Spillman 2004). In particular, the literature has drawn attention to large increases in assistive technology for two common tasks—mobility and bathing. Russell et al. (1997) report increases of over 19 percentage points in the use of mobility equipment among adults from 1980 to 1994 and a consensus report demonstrated agreement in two out of three national surveys that notable increases have occurred in the use of equipment without help for bathing (Freedman et al. 2004). Reliance on such devices is likely to rise further as the number and types of devices available increase. In the last twenty years alone, the number of assistive devices has expanded from 6,000 products to over 29,000 (NIDDR 2004; U.S. Congress Office of Technology Assessment 1985).

Despite these trends, the continuing debate on disparities in health care utilization (e.g., AHRQ 2003) has not yet explicitly recognized assistive technology as a type of care with which to be concerned, and the literature on racial and socioeconomic disparities in forms of assistance remains small, with mixed results. Hence, it remains unclear whether types of assistance among those with difficulty in their daily tasks vary by race/ethnicity and socioeconomic status and whether the aforementioned trends have been experienced broadly, or only by some segments of the older population. Likewise, it remains equally unclear whether the shifts in assistance are similar for less and more advantaged groups and if not, whether differences can be explained by the changing demographic and socioeconomic composition of the older population.

The purpose of this chapter is to explore for the older U.S. population trends in forms of assistance with daily activities, disparities in forms of assistance by race/ethnicity and socioeconomic status, and whether those gaps have changed in recent years. We also explore whether differential patterns between more and less advantaged groups can be explained by recent shifts in the composition of the older population. To the extent that we can identify reasons for and disparities in these phenomena, such analyses may provide insights into explanations for recent declines in late-life disability.

13.2 Background and Framework

13.2.1 Relationship Between Accommodations and Functioning

As shown in figure 13.1, an individual's ability to perform a given activity is related to his or her underlying functional capacity, the demands of a given task (including demands imposed by the physical environment), and accommodations individuals make. Although tasks of interest for younger age groups typically include work and other aspects of social participation, tasks of central interest in late-life have typically been those necessary to live independently such as shopping, cooking, and cleaning (instrumental activities of daily living [IADLs]) and personal care tasks such as bathing and walking (activities of daily living [ADLs]). Personal care limitations are associated with formidable costs, particularly when an individual requires daily assistance for an ongoing, chronic condition. Figure 13.1 also emphasizes the important distinction between disability in the absence of accommodations (that is, *underlying* disability, generally measured as difficulty without help or equipment) and *residual* disability (that is, the level of difficulty with help or equipment if used) (Verbrugge 1990).

Accommodations to age-related changes in functional capacity take various forms. For example, older individuals may change their behaviors by doing a task less frequently or in a different way (e.g., walking across the room by holding onto furniture) (Fried et al. 2001). Accommodations may also consist of two distinct types of assistance: the use of help from another person, whether paid or unpaid, and technological assistance designed to facilitate a specific task or set of tasks (Agree 1999).[1] Although not explic-

---

1. Technology can contribute to the quality of older persons' lives in many ways—for example, through new diagnostic and therapeutic devices or through new information technologies that facilitate telemedicine and telerehabilitation services. Other common household and convenience technologies may not be specifically intended to address disabilities (e.g., microwaves, portable phones, direct deposit) but may be used to compensate for a functional need. To the extent that these technologies may have contributed to recent declines in late-life disability (see Spillman 2004 for discussion of this point) they are of interest; however, measuring their contribution is difficult with currently available data. In this chapter, we therefore concern ourselves with a narrower class of technologies (sometimes referred to as assistive technologies) that are used to increase, maintain, or improve the functional capabilities of individuals for specific tasks.

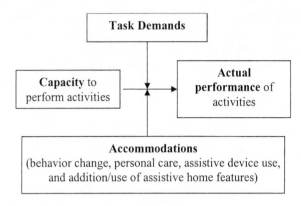

Fig. 13.1   Relationship between accommodations and functioning

itly shown in the figure, changes in behavior may change the nature of the task at hand, whereas assistive technologies either extend an individual's functional capacity or, if in the form of environmental modifications, reduce environmental demands.

Although we recognize that the use of personal care and technological assistance in combination may confer benefits beyond those conveyed by either in isolation, three conceptually distinct groups are germane for our purposes—those who carry out tasks with help from another person (with or without technology), those who use *only* technology in the performance of a task (i.e., use only assistive technology to carry out a task independently), and those who report difficulty but use neither assistive technology nor human assistance in the performance of the task. The latter group is likely heterogeneous in that it consists of individuals with mild difficulty who do not need assistance as well as those who need assistance but do not use any (i.e., those with unmet needs).

Forms of assistance used to cope with functional declines differ by task (Agree and Freedman 2000). Mobility is unique in the sense that it is a central component of many other activities. Consequently, mobility demands are idiosyncratic in timing and length, involving short distances (across a room) or longer ones (walking to the bathroom, or going downstairs, or outside). The ability to walk even short distances involves multiple body systems (including lower body strength, balance, visual acuity, and respiratory, cardiovascular, and cognitive functioning). Because mobility takes place in public as well as private spaces, social stigma may be important in influencing the choice of accommodation for different locations. In addition, environmental barriers such as stairs, inclines, slippery floors, or inadequate lighting may impede the use of certain types of assistance. Assistive devices most often used to bridge difficulty with walking are common and include relatively inexpensive canes and walkers, more expensive wheelchairs or scooters, and home modifications such as ramps, railings, and widened halls and doorways to accommodate wheelchairs.

In contrast, a discrete activity such as bathing can be scheduled at regular intervals, and generally involves one location. The level of physical and cognitive skill required to bathe independently may depend in part on the environment. For example, bathing in a traditional tub (with no environmental modifications) may require climbing over the side, and lowering oneself into the bath whereas using a typical shower (with no equipment or modifications) requires standing and balancing. Most of the technologies designed to facilitate bathing involve a change to the physical environment and include relatively inexpensive tub and shower chairs (for sitting while bathing), grab bars that provide security in the tub or shower, transfer benches (placed in a tub to ease entering and exiting the tub) and relatively more expensive installation of walk-in showers with accessible features or automatic bathtub lifts that facilitate transferring. In contrast to walking, concerns about privacy may be more salient than social stigma in choosing forms of assistance for bathing.

13.2.2   Disparities by Racial/Ethnic and Socioeconomic Status

Both the capacity to perform activities and the demands of those tasks will vary across individuals and can be influenced by race/ethnicity and socioeconomic status. With respect to capacity, previous research has shown that functional limitations tend to be more prevalent among older Hispanics and blacks than older whites, those with fewer years of education, and those with lower incomes (Freedman and Martin 1998; Mendes de Leon et al. 1995; Schoeni, Freedman, and Wallace 2002; Stump et al. 1997), and that many chronic conditions are more prevalent for minorities and those of lower socioeconomic status (Kington and Smith 1997). Less advantaged groups often live in poorer quality older housing and face more environmental barriers and related task demands (Gitlin et al. 2001; Tomita et al. 1997; Newman 2003). At the same time, socioeconomically advantaged groups are more likely to live in homes with features that facilitate aging in place (e.g., retirement communities built with wide hallways, railings, and accessible bathrooms). Other aspects of daily tasks also may vary by socioeconomic status. For example, it may be that more advantaged groups have access to resources that enable them to accomplish tasks more efficiently, such as using private transportation to get to and from places outside the home.

In addition, the relative out-of-pocket costs of assistance are likely to vary in part by socioeconomic status. The out-of-pocket costs faced by an older individual will vary depending on the nature and forms of assistance for a given task. In addition, costs will vary depending on the availability and opportunity costs of informal caregivers and on insurance coverage for personal care and equipment, both of which in turn are linked to socioeconomic status.

Public insurance does not systematically cover assistive technology. Medicare, the primary health insurance program for people aged sixty-five and older, covers personal care assistance only for individuals who cannot leave the home and who also require skilled nursing care. Coverage for durable medical equipment is limited to medically necessary, reusable medical items that are ordered by a physician for use in the home. For example, Medicare generally covers medically necessary walkers and wheelchairs used in the home, but the program does not generally cover stair glides, tub rails, or wheelchair ramps. Medicaid, the insurance program for poor, elderly, blind, and disabled individuals, has a home health benefit similar to Medicare's, which covers nursing, home health aides, and medical equipment suitable for use in the home. In addition, over half of the states have a personal care benefit and almost all states now have a home- and community-based waiver program (LeBlanc, Tonner, and Harrington 2001), the latter of which may be designed to cover assistive technologies and home modifications. Cash and counseling demonstration programs, which provide a cash benefit to Medicaid recipients (as of 2007 implemented or being implemented in fifteen states), may also be used to purchase personal care related goods and services, including assistive technology and home modifications.

Given these complexities, it is not surprising that findings about cross-sectional relationships between socioeconomic status and forms of assistance have been mixed. For example, with respect to race, two studies (Agree, Freedman, and Sengupta 2004; Verbrugge and Sevak 2002) have found that nonwhites are more likely than whites to use assistive technology without help compared to using neither form of assistance. And Agree, Freedman, and Sengupta (2004) also find minorities and persons of Hispanic origin are more likely than others to combine equipment and informal care. Other studies, however, have found that minorities are less likely to use equipment (Hartke, Prohaska, and Furner 1998; Tomita et al. 1997) or that there are no significant racial differences (Norburn et al. 1995). With respect to education, higher levels of education are associated with increased odds of using equipment and/or personal care (Agree, Freedman, and Sengupta 2004; Burton et al. 1995; Hartke, Prohaska and Furner 1998) and with substituting assistive technology for hours of informal care (Agree et al. 2005). Other studies, however, either find a negative relationship between education and informal care (Kemper 1992) or fail to find any relationship between education and the use of assistive technology (Agree 1999; Norburn et al. 1995; Verbrugge and Sevak 2002; Zimmer and Chappell 1994). Several studies have examined aspects of economic status, including percentage of the poverty threshold (in categories), above/below median income, family income and assets, household income, sources of income in addition to Social Security, and subjective measures of economic resources (Agree, Freedman, and Sengupta 2004; Hartke, Prohaska, and Furner 1998; Mathieson, Kronenfeld, and Keith 2002; Norburn et al. 1995; Verbrugge and Sevak 2002). Results from these studies have been mixed, with most studies showing no income effects, and one showing nonlinear effects of percentage of the poverty threshold on the use of mobility devices (Norburn et al. 1995). Another shows income in addition to Social Security increasing the chances of using one, two, or three mobility devices, but the amount of household income inversely related to the chances of using three or more devices (Mathieson, Kronenfeld, and Keith 2002).

There is reason to hypothesize that the relationship between race/ethnicity and socioeconomic status and forms of assistance may be shifting over time, with more advantaged groups benefiting disproportionately from newer technologies. First, although disparities in disability are not well-studied (Freedman et al. 2002), evidence suggests that the risk of needing help with daily activities may be shifting differentially for more and less advantaged groups (Schoeni et al., 2005). To the extent that more advantaged groups are experiencing milder difficulties, they may be more readily able to use assistive devices. In addition, newer technologies may be more expensive relative to older ones, may require learning new ways of performing routine tasks, and may involve adherence to complex instructions. At the same time, newer technologies are not routinely covered by existing and widely held insurance, and those that are may require navigation of the increasingly complex health care system. In addition, the expansion of retirement communities, which often come equipped with advantageous environmental features, may disproportionately favor seniors of higher socioeconomic status. Yet studies to date are based on data that are often at least a decade old and none have attempted to trace changes over time in types of assistance for various racial and socioeconomic groups.

In this chapter we explore trends in forms of assistance with daily tasks, disparities by racial and socioeconomic status, and whether those gaps have changed over time. Building on Agree, Freedman, and Sengupta (2004), we integrate our analysis of predictors of assistance into a cohesive framework with three distinct, nonoverlapping outcomes: use of only assistive technology, any help (from another person with or without assistive technology), and neither form of assistance. In doing so, we focus on individuals reporting difficulty with any ADL, and also investigate these trends for two specific activities for which assistive technology is commonly used, mobility and bathing. Unlike previous studies, we explicitly test for differences by race/ethnicity, education, and income groups as distinct categories of disadvantage and explore changes in these gaps over time.

13.3   Data and Methods

13.3.1   Data and Analytic Samples

The analysis is based on data from the 1992 to 2001 Medicare Current Beneficiary Survey (MCBS). Conducted annually, the MCBS is a continuous survey of a representative national sample drawn from Center for Medicare and Medicaid Service's Medicare enrollment file. The MCBS sample is selected by systematic random sampling with different sampling rates by age (0 to 44, 45 to 64, 65 to 69, 70 to 74, 75 to 79, 80 to 84, and 85 or over) to overrepresent persons with disability who are under sixty-five years of age and people who are eighty-five or older. Newly eligible beneficiaries are added to the sample once a year. Interviews are conducted wherever respondents reside, including long-term care facilities. We focus on the U.S. population aged sixty-five or older living in the community from 1992 to 2001.[2]

In each year, respondents were asked whether because of a health or physical problem they have difficulty by themselves and without special equipment with each of the following activities of daily living: bathing, dressing, eating, transferring, walking, and toileting. Community-dwelling respondents reporting difficulty with or not doing an activity for health reasons were asked whether they received help (hands-on or standby) doing that activity and whether they used special equipment or aids to do that activity. To focus our analysis on the older population at risk for using assistance, we restricted our analytic samples to those reporting difficulty with any ADL (N = 38,603), walking (N = 32,737), and bathing (N = 16,648).

13.3.2   Variables

We examined disparities in the use of assistance by three dimensions of socioeconomic status (SES): race/ethnicity, education, and income quartiles. For race/ethnicity, we contrasted non-Hispanic whites and all other races or ethnicities. Education was classified into three categories: zero to eight years, nine to twelve years (including high school graduates), and more than twelve years. Changes across survey years in the response categories for education did not permit more detailed specification. For 909 cases (0.7 percent of the sample sixty-five and older) that were missing education, we assigned the modal education category by six age-sex groups (females and males age sixty-five to seventy-four, seventy-five to eighty-four, and eighty-five and over).

For our analysis of income differentials and trends, we created a relative

---

2. We excluded 1,970 respondents living in Puerto Rico (80 percent of whom identify themselves as Hispanic), fifty-six cases missing both race and Hispanic origin, and sixty-one cases missing marital status.

rather than absolute measure of income reflecting quartiles. In the MCBS for 1992 to 2001, couple income (and for unmarried respondents, respondent income) was collected in fourteen categories, including a group for missing (n = 4,240 or 3.4 percent of the sample ages sixty-five and older). To create quartiles, we implemented a three-step procedure. First, for each year 1992 to 2001, we used data from the sixty-five and older population from the March Current Population Survey (CPS), which is the U.S. Census Bureau's source for official estimates of income and poverty, to estimate couple income as a continuous function of sociodemographic variables (age, sex, marital status, education, race/ethnicity, region) and the MCBS couple income categories. Second, we used the CPS-based coefficients from this model to estimate an exact couple income within category for each MCBS respondent.[3] Finally, we grouped individuals in the MCBS into income quartiles based on the weighted distribution of the estimated income measure, with quartiles created separately for each year. We evaluated the procedure by comparing the March CPS and estimated MCBS income distributions and trends for the sixty-five and older population and found they were substantially similar (see fig. 13.2).

In multivariate models we controlled for several additional demographic variables previously demonstrated to be related to forms of assistance in this population, including age, sex, marital status, and region. To control for changes over time in underlying capacity, we created a scale reflecting severity of functional limitations. We summed the level of difficulty ranging from 0 (no difficulty) to 4 (unable to do) for three tasks: lifting, reaching, and stooping. The scale ranged from 0–12, with a mean of 5.9 among those reporting difficulty with one or more ADL, and Cronbach's alpha equal to 0.75.[4] Finally, to control for potentially greater access to formal personal care, we included an indicator of Medicaid participation for at least part of the year.

13.3.3   Methods

We first plotted unadjusted trends in the use of any help, only assistive technology, and neither for each outcome (any ADL, walking, and bathing) stratified by socioeconomic status. We tested for trends over time and differences in trends by socioeconomic status using logistic regression

---

3. For a small number of cases the imputation procedure estimated an income that was out of range. Imputed income for thirty-one cases missing on income was less than 0. These values were recorded to 0. For fourteen cases that provided an original response of $25,000 or more, imputed income was less than $25,000 and these values were recorded to $25,000.

4. The MCBS also asked about difficulty with two other tasks: walking two to three blocks and writing. These items were explored but eventually omitted from the scale. We omitted the writing item because it did not correlate with the other items in the scale. We omitted the item about walking two to three blocks because the question did not explicitly refer to the level of difficulty without special equipment and we were concerned the item might be endogenous to the use of assistance, particularly for walking.

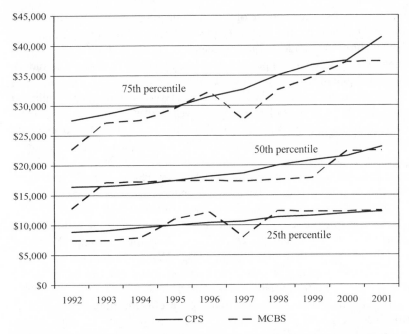

Fig. 13.2   Income quartiles: Current population survey (Actual) versus Medicare current beneficiary survey (estimated)

models with linear terms for year, with standard errors adjusted for the complex design of the MCBS.[5] Departures in the trend from linearity were explored but found not to be consistently significant, so they were not incorporated into multivariate models.

We then fit multinomial logistic regression models predicting the use of any help, only the use of assistive technology, and neither, again adjusting standard errors for sample design.[6] We included in these models a linear trend variable that took the value of 1 in 1992 and increased by 1 in each subsequent year, with maximum value of 10 in 2001. Initially, we fit models including year, race/ethnicity, education, income quartiles, and the control variables as previously discussed. To this main effects model we added an interaction between each of the race/ethnicity and socioeconomic indicators and year (one set at a time). We coded these interactions so that we

5. Ordinary least squares (OLS) regression models were also estimated and in general showed similar patterns but produced statistically significant results in more cases for the more advantaged groups.

6. Standard error adjustments do not take into account the additional gain in precision from overlapping samples and are thus conservative. For one model, standard error adjustments necessitated that seven cases be deleted because they were in primary sampling units (PSU) that were single PSUs within a stratum.

could directly test relative trends separately for each racial/ethnic and socioeconomic group. We then reparameterized the model to test for changes over time in racial/ethnic and socioeconomic differentials (using an adjusted Wald statistic for nested multinomial logit models, adjusted for sample design).

To facilitate the interpretation of the various contrasts from the multinomial logit models, we calculated for each year the predicted probabilities of using each type of assistance by race/ethnicity and socioeconomic status. We calculated the probabilities of each outcome, varying characteristics of interest across the whole data set and averaging the predictions. In doing so, we held all other characteristics constant at the levels observed in the data set.[7] The resulting trends and disparities may be interpreted as changes or gaps for a particular socioeconomic group and activity, net of all other characteristics shown in table 13.1.

13.4   Results

13.4.1   Racial/ethnic and Socioeconomic Composition of the Older Population Reporting Difficulty with Daily Tasks

Distributions for each of the racial/ethnic and socioeconomic indicators and other control variables used in the analysis are shown in table 13.1 for each of the three analytic samples, averaged over the ten years of observation. Compared to the entire population age sixty-five or older, the populations reporting difficulty with any ADL, walking, and bathing overrepresent socioeconomically disadvantaged individuals (with roughly 30 percent reporting zero to eight years of education and 35 to 40 percent falling into the lowest income quartile). The populations reporting difficulty are also substantially older, report more functional limitations, and overrepresent women, unmarried individuals, those living in the South, and Medicaid beneficiaries.

Mirroring increases in educational attainment among the sixty-five and older population, over time the populations reporting difficulty have experienced substantial declines in the percentage with eight or fewer completed years of education and increases in the percentage who have completed thirteen or more years (see table 13.2). Yet, even in 2001, those reporting difficulty with daily activities reported lower levels of educational attainment compared to the entire population ages sixty-five and older. For instance, 28 percent of those with any ADL difficulty had completed eight or fewer years of education compared to only 15 percent of the

---

7. For more details on this methodology, known as the method of recycled predictions, see StataCorp (1997, p. 548).

Table 13.1   **Characteristics of the population ages 65 and older, 1992–2001 (weighted percentages)**

| | Population ages 65+ | Population ages 65+ reporting difficulty with | | |
		Any ADL	Walking	Bathing
Race				
Non-Hispanic white	84.7	82.4	82.0	81.0
Other race	15.3	17.6	18.0	19.0
Education				
0–8 years	20.3	27.8	28.3	31.6
9–12 years	47.8	47.1	47.1	46.4
13+ years	31.8	25.1	25.6	22.0
Income quartiles				
First	25.0	35.6	36.2	41.0
Second	25.0	27.0	27.2	26.9
Third	25.0	21.6	21.3	19.5
Fourth	25.0	15.9	15.3	12.5
Age				
65–74	53.9	39.3	39.0	31.3
75–79	36.1	41.5	41.2	42.4
85+	10.0	19.3	19.9	26.3
Sex				
Male	41.8	34.7	34.7	30.0
Female	58.2	65.3	65.3	70.0
Marital Status				
Married	56.5	45.7	45.1	40.8
Not married	43.5	54.2	54.9	59.2
Region				
Northeast	24.2	19.8	19.9	19.6
South	21.2	25.2	25.0	25.2
Midwest	35.4	36.0	35.8	37.2
West	19.2	19.0	19.3	18.0
Functional limitation Scale				
0	27.0	3.3	2.8	1.5
1–2	30.3	13.7	11.9	5.7
3–5	23.0	30.4	29.3	20.0
6–12	19.7	52.7	56.0	72.8
(weighted mean)	(2.9)	(5.9)	(6.1)	(7.4)
Medicaid participation	8.8	15.3	15.7	19.3
Year				
1992	9.8	10.6	10.7	10.2
1993	9.7	10.1	10.0	10.3
1994	9.7	10.0	10.0	10.4
1995	9.9	10.0	9.9	10.4
1996	10.0	9.5	9.4	10.0
1997	10.1	9.5	9.4	9.7
1998	10.1	9.8	9.8	9.6
1999	10.1	10.2	10.1	10.0
2000	10.2	10.1	10.3	9.7
2001	10.3	10.1	10.3	9.6
N (unweighted)	126,481	38,603	32,737	16,648

Table 13.2   **Racial/ethnic and socioeconomic characteristics of the population ages 65 and older, 1992 and 2001 (weighted percentages)**

| | Population ages 65+ | | | Population ages 65+ reporting difficulty with | | | | | | | | |
| | | | | Any ADL | | | Walking | | | Bathing | | |
	1992	2001	p	1992	2001	p	1992	2001	p	1992	2001	p
Race			***									
Non-Hispanic white	86.6	82.4		84.0	80.5		83.3	80.4		83.7	78.5	
Other race	13.4	17.6		16.0	19.5		16.7	19.6		16.3	21.5	
Education			***			***			***			***
0–8 years	26.2	14.7		34.4	27.8		35.4	20.5		39.2	24.6	
9–12 years	47.8	45.6		46.0	47.2		44.9	48.3		43.5	50.5	
13+ years	26.0	39.7		19.6	25.1		19.7	31.2		17.3	24.9	
Income quartiles						**			***			**
First	25.0	25.0		35.1	36.2		36.3	36.8		39.3	44.3	
Second	25.0	25.0		27.8	26.3		27.7	26.3		28.4	25.0	
Third	25.0	25.0		21.9	21.3		21.7	21.0		19.6	18.7	
Fourth	25.0	25.0		15.3	16.2		14.3	15.9		12.7	12.0	

Note: ** $p<.05$ and *** $p<.001$ for χ^2 test for relationship between year (1992–2001) and variable of interest.

entire population ages sixty-five and older. Income distributions also shifted during this time period, notably toward lower quartiles for those with difficulty bathing, although distributions at the beginning and end of the period were substantially similar among those reporting difficulty with any ADL and with walking.[8]

13.4.2   Unadjusted Trends in Assistance and Disparities by Socioeconomic Status

Figures 13.3–13.5 show the unadjusted trends in assistance among those who reported difficulty with any of the six ADLs, walking, and bathing. Three observations are noteworthy with respect to trends. First, the independent use of assistive technology (indicated "AT only") has increased significantly over the period for select groups—non-Hispanic whites, those with thirteen or more years of education, and those in the lowest income

8. We also explored whether the chances of reporting difficulty with daily activities, which has been previously reported to have declined between 1992 and 2001 for the older population (Freedman et al. 2004), declined differentially by race/ethnicity and socioeconomic status. We found no differentials by race and education; however, there appeared to be important differences by income. The two lowest quartiles demonstrated statistically significant declines in difficulty with any ADL over the ten-year period, whereas the upper quartiles did not. In logistic regression models in which we controlled for demographic and socioeconomic characteristics, we found evidence for smaller declines in the highest quartile compared to the lowest quartile (0.15 percent per year versus 2.3 percent per year). Hence, some narrowing of the differential in difficulty by income over the ten-year period occurred.

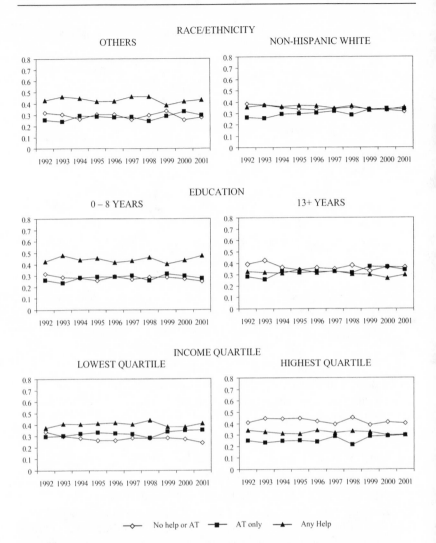

Fig. 13.3   Trends in receipt of assistance with any of six ADLs, population ages 65+ with difficulty in any ADL, by race/ethnicity, education, and income quartiles, 1992–2001

quartile.[9] Second, where significant increases in the use of only assistive technology have occurred, they have in some cases been accompanied by declines in unassisted difficulty (indicated "no help or AT") and in other cases been accompanied by declines in help from another person (desig-

9. Tests based on an OLS specification suggest that the use of AT only for any ADL and for walking also increased significantly among the highest income quartile.

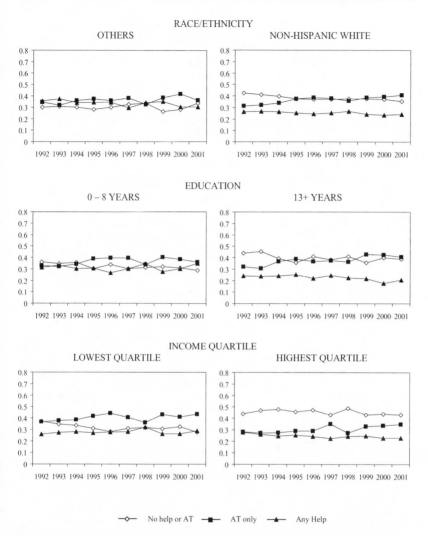

Fig. 13.4   Trends in receipt of assistance with walking, population ages 65+ with difficulty walking, by race/ethnicity, education, and income quartiles, 1992–2001

nated by "any help"). For non-Hispanic whites and the lowest income quartile, assistive technology appears to have offset declines in unassisted difficulty ("no help or AT"). In contrast, those who have completed more than a high school education have become significantly more likely to use only assistive technology and significantly less likely to use any help.

A third observation relates to disparities in assistance by racial/ethnic and socioeconomic status. Less advantaged groups consistently report higher rates of help than more advantaged groups, and more advantaged

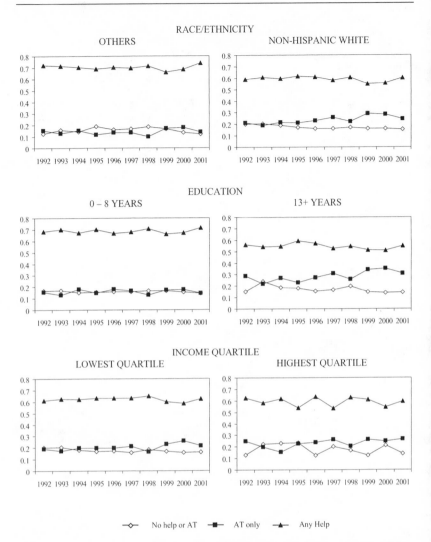

Fig. 13.5   Trends in receipt of assistance with bathing, population ages 65+ with difficulty bathing, by race/ethnicity, education, and income quartiles, 1992–2001

groups consistently report higher rates of unassisted difficulty. This general pattern holds true for all three activity outcomes, although help differentials by income are less pronounced among those reporting difficulty walking and bathing. Gaps in the use of assistive technology for any ADL and walking are in the 4 to 7 percentage point range for the two racial groups and highest versus lowest education groups. In contrast, gaps for bathing equipment are much larger; non-Hispanic whites and those with higher education levels have a 10 and 17 percentage point advantage, respectively, in 2001.

These descriptive figures do not control for differences across racial/ethnic and socioeconomic groups in other factors related to the type of assistance used (such as age, sex, or functional status), nor do they adjust for compositional shifts that have occurred over time. It may be, for example, that assistive technology is increasing in part because of changes in the severity of underlying functional limitations, or that help is declining because of shifts in marital status. Gaps by race/ethnicity and socioeconomic status might not be linked to these characteristics directly, but may be influenced by other demographic differences across groups. To explore whether gaps have changed over time, net of shifts in other demographic factors, we turn to a series of multinomial logit models.

13.4.3   Trends and Disparities Adjusted for Compositional Shifts

Table 13.3 presents the odds ratios predicting assistance among those with difficulty with any of six ADLs, walking, or bathing. The predictors of assistance with any ADL and walking tend to be similar, whereas those for bathing differ in some important aspects, particularly with respect to income effects.

le 13.3   Odds ratios from multinomial regressions for using assistive technology only and receiving any help (versus neither) among those with difficulty with any ADL, walking, or bathing: Main effects models

	Any ADL		Walking		Bathing	
	Any help vs. neither	AT only vs. neither	Any help vs. neither	AT only vs. neither	Any help vs. neither	AT only vs. neither
r	1.008	1.037***	1.013	1.038***	1.022	1.056***
a-Hispanic white	0.794***	0.932	0.793***	0.911	0.795***	1.347**
cation 9–12 years	0.897**	0.988	0.911	0.996	0.928	1.111
cation 13+ years	0.895	1.187***	0.883	1.148**	0.891	1.462***
income quartile	0.993	1.028	0.950	1.012	1.208**	1.196**
income quartile	1.019	0.964	0.977	0.934	1.306***	1.334***
income quartile (high)	0.961	0.886	1.002	0.872**	1.204	1.188
trol variables:						
ge 75–84	1.777***	1.647***	1.743***	1.667***	1.600***	1.340***
ge 85+	5.429***	3.094***	4.999***	3.356***	3.182***	1.233**
emale	1.009	0.971	1.080	0.909**	0.863**	1.288***
larried	1.832***	0.684***	1.852***	0.717***	1.896***	0.700***
idwest	0.826***	1.006	0.721***	1.008	0.731***	0.790
ortheast	1.113	0.950	0.959	0.945	1.322**	0.795
outh	0.913	0.966	0.777***	0.905	0.947	0.840
unctional limitations	1.444***	1.186***	1.363***	1.157***	1.234***	1.014
edicaid participation	1.477***	0.935	1.284***	1.029	1.626***	0.881
ervations	38,603		32,737		16,648	

Significant at less than the 1 percent level.
ignificant at less than the 5 percent level.

Trends in assistance

For all three activity outcomes, among those reporting difficulty there is no trend in the chances of getting any help (relative to using neither help nor AT). In contrast, the chances of using assistive technology (relative to using neither) has steadily increased among those reporting difficulty with any ADL (nearly 4 percent per year), walking (nearly 4 percent per year), and bathing (over 5 percent per year). Significant declines in the chances of using neither type of assistance (relative to using only AT) also occurred (not shown).

Disparities in assistance by socioeconomic status

Significant disparities in assistance are evident by racial/ethnic and socioeconomic status. For all three activity outcomes, non-Hispanic whites have consistently lower risk of using any help (versus neither), and for bathing this group has a significantly higher risk (35 percent higher than minorities) of using only assistive technology. Having completed more than a high school education is associated with an increased risk of using only assistive technology among those reporting difficulty with any ADL (19 percent higher than those with eight or fewer years), walking (15 percent higher) and bathing (46 percent higher). Differentials with respect to income quartiles are more complex and somewhat counterintuitive, with the highest quartile having lower chances than those in the lowest quartile of using only AT for walking (versus nothing). And among those with difficulty bathing, income has an inverse u-shaped relationship with both forms of assistance, so that individuals in the middle quartiles are more likely to use both any help (versus neither) and AT only (versus neither).

13.4.4   Differential Trends by Race/ethnicity and Socioeconomic Status

Tables 13.4 and 13.5 present results from a series of multinomial logit models that allow us to explore differential trends by race/ethnicity (model 1), by education (model 2), and by income quartile (model 3). The models in tables 13.4 and 13.5 contain identical variables but they are parameterized in different ways. For example, model 1 of tables 13.4 and 13.5, which highlights racial/ethnic trends, includes main effects for education and income quartiles and the control variables in table 13.3. However, the interaction between the trend and each race/ethnicity group is parameterized differently depending on the table. Table 13.4 includes parameters representing a *separate* trend line for each of the racial/ethnic groups. This specification allows an explicit test for each group of whether forms of assistance have changed. All three contrasts (any help versus none, AT only versus none, and any help versus AT only) are provided to facilitate interpretation. Table 13.5 includes parameters representing the trend for the

Table 13.4   Odds ratios from multinomial regressions for using assistive technology only, receiving any help, or neither among those with difficulty with any ADL, walking, bathing: Trends stratified by race/ethnicity and socioeconomic status

	Any ADL			Walking			Bathing		
	Any help vs. none	AT only vs. none	Any help vs. AT only	Any help vs. none	AT only vs. none	Any help vs. AT only	Any help vs. none	AT only vs. none	Any help vs. AT only
Model 1: Trend stratified by race/ethnicity									
Trend for Other race/ethnicity	1.00	1.02	0.98	1.02	1.03**	0.99	1.00	1.01	0.99
Trend for Non-Hispanic white	1.01	1.04***	0.97***	1.01	1.04***	0.97**	1.03	1.06***	0.96**
Adjusted Wald statistic (df)	6.68***(4, 2,534)			7.24***(4, 2,433)			3.03**(4, 1,860)		
Model 2: Trend stratified by education groups									
Trend for 0–8 years	1.00	1.02	0.98	1.02	1.03***	0.99	0.99	1.02	0.98
Trend for 9–12 years	1.02	1.05***	0.97***	1.02**	1.04***	0.98	1.04**	1.07***	0.97
Trend for 13+ years	0.99	1.03***	0.96***	0.98	1.04***	0.95***	1.03	1.08***	0.96***
Adjusted Wald statistic (df)	5.27***(6, 2,532)			5.51***(6, 2,441)			2.73**(6, 1,858)		
Model 3: Trend stratified by income quartiles									
Trend for 1st quartile	1.01	1.03***	0.98	1.02	1.03***	0.99	1.01	1.05**	0.96**
Trend for 2nd quartile	1.01	1.04***	0.97***	1.01	1.05***	0.97***	1.04	1.05**	0.99
Trend for 3rd quartile	1.01	1.06***	0.95***	1.02	1.05***	0.97***	1.04	1.08***	0.96
Trend for 4th quartile	1.00	1.00	1.00***	1.00	1.00	1.00***	1.00	1.00	1.00
Adjusted Wald statistic (df)	4.60***(8, 2,530)			4.79***(8, 2,439)			1.82,(8, 1,856)		

Note: Models also control for all main effects shown in table 13.3.

*** Significant at less than the 1 percent level.

** Significant at less than the 5 percent level.

Table 13.5   Odds ratios from multinomial regressions for using assistive technology only, receiving any help, or neither among those with difficulty with any ADL, walking, or bathing: Interaction models

Main effects model with the following interactions:	Any ADL Any help vs. none	Any ADL At only vs. none	Walking Any help vs. none	Walking AT only vs. none	Bathing Any help vs. none	Bathing AT only vs. none
Model 1: Trend interacted with race/ethnicity						
Year	1.00	1.02	1.02	1.03**	1.00	1.01
Non-Hispanic white	0.78**	0.85	0.85	0.85	0.69**	0.99
Non-Hispanic white · year	1.00	1.02	0.99	1.01	1.03	1.06
Adjusted Wald statistic (df) for race · year	0.50 (2, 2,536)		0.83 (2, 2,445)		1.47 (2, 1,862)	
Model 2: Trend interacted with education groups						
Year	1.00	1.02	1.02	1.03***	0.99	1.02
9–12 years of education	0.82**	0.87	0.89	0.96	0.76	0.88
13+ years of education	0.98	1.13	1.08	1.13	0.73	1.08
9–12 years · year	1.02	1.02	1.00	1.01	1.04	1.05
13+ years · year	0.99	1.01	0.97	1.00	1.04	1.06
Adjusted Wald statistic (df) for education · year	1.51 (4, 2,534)		1.69 (4, 2,443)		1.16 (4, 1,860)	
Model 3: Trend interacted with income quintiles						
Year	1.01	1.03***	1.02	1.03***	1.01	1.05**
2nd quartile	1.02	0.95	0.96	0.91	1.05	1.17
3rd quartile	1.07	0.82	0.95	0.80**	1.13	1.14
4th quartile	1.02	0.89	1.06	0.88**	1.27	1.21
2nd quartile · year	1.00	1.01	1.00	1.02	1.03	1.00
3rd quartile · year	0.99	1.03	1.01	1.03	1.03	1.03
4th quartile · year	1.00**	1.00	1.00	1.00	1.00	1.00
Adjusted Wald statistic (df) for income · year	2.04 (6, 2,532)		1.59 (6, 2,441)		0.84 (6, 1,858)	
Observations	38,603		32,737		16,648	

Note: Models also control for all main effects shown in table 13.3.

*** Significant at less than the 1 percent level.

** Significant at less than the 5 percent level.

omitted group (in model 1, nonwhite or Hispanic), the main effect of race/ethnicity (in model 1, non-Hispanic white), and interaction terms between the trend variable and race/ethnicity. This additional parameterization allows an explicit test of the *difference* in trend by the various groups, compared to an omitted group, which may be interpreted as a test for changes in disparities over time. Similar contrasts for education and income groups are provided in the other sections of the two tables.

Trends stratified by race/ethnicity and socioeconomic status

The chances of using assistive technology independently (relative to no assistance) have increased significantly over the period for most groups. For walking, for example, equipment use has increased significantly for all groups except the highest income quartile (column five, table 13.4). At the same time, the chances of using any help versus nothing (for any of the activities) have not changed appreciably for almost all groups. The coefficient is generally close to 1.0 and is not statistically significant except for those completing nine to twelve years of education (for walking and bathing, the chances of any help have increased relative to neither). Taken together, these patterns suggest that the chances of using any help and the chances of using nothing have *both* declined in relation to the use of AT alone. Indeed, as shown in the third column of each panel of table 4, the chances of using any help relative to AT have generally declined for most groups, but these declines typically do not reach statistical significance for groups where AT has increased less than 4 percent per year.

Changes in disparities over time

In testing interactions between each set of racial/ethnic and socioeconomic indicators and year (see table 13.5), only one statistically significant interaction emerged. We found a very small difference between the lowest and highest income quartiles in the trend for receiving help with any ADL. However, because this interaction effect is so small (note that it rounds to 1.00) and because the remaining interactions in the model were not significant, the set of interactions does not rise to significance for the adjusted F-test ($F(26, 2, 532) = 2.04$). Hence we conclude that none of the disparities in forms of assistance by race/ethnicity or socioeconomic status that we observed have changed significantly over the past decade, and none of the trends differ significantly by racial/ethnic and socioeconomic status.

13.4.5 Predicted Probabilities of Assistance by Racial/ethnic and Socioeconomic Status

Table 13.6 shows percentage point changes in assistance between 1992 and 2001, and percentage point differences by racial/ethnic and socioeconomic status in assistance for any ADL, walking, and bathing. The percentages are based on predicted values that are calculated from the main effects model in table 13.3 and isolate the influence of racial/ethnic and socioeconomic status and year on the probabilities of assistance. The estimates differ from those in figures 13.3–13.5 in that they are model-based estimates that control for observed differences across racial/ethnic and socioeconomic groups at-risk for using assistance. In general, adjusting for covariates accentuates the trends in assistance and attenuates the gaps by race/ethnicity and socioeconomic status.

Table 13.6   Percentage point changes from 1992 to 2001 and disparities by race, education, a｜ income in assistance with any ADL, walking and bathing

	Any ADL			Walking			Bathing		
	AT only	Help	Neither	AT only	Help	Neither	AT only	Help	Neit｜
Percentage point change over time (2001 vs. 1992)									
Race									
Other	6	−2	−3	6	−2	−5	4	−1	−｜
Non-Hispanic white	6	−2	−4	6	−1	−5	5	−2	−｜
Education									
0–8 years	6	−2	−4	6	−1	−5	5	−1	−｜
13+ years	6	−2	−4	7	−1	−5	6	−2	−｜
Income									
1st income quartile	6	−2	−4	6	−1	−5	5	−1	−｜
4th income quartile	6	−2	−4	6	−1	−5	5	−2	−｜
Disparities by year									
1992									
Non-Hispanic white vs. Other	1	−4	3	0	−3	3	6	−7	｜
13+ years vs. 0–8 years	4	−4	−1	4	−4	−1	7	−6	｜
4th quartile vs. 1st quartile	−2	0	1	−3	1	2	1	2	−｜
2001									
Non-Hispanic white vs. Other	1	−4	2	0	−3	3	7	−8	｜
13+ years vs. 0–8 years	5	−4	−1	5	−4	−1	8	−7	−｜
4th quartile vs. 1st quartile	−2	1	1	−3	1	2	1	2	−｜

Note: Calculated based on predicted values from model shown in table 13.3. See text for methodolo｜

Trends

Holding all else constant, there is a clear and consistent increase over the decade of about 6 percentage points in the percentage of older adults using only assistive devices for their daily activities. The increase is similar for both racial groups and for more and less advantaged education and income groups. Similarly sized increases were observed among those with difficulty walking (about 6 percentage points) and bathing (about 5 percentage points). Increases in the independent use of assistive technology were offset by declines in both help and neither form of assistance, but declines in using neither (4 to 5 percentage points) were more than twice as large as the declines in help (1 to 2 percentage points).

Disparities

Holding all else constant, disparities by racial/ethnic and socioeconomic status in forms of assistance were similarly sized in 1992 and 2001. However, in both years, having thirteen or more years of education (versus eight or fewer) appears to confer a greater advantage with respect to the independent use of assistive technology than either being non-Hispanic white (versus minority) or in the highest (versus lowest) income quartile.

In 2001, for example, among those with difficulty with any ADL and with walking, individuals who have completed thirteen or more years of education have a 5 percentage point advantage over those who have completed eight or fewer years. Among those with difficulty bathing, those in the highest education group have an 8 percentage point advantage in using technology. At the same time, individuals with the lowest levels of education (zero to eight years) are more likely to use help.

Gaps in assistance by race are most apparent for bathing. In 2001, among those with difficulty bathing, rates of using help for non-Hispanic whites are 8 percentage points lower than for other races and rates of assistive technology use are 7 percentage points higher. Smaller gaps in help are evident for any ADL (4 percentage points) and walking (3 percentage points).

Income disparities are far less substantial. For example, for walking, the significant finding that individuals in the highest quartile have a 13 percent lower risk ($RR = 0.87$) of using only AT relative to individuals in the lowest quartile translates into absolute differences in 2001 of 3 percentage points.

13.5   Discussion

This chapter has provided strong evidence that there has been a substantial increase in recent years in the use of assistive technology by members of the older U.S. population who have difficulty with daily tasks. In general, the increases in assistive technology appear to be widely experienced. Still, some socioeconomic groups are more likely to use assistive technology without help than others. Notably, higher levels of education are associated with higher probabilities of using technology independently to carry out daily activities. Among those with difficulty with one or more daily activities, all else equal, there has been a persistent 5 percentage point gap in the independent use of assistive technology between those with more than a high school education and those with eight or fewer years of completed education. Even larger gaps by education are evident among those reporting difficulty bathing—reaching 8 percentage points in 2001.

We also found descriptive evidence suggestive of different patterns over time among more and less advantaged groups. Among those with more than a high school education, we found that increases in assistive technology have offset declines in the chances of receiving help from another person. In contrast, among low-income groups we found increases in assistive technology have offset declines in unassisted difficulty. However, tests for differences across groups in these patterns (that also took into account differences across groups and over time in the demographic and socioeconomic composition of the population) did not rise to the level of statistical significance. In fact, we found that for most groups increases in assistive technology appear to be offset by decreases *both* in the use of help and in unassisted difficulty, with declines in the latter twice as large as declines in help.

Our analysis is limited in several respects. First, questions about forms of assistance were limited to those individuals reporting that they experienced difficulty with a particular task. As Cornman, Freedman, and Agree (2005) and Pine, Gurland, and Chren (2002) have shown, there is a sizeable group that uses assistive technology, most often canes or environmental features, but does not report difficulty, and this group appears to be increasing in size (Freedman, et al. 2006). Hence, our findings may underestimate the increases in assistive technology that have taken place over the last decade. On a similar note, we have limited our attention to technologies that are specifically designed to assist with functioning in day-to-day tasks, and hence excluded important medical, information, and household technologies that undoubtedly have improved older Americans' quality of life in recent decades. Finally, due to data limitations, we considered only personal care activities in our analysis. In particular, declines in the prevalence of IADL limitations have been much larger than those observed for ADLs; hence, understanding the role of technology in these other activities would be an important next step.

Despite these limitations, our findings have implications for the study of late-life disability trends and disparities therein. A consensus report (Freedman et al. 2004) found agreement across several national datasets (including the MCBS upon which we drew here) that there have been declines during the 1990s in help with ADL activities. Here we have investigated whether declines in help are linked to increases in the use of assistive technology. We found that controlling for compositional shifts, declines in reports of help from 1991 to 2001 among those reporting difficulty amounted to at most 2 percentage points. This figure equals about one-third of the observed decline in help over this period in the entire older population. The rest of the decline in help is the result of fewer people reporting underlying difficulty with daily activities. Indeed, previous studies have demonstrated that the severity of underlying difficulty is the overriding determinant of the types of assistance used (Agree, Freedman, and Sengupta 2004; Verbrugge and Sevak 2002) and that shifts in capacity account for a larger share of declines in dependence than do shifts in forms of assistance (Freedman et al. 2006). Whether the declines among those reporting difficulty have been driven mainly by increases in assistive technology or by other forces not measured in our analysis—such as changes in Medicare home health care or shifts in the causes and extent of underlying difficulty—warrants further attention. Although we were not able to distinguish between paid and unpaid sources of care, future analyses should explore these distinctions, particularly whether the declines in help among more highly educated older adults represent declines in paid or unpaid sources of care.

Our results also have implications for the growing literature on substitution between assistive technology and personal care and on unmet need. We found limited evidence of trade-offs in the aggregate between assistive technology and help in the older U.S. population, and our descriptive findings were consistent with recent evidence that more highly educated seniors may be trading off assistive technology for personal care (Agree et al. 2005). However, this pattern was not dominant, and clearly a greater share of the increase in assistive technology has been offset by declines in unassisted difficulty. At the same time, we found that participation in the Medicaid program is associated with a greater likelihood of receipt of help, but not assistive technology. Hence, for economically disadvantaged seniors participating in this means-tested program, substitution does not appear to be encouraged by the current benefit structure.

With respect to disparities in trends, increasing gaps in the need for help with personal activities have been reported (Schoeni et al. 2005), with lower income seniors and those with fewer years of education not gaining as much as other groups. We did not find increasing gaps in the forms of assistance. However, we found that disparities evident in 1992 persisted a decade later, with better educated individuals more likely than less educated to use assistive technology without help and minorities more likely than others to use help. Racial and education gaps with respect to the use of bathing technology were especially large, all else equal, amounting to 7 to 8 percentage points in 2001—nearly twice the gaps found by education for walking.

These task-specific findings highlight the complex nature of late-life disability and the heterogeneity of the various daily tasks. Although the use of walking and bathing technologies have both increased over the decade by similar amounts, gaps by race/ethnicity and socioeconomic status in the use of technologies to assist in bathing remained notably large. The reason for this pattern is not clear. It may be that technologies to accommodate bathing difficulties involve changes to the physical environment that less advantaged groups may not be in a position to adapt. Currently, national surveys do not provide details on the home environment of older adults with difficulty in daily activities, so further exploration of these kinds of hypotheses will await new data collection efforts.

From a societal perspective, the fact that there have been declines in the proportion of the older population reporting difficulty with ADL activities is undoubtedly good news. However, at the same time, those with difficulty have become increasingly disadvantaged socially and economically over time, even as educational attainment has risen. The especially large and persistent educational disparities in use of assistive technology suggests greater effort in this area—perhaps through public education around access to and benefits of assistive technology—may be warranted. Ultimately, whether the shift toward technological assistance by those experiencing difficulty with daily tasks is judged as beneficial remains to be seen. Technology may enhance independence, but those who use equipment equally or more often report that tasks are tiring, time-consuming, or painful even when they use assistance (Agree and Freedman 2003). Better understanding of the costs and benefits of various forms of assistance for older persons who experience difficulty in their day-to-day tasks is needed for policymaking to keep pace with technological advancements.

References

Agency for HealthCare Research and Quality. 2003. National Health Care Disparities Report. Available at http://www.qualitytools.ahrq.gov/disparitiesreport/download_report.aspx

Agree, E. M. 1999. The influence of personal care and assistive devices on the measurement of disability. *Social Science and Medicine* 48:427–43.

Agree, E. M., and V. A. Freedman. 2000. Incorporating assistive devices into long-term care arrangements: Analysis of the Second Supplement on Aging. *Journal of Aging and Health* 12 (3): 426–50

———. 2003. A comparison of assistive technology and personal care in alleviating disability and unmet need. *The Gerontologist* 43:335–44.

Agree, E. M., V. A. Freedman, J. C. Cornman, D. A. Wolf, and J. E. Marcotte. 2005. Reconsidering substitution in long-term care: When does assistive technology take the place of personal care? *Journals of Gerontology: Social Sciences* 60 (5): S272–80.

Agree, E. M., and V. A. Freedman, and M. Sengupta. 2004. Factors influencing the use of mobility technology in community-based long-term care. *Journal of Aging Health* 16 (2): 267–307.

Burton, L., J. Kasper, A. Shore, K. Cagney, T. LaVeist, C. Cubbin, and P. German. 1995. The structure of informal care: Are there differences by race? *The Gerontologist* 35 (6): 744–52.

Cornman, J. C., V. A. Freedman, and E. M. Agree. 2005. Measurement of assistive device use: Implications for estimates of device use and disability in late life. *The Gerontologist* 45 (3): 347–58.

Freedman, V. A., E. M. Agree, L. G. Martin, and J. C. Cornman. 2006. Trends in the use of assistive technology and personal care for late-life disability, 1992–2001. *The Gerontologist* 46 (1): 124–27.

Freedman, V. A., E. Crimmins, R. F. Schoeni, B. Spillman, H. Aykan, K. Land, J. Lubitz, K. Manton, L. G. Martin, D. Shinberg, and T. Waidmann. 2004. Resolving discrepancies in old-age disability trends across national surveys: Report from a technical working group. *Demography* 41 (3): 417–41.

Freedman, V. A., and L. G. Martin. 1998. Understanding trends in functional limitations among older Americans. *American Journal of Public Health* 88:1457–62.

Freedman, V. A., L. G. Martin, and R. F. Schoeni. 2002. Recent trends in disability and functioning among older adults in the United States: A systematic review. *Journal of the American Medical Association* 288 (24): 3137–46.

Fried, L. P., K. Bandeen-Roche, P. H. Chaves, and B. A. Johnson. 2000. Preclinical mobility disability predicts incident mobility disability in older women. *Journals of Gerontology: Medical Sciences* 55 (1): M43–52.

Fried, L. P., Y. Young, G. Rubin, and K. Bandeen-Roche. 2001. Self-reported preclinical disability identifies older women with early declines in performance and early disease. For the WHAS II Collaborative Research Group. *Journal of Clinical Epidemiology* 54 (9): 889–901.

Gitlin, L. N., W. Mann, M. Tomit, and S. M. Marcus. 2001. Factors associated with home environmental problems among community-living older people. *Disability and Rehabilitation* 23 (17): 777–87.

Hartke, R. J., T. R. Prohaska, and S. E. Furner. 1998. Older adults and assistive devices: Use, multiple-device use and need. *Journal of Aging and Health* 10 (1): 99–116.

Kemper, P. 1992. The use of formal and informal care by the disabled elder. *Health Services Research* 27 (4): 421–51.

Kington, R. S., and J. P. Smith. 1997. Socioeconomic status and racial and ethnic differences in functional status associated with chronic diseases. *American Journal of Public Health* 87 (5): 805–10.

LeBlanc, A. J., M. C. Tonner, and C. Harrington. 2001. State Medicaid programs offering personal care services. *Health Care Financing Review* 22 (4): 155–73.

Mann, W. C., K. J. Ottenbacher, L. Fraas, M. Tomita, and C. V. Granger. 1999. Effectiveness of assistive technology and environmental interventions in maintaining independence and reducing home care costs for the frail elderly. A randomized controlled trial. *Archives of Family Medicine* 8 (3): 210–17.

Manton, K. G., L. Corder, and E. Stallard. 1993. Changes in the use of personal assistance and special equipment from 1982 to 1989: Results from the 1982 and 1989 NLTCS. *The Gerontologist* 33:168–76.

Mathieson, K. M., J. Kronenfeld, and V. M. Keith. 2002. Maintaining functional independence in elderly adults: The roles of health status and financial resources in predicting home modifications and use of mobility equipment. *The Gerontologist* 42 (1): 24–31.

Mendes de Leon, C. F., G. G. Fillenbaum, C. S. Williams, D. B. Brock, L. A. Beckett, and L. F. Berkman. 1995. Functional disability among elderly blacks and whites in two diverse areas: The New Haven and North Carolina EPESE. Established Populations for the Epidemiologic Studies of the Elderly. *American Journal of Public Health* 85 (7): 994–8.

Newman, S. J. 2003. The living conditions of elderly Americans. *Gerontologist* 43 (1): 99–109.

NIDRR (National Institute for Disability and Rehabilitation Research). 2004. National Database of Assistive Technology Information (ABLEDATA). Silver Spring, MD: Macro International, Inc.

Norburn, J. E. K., S. Bernard, T. Konrad, A. Woomert, G. DeFriese, K. Kalsbeek, G. G. Koch, and M. Ory. 1995. Self-care and assistance from others in coping with functional status limitations among a national sample of older adults. *Journals of Gerontology: Social Sciences* 50B (2): S101–9.

Pew, R. W., and S. B. Van Hemel, eds. 2004. *Technology for Adaptive Aging*. Steering Committee for the Workshop on Technology for Adaptive Aging, National Research Council. Washington, D.C.: The National Academies Press.

Pine, M. Z., B. Gurland, and M. M. Chren. 2002. Use of a cane for ambulation: Marker and mitigator of impairment in older people who report no difficulty walking. *Journal of the American Geriatric Society* 50 (2): 263–8.

Russell, J. N., G. E. Hendershot, F. LeClere, L. J. Howie, and M. Adler. 1997. Trends and differential use of assistive technology devices. *Advance Data from*

Vital and Health Statistics, 292. Hyattsville, MD: National Center for Health Statistics.

Schoeni, R. F., V. A. Freedman, and R. Wallace. 2002. Late-life disability trajectories and socioeconomic status. *Annual Review of Gerontology and Geriatrics* 22:184–206.

Schoeni, R. F., L. G. Martin, P. Andreski, and V. A. Freedman. 2005. Persistent and growing socioeconomic disparities in disability among the elderly: 1982–2002. *American Journal of Public Health* 95 (11): 2065–70.

Spillman, B. C. 2004. Changes in elderly disability rates and the implications for health care utilization and cost. *Milbank Quarterly* 82:157–94.

Stump, T. E., D. O. Clark, R. J. Johnson, and F. D. Wolinsky. 1997. The structure of health status among Hispanic, African American, and white older adults. *Journals of Gerontology: Social Sciences* 52: S49–S60.

StataCorp. 1997. *Stata Statistical Software: Release 5.0.* College Station, TX: Stata Corporation.

Taylor, D. H., and H. Hoenig. 2004. The effect of equipment usage and residual task difficulty on use of personal assistance, days in bed, and nursing home placement. *Journal of the American Geriatrics Society* 52 (1): 72–9.

Tomita, M. R., W. C. Mann, L. F. Fraas, and L. L. Burns. 1997. Racial differences of frail elders in assistive technology. *Assistive Technology* 9:140–51.

U.S. Congress Office of Technology Assessment. 1985. Technological change and the U.S. older population. In *Technology and Aging in America.* Washington, D.C.: U.S. Congress Office of Technology Assessment, Report OTA-BA-264.

Verbrugge, L. M. 1990. The iceberg of disability. In *The legacy of longevity: Health and health care in late life,* ed. S. Stahl, 55–75. Newbury Park: Sage Publications.

Verbrugge, L. M., C. Rennert, and J. H. Madans. 1997. The great efficacy of personal and equipment assistance in reducing disability. *American Journal of Public Health* 87 (3): 384–92.

Verbrugge, L. M., and P. Sevak. 2002. Use, type, and efficacy of assistance for disability. *Journals of Gerontology: Social Sciences* 57: S366–79.

Zimmer, Z., and N. Chappell. 1994. Mobility restrictions and the use of devices among seniors. *Journal of Aging and Health* 6 (2): 185–208.

14

How do Medicare Beneficiaries with Physical and Sensory Disabilities Feel About Their Health Care?

Lisa I. Iezzoni, Jane R. Soukup, and Suzanne G. Leveille

Persons with disabilities often experience more problems than others with their health care quality, along various dimensions.[1] *Healthy People 2010*, which sets national health priorities, notes disparities in care for many persons with disabilities, (U.S. Department of Health and Human Services 2000) and in 2005, the U.S. Surgeon General called for concerted efforts to eliminate these disparities (U.S. Department of Health and Human Services 2005). Disability thus joins such patient attributes as race, ethnicity, and nonmajority cultural traditions as targets for health care quality improvement, especially ensuring patient-centered care, perhaps the fundamental guiding principle for improving care according to the Institute of Medicine's seminal report *Crossing the Quality Chasm* (Institute of Medicine Committee on Quality of Health Care in America 2001; Berwick 2002).

Patient-centered care—care that meets patients' preferences, expectations, and needs—requires open and accurate communication between patients and clinicians, as well as ready access to services and other interven-

Lisa I. Iezzoni, M.D., M.Sc., is professor of medicine, Harvard Medical School, and Associate Director, Institute for Health Policy at the Massachusetts General Hospital, Boston. Jane R. Soukup, M.Sc., is a data analyst at Beth Israel Deaconess Medical Center, Boston. Suzanne G. Leveille, Ph.D., is assistant professor of medicine, Harvard Medical School, and a research associate in the Division of General Medicine and Primary Care, Beth Israel Deaconess Medical Center, Boston.

We are grateful for financial support from the National Institute on Aging, grants P30 AG12810 and R01 AG19805, and the Mary Woodard Lasker Charitable Trust and Michael E. DeBakey Foundation.

1. See U.S. Department of Health and Human Services 2000; Rosenbach 1995; Rosenbach, Acamache, and Khandker 1995; Andriacchi 1997; Chan et al. 1999; Lawthers et al. 2003; Iezzoni et al. 2000a; Iezzoni et al. 2001; Iezzoni et al. 2002; Weil et al. 2002; Iezzoni et al. 2003; Iezzoni et al. 2004a; O'Day, Killeen, and Iezzoni 2004; O'Day et al. 2005; Iezzoni et al. 2004b; Iezzoni and O'Day 2006; Iezzoni, Killeen, and O'Day 2006; and McCarthy et al. 2006.

tions. Persons with specific functional impairments, such as vision or hearing deficits, impaired mobility, or limited manual dexterity, confront special communication and physical access challenges within typical medical settings (Iezzoni and O'Day 2006; U.S. Department of Health and Human Services 2005; Kirschner, Breslin, and Iezzoni 2007; Institute of Medicine Committee on Disability in America 2007). Administrative, financial, and organizational factors exacerbate potential barriers to care, as do reduced appointment times and harried physicians. People with disabilities are not necessarily acutely or even chronically ill (e.g., persons who were born blind or deaf and have no active health problems). Nevertheless, many do have narrow margins of health and need extensive time with their physicians to address complex issues (Burns et al. 1990; Gans, Mann, and Becker 1993; Bockenek et al. 1998). Health insurers, including Medicare, typically provide inadequate coverage of items or services required by people with disabilities, such as maintenance physical therapy, personal assistance services, and assistive technologies (Institute of Medicine Committee on Disability in America 2007, Cassel, Besdine, and Siegel, 1999). Discussing options and developing alternative approaches to meet patients' ongoing needs may require additional time with clinicians.

Little work has examined whether persons with specific sensory and physical impairments are receiving patient-centered care (i.e., whether they believe that their care is meeting their expectations and needs). Here, we examine results from the Medicare Current Beneficiary Survey (MCBS), which asks respondents twenty questions about their health care experiences. These questions encompass the technical and interpersonal aspects of care, (Donabedian 1980), as well as measures of access to care. Each dimension holds special implications for persons with visual, hearing, and physical impairments.

14.1 Methods

14.1.1 Database

We examined responses from 15,056 community-dwelling (noninstitutionalized) Medicare beneficiaries interviewed in the 2001 MCBS. As described elsewhere, (Adler 1994, 1995), the MCBS is an ongoing, longitudinal survey of a representative panel of Medicare beneficiaries, with an oversampling of persons under age sixty-five and eighty-five years of age and older. We eliminated persons receiving Medicare under the end stage renal disease entitlement (less than 1 percent of respondents).

Persons typically remain empaneled in the MCBS for four years, with the sample replenished annually (e.g., to replace respondents who died). The MCBS interviews panel members or their proxies in-person three times yearly, tracking participants wherever they reside and using two types of surveys: computer-assisted community questionnaires for persons living in the community, and facility questionnaires for respondents in long-term care or institutional settings. With the facility questionnaire, interviewers query administrators or designated staff, not the Medicare beneficiary, and therefore do not address respondents' perceptions of care. We used results only from the MCBS community survey, which included questions about demographic characteristics, health status and functioning, perceptions of care, and usual source of care. We considered both self- and proxy-reported responses. Overall, 8.9 percent of respondents were proxies: among persons under age sixty-five, proxies supplied 15.3 percent of responses; 8.0 percent of persons over sixty-four years of age had proxies.

14.1.2   Disability Indicators

Annually, the MCBS asks about specific sensory and physical abilities (Adler 1994). We used these responses to identify five categories of potential disabilities pertaining to vision, hearing, walking, reaching overhead, and grasping and writing. For each category, we created two levels based on answers about the extent of difficulties, assigning people to the most severe level for which they qualified. The appendix presents our algorithm for assigning disability categories based on survey responses.

14.1.3   Perceptions of Care

The September–December round of the MCBS includes supplemental surveys on experiences with and perceptions of respondents' usual source of care. Tables 14.2 through 14.4 show the language used in asking about twenty different aspects of care. Questions typically had four response options: strongly agree, agree, disagree, and strongly disagree. We grouped agree and strongly agree responses (likewise disagree and strongly disagree responses). The directionality of the questions varied. Agreement sometimes suggested poor experiences and sometimes good care. We modeled responses bearing negative connotations.

14.1.4   Analyses

All findings employed MCBS sampling weights to produce nationally representative Medicare population estimates. Our analyses used Stata (version 8.2, College Station, Texas).

We used direct standardization methods to adjust for age using seven groupings (eighteen to forty-four, forty-five to sixty-four, sixty-five to sixty-nine, seventy to seventy-four, seventy-five to seventy-nine, eighty to eighty-four, and eighty-five years and over) and sex. For each disability category and each quality dimension, we produced multivariable logistic regression models predicting negative perceptions of care based on: age group, sex, race, ethnicity, residence location (urban versus rural), education (high school or less versus more than high school), household income ($< \$25,000$

and $25,000+), managed care participation, having a specific physician, and proxy respondent. This model adjusts for patient and organizational attributes that could affect perceptions of care to isolate the contributions of disability. We report adjusted odds ratios with 95 percent confidence intervals (CI).

In prior work using the 1996 MCBS, we produced separate multivariable models for persons age sixty-five years and above and younger than sixty-five (Iezzoni et al. 2003). We failed to find consistent, important differences by these broad age groups, although in some instances a nonsignificant trend suggested that younger persons were less satisfied than older persons. Here, we present results from the models combining elderly and younger respondents. Only 92 MCBS respondents reported being blind; because results from this group are statistically unstable, we present results from persons reporting very low vision (1,457 respondents). For brevity in the other impairment categories, we show results only for the most disabled groups. Although generally trends were apparent (i.e., rates of dissatisfaction rose with increasing severity of impairment), this did not always occur across the twenty questions.

14.2   Results

Of an estimated 35.28 million noninstitutionalized Medicare beneficiaries in 2001, 65.6 percent (estimated 23.08 million) reported at least one of five disabling conditions (table 14.1). Among people under age sixty-five (12.8 percent of noninstitutionalized Medicare beneficiaries or 4.52 million), 75.4 percent (estimated 3.31 million) noted at least one of the five disabling conditions.

Among persons over age sixty-five, those with more severe impairments were generally older, on average, than people with less severe limitations (table 14.2). After adjusting for age, higher percentages of women than men typically reported impairments; hearing difficulties was the major exception, where men reported much higher rates than women. After adjusting for age and sex, higher percentages of black than white persons reported all impairments except hearing difficulties. Adjusted percents for Hispanic persons and people of other races varied by disabling condition. Persons with impairments were more likely than others to have only a high school education and annual incomes under $25,000.

Across the five disability categories, from 81.5 percent to 92.8 percent of persons younger than age sixty-five reported having a usual physician (table 14.1). Thus, roughly 10 percent to 20 percent of these younger individuals did not have a usual doctor. Fewer persons older than age sixty-four reported being without a usual physician. Even so, just over 6 percent of older persons with any major disability lacked a usual doctor.

le 14.1   **Population estimates of disabling conditions and having a specific physician**

abling condition	Population estimates millions (population %)[a]			Has a specific physician (%)[b]	
	All	Age < 65	Age 65 +	Age < 65	Age 65+
beneficiaries regardless of presence of disabling condition	35.28	4.52	30.76	87.3	
·on					
·lind	0.19 (0.5)	0.04 (1.0)	0.14 (0.5)	81.5	96.4
·ery low vision	3.16 (9.0)	0.57 (12.7)	2.59 (8.4)	88.8	92.9
·ring					
)eaf/very hard of hearing	2.78 (7.9)	0.28 (6.2)	2.50 (8.1)	88.9	92.4
lard of hearing	12.41 (35.3)	1.21 (26.8)	11.2 (36.5)	89.1	93.2
·king					
·lajor difficulties	6.32 (18.0)	1.22 (27.1)	5.10 (16.6)	92.8	95.0
·loderate difficulties	5.83 (16.6)	1.31 (29.2)	4.52 (14.7)	90.2	92.7
·ching overhead					
·lajor difficulties	3.65 (10.4)	0.96 (21.4)	2.69 (8.8)	92.8	94.7
·loderate difficulties	2.75 (7.8)	0.68 (15.1)	2.07 (6.8)	89.4	94.5
·sping and writing					
·lajor difficulties	2.46 (7.0)	0.72 (15.9)	1.74 (7.3)	90.4	94.0
·loderate difficulties	2.94 (8.3)	0.68 (15.2)	2.25 (5.7)	91.6	93.8
·ne of the 5 disabilities	12.15 (34.5)	1.11 (24.6)	11.04 (35.9)	80.8	90.7
·east one major disability	10.35 (29.4)	2.08 (46.0)	8.27 (26.9)	91.5	93.9

·rce: 2001 Medicare Current Beneficiary Survey.

·weighted population estimates for Medicare beneficiaries, excluding those qualifying because of end-·e renal disease.

·cent adjusted for population weights but not standardized by age and sex.

14.2.1   Perceptions of Health Care Access and Quality

Tables 14.3 through 14.5 show percents (adjusted for age and sex using direct standardization) reporting negative views of various aspects of their care. Table 14.3 examines concerns about costs and access to care: more than 20 percent of persons with major disabilities are dissatisfied with their out-of-pocket costs, compared with 11.8 percent of persons without any of the five impairments. Rates of dissatisfaction for these other cost and access dimensions among persons with major disabilities are two- to three-fold those reported by persons without disability. Table 14.4 addresses perceptions of technical aspects of care. Although persons with major disabilities report higher rates of dissatisfaction along these dimensions, the vast majority of persons report few concerns, with only 1 to 3 percent of persons questioning their doctor's competence and training. The most problematic area involved concerns that the patient has health problems

Table 14.2   Demographic characteristics by disabling condition

Condition	Mean age in years		Demographic characteristic (adjusted %)[a]					
	< 65	65 +	Men	Women	White	Black	Hispanic	Other ra
Vision								
Blind	49.2	80.5	0.7	0.5	0.6	0.7	0.6	0.4
Very low vision	52.3	78.1	8.3	10.5	9.2	9.9	13.3	10.2
Hearing								
Deaf/very hard of hearing	53.1	78.6	11.3	6.3	8.7	5.5	8.3	9.6
Hard of hearing	53.0	76.3	40.7	31.4	37.4	27.7	23.3	34.5
Walking								
Major difficulties	53.3	78.4	15.5	21.5	19.1	23.2	16.3	18.5
Moderate difficulties	52.1	76.6	15.8	18.4	16.6	18.7	20.7	18.2
Reaching overhead								
Major difficulties	53.2	77.2	9.3	12.0	10.6	11.6	11.9	11.3
Moderate difficulties	53.0	76.6	7.0	8.9	7.9	10.4	8.7	8.6
Grasping and writing								
Major difficulties	52.8	77.1	7.0	7.9	7.5	7.8	8.5	8.4
Moderate difficulties	52.6	78.2	8.3	9.0	8.6	10.3	8.6	8.5
None of the 5 disabilities	46.4	73.3	31.2	34.5	32.0	36.6	39.2	35.2
At least one major disability	52.8	77.7	29.4	32.0	31.2	30.8	29.0	32.2

Source: 2001 Medicare Current Beneficiary Survey.
[a] Reweighted population percents. Figures by sex, adjusted by age group (18–44, 45–64, 65–69, 70–75–79, 80–84, and 85+ years). Figures by race and ethnicity adjust for age group and sex using dir standardization.

that should be discussed but are not, with up to 15 percent of persons with major disabilities reporting dissatisfaction.

Interpersonal aspects of care also generated concerns among persons with major disabilities (table 14.5). Nearly 20 percent view their doctor as seeming in a hurry, and almost 15 percent report that their doctor often does not explain medical problems. Nonetheless, less than 10 percent note that their doctor fails to answer all their questions.

Various demographic factors likely influence perceptions of care. Table 14.6 therefore presents odds ratios for being dissatisfied with various aspects of care, after adjusting for demographic characteristics and other attributes. Being without the specific impairment serves as the reference group for each adjusted odds ratio. Virtually every adjusted odds ratio is highly statistically significant (the exception involves the question about physician competence and training). Having any major impairment is associated with adjusted odds ratios generally greater than 2.0, with several surpassing 3.0. Several questions generated especially high adjusted odds ratios across the impairment categories, including: ease of getting to the

Table 14.3   **Concerns about costs and accessing care (%)[a]**

Aspect of care	No DA	Very low vision	Deaf/ HOH	Major difficulties		
				Walking	Reaching	Manual dexterity
Out-of-pocket costs paid for medical services[b]	11.8	21.0	21.4	22.2	23.3	23.1
Ease and convenience of getting to a doctor from where person lives	2.9	12.1	10.8	10.6	11.0	12.3
Getting all medical care needs taken care of at the same location	3.4	10.3	7.8	8.6	9.6	11.4
Availability of medical services at night and on weekends	4.1	11.0	12.4	9.4	10.7	12.7
Ease of obtaining answers to questions over the telephone about treatment or prescriptions	6.2	12.0	12.5	11.9	13.7	14.0

Source: 2001 Medicare Current Beneficiary Survey.
Note: No DA = none of the 5 disabling conditions; HOH = very hard of hearing.
[a] Percent very or somewhat dissatisfied, adjusted for age category and sex using direct standardization.
[b] Phrasing of questions in MCBS.

doctor, having health problems that are not discussed, receiving follow-up care, perceptions that the doctor cares about the patient's overall health, doctors answering all the patient's questions, and concerns about overall quality of care.

14.3   Discussion

The vast majority of Medicare beneficiaries with and without disabilities perceive their physicians as competent and well-trained and hold favorable views of their overall quality of care. Along most other dimensions of care, 80 percent to 90 percent of persons report satisfaction, regardless of disability. However, after accounting for various demographic and other respondent attributes, Medicare beneficiaries with major sensory and physical disabilities are significantly more likely to be dissatisfied with the care they receive, including difficulties accessing care, perceived incomplete understanding by physicians of patients' clinical histories and conditions, lack of thoroughness, and inadequate communication. People with disabilities are also much more likely than others to lack confidence in their doctors. These findings held across disabling conditions.

Given the breadth of quality concerns, devising strategies to improve the

Table 14.4   Concerns about technical aspects of care (%)[a]

				Major difficulties		
Aspect of care	No DA	Very low vision	Deaf/ HOH	Walking	Reaching	Manual dexterity
Doctor is competent and well-trained	1.0	1.6	2.6	1.5	1.6	2.3
Doctor is very careful to check everything when examining you	4.9	7.8	9.1	9.0	9.7	10.6
Doctor has a good understanding of your medical history	3.1	6.3	6.5	5.4	5.8	8.2
Doctor has a complete understanding of the things that are wrong with you	4.8	8.4	7.0	7.5	7.4	10.7
Often has health problems that should be discussed but are not	5.5	11.5	13.9	12.6	14.2	15.4
Availability of care by specialists when needs it	2.8	8.3	7.5	6.8	8.1	8.8
Follow-up care received after an initial treatment or operation	2.4	7.2	6.2	6.7	6.6	7.3
Has great confidence in doctor	4.0	7.8	8.7	7.9	7.6	8.3
Overall quality of the medical services received in the last year	2.6	8.3	8.7	7.7	7.6	9.3

Source: 2001 Medicare Current Beneficiary Survey.

Note: No DA = none of the 5 disabling conditions; HOH = very hard of hearing.

[a]Percent very or somewhat dissatisfied, adjusted for age category and sex using direct standardization.

experiences of patients with disabilities requires careful thought. The fact that persons with disabilities have, on average, lower incomes and educational attainment than do others will likely complicate efforts to relieve their concerns about accessing care and out-of-pocket medical expenses. Making getting to their doctor easier also poses important challenges. Many individuals with disabilities cannot drive, do not own cars, cannot afford taxis, or do not have family or friends who can easily take them to their physicians' offices. Medicaid sometimes covers transportation expenses (e.g., taxi fares) to medical appointments, but Medicare does not.

Concerns related to communication and time might be interwoven, offering opportunities for improvement. Although people with disabilities feel their physicians are competent, they are simultaneously less satisfied

ble 14.5   Concerns about interpersonal aspects of care (%)[a]

Aspect of care	No DA	Very low vision	Deaf/ HOH	Walking	Reaching	Manual dexterity
				Major difficulties		
Concern of doctors for overall health rather than just for an isolated symptom of disease	3.5	9.7	8.8	8.2	9.9	10.1
Doctor often seems to be in a hurry	12.9	17.6	19.8	18.1	18.3	20.1
Doctor often does not explain medical problems	7.4	11.8	12.9	12.7	13.4	15.1
Doctor often acts as though doing you a favor by talking to you	4.9	7.2	8.4	6.6	8.5	9.7
Doctor tells all you want to know about your condition and treatment	6.4	10.5	11.0	9.9	11.7	13.2
Doctor answers all your questions	2.9	5.4	6.8	5.8	6.5	7.7

Source: 2001 Medicare Current Beneficiary Survey.

Note: No DA = none of the 5 disabling conditions; HOH = very hard of hearing.

[a] Percent very or somewhat dissatisfied, adjusted for age category and sex using direct standardization; for "favor" question, percent who completely or somewhat agree.

with their physicians' thoroughness and communication. These latter issues may not reflect reservations about physicians' technical competence, but instead connote worries that physicians do not take the time required to both understand fully patients' clinical concerns and communicate effectively. Although numerous patients, regardless of disability, view physicians as hurried, persons with disabilities and significant health problems may face special risks from time constraints.

Many persons, especially with major disabilities, likely require more time for an average visit than do other patients. Four factors may contribute to extra time demands: complex underlying medical conditions; extra knowledge, skill, sensitivity, or time required by clinicians because of the disabling condition itself; the need to employ special means to ensure effective communication, such as sign language interpreters or assistive listening devices; and discordant perceptions and expectations between physicians and patients, especially around the experience of disability. Examples include informing blind persons about actions during the physical examination or discussing treatment plans with a deaf person through a sign language interpreter (Iezzoni et al. 2003; O'Day, Killeen, and Iezzoni

Table 14.6   Adjusted odds ratios for being dissatisfied with various aspects of care (95%CI)

Aspect of care	Very low vision	Deaf/HOH[a]	Major difficulties Walking	Reaching	Manual dexterity	Any major
Costs and access to care						
Out-of-pocket costs	1.4 (1.2, 1.6)	1.6 (1.4, 2.0)	1.8 (1.6, 2.0)	1.7 (1.5, 2.0)	1.7 (1.4, 2.0)	2.1 (1.8, 2.4)
Ease of getting to doctor	2.1 (1.7, 2.6)	2.1 (1.6, 2.7)	3.0 (2.4, 3.6)	2.2 (1.8, 2.8)	2.4 (1.9, 3.1)	3.8 (3.0, 4.9)
All care at same location	1.9 (1.4, 2.6)	1.8 (1.4, 2.4)	2.4 (1.9, 3.1)	2.2 (1.8, 2.6)	2.6 (2.1, 3.3)	3.1 (2.5, 4.0)
Availability off-hours	1.7 (1.2, 2.3)	2.2 (1.6, 2.9)	1.8 (1.4, 2.3)	1.8 (1.4, 2.3)	2.0 (1.5, 2.6)	2.6 (2.0, 3.3)
Ease of telephone communication	1.4 (1.1, 1.8)	2.0 (1.6, 2.5)	1.9 (1.6, 2.4)	1.9 (1.5, 2.4)	2.0 (1.4, 2.7)	2.3 (1.9, 2.9)
Technical care						
Doctor competent	1.3 (0.7, 2.2)	2.4 (1.4, 4.0)	1.4 (0.9, 2.4)	1.4 (0.9, 2.2)	2.4 (1.5, 3.9)	2.5 (1.6, 3.9)
Doctor checks everything during exam	1.3 (1.0, 1.6)	1.6 (1.2, 2.0)	1.7 (1.4, 2.0)	1.6 (1.3, 1.9)	1.8 (1.5, 2.2)	2.0 (1.6, 2.4)
Doctor understands medical history	1.4 (1.1, 1.9)	1.6 (1.2, 2.2)	1.6 (1.3, 2.1)	1.5 (1.2, 1.9)	2.3 (1.7, 3.1)	2.2 (1.7, 2.8)
Doctor understands what is wrong	1.4 (1.1, 1.8)	1.4 (1.1, 1.8)	1.5 (1.2, 2.0)	1.4 (1.1, 1.8)	2.1 (1.6, 2.8)	1.9 (1.5, 2.4)
Has health problems that are not discussed	1.4 (1.2, 1.8)	2.2 (1.7, 2.8)	2.2 (1.8, 2.7)	2.0 (1.6, 2.4)	2.2 (1.8, 2.7)	2.6 (2.1, 3.1)
Availability of specialists	1.9 (1.4, 2.5)	1.8 (1.4, 2.4)	2.1 (1.6, 2.7)	2.1 (1.6, 2.7)	2.5 (1.9, 3.4)	2.7 (2.1, 3.5)
Follow-up care received	2.0 (1.4, 2.9)	2.0 (1.4, 2.8)	2.7 (2.1, 3.5)	1.9 (1.5, 2.5)	2.1 (1.6, 2.9)	2.8 (2.2, 3.7)
Has confidence in doctor	1.5 (1.2, 1.9)	1.8 (1.3, 2.4)	1.8 (1.5, 2.3)	1.4 (1.1, 1.8)	1.6 (1.2, 2.1)	2.2 (1.8, 2.8)
Overall quality of care	1.9 (1.4, 2.6)	2.3 (1.7, 3.2)	2.8 (2.2, 3.5)	2.0 (1.7, 2.5)	2.4 (1.9, 3.1)	3.3 (2.6, 4.2)
Interpersonal care						
Doctor concerned about overall health	1.7 (1.3, 2.3)	2.1 (1.6, 2.7)	2.2 (1.8, 2.7)	2.2 (1.8, 2.7)	2.4 (1.8, 3.1)	2.8 (2.2, 3.5)
Doctor often in hurry	1.2 (1.0, 1.4)	1.5 (1.3, 1.8)	1.4 (1.2, 1.6)	1.3 (1.1, 1.6)	1.5 (1.3, 1.8)	1.5 (1.3, 1.8)
Doctor does not explain things	1.2 (1.0, 1.4)	1.5 (1.2, 1.9)	1.7 (1.4, 2.1)	1.6 (1.4, 1.9)	1.7 (1.4, 2.1)	1.8 (1.5, 2.1)
Doctor acts as if doing you favor	1.2 (1.0, 1.5)	1.7 (1.3, 2.3)	1.3 (1.0, 1.6)	1.5 (1.2, 1.9)	1.8 (1.5, 2.3)	1.6 (1.3, 2.0)
Doctor tells you all you want to know	1.4 (1.1, 1.7)	1.6 (1.2, 2.0)	1.6 (1.3, 1.9)	1.7 (1.4, 2.0)	1.8 (1.5, 2.3)	1.8 (1.5, 2.1)
Doctor answers all questions	1.6 (1.2, 2.1)	2.0 (1.5, 2.7)	2.3 (1.7, 3.0)	2.2 (1.7, 2.8)	2.4 (1.8, 3.4)	2.4 (1.8, 3.1)

Source: 2001 Medicare Current Beneficiary Survey.

Note: Reference group is persons without the particular condition. Adjustment accounts for: age group, sex, race, ethnicity, residence location (urban versus rural), education (high school or less versus more than high school), household income (< $25 000 and $25,000+), managed care participation, having a spe-

2004; Iezzoni and O'Day 2006). Positioning people with extensive mobility limitations on examination tables generally takes more time than required for other patients.

Studies suggest that patients with longer visits report greater satisfaction than those with shorter appointments (Lin et al. 2001; Gross et al. 1998; Greene et al. 1994). However, persons with substantial health problems generally report less satisfaction with medical care than healthier individuals, possibly because they feel their needs are not fully met (Schlesinger, Druss, and Thomas 1999; Druss et al. 2000). Evidence concerning whether visit lengths have diminished in recent years and the relationship between time spent and managed care insurance remains controversial (Mechanic, McAlpine, and Rosenthal 2001). Nevertheless, average office visits last less than twenty minutes, which is unlikely to offer sufficient time for accommodating persons with significant disabilities and addressing all their health concerns.

Our results support the ideas offered by Wagner and colleagues, who examined the research evidence from the United States and Europe about improving health care outcomes for persons with chronic conditions (Wagner, Austin, and Von Korff 1996; Wagner et al. 2001). Providing complete information was one of four essential elements when designing systems of care, as were practice redesign, patient education, and expert systems (e.g., provider education, consultations). Other investigators have found that patients greatly value communication, respect, and being involved in decision making (Gerteis, Edgman-Levitan, Daley et al. 1993; Cleary et al. 1991; Gerteis, Edgman-Levitan, Walker et al. 1993). Patients who report that their physicians do not always take enough time to answer questions or do not provide sufficient information are likely to consider changing physicians (Keating et al. 2002).

For people with disabilities, many and varied structural accommodations are important to ensure delivery of patient-centered, high-quality care (Institute of Medicine Committee on Disability in America 2007). Some involve removing environmental barriers (e.g., by installing ramps, widened doorways, and automatically-adjustable examination tables [Iezzoni and O'Day 2006; Kirschner, Breslin, and Iezzoni 2007]), while others represent essential tools (e.g., large print and Braille written materials and readily available sign language interpreters [Iezzoni et al. 2003; O'Day, Killeen, and Iezzoni 2004; Iezzoni and O'Day 2006]), and yet others reflect practice policies (e.g., scheduling longer appointment times). Strategies may reach beyond individual practices to the broader health care system, including paying more for routine visits of persons needing interpreters or special physical accommodations.

Our study has important limitations. Although the MCBS offers relatively rich insights about the perceptions of Medicare beneficiaries about their care, the information about specific impairments is limited to self-reports. The MCBS does not inquire about critical disabling conditions, notably mental health disorders, developmental disabilities, and cognitive deficits. We could categorize disability only along sensory and physical impairments, although many persons younger than age sixty-five become eligible for disability because of psychiatric conditions. The use of proxy respondents further complicates interpretation of findings, although research offers contradictory evidence about the direction of potential bias (Iezzoni et al. 2000b; Todorov and Kirchner 2000; Epstein et al. 1989; Rothman et al. 1991; Dorevitch et al. 1992). The MCBS does not indicate the extent of respondents' acute and chronic underlying disease, nor how long they spent with physicians during office visits. Therefore, we could not directly test the hypothesis that disabled patients are especially susceptible to time constraints. Despite these limitations, the MCBS asks more extensive questions about patients' perceptions of care than do most other national surveys.

Reports suggest that rates of disability among older individuals fell substantially during the 1990s (Freedman, Martin, and Schoeni 2002). Multiple factors likely produced improved functional abilities among older persons, including new medical therapies and healthier lifestyles (e.g., decreased smoking). Nonetheless, with the aging population, the absolute number of Americans with functional limitations will rise over 300 percent by 2049 if the age-specific prevalence of major chronic conditions remains unchanged (Boult et al. 1996). The health care system continues to pose significant barriers to obtaining high quality care among persons with disabilities (Institute of Medicine Committee on Disability in America 2007), and our findings from the MCBS suggest that Medicare beneficiaries with sensory and physical impairments are less satisfied with important aspects of their health care than are their nondisabled counterparts. With growing numbers of Medicare beneficiaries with these functional deficits, considering ways to improve their health care experiences will become increasingly pressing in coming decades.

Appendix

Table 14A.1   Questions and Responses From the MCBS to Define Disabling Conditions

Disability questions and responses from the MCBS

Vision
Do you wear eyeglasses or contact lenses? (yes, no, blind)
Which statement best describes your vision (wearing glasses/contact lenses)

Blind	Blind on eyeglasses/contact lens question
Very low vision	A lot of trouble (on vision question)

Hearing
Do you use a hearing aid? (yes, no, deaf)
Which statement best describes your hearing (even with a hearing aid)?

Deaf/very hard of hearing	Deaf on hearing aid question or a lot of trouble (on hearing question)
Hard of hearing	Uses hearing aid or has a little trouble hearing

Walking
How much difficulty to you have walking a quarter of a mile (2 or 3 blocks)
Because of a health or physical problem do you have any difficulty walking by yourself and without special equipment?

Major difficulties	Unable to walk 2–3 blocks or doesn't walk by self without special equipment
Moderate difficulties	A lot of difficulty walking 2–3 blocks or difficulty walking by self without equipment

Reaching overhead
How much difficulty do you have reaching or extending your arms above shoulder level?

Major difficulties	Reports being unable to do or having a lot of difficulty reaching
Moderate difficulties	Reports some difficulty reaching

Grasping and writing
How much difficulty do you have either writing or handling and grasping small objects?

Major difficulties	Reports being unable to do or having a lot of difficulty with hands
Moderate difficulties	Reports some difficulty with hands

References

Adler, G. S. 1994. A profile of the Medicare current beneficiary survey. *Health Care Finance Review* 15 (4): 153–63.

———. 1995. Medicare beneficiaries rate their medical care: New data from the MCBS (Medicare Current Beneficiary Survey). *Health Care Finance Review* 16 (4): 175–87.

Andriacchi, R. 1997. Primary care for persons with disabilities. The internal medicine perspective. *American Journal Physical Medicine and Rehabilitation* 76 (3): S17–20.

Berwick, D. M. 2002. A user's manual for the IOM's "Quality Chasm" Report. *Health Affairs* 21 (3): 80–90.

Bockenek, W. L., N. Mann, I. S. Lanig, G. DeJong, and L. A. Beatty. 1998. Primary care for persons with disabilities. In *Rehabilitation medicine: Principles and practice*, Joel A. DeLisa and Bruce M. Gans, eds. Philadelphia, PA: Lippincott-Raven. 905–928.

Boult, C., M. Altmann, D. Gilbertson, C. Yu, and R. L. Kane. 1996. Decreasing disability in the 21st century: The future effects of controlling six fatal and non-fatal conditions. *American Journal of Public Health* 86 (10): 1388–93.

Burns, T. J., A. I. Batavia, Q. W. Smith, and G. DeJong. 1990. Primary health care needs of persons with physical disabilities: What are the research and service priorities? *Archives of Physical Medicine and Rehabilitation* 71:138–43.

Cassel, C. K., R. W. Besdine, and L. C. Siegel. 1999. Restructuring Medicare for the next century: What will beneficiaries really need? *Health Affairs* 18 (1): 118–31.

Chan, L., J. N. Doctor, R. F. MacLehose, H. Lawson, R. A. Rosenblatt, L.-M. Baldwin, and A. Jha. 1999. Do Medicare patients with disabilities receive preventive services? A population-based study. *Archives of Physical Medicine and Rehabilitation* 80 (6): 642–46.

Cleary, P. D., S. Edgman-Levitan, M. Roberts, T. W. Moloney, W. McMullen, J. D. Walker, and T. L. Delbanco. 1991. Patients evaluate their hospital care: A national survey. *Health Affairs* 10 (4): 254–67.

Donabedian, A. 1980. *Explorations in quality assessment and monitoring.* Ann Arbor, MI: Health Administration Press.

Dorevitch, M. I., R. M. Cossar, F. J. Bailey, T. Bisset, S. J. Lewis, L. A. Wise, and W. J. Maclennan. 1992. The accuracy of self and informant ratings of physical functional capacity in the elderly. *Journal of Clinical Epidemiology* 45 (7): 791–98.

Druss, B. G., M. Schlesinger, T. Thomas, and H. Allen. 2000. Chronic illness and plan satisfaction under managed care. *Health Affairs* 19 (1): 203–9.

Epstein, A. M., J. A. Hall, J. Tognetti, L. H. Son, and L. Conant, Jr. 1989. Using proxies to evaluate quality of life: Can they provide valid information about patients' health status and satisfaction with medical care? *Medical Care* 27 (3): S91–S98.

Freedman, V. A., L. G. Martin, and R. F. Schoeni. 2002. Recent trends in disability and functioning among older adults in the United States: A systematic review. *Journal of the American Medical Association* 288 (24): 3137–46.

Gans, B. M., N. R. Mann, and B. E. Becker. 1993. Delivery of primary care to the physically challenged. *Archives of Physical Medicine and Rehabilitation* 74: S15–S19.

Gerteis, M., S. Edgman-Levitan, J. Daley, and T. L. Delbanco, eds. 1993. *Through the patient's eyes: Understanding and promoting patient-centered care.* San Francisco, CA: Jossey-Bass Publishers, Inc.

Gerteis, M., S. Edgman-Levitan, J. D. Walker, D. M. Stoke, P. D. Cleary, and T. L. Delbanco. 1993. What patients really want. *Health Management Quarterly* 15 (3): 2–6.

Greene, M. G., R. D. Adelman, E. Friedmann, and R. Charon. 1994. Older patient satisfaction with communication during an initial medical encounter. *Social Science and Medicine* 38 (9): 1279–88.

Gross, D. A., S. J. Zyzanski, E. A. Borawski, R. D. Cebul, and K. C. Stange. 1998. Patient satisfaction with time spent with their physician. *Journal of Family Practice* 47:133–37.

Iezzoni, L. I., R. B. Davis, J. Soukup, and B. O'Day. 2002. Satisfaction with quality and access to health care among people with disabling conditions. *International Journal for Quality in Health Care* 14 (5): 369–81.

————— 2003. Quality dimensions that most concern people with physical and sensory disabilities. *Archives of Internal Medicine* 163 (17): 2085–92.

—————. 2004. Physical and sensory functioning over time and satisfaction with care: The implications of getting better or getting worse. *Health Services Research* 39 (6, part 1): 1635–52.

Iezzoni, L. I., M. B. Killeen, and B. L. O'Day. 2006. Rural residents with disabilities confront substantial barriers to obtaining primary care. *Health Services Research* 41 (4): 1258–75.

Iezzoni, L. I., and B. L. O'Day. 2006. *More than ramps: A guide to improving health care quality and access for people with disabilities.* New York: Oxford University Press.

Iezzoni, L. I., B. L. O'Day, M. Killeen, and H. Harker. 2004. Communicating about health care: Observations from persons who are deaf or hard of hearing. *Annals of Internal Medicine* 140 (5): 356–62.

Iezzoni, L. I., E. P. McCarthy, R. B. Davis, L. Harris-David, and B. O'Day. 2001. Use of screening and preventive services among women with disabilities. *American Journal of Medical Quality* 16 (4): 135–44.

Iezzoni, L. I., E. P. McCarthy, R. B. Davis, and H. Siebens. 2000a. Mobility impairments and use of screening and preventive services. *American Journal of Public Health* 90 (6): 955–61.

—————. 2000b. Mobility problems and perceptions of disability by self-respondents and proxy respondents. *Medical Care* 38 (10): 1051–57.

Institute of Medicine Committee on Disability in America. 2007. *The future of disability in America.* Washington, D.C.: National Academies Press.

Institute of Medicine Committee on Quality of Health Care in America. 2001. *Crossing the quality chasm: A new health system for the 21st century.* Washington, D.C.: National Academies Press.

Keating, N. L., D. C. Green, A. C. Kao, J. A. Gazmararian, V. Y. Wu, and P. D. Cleary. 2002. How are patients' specific ambulatory care experiences related to trust, satisfaction, and considering changing physicians? *Journal of General Internal Medicine* 17 (1): 29–39.

Kirschner, K. L., M. L. Breslin, and L. I. Iezzoni. 2007. Structural impairments that limit access to health care for patients with disabilities. *Journal of the American Medical Association* 297 (10): 1121–25.

Lawthers, A. G., G. S. Pransky, L. E. Peterson, and J. H. Himmelstein. 2003. Rethinking quality in the context of persons with disability. *International Journal for Quality in Health Care* 15 (4): 287–99.

Lin, C.-T., G. A. Albertson, L. M. Schilling, E. M. Cyran, S. N. Anderson, L. Ware, and R. J. Anderson. 2001. Is patients' perception of time spent with the physician a determinant of ambulatory patient satisfaction? *Archives of Internal Medicine* 161 (11): 1437–42.

McCarthy, E. P., L. H. Ngo, R. G. Roetzheim, T. N. Chirikos, D. Li, R. E. Drews, and L. I. Iezzoni. 2006. Disparities in breast cancer treatment and survival for women with disabilities. *Annals of Internal Medicine* 145 (9): 637–45.

Mechanic, D., D. D. McAlpine, and M. Rosenthal. 2001. Are patients' office visits with physicians getting shorter? *New England Journal of Medicine* 344 (3): 198–204.

O'Day, B. L., M. B. Killeen, and L. I. Iezzoni. 2004. Improving health care experiences of persons who are blind or have low vision: Suggestions from focus groups. *American Journal of Medical Quality* 19 (5): 193–200.

O'Day, B. L., M. B. Killeen, J. Sutton, and L. I. Iezzoni. 2005. Primary care experiences of people with psychiatric disabilities: Barriers to care and potential solutions. *Psychiatric Rehabilitation Journal* 28 (4): 339–45.

Rosenbach, M. L. 1995. Access and satisfaction within the disabled Medicare population. *Health Care Finance Review* 17 (2): 147–67.

Rosenbach, M. L., K. W. Acamache, and R. K. Khandker. 1995. Variations in Medicare access and satisfaction by health status: 1991–1993. *Health Care Finance Review* 17 (2): 29–49.

Rothman, M. L., S. C. Hedrick, K. A. Bulcroft, D. H. Hickam, and L. Z. Rubenstein. 1991. The validity of proxy-generated scores as measures of patient health status. *Medical Care* 29 (2): 115–24.

Schlesinger, M., B. Druss, and T. Thomas. 1999. No exit? The effect of health status on dissatisfaction and disenrollment from health plans. *Health Services Research* 34 (2): 547–76.

Todorov, A., and C. Kirchner. 2000. Bias in proxies' reports of disability: Data from the National Health Interview Survey on disability. *American Journal of Public Health* 90 (8): 1248–53.

U.S. Department of Health and Human Services. 2000. *Healthy people 2010, vols. 1 and 2, 2nd ed.* Washington, D.C.: Government Printing Office.

———. 2005. The surgeon general's call to action to improve the health and wellness of persons with disabilities. Washington, D.C.: U.S. Department of Health and Human Services, Office of the Surgeon General.

Wagner, E. H., B. T. Austin, and M. Von Korff. 1996. Organizing care for patients with chronic illness. *The Milbank Quarterly* 74 (4): 511–44.

Wagner, E. H., R. E. Glasgow, C. Davis, A. E. Bonomi, L. Provost, D. McCulloch, P. Carver, and C. Sixta. 2001. Quality improvement in chronic illness care: A collaborative approach. *Joint Commission Journal on Quality Improvement* 27 (2): 63–80.

Weil, E., M. Wachterman, E. P. McCarthy, R. B. Davis, B. O'Day, L. I. Iezzoni, and C. C. Wee. 2002. Obesity among adults with disabling conditions. *Journal of the American Medical Association* 288 (10): 1265–68.

15

Inter-Spousal Mortality Effects
Caregiver Burden Across the Spectrum of Disabling Disease

Nicholas A. Christakis and Paul D. Allison

The health of two people connected by a social tie may be interdependent. The impact of the *death* of one spouse on the risk of death of the other, known as the widow/er effect, is a classic example (Parkes and Fitzgerald 1969; Lillard and Waite 1995; Martikainen and Valkonen 1996a; and Schaefer, Quesenberry, and Soora 1995). The impact of *illness* in one spouse on the risk of ill health or death in the other spouse (the proband under study), is another example. This latter phenomenon, often termed caregiver burden, is typically studied as if it were unrelated to the widower effect (Clipp and George 1993; Dunkin and Anderson-Hanley 1998; Shaw et al. 1997; Schulz et al. 2003)—as if ill health in a spouse affects the morbidity, but not necessarily the mortality, of caregiving probands.

Indeed, most prior work on caregiver burden has focused on how spousal illness worsens the health of probands, but not on whether it increases their mortality, with the exception of one influential study that suggested that caregiving to dementia patients was a risk factor for death (Schulz and Beach 1999). Moreover, comparisons across different types of spousal diseases, in terms of how they may affect caregiver health, are lacking. Some studies have found that worse physical health in a spouse is

Nicholas A. Christakis is a Professor in the Departments of Health Care Policy and of Sociology at Harvard University, and an attending physician at Massachusetts General Hospital. Paul D. Allison is a Professor in the Department of Sociology at the University of Pennsylvania.

The authors thank Laurie Meneades for the expert data programming required to build the analytic data set and Felix Elwert for statistical programming and for comments on the manuscript. We also thank participants in the NBER Disability Workshop for helpful feedback. We are grateful for financial support from the National Institute on Aging grants P30 AG12810 and R01 AG19805, and the Mary Woodard Lasker Charitable Trust and Michael E. DeBakey Foundation.

linked to worse physical health in the proband, perhaps due to greater caregiving demand (Clipp and George 1993; Shaw et al. 1997; Pruchno and Resch 1989). Poor mental health in the spouse also appears to adversely influence the physical health of the caregiver (Zarit et al. 1986; Barusch and Spaid 1989; Pruchno and Resch 1989; Scholte op Reimer et al. 1998; Shaw et al. 1997). Indeed, it has been suggested that mental impairment in the patient may induce more caregiver burden than physical impairment. Very few studies, however, compare diseases in terms of the health consequences they impose on caregivers (Clipp and George 1993; Dura, Haywood-Niler, and Kiecolt-Glaser 1990).

Prior work on the widower and caregiver effects has suffered from a variety of further limitations that have complicated efforts to understand the effect on a proband's mortality risk of having a spouse fall ill or die. First, there is the challenge of separating the impact of spousal illness on proband death from the impact of spousal death on proband death; that is, we are interested in understanding how spousal illness itself, whether accompanied by subsequent spousal death or not, affects proband health.

Second, there is the problem of confounding. That is, if one spouse falls ill or dies, the next one may also fall ill or die, but not because the latter spouse is affected by caring for the first spouse. Rather, the second may fall ill because the two spouses share some traits that determined the health outcomes of both. Illness or death of one spouse could be associated with the death of the other because of (a) a common accident, (b) shared environmental exposures (such as environmental toxins, poor dietary practices, or poverty), or (c) selection because of assortative mating (e.g., the tendency of the unhealthy to marry the unhealthy). This problem, which is typically overlooked in studies of caregiver burden, requires special statistical methods and data to be addressed.

Third, prior work on the caregiver burden has typically focused on outcomes at a single point in time. But the effect of having a spouse fall ill might vary across time. The health consequences of being in the caregiving role might be demonstrably worse for probands at particular points in time after the occurrence of spousal illness.

Our work addresses the foregoing concerns, using data and methods that allow us to investigate caregiver mortality effects across the spectrum of disease and across time in the caregiving role. In addition, our study uses a reliable measure of caregiver burden (i.e., the risk of death) and a large, nationally representative sample with very long follow-up. We hypothesize that being in a caregiving role will: increase the mortality risk of probands; that this effect will be distinct from the effect of being widowed; that this effect will vary in patterned ways across different spousal illnesses; and that, moreover, this effect will depend upon the amount of time the proband is in the caregiving role.

15.1 Methods

15.1.1 Data

To assemble a suitably large, population-based inception cohort of elderly couples with sufficient temporal and diagnostic detail and with sufficient follow-up, we extracted and linked raw Medicare claims at an individual level (Lauderdale et al. 1993; Mitchell et al. 1994). In the first step of data development, all Medicare beneficiaries older than sixty-five as of January 1, 1993, as noted in the so-called Denominator File, were examined and subjected to a spousal identification algorithm (Iwashyna et al. 1998; Iwashyna et al. 2002). Notably, the Denominator File, which contains all Medicare beneficiaries, consequently captures 96 percent of all Americans older than sixty-five (Hatten 1980). We estimate that, among the 32,180,588 elderly people in this file, there are 6.6 million elderly couples where both partners are older than sixty-five, and we detected 5,496,444 (83 percent) of them. Of these, 4,874,817 were couples where both parties were sixty-five to ninety-eight years old and resided in the fifty states. From this group, we chose a simple random sample of 540,793 couples identified with one of two methods of detection (Iwashyna et al. 1998). The Denominator file provides demographic information (e.g., age, sex). A separate Vital Status file gives precise death dates, here censored at January 1, 2002. As a marker for co-residence, we observed whether both members of each couple had an address within the same zip code; 4.2 percent of the couples ($N = 22,553$) lived in different zip codes, and we excluded these couples from further analysis, leaving an analytic sample of 518,240.

Using so-called MEDPAR records for 1993–2002, we obtained the dates of all hospitalizations and also the reasons for hospital admission in the form of ICD-9 diagnostic codes. That is, we measured the occurrence of a serious disease in spouses during the follow-up period by using the principal diagnosis noted on inpatient claims, as categorized by using a 49-category indicator variable based on a Centers for Disease Control and Prevention (CDC) taxonomy of ICD-9 codes used in hospitalizations (Hall and DeFrances 2003). In the present analyses, for parsimony, the diagnoses were collapsed into sixteen categories, as shown in table 15.1. Other analyses (not shown here) using the 49-category system did not yield different results.

By using hospitalization claims, it is possible to detect the occurrence of serious diseases at least as accurately as asking people directly (Zhang, Iwashyna, and Christakis 1999). Given the seriousness of the diagnoses at hand (e.g., sepsis, stroke, Myocardial Infarction [MI], lung cancer, abdominal surgery, etc.), and given prior work on using hospitalizations to detect disease incidence, we used hospitalization as a marker for the occurrence of

Table 15.1   Percentage of spouses and probands dying within a year of spousal hospitalization, by condition, separately for husbands and wives

Wife's diagnosis	Number of couples with this disease occurring in the wife	Percentage of husbands dead within one year of the wife's diagnosis	Percentage of wives dead within one year of the wife's diagnosis
Sepsis	3,971	7.38	27.73
Pneumonia	15,884	7.17	17.92
Colon cancer	5,056	6.39	19.44
Pancreas cancer	641	6.86	80.97
Lung cancer	2,416	5.55	55.09
Leukemia or Lymphoma	1,538	7.54	52.93
All Other Malignancies	18,158	5.06	27.57
Stroke	24,674	6.90	18.59
Dementia	2,642	8.55	21.23
Psychiatric disease	4,893	7.50	7.26
Ischemic heart disease	30,188	6.19	13.39
Congestive heart failure	13,261	7.46	25.60
COPD	8,335	6.37	13.95
Abdominal surgical disease	27,042	6.29	8.02
Hip and serious fractures	18,087	8.59	12.63
All other diagnoses	170,483	5.91	9.76
Total	347,269	6.33	13.76

Husband's diagnosis	Number of couples with this disease occurring in the husband	Percentage of wives dead within one year of the husband's diagnosis	Percentage of husbands dead within one year of the husband's diagnosis
Sepsis	5,022	4.04	34.87
Pneumonia	23,594	4.51	30.23
Colon cancer	6,559	2.99	23.65
Pancreas cancer	678	3.54	82.01
Lung cancer	4,329	3.44	66.20
Leukemia or Lymphoma	2,121	3.35	65.11
All other malignancies	21,263	2.82	36.66
Stroke	31,471	3.65	22.73
Dementia	3,348	4.99	37.81
Psychiatric disease	2,666	5.74	19.50
Ischemic heart disease	50,596	2.94	15.89
Congestive heart failure	18,644	4.25	34.47
COPD	9,532	4.12	24.12
Abdominal surgical disease	26,623	3.46	12.81
Hip and serious fractures	9,800	5.09	28.10
All other diagnoses	167,234	3.39	17.22
Total	383,480	3.53	21.83

the diagnoses of interest. Of course, in some cases, the disease in question could have been noted prior to the time of hospitalization during the follow-up period (e.g., during outpatient visits), but we nevertheless regard hospitalization as a marker for a particularly burdensome stage of the diseases in question. We treated the date of first hospital admission during the time period after January 1, 1993 as the anchoring date of disease occurrence for the purpose of assessing impact of spousal illness on probands. Each person in each couple in our cohort could have multiple hospitalizations (though most, 60 percent, had zero, one, or two) over the nine-year follow-up, but we marked each spouse only upon the occurrence of their *first* hospitalization.

For each individual, we also looked back through three years (1990–1992) of prior inpatient claims in order to detect what illnesses, if any, they had at baseline and thus establish a morbidity burden as of January 1, 1993. The necessity of determining baseline morbidity at cohort inception is the reason for the criterion of greater than sixty-eight years of age for certain analyses (i.e., the Cox models in table 15.2), because patients who were less than sixty-eight in 1993 could not have had Medicare claims filed for a full antecedent three-year period. This three-year duration of retrospective ascertainment of health problems has been shown to be adequate for the detection of prevalent chronic conditions (Zhang, Iwashyna, and Christakis 1999; McBean, Warren, and Babish 1994). We used the Charlson score to summarize baseline morbidity (Zhang, Iwashyna, and Christakis 1999), and we trichotomized it as 0, 1, or ≥ 2. As a further measure of baseline health, we also counted the number of weeks each individual had spent in the hospital in the prior three years.

All of the variables used here have been previously validated or extensively exploited. Investigators have assessed, for example, the optimal use of Medicare data for measuring age (Kestenbaum 1992) and race (Lauderdale and Goldberg 1996). We determined whether the couple was below the state poverty line using previously described methods (Carpenter 1998; Clark and Hulbert 1998; Escarce et al. 1993; Pope et al. 1998). With respect to reliability of claims for detection of specific diseases, prior work has shown that claims have a sensitivity ranging from 89 percent to 93 percent for the detection of a wide variety of conditions in medical charts (e.g., cancers of various kinds, congestive heart failure, hip fracture, etc.) (Fisher et al. 1992; Romano and Mark 1994; Bergmann et al. 1998; Krumholz et al. 1998; Cooper et al. 1999; Benesch et al. 1997). Specificity for these conditions is also very high and ranges from 99 percent to 100 percent (Romano and Mark 1994). The properties of claims in the more global assessment of overall morbidity burden have also been validated (Zhang, Iwashyna, and Christakis 1999).

For certain results, there is one further proviso, namely, that neither member of the couple be a member of a staff-model HMO. This restriction

Table 15.2	Hazard of proband death depending on spousal death or hospitalization		

		Hazard ratio of death (95% CI)	
		Male probands	Female probands
Spousal death			
Widowhood		1.205***	1.169***
		(1.189–1.221)	(1.151–1.187)
Spousal hospitalization (diagnosis)			
Sepsis		1.089**	1.071
		(1.012–1.172)	(0.979–1.171)
Pneumonia		1.062***	1.058***
		(1.025–1.100)	(1.015–1.103)
Colon cancer		1.016	1.012
		(0.949–1.087)	(0.933–1.096)
Pancreas cancer		0.863	1.18
		(0.536–1.388)	(0.654–2.132)
Lung cancer		0.939	1.135
		(0.800–1.103)	(0.958–1.344)
Leukemia or Lymphoma		1.077	1.081
		(0.911–1.273)	(0.869–1.344)
All other cancers		0.988	0.956
		(0.950–1.028)	(0.908–1.007)
Stroke		1.061***	1.047**
		(1.030–1.092)	(1.009–1.085)
Dementia		1.215***	1.279***
		(1.115–1.323)	(1.143–1.433)
Psychiatric disease		1.191***	1.315***
		(1.122–1.265)	(1.182–1.462)
Ischemic heart disease		1.045***	0.966**
		(1.018–1.072)	(0.938–0.995)
Congestive heart failure		1.115***	1.146***
		(1.071–1.162)	(1.092–1.204)
Chronic obstructive pulmonary disease		1.118***	1.131***
		(1.065–1.175)	(1.061–1.207)
Abdominal surgery		1.038***	1.026
		(1.011–1.065)	(0.990–1.062)
Hip and other serious fractures		1.146***	1.106***
		(1.112–1.182)	(1.043–1.173)
All other diagnoses		1.019***	1.008
		(1.006–1.032)	(0.990–1.026)
Covariate controls			
Age of husband (years)		1.093***	1.001
		(1.091–1.094)	(0.999–1.003)
Age of wife (years)		1.001	1.096***
		(1.000–1.003)	(1.094–1.098)
Wife older than husband		1.051***	1.042***
		(1.037–1.065)	(1.025–1.059)
Couple below poverty line		1.341***	1.433***
		(1.318–1.364)	(1.404–1.462)

Table 15.2   (continued)

	Hazard ratio of death (95% CI)	
	Male probands	Female probands
Charlson score of husband = 1	1.520***	0.977**
	(1.500–1.540)	(0.960–0.994)
Charlson score of husband = 2	2.205***	0.972***
	(2.181–2.230)	(0.956–0.988)
Charlson score of wife = 1	1.01	1.936***
	(0.995–1.026)	(1.904–1.968)
Charlson score of husband = 2	0.99	2.959***
	(0.975–1.007)	(2.915–3.004)
Number of weeks husband in hospital in 1990–1992	1.030***	0.995***
	(1.030–1.031)	(0.993–0.997)
Number of weeks wife in hospital in 1990–1992	0.998***	1.030***
	(0.996–0.999)	(1.029–1.031)
Race of husband: black	1.096***	1.120***
	(1.025–1.171)	(1.032–1.216)
Race of husband: Asian	0.818***	0.923
	(0.757–0.883)	(0.839–1.015)
Race of husband: Hispanic	0.879***	1.01
	(0.852–0.906)	(0.973–1.048)
Race of husband: other	1.039	0.910
	(0.958–1.127)	(0.822–1.008)
Race of husband: unknown	2.028***	0.837***
	(1.953–2.105)	(0.795–0.882)
Race of wife: black	0.953	0.96
	(0.892–1.018)	(0.884–1.042)
Race of wife: Asian	0.877***	0.720***
	(0.807–0.953)	(0.646–0.802)
Race of wife: Hispanic	0.954	0.735***
	(0.907–1.002)	(0.689–0.785)
Race of wife: other	0.99	1.210***
	(0.929–1.054)	(1.125–1.302)
Race of wife: unknown	0.819***	1.834***
	(0.783–0.855)	(1.753–1.920)

Notes: The table shows Cox regression models of survival, separately for husbands and wives, with hazard ratios and 95% confidence intervals. Subjects were followed from January 1, 1993 to January 1, 2002. Widowhood and spousal hospitalizations are treated as time-varying covariates during the follow-up period. Spousal hospitalizations were the principal diagnosis for the first hospitalization, if any, noted during follow-up. All covariates measured at baseline at January 1, 1993. The omitted category for Charlson score measures is zero and for race is white.

*** Significant at less than the 1 percent level.
** Significant at less than the 5 percent level.

is required since such individuals cannot have their complete health histories ascertained in the claims. This exclusion accounts for less than 7.0 percent of the impaneled sample.

15.1.2   Statistical Methods

We employ both conventional survival models (Cox regression) and also fixed effects methods to analyze our data. The former offer the advantage of explicitly estimating the effects of measured attributes (e.g., age) on the outcomes of interest and, more importantly, permit a more flexible parameterization that allows us to separately estimate the effects of caregiving and widowhood. The latter offer the substantial advantage of controlling for time-invariant factors that might confound the effects of interest, whether they are measured or not.

In the Cox regression models, the dependent variable is the duration of survival of the proband, from January 1, 1993 until January 1, 2002. Pertinently, we treat spouse's diagnosis with a disease and spouse's death as *separate* time-varying covariates, with the result that the estimate of the impact of a spouse being hospitalized with one of the sixteen conditions upon a proband takes into account whether the spouse does or does not subsequently die. These models are restricted so that all subjects are a minimum of sixty-eight years old. We used a Wald test to evaluate the difference between the time-varying indicators of spousal hospitalization and spousal death in the same model. Tests for violations of the proportionality assumption for key variables revealed no problems.

Fixed effects models permit the estimation of the effect of factors such as the occurrence of a particular diagnosis in a spouse, which does change over the longitudinal follow-up, while accounting for any measured or unmeasured factors that do not change—whether these factors pertain to the spouse, the proband, or the couple. This is accomplished by using each couple as its own control, comparing the time at which a spousal diagnosis occurred with times at which it had not. While it is true that the measured and unmeasured variables we wish to control for (e.g., poverty, smoking, education, toxic exposure history, marital happiness) might indeed not be absolutely stable over time, their temporal variability (which we cannot control) is likely to be very small relative to their between-couple variability (which we can control).

Hence, taking a discrete-time approach with couple-days as the units of analysis, we performed a conditional logistic regression predicting whether or not a death occurs on a given day. Each couple is treated as a separate stratum, thereby controlling for all stable differences between couples. This approach has seen several methodological and applied articles in the epidemiology literature, where it is called the case-crossover design (Maclure 1991; Marshall and Jackson 1993; Redelmeier and Tibshirani 1997), and we used a modification called the case-time-control design (Suissa 1998).

Despite its salient advantages, this method has some limitations. For example, the covariates of interest cannot be monotonic functions of time. Consequently, our modeling approach uses dummy variables for spouse hospitalized for disease X within the last 30, 60, 90, 180, 360, and so on, days. This feature also offers the advantage of allowing us to explicitly investigate the shape of the effect of a spouse's illness (and/or death) on a proband's death across time (Allison and Christakis 2006). As implemented, these models estimate the effect of spousal diagnosis, with or without subsequent death, on proband death.

15.2 Results

15.2.1 Cohort Attributes

At cohort inception ($N = 518,240$), the mean age of the husbands was 75.4 years and of the wives 72.9 years; in 79.1 percent of the couples, the husband was older than the wife; 90.1 percent of the husbands and 92.1 percent of the wives were white; 5.4 percent of the couples were below their state poverty line. The mean Charslon comorbidity score of the husbands at cohort inception was 0.50 and of the wives, 0.30. From January 1, 1993 to January 1, 2002, 383,480 (74.0 percent) of the husbands and 347,269 (67.0 percent) of the wives were hospitalized at least once. Over the same time period, 252,557 of the husbands (48.7 percent) died and 156,004 (30.1 percent) of the wives died; in 95,330 couples, both parties died.

15.2.2 Spousal Illness and Proband Death
in the Elderly: Unadjusted Results

Table 15.1 shows the percentage of probands who die within one year of their spouse being hospitalized with one of sixteen disease categories at any time during the nine-year follow-up. For example, whereas 6.39 percent of husbands die within a year of their wife being hospitalized with colon cancer, 6.90 percent die within a year of their wife being hospitalized with a stroke, 8.55 percent die within a year of their wife being hospitalized with dementia, and 7.50 percent die within a year of their wife being hospitalized for psychiatric disease. Symmetrically, whereas 2.99 percent of wives die within a year of their husband being hospitalized with colon cancer, 3.65 percent with a stroke, 4.99 percent with dementia, and 5.74 percent with psychiatric disease.

The median number of days between a wife's hospitalization and a man's subsequent death, in those couples with both these events, was 1,103, and between a husband's hospitalization and a woman's death was 1,287.

Table 15.1 also reports the percentage of spouses who themselves die within a year of their own hospitalization; the disease categories show substantial and plausible variation in their lethality. For many diseases, the majority of patients themselves die within a year of hospitalization, further supporting the importance of separating the impact on probands of the occurrence of disease versus death in spouses.

15.2.3   Cox Regression Models: Adjusting for Measured Covariates

The Cox models in table 15.2 provide estimates of the effect of spousal illness on proband risk of death after adjusting for whether the spouse dies and after adjusting for other measured attributes of both parties, including their age and baseline morbidity. For example, the occurrence of colon cancer in a wife does not itself affect the husband's risk of death (HR 1.02, 95 percent CI: 0.95–1.09), whereas the occurrence of a stroke in a wife raises the husband's risk by 6 percent (HR 1.06, 95 percent CI: 1.03–1.09), CHF by 12 percent (HR 1.12, 95 percent CI 1.07–1.16), dementia by 22 percent (HR 1.22, 95 percent CI: 1.12–1.32), and psychiatric disease by 19 percent (HR 1.19, 95 percent CI: 1.12–1.27). Similarly, the occurrence of colon cancer in a husband has no effect on a wife (HR 1.01, 95 percent CI: 0.93–1.10), whereas a husband's stroke raises a wife's risk of death by 5 percent (HR 1.05, 95 percent CI: 1.01–1.09), CHF by 15 percent (HR 1.15, 95 percent CI: 1.09–1.20), dementia by 28 percent (HR: 1.28, 95 percent CI: 1.14–1.43), and psychiatric disease by 32 percent (HR 1.32, 95 percent CI: 1.18–1.46).

The results in table 15.2 also reveal that in the case of both husbands and wives, the death of a spouse is associated with 20 percent and 17 percent increase, respectively, in the hazard of death net of the health burden imposed by the spouse's anteceding illness as marked by their hospitalization. Moreover, for men, their hazard of death (over the following nine years) is higher if they are older in age, their wife is older than they are, they are black, they have a higher baseline morbidity (measured either as a Charlson score or number of days spent in the hospital), or they are poor. For women, their hazard of death is higher for the same reasons.

A reduced form Cox model (not shown) with an indicator for the occurrence of any disease at all showed that the occurrence of any hospitalization in a wife increases a husband's risk of death by 4.2 percent and the occurrence in a husband increases a wife's risk of death by 2.3 percent, even after controlling for whether the hospitalized person subsequently dies. Moreover, comparison of the effect of any hospitalization to a death reveals that a spouse's (husband's or wife's) recent diagnosis (within the past thirty days) is about 75 percent as bad for a proband's mortality as a spouse's death within the past thirty days.

15.2.4   Fixed Effects Models: Adjusting for
Measured and Unmeasured Attributes

Table 15.3 gives the relative odds of a proband dying on a particular day within six months of a spouse's hospitalization, depending on whether a

le 15.3   Odds ratios for proband death within six months conditional on new spousal hospitalization, by spousal diagnosis

ease category	Impact of wife's diagnosis on husband's odds of death within six months	95% CI		Impact of husband's diagnosis on wife's odds of death within six months	95% CI	
sis	1.198	1.006	1.427	1.142	0.924	1.411
umonia	1.325	1.213	1.448	1.232	1.122	1.353
on cancer	1.153	0.970	1.371	0.974	0.780	1.215
creas cancer	1.310	0.818	2.098	1.658	0.936	2.937
ng cancer	0.963	0.742	1.252	1.271	0.995	1.624
kemia/Lymphoma	1.605	1.231	2.093	1.101	0.768	1.579
other cancers	1.033	0.934	1.143	1.060	0.933	1.205
oke	1.105	1.024	1.191	1.102	1.006	1.207
mentia	1.472	1.217	1.780	1.381	1.105	1.725
chiatric disease	1.584	1.356	1.851	1.771	1.389	2.256
hemic heart disease	1.119	1.041	1.203	1.132	1.045	1.226
F	1.105	1.003	1.217	1.272	1.144	1.416
PD	1.212	1.064	1.381	1.364	1.172	1.587
dominal surgery	1.124	1.042	1.213	1.189	1.075	1.315
and other Serious fractures	1.352	1.253	1.460	1.178	1.026	1.352
other diagnoses	1.140	1.105	1.175	1.178	1.131	1.226

spouse is hospitalized with one of the sixteen conditions at any time between 1993 and 2001, separately for male and female probands. Hospitalization for a variety of serious conditions in wives increases the risk of a husband's death within six months of the diagnosis: the diagnosis of acute events such as a stroke, heart attack, pneumonia, or hip fracture in a woman will increase a husband's odds of death within six months, net of all stable attributes of both partners, between 10 percent and 35 percent. The diagnosis of diseases such as dementia or psychiatric conditions increase the odds of a husband's death within six months by 47 percent and 58 percent, respectively. The diagnosis of most cancers in a wife does not appear to affect her husband's risk of death within six months.

Similarly, hospitalization for a variety of serious conditions in husbands increases the risk of wife's death within six months of the diagnosis: the diagnosis of acute events such as a stroke, heart attack, pneumonia, or hip fracture in a woman will increase a husband's odds of death within six months, net of all stable attributes of both partners, between 10 percent and 23 percent. The diagnosis of diseases such as dementia or psychiatric conditions increase the odds of a husband's death within six months at 38 percent and 77 percent, respectively. The diagnosis of any cancer in a husband does not appear to affect his wife's risk of death within six months.

Expanding to a broader time window than just six months, figure 15.1 shows the impact of the occurrence of a spousal hospitalization in general, without regard to spouse's particular diagnosis, upon a partner's risk of death. When one person is hospitalized with any disease, the other's risk of death shows a statistically significant increase above baseline and remains elevated for at least two years. This is the case even after accounting for all stable measured or unmeasured attributes of the couples, which are controlled for in this model, and without regard to whether the hospitalized spouse lives or dies. For both men and women, the effect of spousal diagnosis is greatest just after the hospitalization and lowest at roughly six months after the occurrence.

Figures 15.2 and 15.3 graphically show the impact of spousal diagnosis on proband risk of death across a two-year horizon for a selection of eight of the sixteen conditions, separately for male and female probands. In general, these graphs have a U shape with a nadir at 90–180 days.

15.3 Discussion

Prior work on the widower effect and caregiver burden may conflate the two phenomena. It is important, in studies of caregiver burden, to parse out the adverse health impact of widowhood itself and, in studies of the widower effect, to parse out the impact on a proband of a spouse's pre-death illness or disability. Indeed, we find that it may be roughly as bad for a proband's health, relatively speaking, to have a partner be hospitalized with a serious disease as it is for that partner to die. Our diagnosis-specific results suggest that possibly a substantial part of the widower effect may be related not to the death of the spouse, but to the fact that they were ill with particular kinds of diseases before they died. Moreover, independent of the foregoing, the temporal pattern of the caregiver burden effect also suggests that the impact of caregiving may involve both the acute stress of the occurrence of the spouse's illness and a longer-term effect of losing the ongoing support of the spouse.

We specifically hypothesized that particular spousal diagnoses could vary in how burdensome they are to probands and hence the extent to which they affect proband health and mortality. The more a disease interferes with a person's physical or mental ability, regardless of the extent to which it is deadly, the worse for the partner of the ill person. There are a number of possible ways that diseases might be assessed in terms of their impact on the afflicted person's health status and consequently their burdensomeness. For example, prior work has documented that diseases vary in their impact on the activities of daily living (ADL) score (Ferrucci et al. 1997; Rosen et al. 2000; Covinsky et al. 1997). Other studies have specifically examined disability rates in individuals at various time intervals after hospitalization with various diseases (Gill et al. 2004; Landrum and

All Diagnoses

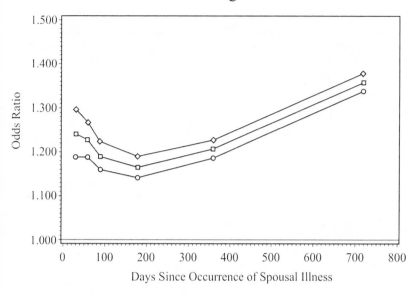

All Diagnoses

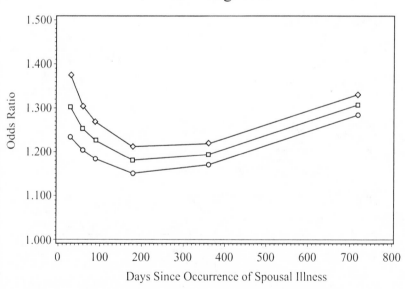

Fig. 15.1   Proband risk of death over various time intervals after spousal hospitalization with any condition (fixed effects estimates), for husbands and wives

Notes: The top panel shows the husband's risk of death (odds ratio and 95% time intervals) on days falling within certain time periods, depending on whether his wife has been hospitalized in the relevant time period, compared to days when his wife had not died within the relevant time period, as generated by fixed effects models. The bottom panel shows the wife's risk of death.

Steward 2004). One study found that stroke or hip fracture are more likely to cause new and serious disability than Congestive Heart Failure (CHF) or cancer (Ferrucci et al. 1997). Yet another way to rank diseases relies on SF-36 measures of physical or mental function, and one meta-analysis of over 15,000 patient reports ranked disease groups in the following order,

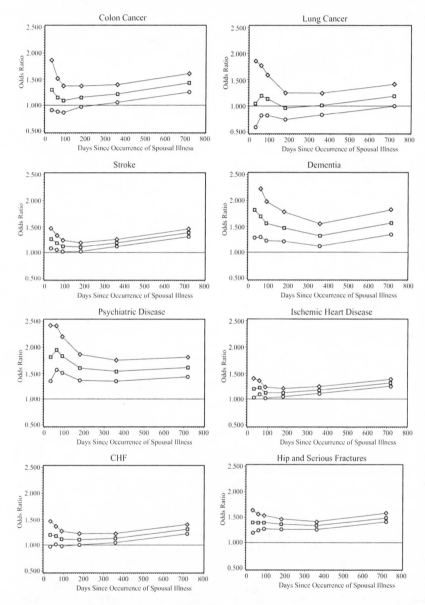

Fig. 15.2   Husband's risk of death over various time intervals depending on occurrence of illness in wife

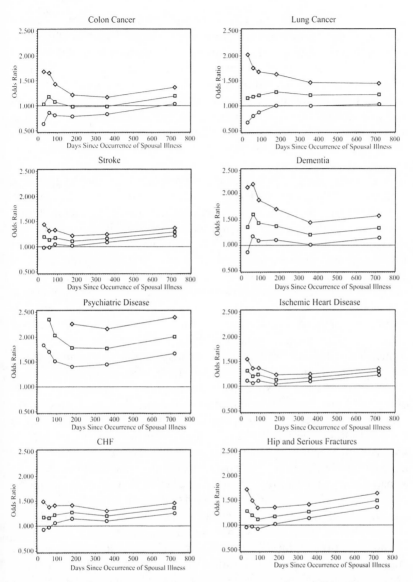

Fig. 15.3   Wife's risk of death over various time intervals depending on occurrence of illness in husband

from most to least impact: cerebrovascular conditions, cardiovascular conditions, respiratory conditions, and cancer (Sprangers et al. 2000).

The purpose of ranking diagnoses according to such measures is not to adjudicate among the various ways of ranking diseases, nor to directly estimate the effect of ADL or other decrements per se on a partner's health. For such a purpose, it would clearly be ideal (though impossible, given our sample size requirements) if we could have, for each patient regardless of their diagnosis, more detailed measures of their health or disability status or even the actual demands they make of their partner. Rather, the object in using this prior work is to provide support for the contention that diagnoses do indeed vary in their burdensomeness and therefore to assist in interpreting our results. In general, our results confirm that diseases do vary and that cancer diagnoses appear especially nonburdensome. While dementia, the most frequently studied diagnosis with respect to caregiving, is on the upper end of burdensomeness (at least as we have measured it here, in terms of risk to a proband's life), other diseases, such as chronic obstructive pulmonary disease (COPD) and psychiatric conditions appear to rival it even though they are less lethal.

Both the widow/er and caregiver effects conform to theories and findings regarding the role of stress and social support in health and mortality (House, Landis, and Umberson 1988; Berkman and Syme 1997; Thoits 1995; Berkman, Geo-Summers, and Horwitz 1992; Berkman and Glass 2000; Cohen et al. 1997; Esterling, Kiecolt-Glaser, and Glaser, 1996). As such, it is possible to postulate two broad mechanisms whereby illness in one spouse might affect the health and risk of death of the other: illness or death in a spouse may impose stress on the proband, and illness or death in a spouse may deprive a proband of social support previously offered by the spouse. These two effects, while both negative, may, however, operate over different time frames. For example, the stress effect might last for a few weeks or months and the support effect might last for several years. Moreover, the former might have immediate onset and decrease with time (as the proband recovers from the acute shock of the onset of serious illness in the spouse) and the latter might increase with time (as the absence of spousal support cumulates). Once a spouse falls seriously ill (or dies), probands might begin to exhibit harmful behaviors, ranging from drinking to bad dietary practices to accident-prone activities with an attendant increase, over the longer term, in the hazard of death (Umberson 1987, 1992; Iwashyna 2001). Stress and the lack of social support may also adversely affect biological parameters (Cohen et al. 1997).

Thus, we also hypothesized that the impact of being in a caregiving role might vary according to the duration in that role and we found, across a broad range of diagnoses, a U-shaped function with a nadir at 90–180 days. One interpretation of this shape is that early in the course of a spouse's illness, a proband experiences a stress effect, to which he or she eventually adapts such that the health risks of being a caregiver decline; eventually, however, the lack of social support from the newly seriously ill spouse becomes a problem, and health risks in the proband increase again. Interestingly, some prior work on the risk of death in probands depending on the duration of bereavement (i.e., time since the death of their spouse) has suggested a similar U-shaped function with a nadir between 0.5 and 1.0 years

(Martikainen and Valkonen 1996b), and work on how duration of awareness of a husband's impending death affects a wife's long-term anxiety reveals a similar U-shape (Vadimarsdottir et al. 2004).

Although wives are more likely than husbands to be caregivers (for numerous reasons, ranging from longer female life expectancy to the pressure
to fill a social role), most studies have suggested that wives report higher
levels of burden than husbands who are caregivers or than control populations (Barusch and Spaid 1989; Pruchno and Resch 1989; Russo and
Vitaliano 1995; Dunkin and Anderson-Hanley 1998), with attendant psychological consequences. Our work shows that, over a broad range of
diseases, and when burden is measured as the risk of death, husbands suffer as much, marginally speaking, as wives from having a seriously ill partner. However, some of these effects may be gendered in ways that warrant
further exploration. Since husbands and wives bring different benefits to a
marriage, husbands and wives may rely on each other for different kinds of
assistance (Waite and Gallagher 2000); therefore, different health deficits
in partners might affect husbands and wives differently. Thus, for example,
mental deficits in husbands may be worse for wives than mental deficits
in wives are for husbands; physical deficits in wives may be worse for husbands than physical deficits in husbands are for wives. We found some suggestive evidence of disease heterogeneity in this regard, but more work is
needed to clarify any such gendered effects.

We used observational epidemiological methods to evaluate the effects
of interest since a randomized controlled intervention trial—involving assigning spouses to different diseases—clearly would be impossible. In such
circumstances, observational studies are our best source of clinical evidence (Abel and Koch 1999, Concato, Shah, and Horwitz 2000). Epidemiological studies, however, raise unavoidable concerns regarding confounding or selection. In order to get the large size and long follow-up needed to
evaluate the phenomena of interest here, we had to forego other information about cohort members that would have been useful. Moreover, we
lack information about time-varying traits of probands and couples other
than the occurrence of spousal disease or death. Such a lack of information, and the non-random assignment of couples to different spousal illness conditions, is unavoidable.

However, the implementation of fixed effects models helps to partly mitigate this concern. This method also helps mitigate concerns regarding the
possible endogeneity of the processes leading to a spouse's hospitalization
and the proband's likelihood of dying. For example, there might be *unmeasured* traits that make a proband unable to care for a spouse, that therefore increase the spouses' probability of being hospitalized (given the onset of a particular condition), and that are correlated with the proband's
own risk of death during the caregiving period. In addition to the fact that
our fixed effects models can adjust for such (unmeasured) traits, it is also

worth noting that the probability of being hospitalized for most of the diseases we are considering here (e.g., MI, stroke, sepsis, hip fracture, abdominal surgery) is unlikely to depend much on attributes of a proband. Finally, such fixed effects models seem especially appropriate in the present setting because once people reach the age of sixty-five, their educational status, wealth, taste for health care, and health habits tend to be stable, and such attributes can be seen as having a fixed effect on individual's propensity to fall ill or die.

The supposition that being in a caregiver role is causally associated with subsequent harm to the health of a proband is supported by additional aspects of our findings, not limited to the magnitude of the effects we observe. For example, our data suggest a kind of dose/response relationship whereby different diseases, of different burdensomeness (as described by prior work), have different marginal risks of death. In addition, our findings comport with other customary criteria regarding the likelihood of causation based on epidemiological data, including the temporal order, consistency with past studies, and biological plausibility of the association. Nevertheless, further study will be needed.

Our work has a number of other limitations. We use "caregiver" to signify being in the caregiving role. But we cannot actually be sure that the proband provided any care to the spouse. The kind of data required for our study of mortality effects (e.g., the sample size) necessarily lacks detail on caregiving activities and on whether caregivers other than the spouses are also involved. Nevertheless, we do document an effect on the partners of ill persons. We also focus here on a single (hard) endpoint, namely, proband death. However, we see this as an advantage. That is, whereas in prior studies of widowhood both the exposure (death of a spouse) and the outcome (death of a proband) have been unambiguously and consistently defined, prior studies of caregiver burden—or the effect of illness of one party on the health of the other—have used variable outcomes that make comparisons across populations and diseases difficult and have typically been conducted with one disease or one type of couple. Our work avoids this problem by focusing on death as an outcome.

Though inter-individual health effects of the kind investigated here are frequently overlooked, they may have substantial clinical and policy significance. Most generally, illness and death in individuals who, being embedded in social networks, are connected to their spouses and to others, can impose health externalities on these other people (Christakis 2004; Christakis and Iwashyna 2003). Whatever the adverse health consequences to a person from falling ill, and whatever the mitigation of these consequences attributable to the receipt of medical care, there may be health consequences that also accrue to those to whom the sick person is connected. This in turn means that efforts to reduce disease, disability, and death can be self-reinforcing as a decrease in the burden of these events in one individual can have cascading benefits for others. Therefore, health care might indeed be more socially efficient than an individual, patient-level perspective might suggest (Christakis and Iwashyna 2003). For example, there is evidence that disability rates among the elderly have been falling at 0.5 percent to 2.5 percent per year over the last decades (Freedman, Martin, and Schoeni 2002). It is conceivable that some fraction of the decline in disability may be related to positive health externalities or may be self-reinforcing. That is, if disability or death in one person can contribute to disability or death in others, then reductions in disability may have multiplicative effects because of social network ties.

Our findings therefore have implications for the assessment of cost-effectiveness of medical interventions. There may be collateral benefits of health care interventions upon the relatives of patients, and these benefits may enhance the cost-effectiveness of the intervention. Thus, in the present case, medical care delivered to patients that alleviates the burdensomeness of their condition may benefit not only the patients, but also their spouses or other loved ones, and this may increase the overall cost-effectiveness of medical care.

Our findings can also inform the delivery of support services to caregivers. A recent randomized controlled trial of 300 stroke patients and their caregivers found that training the caregivers in caregiving lowered the costs of care for the patients and decreased their anxiety; moreover, trained caregivers experienced less caregiver burden, anxiety, and depression, and they had a superior quality of life (Kalra et al. 2004). Our work suggests that such interventions to assist caregivers are especially likely to be useful in diseases like stroke and selected others, but less so in cancer. Moreover, the timing of such interventions might be optimally matched to the time of greatest risk of caregivers: for example, just after the initial occurrence of the disease.

Finally, patients themselves care about how their illness affects others to whom they are connected (Steinhauser et al. 2000). The fact that illnesses can have palpable effects on the health of others to whom patients are connected will likely interest patients as they seek to maintain their social relations and seek to avoid imposing burdens on their loved ones throughout their own experience of their condition.

References

Abel, U., and A. Koch. 1999. The role of randomization in clinical studies: Myths and beliefs. *Journal of Clinical Epidemiology* 52:487–97.

Allison, P. D., and N. A. Christakis. 2006. Fixed effects methods for the analysis of non-repeated events. *Sociological Methodology* 36 (1): 155–72.

Barusch, A. S., W. M. Spaid. 1989. Gender differences in caregiving: Why do wives report greater burden? *The Gerontologist* 29 (5): 667–76.

Benesch, C., D. M. Witter, Jr., A. L. Wilder, P. W. Duncan, G. P. Samsa, and D. B. Matchar. 1997. Inaccuracy of the International Classification of Disease (ICD-9-CM) in identifiying the diagnosis of ischemic cerebrovascular disease. *Neurology* 49:660–64.

Berkman, L., and T. Glass. 2000. Social integration, social networks, and health. In *Social epidemiology*, eds. L. F. Berkman and I. Kawachi, 174–90. Oxford: Oxford University Press.

Berkman, L., R. Horwitz, and L. Leo-Summers. 1992. Emotional support and survival after myocardial infarction: A prospective, population-based study of the elderly. *Annals of Internal Medicine* 117:1003–9.

Berkman, L., and L. Syme. 1997. Social networks, host resistance, and mortality: A nine-year follow-up study of Alameda County residents. *American Journal of Epidemiology* 109:186–204.

Bergmann, M. M., T. Byers, D. S. Freedman, and A. Mokdad. 1998. Validity of self-reported diagnoses leading to hospitalization: A comparison of self-reports with hospital records in a prospective study of American adults. *American Journal of Epidemiology* 147:969–77.

Carpenter, L. 1998. Evolution of Medicaid Coverage of Medicare Cost Sharing. *Health Care Financing Review* 20:11–18.

Christakis, N. A. 2004. Social networks and collateral health effects. *British Medical Journal* 329:184–85.

Christakis, N. A., and T. J. Iwashyna. 2003. The health impact on families of health care: A matched cohort study of hospice use by decedents and mortality outcomes in surviving, widowed spouses. *Social Science and Medicine* 57:465–75.

Clark, W. D., and M. M. Hulbert. 1998. Research issues: Dually eligible Medicare and Medicaid beneficiaries, challenges and opportunities. *Health Care Financing Review* 20:1–10.

Clipp, E. C., and L. K. George. 1993. Dementia and cancer: A comparison of spouse caregivers. *The Gerontologist* 33 (4): 534–41.

Cohen, S., W. J. Doyle, D. P. Skoner, B. S. Rabin, J. Gwaltney, and M. Jack. 1997. Social ties and susceptibility to the common cold. *Journal of the American Medical Association* 277:1940–44.

Collins, C., and R. Jones. 1997. Emotional distress and morbidity in dementia carers: A matched comparison of husbands and wives. *International Journal of Geriatric Psychiatry* 12:1168–73.

Concato, J., N. Shah, and R. I. Horwitz. 2000. Randomized, controlled trials, observational studies, and the hierarchy of research designs. *New England Journal of Medicine* 342:1887–92.

Cooper, G. S., Z. Yuan, K. C. Stange, L. K. Dennis, S. B. Amini, and A. A. Rimm. 1999. The sensitivity of Medicare claims data for case ascertainment of six common cancers. *Medical Care* 37:436–44.

Covinsky, K. E., A. C. Justice, G. E. Rosenthal, R. M. Palmer, and C. S. Ladnefeld. 1997. Measuring prognosis and case mix in hospitalized elders: The importance of functional status. *Journal of General Internal Medicine* 12:203–8.

Dunkin, J. J., and C. Anderson-Hanley. 1998. Dementia caregiver burden: A review of the literature and guidelines for assessment and intervention. *Neurology* 51 (Suppl. no. 1): S53–S60.

Dura, J. R., E. Haywood-Niler, and J. K. Kiecolt-Glaser. 1990. Spousal caregivers of persons with Alzheimer's and Parkinson's Disease dementia: A preliminary comparison. *The Gerontologist* 30 (3): 332–36.

Escarce, J. J., K. R. Epstein, D. C. Colby, and J. S. Schwartz. 1993. Racial differences in the elderly's use of medical procedures and diagnostic tests. *American Journal of Public Health* 83:948–54.

Esterling, B. A., J. K. Kiecolt-Glaser, and R. Glaser. 1996. Psychosocial modulation of cytokine-induced natural killer cell activity in older adults. *Psychosomatic Medicine* 58:264–72.

Ferrucci, L., J. M. Furalnik, M. Pahor, M. C. Corti, and R. J. Havlik. 1997. Hospital diagnoses, Medicare Charges, and nursing home admissions in the year when older persons become severely disabled. *Journal of the American Medical Association* 277:728–34.

Fisher, E. S., F. S. Whaley, M. Krushat, D. J. Malenka, C. Fleming, J. A. Baron, and D. C. Hsia. 1992. The accuracy of Medicare's hospital claims data: Progress has been made, but problems remain. *American Journal of Public Health* 82:243–48.

Fitting, M., P. Rabins, M. J. Lucas, and J. Eastham. 1986. Caregivers for dementia patients: A comparison of husbands and wives. *The Gerontologist* 26 (3): 248–52.

Freedman, V. A., L. G. Martin, and R. F. Schoeni. 2002. Recent trends in disability and functioning among older adults in the United States: A systematic review. *Journal of the American Medical Association* 288:3137–46.

Gill, T. M., H. G. Allore, T. R. Holford, and Z. Guo. 2004. Hospitalization, restricted activity, and the development of disability among older persons. *Journal of the American Medical Association* 292:2115–24.

Hall, M. J., and C. J. DeFrances. 2003. 2001 National Hospital Discharge Survey. Advance Data from Vital and Health Statistics, no. 332. Hyattsville, MD: National Center for Health Statistics.

Hatten, J. 1980. Medicare's common denominator: The covered population. *Health Care Financing Review* Fall: 53–64.

House, J. S., K. R. Landis, and D. Umberson. 1988. Social relationships and health. *Science* 241:540–45.

Iwashyna, T. J. 2001. In sickness and in health: Understanding the effects of marriage on health. Chicago: University of Chicago, Dissertation Library.

Iwashyna, T. J., G. Brennan, J. X. Zhang, and N. A. Christakis. 2002. Finding married couples in Medicare claims data. *Health Services and Outcomes Research Methodology* 3:75–86.

Iwashyna, T. J., J. Zhang, D. Lauderdale, and N. A. Christakis. 1998. A methodology for identifying married couples in Medicare data: Mortality, morbidity, and health care use among the married elderly. *Demography* 35:413–19.

Kalra, L., A. Evans, L. Perez, A. Melbourne, A. Patel, M. Knapp, and N. Donaldson. 2004. Training caregivers of stroke patients: Randomised controlled trial. *British Medical Journal* 328:1099–1101.

Kestenbaum, B. 1992. A description of the extreme aged population based on improved Medicare enrollment data. *Demography* 29:565–80.

Kiecolt-Glaser, J. K., J. R. Dura, C. E. Speicher, O. J. Trask, and R. Glaser. 1991. Spousal caregivers of dementia victims: Longitudinal changes in immunity and health. *Psychosomatic Medicine* 53:345–62.

Krumholz, H. M., M. J. Radford, Y. Wang, J. Chen, A. Heiat, and T. A. Marciniak. 1998. National use and effectiveness of the beta-blockers for treatment of elderly patients after acute Myocardial Infarction. *Journal of the American Medical Association* 280:623–29.

Landrum, M. B., and K. Steward. 2004. Pathways to disability. NBER Working Paper no. 13304. Cambridge, MA: National Bureau of Economic Research.

Lauderdale, D., S. E. Furner, T. P. Miles, and J. Goldberg. 1993. Epidemiological uses of Medicare data. *American Journal of Epidemiology* 15:319–27.

Lauderdale, D. S., and J. Goldberg. 1996. The expanded racial and ethnic codes in the Medicare data files: Their completeness of coverage and accuracy. *American Journal of Public Health* 86:712–16.

Lillard, L. A., and L. J. Waite. 1995. 'Til death do us part: Marital disruption and mortality. *American Journal of Sociology* 100:113–56.

Maclure, M. 1991. The case-crossover design: A method for studying transient effects on the risk of acute events. *American Journal of Epidemiology* 133:144–53.

Marshall, R. J., and R. J. Jackson. 1993. Analysis of case-crossover designs. *Statistics in Medicine* 12:2333–41.

Martikainen, P., and T. Valkonen. 1996a. Mortality after the death of a spouse: Rates and causes of death in a large Finnish cohort. *American Journal of Public Health* 8:1087–93.

———. 1996b. Mortality after death of spouse in relation to duration of bereavement in Finland. *Journal of Epidemiology and Community Health* 50:264–68.

McBean, A. M., J. L. Warren, and J. D. Babish. 1994. Measuring the incidence of cancer in elderly Americans using Medicare claims data. *Cancer* 73:2417–25.

Mitchell, J. B., T. Bubolz, J. E. Paul, C. L. Pashos, J. J. Escarce, L. H. Muhlbaier, J. M. Wiesman, W. W. Young, R. S. Epstein, and J. C. Javitt. 1994. Using Medicare claims for outcomes research. *Medical Care* 32: JS38–JS51.

Mittelman, M. S., S. H. Ferris, E. Shulman, G. Steinberg, A. Ambinder, J. A. Mackell, and J. Cohen. 1995. A comprehensive support program: Effect on depression in spouse-caregivers of AD patients. *The Gerontologist* 35 (6): 792–802.

Parkes, C. M., B. Benjamin, and R. G. Fitzgerald. 1969. Broken heart: A statistical study of increased mortality among widowers. *British Medical Journal* 1:740–43.

Pope, G. C., K. W. Adamache, E. G. Walsh, and R. K. Khandker. 1998. Evaluating Alternative Risk Adjusters for Medicare. *Health Care Financing Review* 20:109–29.

Pruchno, R. A., M. H. Kleban, E. Michaels, and N. P. Dempsey. 1990. Mental and physical health of caregiving spouses: Development of a causal model. *Journal of Gerontology* 45 (5): P192–99.

Pruchno, R. A., and S. L. Potashnik. 1989. Caregiving spouses: Physical and mental health in perspective. *Journal of the American Geriatrics Society* 37:697–705.

Pruchno, R. A., and N. L. Resch. 1989a. Abberrant behaviors and Alzheimer's Disease: Mental health effects on spouse caregivers. *Journal of Gerontology* 44 (5): S177–82.

———. 1989b. Husbands and wives as caregivers: Antecedents of depression and burden. *The Gerontologist* 29 (2): 159–65.

Redelmeier, D. A., and R. J. Tibshirani. 1997. Association between cellular-telephone calls and motor vehicle collisions. *New England Journal of Medicine* 336:453–58.

Romano, P. S., and D. H. Mark. 1994. Bias in the coding of hospital discharge data and its implications for quality assessment. *Medical Care* 32 (1): 81–90.

Rosen, A., J. Wu, B. Chang, D. Berlowitz, A. Ash, and M. Moskowitz. 2000. Does diagnostic information contribute to predicting functional decline in long-term care? *Medical Care* 38:647–59.

Russo, J., and P. P. Vitaliano. 1995. Life events as correlates of burden in spouse caregivers of persons with Alzheimer's Disease. *Experimental Aging Research* 21:273–94.

Russo, J., P. P. Vitaliano, D. D. Brewer, W. Katon, and J. Becker. 1995. Psychiatric disorders in spouse caregivers of care recipients with Alzheimer's Disease and matched controls: A diathesis-stress model of psychopathology. *Journal of Abnormal Psychology* 104 (1): 197–204.

Schaefer, C., C. P. Quesenberry, and W. Soora. 1995. Mortality following conjugal bereavement and the effects of a shared environment. *American Journal of Epidemiology* 141:1142–52.

Scholte op Reimer, W. J. M., R. J. de Haan, P. T. Rijnders, M. Limburg, and G. A. van den Bos. 1998. The burden of caregiving in partners of long-term stroke survivors. *Stroke* 29 (8): 1605–11.

Schulz, R., and S. R. Beach. 1999. Caregiving as a risk factor for mortality: The caregiver health effects study. *Journal of the American Medical Association* 282 (23): 2215–19.

Schulz, R., A. B. Mendelsohn, W. E. Haley, D. Mahoney, R. S. Allen, S. Zhang, L. Thompson, and S. H. Belle. 2003. End-of-life care and the effects of bereavement on family caregivers of persons with dementia. *New England Journal of Medicine* 349:1936–42.

Shaw, W. S., T. L. Patterson, S. J. Semple, S. Ho, M. R. Irwin, R. L. Hauger, and I. Grant. 1997. Longitudinal analysis of multiple indicators of health decline among spousal caregivers. *Annals of Behavioral Medicine* 19 (2): 101–9.

Siegel, K., V. H. Raveis, V. Mor, and P. Houts. 1991. The relationship of spousal caregiver burden to patient disease and treatment-related conditions. *Annals of Oncology* 2:511–16.

Sprangers, M. A. G., E. B. De Regt, F. Andries, H. M. E. Van Agt, R. V. Bijl, J. B. De Boer, M. Foets, et al. 2000. Which chronic conditions are associated with better or poorer quality of life? *Journal of Clinical Epidemiology* 53:895–907.

Steinhauser, K. E., N. A. Christakis, E. C. Clipp, M. McNeilly, L. McIntyre, and J. A. Tulsky. 2000. Factors considered important at the end of life by patients, family, physicians, and other care providers. *Journal of the American Medical Association* 284:2476–82.

Suissa, S. 1998. The Case-Time-Control Design: Further assumptions and conditions. *Epidemiology* 9:441–45.

Thoits, P. A. 1995. Stress, coping, and social support processes: Where are we? What next? *Journal of Health and Social Behavior* (Extra Issue): 53–79.

Umberson, D. 1987. Family status and health behaviors: Social control as a dimension of social integration. *Journal of Health and Social Behavior* 28:306–19.

———. 1992. Gender, marital status and the social control of health behavior. *Social Science and Medicine* 34:907–17.

Vadimarsdottir, U., A. R. Helgason, C. J. Furst, J. Adolfsson, and G. Steineck. 2004. Awareness of husband's impending death from cancer and long-term anxiety in widowhood: A nationwide follow-up. *Palliative Medicine* 18:432–43.

Waite, L., and M. Gallagher. 2000. *The case for marriage.* New York: Doubleday.

Zarit, S. H., P. T. Todd, and J. M. Zarit. 1986. Subjective burden of husbands and wives as caregivers: A longitudinal study. *The Gerontologist* 26 (3): 260–66.

Zhang, J., T. J. Iwashyna, and N. A. Christakis. 1999. The performance of different lookback periods and sources of information for Charlson comorbidity adjustment in Medicare claims. *Medical Care* 37:1128–39.

Contributors

Emily M. Agree
Population, Family, and Reproductive
   Health
Bloomberg School of Public Health
Johns Hopkins University
615 North Wolfe Street
Baltimore, MD 21205

Paul D. Allison
Department of Sociology
University of Pennsylvania
3718 Locust Walk
Philadelphia, PA 19104

James Banks
Institute for Fiscal Studies
7 Ridgmount Street
London WC1E 7AE England

Ernst R. Berndt
Sloan School of Management, E52-452
Massachusetts Institute of Technology
50 Memorial Drive
Cambridge, MA 02142

Axel Börsch-Supan
Mannheim Research Institute for
   Economics of Aging
University of Mannheim
Building L13, 17
D-68131 Mannheim, Germany

Paula Canavese
Deloitte Tax LLP
111 S Wacker Drive
Chicago, IL 60606

Amitabh Chandra
John F. Kennedy School of
   Government
Harvard University
79 John F. Kennedy Street
Cambridge, MA 02138

Michael E. Chernew
Department of Health Care Policy
Harvard Medical School
180 Longwood Avenue
Boston, MA 02115

Nicholas A. Christakis
Department of Health Care Policy
Harvard Medical School
180 Longwood Avenue
Boston, MA 02115

Rena M. Conti
Advanced Pediatric Health Services
The University of Chicago
5841 South Maryland Avenue,
   MC6082
Chicago, IL 60615

Jennifer Cornman
Department of Health Systems and
 Policy
University of Medicine and Dentistry
 of New Jersey School of Public
 Health
335 George Street, Suite 2200
New Brunswick, NJ 08903

Dora L. Costa
Department of Economics
University of California, Los Angeles
Box 951477
Los Angeles, CA 90095-1477

David M. Cutler
Department of Economics
Harvard University
1875 Cambridge Street
Cambridge, MA 02138

Mark Duggan
Department of Economics
3115L Tydings Hall
University of Maryland
College Park, MD 20742

Robert W. Fogel
Center for Population Economics
Graduate School of Business
The University of Chicago
5807 South Woodland Avenue
Chicago, IL 60637

Richard G. Frank
Department of Health Care Policy
Harvard Medical School
180 Longwood Avenue
Boston, MA 02115

Vicki A. Freedman
Department of Health Systems and
 Policy
University of Medicine and Dentistry
 of New Jersey School of Public
 Health
335 George Street, Suite 2200
New Brunswick, NJ 08903

Dana Goldman
RAND Corporation
1776 Main Street
Santa Monica, CA 90407-2138

Florian Heiss
Department of Economics
University of Munich
Ludwigstr. 28 (RG)
D-80539 Munich, Germany

Michael Hurd
RAND Corporation
1776 Main Street
Santa Monica, CA 90407

Lisa I. Iezzoni
Institute for Health Policy
Massachusetts General Hospital
50 Staniford Street
Boston, MA 02114

Scott A. Imberman
Department of Economics
204 McElhinney Hall
University of Houston
Houston, TX 77204-5019

Arie Kapteyn
RAND Corporation
1776 Main Street
Santa Monica, CA 90407

Mary Beth Landrum
Department of Health Care Policy
Harvard Medical School
180 Longwood Avenue
Boston, MA 02115

Suzanne G. Leveille, PhD RN
Division of General Medicine and
 Primary Care
Beth Israel Deaconess Medical
 Center
1309 Beacon St., CO-219
Brookline, MA 02446

Linda G. Martin
RAND Corporation
1200 South Hayes Street
Arlington, VA 22202-5050

Feng Pan
United BioSource Corporation
7101 Wisconsin Avenue, Suite 600
Bethesda, MD 20814

Andrew A. Samwick
Department of Economics
6106 Rockefeller Hall
Dartmouth College
Hanover, NH 03755-3514

Robert F. Schoeni
Institute for Social Research
University of Michigan
426 Thompson Street
Ann Arbor, MI 48104-2321

Baoping Shang
Health Policy Center
The Urban Institute
2100 M Street, NW
Washington, D.C. 20037

James P. Smith
RAND Corporation
1776 Main Street
Santa Monica, CA 90401-3208

Jane R. Soukup
General Medicine and Primary Care
Beth Israel Deaconess Hospital
330 Brookline Avenue
Boston, MA 02215

Kate A. Stewart
Mathematica Policy Research, Inc.
600 Maryland Ave, SW, Suite 550
Washington, D.C. 20024-2512

Arthur van Soest
Department of Econometrics and
    Operations Research
Tilburg University
P.O. Box 90153
5000 LE Tilburg, the Netherlands

Christina C. Wee
Division of General Medicine and
    Primary Care
Beth Israel Deaconess Medical Center
1309 Beacon Street, CO-222
Brookline, MA 02446

David A. Wise
John F. Kennedy School of
    Government
Harvard University
79 John F. Kennedy Street
Cambridge, MA 02138

Richard G. Woodbury
Maine House of Representatives
2 State House Station
Augusta, ME 04333

Author Index

Subject Index